MODERN EUROPEAN SOCIAL HISTORY

SELECTIONS BY

James J. Sheehan
T. William Heyck
Judson Mather
Robert J. Bezucha
Louise A. Tilly
Glen Waggoner
Edward E. Malefakis
Edward Shorter
Robert Neuman
Anthony Esler
Michael Marrus
Amy Hackett

MODERN EUROPEAN SOCIAL HISTORY

EDITED BY

Robert J. Bezucha
Northwestern University

D. C. HEATH AND COMPANY
Lexington, Massachusetts Toronto London

Clothbound edition published by Lexington Books.

Engraving on cover of paperbound edition is by Gustave Doré.

Published simultaneously in Canada.

Printed in the United States of America.

Paperbound International Standard Book Number: 0–669–61143–3
Clothbound International Standard Book Number: 0–669–81117–3

Library of Congress Catalog Card Number: 79–172910

Acknowledgments

It makes no sense to pretend that any persons but the contributors, many of them close friends, are responsible for this book. I would like to thank a few others, however: Bertrand Lummus of D. C. Heath and Company, who was willing to invest in the future of social history; John Bowditch, Raymond Grew, and Sylvia Thrupp, who introduced me to the field; James Sheridan, a prince of a chairman, who arranged for me to have a quarter's leave; Susan Bogie, who did much of the typing; and my family, which happily has little interest in social history.

R. J. B.
Evanston, Illinois
May 1971

CONTENTS

V.   FORMS OF SOCIAL PROTEST

INTRODUCTION

In every profession there is a risk of talking for so long about one's task that the job itself is never accomplished. Historians are prone to their own version of this hazard. Their students have likely already discovered that for every masterpiece of the historiographer's art there are at least ten dreadful little essays called "What is History?" With this spectre weighing on our minds, we begin this book by discussing the question, What is social history?

There is good reason to ask this question. During the past decade, courses on social history, journals devoted to studying it, and most important, people calling themselves social historians have appeared increasingly on American campuses. But what is social history? Where can a student turn to learn what it is about? This introductory essay along with the rest of the book is an attempt at providing the answers. The reader should not expect to come away from these pages, however, with a precise definition of social history or the sort of answer that would be marked correct on a multiple choice examination. Rather it is hoped that he or she will have gained some sense of the fact that social history is a flourishing, richly various discipline in which the disagreements among its practitioners signal, at the very least, that they are asking important questions about the past.

I

A survey of definitions, both past and current, might give the false impression that social history is a poor stepchild among academic disciplines. G. M. Trevelyan described the intent of his *English Social History* (London and New York: Longmans, Green and Co., 1942, p. vii) to be "the history of a people with the politics left out." Seeking to demur, another British historian, Asa Briggs, writes, "I want to consider social history not as history with the politics left out but as economic history with the politics put in." (*British Journal of Sociology* 1 [1950]: 68.) Even one of its most influential American practitioners, Charles Tilly, recently reviewed the textbook of another, Peter Stearns, by telling us that it is "bitter hard . . . to write the history of remainders." (*Journal of Modern History* 42 [1970]: 576.) A long list of other quotations could be offered to the same effect. The question, therefore, is raised: Will Cinderella ever get to the ball?

She will never arrive until she resolves to stop gathering the scraps of material that have been discarded by her sister disciplines and sets about the serious business of making a new dress for herself. Social history often has been considered a poor stepchild because it was conceived of by those who wrote it as being a kind of history rather than a way of looking at history. The idea that there exists a limited range of subjects appropriate to the field—a snug place alongside the hearth—is one for which many social historians are themselves responsible. Let us take a brief look at three of the most frequently encountered of these approaches; although valuable work continues to emerge from them, they are a virtual cul-de-sac for the future of the discipline as a whole.

1. Social history as the history of culture. At its best, this is the approach represented by Trevelyan ("history with the politics left out"), the study of the daily lives of members of different social classes in different periods. At its worst, this is the history of "pots and pans," that is to say of furniture, costumes, coiffures, and other cultural artifacts, without reference to how and where they fit into the structure of the surrounding society. To consider this approach satisfactory would be to accept a permanent residual position for social history.

2. Social history as the history of "the social question." This approach has been most influential on the European continent and in Britain and is closely tied to the existence of a strong Marxist intellectual tradition. Readers may turn to two journals, *The International Review of Social History* (Amsterdam) or *Le Mouvement Social* (Paris), although both have recently begun to broaden their horizons, to find numerous illustrations of Arthur Lehning's prescription that "what is *mainly* involved" in social history "is the history of the working classes, of social conditions, of the workers' movements, and the theories and ideologies associated with these" (The *Times Literary Supplement,* September 8, 1966, p. 809). The inherent limitations of this approach are apparent when one considers the masterpieces of social history that have been produced recently on the peasantry (E. Le Roy Ladurie), the aristocracy (Lawrence Stone), and the middle classes (A. Daumard). History may well be the chronicle of class struggle, but it is clearly not that of the working classes alone.

3. Social history as the "old" economic history. Social and economic history have been closely related for nearly half a century. When Lucien Febvre and Marc Bloch sought to break with traditional political history and founded their journal *Annales d'histoire* (1929), they added the subtitle *"économique et sociale."* In most cases, however the "social" dimension was clearly subservient to the "economic" one. This situation has been recently reversed as the result of a schism in the ranks of economic historians. While some have sought to re-

spond to the growth of a systematic mathematical orientation in economics (econometrics) by developing a quantitative method of their own (called cliometrics by such exponents as Robert Fogel), others have had either to weather the epithet that they were writing "old" economic history, or else to run for shelter under the broad umbrella of social history. Their arrival has been welcome, since virtually all social historians recognize the fundamental importance of economic factors. But there has been a certain danger that the result would be like pouring old wine into new bottles—or perhaps the same old bottles with a new label.

Leaving aside for the moment the explanation for its sudden popularity, there has been mounting pressure for general statements concerning social history. The most successful have been those which shunned both defensiveness and parochialism and positively asserted that it is a particular way of looking at history. In the words of Harold Perkin: "The social historian differs from other historians only in the questions he asks and the answers he seeks" (1962).* Many would now agree that the questions to be asked and the answers sought revolve around an interest in the history of society, or to cite Perkin again, "the understanding of the life of men in the past, in its setting of society and institutions." This being the case it is evident why no subject or set of subjects can be isolated and presented as appropriate to social history; neither can any be thought inherently inappropriate. Since all social phenomena are organically related, we must rather think of social history as the area where political, economic, intellectual (and one would hope eventually diplomatic and military) history meet, interconnect, and overlap. To state matters boldly, it is unlikely that there is anything that can be studied about the past that lies outside the perimeters of social history. That is what makes the field currently so exciting and challenging.

Social history is naturally eclectic. Its subject matter has subsumed other, more traditional categories of history. But it is also eclectic in the fact that it has borrowed heavily from the methods and techniques (and the questions) of the other social sciences, that is to say from anthropology, demography, economics, psychology, and sociology. The very concept of "society" around which the practitioners of social history propose to build their subject has been taken from these sister disciplines. Social history as it is currently being written differs from that of earlier generations principally in its interdisciplinary approach to the past. This is at once the key to the strength of its popularity and the explanation for much of the criticism that has been leveled against it.

Critics frequently accuse social historians of abandoning traditional

* All literary references in the introduction are elaborated in a bibliography at the end of the introduction.

topics, swallowing crude concepts from the social sciences without digesting them, heaping on statistics, tables, and graphs with little concern for their appropriateness or usefulness, so that their final products are so riddled with jargon that history is not only no longer a narrative but also no longer prose. Let us consider each of these points in more detail.

First, social historians have not so much abandoned traditional topics as they have found new ways to study them. In addition, they have opened to systematic research whole areas that were once considered outside the historian's province. Certainly there should be no penalty for extending the range of a discipline. Second, while some individuals may be guilty of understanding very little about the concepts or models they have adopted, it is time to drop the illusion that traditional historical explanations of causation are somehow less subject to crude reductionism or personal bias. There is also little merit in continuing the debate as to whether or not some social sciences are interested in establishing "general laws" while history is principally concerned with "particular instances"; all treat the particular and the general, and have much to share with one another. Third, the attack on quantification is misdirected as a criticism of social history as a whole. It is a valuable warning, on the other hand, to those who believe that mastery of a particular technique automatically makes them master historians. They should remind themselves that Marc Bloch's great work *Feudal Society* can be readily understood by any intelligent reader. Fourth, the response to the criticism of jargon in social history must be made in two stages. Historians should rightfully exhort their fellows to a concern for style and must resist obfuscation wherever it appears. But wretched style and resort to arguments that on reflection prove to be less than meritorious are not the unique sins of social historians. What some may consider to be jargon, others will recognize as a legitimate and valuable mode of expression. Perhaps the real danger is that social history will have less appeal to the general public; that is an enormous problem which plagues all of the social sciences. Yet there are already enough examples of works that have received wide acceptance, such as those of Peter Laslett and George Rudé, to suggest that this problem is not insoluble.

A fifth criticism has been raised among social historians themselves: there has been little progress toward actually writing the history of society. The explanation lies in the fact that the field, as so defined, is still in an early stage of its development and there is not yet even agreement as to its basic contours. Should one accept the periodization developed in political history (Europe, 1815–1914, for example) or are there other divisions more appropriate to the history of society? Will the basic unit for study remain the nation-state or must other kinds of units be found? Much frustration, confusion, and impatience has arisen from the fact that social historians have proceeded (one may argue with good reason) to work from a specific center out toward eventual general statements. Their results to date are often more promising than conclusive.

But what has been accomplished? What kinds of questions or topics have proven valuable in the task of writing the history of society? Eric Hobsbawm has recently compiled a list (*Daedalus,* Winter 1971): (1) demography and kinship; (2) urban studies; (3) classes and social groups; (4) the history of "mentalities" or collective consciousness or "culture" in the anthropologist's sense; (5) the transformation of societies (for example, modernization or industrialization); (6) social movements and phenomena of social protest. Each of these clearly reflects the influence of the other social sciences and the movement toward interdisciplinary research.

Social history is not a poor stepchild, a kind of history concerned with subjects other historians consider marginal or unimportant. Neither is it concerned with the history of everything. It is instead a way of looking at the past that reflects and represents the attempt of present-day scholars to bring a variety of tools to the task of studying "society," in this case the history of society. The growing popularity of social history is not a fad, for it does not rely on gimmicks. And, while one must be wary of making inflated claims for what has so far been accomplished, there is good reason to be confident about the future. To cite Eric Hobsbawm again: "It is a good moment to be a social historian. Even those of us who never set out to call ourselves by this name will not want to disclaim it today."

II

Every history book has its own history. This volume perhaps began with the realization that there is precious little a teacher can assign for reading and discussion to students interested in the social history of modern Europe. But how to fill the gap? The prospect of writing a textbook in such a rapidly changing field is enough to discourage all but the bravest or most determined scholar. The few who have tried have sometimes produced admirable results, although many of their arguments have been laid open to revision or outright rejection almost before they appeared in print. Perhaps, because there is still insufficient agreement as to the basic contours of social history, it is too soon for a completely successful textbook. What about a reader? Collections of reprinted articles, some organized around themes and others around methodology, are now flooding the market. Many are serious endeavors and creative contributions to teaching or learning about history; others, it must be admitted, are a bit stale. All too often "putting together a reader" is something scholars do for profit (albeit a modest one) or because they are between research and writing projects of their own. A collection of some of the brilliant articles that have appeared in American, British, and European academic journals in the last few years might well fill the students' need; but any diligent teacher can refer students to the library for such articles, and such a reprinting project did not strike this editor as very enjoyable.

Modern European Social History is a collection of original essays and is intended to introduce students to a substantial part of "what is happening" currently and to suggest the direction that historical studies are likely to take in the next decade. It is not an easy book, nor is is meant to be one. The authors presume that students are willing to read carefully and think hard about history, particularly if they are anxious to learn more about the past than the traditional "kings and battles."

But what is this book about? What kinds of people wrote it? Readers are justified in demanding answers to these questions before going further.

To say that all of the essays are concerned with modern European social history is clearly not enough. While they cover a wide range of time (1750–1939) and geographical area (England, France, Germany, Italy, and Spain), they have been organized in five topical sections representing some of the important subcategories of social history. These sections on political and social elites, the working classes, the peasantry, personal behavior and social change, and forms of social protest, are preceded by a brief editorial introduction that outlines general problems and points out the contribution of the individual essays.

It is certain that some will think this collection is a "mixed bag." Others may lament that the book has no central, unifying theme. It will be valuable, therefore, to respond to these criticisms in advance. First, social history as we have defined it is the history of society. At present by its very nature it is a mixed bag, drawing on other historical fields and a variety of academic disciplines for its subject matter and methodology. Furthermore, while some of its practitioners already feel confident to make general statements about their specialities, others are still inclined to limit their scholarly horizons to specific studies, to build blocks of information and interpretation for the future. The current state of social history as a discipline, as well as the editor's intention that the essays should exhibit geographical, chronological, and topical variety, go far toward explaining the final product. It is hoped that the present volume will add to the precision of those that may follow it.

Second, while there is no explicit theme binding these twelve essays together, all are concerned with examining at least a part of the process by which Europe passed from a traditional to a modern society. An interest in the modernization of European society in the nineteenth century (many of the authors also refer to industrialization and secularization) is, therefore, an implicit theme present throughout the book.

The twelve contributors to this volume were not chosen because they were partisan members of any "school" of social history. Neither are they seeking to create one now. Some, much like the man who did not realize he had been speaking prose all along, did not begin their work with the intention of writing social history. Others do not today consider themselves exclusively "social" historians. This is as it should be. It reflects the newness of the discipline in American universities on the one hand, and the manner in which social history has subsumed more established categories of history on the other.

If the authors are not a self-conscious "school," they probably do represent an academic generation of Americans interested in the social history of Europe. All are in their early or middle thirties and received their advanced training during the 1960s. Their graduate degrees are testimony to the extraordinary diversity of American higher education: three from Columbia University, two each from the University of California at Berkeley and the University of Michigan, and one each from the University of Texas, the University of Toronto, and Harvard, Duke, and Northwestern universities. Unlike the decades that preceded them (and apparently the one that follows), the 1960s were a period when there was wide opportunity for fledgling historians to begin their research abroad. This was fortuitous because social history, perhaps more than other fields, often requires access to materials impossible to obtain on this side of the Atlantic. So it was that the research reflected in most (but not all) of these essays was carried out in the libraries and archives of Amsterdam, Berlin, Cologne, London, Lyon, Paris, Madrid, Milan, and Munich. Readers should not consider for a moment that these particular contributors are the only ones doing important work in social history; the point here is quite the opposite. Were an editor to select twelve other young Americans to write another book such as this one, there would be differences in specific topics and interpretations, but the general results with regard to broad areas of research and methodology would be much the same. In this sense it is a representative collection.

What are the subjects covered in the book? What kinds of sources and historical methods will the reader encounter? The individual essays reflect a number of issues currently being debated in the academic world; there are studies of bureaucratic co-option, social, political, and religious movements, collective violence, the "new" urban history, rural uprisings and peasant land reform, population growth, the family and individual sexual behavior, youth rebellion, and even women's liberation. Throughout all there is an attempt to demonstrate that history should not be partitioned into exclusive boxes, and that social change must be organically explained. Such variety should be rich enough to satisfy even the most sated palate.

The sources, historical methods, and writing styles found here are as various as the subject matter. Attention to the footnotes reveals the authors' ability to find new use for familiar sources as well as value in others formerly considered useless. Printed material such as newspapers, books, pamphlets, records of debates and interviews, archival documents including police reports, dossiers of accused criminals, private and official correspondence, and statistical information drawn from surveys, population censuses, and tax rolls have all been marshaled to the task. In addition, the notes which appear at the end of each essay include a detailed bibliographical guide to secondary literature on the subject.

The range of historical methods is equally striking. While some authors have written in a traditional narrative style, others, exponents of a more quantitative approach to history, have presented much of their research in the form of graphs, charts, and tables. Some make reference to concepts drawn from classical sociology; others have used more recently developed models to explain and describe social change; and a third group has employed a computer to organize and analyze its material. At a time when the social sciences are increasingly divided between the "counters" and the "noncounters," this collection illustrates that there is 'room for both in social history.

Modern European Social History is offered to students as a serious introduction to a new and exciting discipline. Upon reading it, some will surely long for the good old days when history was still the story of "kings and battles." Perhaps they will even agree with the opinion reported by Peter Laslett in *The World We Have Lost* (p. 239) that "it is sometimes said that Clio the Muse is dead and that history is no longer written as literature." They should be reminded that Laslett quickly adds: "Certainly the imaginative reconstruction of a former society can only foster an interest in its people as people." And that, after all, is the goal of social history.

III

Here is a guide to further reading in social history. It is intentionally brief and generally confined to works in English. Readers will find literally hundreds of other references in the notes of the individual essays.

1. Historiography

ARTICLES

J. H. Hexter, "A New Framework for Social History," in *Reappraisals in History* (Evanston: Northwestern University Press, 1961).

Eric J. Hobsbawm, "From Social History to the History of Society," *Historical Studies Today* (*Daedalus*, Winter 1971).

"New Ways in History," *Times Literary Supplement* (London), 7 April, 28 July, and 8 September 1966.

Harold J. Perkin, "Social History," in H. P. R. Finberg, ed., *Approaches to History* (London: Routledge and K. Paul, 1962).

Peter N. Stearns, "Some Comments on Social History" and Werner Conze, "Social History," *Journal of Social History*, vol. 1, no. 1 (1967).

Charles Tilly, "Clio and Minerva," in J. C. McKinney and E. A.

Tiryakian, eds., *Theoretical Sociology: Perspectives and Developments* (New York: Appleton-Century-Crofts, 1970).

BOOKS

Martin Ballard, ed., *New Movements in the Study and Teaching of History* (Bloomington, Ind. and London: University of Indiana Press, 1970).

Fernand Braudel, *Écrits sur l'histoire* (Paris: Flammarion, 1969).

Paul Conkin and Roland N. Stromberg, *The Heritage and Challenge of History* (New York and Toronto: Dodd, Mead and Co., 1971).

J. H. Hexter, *The History Primer* (New York: Basic Books, 1971).

John Higham, Leonard Krieger and Felix Gilbert, *History* (Princeton, N.J.: Princeton University Press, 1965).

David Landes and Charles Tilly, eds., *History as a Social Science* (New York: Prentice-Hall, Inc., 1971).

L'histoire sociale: sources et methodes (Paris: Presses Universitaires de France, 1967).

Walter Laquer and George Mosse, eds., *The New History: Trends in Historical Research and Writing Since World War II* (New York: Harper & Row, 1966).

Seymour Martin Lipset and Richard Hofstadter, eds., *Sociology and History: Methods* (New York: Basic Books, 1968).

Robert A. Nisbet, *Social Change and History: Aspects of the Western Theory of Development* (New York: Oxford University Press, 1969).

2. *Journals Concerned with Social History*

Annales, Économies, Sociétés, Civilisations (Paris)
Comparative Studies in Society and History
History and Theory
International Review of Social History (Amsterdam)
Journal of Economic History
Journal of Interdisciplinary Studies
Journal of Social History
Le Mouvement Social (Paris)
Past and Present (Oxford)
Revue d'histoire économique et sociale (Paris)
Societas

3. *Select List of Important Works*

Philippe Aries, *Centuries of Childhood: A Social History of Family Life* (New York: Vintage Books, 1962).

J. A. Banks, *Prosperity and Parenthood: A Study of Family Planning*

Among the Victorian Middle Classes (London: Routledge and K. Paul, 1954).

Marc Bloch, *Feudal Society* (Chicago: University of Chicago Press, 1961).

Fernand Braudel and Ernest Labrousse, eds., *Histoire économique et sociale de la France, 1660–1789* (Paris: Presses Universitaires de France, 1970).

Richard Cobb, *The Police and the People: French Popular Protest, 1789–1820* (Oxford: Clarendon Press, 1970).

Alfred Cobban, *The Social Interpretation of the French Revolution* (Cambridge: Cambridge University Press, 1965).

Adeline Daumard, *Les bourgeois de Paris au XIXᵉ siècle* (Paris: Flammarion, 1970).

Georges Dupeux, *Aspects de l'histoire sociale et politique du Loir-et-Cher, 1848–1914* (Paris: Mouton, 1962).

J. F. C. Harrison, *The Early Victorians, 1832–1851* (New York: Praeger Publishers, 1971).

Patrice L-R Higonnet, *Pont-de-Monvert: Social Structure and Politics in a French Village, 1700–1914* (Cambridge, Mass.: Harvard University Press, 1971).

Eric J. Hobsbawm, *Industry and Empire: The Making of Modern English Society, 1750 to the Present Day* (New York: Pantheon Books, 1968).

————. *Primitive Rebels: Studies of Archaic Social Movements in the 19th and 20th Centuries* (New York: W. W. Norton & Co., 1965).

Eric J. Hobsbawm and George Rudé, *Captain Swing: A Social History of the Great English Agricultural Uprising of 1830* (New York: Pantheon Books, 1968).

Peter Laslett, *The World We Have Lost: England Before the Industrial Age* (New York: Charles Scribner's Sons, 1965).

Emmanuel Le Roy Ladurie, *Les Paysans de Languedoc* (Paris: Flammarion, 1969).

John McManners, *The French Revolution and the Church* (New York: Harper & Row, 1969).

Arthur Marwick, *Britain in the Century of Total War: War, Peace and Social Change, 1900–1967* (Boston and Toronto: Little, Brown and Co., 1968).

Harold Perkin, *The Origins of Modern English Society, 1780–1880* (Toronto: University of Toronto Press, 1969).

George Rudé, *The Crowd in the French Revolution* (Oxford: Clarendon Press, 1959).

————. *The Crowd in History, 1730–1848* (New York: John Wiley & Sons, 1964).

Albert Soboul, *The Parisian Sans-Culottes and the French Revolution*
(Oxford: Clarendon Press, 1964).

Peter Stearns, *European Society in Upheaval: Social History Since
1800* (New York: The Macmillan Co., 1967).

Lawrence Stone, *The Crisis of the English Aristocracy, 1558–1641*
(Oxford: Clarendon Press, 1965).

Neil Smelser, *Social Change in the Industrial Revolution* (Chicago:
University of Chicago Press, 1959).

Charles Tilly, *The Vendée* (Cambridge, Mass.: Harvard University
Press, 1964).

Stephan Thernstrom and Richard Sennett, eds., *Nineteenth-Century
Cities* (New Haven: Yale University Press, 1969).

E. P. Thompson, *The Making of the English Working Class* (New
York: Vintage Books, 1966).

Hans-Ulrich Wehler, ed., *Moderne deutsche sozialgeschichte* (Cologne
and Berlin: Kiepenhauer and Witsch, 1966).

E. A. Wrigley, *Industrial Growth and Population Change* (Cambridge:
Cambridge University Press, 1962).

MODERN
EUROPEAN
SOCIAL
HISTORY

I. POLITICAL AND SOCIAL ELITES

Elites are the backbone of history. A biography of the British statesman Disraeli, a study of the German General Staff, or a history of court life under the emperor Napoleon share an implicit interest in those powerful individuals and groups who dominate the life of a particular society. At the same time as such traditional (and often important) work continues, a common explicit concern for the study of elites has resulted in the construction of methodological and conceptual bridges between history and other social science disciplines. The political scientist interested in discovering who governs in the local and national community or the sociologist seeking to learn how power and authority are translated into social action have much to tell the historian, who has a great deal to say in return.

Social theorists of the period from Gaetano Mosca's The Ruling Class *(1896) to C. Wright Mills'* The Power Elite *(1956) and beyond have convincingly demonstrated that elites have not disappeared, as once predicted, but continue to play an important role in the operation of an industrial-democratic society. To be sure, their authority no longer rests as it once did on noble birth or the ownership of landed estates. There are new prerequisites for elite status in modern society, and most current work on the subject has sought to explain how leaders are recruited and wield power today. The questions of the social historian take another direction.*

The central task confronting those interested in the role of elites in nineteenth-century European history is to explain why certain social groups retained or gained status, power, and authority at the same time that others lost or failed to gain them during the transition from the traditional world of the eighteenth century to the modern one of the twentieth century. The three essays in this section differ widely in their sources, methodology, and range of inquiry. Each, however, addresses itself to the same difficult question.

James J. Sheehan's "Conflict and Cohesion among German Elites in the Nineteenth Century" examines the reasons that the landed nobility was not destroyed by the twin revolutionary forces of industrialization and liberalism, but instead retained much of its political and social influence until the eve of war in 1914. Focusing on the state institutions of the bureaucracy and the military, Sheehan describes how the German nobility was able to transfer its own values to the wealthy middle class (the Bürgertum*) with which it otherwise would have had to contend for real power. Readers*

1

should note how Sheehan, using Max Weber's model of social stratification, explains the fusion of premodern and modern elites into what he calls "the conservative coalition," united by the "threat of social and political demo-cratization to the entire system of privilege, property, and power. . . ."

T. W. Heyck's "British Radicals and Radicalism, 1874–1895: A Social Analysis" suggests some important ways in which politics can be studied as an aspect of social history. Since Radicals were members of a social move-ment that flourished within the Liberal party, Heyck has used a special computer program and a statistical analysis of voting in the House of Com-mons to identify their leaders and tell us about their geographic, economic, religious, and educational background. Building upon this information, he first studies the structure and organization of Radicalism on the local and national levels and then examines its ideology and program, the social ideals supported by the members of the movement. Heyck's purpose is to explain why the supposedly irresistible force of British politics collapsed on the road to power. He finds his answer in the fact that Radicalism, the sublimation of middle-class interests into a social movement, was unable to transform its basic character in order to meet the challenge of the working-class Labor party.

Judson Mather's "The Assumptionist Response to Secularization, 1870–1900" describes how a militantly conservative order of the Roman Catholic Church used a modern medium to deliver its reactionary message. Mather repeatedly emphasizes the Assumptionists' remarkable ability to combine the old with the new, an intransigent theological position with social and politi-cal flexibility; their popular newspaper, La Croix, *he points out, "used politics for its own purpose." The key to the essay lies in Mather's subtle argument that what he calls* La Croix's *"cultic outlook" reflected a concern with the social impact of modernization, which also preoccupied early sociol-ogists such as Emile Durkheim. The Assumptionists struck a sensitive chord in French society, he concludes, because "they encapsulated modernization in a form that Catholics could understand and handle with some confidence."*

Sheehan, Heyck, and Mather have studied three different types of elites in three separate nations. What binds their work together is the theme of adaptability, the success or failure of a social group in imparting its own values to others in a rapidly changing world. The adoption of aristocratic values by the German Bürgertum, *the Radicals' inability to retain the alle-giance of the British worker, and the Assumptionists' influence on sectors of both the Catholic bourgeois and working classes suggest some partial answers to the question of why particular elites gained or retained, lost or failed to gain status, power, and authority during the nineteenth century.*

CONFLICT AND COHESION AMONG GERMAN ELITES IN THE NINETEENTH CENTURY

James J. Sheehan

This essay seeks to provide a rough sketch of the changing character and relationships of certain elites in nineteenth-century Germany.[1] In order to deal with some very complex issues as concisely as possible, I have had to limit the focus in two important ways: first, I have not tried to confront Germany's regional diversity, but rather I have emphasized Prussian developments in the period before national unification and Prussia together with the Reich after 1871; second, I have concentrated on the landed aristocracy, the bureaucracy, and the army, and on the relationships of these institutions to propertied and educated elites. Any endeavor to include an account of other institutions such as political parties, local government, universities, and business enterprises would have raised more analytical and evidential problems than could be handled in one historian's lifetime, let alone in one brief essay.[2]

Before we begin to consider the historical dimensions of our problem, it may be useful to recall the distinctions about social stratification offered by Max Weber.[3] There are, Weber maintained, three distinct hierarchies in the modern social system: first, there is an economic hierarchy, which is determined by the relationship of individuals to the market and defines what Weber called "class"; second, there is a prestige hierarchy, which is based on the possession of social power and defines status; third, there is a political hierarchy, which is based on the possession of power.

In the premodern era, which in German central Europe lasted until the second half of the seventeenth century, these three hierarchies tended to coincide, especially at their upper levels. The nobility possessed the most important economic resource, the land, and also held a near monopoly on prestige and power. In fact, as Otto Brunner and others have pointed out, premodern political and social concepts do not clearly distinguish between economic, social, and political power.[4] In what Brunner has called the world of *Herrschaft,* the key authority relationship was that between the lord *(Herr)* and his dependents, a relationship that was based on a fusion of the lord's mastery over the means of production, his unchallenged role as social leader, and his preeminence in the political system. In this social setting, the

James J. Sheehan received his Ph.D. from the University of California at Berkeley, and is now teaching at Northwestern University.

state as an exclusively political institution did not exist, nor did a market economy based exclusively on economic factors.

Brunner's image of the world of *Herrschaft* is, of course, an ideal type. In practice, economic, social, and political power were never entirely fused. But they were closely linked, and when in the course of the eighteenth century men began to sense that they were drifting apart, the proper relationship between wealth, status, and power became a central theme in German social thought and literature.[5] By the first decades of the nineteenth century it had become conventional for the defenders of the old aristocracy to lament the passing of wealth and power into the hands of baseborn individuals who were ill prepared to lead society. These laments were answered by those who regarded the nobility's residual privileges as anachronisms and called for the assumption of power and status by men who represented the "productive forces" in social and economic life.

During the middle decades of the nineteenth century, many of those who identified with the forces of "progress" believed that a new synthesis of class, status, and power was emerging. These men were confident that economic growth and social progress were inexorably intertwined. For them, the spread of cities, the modernization of the economy, and the increasing level of education would provide the basis for a new economic, social, and political elite. As the industrialist Friedrich Harkort put it in the 1840s: "The locomotive is the hearse which will carry absolutism and feudalism to the graveyard."[6]

The obituary proved premature. By the end of the nineteenth century, Germany had locomotives aplenty, indeed the German economy was the most advanced in Europe, but there had not been congruent changes in a number of important social and political institutions. Premodern social groups continued to occupy key positions in the political system and their values continued to flourish. The result was that in a number of German institutions there was a mixture of modern and premodern groups and values. We can now follow the development of this situation among German elites, where, in Robert Michels' concise phrase, "we find less a replacement of the old ruling groups by new groups coming to power than an amalgam and fusion of the two."[7]

I

When Harkort spoke of the demise of "feudalism," he had in mind the social and political power of the landed nobility. It seemed to him, and to many of his contemporaries, that just as aristocrats had been the chief beneficiaries of traditional social institutions, so they would be the chief casualties when these institutions gave way to an urban, industrial world. Indeed, an observer in the 1840s could not overlook the important ways in which the power of the aristocracy had declined; the expanding institutions of the state had cut into the nobility's control over local institutions, while the growth of commerce and industry had threatened both the economic position of many estate-owners and their unchallenged monopoly of social status.[8] In retrospect we can see that the decline of the aristocracy was neither as complete nor as irreversible as many hoped or feared in the middle of the century. To be sure, many nobles did collapse in the face of change, lost their ancestral homes, and slipped into the shadowy world of the declassé. Others maintained their social standing by accepting the dependent status of a landless bureaucrat or officer. But the aristocracy as a privileged and powerful group in German society did not disappear. Many nobles were able to acclimate themselves to the new world and bend its forces to their will. For these men, who could augment the residual privileges of their caste with an understanding of new techniques of political and economic exploitation, the path to power was broad and the rewards great. The history of the landed nobility east of the Elbe river, that group conventionally called the "Junkers," provided the most striking example of challenge and response in the German aristocratic community.[9]

Until the second half of the seventeenth century, the Junkers enjoyed that economic, social, and political preeminence that belonged to the landed elites in the world of *Herrschaft*. They ruled their peasants with most of the powers of a sovereign, they staffed the diffuse organs of local administration, and they controlled the *Stände,* corporate representative institutions that limited the financial autonomy of the ruling Hohenzollern. Beginning in the 1640s, the Junkers' position began to be challenged from two directions. First, the Hohenzollern rulers gradually developed administrative and military institutions that freed them from the fetters imposed by the *Stände* and created independent centers of political power. Second, in the course of the eighteenth century, economic pressures on the estate-owners drove many nobles off the land. Although until 1807 it was impossible for a commoner to own an estate legally, by the end of the eighteenth century the relentless logic of the market had seriously eroded the economic position and social power of many old families.[10]

During the opening decades of the nineteenth century, pressures from both the state and the market increased. During the reform era (1806–1819), some of the most important legal foundations of noble privileges were removed by progressive bureaucrats eager to expand their own power and modernize Prussian society. At the same time, an increasingly fluid economic situation increased the dislocation of the aristocratic estate owners. In 1847, for example, commoners owned 1,100 estates in Silesia, while aristocrats owned 1,856.[11] Nevertheless, despite the erosion of their privileges, despite the growing social heterogeneity of the estate-owning class, despite the dangers of political heterodoxy, the Junkers managed to survive as a self-conscious social group whose power and prestige in German society was in no way proportionate to its size, collective talents, or relative economic importance.

In the next two sections of this essay we will consider in some detail how the evolution of the state's bureaucratic and military institutions at first threatened, but eventually came to reinforce the Junkers' position in the state and society. For the moment it is sufficient to call attention to one general feature of the Junkers' relationship to the state that influenced their ability to accommodate themselves to the challenges they faced. As the state evolved in Prussia, it reduced the political autonomy of the Junkers on both the national and local levels, but it also provided them with new avenues to power and influence. In the course of the eighteenth century, many Junkers made their careers in the bureaucracy, and it became customary for most of them to spend at least a brief period in military service. These experiences gave them access to new forms of political power denied to those aristocratic groups that remained outside of the nexus of state institutions. Moreover, state service may have instilled in the Junkers a certain respect for efficiency, a kind of "rationality" that was often so conspicuously absent among aristocratic groups who lived in idle but diminishing grandeur or became ceremonial appendages to a princely court. In the long run therefore, the growth of the Prussian state gave the Junkers opportunities and a taste for power that remained among their most prominent characteristics as a social group.

The same combinations of short-run danger and long-run opportunity obtained in the Junkers' relationship to the economic market. To understand this relationship we must keep in mind that the income the Junkers derived from their estates was not in the form of rents but was rather the profit they earned as agricultural entrepreneurs.[12] This gave them a direct and powerful relationship to their peasant dependents, and it also involved them directly in the struggle to defend their economic self-interest. In the second half of the nineteenth century the Junkers became the chief spokesmen for agrarian interests in Germany; they were able to identify themselves and their values with the good of German agriculture as a whole. This process helped the Junkers to absorb the "new men" who bought estates and to make them part of a group with a strong sense of collective purpose and self-interest, a group whose tone and direction was set by the representatives of the Junker class. The result was a new social group, composed of old families and recent arrivals, of nobles and commoners, but a group whose political uniformity represented the persistence of old values in the face of growing social heterogeneity.[13]

The Junkers' survival, therefore, depended on their ability to deflect the impact of both economic and political challenges to their position. By becoming the spokesmen for German agriculture, they were able to turn the economic conflicts of the late nineteenth century to their advantage. And by becoming part of the expanding state institutions, they were able to attenuate, or at least to delay, the erosion of the substance of their political power. We can now follow this latter theme more closely by turning to the growth of administrative institutions in Prussia and their highly complex relationship to the landed elite.

II

As we have seen, the growth of a bureaucratic apparatus in Prussia can be traced to the mid-seventeenth century when a series of energetic Hohenzollerns, beginning with the so-called Great Elector, Frederick William (1640–1688), began to build a powerful set of central administrative institutions. These institutions were meant to help the ruler extract resources (mainly human and financial support for the army) from his territory and to enable him to employ these resources without interference from the landed nobility. Princely ambitions for power and independence conditioned the character of the emerging bureaucracy: the ruler's desire for efficiency led him to consider an official's ability and performance as well as his lineage for recruitment and promotion; similarly, the ruler's desire for independence often led him to encourage the ambitions of able commoners, who tended to be more responsive to the royal will than the less dependent nobility.[14]

From the first, therefore, the bureaucracy was directed against the landed aristocracy's autonomy and traditional authority. Especially in the century between the reign of the Great Elector and that of Frederick II ("the Great," 1740–1786) clashes between the nobility and the central power were frequent and often bitter. However, the relationship was never one of unremitting hostility. The enmity between monarch and noble was always qualified by the knowledge that they belonged to the same social world and that neither could destroy the other and survive. Moreover, aristocratic and bureaucratic institutions tended to overlap and coexist. Prominent noblemen often held high administrative posts, while successful commoners in the bureaucracy were frequently ennobled and absorbed into the aristocracy. The mixed character of the administrative elite is suggested by the term *Amtsaristokratie,* which came to be used to refer to the leaders of the bureaucracy. This group was defined both by office *(Amt)* and by high social status; it embodied both bureaucratic and aristocratic values, and it was recruited and judged according to a blend of ascriptive and achievement standards.[15]

On the local level, the overlapping of bureaucratic and aristocratic institutions was even more apparent. The Hohenzollerns were always more interested in securing their own freedom of action at the head of the state than in interfering with the nobles' domination over their dependents. Even during the reign of the Great Elector, therefore, nobility and prince forged a fragile but significant compromise by which noble acquiescence in princely ambitions was exchanged for the central government's support for the persistence of the nobles' control over the peasantry.[16] The institutional expression of this arrangement became the office of *Landrat,* the chief administrative officer in rural Prussia, who was at once an agent of the state and a part of the local aristocratic establishment.[17] Until the end of the Prussian monarchy in 1918, the *Landrat* served as a boundary figure between the central government and the local interests of the nobility. His appointment was never simply a bureaucratic decision, as this account of the *Landrat*'s role in Silesia around 1900 makes clear:

The selection of a Landrat *involved many considerations in addition to personal ability: political views, connections in his district, and family ties to influential people who could facilitate and enrich the fulfillment of his duties but also could limit his absolutely necessary freedom of action.*[18]

The final phrase is worth noting because it hints at the tension inherent in the *Landrat*'s role; appointed by the state, but tied to the local elite, he could face some difficult choices when the interests of these two forces came into conflict. This tension continued to emerge again and again through the life of the Prussian state.[19]

The role conflict built into the *Landrat*'s position was felt to some extent by other eighteenth-century bureaucrats whose function as instruments of the royal will did not always coincide with their interests and loyalties as members of the aristocracy. This problem was complicated during the second half of the eighteenth century when bureaucrats began to develop a sense of institutional self-esteem and self-interest that transcended their earlier self-image as agents of the king. During this period officials gradually came to regard themselves as "state servants" instead of "royal servants," a shift in terminology that reflected their conviction that they were the proper guardians of the public interest.[20] In the reigns of the weak kings who followed Frederick II, the bureaucracy increased its autonomy from its royal master and began to function more and more as an independent center of political power.

Many of the same men who began to view the bureaucracy as the proper center of political power also became convinced that the administration should play an active role in the modernization of Prussian politics and society. These officials became the advocates of a "revolution from above," which was of great significance for the history of modern Germany.[21] From the outset, there was a latent ambivalence in the work of these bureaucratic reformers. On the one hand, they wanted to release "the inexhaustible power that slumbers unused and undeveloped in the nation"[22]; but on the other hand, their own position depended on the existence of an essentially authoritarian system of bureaucratic control. This ambivalence shaped the experience of modernization in Prussia, a process that combined the loosening of traditional inhibitions of economic growth and social mobility with the tightening of bureaucratic control over political power.

The connection between reform and bureaucratic power was apparent in the Prussian Legal Code, which was formulated under the influence of progressive officials during the last decades of the eighteenth century,[23] and it remained a prominent feature of the political, social, and economic changes introduced after 1806, when the defeat of Prussia by Napoleon gave reform-minded officials an opportunity to dominate the Prussian adminis-tration. Taken together, these reforms made some significant steps towards economic and social emancipation, but they also bolstered the power and independence of the bureaucratic apparatus.[24]

During the era of reform the conflict between the leading reformers in the bureaucracy and the majority of landed aristocrats once again reached crisis proportions. The Junkers objected to the social and economic eman-cipation being pushed by the reformers and to the steps being taken to in-crease the bureaucracy's political power. It was with considerable relief, therefore, that the aristocracy viewed the waning of the reform impulse that followed the defeat of Napoleon in 1815. Some of the high-ranking reformers were forced from office, while the influence of men with ties to the landed nobility increased within the administration.[25] However, despite the name conventionally given to the era following 1815, these years did not see a "restoration" of prereform institutions. Bureaucratic power was not significantly weakened, nor were the social and economic reforms un-done. There was, however, a new set of tensions built into the administra-tion by a continuing conflict over reform. After 1815 the conflicts already apparent within the administration—between loyalty to the state and to the nobility, between obedience to the king and institutional self-interest— were overlaid by conflicts between those who wanted to continue the "rev-olution from above" and those who saw the bureaucracy as a dike against the further spread of economic change, social dislocation, and secular cul-ture into Prussia.[26]

This conflict within the bureaucracy was reflected in the extremely ambiguous relationship between the state and society, which was one of the central themes in the period 1815–1848. In some respects, the state played a clearly repressive role, censoring news, inhibiting political organization, and interfering in economic and social life. But in other ways the state was a source of progress and enlightenment; bureaucrats encouraged the growth of schools, steered government investment towards productive enterprises, built highways and railroads, and so on. This ambiguity helps to explain why the state was attacked from both the left and right before 1848, when Junkers like the young Bismarck viewed the state as too liberal and lib-erals like the Rhenish businessman David Hansemann viewed it as too reac-tionary. In a sense, both were right, because in the period following the great reforms both tendencies coexisted within the administrative establish-ment.[27]

The revolution of 1848 significantly changed both the relationship between the state and society and the alignment of forces within the bu-reaucracy itself. In the first place, the outbreak of revolution greatly strengthened the hands of those officials who had long maintained that to sponsor social and economic change was to undermine political stability. Second, the political movements and parliamentary institutions that began in 1848 provided a new set of competitors for the bureaucracy and thereby an impetus for greater political conformity within it. Finally, leading bureaucrats were deeply shaken by the degree to which men from their own institution had joined opposition movements during the revolution. Taken together, these developments convinced officials that the relative tolerance of political diversity within the bureaucracy might have been possible when political authority of officials had been unchallenged, but that such tolerance was a luxury they could not afford in the turbulent political world born in 1848.[28]

Beginning in the 1850s, therefore, the pressures for political conformity within the bureaucracy increased significantly. These pressures did not bring about a sudden destruction of the progressive impulse within the administration; but this impulse was quickly blunted, and there was a clear shift of the initiative into the hands of the more conservative elements. Fewer and fewer officials now regarded the administration as a quasi-parliament in which a variety of opinions could be expressed and synthesized, nor was there much talk of the need for "intellectual freedom in order to create what is needed" for the state.[29] Instead, the primary task of the official was now seen as the loyal and unquestioning defense of the status quo.

The struggle against independence and progressive views in the bureaucracy was intensified when Otto von Bismarck became Minister President of Prussia in 1862. Bismarck took vigorous action against those officials who joined the liberal opposition during the constitutional conflict in the 1860s.[30] After national unification in 1871, he moved against those men who seemed to endanger his own personal authority as well as against those who did not fit into the emerging conservative coalition he was attempting to create.[31] Even some of his admirers regretted the changes in the character of the administration that resulted from Bismarck's ruthless demands for obedience:

The domination of this Jupiter has meant that independence increasingly disappears. Every day men assume the highest offices who are undoubtedly efficient, but from whom no one expects an independent opinion or action. Rather, these men belong to the most subserviently obedient cohorts of Prince Bismarck.[32]

By the time Bismarck was forced from office in 1890, therefore, the Prussian and the imperial bureaucracies had become obedient but largely directionless institutions. His successors could not match his mastery of the administration, nor could they provide it with energy and direction. By 1914, the bureaucracy of both Prussia and the Reich was governed by a persistent inertia, a lack of positive goals, and a tendency to break down into conflicting departments each with its own particular interests and orientation.[33] These structural weaknesses of the administration inhibited the government's ability to respond to the needs of a rapidly growing industrial society. At the lower levels of the administration, honesty, a relatively high degree of efficiency, and adequate technical skills helped to compensate for the failures in the upper ranks, but these virtues could at best postpone a confrontation with the main problems of German society.

It is important to emphasize that the weaknesses of the bureaucracy during the imperial era came less from individual failings than from institutional training and recruitment policies that aimed more at finding reliable defenders of the established order than at finding men who might successfully guide a complex society. The training of politically important bureaucrats, for example, was meant to insure that only conservatively oriented men could gain access to significant positions of power. The content of an official's education put emphasis on legal studies, which had a predominantly conservative cast in German universities. This was reinforced by the conservative ideology of the university community, as well as by the prevailing values in the student fraternities, which played a central role in the social and professional life of many bureaucrats.[34]

Even more explicitly than the form of training, modes of recruitment were designed to avoid both social and political heterodoxy. In the face of a steadily expanding state apparatus and an increasingly insistent need for technically competent personnel, the leaders of the bureaucracy after 1870 could not avoid recruiting from a wide range of social groups. Nevertheless, there was a concerted effort made to keep the most important positions in the hands of "reliable" individuals from establishment backgrounds. In view of the overall growth of the bureaucracy in the course of the nineteenth century, this effort at frustrating the bureaucratic "tendency towards leveling" was surprisingly successful.[35] The recruiting mechanism for leading positions screened out men with inferior social credentials or questionable political views since after candidates had passed the necessary examinations they could still be rejected by the responsible district governor, or *Regierungspräsident,* if he felt that the candidates did not fit in. Otto Hintze, who was not one to dwell on the bureaucracy's shortcomings, pointed out that this system opened the way for personal as well as political prejudices. In fact, it formalized what Max Weber called a system of "unofficial patronage," by which family ties, personal influence, fraternity membership, and a reserve officers' commission influenced appointment and promotion.[36] The results of this system are made clear if we consider the social composition of the upper ranks of the administration, the majority of whom came from social groups traditionally tied to the political and social order. In 1910, for example, 75 percent of the leading officials in Prussia were the sons of army officers, landowners, or other officials. Equally apparent is the tendency to maintain the identification of ascriptive status and political power. The number of titled individuals was disproportionately high in the upper ranks of the administration, a disproportion that suggests the degree to which a *von* before one's name could help to level the climb up the ladder of success. Indeed it is remarkable that the percentage of nobles among district and provincial governors declined less than 10 percent in the century before 1914 despite the transformation of German society that occurred in that period.[37]

Although, as already mentioned, the tensions between the bureaucracy and the landed nobility were by no means totally dissolved in the late nineteenth century, the cooperation between these two elites was tightened by the common danger posed by forces for social and political democratization. The careful nurturing of conservative ideology within the administration and the continued association of rank and aristocratic title tended to buttress the nobility's position, as well as to block the way for political reform. "How would it be possible for us to have a liberal government," asked one official in 1910, "We are caught in an iron net of conservative administration and local government (*Selbstverwaltung*)."[38]

III

Like the bureaucracy, the Prussian army originated as part of the Hohenzollerns' efforts to widen the circle of their own power over Prussian society.[39] After the middle of the seventeenth century, the army played a key role in the process of state building, absorbed a large part of the state's income, and to a degree shaped the civil administration. Until about 1700, the army was an instrument of the central power. In the early eighteenth century, however, two developments turned the army into a key institution for the Prussian social system. First, during the reign of King Frederick William I (1713–1740) the officer corps began to be recruited largely from the Prussian nobility since the monarch was convinced that military service would inculcate obedience to the state and sovereign. By the middle of the century a rather large percentage of the landed nobility spent some time in the officer corps, where their loyalty to the king as feudal overlord was reshaped into the obedience owed by an officer to his commander-in-chief. Second, the introduction of the so-called Canton System greatly increased the army's role in the life of the Prussian peasantry. By this system, rural Prussia was divided into cantons, which were held responsible for the recruitment and maintenance of a certain number of troops. So that a shortage of agricultural labor would be avoided, eligible peasants spent part of the year on active duty and then returned home to take part in planting and harvesting the crops. The local military authority controlled not only those in military service, but also aspects of social and economic life in the canton. Since the military authorities were often estate-owners or the relatives of estate-owners, this system reinforced the obedience of the peasant for his lord with the obedience of the soldier for his military superior. In effect, therefore, during the first half of the eighteenth century, both the relationship between monarch and aristocracy and the relationship between aristocracy and peasantry tended to take on a military cast.[40]

During the reign of Frederick II the domination of the officer corps by the aristocracy was firmly established. In the 1780s, at least 90 percent of the corps had titles; commoners were usually relegated to unfashionable branches that required some kind of technical training.[41] Unfortunately, hereditary privileges and family connections are usually not the best criteria for selecting military leaders. After Frederick's death the Prussian military establishment became ossified and a little senile, combining ineptness and overconfidence in disastrous proportion. These frailties were revealed with painful clarity on the battlefield of Jena in 1806, when Napoleon's army reduced the Prussian forces to a disorderly and retreating mob.

In the army, as in the bureaucracy, the defeat of 1806 opened the way for a progressive minority of officers to effect reforms. In the next few years, aristocratic privilege was formally removed, educational requirements were tightened, and competence was made an important criterion for promotion.[42] However, the power of the army's traditional leadership was not broken during the era of reform. In some ways the officer corps was modernized, but aristocratic status continued to play an important role in recruitment and advancement, while premodern aristocratic ideals continued to set the tone for military life.[43]

After the middle of the nineteenth century, new pressures for modernization were generated by the need to expand the military establishment into a mass army and by the increasingly technical character of modern warfare. These demands had to be met if the army was to be an effective instrument of foreign policy. However, the army had another, equally important role to play. It had to be not only the defender of the state against foreign enemies, but also the defender of the established order against domestic unrest.[44] This duality of function meant that the army, to an even greater degree than the bureaucracy, faced the need of synthesizing operational efficiency and political reliability; it had to be able to put together modern skills and premodern values; it had to prevent social heterogeneity from generating political heterodoxy.

In their attempt to escape the dangers attendant on institutional expansion and technical modernization, the leaders of the army used many of the techniques employed by the bureaucracy for similar purposes. For example, when it became clear that the number of men required for the officer corps was simply too large to be recruited solely from the nobility, the military leadership made sure that the expansion of the corps involved only those commoners from "reliable" social and political backgrounds. The results of this policy are clear when we consider that in the 1860s, although more than half of the newly commissioned officers were commoners, 80 percent were from families whose social position as landowners, officers, and officials tied them to the old social order.[45] Even after a candidate had passed the formal requirement for a commission, he had to be elected by the officers of the regiment to which he aspired. This mechanism, the military analogue to the power of the district governor in the administration, insured that socially and politically "unacceptable" individuals were excluded. After an individual joined the corps, everything was done to insure that he conformed to the army's traditional values. Even the mildest form of political opposition was prohibited, and officers were encouraged to center their social life within the corps, lest they become infected with the dangerous ideas prevalent in the civilian world.[46]

As in the bureaucracy, the continued importance of aristocratic status in the officer corps was one result of the need for maintaining political reliability in the face of rapid social change. The Prussian nobility continued to set the tone for the corps. They dominated the "best" regiments and their values informed the semifeudal code of military honor. Moreover, although the aristocracy was no longer formally advantaged, their names appeared with increasing frequency at each step up in the military hierarchy. The data on the social composition of the corps leave no doubt that the possession of a *von* greatly facilitated professional success. Thus in 1886, 35 percent of the corps were nonnoble; in 1895, 66 percent, and in 1913, 70 percent. However, in 1866, 86 percent of those with the rank of colonel and above had titles; in 1900, 61 percent; and in 1913, 52 percent.[47] Therefore, despite a growing emphasis on technology, despite more stringent educational requirements, and despite the increasingly mixed social composition of the military elite, aristocratic status continued to be associated with high rank, and traditional social values continued to be cherished in the corps.

The social significance of the army as a bastion of aristocratic values and power was increased by the fact that the army's influence extended beyond those who served on active duty. The key institution in this was the reserve officer corps. In the reserves, as in the regular army, regimental officers controlled the selection of their colleagues. Moreover, reserve officers were subject to many of the same pressures for social and political conformity that existed in the army as a whole. The impact of these pressures after 1871 was considerable because membership in the reserves became a highly valued sign of social status, and in some professions, almost a prerequisite for a successful career. As one father advised his son in the 1890s: "To be a successful German these days, one must be a successful soldier."[48] During the imperial era, therefore, the officer corps helped to institutionalize the reconciliation of the *Bürgertum*[49] and the established order, as in the eighteenth century it had furthered the reconciliation of the landed nobility and monarchical authority.[50]

IV

In each of the elites we have discussed, the process of modernization produced a marked social heterogeneity. This was true of the Junkers, whose social diversification was caused by the subjection of estate-owning to the demands of the economic market. In the army, and to a lesser degree in the bureaucracy, the need to expand in size and technical competence opened the way for a variety of social groups. However, as we have noted, all three of these elites were at least partially successful in maintaining traditional social and political values in the face of this increasing social diversification. The prestige of the nobility and the economic interests common to all estate-owners enabled the Junkers to absorb the new arrivals. Indeed, after 1871 many of these new men played an active role in the political movements that developed to defend the privileges and powers of the landed elite. In the army and bureaucracy, carefully established modes of recruitment and well-nourished corporate ideals accomplished analogous results. We must now attempt to put this process of social fusion into its proper historical setting by examining the shift in values that occurred among the propertied and educated strata of German society during the last third of the nineteenth century.

Before considering the shift in the attitudes of the German *Bürgertum,* we must make the obvious but often forgotten point that the values of social groups do not change like soldiers on parade, suddenly and with uniformity. Throughout the imperial period, many German burghers did not participate in the process we shall describe, but remained faithful to the ideals of freedom and equality that had characterized the best of the liberal movement. Others participated, but in subtle and elusive ways that are difficult to measure and document. Still others wavered according to specific issues and changing interests. The following pages seek only to illuminate the most prominent features of a diverse social landscape, a landscape still insufficiently explored by sustained historical research.

The clearest expression of a shift in attitude among the *Bürgertum* was their reconciliation with the Prussian monarchy after the military victories of 1866 and 1871. This reconciliation involved an enthusiastic acceptance of the imperial political system and a retreat from the political ambitions articulated by the liberal movement during the middle third of the century. The changing political behavior of the *Bürgertum* was part of a broader change in values that included a basic shift in the relationship between propertied and educated commoners and the aristocracy. Among many burghers, acceptance of the imperial political system was accompanied by a desire to share in the traditional prestige of the landed nobility. Such ambitions were not new in German society, but after the formation of the Reich they became notably more widespread and intense. Rhenish manufacturers, Berlin bankers, even proud Hamburg patricians rushed to buy estates, less as an investment than as an attempt to acquire the environment within which the habits of the aristocracy might gracefully be emulated.[51] Some of these men were able to marry into noble families, usually those families in need of financial resuscitation. The more perceptive members of the government viewed this process with some satisfaction and furthered it by catering to the *Bürgertum*'s appetites for titles and honors. Bismarck, for example, came to regard ennoblement not as a reward for service, but as a political means of widening the base of the conservative coalition in German society.[52]

The ambition to emulate and even to be absorbed into the world of the aristocracy could only be sustained by the upper stratum of the *Bürgertum*, which tended to become—in Robert Michels' words—"merely the threshold to the nobility."[53] However, we can trace the effects of this attitudinal shift in circles beyond the relatively small group that could acquire titles and estates. Thus, many who could not presume to a patent of nobility could still hope for one of the many orders granted by the monarch, which carried some patina of traditional prestige. Also, membership in a fashionable regiment, a prestigious student fraternity, or the reserve officer corps broadened the range of opportunity for men to bask in the reflected glory of the aristocratic establishment.[54] For those denied the chance to wear the king's coat as an officer or to acquire a facial scar in a dueling fraternity, there remained the vicarious satisfaction of following the affairs of the court and aristocracy in literature and periodicals. Our knowledge of this diffusion of values among the lower strata of the *Bürgertum* is very slim, although E. K. Bramsted's work on the popular magazine *Die Gartenlaube* is a suggestive beginning.[55]

The most obvious cause for the redirection of the *Bürgertum*'s sociopolitical attitudes was the effect of the unification of Germany under Prussian leadership in 1871. The victories of Bismarck's diplomacy and Moltke's army earned the admiration of many who months before had been vowing undying enmity to the reactionary regime of Junkers. The events of dramatic years of the *Reichsgründung* crystallized a sense of insecurity and uneasiness that had been part of the German *Bürgertum*'s self-image for decades, and that was deepened by the failure of the revolution of 1848 and the inconclusive course of the Prussian constitutional conflict. The achievements of the 1860s possessed such psychological power over the *Bürgertum* because these triumphs contrasted so sharply with German liberalism's lame efforts at political action. For many, this contrast induced a permanent rejection of political opposition and an unwavering allegiance to Bismarckian politics. For some, the *Reichsgründung* called into question not only the political goals of liberalism, but the social values on which these goals had rested. Herman Baumgarten, for example, drew from the events of 1866 the lesson that "it is a ruinous error . . . to believe that any competent scholar, lawyer, merchant, or official, who is interested in public affairs and who reads the newspapers carefully, has the ability to become actively involved in politics . . . ."[56]

If the triumphs of the *Reichsgründung* played on the *Bürgertum*'s sense of inferiority, the formation of the German Social Democratic party and the example of the Paris Commune deepened their fear of social unrest.[57] Once again, the events of the period 1866–1871 tended to crystallize long-term developments: the deep-seated social and cultural cleavages in German society and the *Bürgertum*'s long-standing anxiety about the threats to social order from the lower classes. By the 1870s, many burghers saw royal power and even aristocratic influence as necessary allies against the dangers of social and political democracy. For these men, the danger of radical change converted the nobility from a rival into an ally in the defense of property and order, agrarian Germany from a bastion of backwardness into a necessary source of stability, the Prussian army from an instrument of tyranny into the most reliable guarantee of domestic tranquility.[58]

The third element that helped to forge new ties between sectors of the *Bürgertum* and the conservative forces in the empire was produced by the growing sense among these groups that they shared certain common economic interests. One aspect of this was the increasing interrelationship of the state and some industrial enterprises, especially in the field of armaments, that made it economically essential for industrialists to have close and amicable ties to the bureaucratic and military establishments. Moreover, beginning with the period of economic dislocation following the depression of 1873, agricultural and industrial interests found that they shared a common need for state help in the form of tariff protection. These common interests, reinforced as they were by closer social ties and by a sense of common threat from the left, helped to provide the basis for a discontinuous and tension-filled but enormously significant alliance between heavy industry and landed wealth.[59]

These three elements—common commitment to the new Reich, sense of common peril, and awareness of mutual economic interests—helped to close the political and social gap between the old aristocracy and the *Bürgertum* and to forge a conservative coalition between the representatives of economic "progress" and those forces of "absolutism and feudalism" that Friedrich Harkort had consigned to an early extinction. The defenders of the status quo recognized that this coalition of forces provided the best defense for the imperial social and economic system. It was from this coalition that the most reliable parliamentary support for the government was to be found and it was from the social groups that composed this coalition that the leaders of the bureaucracy and army were recruited.[60]

This is not the time to give a detailed picture of how this sociopolitical alignment shaped German history between the *Reichsgründung* and the war. It is enough for our purposes to recall that in 1878–1879 Bismarck presided over its first great parliamentary manifestation in a series of moves that included the adoption of a protective tariff policy and the passage of vigorous laws against Social Democracy. During the 1880s Bismarck added an element that was to become increasingly important in the persistence of the conservative coalition, namely, support for an expansionist foreign policy. Under Bismarck's successors after 1890, economic protection, antisocialism, and imperialism continued to serve as the political focus for the cooperation of the defenders of the Reich.[61] Throughout the imperial period, in the parliaments and in other key institutions, these factors mobilized some of Germany's most vigorous and powerful social groups against meaningful reform, and in the process they facilitated the persistence of aristocratic ideals and influence well into the twentieth century.

V

In conclusion, let us return briefly to the Weberian distinction between class, status, and power with which we began. We have traced how the fusion of these hierarchies in the landed aristocracy was shattered by the growth of a bureaucratic state and the development of a modern economy. And yet a new progressive synthesis did not emerge. The modernization of Prussia did not bring to an end the forces of "feudalism and absolutism," as men like Harkort hoped and expected. Instead, Germany before 1914 was hallmarked by a pervasive institutional incongruence: the German economy was the most dynamic and innovative in Europe, but premodern elites and values continued to be important in German political and social life. The great estates east of the Elbe, the bureaucracy, and the army continued to provide institutional support for those who defended the need for a hierarchical social system and the virtues of an authoritarian polity.

The persistence of these values is even more striking when we consider that they were defended not merely by remnants of the old aristocracy, but by a fusion of the traditional nobility and significant sectors of the propertied and educated *Bürgertum*. Indeed, this fusion of old and new elites into a conservative coalition was the key element in the persistence of premodern values in the political and social systems. This coalition was able to play such a formidable role in the defense of the status quo only because the Junker landowners, bureaucrats, and officers were joined by a significant number of bankers, industrialists, and professors. Knitted together by common fears and common interests, these forces, and the institutions they dominated, formed an almost irresistible barrier to substantial social and political reform.

It would, of course, be a mistake to overestimate the cohesion of this conservative coalition and to overlook the conflicts that continued to erupt both within and among its components. In the fast-changing social and economic world of the late nineteenth and early twentieth centuries, industrialist and landowner, civilian and officer, aristocrat and burgher frequently found their interests in conflict. But these conflicts were always attenuated by the common interests and dangers we have described. The same complex of social, economic, and political forces that created the sources of conflict within the conservative coalition, also produced the common perils that kept the alliance together. The threat of social and political democratization to the entire system of privilege, property, and power always overshadowed the intramural struggles within the ranks of the privileged, the propertied, and the powerful.

On the eve of war in 1914, there were signs that this blend of conflict and cohesion was becoming unstable. Labor unrest, the growing strength of Social Democracy, and a widespread sense of political frustration combined to provide an impetus for considering new solutions to Germany's discontents. On the one hand, there were those who argued for a broad reformist coalition that would include progressive elements in the *Bürgertum* and also moderate Social Democrats. On the other hand, there were those who saw no way out of the Reich's political problems but by means of an authoritarian regime to be produced by a right-wing coup.[62] The war gave both of these groups opportunities undreamed of before 1914. By 1917 they had begun to coalesce into the moderate and right-wing movements whose long struggle for power conditioned the course and sealed the fate of Germany's democratic experiment after 1918.[63]

However, if we look back from 1914 rather than ahead into the turmoil unleashed by the war, the conservative coalition emerges as impressively adept in its struggle to contain pressures for social and political change. But we should not forget that the cost of their success was high: the alienation of lower income and status groups from the imperial system; the persistance of anachronistic groups and values in key positions of power; the loss of a creative impulse at the heart of the political apparatus; and the recurrent need to use foreign political antagonisms for domestic political purposes. The prosperous and powerful Reich of 1914 was able to defer payment of these costs, but in the decades following, a bill of great magnitude would come due.

NOTES

1. The term *elite* here refers to the ordinary-language meaning of a group at the top of the social, economic, or political hierarchies. For further information and analysis of the concept, the following books and articles can be consulted: G. D. H. Cole, *Studies in Class Structure* (London, 1955); R. Aron, "Social Structure and the Ruling Class," *British Journal of Sociology* 1 (1950):1–16 and 126–43; S. Langer, *Beyond the Ruling Class* (New York, 1963); T. Bottomore, *Elites and Society* (New York, 1965); U. Jaeggi *Die gesellschaftliche Elite* (Bern, 1969); and H. Dreitzel, *Elitebegriff und Sozialstruktur* (Stuttgart, 1962). R. Bendix and S. M. Lipset have collected some important essays on elites in *Class, Status, and Power*, 2nd ed. (New York, 1966).

2. Wolfgang Zapf has attempted to analyze the whole elite structure of twentieth-century Germany in his *Wandlungen der deutschen Elite, 1919–1961* (Munich,

1965). There are some articles on a variety of elites in *Führungsschicht und Eliteproblem, Jahrbuch der Ranke Gesellschaft,* vol. 3 (1957). A guide to statistical material on elites may be found in my article "Quantification in the Study of German Social and Political History," to be published by Yale University Press in 1972 in Val Lorwin and Jacob Price, eds., *Dimensions of the Past.*

3. There is a convenient summary of Weber's views in *From Max Weber: Essays in Sociology,* ed. H. Gerth and C. W. Mills (New York, 1958), pt. 2.

4. Brunner's concept of *Herrschaft* is given in the conclusion of his *Adeliges Landleben und europäischer Geist* (Salzburg, 1949), pp. 313–39 and in his essays collected under the title *Neue Wege zur Sozialgeschichte,* 2nd ed. (Göttingen, 1968). An astute critique of Brunner's work can be found in David M. Nicholas, "New Paths of Social History and Old Paths of Historical Romanticism. An Essay Review on the Work and Thought of Otto Brunner," *Journal of Social History* 3 (1970):277–94.

5. For an introduction to this problem, see J. Schultze, *Die Auseinandersetzung zwischen Adel und Bürgertum in den deutschen Zeitschriften der letzten drei Jahrzehnte des 18. Jahrhunderts* (Berlin, 1925) and R. Pascal, *The German Sturm und Drang* (Manchester, 1955). The impact that social conflict between the aristocracy and new social groups had on progressive theologians can be seen in the useful monograph by Alexandra Schlingensiepen-Pogge, *Das Sozialethos der lutherischen Aufklärungstheologie am Vorabend der Industriellen Revolution* (Göttingen, 1967).

6. Quoted by F. Zunkel, *Der Rheinisch-westfälische Unternehmer, 1834–1879* (Cologne and Opladen, 1962), pp. 89–90. For·some interesting remarks on the cultural impact of the railroad, see M. Riedel, "Vom Biedermeier zum Maschinenzeitalter. Zur Kulturgeschichte der ersten Eisenbahnen in Deutschland," *Archiv für Kulturgeschichte,* 43 (1961):100–23.

7. *Umschichtungen in den herrschenden Klassen nach dem Kriege* (Stuttgart, 1934), p. 39. For some stimulating ideas on the origins and implications of Germany's peculiar mixture of modern and premodern forms, see T. Veblen, *Imperial Germany and the Industrial Revolution* (New York, 1954); T. Parsons, "Democracy and Social Structure in Pre-Nazi Germany" (1942), reprinted in *Essays in Sociological Theory* (Glencoe Ill., 1954); G. Lukács, "Einige Eigentümlichkeiten der geschichtlichen Entwicklung Deutschlands," in *Die Zerstörung der Vernunft* (Neuwied, 1962), pp. 37–83; and R. Dahrendorf, *Society and Democracy in Germany* (New York, 1967).

8. For a contemporary statement of the dangers facing the aristocracy, see the quotation from von der Marwitz in F. von Oertzen, *Junker. Preussischer Adel im Jahrhundert des Liberalismus* (Berlin, 1939), p. 68. Ferdinand Toennies has a brief but incisive introduction to the problem of the nobility in "Deutscher Adel im 19. Jahrhundert," *Neue Rundschau,* 23 (1912):1041–63.

9. For an introduction to the Junkers in the eighteenth century, see the essay on Prussia by A. Goodwin in the volume he edited on *The European Nobility*

in the Eighteenth Century (London, 1953). A rather sympathetic picture of this social group can be found in W. Görlitz, *Die Junker* (Glücksburg/Ostsee, 1956). My account has been most influenced by the writings of Robert Michels and Otto Hintze, and especially Hans Rosenberg: Michels, "Zum Problem der Zeitlichen Widerstandsfähigkeit des Adels," in *Probleme der Sozialgeschichte* (Leipzig, 1914); Hintze, "Die Hohenzollern und der Adel," in *Regierung und Verwaltung, Gesammelte Abhandlungen*. vol. 3 (Göttingen, 1967) and *Die Hohenzollern und ihr Werk* (Berlin, 1916); Rosenberg, "The Rise of the Junkers in Brandenburg-Prussia, 1410–1653," *American Historical Review*, 49 (1943–44):1–22 and 228–42 and "Die Pseudodemokratisierung der Rittergutsbesitzerklasse," in Hans-Ulrich Wehler, ed. *Moderne Deutsche Sozialgeschichte* (Cologne, 1966).

10. On this point, see J. Ziekursch, *Hundert Jahre schlesischer Agrargeschichte* (Berlin, 1927) and F. Martiny, *Die Adelsfrage in Preussen vor 1806 als politisches und soziales Problem* (Stuttgart and Berlin, 1938). For the economic situation of the Junkers in the early nineteenth century, see E. Jordan, *Die Entstehung der Konservativen Partei und die preussischen Agrarverhältnisse von 1848* (Munich and Leipzig, 1914).

11. Reinhart Koselleck, *Preussen zwischen Reform und Revolution* (Stuttgart, 1967), p. 347. Johannes Ziekursch studied 355 Silesian estates and found that in the 1850s only 59 of them had been in the same family for more than 40 years. Ziekursch, *Agrargeschichte,* p. 385.

12. The classic statement on this issue is in the work of Georg Friedrich Knapp. See, for example, his *Grundherrschaft und Rittergut* (Leipzig, 1897). See also Max Weber's famous article "Capitalism and Rural Society in Germany," reprinted in Gerth and Mills, *From Max Weber,* pp. 363–85. For some useful data on the concentration of land in Prussia, see Weber's "Agrarstatische und sozialpolitische Betrachtungen zur Fideikommissfrage in Preussen," in *Gesammelte Aufsätze zur Soziologie und Sozialpolitik* (Tübingen, 1924).

13. This point is made forcefully in Rosenberg's article on "Die Pseudodemokratisierung." See also the excellent monograph by Hans-Jürgen Puhle, *Agrarische Interessenpolitik und preussischer Konservatismus im wilhelminischen Reich* (Hanover, 1967). Ursula Lindig's dissertation "Der Einfluss des Bundes der Landwirte auf die Politik des wilhelminischen Zeitalters, 1893–1914" (Hamburg, 1954) is greatly inferior to Puhle's book, but it has some useful data. The best account in English is S. Tirrell, *German Agrarian Politics After Bismarck's Fall* (New York, 1951).

14. The best introduction to the process of bureaucratic state-building in Prussia is Hans Rosenberg, *Bureaucracy, Aristocracy, Autocracy: The Prussian Experience, 1660–1815* (Cambridge, Mass., 1958). Those who know Rosenberg's profound contribution to Prussian history will recognize the extent of my debt to his work in this section and indeed throughout this essay. The classic formulation of a definition of bureaucratic authority can be found in Max Weber, *The Theory of Social and Economic Organization* (Glencoe, Ill., 1947), pp. 329 ff. Hanns Hubert Hofmann has edited a most useful collection of

essays on the emergence of the state, *Die Entstehung des modernen souveränen Staates* (Cologne and Berlin, 1967).

15. Rosenberg, *Bureaucracy,* pp. 70 ff., 107, and 139 ff.

16. Hintze, "Die Hohenzollern und der Adel," p. 39.

17. For an account of the specific development of the office in one region, see Hintze, "Der Ursprung des preussischen Landratsamts in der Mark Brandenburg," in *Gesammelte Abhandlungen,* 3:164–203.

18. Georg Michaelis, *Für Staat und Volk. Eine Lebensgeschichte* (Berlin, 1922), p. 187.

19. For a dramatic example of this conflict in the 1890s, see H. Horn, *Der Kampf um den Bau des Mittellandkanals* (Cologne and Opladen, 1964).

20. O. Hintze, "Das preussische Staatsministerium im 19. Jahrhundert," in *Gesammelte Abhandlungen,* 3:534.

21. On the "revolution from above," see Koselleck, *Preussen,* passim and also L. Krieger, *The German Idea of Freedom* (Boston, 1957), especially pp. 139 ff.

22. The phrase is from the military reformer Gneisenau, as quoted by Friedrich Meinecke, *Das Zeitalter der deutschen Erhebung* (Göttingen, 1957), p. 70.

23. The best account of the Legal Code is in Koselleck, *Preussen.* See also Hintze's essay "Preussische Reformbestrebungen vor 1806," in *Gesammelte Abhandlungen,* 3:504–29; Rosenberg, *Bureaucracy,* pp. 190 f; and two recent articles by Günter Birtsch, "Zum konstitutionellen Charakter des preussischen Allgemeinen Landrechts von 1794," *Politische Ideologien und Nationalstaatliche Ordnung (Festschrift für Theodor Schieder)* (Munich and Vienna, 1968) and "Gesetzgebung und Repräsentation im späten Absolutismus," *Historische Zeitschrift,* 208(1969):265–94.

24. There is an enormous literature on the Prussian reforms, which included fundamental changes in the legal position of serfs, structural changes in the educational system, and shifts in the legal restrictions on trade and commerce, as well as administrative and military reforms. The best introduction to what the reformers did is in E. R. Huber, *Deutsche Verfassungsgeschichte,* vol. 1 (Stuttgart, 1957). Huber is much less help in explaining the motives of the reformers and the implications of their reforms. On these problems, see Koselleck, *Preussen;* Rosenberg, *Bureaucracy,* pp. 202 ff.; E. Kehr, "Zur Genesis der preussischen Bürokratie und des Rechtsstaats," in Hans-Ulrich Wehler, ed. *Der Primat der Innenpolitik* (Berlin, 1965), pp. 31–52; and H. Heffter, *Die Deutsche Selbstverwaltung im 19.Jahrhundert* (Stuttgart, 1950).

25. See the data on the social composition of the bureaucracy in Koselleck, *Preussen,* pp. 434–35, n. 155.

26. A good example of this conflict can be seen in Thomas Nipperdey's interesting account of educational policy in early nineteenth-century Prussia, "Volksschule und Revolution im Vormärz," *Politische Ideologien und Nationalstaatliche*

Ordnung (Festschrift für Theodor Schieder) (Munich and Vienna, 1968), pp. 117–42. There are some excellent essays on this and related problems in W. Conze, ed. *Staat und Gesellschaft im deutschen Vormärz* (Stuttgart, 1962).

27. For a characteristic critique of the bureaucracy, see the memorandum written in 1840 by Hansemann and reprinted in J. Hansen, ed., *Rheinische Briefe und Akten,* new ed., vol. 1 (Osnabrück, 1967), pp. 197 ff. The ambivalent character of the state, especially in its relationship to economic development, is reflected in the debate over whether the state promoted or retarded economic growth. For the former view, see W. O. Henderson, *The State and the Industrial Revolution in Prussia* (Liverpool, 1958), and for the latter, R. Tilly, *Financial Institutions and Industrialization in the Rhineland, 1815–1870* (Madison, 1966). It seems to me that to some extent both Henderson and Tilly are correct, since government policy did impede and also encourage economic development.

28. On the Prussian bureaucracy at midcentury, see the monograph by John Gillis, *The Prussian Bureaucracy in Crisis, 1840–1860* (Stanford, 1971). For some remarks on the reasons for discontent within the bureaucratic ranks, see L. O'Boyle, "The Problem of an Excess of Educated Men in Western Europe, 1800–1850," *Journal of Modern History,* 42(1970):471–95.

29. The phrase is Leopold von Ranke's and is quoted in H. Holborn, "Der deutsche Idealismus in sozialgeschichtlicher Beleuchtung," in Hans-Ulrich Wehler, ed., *Moderne Deutsche Sozialgeschichte* (Cologne, 1966), p. 92.

30. See E. Anderson, *The Social and Political Conflict in Prussia, 1858–1864* (Lincoln, Neb., 1954) and A. Hess, *Das Parlament das Bismarck widerstrebte* (Cologne and Opladen, 1964).

31. The classic account of the conservative shift in Bismarckian Germany and its relationship to the bureaucracy is E. Kehr, "Das soziale System der Reaktion in Preussen unter dem Ministerium Puttkamer," in Hans-Ulrich Wehler, ed., *Der Primat der Innenpolitik* (Berlin, 1965), pp. 64–86. For an account of Kehr and his contribution to German historiography, see Wehler's introduction to this volume and James J. Sheehan, "The Primacy of Domestic Politics: Eckart Kehr's Essays on Modern German History," in *Central European History,* 1(1968):166–174.

32. Karl Oldenburg, *Aus Bismarcks Bundesrat. Aufzeichnungen des Mecklenburg-Schwerinschen Bundesrats-Bevollmächtigten Karl Oldenburg aus den Jahren 1878–1885* (Berlin, 1929), p. 10.

33. For some remarks on this tendency in bureaucracies in general, see G. Almond and C. B. Powell, *Comparative Politics: A Developmental Approach* (Boston, 1966), p. 156. In the German case the situation was aggravated by the problems arising from the unclear division of powers between the Prussian and the Imperial administrations. On this problem, see R. Morsey, *Die oberste Reichsverwaltung unter Bismarck, 1867–1890* (Münster, 1957) and E. Klein, "Funktion und Bedeutung des Preussischen Staatsministeriums," *Jahrbuch für die Geschichte Mittel- und Ostdeutschlands* 9/10(1961):195–261.

34. For the importance of fraternity membership in a bureaucrat's career, see Ernst von Ernsthausen, *Erinnerungen eines preussischen Beamten* (Berlin and Leipzig, 1894), pp. 32 ff. and 54 ff. and H. Holborn, ed., *Aufzeichnungen und Erinnerungen aus dem Leben des Botschafters Joseph Maria von Radowitz* (reprinted ed., Osnabrück, 1967), 1:24.

35. Max Weber argued that bureaucratic institutions produced a "tendency towards leveling" because they were forced to seek competent individuals from all sectors of society. See *Social and Economic Organization*, p. 340. For some data on the overall growth of the bureaucracy, see John Cullity, "The Growth of Governmental Employment in Germany, 1882–1950," *Zeitschrift für die gesamte Staatswissenschaft*, 123(1967):201–17.

36. See O. Hintze, *Der Beamtenstand* (*Vorträge der Gehe-Stiftung*, vol. 3) (Dresden, 1911), p. 48 and M. Weber, "Parlament und Regierung im neugeordneten Deutschland," *Gesammelte Politische Schriften* (Tübingen, 1958), p. 355. L. Schücking claimed that in 1903–05 almost 750 candidates for a bureaucratic post in Prussia were refused and that the majority of them were rejected because their backgrounds did not give sufficient guarantee of conservative views: *Die Reaktion in der inneren Verwaltung Preussens* (Berlin, 1908), p. 44.

37. On the social composition of the Prussian bureaucracy, see the figures released by the Minister of the Interior in 1910 and reprinted in W. Koch, *Volk und Staatsführung vor dem ersten Weltkriege* (Stuttgart, 1935), p. 78. The problem has been analyzed in more general terms in the following works: F. von Schulte, "Adel im deutschen Offizier- und Beamtenstand. Eine soziale Betrachtung," *Deutsche Revue*, 21(1896):181–92; N. von Preradovich, *Die Führungsschichten in Österreich und Preussen (1804–1918)* (Wiesbaden, 1955); Morsey, *Die oberste Reichsverwaltung*; J. C. G. Röhl, "Higher Civil Servants in Germany, 1890–1900," *Journal of Contemporary History*, 2(1967): 101–21; and L. Muncy, *The Junker in the Prussian Administration under William II, 1888–1914* (Providence, R.I., 1944).

38. As quoted in J. Bertram, *Die Wahlen zum deutschen Reichstag vom Jahre 1912* (Düsseldorf, 1964), p. 131.

39. As in so many problems of Prussian institutional history, the best place to begin a study of the army and Prussian society is the work of Otto Hintze. See, for example, Hintze's essay "Staatsverfassung und Heeresverfassung," *Staat und Verfassung, Gesammelte Abhandlungen*, vol. 1, 2nd ed. (Göttingen, 1962), pp. 52–83. There is a great deal of information in Curt Jany, *Geschichte der königlich-preussischen Armee*, 4 vols. (Berlin, 1928–33). Also useful is Gordon Craig, *The Politics of the Prussian Army, 1640–1945* (New York and Oxford, 1956) and the first volume of Gerhard Ritter's *Staatskunst und Kriegshandwerk* (Munich, 1954), which has recently appeared in an English translation.

40. These developments are skillfully analyzed in O. Büsch, *Militärsystem und Sozialleben im alten Preussen, 1713–1807* (Berlin, 1962).

41. Karl Demeter, *The German Officer-Corps in Society and State, 1650–1945* (New York and Washington, 1965), pp. 3 ff. This is an abridged translation of *Das Deutsche Heer und seine Offiziere*, 2nd ed. (Berlin, 1961).

42. On the military reforms, see Ritter, *Staatskunst*; Craig, *Politics of the Prussian Army*; W. O. Shanahan, *Prussian Military Reforms, 1786–1813* (New York, 1954); and P. Paret, *Yorck and the Era of Prussian Reform, 1807–1815* (Princeton, New Jersey, 1966).

43. See the data in Koselleck, *Preussen*, pp. 434–35, n. 155.

44. For an intelligent treatment of the general problem of foreign and domestic functions of armies, see A. Vagts, *A History of Militarism*, rev. ed. (n. p., 1959).

45. Demeter, *The German Officer-Corps*, pp. 20 ff. See also the following for the army in late-nineteenth-century Germany: E. Obermann, *Soldaten, Bürger, Militaristen* (Stuttgart, 1958); G. Ritter, *Staatskunst und Kriegshandwerk*, vol. 2 (Munich, 1960); F. Endres, "Soziologische Struktur und ihre entsprechende Ideologien des deutschen Offizierkorps vor dem Weltkriege," *Archiv für Sozialwissenschaft und Sozialpolitik*, 58(1927):282–319; and the essays on the army by Manfred Messerschmidt and Wilhelm Diest in *Das kaiserliche Deutschland: Politik und Gesellschaft 1870–1918* (Düsseldorf, 1970).

46. M. Kitchen, *The German Officer Corps, 1890–1914* (Oxford, 1968), pp. 115 ff.

47. Demeter, *German Officer-Corps*, pp. 22 ff. and Schulte, "Adel im deutschen Offizier- und Beamtenstand." On the value of a title, see the remark by Leopold von Ranke cited in Vagts, *Militarism*, p. 195 and B. von Hutten-Czapski, *Sechzig Jahre Politik und Gesellschaft* (Berlin, 1936), 1:146.

48. Carl Mönckeberg, ed., *Bürgermeister Mönckeberg. Eine Auswahl seiner Briefe und Aufzeichnungen* (Stuttgart, 1918), pp. 25 and 97–99.

49. I have decided to use the German term *Bürgertum* here because to substitute *bourgeois* or *middle class* is to imply a set of social similarities that do not exist. *Bürgertum* has a more traditional and somewhat more exclusive connotation than either the French or the British terms. I will use it to mean nonaristocratic groups with a comfortable income and a secure place in an economic, cultural, or governmental institution.

50. See E. Kehr, "Zur Genesis des königlich-preussischen Reserveoffiziers," in *Primat der Innenpolitik*, pp. 53–63. The works cited in Note 45 are also useful on the social significance of the army.

51. F. Zunkel, *Der Rheinisch-westfälische Unternehmer*, pp. 128 ff. and P. E. Schramm, *Hamburg, Deutschland, und die Welt* (Munich, 1943), pp. 615 ff.

52. On Bismarck's views of ennoblement, see Morsey, *Die oberste Reichsverwaltung*, p. 247. Lamar Cecil has done a statistical study of ennoblement that emphasizes the continued importance of traditional considerations such as service at court, and so on. L. Cecil, "The Creation of Nobles in Prussia, 1871–1918," *American Historical Review*, 75(1970):757–95.

53. Michels, "Zum Problem der zeitlichen Widerstandsfähigkeit des Adels," *Probleme der Sozialphilosophie* (Leipzig, 1914), p. 151. See also Werner Sombart, *Die deutsche Volkswirtschaft im neunzehnten Jahrhundert*, 2nd ed. (Berlin, 1909), p. 508.

54. Note novelist Theodor Fontane's remark on the occasion of his receiving a Hohenzollern order in 1889: "If I were a man with a social position . . . this distinction would have practically no meaning for me. But in view of the fact that in Germany, and particularly in Prussia, you count for something only if you are 'government-graded' such a medal has some real practical value: people look at you with great respect and treat you decently." Quoted by J. Remak in *The Gentle Critic: Theodor Fontane and German Politics, 1848–1898* (Syracuse, N.Y., 1964), p. 67. It was generally recognized that a title was helpful in most careers as well as in elevating one's social position. See, for example, Robert von Mohl, *Lebenserinnerungen, 1799–1875* (Stuttgart and Leipzig, 1902), 1:64.

55. E. K. Bramsted, *Aristocracy and the Middle Classes in Germany: Social Types in German Literature, 1830–1900*, rev. ed. (Chicago and London, 1964), pp. 203 ff.

56. H. Baumgarten, "Der deutsche Liberalismus: Eine Selbstkritik," *Preussische Jahrbücher*, 18(1866):472. Heinrich von Treitschke wrote about the same time that "if you watch our middle class at close range . . . you can't help seeing that as a rule only aristocrats (of birth or mind) make good statesmen." Quoted in A. Dorpalen, *Heinrich von Treitschke* (New Haven, 1957), p. 114. For a useful analysis of the impact of the *Reichsgründung* on German politics, see Karl Georg Faber, "Realpolitik als Ideologie: Die Bedeutung des Jahres 1866 für das politische Denken in Deutschland," *Historische Zeitschrift*, 203(1966): 1–45.

57. For the impact of the Commune, see J. J. Sheehan, *The Career of Lujo Brentano: A Study of Liberalism and Social Reform in Imperial Germany* (Chicago and London, 1966), pp. 46 ff., and the literature cited there.

58. For a provocative interpretation of the relationship between German socialism and society, see G. A. Ritter, *Die Arbeiterbewegung im wilhelminischen Reich* (Berlin/Dahlem, 1959).

59. The interaction of economic interests and political alignment has recently become a central issue in the historiography on the empire. Much of this new work builds on some classic accounts on political developments that had until a few years ago been on the fringes of German scholarship: E. Franz, *Der Entscheidungskampf um die wirtschaftspolitische Führung Deutschlands (1856–1867)* (Munich, 1933); E. Kehr, *Schlachtflottenbau und Parteipolitik, 1894—1901* (Berlin, 1930); and Hans Rosenberg, "Political and Social Consequences of the Great Depression in Central Europe, 1873–1896," *Economic History Review*, 12(1943):58–73. Especially noteworthy among the recent works are H. Böhme, *Deutschlands Weg zur Grossmacht* (Cologne and Berlin, 1966); Ivo Lambi, *Free Trade and Protection in Germany, 1868–1879*, Beiheft 44 *Vierteljahrsschrift für Sozial- und Wirtschaftsgeschichte* (Wiesbaden, 1963); Karl

Hardach, *Die Bedeutung wirtschaftlicher Faktoren bei der Wiedereinführung der Eisen- und Getreidezölle in Deutschland, 1879* (Berlin, 1967); H. Rosenberg, *Grosse Depression und Bismarckzeit* (Berlin, 1967); W. Steglich, "Beitrag zur Problematik des Bündnisses zwischen Junker und Bourgeoisie in Deutschland, 1870–1880," *Wissenschaftliche Zeitschrift der Humboldt Universität Berlin,* 9(1959–60):323–40; H-J. Puhle, *Agrarische Interessenpolitik;* H. Kaelble, *Industrielle Interessenpolitik in der Wilhelminischen Gesellschaft* (Berlin, 1967); D. Stegmann, *Die Erben Bismarcks. Parteien und Verbände in der Spätphase des Wilhelminischen Deutschlands* (Cologne and Berlin, 1970). For additional citations and an excellent summary, see H-J. Puhle, "Parlament, Parteien und Interessenverbände, 1890–1914," in M. Stürmer, ed., *Das Kaiserliche Deutschland* (Düsseldorf, 1970), pp. 340–77.

60. For two striking examples of this process, see the material on the Hansemann family in Böhme, *Deutschlands Weg,* pp. 203, 426, and 429, and the career of Johannes Miquel described by Hans Herzfeld in *Johannes von Miquel,* 2 vols. (Detmold, 1938).

61. On the domestic uses of foreign policy, see Kehr's essays in *Primat der Innenpolitik* and *Schlachtflottenbau;* Hans-Ulrich Wehler, *Bismarck und der Imperialismus* (Cologne and Berlin, 1969); V. Berghahn, "Flottenrüstung und Machtgefüge," in Stürmer, *Das Kaiserliche Deutschland* (Düsseldorf, 1970), pp. 378–96; Stegmann, *Erben Bismarcks;* F. Fischer, *Krieg der Illusionen: Die deutsche Politik von 1911 bis 1914* (Düsseldorf, 1969); K. Wernecke, *Der Wille zur Weltgeltung* (Düsseldorf, 1970); and Pauline Anderson, *The Background of Anti-English Feeling in Germany, 1890–1902* (Washington, 1939).

62. For the political situation on the eve of the war, see Fischer, *Krieg der Illusionen;* Stegmann, *Erben Bismarcks;* Hans-Ulrich Wehler, *Krisenherde des Kaiserreiches. Studien zur deutschen Sozial- und Verfassungsgeschichte* (Göttingen, 1970); G. Schmidt, "Deutschland am Vorabend des Ersten Weltkriegs," in Stürmer, ed., *Das kaiserliche Deutschland,* pp. 397–433. For additional literature and a brief statement of the alternatives facing the Reich in 1914, see J. Sheehan, "Germany, 1890–1918: A Survey of Recent Research," *Central European History,* 1(1968):345–72.

63. On the relationship between imperial and republican politics, see G. A. Ritter, "Kontinuität und Umformung des deutschen Parteisystems, 1918–1920," in *Entstehung und Wandel der modernen Gesellschaft, Festschrift für Hans Rosenberg* (Berlin, 1970), pp. 342–84. On the formation of the radical right-wing movement during the war, see Stegmann, *Erben Bismarcks,* pp. 449 ff.; F. Fischer, *Griff nach der Weltmacht* (Düsseldorf, 1961), pp. 419–620; and G. Feldman, *Army, Industry and Labor in Germany, 1914–1918* (Princeton, 1966). On the moderates, see K. Epstein, *Matthias Erzberger and the Dilemma of German Democracy* (Princeton, 1959) and the documents in E. Matthias and R. Morsey, eds., *Der Interfraktionelle Ausschuss 1917/18,* 2 vols., (Düsseldorf, 1959).

BRITISH RADICALS AND RADICALISM, 1874–1895: A SOCIAL ANALYSIS

T. William Heyck

Radicals were the irresistible force of nineteenth-century British politics. Constitution and society seemed inexorably to move in their direction, and by the late-Victorian period they had grown in numbers and influence to the point that they threatened to dominate the political arena. After the general election of 1885, a conservative Kentish newspaper warned: "It is no longer a question between Liberal and Conservative, but between Radicals, or rather Jacobins, and Anti-Radicals. . . .[1] Yet by 1895 it was clear that the Radicals were not going to be able to seize the reins during the nineteenth century, and might not even in succeeding years. Clearly it is necessary to understand Radicalism to know the course and content of late-Victorian British politics. Unfortunately it is not as easy a task as it might first seem. When one calls to mind the very different kinds of people who made up Radicalism, the task seems just about impossible. How can one make any sense of a group that included such opposites as the atheist Charles Bradlaugh and the ardent Puritan John Bright? Or the imperialist Joseph Chamberlain and the little-Englander John Morley? Or the capitalist J. T. Brunner and the coal miner Thomas Burt? The difficulty is not in describing the political views and behavior of well-known men like these; it is rather in knowing the main stream of the movement, in explaining what was common to its members, and in analyzing the ways they organized and expressed themselves. One needs a mode of analysis that can make coherent a mass of inchoate information and give meaning to the pattern that emerges.

A number of analytical methods could be used. Perhaps the one that comes to mind first is to define modern Radicalism, then look into the late-Victorian period to find and describe those who fit the a priori definition. Unfortunately, this method is unhistorical and would no doubt miss practically all of the people who would have been regarded as Radicals in the late nineteenth century. For example, the most common modern definition of Radicalism is that Radicals are people who work for change outside the "the system"; and such a view would not include a single one of the worthies named above. One might look for an orientation of extremism, for the word

T. William Heyck received his Ph.D. from the University of Texas, and is now teaching at Northwestern University.

radical connotes getting to the root of something. This approach has the virtues of being comprehensive and of catching the missionary spirit of most radicals. It also was used by late-Victorians themselves. Gladstone, for instance, once said that Radicals were people who were in earnest.[2] But such concepts are apt to be *too* comprehensive: Gladstone himself was no Radical but he was at least as earnest as anyone else. One must be more specific. Another method, which might be called historical, would be to look to the early history of Radicalism (say, from 1760) and trace the life of the leading Radical doctrines into the 1870s and 1880s. This technique would tell us what the Radicals wanted, and give an opportunity to study their demands in relation to the changing political and social context. But it might also mislead the investigator into looking in the late-Victorian period for the wrong things. The briefest glance at the late-nineteenth-century Radicals shows that on the whole they were more democratic than the Wilkites and early parliamentary reformers, less revolutionary than the British Jacobins, and less intellectualized than the Philosophic Radicals of the 1830s. But one thing can be learned from the early history of Radicalism that is invaluable for understanding its successors: Radicalism was more than a political faction; it was a general movement against privilege in the particular forms that privilege took in the late eighteenth and early nineteenth centuries.

This generalization leads us toward a more satisfactory analysis. Many historians today are dissatisfied with political history that simply treats political phenomena as events separate from society at large. This does not mean that we should abandon political history as irrelevant, but that we should regard politics as an aspect of social history. Politics has to do with the distribution and use of power within a nation or community; therefore it is one expression of the conflict of social forces. As Samuel Hays puts it, "Political history is concerned with the conflicts among the varied goals and values which arise in society. . . ."[3] Certainly the late-Victorian Radicals are best understood as one side in the clash of values or social ideals, the landed versus the entrepreneurial, that forms the main theme of Victorian political history. They were in fact what sociologists call a social movement, or a number of people banded together to alter or supplant portions of the existing social order.[4] This is a mode of analysis that will enable us to answer some of the important questions about Radicalism: Who were its proponents? Why did they enter the movement? Who formed the Radical elite? How did Radicals relate to each other? What was the structure of the movement? What did the supporters want, and how did they justify it? What was their view of the good society?

I. Personnel

The first problem is to discover who the late-Victorian Radicals were. It is easy to name a few of the well-known Radicals, but it is much more difficult to uncover the general membership of such a large and varied movement. The records are at once voluminous and spotty. There is, however, one important and accessible path to learning about Radicalism: a study of the Radical Members of Parliament, the elite of the movement. Through knowing about them, one can understand the social composition of the leadership, get a feel for what the most influential Radicals were like, and then infer certain things about the movement as a whole. Unfortunately, even the task of identifying the parliamentary Radicals is not easy. The method used here has two stages. First, from contemporary sources were compiled the names of men who were called, or called themselves, Radicals. This simple approach has the advantage of taking the past at its own word; furthermore, enough information is available to list most M.P.s who were commonly regarded as Radicals. However, on grounds that such a compilation would likely be incomplete, a second stage involving a new kind of statistical analysis of voting in the House of Commons was used. This technique selected the divisions (that is, votes) best discriminating between M.P.s known to have been Radical and those known as other-than-Radical, then pointed out the obscure M.P.s who voted with the known Radicals on the decisive divisions. This computer method provided a list of M.P.s who effectively were Radicals. It is this group who are here considered to be Radical M.P.s.[5]

The figures gained in this two-stage procedure conform remarkably well with such contemporary estimates as exist.[6] Table I shows the number of Radical M.P.s of the late-Victorian period.

TABLE I. NUMBER OF RADICAL M.P.s, 1874–1895

	1874–80	1880–85	1886	1886–92	1892–95
Total number of Radicals sitting in each Parliament	89	130	165	159	207
Number of Radicals gaining or losing seats during each Parliament	12	15	5	34	10
Average number of Radicals sitting at any one time, rounded to the nearest five	80	120	160	145	200
Rate of increase		50%	33%	−9%	38%
Radical M.P.s as a percentage of the Liberal M.P.s	32%	34%	48%	73%	74%
Radical M.P.s as a percentage of the House of Commons	12%	18%	25%	?2%	30%

Two significant observations can be made from this table. First, with the exception of the general election of 1886, the Radicals increased their numbers in Parliament in every general election from 1874 to 1895. This accounts both for the widespread fear of Radicalism among the more conservative members of the Tory and Liberal parties, and for the eagerness with which Radicals anticipated victory over the defenders of traditional institutions, including the moderate members of the Liberal party. Especially in 1885, Radicals felt closer to gaining power than at any time in their history. Second, though it is clear that the general election of 1886, which was conducted largely over the issue of Irish Home Rule, slowed the Radical advance in the nation at large, that same election contributed to the rapid accession of Radicals to power within the Liberal party, of which they formed the left wing. Home Rule tended to drive Whigs and moderates out of the party, not the Radicals, who gained relatively from the issue.[7] The table shows that by 1892 the parliamentary Liberal party was essentially made up of Radicals. That this development imposed itself on the policies of the party is shown by the fact that statistical analysis of voting within the parliamentary Liberal party distinguishes Radicals from moderates much less clearly after 1892 than before.[8]

Most of these Radical M.P.s were big businessmen and wealthy lawyers. Very few of them obtained their income from the traditional sources of the British political elite (land and the public services), but they were not men of the masses. Most were owners or directors of large operations, such as collieries, iron foundries, textile mills, mercantile houses, and so forth. Table II shows the occupations of the Radical M.P.s.

TABLE II. OCCUPATIONS OF RADICAL M.P.s, 1874–1895

Occupation	1874–80	1880–85	1886	1886–92	1892–95
Commerce and industry	48	64	75	71	89
Law	21	26	31	35	53
Professions (other than law)	0	3	5	4	4
Writing and journalism	5	11	13	13	19
Teaching	0	4	7	5	7
Civil service	1	0	2	3	3
Workers	2	3	11	10	11
Armed forces	2	1	2	0	1
Land	5	8	8	9	6
Others	1	1	4	2	3
Unknown	4	9	7	7	11
Totals	89	130	165	159	207

Like Dickens' Josiah Bounderby, these were the kind of men who made things go in the great commercial and industrial centers of the British provinces. And like Bounderby, they worked hard and regarded themselves as self-made men. Their biographies show that they felt compelled to take part in some productive enterprise, even though most of them were born into wealthy families. Clearly the norms of their subculture, as well as a simple desire for wealth, demanded hard work from them.[9]

These observations raise the question of why such men would enter active politics. They did not need political power as a gateway to wealth; moreover, only a few of them were reared in circles that expected as a matter of course that their young men would take part in ruling the country. It may have been partly an attempt by them to gain public recognition of their personal worth, for as Table III shows, the usual badges of status did not come as easily to them as their economic power warranted.

TABLE III. SYMBOLS OF SOCIAL ACHIEVEMENT BY RADICAL
         M.P.s, 1874–1895

Type of Achievement	1874–80	1880–85	1886	1886–92	1892–95
Oxford and Cambridge					
graduates	19	29	40	42	63
Other university graduates	18	28	31	25	37
Public school only	2	3	2	5	8
Large landowners	17	31	25	13	14
Magistrates and deputy					
lieutenants for the					
counties	36	62	56	50	58
Aldermen and mayors	15	22	29	29	43
Chamber of commerce					
officers	5	12	7	11	12
Members of Whig families	4	5	2	3	3
Patrons of church livings	1	3	3	2	0
Ability to live well with no					
visible means of income	4	9	7	7	11

For the most part, the status that they enjoyed was hard-won: magistracies, civic offices, Chamber of Commerce directorships, and so forth. Political activity could give them a sense of public power usually ascribed by birth to the traditional elite. But the biographies of these men reveal a more important objective for them; most Radical M.P.s entered politics in order to correct some specific grievance imposed on them by existing political or social arrangements, and more generally to give political expression to a stridently middle-class perspective of British life. To use Professor Smelser's categories, they formed a movement that was both norm-oriented and value-oriented.[10] Of course not all middle-class men in late-Victorian Britain were Radicals, nor were all Radicals outside Parliament of the

middle class. Yet it is clear that most Radical M.P.s were middle-class men
who for one reason or another felt that some oppressive privilege associated
with landed society needed reforming, and that the principle of competition
ought to be made to prevail over all others, paternalist or cooperative,
throughout British life. Radicalism thus differed from Liberalism in its intent—not simply to make social institutions tolerate middle-class values, but
to reorder society strictly according to their tenets. Radicalism can be seen
as latent in the middle class; it was activated by the particular circumstances
of some individuals who felt unable to assimilate to the social order.[11]

The factor that at once raised specific grievances and imparted to the
Radical M.P.s their middle-class values was religion. Most of them were
Nonconformists.[12] Table IV is a listing of their religious affiliations. In-

TABLE IV.   RELIGION OF RADICAL M.P.s, 1874–1895

Denomination	1874–80	1880–85	1886	1886–92	1892–95
Church of England	99	18	14	19	20
Church of Scotland	4	5	4	4	3
Baptist	4	8	10	7	10
Congregationalist	7	20	17	18	24
Methodist (including Calvinistic)	9	12	17	13	24
Primitive Methodist	1	1	5	3	3
Quaker	9	9	7	7	5
Unitarian	7	11	19	16	15
Scottish Dissenting Presbyterian (Free or United Church)	3	6	5	3	2
Presbyterian, unspecified type	5	2	2	3	5
Nonconformist, unspecified type	11	13	22	25	29
Roman Catholic	1	1	2	0	1
Jewish	2	1	4	3	3
No religion	4	7	7	6	6
Unknown	13	16	30	32	57
Totals	89	130	165	159	207

cluding Jews, Roman Catholics, and atheists, about 80 percent of all Radical M.P.s stood outside the established churches. This was true even after
Home Rule, which caused much debate within Nonconformist circles, had
shouldered its way to the forefront of British politics. As for the Radical
M.P.s who belonged to either the Church of England or the Church of Scotland, some were Evangelicals, like Sir Wilfrid Lawson, who differed very
little in religious spirit from the Nonconformists, and others, like G. O.

Morgan, had intellectually turned away from the principle of establishment; in Morgan's case, the reason was his reaction against the ritualism he saw as an Oxford undergraduate. Still others were led by their constituents to take a more radical stance; this was particularly true in Wales and Scotland, where religious feelings ran very hot, but it also applied in some of the predominantly Nonconformist areas of England.[13]

A prototype Radical M.P. emerges from the statistical and biographical data. The Radical M.P. was a successful businessman. He regarded himself as a self-made man, though most likely he was of the second or third generation of the family firm. He received education beyond the national average, but not usually an Oxbridge degree. As a young man he devoted himself completely to his business. He was a strong Dissenter, regularly pious in his home life. After accumulating a large fortune, he won some civic honors, but only rarely entered the landed gentry. He belonged to the local Liberal association, but first became politically active through one of the many moral issues so important to Nonconformists—unsectarian education and the school boards, temperance, the Eastern question, among others. His feeling that British society did not accord him the influence his achievements entitled him to, and his belief that the political and social systems did not reflect his pious, work-oriented values made him a Radical. He became a candidate for Parliament because his wealth and ability attracted the attention of local party leaders, who shared his view of the world, and because his sense of grievance at the hands of the Established Church and the landed orders led him to seek power. Entering the House of Commons at the age of forty-five, he devoted himself to one or two of the numerous causes that constituted the Radical program, accepted the Liberal whip on many issues, but reserved the right of independent action on matters involving political and religious equality. He shared with his fellow Radicals the myth that the enemy was privilege, and that British society was not already achievement-oriented.[14] He sought the support of Radical workingmen, but did not actively recruit them into his organizations. He detected a kindred spirit in Gladstone, but hated the Whigs.

The career of Henry Joseph Wilson typifies parliamentary Radicalism. Wilson was born in Nottinghamshire in 1833, the son of a prosperous cotton spinner. His mother and father, strong Congregationalists, actively supported antislavery and foreign missionary work; their austere Nonconformity dominated his early life. Wilson attended a Dissenters' school in Taunton and, briefly, University College, London. Thereafter he joined a Sheffield smelting business, which he built into a large operation. According to the standards of the day, he was a model employer, cutting the weekly hours of labor in his factory to forty-eight and even providing a bathhouse for his workers. Bentham's utilitarianism and Samuel Smiles's *Self Help* were his intellectual guides. But Puritanism was the most powerful influence in his life. Both Wilson and his wife were fervent Dissenters. They took a deep interest in

Josephine Butler's agitation to repeal the contagious (venereal) diseases laws, which they regarded as sanctioning prostitution by the provision for medical inspection of prostitutes in army garrison towns. In 1870, they organized the Sheffield branch of the crusade. At the same time, Wilson became disturbed by Forster's education act of 1870. In 1872, he and a few others formed the Sheffield Nonconformist Committee, with the object of reforming the act and controlling the new school board. By 1874, Wilson had plunged into Radical politics in Sheffield, first as secretary of the Sheffield Liberal Association and electoral agent for Joseph Chamberlain, then in 1885, as M.P. for Holmfirth, eager to enact purity into law. Wilson never won great prominence, but the Radicals in parliament consisted of row on row of men like him.[15]

To what extent was the Radical M.P. representative of Radicals in the country at large? A study of Radical organizations and programs, the subjects of the next two sections, will be necessary to answer this question, but a look at Radical constituencies now can provide a basis for a few generalizations. The Radical M.P.s most often represented constituencies in the Nonconformist areas of Britain: Scotland and Wales; the North, Northwest, and Midlands of England; East Anglia; and the Southwest of England from Bristol to Cornwall. Even after 1886, the strongly Nonconformist areas remained Radical, except in Cornwall and near Birmingham, the former being explained by the proximity of Ireland and the consequent urgency of an imagined Irish threat, the latter by the influence of Joseph Chamberlain, staunch Unionist and political czar of Birmingham.[16] The dependence of Radicalism on the Celtic fringe, already pronounced by 1874, was strengthened after 1886 (see Table V).

TABLE V. REGIONAL DISTRIBUTION OF RADICAL CONSTITUENCIES, 1874–1895
(Percentage)

Geographical Area	1874–80	1880–85	1886	1886–92	1892–95
English	74	75	75	65	68
Welsh	9	10	10	13	13
Scottish	17	15	15	22	19

Another important pattern can be seen in the type of constituencies represented by Radicals. About half of the Radical M.P.s (46 percent in 1874–80 and 50 percent in 1880–85) represented great industrial constituencies. Another 37 percent in both parliaments sat for medium-sized provincial boroughs. In both kinds of constituencies, Nonconformist and working-class voters were more influential than in rural areas. The reform acts of 1884 and 1885, which generally honored the principles of manhood suffrage and single-member constituencies of equal size, were expected to enable Radicals to increase their strength in the large cities. In the general election of 1885, however, Radical success in the cities fell far short of expectations, partly because the Irish vote went to the Conservatives, but also because there were surprisingly large reserves of Conservative workingmen and because the suburbs were staunchly Tory.[17] Though the Irish vote in 1892 and 1895 went to the Liberals and Radicals, the other patterns remained constant. At the same time, the Radical performance after 1885 in the counties, even the rural county constituencies, exceeded most predictions. Before 1885, the only people in the rural areas of England to show substantial Radicalism were the farm laborers organized by Joseph Arch in the Agricultural Labourers' Union. But the reform acts of 1884 and 1885, by extending the county franchise and by marking out electoral divisions made up of rural villages, uncovered considerable Radicalism among village artisans as well as farm laborers, especially in the villages of strongly Nonconformist traditions.[18] Tables VI and VII illustrate these points.

TABLE VI.   RADICAL CONSTITUENCIES, BY SIZE AND TYPE,
            1874–1885

Size and Type	1874–80	1880–85
Small boroughs (0–1,999 electors)	12	7
Provincial boroughs (2,000–9,999 electors)	33	48
Big city boroughs (10,000+ electors)	40	60
Rural county seats	3	6
Industrial county seats	1	5
Part rural, part industrial county seats	0	4

TABLE VII. RADICAL CONSTITUENCIES, BY SIZE AND TYPE,
            1886–1895

Size and Type	1886	1886–92	1892–95
Small boroughs (0–5,000 electors)	4	9	14
Medium-sized boroughs (5,001–9,000 electors)	11	7	14
Large boroughs (9,000+ electors, plus all borough constituencies that were part of a large city)	71	62	67
Rural county	25	25	47
Industrial county	42	41	49
Part rural, part industrial county	12	15	16

Obviously, there is a great deal that a simple enumeration of Radical constituencies cannot say about the nature of Radicalism in the country at

large. It cannot, for example, tell us anything about Radicalism within the
nonvoting population, including all women and perhaps half of the less
prosperous adult males. Nor can it indicate how many of the votes for
Radical M.P.s came from genuine Radicals, for the power of deference
worked even for Radical candidates, particularly where they were industrialists running in a locality dominated by their own industries.[19] But if one
adds to the breakdown of Radical constituencies certain other information,
some useful conclusions can be drawn. For one thing, the Radical M.P.
must have been very much like his middle-class constituents in religion and
in perception of being excluded from orthodox society, though no doubt he
was richer and more politically astute than they. Radicalism was strong
where the middle class felt geographically and socially distant from the
center of Anglican, landed, fashionable, cosmopolitan orthodoxy. It was weak
where landed society was strong, and where new suburbs were providing
the means of assimilation for middle-class people into conservative society.
Radicalism throughout Britain was dominated by a core of hard-driving,
wealthy, moralistic businessmen, indistinguishable from the Radical M.P.

Of course the Radical M.P. was nothing like his working-class constituents in social status, life styles, or career patterns. But a number of factors
worked to create strong similarities between them in basic values, in identification of the political and social enemy, thus in policies. One thing was
religion. Clearly, workingmen tended to be Radicals where they were themselves Nonconformists. The only exception to this rule was in London, where
secular Jacobin traditions remained from earlier Radical history.[20] Nonconformity not only provided an organizational link to middle-class Radicals,
but also imparted to workingmen essentially middle-class values—hard
work, prudence, thrift, sobriety, self-help.[21] Another factor was trade unions,
which before 1889 were exclusive, businesslike organizations devoted to
securing a place for skilled workers in a capitalist society. Their values and
their politics were Radical, and their members readily accepted, until the
1880s, middle-class spokesmen in parliament.[22] Prosperity itself provided
basic resemblances between working-class Radicals and their bourgeois M.P.s.
For one thing the "Aristocracy of Labour" were more literate, thus politically
and socially less deferential and conservative than the laboring poor; for
another, they more freely consorted with people of the lower middle class.[23]
During the 1880s, when the depression in trade and industry was causing
severe hardship among some sections of the working class, and when class
consciousness and socialism were growing, the identity of values between
middle-class and working-class Radicals increasingly deteriorated. Still, to a
remarkable degree, the outlook and goals of the parliamentary elite and the
working-class rank and file of Radicalism were very similar. The estimate
of H. J. Wilson of his constituency, Holmfirth, which consisted largely of industrial villages, coal mines, and small farms, illustrates the point. He wrote
to his family in 1885 that his constituents were bright and cheerful: "And

they are good Radicals, very ready for any hit at aristocracy or land-grabbing. I don't think they are so well taught on Temperance as Sheffield people; but of course I don't conceal my opinions."[24]

II. Structure

Paradoxically, the late-Victorian Radicals organized too much and too little. Three things stand out concerning the structure of their movement. First, since most middle-class Radicals entered politics out of commitment to some special crusade, innumerable middle-class Radical organizations existed in the Commons and in the country. The multiplicity of these societies before 1886 operated against the formation of a single agency of Radicalism and constituted one of the principal, and most revealing, weaknesses of the movement. Second, after 1886, when the Home Rule crisis had forced organizational changes on Radicals, this weakness appeared in a different form—the fragmented nature of the Liberal-Radical program. Third, Radicalism had another crucial weakness in the unwillingness of the bourgeois Radicals to incorporate their working-class allies into the structure of the movement. There were hundreds of working-class Radical organizations that remained unconnected with the national middle-class agencies. Middle-class Radicals also made little attempt to recruit workingmen into influential positions within their organizations. Late in the 1880s, the demands of working-class Radicals became more obtrusive, but still workers were not absorbed into the middle-class structure, and this set the stage for the eventual departure of workingmen from the movement. These factors help explain the influence, functions, and ultimate failure of Radicalism.

Throughout the late-Victorian period, the Radicals were part of the Liberal party, but only in an informal and inconstant way. Before 1886, Radicals in Parliament had little influence in the central organizations of the party. They had no control over the party whips and little over the party's main electoral office, the Liberal Central Association. Moreover, they had no effective parliamentary organization of their own. From time to time, each group of Radical M.P.s put forward its one main idea, but there was no central agency to marshal the full Radical strength. Instead, Radical M.P.s dissipated their efforts in a kaleidoscope of temporary alliances and associations. Joseph Chamberlain, with his simmering impatience with ineffectiveness, sought to unify the Radicals as soon as he entered the House of Commons in 1876. He and Sir Charles Dilke formed what they called the "new party," a hard core of Radicals that was to be independent of the party whips. But it was soon reduced to two leaders and one follower.[25] The only other Radical organization at the parliamentary level was the Radical Club, founded in 1870 by the intellectual elite of the movement. It began to lose members in 1874 when some were defeated in the general election and others became disillusioned with democracy; it dissolved in 1880.[26] From the late 1870s, Radicals increasingly tended to exercise their influence through the Liberal party.

Until the founding of the National Liberal Federation in 1877, middle-class Nonconformist societies were the main Radical organizations outside Parliament. Each of these, like the Peace Society, the United Kingdom Alliance, the Liberation Society, the National Education League, and the Central Nonconformist Committee, had a specific goal and made no attempt to unify Radicals in support of a comprehensive program. They wanted the votes of workingmen, but did not try to recruit a general working-class membership. Insofar as they dealt with workers, it was to seek the support of a few influential trade union organizers, who presumably could sway the votes of wider circles.[27] Thus both the members and the leaders of these societies were bourgeois; indeed, the memberships overlapped to a considerable degree and had similar goals. Yet they cooperated very little, each preferring to operate as the Anti-Corn Law League had in the 1840s, as a pressure group to relieve some specific grievance.

Chamberlain recognized the potential power in such organizations and wanted to make it effective through a comprehensive program, in other words, to go beyond the Anti-Corn Law League model. Although he was a founder of the National Education League and the Central Nonconformist Committee, he did not think that their special issue, the establishment of a free, unsectarian, compulsory system of elementary education, was sufficient to weld the Radicals together. On the suggestion of another Birmingham Radical, Chamberlain decided to organize middle-class Radicalism through a federation of local Liberal associations. These had been established on open, democratic lines after 1867 to organize the newly enfranchised urban electorate. In May 1877, Chamberlain and his fellow Birmingham Radicals established the National Liberal Federation, an affiliation of all Liberal associations they regarded as democratic in structure. The Education League dissolved into the new Federation, but the other Nonconformist societies retained their independence.[28]

The National Liberal Federation became an important organization, but at least before 1886 it did not serve the unifying purpose it was supposed to. It was feared by the Whigs, who recognized that it would put local and national party management into the hands of the Radical activists, but it did not harness the energy of the Nonconformist Radical societies or destroy Whig influence within the party (that influence was destroyed mainly by Whig abandonment of the party). It was unable to tap working-class Radical strength, partly because no attempt was made to attract workers into its power structure, and partly because workingmen recognized its essentially bourgeois character. As one labor organizer (a firm Radical) put it, the "borough caucuses would work admirably as traps in which to shut up the working men of the country, allowing them only political action as their masters and managers permit."[29]

The Home Rule crisis of 1886 had a marked impact on the structure of middle-class Radicalism. After 1886, because of the importance of Home Rule, the independent parliamentary and extra-parliamentary associations, like the Liberation Society, were less significant to the movement than before. At the same time, however, because Radicals numerically had become so important within the Liberal party, the institutions of the party tended to reflect Radical attitudes, and in some cases central party agencies merged with Radical organizations. The kaleidoscopic nature of middle-class Radical activities was not changed, but now Radical groups competed with each other for official party sanction. The party whips, and their agency, the Liberal Central Association, now functioned largely for Radical policies; Radical M.P.s were appointed whips in 1886 and 1892. This merging of Liberal and Radical parliamentary agencies tended to bureaucratize Radicalism, and in reaction to this process, the irrepressibly crankish temperament of Radical M.P.s spawned small parliamentary ginger groups. For instance, a few young men, new to the House of Commons and consciously more "modern" than the usual provincial Radicals, formed a working alliance known as the Articles Club. This group, including R. B. Haldane, Sir Edward Grey, and H. H. Asquith, later became known as the New Liberals or the Liberal Imperialists.[30] They acted in opposition to the Radical malcontents organized, complete with whips and caucuses, by the chronic troublemaker, Henry Labouchere.[31] Still another alliance grew out of the nationalist sentiment felt by the young Welsh M.P.s, who hovered in near revolt against the Liberal party, not because of the party's refusal to accept Radical policies, but because of the primacy given to rival Radical claims. In 1894, four Welsh Radicals even for a time rejected the party whips.[32] This chaotic situation has been blamed largely on Gladstone, but it was, in fact, the result of the absorption of Radicalism by the party institutions.

Outside Parliament, the National Liberation Federation underwent crucial developments after 1886, all tending to increase Radical influence within the party. Inasmuch as Radicals had fared better than Liberals in the general election of 1886, the Federation was given more electoral and policy control at the expense of the Liberal Central Association. In addition, since Chamberlain had left the party, the Federation was moved by its professional secretary, Francis Schnadhorst, from Birmingham to London, into offices adjacent to the Central Association. Schnadhorst became secretary to the Association as well as to the Federation.[33] These alterations effectively installed middle-class Radical views in the party's central headquarters. The distinctions between the functions of the parliamentary and the extra-parliamentary organizations became much less clear. Both had electoral duties, and both advised party leaders on policy. The party propaganda agency, the Liberal Publication Department, established in 1887, was the product of combined party headquarters, and controlled by Radicals.[34] These steps amounted to a considerable advance of Radicalism within the Liberal party.

Meanwhile the Federation also greatly expanded its organization outside the offices in Parliament Street. In October 1886, in a drive to carry

Home Rule, Schnadhorst set out to establish Liberal associations of the democratic type in every part of Britain, all to be connected by a network of regional federations or by direct association with national party head-quarters. Regional conferences in nine areas were staged, and a carefully coached speaker from party headquarters was sent to each one to speak for a package consisting of Irish Home Rule and the reforms especially desired in that area.[35] In this way, the National Liberal Federation was converted into an agency for the formulation of official party policy. Leaders of the parliamentary Liberal party depended on the Federation to stimulate popu-lar support, and in return they accepted the demands of the Federation as the official party program. The process of gathering these demands, area by area, was quite deliberate, and the endorsement of them by party leaders at the annual conference of the Federation was quite explicit. Invariably, the programs were compilations of the desires of the most active and Radical members of the Federation—in other words, the Liberal party program became a summary of the well-established goals of middle-class Radicalism.[36]

The crystallization of the organizational structure increased middle-class Radical influence, but it also tended to confirm the imperviousness of Radicalism to working-class influence. Throughout the late-Victorian period there were organizations of working-class Radicals at the national level but they remained separate from middle-class societies. The largest of these were made up of influential trade union leaders, who were not militantly class-conscious, for they, writes Henry Pelling, "felt themselves to be more closely akin to the Liberal middle class, whose sober habits and dissenting religion they commonly shared."[37] The first of these was the Labour Representation League, founded in 1869 by London union leaders in order to promote working-class representation in the House of Commons. The League, though active in the general election of 1874, had dwindled away by 1880. It never established a broad base of support among workers, for its membership was made up of individuals and not unions. Its secretary, Henry Broadhurst, won a seat in the House in 1880, but was in every way except occupational back-ground an orthodox middle-class Radical.[38] The Trades Union Congress established in 1871 a Parliamentary Committee to promote favorable labor legislation, but it did not enter into electoral work. From the time of its founding through the 1870s, it was dominated by union leaders who agreed completely with middle-class Radicals and who were content with the secondary role assigned to them by the parliamentary leadership. Partly in reaction to its passivity, more aggressive workingmen in 1886 caused the establishment by the T.U.C. of the Labour Electoral Association, which was to work for the return of laborers to the House of Commons. It, too, soon became tied to the liberal party through its advocacy of standard Radical policies, and resisted pressure to support socialist candidates.[39] Thus two features of these working-class organizations stand out: first, that they espoused policies based on values identical to those of the middle-class

societies; and second, that they had little influence in those societies; they
were used but not absorbed by middle-class Radicals.

In London, however, there was among some workingmen a different
inclination. Since it was essentially secularist the London working class did
not function in the usual alliance with Dissent. London Radicals drew on
Jacobin rather than Nonconformist traditions. They had numerous clubs
that were separate from the Liberal party, the National Liberal Federation,
and the trades unions. Although these clubs were mainly social organizations,
in the late 1870s and early 1880s their political activity increased, owing to
their interest in the Eastern question, Irish coercion, and land reform. As a
result of this political intensification, the Radical clubs, which were very
suspicious of the bourgeois National Liberation Federation, took part in
forming the Democratic Federation.[40] This organization could have unified
all Radicals of the working class who desired independence from the N.L.F.
wire-pullers. However, shortly after its founding, H. M. Hyndman, the
socialist leader of the Democratic Federation, denounced "capitalist Radicalism" and in 1882 changed the society's name to the Social Democratic Federation. All but one of the Radical clubs withdrew. In 1885 and 1886, most of
the Radical clubs joined some secular societies in establishing the Metropolitan Radical Federation, which, though not professing socialism, doggedly
maintained its independence from Liberal party agencies and the National
Liberation Federation.[41]

Below the national level the structure of late-Victorian Radicalism is
very blurry. Probably the most effective organizations were the local Liberal
associations, many of which were dominated by Radicals. These associations
undoubtedly had as members nearly all of the active middle-class Radicals,
and depending on the constituency, many working-class Radicals as well.
Theoretically, these local associations were to be open without fee to any
Liberal, and through an elaborate system of ward meetings and general conferences would bring the Liberal working class into the organization. In
practice, however, they were dominated by the substantial bourgeois leaders,
who paid the bills, set the policies, and selected the candidates. In many
places it soon became clear that there were not enough members to sustain
ward meetings or warrant a distinction between general conferences and
the meetings of the ruling body.[42] Many of these same middle-class Radicals
formed the membership of local branches of the great Nonconformist societies—the United Kingdom Alliance, the Liberation Society, and so on.
This meant that a relatively few active men were called on to carry heavy
burdens in each locality. Thus on the local level as on the national, the
middle-class Radicals tended to dissipate their strength.[43]

The outlines of local working-class Radicalism are even less clear.
There were numerous working-class clubs and associations throughout the
country. Some of these associations were identical to the local Liberal associations, except that they had working-class memberships; class consciousness

alone kept them separate. They also seem to have been made up of comparatively well-off workers, the most secure of the working class; in Aberdeen, for example, the Aberdeen Radical Association was indistinguishable from the local Trades Council.[44] Radical clubs seem to have been more numerous and varied. They were spread across Britain, some being, as Hanham says, "lingering remnants of Chartism, some no more than trade union lodges or friendly societies which met in a congenial public house, some semi-revolutionary underground organizations with mysterious continental connections."[45] Most of them were mainly social clubs, some sponsored from the outside by religious groups and having a moral purpose—teetotaling habits, self-education, wholesome recreation, for example. The best established of these were connected with the Working Men's Club and Institute Union, which could claim 66 clubs in 1874, 206 in 1885, and 518 in 1895, each with perhaps 250 members; of these about one-third had Radical political purposes.[46] There were other Radical clubs independent of this Union, but their number and effectiveness is debatable: Charles Booth recorded that in London the independent Radical clubs were little more than iniquitous drinking societies.[47] These working-class clubs and associations could on occasion raise big crowds for public demonstrations and provide voters and electoral workers for middle-class party managers, but otherwise they were ineffective, both as agencies defending working-class interests and as organizations for recruiting, training, and promoting workingmen to the bourgeois structure.

The career of a professional Radical organizer named Howard Evans illustrates many of the salient points about the Radical structure. The son of a Puritan chartist, Evans as a young man worked for labor representation in Parliament with two trade union officials, Randall Cremer and George Howell. These men were loyal allies of middle-class Radicals, and in 1869, at Howell's suggestion, Evans became secretary to George Dixon, mayor of Birmingham, a founder of the National Education League and Radical M.P. Howell soon was engaged in Education League business, and in the 1870s managed its London office. At that time the Education League shared rooms with another middle-class Radical society, the Land Tenure Reform Association, whose president was John Stuart Mill. Evans served as secretary of the Association. Mill and his circle introduced Evans to their campaigns for women's suffrage, prohibiting vaccination, and abolishing the game laws. In 1872, Evans helped coordinate the work of Joseph Arch's National Agricultural Labourers' Union, through which he met two of the Union's middle-class supporters, Joseph Chamberlain and Samuel Morley. He had connections with other middle-class Radicals through the Leaseholds Franchise Association and through Howell, who knew many Radical M.P.s and the leaders of British positivism, themselves staunch Radicals. Late in the 1870s Evans went to work for the *Echo,* a London Radical paper owned by Passmore Edwards and Arthur Arnold, two Radical M.P.s devoted to land reform, franchise extension, and various moralistic Nonconformist crusades. Evans edited the *Echo* in the 1880s. He ended his career as an administrator for the Liberation Society.[48]

It is interesting how easily Evans moved between very different Radical circles: trade unions, Nonconformist societies, middle-class intellectual groups. The middle-class agencies he worked for were connected by inter-locking directorates and memberships; they had close relations with the leaders of working-class Radicalism. Clearly the materials existed for a uni-fied Radical movement, yet the organizations remained independent of each other; middle-class groups kept separate from each other and from working-class institutions. Organizational diffusion was a fundamental characteristic of the movement. Perhaps this was due to the function of these organiza-tions and of the movement as a whole. For middle-class people each organiza-tion was a way not only to relieve a specific grievance, but also to satisfy a need to relate to a society from which they felt excluded. The grievances might be eased by unification of the organizations, but the need could not. For the working-class Radicals, their organizations had several functions: to organize the power of the working-class voter, to satisfy a need for congre-gation, and to help laboring men to relate to middle-class society, the basic outlines and values of which they had accepted. When the functions of the organizations are viewed in this way, it becomes clear why bourgeois Radicals diffused their organizational efforts and failed to integrate them with those of workingmen, and why working-class Radicals were unable either to move up through middle-class organizations to elite status or to mobilize the masses in support of a value system produced by another class.

Beginning in the 1880s, the most important organizational problem faced by the Radicals was to respond constructively to growing demands by the working class for parliamentary representation. After the depression in trade and industry began to affect the working population, social criticism and working-class consciousness began to increase. The old claim of middle-class Radicals to represent labor in the House satisfied an ever-smaller num-ber of workingmen, and this fact presented Radicals with a crucial test of flexibility. They failed the test. In London, the situation was particularly significant, because the Liberal and Radical associations and clubs of the metropolis, with strong traditions of working-class membership and inde-pendence from provincial Nonconformity, attracted broader ranges of ideas and people than the Liberal associations in the country. Fabian socialists "permeated" some London organizations, and in 1889 Sidney Webb was appointed to the executive committee of the London Liberal and Radical Union, which was the metropolitan branch of the National Liberal Federa-tion. But the organization of the Radical clubs, the Metropolitan Radical Federation, remained independent of the Liberal and Radical Union, still mistrusting middle-class managers; and with the growth of doctrinaire social-ism, new unionism, and labor militance, the Liberal and Radical associations of London, including the Radical clubs, lost their working-class support by the mid-1890s.[49]

On the national level, this tendency took the form of demands by workingmen for seats in Parliament. These demands often had little to do with ideology or specific policies. It was mainly that workingmen wanted to see their own kind in the House of Commons. Schnadhorst and other Radical leaders, having long insisted that Radicalism cut across class lines, said that they would welcome more working-class M.P.s, but that decisions to adopt labor candidates must remain with the local Liberal associations. They felt that they could not deprive their loyal constituency chiefs of the time-honored right to choose candidates. In November 1890, James Tims, secretary of the Metropolitan Radical Federation, formally asked Schnadhorst to have fifty Liberal candidates across the country withdrawn, so that laboring men, with N.L.F. support, could contest the seats. Schnadhorst refused to dictate to the local associations or promise financial support.[50]

This attitude by the Radical chiefs effectively precluded much working-class representation through the institutions of Radicalism. It showed that the Radical parliamentary leaders ultimately acted on the assumption that their organizations were of, for, and by the middle class. The leaders of late-Victorian Radicalism were of a social type that prevented understanding and flexibility in dealing with new kinds of labor spokesmen. Schnadhorst wrote to Gladstone of Sidney Webb:

He is quite a new man & has little means of knowing the sentiments of London workmen. London to him & others means the few noisy impracticables who meet in a few Clubs, a class whom no programme can ever satisfy—they are the men who keep London Liberals divided and weak. Cooperation with them is almost impossible. There is a wide gulf between the sober, intelligent hardheaded men of the provinces and these men.[51]

There was a wide gulf indeed! The sober, hardheaded men of the provinces were the representatives of a social ideal that had since the mid-nineteenth century united Radicalism; but the unity which that ideal had imposed on the Radical movement was decaying.

III. Ideology

Despite their difficulty in organizing themselves effectively, the late-Victorian Radicals did agree on the target and objectives for a Radical program. This program reflected the social ideal that defined the movement. The Radicals believed in competition in all aspects of society, for they assumed that the natural action of social and economic forces, if unimpeded, would generate progress. To a greater or lesser degree, all groups in the political spectrum— Conservatives and Liberals as well as Radicals—shared this assumption.[52] The distinctions between these groups lay in their different perceptions of social reality and thus in their identification of the enemies of progress. The

Tories thought that social forces already were in balance, and that further weakening of traditional institutions would bias the equation heavily in favor of nonlanded orders. Liberals by the late nineteenth century did not see landed institutions in so precarious a position, and considered that minor adjustments should be made to give middle- and working-class factors a fair influence. Radicals, however, contended that British society was still dominated by the privileges of the landed elite, and that institutions would have to be purged of these impeding elements to allow the free play of political, social, and economic forces to take place. Thus they would have replaced the traditional, particularist, and ascriptive elements in society with rational, egalitarian, and achievement-oriented components.[53] To accomplish this, they would have abolished the privilege in political and religious arrangements. They would have struck at the power of the landed orders by breaking their ancient monopoly in land.

Though this ideology was supported by large numbers in the working class, it was essentially a middle-class product. What James Mill had written in 1826 was still regarded as true in the 1880s:

The value of the middle classes in this country, their growing numbers and importance, are acknowledged by all. These classes have long been spoken of, and not grudgingly, by their superiors themselves, as the glory of England; as that which alone has given us our eminence among nations; as that portion of our people to whom every thing that is good among us may with certainty be traced.[54]

This is the idea that lay behind Joseph Chamberlain's classic remark that the aristocracy as a class "toil not neither do they spin."[55] Yet the Radicals could not see that their ideology might entrench privileges of the bourgeoisie. Before 1885 they had remarkably little in the way of a program designed for the working class, and they became interested in urban social problems only very slowly. Their reluctance to reshape their program to meet the demands of socialists and militant workingmen, and to refurbish the dwindling attractiveness of their old policies, illuminates at once the social origins of the movement and the causes of its decline.

According to the *Fortnightly Review*, if there was a common denominator to Radicalism, it was "a belief in the right and ability of the people to govern themselves."[56] This belief did not apply to women, for the Radicals (with a few exceptions) thought solely in terms of men; but otherwise they would establish a democratic franchise. Before 1885 they sought to extend the county franchise to include agricultural laborers and to equalize electoral districts; after passage of the 1884–85 reforms, they advocated things like the abolition of plural voting (that is, establishing "one man, one vote"), simplification of electoral qualification and registration, and payment of electoral expenses from the rates. Increasingly after 1880 they sought elective county councils. The principle of political democracy demanded all of these items. Furthermore, the Radicals expected these measures to end the great landowners' domination of the Liberal party and the House of Commons. The same objective put limitations of the power of the House of Lords in their program. This issue became important to them in 1884, when the Lords initially rejected the 1884 reform bill, and crucial after 1893, when the Lords began to ruin much Liberal legislation.[57] Only the ambiguity and division in the leadership of the Liberals in 1895 and the subsequent weakness of the party postponed the problem until the twentieth century.[58]

Policies arising from religion constituted a significant part of the Radical program. Disestablishment of the Churches of England, Wales, and Scotland stood very high with every Radical.[59] Their campaign was successful in that the number of M.P.s who were pledged to disestablishment increased after the general elections in both 1880 and 1885. The Home Rule issue diverted attention from disestablishment in the late 1880s, and the rising nationalism of Welsh and Scottish Radical M.P.s, who expressed their aims in terms of regional disestablishment, left disestablishment in England to the more distant future.[60]

But disestablishment was not the only issue arising from religion to concern Radicals. Throughout the 1870s, they felt that education presented the most pressing problem, for they thought that the education act of 1870 had erected a new state school system afflicted with the worst features of denominational education. They also thought that the schools should be made free.[61] Another religious issue, winning support from a circle of Liberals larger than Radicalism, was the burials question, in which Nonconformists demanded the right to burial with their own ceremonies in Anglican cemeteries.[62] Finally, the Radicals were enthusiastic for temperance legislation. Though they could not agree until the 1880s on a specific plan, they regarded temperance reform as an important social issue, for if adopted it would enable working people to practice that prudence and self-help so crucial to the Radical social ideal. By 1890 their pressure had forced the leaders of the Liberal party to accept temperance legislation as official policy.[63]

The land question concerned all Radicals, regardless of class. Working-class Radicals thought that the monopoly in land was the main source of their own economic difficulties. In this belief, they drew on a long hostility to industrial society and a nostalgia for the rural past: for them the good life would be that of a small proprietor. Their policies tended to be extreme —nationalization and redistribution. They greeted the single-tax idea of Henry George, though it did not envision small proprietorships, with great enthusiasm.[64] By the 1870s, however, middle-class Radicals dominated the protest against landowners. They regarded Britain's land laws as anachronistic, unbusinesslike, and irrational bulwarks of the landed orders.

The land laws of England [wrote one Welsh Radical] are wrapt in a fog so dense as to make the subject intensely unattractive to the general public. Unlike our

commercial code, they have their origin in remote and semi-barbarous times, and
are overlaid by a mass of medieval rubbish, a legacy from that wonderful Norman
race. . . .[65]

Unfortunately, the myth of aristocratic privilege was so strong that few
Radicals understood what the land laws were, and even fewer could agree on
the kind of scheme that would break the power of the landowners. Many
thought that the monopoly in land could be broken simply by the abolition
of entail and primogeniture, little realizing that the former existed only in
the form of family settlements, and the latter only in the very rare cases of
intestacy.[66] Others wanted to set the free market operating in land, believing
that the laws of land transfer allowed settlements and legal obligations to
obstruct the sale of land. By cutting away the undergrowth of "unbusinesslike" property laws, the Radicals could expose landowners to the rigors of
the free market. But their idea of "Free Trade in Land" would have worked
no better than abolition of entail or primogeniture. Landowners held on to
their property for social reasons; greater ease of sale alone would not have
caused them to break up their estates. The issue gradually settled itself. With
the rapid collapse of agricultural prosperity in the late 1870s and 1880s, the
demand for land diminished, landlords began to grant tenancies on more
favorable terms, and the need for the swift flow of land through the market
dwindled.[67] Lloyd George in his famous 1909 budget adopted the old Radical tradition of attacking landlords, but the issue in reality had become
much less central to British society.

This fact was tacitly recognized by the editors and authors of *The
Radical Programme,* which began to appear in the *Fortnightly Review* in
1883. Chamberlain, who edited the volume, since the early 1870s had worked
to unify the scattered Radical goals, and after 1875 he turned to land reform
as the solidifying agent. He found that his problem was to select from all
the possible formulas the one most likely to be politically effective: tenant
right, free trade in land, a single tax on land, or nationalization.[68] The land
policy in *The Radical Programme* consisted of a combination of reforms, all
with the intent of multiplying the number of landowners. But by that time,
Chamberlain had submerged the land question into the more general problem of the condition of the working class. He recognized rather earlier than
most middle-class Radicals that modern democratic politics would require
the sublimation of old Radical policies into a program likely to be popular
with working people.

Thus, *The Radical Programme* reflected a new social concern by Radicalism. The old Radical policies had social implications in that ideally they
would have transformed Britain into a middle-class Nonconformist society,
but they had no significant urban social plan. But the social orientation of
The Radical Programme is obvious. As Chamberlain put it in a complementary essay, the central problem of the age was the great disparity between

the wealth of the nation as a whole and the misery of the poor.[69] This problem essentially concerned the rights of property versus the rights of the community. Property had obligations that went with ownership, and owners should pay for their rights.[70] In accordance with these new assumptions, the authors of *The Radical Programme* called for improvement of the public health and artisans' dwellings acts to make them effective and to shift the burden of improvements to the landlords. They argued that landlords had profited from an "unearned increment" caused by the general growth of population in the towns, for which the community at large should receive compensation. The machinery for urban improvement would 'consist of stricter allowances for payment of landlords who had been bought out by improving authorities, and taxation of real property owners to pay for improvements. For agricultural laborers, the authors proposed to compel landlords to attach a small plot of land to every cottage they rented, and to give powers of compulsory appropriation to local authorities in rural districts.[71]

In its consideration of problems of the urban masses beside the grievances of the middle-class Nonconformists, *The Radical Programme* represented a considerable advance in Radical thinking. Naturally this could have raised serious difficulties in attracting support from middle-class Radicals, who might be suspicious of attacks on property on the one hand and a shift of attention from their special issues on the other. Chamberlain attempted to overcome this difficulty by including in *The Radical Programme* most of the old, narrow Radical causes: religious equality, free schools, democratic local government, and equalization of tax burdens on real and personal property owners; and by putting the new proposals firmly in the framework of old Radical principles.[72] Chamberlain's social policy was far from socialism. It emphasized the local authority, not the central government. It continued the traditional hostility to landlords, but did not raise the issue of the privileges of personal property owners, and raised only vaguely that of the primacy of the community as against the individual. The new program would simply subject the property owners in towns to the same attacks that Radicals had long aimed at owners of landed estates. It was a new formulation of the old Radical social ideal.

After 1885, the idea of making owners of real property pay a fair share of social expenses formed the main theme of Radical social policy. Increasingly Radicals adopted from Henry George the idea and the rhetoric of the "unearned increment," and urged that the full value of it ought to go to the local authorities. In urban affairs, they wanted to give city officials the right to tax the urban unearned increment, to take land for housing, sanitation, and beautification, and to force landlords as well as occupiers to pay the rates.[73] This set of policies stretched the Radical ideology—individualistic, competitive, and achievement-oriented—about as far as it would go. In some respects it caused considerable unrest among Radicals. Certain Radi-

cals in London, more subject to innovative influences and less bound by
provincial Nonconformist attitudes, enthusiastically embraced and elaborated the new urban social concern, much to the consternation of older,
more conventional Radicals. The London Radicals sought to amalgamate
London's obsolete and complicated system of vestries, districts, and corporations into one representative government. They would use this central authority the way Chamberlain had once used the Birmingham City council
—to improve gas, water, and sanitation services, and to raise the standards
of working-class housing. They would tax ground owners instead of occupiers, and through "leasehold enfranchisement" would enable occupiers
to become owners. For the country at large, the London Radicals advocated
improvement of wages and hours for government employees, and abolition
of taxes on common items of the breakfast table.[74] All of this they couched
in tones of criticism of rigid laissez-faire attitudes that frightened other
Radicals. John Morley, for instance, wrote Chamberlain in 1888:

*The anarchic follies of the London Radicals are playing the Tory game to a marvel.
Indeed if these men are Radicals I'm a Tory. We cannot win without accession of
strength from the London constituencies, and that strength will never come so long
as these blatant democrats persist in frightening the small shopkeeper, for one
thing, and in standing aloof from organization for another.*[75]

The small group of Radicals who eventually earned the label of the
"New Liberals" were perhaps even more impressed by the urgency of urban
social problems than the London men. They were responding to the growing
social concern of the 1880s, of which one form was the revival of socialism.
Various socialists and other social critics were raising fundamental questions
about the nature of industrial society.[76] To some of the younger Radicals
these questions demanded a more positive program than Radicals had traditionally pursued. R. B. Haldane, who had been trained in German idealism
rather than Benthamite empiricism, was the intellectual leader of this
progressive group. He wrote:

*The mere removal of the obstacles which used to block the highway of human
progress has been pretty well completed. We are face to face with a new kind of
social problem. Liberalism has passed from the destructive to the constructive stage
in its history.*[77]

Implicit in this remark was a new view of the world. Unlike Radicals
of an older generation, the New Liberals did not believe that the unimpeded
action of social and economic forces led to progress; indeed, most of the
impediments were gone, they believed, and the social problem was greater
than ever. Like all Victorian Radicals, the New Liberals wanted to establish
conditions in which the individual would have maximum freedom of action.
But they now felt that positive action by the state would be necessary to

bring about the optimum environment. Thus they were severely critical of
unrestrained capitalism and regarded some of the older Radicals as obsolete
individualists. For instance, to a few Radicals, John Morley represented the
"individualist tail" of old-fashioned Radicalism; he was the "bondslave of
Political Economy."[78]

There is no doubt that men like John Morley and Charles Bradlaugh
did not share the New Liberals' sense of urgency about social issues, or look
upon new spokesmen of the working class with much understanding.[79] Yet
if the old Radicals differed in attitude very sharply from the New Liberals,
in specific policies they differed very little. All of the Radicals rejected the
cooperative ideal underlying socialist programs and affirmed their belief in a
competitive system. Arthur Arnold, a land reformer who stood at about the
middle of the Radical spectrum, explained that Radicals wanted to regulate,
not replace, the capitalist system: "We seek to establish a well-ordered competition, because we find that in some form competition is the mainspring of
production, and that moral and material stoppage and decline follow upon
removal of this mainspring."[80] As Haldane put it, the state provides a civilized environment for capitalists, and the state has a right to charge a "rent"
for its services.[81] But for all the idealist rhetoric, Haldane's sentiment was
only an extension of Chamberlain's old doctrine of "ransom" to property of
all kinds. Most Radicals could accept it, for it was old Radical wine in New
Liberal bottles.

If the Radicals agreed in rejecting socialism, in terms of practical policies they did not agree on where to draw the line. The issue that often
divided Radicals from socialists and from militant workingmen was the
eight-hour day. In the belief that competition should operate throughout
society, Radicals like Morley, Bradlaugh, Mundella, and even Thomas Burt
(a former coal miner) rejected proposals for legislation for an eight-hour day.
They would accept legislative limitation of adult working hours only if the
health and safety of the workers were at stake; otherwise, they thought, free
and fair bargaining between employers and well-run unions could win the
conditions desired by labor yet still be compatible with the existence of industry.[82] This essentially was the policy of the 1870s, prominently displayed
in the work of the positivists like Fredric Harrison and E. S. Beesly, and it
was shared by the New Liberals in the 1880s and 1890s.[83] Haldane, for example, rejected the eight-hour day and declared that "cowardice and apathy
alone" kept workers from winning the hours they wanted.[84] Though a number of Radicals gradually took up the cudgels for the eight-hour day, especially in regard to the mining industry, not enough did so quickly as to
retain the adherence of workingmen. In their slowness, the Radicals revealed the class orientation of their movement and invited the end of the old
middle- and working-class alliance, which was largely accomplished by 1914.

The foregoing analysis of the Radical ideology shows that it, like all
political ideals, was largely a sublimation of class interests. Like the elite and

the structure of the movement, the ideology was dominated by bourgeois views and needs. Eventually the working-class Radicals seceded from the Radical movement and joined other workers in establishing an independent Labour party. The cause of this great political transformation did *not* lie in the attachment of Radicalism and Liberalism to Irish Home Rule, or in subordination to the policies of Gladstone, still less in the split in Liberal leadership during World War I. Rather, the cause was that the Radicals by their very nature were unable to deal with working-class demands for power and policies that reflected a different social ideal. The movement was not able to transform its basic character in order to hold a section of its constituents; indeed, it is doubtful that any social movement ever has. And at the same time that the divergence from labor was growing, economic and social change was soothing the aggravations that had long produced Radicalism in certain sections of the middle class. With their religion growing dim, with the demands for political democracy largely accomplished, and with the social status of land diminished, the British middle class gradually moved to conservatism. By the 1920s, Radicalism as a political force had dissipated, for its social functions were no longer needed.

NOTES

1. From Viscount Chilston, *Chief Whip: The Political Life and Times of Aretas Akers-Douglas, 1st Viscount Chilston* (London, 1961), p. 59.

2. J. Morrison Davidson, *Eminent Radicals in Parliament* (London, 1879), p. 1.

3. Samuel P. Hays, "New Possibilities for American Political History: The Social Analysis of American Political Life," in Seymour M. Lipset and Richard Hofstadter, eds. *Sociology and History: Methods* (New York, 1968), p. 182.

4. This is a paraphrase of the definition given in W. Bruce Cameron, *Modern Social Movements: A Sociological Outline* (New York, 1966), p. 7. Two other good discussions of social movements are Herbert Blumer, "Social Movements," in A. M. Lee, ed., *Principles of Sociology* (New York, 1967), pp. 199–220, and Rudolf Heberle, *Social Movements: An Introduction to Political Sociology* (New York, 1951).

5. The method will be described in greater detail in a forthcoming article I have written with William Klecka of Northwestern University: "Late-Victorian Radical M.P.'s: New Evidence from Discriminant Analysis." The computer program utilized in the statistical analysis is "EIDISC, Stepwise Multiple Discriminant Analysis," designed by Donald Morrison, available from Vogelback Computing Center, Northwestern University, Library Number NUCC068. Complete lists of the Radical M.P.s are included in the appendices of my forthcoming book, *British Radicals and the Irish Question, 1874–1895*.

6. Contemporary estimates set the number of Radical M.P.s at about 70 for the 1874–80 parliament, 110 for the 1880–85 parliament, and between 60 and 150 for the 1886 parliament. No reliable estimates exist for the two parliaments following, but it is worth noting that such establishment newspapers as *The Times* from 1886 on regarded all of the parliamentary Liberal party as "Radical." See F. W. Hirst, *Early Life and Letters of John Morley*, 2 vols. (London, 1927), 2:19; Bernard Holland, *The Life of Spencer Compton, Eighth Duke of Devonshire*, 2 vols. (London, 1911), 1:141–42; S. Maccoby, *English Radicalism, 1853–1886* (London, 1953), p. 254; Winston S. Churchill, *Lord Randolph Churchill*, 2nd ed. (London, 1952), pp. 227 and 406; *The Times*, 19 December 1885; and Lord Richard Grosvenor to Gladstone, 12 December 1885, Gladstone Papers, BM 44:316.

7. This conclusion is directly contrary to the usual accounts, such as that in G. D. H. Cole, *British Working Class Politics, 1832–1914* (London, 1941), pp. 82–83; I have developed it further in my forthcoming book, *British Radicals and the Irish Question, 1874–1895*.

8. That is, analysis by the EIDISC program of Liberal party voting patterns from 1874 to 1892 distinguishes quite clearly a group of M.P.s on the left of the party spectrum, with the Whigs equally clearly distinguished on the right, and a large body of moderates in between. But that same kind of analysis for the 1892–95 parliament results in a pattern having most of the Liberal party bunched at the Radical end. One can mark out Radicals from moderates only by drawing perhaps an indefensibly fine line between the two groups.

9. Biographical data for Tables II and III come from John Bateman, *The Great Landowners of Great Britain and Ireland* (London, 1878 and 1883); *Burke's Landed Gentry; D.N.B.; Dod's Parliamentary Companion* (London, 1874–95); Joseph Foster, *Members of Parliament, Scotland* (London, 1881); Joseph Foster, *Men at the Bar* (London, 1885); *Men of the Times; The Parliamentary Directory of the Professional, Commercial, and Mercantile Members of the House of Commons* (London, 1874); and *Who Was Who.*

10. Neil J. Smelser, *Theory of Collective Behavior* (New York, 1962), chap. 9 and 10.

11. The best discussion of middle-class ideals and values is Harold Perkin, *The Origins of Modern English Society, 1780–1880* (Toronto, 1969), chap. 6–8.

12. Information on the religion of M.P.s is very difficult to find. The data for Table IV come from biographies, plus files of *The Nonconformist, The Baptist, The Methodist Times, The Congregationalist,* and obituaries in *The Times.*

13. For Wales, see Kenneth O. Morgan, *Wales in British Politics* (Cardiff, 1963), passim; for Scotland, see James G. Kellas, "The Liberal Party in Scotland, 1876–1895," *Scottish Historical Review* 64 (April 1965):1–16; and D. C. Savage, "Scottish Politics, 1885–86," *Scottish Historical Review* 40 (October 1961):118–35.

14. Harold Perkin argues that by midcentury, the middle-class achievement ideal

already prevailed in British society: *Origins of Modern English Society,* chap. 8.

15. W. S. Fowler, *A Study in Radicalism and Dissent: The Life and Times of Henry Joseph Wilson, 1833–1914* (London, 1961). There is much biographical material on Wilson in the Wilson Papers in Sheffield University and the Sheffield Central Library.

16. These conclusions, along with much of the information on constituencies, are drawn from Henry Pelling, *Social Geography of British Elections, 1885–1910* (New York, 1967), especially pp. 163 and 179–203.

17. Pelling, *Social Geography of British Elections,* pp. 418–20.

18. Ibid., pp. 426–29, 432–33; H. J. Hanham, *Elections and Party Management: Politics in the Time of Disraeli and Gladstone* (London, 1959), pp. 29–32. In Wales, practically all of the rural population was Nonconformist and Radical. In Scotland, the crofters of the highlands formed an important segment of Radicalism.

19. Hanham, *Elections and Party Management,* pp. 77–78.

20. Paul Thompson, *Socialists, Liberals and Labour: The Struggle for London, 1885–1914* (Toronto, 1967), chap. 5.

21. Perkin, *Origins of Modern English Society,* pp. 347–64.

22. H. A. Clegg, Alan Fox, and A. F. Thompson, *A History of British Trade Unions Since 1889* (Oxford, 1964), pp. 49–50; Henry Pelling, *The Origins of the Labour Party, 1880–1900* (Oxford, 1965), p. 6.

23. Henry Pelling, *Popular Politics and Society in Late Victorian Britain* (New York, 1968), pp. 18, 54–57. Pelling questions whether a "labour aristocracy" really existed, though he makes it clear that there was a wide range of incomes in the working class.

24. June 14, 1885, Henry J. Wilson Papers, Sheffield Central Library, MD 2615–3.

25. Dilke Memoirs, BM 43,932, fols. 248–49.

26. Ibid., BM 43,933 fols. 44–45 and 269; and BM 43,934, fol. 156.

27. A. W. Humphrey, *Robert Applegarth: Trade Unionist, Educationist, Reformer* (London, n.d.), pp. 198–99; Hanham, *Elections and Party Management,* pp. 327–43.

28. Francis H. Herrick, "The Origins of the National Liberal Federation," *Journal of Modern History* 17 (June 1962):116–26; Joseph Chamberlain to John Morley, 19 April 1873, Chamberlain Papers, University of Birmingham Library, JC 5/54/13.

29. Quoted in Clegg, Fox, and Thompson, *History of Trade Unions Since 1889,* p. 51.

30. John Morley, *Recollections,* 2 vols. (New York, 1917), I:323–24; R. B. Haldane, *An Autobiography* (London, 1929), pp. 100–103.

31. Henry W. Lucy, *A Diary of the Salisbury Parliament, 1886–1892* (London, 1892), p. 215.

32. Morgan, *Wales in British Politics*, pp. 141–44.

33. Barry McGill, "Francis Schnadhorst and Liberal Party Organization," *Journal of Modern History*, 34 (March 1962):29; R. Spence Watson, *The National Liberal Federation: From Its Commencement to the General Election of 1906* (London, 1907), pp. 54–66.

34. National Liberal Federation, *Tenth Annual Report* (London, 1887), pp. 28–29.

35. Ibid., pp. 11–25; Percy Corder, *The Life of Robert Spence Watson* (London, 1914), pp. 244–47; Watson, *National Liberal Federation*, pp. 65–69.

36. See *Annual Reports* of the National Liberal Federation from 1886 to 1891.

37. *Origins of the Labour Party*, p. 6.

38. Cole, *British Working Class Politics*, chap. 5 and 6. B. C. Roberts, *The Trades Union Congress, 1868–1921* (London, 1958), p. 101.

39. Cole, *British Working Class Politics*, chap. 8; Roberts, *Trades Union Congress*, pp. 109–90.

40. Paul Thompson, *Socialists, Liberals and Labour*, p. 93.

41. Pelling, *Origins of the Labour Party*, pp. 22–23.

42. Hanham, *Elections and Party Management*, p. 135.

43. Ibid., p. 121.

44. Kenneth D. Buckley, *Trade Unionism in Aberdeen, 1878 to 1900* (Edinburgh, 1955), p. 100.

45. Hanham, *Elections and Party Management*, p. 325.

46. Working Men's Club and Institute Union, *Twenty-fifth Annual Report* (London, 1887), pp. 5, 25–26; *Twenty-seventh Annual Report* (London, 1889), pp. 24, 69–70; George Tremlett, *First Century of the Working Men's Club and Institute Union* (London, 1962), p. 40.

47. Charles Booth, *Life and Labour of the People in London, Final Volume* (London, 1903), p. 77.

48. See Howard Evans, *Radical Fights of Forty Years* (London, 1913).

49. Paul Thompson, *Socialists, Liberals, and Labour*, chap. 5.

50. National Liberal Federation, *Eleventh Annual Meeting* (London, 1888), p. 29; *Proceedings of the Fourteenth Annual Meeting* (London, 1891), pp. 18–20.

51. September 10, 1888, Gladstone Papers, BM 44,295.

52. Perkin, *Origins of Modern English Society*, chap. 8. It is also quite evident in Matthew Arnold's *Culture and Anarchy*.

53. See Perkin, *Origins of Modern English Society*, chap. 7; and Seymour M. Lipset, "Value Patterns, Class, and the Democratic Polity: The United States and Great Britain," in *Class, Status and Power*, 2nd ed. (New York, 1966), pp. 161–71.

54. Quoted in Perkin, *Origins of Modern English Society*, p. 230.

55. From a speech in Birmingham, 30 March 1883; see J. L. Garvin and Julian Amery, *The Life of Joseph Chamberlain*, 6 vols. (London, 1932–69), 1:392.

56. "The Future of the Radical Party," *Fortnightly Review* 199 (July 1883):6. The article is unsigned, but it seems reasonable to assume that T. H. S. Escott, the editor of the *Fortnightly*, wrote it.

57. See, for example, T. H. S. Escott, "The Radical Programme. ii. Measures," *Fortnightly Review* 201 (September 1883):439–41; J. E. T. Rogers, "The House of Lords," *Fortnightly Review* 212 (August 1884):257–70; Andrew Reid, ed., *The New Liberal Programme* (London, 1886), passim; *The Speaker*, 11 and 24 January 1890; and T. Wemyss Reid, "The Leeds Conference," *The Liberal Magazine* 11 (July 1894):200–202.

58. See Peter Stansky, *Ambitions and Strategies: The Struggle for Leadership in the Liberal Party in the 1890s* (Oxford, 1964), pp. 175–80.

59. Joseph Chamberlain, "The Liberal Party and Its Leaders," *Fortnightly Review* 81 (September 1873):287–302; R. W. Dale, "The Disestablishment Movement," *Fortnightly Review* 111 (March 1876):311–39; John Morley, "The Radical Programme. vi. Religious Equality," *Fortnightly Review* 209 (May 1884): 569–92.

60. Morgan, *Wales in British Politics*, pp. 77–140; James G. Kellas, "The Liberal Party and the Scottish Church Disestablishment Crisis," *English Historical Review* 79 (January 1964):31–46.

61. *The Congregationalist* (January 1874), p. 128; Joseph Chamberlain, "Free Schools," *Fortnightly Review* 221 (January 1877):54–72; Francis Adams, "The Radical Programme. v. Free Schools," *Fortnightly Review* 205 (January 1884): 1–20; Garvin and Amery, *Chamberlain*, 1:116–18.

62. Owen Chadwick, *The Victorian Church*, Part II (London 1970), pp. 202–207.

63. G. W. E. Russell, ed., *Sir Wilfrid Lawson, A Memoir* (London, 1909), passim; *Hansard* 120 (17 June 1874):2; and *Hansard* 151 (5 March 1880):441; W. S. Caine, "The Attitude of the Advanced Temperance Party," *Contemporary Review* 63(January 1893):48–52.

64. Sidney and Beatrice Webb, *The History of Trade Unionism* (London, 1894), pp. 361–62; Pelling, *Origins of the Labour Party*, pp. 9–10.

65. George Osborne Morgan, "Land Law Reform," *Fortnightly Review* 156 (December 1879):805.

66. F. M. L. Thompson, "Land and Politics in England in the Nineteenth Century," *Transactions of the Royal Historical Society*, 5th ser., vol. 15 (London,

1965), passim; G. J. Shaw Lefevre, *English and Irish Land Questions* (London, 1881), passim.

67. F. M. L. Thompson, "Land and Politics," pp. 40–42.

68. Joseph Chamberlain, "The Liberal Party and Its Leaders," pp. 287–302; Chamberlain, "The Next Page of the Liberal Programme," *Fortnightly Review* 94 (October 1874):405–29; John Morley to Chamberlain, 24 December 1882, Chamberlain Papers, University of Birmingham, JC 5/54/466; Chamberlain to Dilke, 31 December 1882, Dilke Papers, BM 43,885.

69. "Labourers' and Artisans' Dwellings," *Fortnightly Review* 204 (December 1883): 761.

70. Escott, "The Radical Programme. II. Measures," p. 446.

71. Frank Harris, "Housing of the Poor in Towns," *Fortnightly Review* 202 (October 1883):599–600; Jesse Collings, "The Radical Programme. IV. The Agricultural Labourer," *Fortnightly Review* 203 (November 1883):620–21.

72. Joseph Chamberlain, ed., *The Radical Programme* (London, 1885), passim. This book consisted of the essays published in the *Fortnightly* from 1883 to 1885 under the title "The Radical Programme," plus two essays on local government in England and Ireland. For the names of the contributors, see Joseph Chamberlain, *A Political Memoir, 1880–1892*, ed. C. H. D. Howard (London, 1953), p. 108.

73. A. J. Williams, "A Model Land Law," *Fortnightly Review* 244 (April 1887):569; *The Speaker*, 9 August 1890; and J. F. Moulton, "The Taxation of Ground-Rents," *Contemporary Review* 57 (March 1890):413–14.

74. Thompson, *Socialists, Liberals and Labour*, pp. 90–111; A. M. McBriar, *Fabian Socialism and English Politics, 1884–1918* (Cambridge, 1962), pp. 187–98 and 234–42; James Stuart, "The London Progressives," *Contemporary Review* 61 (April 1892):530–31.

75. February 8, 1888, quoted in Garvin and Amery, *Chamberlain*, 2:515.

76. See Helen M. Lynd, *England in the 1880's: Toward a Social Basis for Freedom* (New York, 1945); Pelling, *Origins of the Labour Party*, chap. 2.

77. "The Liberal Creed," *Contemporary Review* 54(October 1888):463.

78. G. W. E. Russell, "The New Liberalism: A Response," *Nineteenth Century* 151 (September 1889):498. See also L. A. Atherley-Jones, "The New Liberalism," *Nineteenth Century* 150 (August 1889):189.

79. Morley wrote to Haldane: "The Fabians interest and stimulate and suggest—but they are loose, superficial, crude, and impertinent. Does that satisfy you?" September 28, 1891, Haldane Papers, National Library of Scotland, MS 5903. For Bradlaugh, see H. B. Bonner and J. M. Robertson, *Charles Bradlaugh, A Record of His Life and Work*, 2 vols. (London, 1894), 2:382–83.

80. "Socialism and the Unemployed," *Contemporary Review* 53 (April 1888):561.

81. "The Liberal Creed," p. 466.

82. D. A. Hamer, *John Morley: Liberal Intellectual in Politics* (Oxford, 1968), pp. 255–70; Charles Bradlaugh, "Regulation by Statute of the Hours of Adult Labour," *Fortnightly Review* 279 (March 1890):440–54; Thomas Burt, "Mr. Chamberlain's Program," *Nineteenth Century* 190 (December 1892):868.

83. For the policy of the positivists, see Royden Harrison, *Before the Socialists: Studies in Labour and Politics, 1861–1881* (London, 1965).

84. "The Liberal Creed," p. 468. Also R. B. Haldane, "The Eight Hours Question," *Contemporary Review* 57 (February 1890):240–55.

THE ASSUMPTIONIST RESPONSE TO SECULARIZATION, 1870–1900

Judson Mather

The Augustinians of the Assumption, or Assumptionists, were a religious congregation established in 1850 by Father Emmanuel d'Alzon, the vicar general of the diocese of Nîmes. In most particulars, the order was very similar to dozens of other new congregations established in France during the nineteenth century. Yet during the last quarter of the century, the impact of this small congregation on French Catholicism was unparalleled. René Rémond calls the period between 1871 and 1901 the era of Assumptionist Catholicism in France. The Assumptionists, as he points out, not only epitomized the distinctive religious sensibilty of the era; they also organized and publicized it in a striking and effective way.[1]

In large measure, the Assumptionists' success was grounded on their ability to combine the old and the new. From the standpoint of their rule and style of life, the Assumptionists were a thoroughly conservative religious order. Their attachment to traditional social and political views was not merely a theoretical one; it was part of their daily experience.[2] Yet this conservatism did not extend to their activities. They adopted the techniques of large-scale organization and mass communication with great skill. Indeed, they utilized these techniques far more effectively than any French Catholic group more sympathetic to democratization and modernization.

The foremost instrument of the Assumptionists' response to secularization was their daily tabloid paper, *La Croix,* launched in 1883. *La Croix* cast a wide net; by the end of the century it had over 150,000 subscribers. It was the center of a vast network of regional supplements and subscription committees. Furthermore, as a paper competing with the secular as well as the religious press, *La Croix* became involved in a broader range of secular interests than any other Assumptionist activity.

It was these secular involvements that brought *La Croix* its greatest fame and notoriety. At the end of the century, the paper was credited widely with being the loudest and most violent Catholic voice in the anti-Dreyfusard camp. In the aftermath of the Dreyfus affair, the government raided Assumptionist houses throughout France and dissolved the order.

Judson Mather received his Ph.D. from the University of Michigan. He is currently teaching at Michigan State University.

It was, in retrospect, the opening shot in the campaign to separate the Church and the State.

All this suggests something about the real touchstone of the Assumptionist response to secularization: it involves their distinctive way of relating the sacred to the secular in their propaganda and activities. Why was it that the Assumptionists first turned to modern secular techniques in communicating their religious message? How did they make their innovations acceptable to conservative militant Catholics, and how did they handle the inevitable tensions between their medium and their message? Perhaps most important, how and why did the Assumptionist response to secularization change in the course of a generation? What did their reactionary politics, anti-Semitism, and xenophobic nationalism during the Dreyfus affair have to do with the distinctive religious sensibility that marked their appearance on the public scene? These are some of the questions that will be examined in the following pages.

The Assumptionist response to secularization was in many ways innovative and unique. But it grew out of an earlier militant Catholic response to the post-Revolutionary world. The aging Pius IX epitomized this response in an address to a group of French Catholics visiting Rome in 1871:

What I fear for you is not that miserable band of Communards—demons escaped from Hell—but Catholic liberalism. I do not mean those Catholics once called liberal (they often have deserved well of the Holy See) but that fatal system which dreams of reconciling two irreconcilables—Church and revolution. I already have condemned it, but if need be, I would condemn it forty times over.[3]

Perhaps the most remarkable aspect of the Pope's statement was his sense of the direction from which the most serious threat came. The Church was endangered far more by compromise, or "reconciliation," than by frontal assault. The worst enemy was the enemy within. This was a basic feature of militant Catholic psychology. They saw themselves as imprisoned by modernity, constrained, harassed, and tempted by it. Under such conditions, defiance and aloofness were viewed as primary needs. Their first task was to protect the Church's integrity.

This outlook had a formative influence on the ultramontane program of the militant Catholics between 1830 and 1870. Against the traditional "Gallican" or national liberties of the Catholic Church in France, ultramontanism proclaimed the authority of the Pope to regulate the details of the Church's life from "over the mountains." In practice, ultramontanism was a many-sided undertaking. It involved the centralization and tightening of authority in the Church. It worked for the standardization of the liturgy and of devotional tastes in the Roman pattern. It enthusiastically elaborated doctrines, such as the Immaculate Conception and papal infallibility, which underlined the militants' disdain for modern views and naturalistic explanations. Underneath this diversity of projects, however, there was a common theme. The militants were working to give the Church the kind of autonomy and distinctiveness they regarded as essential.

Quite early in this period, militant Catholics turned to journalistic publicity as one of their primary tools in implementing their program. Their main concern was that of arousing Catholic zeal and esprit de corps. Louis Veuillot, the editor of the militant Catholic daily, *L'Univers,* and one of the most dedicated and powerful churchmen in France, put it bluntly in 1850.

I am . . . very little troubled by the evil of not converting the impious; it is not to them that I devote myself; I devote myself to awakening, encouraging, and converting the faithful, to making them march into combat, to engaging them in it in spite of themselves. . . . These are the workers who will convert the impious.[4]

But militant Catholic publicity also had important secondary functions. It was an expression of zeal as well as a call thereto. It was a form of attack on secularization that minimized the risk of counterattack. This, indeed, was one of Veuillot's strategic advantages as a lay publicist. Militant Catholicism could speak through him without officially being responsible for what he said.

Furthermore, publicity was one of the most important means the militant Catholics had for insulating themselves from the world. Their mixture of piety and invective led to what Raymond Carr has called their "paranoid style." The metaphor is a suggestive one. Paranoia has its own inner logic; because militant Catholics viewed compromise as the greatest threat facing the Church, they saw the Church's isolation as an advantage to be protected rather than a difficulty to be overcome. The paranoid style enhanced this isolation. By being outrageous, militant Catholics could avoid the sympathy, and therefore the subtle interference, of the outside world. Publicity helped them to create the "space" necessary for shaping the internal affairs of the Church with relative freedom.

The character of militant Catholic publicity was closely related to the nature and purpose of militant Catholic politics. The militants faced a serious dilemma in their political response to the postrevolutionary world. On the one hand, they were genuinely preoccupied with politics. This was, at least in part, a consequence of their institutional perspective: the Church, rather than ideas or beliefs, was the category by which they measured everything. And the most obvious foil to the Church was the State. It was the State that assaulted the Church's property and freedom. And it was the State, through such devices as secular education and liberty of the press, that was the source of the insidious corruption that threatened the Church more subtly and pervasively. Yet the militant Catholics could not respond to this threat directly, through effective political participation. To do so would be to work within "the system"; it would be tantamount to an admission of the validity of the Revolution and the pluralistic world it had created.

The usual militant Catholic solution to this dilemma was to subordinate politics to publicity. That is, militants would use political issues and occasions more to gain exposure than to seek victories in elections. Veuillot sounded the authentic note of militant Catholic politics when he wrote to Albert de Mun in 1876, praising the latter's political platform: "Defeat on such a horse is worth more than success obtained by cringing. Such a defeat can only serve the cause; such a success could only jeopardize it."[5]

By the time of this letter, however, and in spite of Veuillot's assurances, the strategy of serving the cause was less certain than it had been a decade or two earlier. The impetus of militant Catholicism, the cause of ultramontanism, had succeeded. The Vatican Council's declaration of papal infallibility had been the capstone to a generation of effort. Furthermore, the crisis of the Franco-Prussian war had mitigated the sense of alienation from the nation felt by French Catholics. Seminarians, brothers from the religious houses, and papal zouaves fought for France on French soil. More than at any time since 1830, Catholics felt themselves to be a part of France.

The combination of doctrinal victory and national disaster pushed militant Catholics toward a more active participation in public affairs. They were predisposed to see the hand of God in history, and for them the message of the moment was clear. France had felt not the wrath of Bismarck but the wrath of God. Eighty years of sin and infidelity had had their reward. It was a warning and a call to national repentance and reparation. "We believe," wrote Veuillot, "that it is not by a revenge against the Prussians that France will regain its glory, but by a revenge against its sin."[6]

The leadership of the militant Catholic wing of the Church, men such as Veuillot and Cardinal Pie, tended to treat repentance as a political issue. There was, first of all, the plight of the Pope. To their mind, the events of 1870 had underlined the deep connection between France and Rome. The fates of the nation and the city were intertwined; the two had fallen together; they would rise together again. By petition and publicity, they mounted a vast campaign to have France come to the aid of "the prisoner in the Vatican."[7]

Militant Catholics also saw the hand of God in the opportunity France then had to restore the Bourbon monarchy. More than just their general royalist perferences were at work in this campaign. Catholic militants saw in the comte de Chambord one of their very own. The Pretender's rejection of the tricolor was a potent symbol of the militant Catholic attitude toward the Revolution, and their attachment to his cause grew as his opportunity to return vanished.

It mattered little to the militant Catholics that the causes of the

Pope and the Pretender were immensely unpopular. "My *métier*," wrote Veuillot, "is not to favor at any price the good personal relations between diplomats resolved to sacrifice principles to difficulties at any price."[8] Militant Catholics were accustomed to read unpopularity as a sign of integrity. What they failed to recognize was that these causes, for all their unpopularity, were basically secular issues. They were not adequate substitutes for the broad internal and religious concerns that ultramontanism had cultivated and expressed. To this extent, they were undercutting the "independence" of the Church so prized by the militants.

The Assumptionists were not yet publicists in the early seventies, and hence they avoided any deep involvement in the royalist and ultramontane politics of that period. They were, however, in a position to respond to and cultivate some the religious opportunities created by the postwar situation. They made the new religious sensibility of the era their own, and they made the organization and popularization of this sensibility into the kind of religious concern that ultramontanism had been during the previous generation. This fundamental concern provided the Assumptionists with an incentive to make improvements in established militant Catholic techniques. By the late seventies, they had begun to develop new forms of publicity to propagate their religious concerns.

Certain aspects of the Assumptionists' early development sensitized them to the need and the opportunities for popularization. The founder of the order, Father Alzon, saw organization as the key to forwarding the Church's interests. He himself was an indefatigable organizer, creating a dizzying succession of societies, committees, confraternities and clubs—to convert Protestants, observe Sunday rest, petition for Catholic universities, recruit papal zouaves, moralize the youth, pray for workingmen. It was a passion and a talent that he instilled in his followers.

A second factor was the means of recruitment established by the Assumptionists. A member of the elite himself, Alzon had hoped to attract his kind to the congregation. But though the aristocrats and the haute bourgeoisie in the Midi sent their sons to his college, the students did not become Assumptionists. In the mid-sixties, the Assumptionists reacted to this situation by creating a free seminary for poor boys. Graduates were free to become diocesan priests or to enter another religious order, but about half of them became Assumptionists. After 1870, the majority of the Assumptionists entered the order by way of these seminaries.[9] For themselves at least, the Assumptionists were finding the future of militant Catholicism among the people rather than among the elite.

The political conditions in the department of the Gard were a third factor that sensitized the Assumptionists to the importance of popularization. Of all the regions in France, the Gard was probably the one most polarized along religio-political lines. Religion really did determine politics there; Catholic "whites" confronted Protestant "reds" in every election.

Alzon was one of the most important political power brokers in the region. He was both a vicar general and a wealthy local aristocrat: a permanent fixture in a way that even successive bishops of Nîmes were not.[10] Thus the Assumptionists arrived on the public scene in France with more practical political experience and sophistication than most monks possessed. Perhaps most important, they had some practical preparation for coping with anticlericalism as a live and continuing political issue.

. Timing was also important. By 1870, the Assumptionists had been in existence for twenty years, and new men were moving into responsible positions in the order. These men were steeped in the ultramontane zeal of the earlier generation. But this meant that they had internalized ultramontanism to a considerable degree. Their chief concern was less one of defending new ideas than one of implementing established principles.

The key figure in the Assumptionists' work of popularization was Father Vincent de Paul Bailly. Bailly had a rather unusual background for a nineteenth-century monk. He came from a Parisian bourgeois family; his father had been an important if not famous Catholic activist in the thirties. Bailly had entered government service, and by the time of the Crimean War he had become Napoleon III's personal telegrapher. Shortly after the war he resigned, became an Assumptionist, and was ordained to the priesthood.

In 1870, Father Bailly was assigned to the Assumptionist house in Paris. He made himself useful to various Catholic organizations and committees, but it was not until 1872 that his real talent for organization became apparent. More or less by accident, the Assumptionists became responsible for organizing a large pilgrimage to La Salette.[11] Bailly made a great success of it, and moved quickly to turn the initial success into a permanent organization. By 1874, an important ecclesiastic, Mgr. Ségur, could write to an interested correspondent that

the Augustin Fathers of the Assumption [are] charged by the Pope with the great general work of pilgrimages. . . . It is very probable that the committees you mentioned to me and which are already in touch with those at Avignon are their pilgrimage committees; they are everywhere.[12]

The Assumptionists' involvement in the organization of pilgrimages meant that they were at the center of one of the most significant elements in the new religious sensibility of the seventies. The militant Catholic call for repentance and renewal was not, at its root, a political ploy. It had touched a responsive chord in France. The permanent monument to this postwar sensibility was the church of the Sacré Coeur on Montmartre, in Paris. It was built with subscriptions that poured in from everywhere in France: for chapels, for pillars, and even for stones. But the expressions of this sensibility that involved the greatest number of people most directly were the pilgrimages. Between 1870 and 1878, for example, almost a thousand pilgrimages, involving more than half a million pilgrims, were conducted to Lourdes alone.[13]

Had the Assumptionists limited themselves to popularizing and organizing pilgrimages, their influence would have been ephemeral. But they recognized that the pilgrimages were the form rather than the substance of the new sensibility; as the original enthusiasm for pilgrimages waned, they looked for other mediums through which the sensibility could be cultivated and expressed. In the mid-seventies, they turned to publication as a means for implementing this aim. Since the summer of 1872, the pilgrimage committees had distributed a glorified newsletter, *Le Pèlerin*. It carried, besides news of pilgrimages, innocuous legends and novels, and accounts of miraculous occurrences. In December 1876, Bailly took charge of *Le Pèlerin*. He immediately increased its size, added pictures, and made its tone and content more lively. The result was one of the first illustrated weekly magazines in France. Its success was impressive. By 1879, *Le Pèlerin* had 48,000 subscribers.[14]

Alzon originally had hoped that *Le Pèlerin* would "give a solid direction to Christian spirits." Hence he was somewhat disappointed with the way in which the magazine developed. "Let us not forget," he wrote in 1879, "that *Le Pèlerin* pleases because it deals in *le genre zozo* [the lisping style]. . . . It succeeds by . . . a deplorable propensity: the lowering of the spirit" and "the waste of it. Frenchmen are not capable of more."[15]

Alzon might have been disillusioned with *Le Pèlerin*, but he was pointing out one of the fundamental and distinctive characteristics of Assumptionist publicity. Their publicity served the same basic goals as earlier militant Catholic propaganda. Its aim was to mobilize the troops and to manifest the Church's distinctiveness and integrity to a hostile world. What differed was the role that the Assumptionists gave to ideas. Earlier militant Catholic publicity generally had reflected the view that right ideas are the basis of right actions. Though its concern was institutional, its approach was intellectual. It was heresy—theological, philosophical, historical, and political—that it condemned, and orthodoxy on these matters that it asserted.

The Assumptionist approach to publicity was the opposite. The Assumptionists took the stand that if the right enthusiasms were cultivated, the right ideas, in some form, would take care of themselves. The essential point was to get people to think of themselves as fervent Catholics, and to get others to see them in this way. Such an approach was realistic in two ways. It accepted the success of ultramontanism; it recognized that to be fervently Catholic was to be ultramontane, no matter what the quality of one's ideas. It also accepted the fact that the Church now had to defend its autonomy and integrity in a democratic and literate milieu. The enemy within that Pius IX had warned against had not disappeared. But it had changed. The threat no longer came from the cultivated Catholic liberalism that tried to reconcile the ideas of the Church and the Revolution. Now

it came from the ordinary Catholic who had no qualms about voting republican and reading secular republican papers.

Essentially, Assumptionist publicity was doing what older militant
Catholic publications once did, but by the seventies failed to do. It cultivated, supported, and extended militant Catholic organization. While Alzon
lived, there was a certain restraint on developing this approach further.
But three years after his death, Bailly went beyond *le genre zozo* of *Le
Pèlerin* and established a four-page tabloid daily, *La Croix*. The purpose
of the new paper was spelled out in the lead editorial of the opening number, written by Alzon's successor as Superior General of the Assumptionists,
Father Picard:

*We submit to a sad necessity. . . . In our opinion, the daily press is the scourge of
the epoch. The best of the dailies can do nothing, because it accustoms man to no
longer reflect, and to create a superficial society which laughs at everything and
can find a subject for amusement even in public mourning. . . . The review has
killed the book; the serious daily has killed the review; the newspaper has killed
the serious daily.*

*Why then, you ask, create one of these little dailies? Because there is no other
means to strike the enemy on the grounds that he ravages.*[16]

Picard's emphasis on the importance of the daily press had a real
basis in fact. Adult literacy in France went from 60 percent in 1870 to 95
percent in 1900, and the popular newspapers were at once the beneficiary
and the chief means of this increase.[17] *La Croix* sought to attract the Catholic element in this market. Its launching involved a recognition that for
Catholics as for other Frenchmen, new attitudes and new interests followed
in the wake of new skills. Bailly put it perceptively; *La Croix,* he said, was
addressed to "Catholics who need to know the news every day."[18]

What indications there are of *La Croix*'s readership suggest that it
reached the market for which it was intended. Its circulation was limited
not only in Paris and in the center of France but also in the traditionally
Catholic West. It was strongest in the North and (to a lesser extent) in the
Southwest and the Southeast.[19]

The workers were the showpiece of *La Croix*'s subscription lists. Because the paper wanted to cultivate a broad popular appeal, it characterized
itself as a paper of the workingman.[20] In the one social analysis of its subscribers that the paper published (dealing with a locale in the North), *La
Croix* found that its readers were 75 percent workers and 25 percent bourgeois.[21] It seems unlikely, however, that this pattern prevailed everywhere.
The Catholic workers in the North were a large and well-organized minority in a region where "reds" made up the majority. It was the kind of
situation in which La Croix could be an important voice.

Although *La Croix* pictured itself as a workingman's paper, it had
little to say about the particular interests, grievances, and aspirations of the

workers as a social class. Its emphasis was rather on the *character* of workers: their frankness and openness, their hatred of cant. *La Croix*'s typical workingman was not the victim of exploitation; he was the salt of the earth. The quality of his life was threatened not so much by bad employers as by bad fellow workers.[22]

This indicates something about *La Croix*'s appeal to its bourgeois readers.[23] The paper vociferously attacked the "bourgeoisie" for its spinelessness, its self-indulgence, and its lack of principles. But underneath the pyrotechnics, it shared the values of the bourgeois world in a very fundamental way. It stood for frugality, hard work, morality, and order. This distinction between the paper's rhetoric and its values is illustrated by one of Bailly's editorials in 1884.

The bourgeois atheist affirms that there is no other life, that no Providence keeps watch, that it is thus for each one to make his own place in the sun. Here is a doctrine that absolutely condemns the inequality of fortunes, and that incites the destitute to eat the bourgeois.

The editorial then launched into a witty dialogue between the bourgeois and the destitute. The bourgeois offer a substitute dish: "Eat priest! it's excellent." The destitute reply that they have done so already, and they still are hungry. So the bourgeois offer them "the magistracy" for a second course, and for a third tell them, "You have divorce; eat your family: it's excellent." But the destitute reply, "We would much rather eat the bourgeois." The editorial concludes by suggesting a "remedy to this voracity . . . ."

On the one side, it is necessary to instruct the bourgeois who "has" and to teach him to believe in the God of charity; then he will leave his belly and be an apostle to the truth. . . . On the other side, it is necessary that the destitute be lured to the truth by love, and that they be given those only riches which can salve misfortune here below: the certitude of another life and the eternal enjoyment of his God.[24]

It was hardly the kind of remedy that would fill the paper's bourgeois readers with consternation.

La Croix's position, then, was considerably different from that of the contemporary movement of Social Catholicism. The paper honored the leader of the Social Catholics, Albert de Mun, as a great politician and orator. But, as far as possible, it was discreetly silent about his ideas and programs. Its differences with him came into the open on the question of factory inspection for the protection of women and children:

We are absolutely in accord with our holy and eloquent friends in being against the crying abuse that women and children suffer in certain factories, and our indignation is increased by the description that has been made of it. But much more than this abuse, we dread that devouring monster which is called the socialism of the State.

Interventionism might be necessary in England, which had to cope with "the egotism of the Protestant Religion." But for France, *La Croix* acknowledged that it agreed with "the liberals": it reckoned "that the intervention of the State would be a greater evil than liberty."[25]

By the late nineteenth century, the lower clergy were coming to number among the Catholics who needed to know the news every day. *La Croix* was both cheaper and livelier than the old daily of the presbytery, *L'Univers*. Furthermore, it directed itself specifically to the lot and the potential of the lower clergy. It recognized their sense of intimidation:

One no longer says, as in '93, "The priests to the lamppost!" but rather, "The priests to the sacristy!" The formula is new, but the hatred it expresses is the same . . . and the persecution it foments is no less fierce.

But the paper did more than commiserate. It counseled the clergy to meet the attack directly:

If the enemy only wanted a political party out of it, the priest could hesitate. But it is a matter of defending the faith of a whole people, it is his raison d'être, *it is his life. Leave the sacristy. Go fight the enemy everywhere he is found. Pursue him into his last entrenchments . . . , mix in public affairs . . . , counsel and direct your troops.*[26]

La Croix's support for militant clergy went beyond good advice. The paper raised substantial sums for the "robbed curés"—or the clergy who were deprived of their salary by the Minister of Cults, usually for political indiscretions. But perhaps most important, *La Croix* offered the clergy a means of coming out of the sacristy. Circulating *La Croix* was presented to them as an evangelical enterprise.[27] The lower clergy became the salesmen of *La Croix* and the organizers of its salesmen. "I am among those," wrote one priest, "who regard the obligation of propagating the good newspaper as an obligation as grave . . . as those of saying my breviary, preaching the Gospel, and administering the sacraments."[28] Even the clergy who did not respond so enthusiastically found the paper appealing. In 1896, Picard estimated that *La Croix* had 25,000 readers among the priests.[29]

Although there was diversity among *La Croix*'s subscribers, the most important consideration in the paper's development was the common interests and concerns of its readers. Here the editors were faced with the old problem of militant Catholic politics. Catholics who needed to know the news every day were, if not politically sophisticated, at least politically sensitized and discontent. *La Croix* needed to meet this political interest if it was to succeed. But it also needed to control this aspect of its appeal, and subordinate it to the paper's fundamental religious concerns. It had to use politics for its own purposes.

La Croix's basic device for avoiding constraining political commitments was its thoroughgoing political negativism. It cultivated a mordant, implacable antigovernmentalism that seemed to suggest that almost any alternative to the current state of affairs in France would be an improvement. "We don't want to say," claimed one editorial,

that in itself the republic is an absolutely bad form of government, when the Church itself has not condemned it; but without the unity of the faith and the basis of the conscience, a parliamentary way, constituted with free-thinking, free-living members, without faith or law other than that fabricated by themselves, and over which the one just God does not reign, is a monstrous entity.[30]

This was as much as the paper would concede. It saw France becoming more and more like America, the "fatherland of self-government," where the "politicians are recruited from among the worst citizens, from the moral point of view." As a substitute for competence in government, universal suffrage "is a silliness that will astonish future ages." For a constitutional ruler cannot really rule; he himself is ruled by a majority and he "must leave his conscience in the privy" when he enters office.[31] *La Croix*'s political propaganda depended on the substance, if not the label, of antirepublicanism.

At the times of national elections, *La Croix* was fairly careful to avoid the risks of political alliances and involvements. In 1885, the first election year after the paper's founding, it made a rather clumsy attempt to establish a clerical party and program. But its main effort was to channel political interest and energy into devotional activities. *La Croix* claimed that prayer and not campaigning was the real key to victory. When the results of the first round of the election appeared encouraging, the paper contended that

prayer has had all the triumphs that it promised and it will be ever thus. . . . It is important to continue this month of the Rosary with great fervor, because God seems to have adjourned this run-off election in order to prove [our] perseverance. If this movement grows instead of declining from now to the 18th, God will reenter his country of France freely.

What could be treated as the potential source of victory could also, in the aftermath, be seen as the cause of defeat. "In place of the 112 deputies necessary to give a majority to the partisans of God," wrote Bailly, "we can count only about twenty of them. . . . All of those fine conservatives who have not put their effort into public prayer but . . . have put their belly at the table merit no salvation at all."[32]

La Croix's devotional emphasis was even more prominent in its handling of the next national election, in 1889. The paper created a front organization for the occasion, the Ave Maria League, which enabled it to claim that it was speaking "for" instead of "to" Catholic voters. In the teeth of the centenary of the Revolution, the League and the paper celebrated the bicentennial of St. Margaret Mary's call for the consecration of France to the Sacred Heart. Even the paper's platform for the election, which was published as the League's program, focused less exclusively on clerical politics than it had in 1885:

No more thieves. No more laicizers. No more persecutors. No more Freemasons. No more Jews. No more Prussians. No more foreigners to govern France. Nothing but honest men. Nothing but Catholics. Nothing but Frenchmen.[33]

This 1889 manifesto indicates a further important ingredient in *La Croix*'s political propaganda: its nationalist emphasis. Nationalism was useful to *La Croix* in at least two ways. On the one hand, it had provided a surrogate for the "party politics" the paper professed to scorn. On the other hand, it transcended the narrowness of the paper's fundamentally clerical interests. On the level of apologetics, nationalism provided a way of forwarding the institutional aims of the Church at the same time that it claimed its concern was for the common good: the broad concerns and high aims of the nation.

To some extent, *La Croix*'s nationalistic emphasis was a part of a general development on the political Right in France. As Raoul Girardet has pointed out, nineteenth-century nationalism in France was typically the preserve of political dissidents.[34] Through the first three quarters of the century, patriots on the Left could look back with nostalgia on the unity and glory of the Revolution. But after 1877, the Republic was the established regime, and antirepublicans could deplore the gulf between "the Republic" and "the nation." "Clearly the Republic is disintegrating the last forces of France more and more," said *Le Correspondant* in 1882; "it is religion that it attacks, it is the State that it weakens; it is society that it dissolves; it is the fatherland that it compromises."[35]

In the mid-eighties, however, *La Croix*'s nationalism went well beyond the conservative patriotism of the Right. It developed a distinctive form of Catholic nationalism centered on French imperialism. The key to the paper's position was the idea of mission. "France only exists by virtue of the people of God. . . . Each time France has been faithful to its mission, it has been filled with blessings." The "role of France," if it would accept it, was "the extension of the reign of Jesus Christ, of whom it is the lieutenant on earth." Thus there was an important element of providentialism in the paper's view of French imperialism. France was acquiring an empire not in a fit of absentmindedness, but in the grasp of unrecognized, beneficent forces. "We see," wrote Bailly, "the Cross and not the steamboat invading new regions. The steamboat is made to aid the missionaries and the saints; the best of packet boats is only an ass for relics."[36]

There is no doubt that imperialism was an appropriate interest for Catholic nationalism to pursue. French missionaries *were* an important arm of French imperialism in the Middle East, Africa, the Far East and the Pacific. Even such men as Gambetta and Paul Bert admitted that their anticlericalism was not for export to the colonies.

Furthermore, *La Croix*'s approach to nationalism was a good deal more appealing than the pessimistic revanchardism of the Right. It focused on future glory rather than past defeat, exotic adventure rather than present danger. In many ways, *La Croix*'s view was akin to the revolutionary, Jacobin nationalism of the earlier part of the century. Both were aggressive rather than defensive. And in both, the rhetoric of universalism only thinly veiled an underlying cultural chauvinism.

Yet although *La Croix*'s ideology was cogent and appealing, it was a serious political embarrassment. For imperialism was a Republican cause during the eighties; the Right considered imperialism to be dangerously irresponsible. It held that France could no longer "practice a national policy and a colonial policy at the same time. . . . It must concentrate its forces and its hopes" at the frontier with Germany rather than "spread them around the oceans."[37] The issue came into sharpest focus at the end of 1885, when the Chamber voted on the funding of the war in Indochina. On the Right, only one deputy, a bishop, voted with the government. *La Croix* was furious:

Mgr. Freppel . . . has dared to raise the flag of Catholic and French interests against the extreme Left and the entire Right: alone . . . , he has refused to be intimidated. . . . We counted on certain friends to the Right, and we are constrained by conscience to say that they have offered the saddest, the most unpatriotic spectacle that we have ever seen in a French Chamber. . . . Yes, today we have had the misfortune of seeing the cause of God and of our fatherland defended with intelligence by M. Paul Bert, against the greatest names of France.[38]

This editorial marked the apogee of *La Croix*'s imperialist emphasis. In the long run, the paper's antirepublicanism was too deep and its connections with the Right too strong for it to sustain this kind of singular opposition. By the end of the eighties, too, Boulangism had lent a certain swagger and popularity to revanche, and *La Croix* responded to this shift in popular taste. As can be seen in the paper's manifesto for the election of 1889, cited above, its nationalism had become more conventional, defensive, and xenophobic by the end of the decade.

Yet *La Croix*'s imperialist phase had more than a passing significance for the paper's development. As it has often been noted, nationalism can function as a surrogate for religion. In this sense, it was one of those compromises with the Revolution that militant Catholics most wanted to avoid. *La Croix*'s approach to nationalism helped to minimize, or at least obscure, this difficulty. Because the paper first had justified nationalism in a "Catholic" way, the ground had been prepared for its later shift to a more conventional nationalistic stand.

Beyond this, *La Croix*'s early nationalistic propaganda is indicative of the way the paper integrated its broad secular interests into its claim to be a purely Catholic journal. *La Croix*'s outlook was what might be called cultic; it tended to view all matters from the standpoint of their cultic function. France's empire was a reflection of the nation's Catholic vocation. Even steamboats, it claimed, had been invented to carry missionaries.

This kind of cultic emphasis and outlook was at the heart of the Assumptionist response to secularization. The Assumptionists viewed the conflict between the Church and the world not as a war between right and wrong ideas or even as a war between the sacred and the secular. Rather they saw it as a conflict between two opposed religious cults: each with its own creed, organization, and ceremonial, each making the effort to win the adherence of Frenchmen. The danger confronting France, they held, was not irreligion but a new religion. Secularization was a hoax, a mask for a new, satanic religion. *La Croix*'s task was to strip away this mask and expose the real, sacral character of secularization.

La Croix's emphasis enabled it to make a religious issue out of the most unpromising sort of material. But it could dramatize the peril confronting France best in issues where the religious question was obvious. The most striking instance of such a situation in the eighties was the furor surrounding the funeral of Victor Hugo, in late May and early June, 1885. It was a time of large type and black-bordered boxes on the front page of the paper. The "laic god," it proclaimed, "is Satan," and France could "look forward to a series of abominable feasts destined to establish the cult of Satan." The paper pictured the State as the incarnation of Satan; with Hugo's funeral, the cult of the *"Dieu-Etat . . .* is established as under the Terror," except that "the courtesan, the goddess of Reason, has been replaced by a cadaver."[39]

Elsewhere, *La Croix* tended to treat the Republic as the "Church" of the new, satanic religion. The deputies were "theologians . . . inspired by the devil," and the Chamber was described as the devil's headquarters; parliament, like hell, was the epitome of disorder and division. This religion also had its devotions: God, the family, the fatherland and good sense were suppressed "in order to adore the urn"—the ballot box.[40]

In the paper's view, the new religion worked through occult forces and key institutions as well as in a directly political way. The "princes and ministers" were not the real leaders of the day, wrote Picard in an editorial attacking Freemasonry. The real chiefs remained behind the scenes. "When one seeks them, when one goes to the bottom of it if he can, he finds the Jew or the enemy of Christ." Freemasonry, according to the paper, was the religion of Moloch, the god who demanded "blood in quantity" and "all the children of the nation."[41]

La Croix often saw the blood in quantity as being provided by the laicized hospitals. The paper attacked these institutions through a kind of running anti-anticlerical campaign. Nurses were not just nurses; they were *les religieuses laiques* or the new sisters of charity. Let one of them be arrested, and the whole story would be detailed on the front page of the paper. In the hospitals, the chapels were replaced by operating rooms; "dissection replaces services for the dead." Logically, laicized hospitals should provide patients with a rope for hanging themselves: "those who suffer interminably, and do not pray at all, find a supreme consolation in finishing with life by means of it." Indeed, "statistics have established that since laicization the average number of deaths, outside of all epidemics, has grown in an immense proportion in Paris."[42]

However bad laicized hospitals might be, they did not approach the evil being done by state education. In part, La Croix was frightened by the presumed effectiveness of "the neutral or atheistic State education." It was reaching the children of France and thus shaping the nation's future. But the crux of La Croix's grievance was with this education's "neutrality." Neutrality was the paper's word for pluralism, and there was no aspect of secularization that it hated and feared more. Pluralism did not simply arrive at the wrong answers; it undermined the whole framework of right and wrong answers. There was a radical falsity to pluralism, for it put truth on the same level as error. "There is no neutrality," the paper asserted. "There can be neutrality between two errors, but when the truth is in play, to put it in the same sack is a supreme outrage." Indeed, neutrality was a supreme outrage not only in principle but also in effect. The end product of pluralism was nihilism:

The nothing at all *is the latest style in making doctrine; the world tends to return into nothingness. . . . That which is called materialism, nihilism, atheism . . . prevails, even outside of madhouses. . . . The supreme genre of innovators [is] the suicides. . . . The world of the adversaries of God has arrived at the bottom of negations. . . . To be logical and practical . . . it kills itself.*[43]

There were a number of tactical advantages to La Croix's cultic emphasis. If the problems facing France were (as the paper claimed) essentially cultic, then they demanded the kind of cultic solutions the Church could offer. One of Bailly's editorials, for example, provided statistics on the alcohol problem in France and an intelligent discussion of the various schemes proposed for an alcohol tax. "Our advice," he concluded, "would be to double the price of small bottles, in order to provide a billion for the payment of . . . debts, and to build churches . . . where one would preach against drunkenness."[44]

More broadly and significantly, La Croix's cultic outlook provided a way of connecting its religious concerns with the sine qua non of popular journalism: sensationalism and an emphasis on crime and disaster. La Croix frequently treated both crime and punishment as rituals of the new religion. Anarchists' bombs were the laic equivalent of divinely ordained earthquakes; prisons were laic convents.[45] Executions, a stock-in-trade for sensational papers, were treated in great detail, but treated almost as liturgical events. Electrocutions were described as "infernal": an example of "the pretended humanity of our century." The paper strongly opposed the suppression of the death penalty or even of public executions. It was not happy, however, with the way executions were carried out in France. "We protest against the progressive laicizing of the death penalty as we have protested against the laicizing of the school." Proper executions should have a religious character:

In Spain, where the Catholic tradition is still vital, the death penalty is, on the one hand, singularly sweetened for the victim. On the other hand, the spectacle of executions preserves the great characteristic of dignity, and for everyone the lesson is profoundly moralizing. Thanks to the same religious sentiment, it was thus in the Papal States. . . . What moral beauty, what a beginning of rehabilitation on earth, for those whom justice must brand, and do you not see that religion gives incomparable grandeur to that which becomes ignoble and odious without it?[46]

There was another and even broader advantage to the paper's cultic emphasis. By sacralizing the secular in this way, it could offer a reassuring explanation for many of the unsettling changes that were taking place around the Church in France. The cultic view carried the implication, and often made the assertion, that God was in control.

This element is most obvious in the unvarying background of providentialism found in the paper. Do the enemies of the Church seem to have triumphed? It is only by God's permission:

Rebellious children, the greatest chastisement of your irritated Father has been to let you touch the fire from which He guarded you. Laicize, infect, manufacture [your] explosives, and when your volcano works, come crying for mercy at the feet of the Church; it alone can dress your wounds.

Nor is God's permissiveness without its warnings. Droughts and fires, epidemics and earthquakes are messages from God:

Law is changed; the Revolution is complete. . . . Does not God respond to these tremors of hatred with earth tremors? Have they ever been as terrible and as universal as in recent years . . . ? France will be terribly chastized along with all the neighboring nations which have drawn back from God and his Church. The unwonted phenomena which are happening in the world are the harbingers of appalling desolations.

If providentialism warned the evil it also comforted the just. It served as a justification for the cultic activity that the paper was constantly recommending to its readers. Novenas, pilgrimages, and pious organizations devoted to reparation were presented as the nation's last line of defense. Here were loyal French Catholics standing in the breach between the wrath of a just God and the defenselessness of a culpable, indifferent nation. Indeed, if the Church and the nation seemed weak and disorganized, that too had a purpose. It created the opportunity for God's providential intervention:

Humiliated from without, persecuted from within, prayers and tears are all that remain to you, O well-beloved France. Who knows? By the strength of prayer and suffering you soon may be the mother of some great Christian destined to enlighten and renew the whole West, like the converted Augustine. That this desired hero may come![47]

On the surface, *La Croix*'s journalistic style and technique do not appear to be much more than a crude foil to militant anticlericalism. This is true in part, but it is insufficient. There was a good deal of perceptiveness and imagination at work underneath the bluster. *La Croix,* in its noisy, popular way, reflected some of the insights of the most sophisticated contemporary conservatism, as it was being developed by Emile Durkheim. That is, the preoccupations that animated *La Croix*'s practical concerns were very similar to those behind Durkheim's theoretical interests.

In his first book, *The Division of Labor,* Durkheim took up the question of the social impact of modernization. The direct criticism in the book was leveled against the oversanguine optimism of Spencer's evolutionary sociology. But the implicit and overall polemic was against the nostalgia of Tonnies' *Gemeinschaft/Gesellschaft* distinction: the idea that the 'organic' solidarity of rural life had degenerated into the impersonal mechanical organization of the urbanized world. The parallel to *La Croix*'s program here is striking. The paper continually attacked optimism about modernity. But at the same time, with much less fanfare, it accepted and used the social changes that were taking place in France. It had a clear, practical understanding of the point that Durkheim was making theoretically: that physical density and mobility increase interaction, and interaction increases moral influence. That, in a sense, was what the pilgrimages and the newspaper subscription campaigns were all about. The Assumptionists recognized the new forms of association that were operative in France; their interest was in making these forms operate in the Church and for the Church.

The parallel between *La Croix*'s program and Durkheim's studies extended to the latter's pioneering work on suicide. Durkheim's *Suicide* was not "about" social problems any more than *The Division of Labor* was "about" Tonnies. But implicitly *Suicide* indicated the types of social situations that led to personal disintegration. Suicide rates were high where social solidarity was either too tenuous or too suffocating, or where life conditions were changing too rapidly. Clearly, at the end of the nineteenth century in France, the second "type" of suicide was far less a problem than the first and the third.

The significant social problem from this perspective, then, was that of giving sufficient social support to the individual while mitigating the impact of change upon him. This was something *La Croix* did very well for its readers. The paper's cultic emphasis and its technique of sacralizing the secular encapsulated modernization in a form that Catholics could understand and handle with some confidence. Furthermore, *La Croix* was not just something one could read; it was something one could belong to. Simply to be a reader of *La Croix* conferred a status—evoked a sense of belonging and of purpose. In spite of the paper's authoritarian outlook, it managed to communicate to its reader an image of himself as an admirable and self-possessed individual. He was courageous enough to march to the beat of a different drummer, acute enough to see through the fabrications of secular propaganda. Beyond this, belonging to the paper's readership opened up a further range of reassuring memberships and purposeful activities: committees, conferences, novenas and pilgrimages, subscriptions for the needy, and even occasionally a place in the sun through a printed letter to the editor.

The most obvious parallel—and distinction—between *La Croix* and Durkheim was the connection both saw between religion and society. Durkheim's view, presented in its developed form in *The Elementary Forms of the Religious Life,* was that the sacred was the mask, the cultic expression, of society itself. *La Croix*'s position was precisely the opposite. In its program of sacralizing the secular, it pictured society as an all-too-accurate and immediate reflection of a group's relation to the sacred. Setting out in opposite directions, the paper and Durkheim arrived at very similar positions. Both saw social solidarity as a function of religious unity, practice, and belief. "When the fatherland no longer has altars," wrote Bailly,

it no longer exists; it is a body without a soul. It still can be defended as strangers, brought together by chance at a hostelry, defend themselves against murderers in the hour of danger. But hostelry is not a family hearth. It has no soul.

The highest motives of union between men are the community of spiritual interests, and the greatest cause of disunion is not to agree on the means of preparing for eternity, that is to say, on the goal of life, since in the final analysis it is, above all, to guarantee menaced means of salvation that a family becomes a society, a fatherland.[48]

From a Durkheimian viewpoint, *La Croix*'s cultic emphasis might be retrograde, upside down. But it focused on the real hinges on which social organization turned.

The appeal and attractiveness of *La Croix*'s approach to a wide circle of readers is evident in the paper's success. In a period of a few years, it was transformed from an innovative experiment in popular religious com-

munication into French Catholicism's largest and most powerful journalistic institution, and indeed one of the larger dailies in France.[49] The
paper's most spectacular growth came in the late eighties. In April 1888, *La
Croix* had 60,000 subscribers. Six months later, this had risen to 85,000; a
year later to 109,000. By October 1889, the number stood at 128,000. The
growth of the paper is reflected in other ways. Early in 1887, it acquired a
high-speed rotary press. In 1889, it bought the printing plant it had been
renting since 1884. Its staff grew from thirty in 1885 to more than two
hundred and fifty in 1892.[50]

La Croix's rapid growth was in large part a result of the Assumptionists' genius for effective, large-scale organization. In the past, they had
applied this talent to the leadership of pilgrimages. Now they brought it to
bear on the matter of selling newspapers. The subscription campaign inaugurated at the end of 1887 differed from the paper's earlier ones; its focus
was on the organization of subscription committees. Papers were sent in
bulk to individuals or committees who would distribute them and solicit
subscriptions, at a profit to themselves. Six months after launching the
campaign, the paper still was pressing for more committees: "We are only
at the beginning of our campaign. . . . The efforts that have been made are
individual and local. The great force of association still has not been applied." An employee of *La Croix*, Abbé Garnier, traveled around the country organizing conferences and publicizing the paper. By March 1889, a
special periodical, *La Croix des Comités,* was being published. The campaign drew to a close at the end of 1889: "It was two years ago," wrote
Bailly, "that our subscribers, who were numerous but isolated, conceived
of founding committees. . . . They have surpassed all hopes." The organization was indeed an impressive one: by March 1893, there were 1,849 local
committees.[51]

In addition to the subscription committees, a network of regional
supplements to *La Croix* began to be developed at this time. The first of
these was established at Reims early in 1888; by 1895, there were almost one
hundred regional *Croix*, most of them weeklies. The most important of
them, however, were dailies; *La Croix du Nord* was publishing more than
20,000 copies a day in the early nineties.[52]

The rapid growth of *La Croix* had a number of consequences for the
paper. In the first place, it entailed a certain loss of editorial autonomy. In
the mid-eighties, *La Croix* was an instrument in the hands of its directors;
they *were* the institutional structure of the paper. But by the beginning of
the nineties, *La Croix* had become a complex organization, with a number
of interdependent, semiautonomous parts. The powerful committees and
supplements, especially in the Nord, had a voice in shaping the paper's
policy.

The rapid expansion and then leveling off of *La Croix's* circulation
also had the effect of fixing the paper's readership in a permanent way. This

did not change the paper immediately, but it did affect subtly the paper's potential for change. One of the factors behind *La Croix*'s growth in the eighties was the confidence of the Assumptionists in their enterprise. Its editors were convinced that *La Croix* would appeal to the great mass of Frenchmen, and that the great mass of Frenchmen would respond to it eventually. By the early nineties, it was apparent that this was not the case; *La Croix*'s world was that of a narrower, more reliable public than originally it had hoped for.[53]

Under ordinary circumstances, the inflexibility of *La Croix*'s established position would have mattered little. But just at the time that the paper's organization and clientele had crystalized, it was confronted with the necessity of changing its political stand. In an encyclical promulgated on February 16, 1892, Pope Leo XIII inaugurated the policy known as the Ralliement. Officially at least, the tacit alliance between the Church and the royalists in France was brought to an end. The Pope directed French Catholics to forego their opposition to the established regime and accept the Republic.

The ultramontane loyalties of the Assumptionists themselves might have been strong enough for them to swallow their preferences and do a political about-face. But *La Croix* could not count on its readers doing the same. In a sense, *La Croix* was caught by the political anachronism of the papal policy. For the Church to have a political line dictated from Rome was a step backward, however enlightened that line might be. *Le Temps* did not miss this point: "Ultramontanism exercised in favor of the Republic is no less dangerous than ultramontanism directed against it, and we have no more taste for the one than for the other."[54] In fact, the "danger" was rather small; the idea that the Church could legislate political behavior was out of date in France. Frenchmen had been showing this at the ballot box for twenty years.[55] The Ralliement was a reiteration of the illusion that a significant portion of the electorate could be enticed into "voting Catholic." The effect of this reiteration was to goad the royalist Catholic leadership into articulating what the republican Catholic troops undoubtedly felt:

The royalists yield with respect before the infallible authority of the Holy Father in matters of faith. As citizens, they claim the right that all peoples have, to speak out in liberty on all the questions which concern the future and the grandeur of their country. The form of government is one of these questions par excellence. *It is in France, and among Frenchmen, that it must be resolved.*[56]

La Croix understood and tacitly accepted the viewpoint expressed here. Hence it responded to the Ralliement with the utmost reluctance. It published the encyclical, but without any comment.[57] Early in May 1892, when the Pope went further and made it clear that he was demanding more than neutrality, *La Croix* characterized his demand as a "new and more pressing invitation to put religious interests above all others." But this would not do, and finally, some three weeks later, *La Croix* made its submission in an editorial written by Picard:

Let us attack none of our friends. . . . Let us say to all: the Pope wants unity: let us be united as he wishes. He tells us to accept the Republic; let us accept it. Let us march resolutely against bad institutions . . . , loyally attempting to establish a Christian republic in France.

If events do not respond to our efforts, what have we lost? Nothing. The merit of having obeyed the Pope and of not having despaired over our country will remain with us always.[58]

The paper's distaste hardly could have been communicated more effectively.

The Ralliement, in a sense, was even more damaging to *La Croix*'s style than to its position. "Speak little, work much, pray even more: that is our motto," wrote Picard shortly after *La Croix* had rallied.[59] Working much and praying more were possible, but speaking little could not last. Prudence was the one thing *La Croix* could not long afford. The impetus behind the whole enterprise was the militant communication of the Assumptionists' grievances and enthusiasms. New channels for this impetus had to be found. As *La Croix* was forced to curtail some of its antirepublicanism, it developed the anti-Semitic and nationalistic themes that were already present in its propaganda.

These changes in emphasis affected *La Croix*'s propaganda more drastically than might have been expected. For it was a shift from a genuine to an artificial emphasis. Catholic grievances against the State were real grievances; the State in fact was abusing the Church in some ways. But Catholic grievances against Jews and foreigners were largely manufactured ones. And perhaps most to the point, an animus against Jews and foreigners was hard to justify on purely religious grounds.

The problem was most clear-cut in the paper's anti-Semitism. In the eighties, *La Croix*'s formal position with regard to the Jews was "religious"; it disavowed pogroms; it was only concerned with the conversion of Jews. But this was not the aspect of the paper's anti-Semitism that appealed to its readers. With the enormous quantitative increase in *La Croix*'s invective against the Jews during the nineties, the restraining effects of its formal position were overwhelmed. The demagoguery and its justification became a kind of closed circle. The demagoguery spoke of the enormous threat posed by the Jews; the enormous threat justified the demagoguery. In 1892, for example, a Jewish army officer, Captain Mayer, was goaded into a duel by *La Libre Parole* (an anti-Semitic newspaper) and killed. Bailly was disturbed by the outcry this raised, and told *La Croix*'s readers:

Do not let them exploit the deviations of La Libre Parole *for the purpose of checking the legitimate defense of Catholics, outraged everywhere by the Semitic press, and let them also consider, even while blaming* [La Libre Parole], *the mission it has been given of raising one of the most formidable problems of our times.*[60]

Clearly, the connection here between fervent Catholicism and vicious anti-Semitism was very strained. Journalistic outrage did not justify murder. Increasingly, *La Croix* found itself forced to fill in the picture of the "formidable problem" posed by the Jews. By 1894, it was publicizing a picture of the threat of a vast secular conspiracy. Jews and socialists, Protestants and Freemasons, England and Germany were working hand in hand for the overthrow of France.[61]

The Dreyfus affair had the effect of crystalizing this aspect of *La Croix*'s propaganda. The affair seemed to provide a vindication for the paper's new emphasis; it "showed" that all *La Croix* had been warning against was true. Beyond this, the affair gave the paper's nationalism and anti-Semitism a cause and focus they previously had lacked. The effect of this, however, was an extensive alteration of the paper's response to secularization. In the heat of the Dreyfus affair, *La Croix* abandoned its old penchant for sacralizing the secular. It had, in a sense, turned away from its original cause.

Most obviously, the paper seemed to lose its sense of the unique and superior importance of the Church. This change was most visible in the role the paper attributed to the army. During the eighties, *La Croix*'s attitude toward the military was ambivalent. It admired "the sacrifice and patriotism of soldiers . . . , the ideas of energy and devotion." But it found the current organization of the military to be odious: "We envisage universal obligatory military service in a completely different way."[62] By late 1898, however, the paper explicitly repudiated its distinction between the army in theory and the army in practice. For "too long," it said, "we have been content with vehement exclamations on the severities of the conscription law, the dangers of the barracks, on the disaster to faith and morals, on the scorn of the rights of the Church." It was time for "all Catholics to unite and devote themselves to giving the army conscripts well steeped in the love of the fatherland." The paper exalted in "the alliance of the saber and the holy water sprinkler," and Bailly went so far as to claim, "The Army is France!"[63]

The development of *La Croix*'s nationalism went hand in hand with its militarism. By the late nineties, the paper was claiming an intrinsic connection between Catholicism and nationalism. All the delegates attending an anti-Semitic congress at Trent, it said, showed "the most sincere and ardent patriotism"; it was a "new revelation of the Christian spirit." Later, it claimed that "everywhere one sees the Church arising as the bulwark of nationalities against the invasion of internationalism. . . . Everywhere Catholics affirm themselves to be patriots, and in each country the most Catholic are the most patriotic." In *La Croix*'s ideology, the army and the nation had come to a kind of coequality with the Church. "The hour is critical," said one of the paper's manifestos, "but we do not doubt the salvation of our dear country, because we hold that France must participate in the immortality of the Church."[64]

The secularization of *La Croix*'s enthusiasms carried over into a profound secularization of the attitudes it expressed. It no longer tried so hard to find a sacred meaning in secular situations. Indeed, it tended to take a leaf from the book of the anticlericals, and turned to the debunking of its religious opponents. It called Protestantism "a dead form, galvanized solely by interest." Most Protestants were free "of all vestiges of Christianity." Their religion had become "the religion of money. . . . Everyone knows today that Protestantism is not a religion but a party"; its power resides in "the money received from the full hands of England, Germany, and perhaps also the Jews."[65]

This kind of cynicism deeply affected not only the paper's enmities, but also its view of the interests and prospects of Catholicism. In one of its most widely noted editorials, it rejoiced over the "reaction in favor of Catholicism" displayed in the anti-Semitic riots in Algeria; shopkeepers were writing on their windows, "Catholic firm; no Jews here." Bailly claimed that "the royalty of Christ in Algiers is . . . manifested . . . by the protection and immunity that the title of French and Catholic assured to all the stores which did it the honor of carrying it publicly."[66]

By the end of 1899, *La Croix*'s cynicism sometimes lost even the trappings of piety. The flavor of the paper's outlook was captured in Bailly's remarks on the attempted assassination of Dreyfus's lawyer, Labori, at the Rennes trial: "We couldn't resign ourselves, last Saturday, to write the little article of reprobation that an assassin merits, because we suspect that Labori was playing a new act in his comedy."[67] This came very close to the kind of nihilistic attitude that *La Croix* once had reprobated as the end product of secularization.

La Croix's changed response to secularization had the effect of playing into the hands of its enemies. Politicized and violent, *La Croix* was the epitome of what the anticlericals found odious about Catholics in general and monks in particular. Powerful and widely read, *La Croix* could be treated as a threat in the very way that it had treated Dreyfus: nefarious in itself, and at the same time "only a flag" for a wider and deeper danger.[68]

Yet *La Croix*'s slide into secularized propaganda was not so inadvertent as its response to the Dreyfus affair might suggest. The paper's fundamental religious concerns did not disappear. But these concerns were altered drastically in the mid-nineties, chiefly in the course of the paper's response to a particular piece of anticlerical legislation.

Early in 1895, the government enacted a new tax on religious orders, the so-called Ribot Law. The Catholic reaction was vociferous; even journals that genuinely supported the Ralliement, such as *L'Univers* and *La*

Quinzaine, were outraged. *La Croix* treated the new law as a fresh revelation of the fundamental anticlericalism of the Republic; it was an opportunity for the paper to revive its old antirepublicanism. But in its anxiety to exploit the issue to the full, the paper abandoned some of the most important cautions it had observed in its earlier response to secularization.

From the start, *La Croix* claimed that the new law was not only odious but also unconstitutional. By taxing the religious differently, the government was denying their equality before the law. Hence civil disobedience was not merely permissible; it was a duty: "If the religious, by paying however little it might be, were to accept . . . the law," they "would be making a coup d'etat with M. Ribot."[69] This was further than the paper ever had gone in the past. It had engaged in violent polemic against anticlerical legislation, but a serious call—and commitment—to resistance was unprecedented. In one stroke, *La Croix* put itself in a position that it had managed to avoid during the previous twelve years of its existence. It became involved in an important controversy within the Church, the voice of an organized and powerful faction. *La Croix*'s polemic, formerly reserved for the "world," was turned on fellow churchmen. The paper attacked bishops and religious orders, which decided, reluctantly, that the tax had to be paid. And it insinuated constantly that the Pope's neutrality on the issue was not genuine. "What is certain is that the *Pope does not command paying*. The Holy Father does not defend paying either. . . . Heroism is not imposed."[70] With considerable justification, *L'Univers* accused *La Croix* of making "Rome speak when Rome says nothing," of using "ruse and equivocation" in reporting "deductions, appreciations and desires as facts."[71]

In addition to this new adventure in Church controversy, the Ribot Law supplied a justification for *La Croix*'s turning to direct political action. If this particular law was as decisive and important as the paper claimed, then the Church's ability to put political pressure on the government became equally important. "*If you had good deputies you would not have these detestable laws;* the electoral work is thus the work of works."[72]

The Assumptionists brought to this new concern for political action not only their abilities as propagandists but also their formidable organizational talents. Using *La Croix*'s hundreds of circulation committees as a base, they launched a new organization, the Justice-Equality Committees, early in 1896. Within a few months, the Committees were the most powerful and best-organized Catholic political group in France. Thus divisiveness of action was added to divisiveness of word. By focusing on anticlerical legislation, the Justice-Equality Committees were working at cross purposes to the Pope's efforts to effect a reconciliation between the government and the Church in France.

The éclat surrounding *La Croix*'s political activities tended to obscure an even more fundamental change occasioned by the Ribot Law controversy. *La Croix* claimed that the real issue at stake in the controversy was religious; it was not money or property or even the constitution, but the integrity of the religious orders. We defend the property of the congregations, said Bailly, "as a supreme reserve of the fatherland, and we have so little concern for their walls and their pocketbooks that we congratulate them for letting themselves be sold, led into prison and strangled, if it is necessary, rather than accept the slow poison" of the Ribot Law.[73] The integrity of the religious life was not, of course, a new concern with the Assumptionists. But with the Ribot Law, this concern came to be handled in a completely different way. What had been previously the source of Assumptionist activities came to be seen as the object of those activities. The Assumptionists were retreating into a narrower and safer position.

This is a crucial point, which deserves some elaboration. For "active" religious orders, or those engaged in work outside the cloister, there has always been a certain amount of tension between life and work. During the nineteenth century, this tension was reenforced by the deliberate archaism of the religious life. The archaism was not inadvertent; confronting the present with the past was part of the nineteenth-century monastic response to secularization. In this, however, the nineteenth-century orders differed from the most successful monastic responses to secularization in previous eras. The seventh-century Benedictines, the twelfth-century Canons, the thirteenth-century Friars and the sixteenth-century Jesuits all had altered their monastic life style in response to changes in the contemporary secular social order. They fitted their life to their work in a way that most nineteenth-century congregations did not.

A crucial part of the Assumptionists' achievement was their ability to turn this limitation into an advantage. They were not intimidated by the tension between past and present, life and work: they gloried in it. They did not regard their traditional monastic culture as a protection against the world. Rather it was their indispensable resource in confronting the world. The confidence and enthusiasm with which they did battle had much to do with their appeal and persuasiveness in Catholic circles.

Yet this distinctively extroverted stand taken by the Assumptionists was really a rather precarious one. It had little support in the Church beyond the Assumptionists' own sense of self-confidence. And by the early nineties, the "evidence" that supported this confidence was less compelling than it had been in the past. *La Croix*'s circulation had reached a plateau; publicity, mass communication, and mass organization were not tranforming and revitalizing the Church in France. The Assumptionists faced a double problem. From the viewpoint of outsiders, there was the question of whether they were doing too much: Was sensational journalism really an appropriate monastic activity? From their own viewpoint, there was the question of whether they were doing enough: Were "mere words" sufficient for their task, and a sufficient witness to their dedication and zeal?

The Ribot Law controversy presented an opportunity to deal with both these problems at the same time. The Assumptionists were able to authenticate their words with an act. By their gesture of defiance, they were putting their work and enterprise on the line. They were risking prosecution and possible expropriation as a witness to their integrity. By the same token, their intransigence downgraded the religious importance of their activity; their enterprise become detached from their central religious preoccupations and auxiliary to them. There was a certain finality to the gesture of defiance. It had no progam; it involved no need to adapt to changing circumstances. Although there was a great deal of scope left for explanation and justification, nothing could be added to the gesture itself. The initiative was forced deliberately back into the hands of the State.

La Croix, in effect, was trying to create a situation in which the Church, at least by its own standards, could not lose. Defiance of the Ribot Law created two possible futures. On the one hand, the balance of power within the government might be changed, the law dropped, and the orders' intransigence vindicated. On the other hand, the law might be enforced, and the benefits of persecution would be reaped by the Church. "They will plunder, possibly, but then they will plunder by force, and whatever they say, this conspicuously changes the role of the State. This above all can change the future." "One can only remember with confidence that the destruction" of the religious orders during the Revolution "created a religious vitality twenty times more intense" and "multiplied works and vocations."[74]

The religious stand *La Croix* reflected after 1895, then, was one that combined withdrawal and extremism. The paper cultivated an atmosphere of impending martyrdom: "On entering their chapel these days, the religious say, 'Now it is ready; the hour of God will sound. . . . The victim is prepared and ready.'" Frequently the paper spoke of St. Lawrence, the deacon who had been grilled alive for his defense of Church property, as the patron and exemplar of the religious orders in France.[75]

This extremism in *La Croix*'s religious outlook in the late nineties ran parallel to the paper's extremism in secular polemic, and served as a justification for it. *La Croix* had come to hold that polarization and confrontation best could serve the interests of the Church in France. In anti-Dreyfusardism and political activity, as in its religious response to the Ribot Law, the paper worked to bring about the kind of polarization and "choice" it saw as essential.

Through all the extensive changes in the Assumptionists' response to secularization, there was one important and central element of continuity. For the Assumptionists as for Pius IX, the refusal to "reconcile the Church and the Revolution" remained fundamental. And for both, at the core of this refusal was the rejection of pluralism, and above all the pluralism of the modern State. Militant Catholics saw in the modern State the subversion of the Church's traditional normative role in society. The Church, of course, continued to speak as if it were the arbiter of social morality and personal ethics. But it was competing with other outlooks in these matters, and the State was acting as referee in this competition. Thus from the standpoint of the militant Catholics, the State had both usurped the Church's function and corrupted its own. It had abdicated the role of enforcing the Church's truth and had debased its own activity into the mere allocation of influence. It was, in *La Croix*'s phrase, "the supreme outrage."[76]

The reaction of militant Catholics to this outrage was ambivalent. On the one hand, they attempted to gain and hold onto a kind of privileged access to the State: the solution of clerical politics. On the other hand, they tended to dismiss the modern world as hopelessly benighted, and to pre-occupy themselves with internal, institutional concerns. *La Croix*'s initial program was an imaginative and cogent departure from these tendencies. It recognized that ultimately public opinion rather than the State itself had become the source of value judgments. Hence though it used political rhetoric, it bypassed politics; it made its appeal directly to public opinion. *La Croix* was attempting to bring indirect but effective pressure to bear on the State.

A number of factors entered into the breakdown of this initial response, but the most decisive was the coming of the Ralliement. In one way, the program of the Ralliement was the precise opposite of *La Croix*'s program. *La Croix* was using innovative means to achieve traditional ends. The Ralliement used traditional means—the dictation of political norms by religious authority—to achieve a new and (to the militants) threatening end: the acceptance of the modern, pluralistic state.

La Croix first tried to temporize. But when the Assumptionists felt the integrity of their religious life to be threatened, they turned their energies to the old militant Catholic effort of keeping the Church pure and uncompromised. This involved the remobilization of clerical politics. Yet *La Croix* was not really concerned with winning a voice for the Church in public affairs. Rather it was concerned that if any voice were heard from the Church, it would be the right voice. Its aim was to drown out those Catholics who would make the fatal compromise with pluralism.

If *La Croix*'s political program in the nineties was a reflection of its basic concerns, so were its alliances. The old political foil to republican pluralism, that of royalism, had been authoritatively rejected by the Pope. Both because of the connections *La Croix* had been cultivating since its founding, and because of a lack of alternatives, the paper moved decisively into the nationalistic and anti-Semitic camp. Yet there was more than sheer opportunism in this emphasis. The alliance fitted the paper's real concerns. For nationalism and anti-Semitism were inherently integral. They pushed pluralistic divisions into the background; they asserted that the basis of self-identification and belonging was not divisive. It was not social class or political party, or ultimately even religious affiliation, that mattered. It was patriotism, Frenchness.

The shifts in La Croix's emphases answered some of the paper's most pressing and immediate problems. But the Assumptionists' success as a force in secular politics and publicity was a dubious one. Once involved in broad secular causes, all the paper had to offer was the politics of martyrdom: a final if negative way of manipulating the State to treat the Church as a unique and important institution. As best, La Croix prepared the ground for the Church's official response to the separation controversy, namely, the position that victimization was better than compromise. At worst, it did much to forward a cause it would have reprobated in earlier years: Maurras' "politics first of all" and his "clericalism without God."

What was lost in the midst of these changes undertaken by La Croix was the distinctive religious sensibility that the Assumptionists had epitomized, publicized, and organized. La Croix maintained its old techniques and involvements, but it lost its original inspiration. It had become a noisy and obtrusive advocate of conventional anti-Semitism, nationalism, militarism, and political activity—and of conventional militant Catholicism. It had abandoned its original innovative goal of popular religious communication for the limited one of intransigent institutional defense. Thus the government's dissolution of the Assumptionists at the end of 1899 was in one way anticlimactic. The Assumptionist era in French Catholicism already had come to an end.

NOTES

1. René Rémond, *The Right Wing in France from 1815 to De Gaulle* (Philadelphia, 1966), pp. 184–88.

2. P[olyeucte] Guissard, *Un Siècle d'histoire assomptioniste* (Worcester, Mass., 1950), pp. 55–58.

3. Cited in Philip Spencer, *Politics of Belief in Nineteenth-Century France: Lacordaire, Michon, Veuillot* (New York, 1954), p. 244.

4. Louis Veuillot, *Oeuvres completes* (Paris, 1932) 18:215.

5. Veuillot, *Oeuvres*, 26:103.

6. Cited in Eugene Veuillot, *Louis Veuillot* (Paris, 1901–1913), 4:181–82.

7. See Eber Malcolm Carroll, *French Public Opinion and Foreign Affairs, 1870–1914* (Hamden, Conn., 1964), pp. 50–52.

8. Veuillot, *Oeuvres*, 25:262.

9. Guissard, *Histoire assomptioniste,* p. 82. See the same author's *Histoire des alumnats, le sacerdoce des pauvres* (Paris, 1955).

10. Jean Maurain, *La Politique ecclésiastique du Second Empire de 1852 à 1869* (Paris, 1930), pp. 300, 302, 390–91, 505.

11. Michael Guy, *Vincent de Paul Bailly, fondateur de La Croix, cinquante ans de luttes religieuses* (Paris, 1955), pp. 66–68.

12. Cited in Marthe de Hédouville, *Monseigneur de Ségur, sa vie, son action, 1820–1881* (Paris, 1967), p. 603.

13. E. Lecanuet, *L'Eglise de France sous la Troisième République* (Paris, 1910), 1:380–82.

14. Guy, *Vincent de Paul Bailly,* pp. 83, 88. Pierre Sorlin, *La Croix et les Juifs, 1880–1899: contribution à l'histoire de l'antisémitisme contemporaine* (Paris, 1967), p. 26.

15. Letter to F. Picard, 19 December 1876: cited in Adrien Pépin, *L'Ame d'un grand apôtre, le père d'Alzon* (Paris, n.d.), p. 342. Letter to F. Picard, 9 December 1879: cited in Sorlin, *La Croix et les Juifs,* pp. 27–28.

16. *La Croix,* 16 June 1883.

17. Robert F. Byrnes, "The French Publishing Industry and Its Crisis in the 1890's" *Journal of Modern History* 23 (September 1951):232.

18. Cited in Guy, *Vincent de Paul Bailly,* p. 108.

19. See maps in Sorlin, *La Croix et les Juifs,* pp. 49–52.

20. *La Croix,* 13 March 1888; 8 February 1889.

21. *La Croix,* 20 August 1888.

22. *La Croix,* 23 May 1888.

23. The fact and the extent of *La Croix*'s bourgeois readership has been shown by Sorlin's research in the police files at the *Archives nationales.* See *La Croix et les Juifs,* pp. 48, 53.

24. *La Croix,* 4 July 1884.

25. *La Croix,* 17 June 1888; 13 September 1890.

26. *La Croix,* 11 December 1884; 26 April 1890.

27. By the late eighties, it also could be a way to add to their income: see below, page 77.

28. *La Croix,* 6 March 1896.

29. Sorlin, *La Croix et les Juifs,* p. 36

30. *La Croix,* 10 May 1885.

31. *La Croix,* 16 April 1885; 21 June 1885; 28 October 1884.

32. *La Croix*, 7 October 1885; 20 October 1885.

33. *La Croix*, 9 October 1888; 2 April 1889; 1 June 1889; 7 June 1889; 4 July 1889.

34. Raoul Girardet, "Introduction à l'étude du nationalisme française," *Revue Française de Science Politique* 8 (1958):519.

35. *Le Correspondant*, 10 April 1882, p. 186.

36. *La Croix,* 22 March 1884; 26 November 1885; 28 January 1886.

37. *Le Correspondant*, 25 February 1888, p. 764.

38. *La Croix*, 23 December 1885.

39. *La Croix,* 30 May 1885; 28 May 1885; 3 June 1885.

40. *La Croix*, 6 June 1884; 5 November 1888; 1 March 1889; 17 June 1884.

41. *La Croix*, 2 May 1884; 31 May 1884.

42. *La Croix*, 23 September 1886; 6 February 1885; 13 March 1886; 6 December 1885.

43. *La Croix*, 28 April 1885; 23 March 1886; 19 March 1885.

44. *La Croix*, 26 January 1886.

45. *La Croix*, 6 June 1884; 16 December 1885.

46. *La Croix*, 8 August 1890; 22 May 1894; 26 June 1898; 22 May 1894.

47. *La Croix,* 28 January 1885; 6 June 1884; 5 May 1885.

48. *La Croix*, 2 July 1884.

49. In the early nineties, the *Petit Journal* had a circulation of over a million, the *Petit Parisien* about half that. But *Le Figaro,* for example, had a circulation of only 30,000. See Sorlin, *La Croix et les Juifs*, p. 254.

50. Sorlin, *La Croix et les Juifs*, pp. 41, 30, 252.

51. *La Croix*, 18 December 1887; 29 May 1888; 1 December 1889. Sorlin, *La Croix et les Juifs*, pp. 44, 255–56.

52. Sorlin, *La Croix et les Juifs*, pp. 45, 255, 257.

53. In the early nineties, *La Croix*'s emphasis on being a workingman's paper practically disappeared.

54. *Le Temps*, July, 1891.

55. See Charles de Lacombe, *Journal politique* (Paris: 1908), 2:41. Entry for April, 1874. "The peasants say to me, 'It is necessary to wed the Republic with Napoleon!' . . . because according to them the Republic is not strong enough to protect them against the *ancien régime* and the regime of priests."

56. Declaration of the royalist deputies, 9 June 1892. Cited in Lecanuet, *L'Eglise de France*, 2:547–48.

57. *La Croix*'s silence was not atypical. Only a quarter of the episcopate made a favorable pronouncement on the encyclical.

58. *La Croix*, 7 May 1892; 25 May 1892.

59. *La Croix*, 12 June 1892.

60. *La Croix*, 28 June 1892.

61. *La Croix*, 5 November 1891; 6 May 1892; 3 May 1893; 25 October 1893; 28 November 1893; 6 January 1894.

62. *La Croix*, 1 October 1893.

63. *La Croix*, 13 October 1898; 16 July 1898; 15 December 1898.

64. *La Croix*, 7 October 1896; 16 February 1899; 22 January 1899.

65. *La Croix*, 23 December 1897; 7 August 1898; 9 May 1899.

66. *La Croix*, 3 April 1898; 19 December 1899.

67. *La Croix*, 17 August 1899.

68. *La Croix* publicized the attacks made on it. See 1 March 1899; 20 May 1899; 22 September 1899; 29 September 1899; 3 October 1899.

69. *La Croix*, 21 March 1895.

70. *La Croix*, 2 August 1895. See also *La Croix*, 16 May 1895; 1 June 1895; 11 August 1895; 10 September 1895; 14 September 1895; 12 October 1895.

71. *L'Univers*, 15 August 1895. See also *L'Univers*, 28 July 1895; 4 September 1895; 12 September 1895; 3 October 1895; 18 October 1895; 20 October 1895.

72. *La Croix*, 11 November 1896.

73. *La Croix*, 4 December 1898.

74. *La Croix*, 22 October 1895; 18 March 1899.

75. *La Croix*, 18 March 1899; 1 May 1895; 5 May 1895; 6 June 1895; 11 August 1898.

76. *La Croix*, 23 March 1886.

II. WORKING CLASSES

The essays in this section are concerned with two distinct types of working classes, a "preindustrial" artisan community on the one hand, and a factory labor force on the other. They are bound together by a mutual interest in re-creating the social structures of specific urban environments. As such, they are representative of the importance of local studies in social history, and also they mark the influence of what has been called the new urban history. Both essays use examples of collective violence—the Lyon uprisings of 1831 and 1834 and the Milan revolt of 1898—as the lens through which our attention is focused on the development of the working classes. The explanation for this emphasis rests not only on the authors' desire to extend our knowledge concerning the role of violence in European history, but also on the acknowledgement that historians are most likely to find information about the lives of ordinary persons from accounts of their extraordinary activities. Success in writing "history from below" very often depends on events that catch the attention of the police and other public officials who keep written records in our society. In order to control for the bias (sometimes intentional, but often unintentional) in such evidence, both essays attempt to place these violent events in a broader context of information about the community, much of it gathered from fiscal and population censuses. While they differ sharply as to the weight that statistical data are made to bear in the presentations, both authors suggest that social, economic, and urban history should be considered as complementary rather than competing or exclusive disciplines.

Robert J. Bezucha's "The 'Preindustrial' Worker Movement: The Canuts of Lyon" focuses on the economic and social structure of one of Europe's most important manufacturing centers in an era before the effects of industrialization were broadly felt on the Continent. In re-creating the world of the canuts, the Lyonnaise silk weavers, his purpose is to explain why this hierarchical community of artisans became synonymous with labor agitation and violence in the first half of the nineteenth century. After describing the manner in which the silk industry was subtly transformed by a combination of technological innovation and the institutional, legal, and social results of the French Revolution, Bezucha traces the canuts' attempt to organize their community and break the power of the silk merchants, and then examines the uprisings of 1831 and 1834 within what he calls "the

Lyonnaise context of violence." Readers should find in this essay some explanation of the fact that it was artisans, not factory workers, who fathered the European labor movement.

Louise A. Tilly's "I Fatti di Maggio: The Working Class of Milan and the Rebellion of 1898" transfers our attention to an industrial city at the end of the nineteenth century and reconstructs in detail the structure and characteristics of its working class. Readers cannot fail to notice the scrupulous care with which Tilly explains the nature of her sources and submits them to statistical analysis in order to present a multidimensional picture of the community; the use of population pyramid charts enhances the clarity of her argument to a degree that would be impossible to attain by narration alone. Her next step, taken by means of the admittedly less accurate information regarding arrests and casualties in the rebellion of 1898, leads to the conclusion that "the persons involved in the Fatti di Maggio *were not a random assortment of the population of Milan." In explaining the reasons for this fact, Tilly not only demonstrates how social historians can go beyond the biased accounts of riots offered by contemporary observers, but also sets the events of 1898 within the larger picture of the development of Milan and the Italian working class.*

THE "PREIENDUSTRIL" WORKER MOVEMENT: THE CANUTS OF LYON

Robert J. Bezucha

The working class was born in the workshop, not the factory. It is one of the cherished dogmas of social history that artisans, their status and jobs threatened by economic change, fathered the labor movement.[1] Outside of the capital cities such as Paris and Berlin, there was no more important European incubator than Lyon. Twice within three years, in November 1831 and April 1834, the second city of France was the scene of bloody insurrection. These uprisings of the Lyon silk workers, or *canuts* as they were called, presented the rulers of Metternich's Europe with a frightening spectacle. The young Karl Marx believed that the *canuts,* with their motto "Live Working or Die Fighting," had launched the inevitable class warfare.[2]

Riot and revolt hold a constant fascination for students of modern European history, but until recently much of the work on these subjects has been methodologically crude, so that simple, value-laden terms such as "the mob" and "the people" have passed as descriptions of complex phenomena. All this is now changing. Some of the most significant contributions to social history have dealt with the study of crowds and the role of collective violence.[3] As historians have learned new ways to do their work, they have also come to recognize that violence registers only that moment when a volatile social compound has reached the flash point. But what elements made up its formula? What sorts of antagonisms heated it to explosion? The answers to questions such as these seem critical for understanding the context of violence, whether in Lyon or elsewhere.

The present essay is meant to serve a triple purpose: First, to trace the operation of the Lyon silk-weaving industry about the year 1830 and to indicate the economic and social antagonisms that developed as it changed in the half-century after 1789; from this will emerge a definition of the term *"preindustrial" worker movement.* Second, to describe the *canuts'* attempt to organize their community and break the economic power of the silk merchants. Third, to explain the uprisings of 1831 and 1834 within the particular Lyonnaise context of violence. We shall discover along the way that the *canuts* were a unique community of workingmen, whose organization

Robert J. Bezucha received his Ph.D. from the University of Michigan. He now teaches at Northwestern University.

and ideology were remarkable for their time. Nevertheless, this essay should not be consigned to that unjustly denigrated corner of the profession called local history. Social historians must go "inside" a number of worker communities and examine how their members perceived themselves, their work, and their future in order to understand better exactly how and why artisans fathered the labor movement.

I

As Detroit is linked with the automobile industry in the minds of modern Americans, so nineteenth-century Europeans associated Lyon with the production of silk cloth. More than a quarter of her nearly two hundred thousand residents were employed by the *Fabrique,* the traditional name for the local silk industry. In 1830, there were approximately twenty-five thousand looms in Lyon, and silk and silk-related products accounted for almost half of the city's total commercial income and a third of the value of all French exports.[4] Lyon, in other words, was one of the largest and most important manufacturing centers in the world.

Textiles were in the vanguard of the Industrial Revolution. The production of silk cloth, however, was an exception. In 1830, the structure of the Lyonnaise *Fabrique* appeared on the surface to be essentially the same as in 1730. Although manufacturing was concentrated in an urban environment, there were no large-scale factories. The hand production was divided between three basic groups: the merchants (popularly but inaccurately called *fabricants*), who purchased raw silk, let it out for weaving on contract, and marketed the finished cloth; the master weavers *(chefs d'atelier),* who owned the looms and wove the cloth in their workshop in return for payment from the merchants; and the journeymen *(compagnons or ouvriers en soie),* who labored at the looms under the masters' supervision and received half of the contracted payment for the cloth. This archaic system seems simple and static in description, but in reality it was highly complex and fluid. The social and economic antagonisms produced by precisely these complexities, moreover, generated the worker movement in Lyon. Let us move "inside" the *Fabrique* as it was around 1830, and follow the three basic groups through the manufacturing process. Our purpose will be threefold: to learn how the industry was changing over time, to see how each group perceived its own role and those of the others, and to understand how they defined the problems of the industry and their possible solution.

The silk merchants were commercial capitalists seeking to market goods of high quality at the lowest possible cost. Most of them, however, were not French counterparts of the infamous Mr. Bounderby in Dickens' novel *Hard Times,* grinding out large profits by the ruin of the weavers. Silk, unlike cotton cloth, was a luxury product constantly at the mercy of the sensitive mechanisms of world trade. One report on economic prospects issued by the local chamber of commerce noted the cholera epidemic in Paris, revolutions in Latin America, the banking crisis in the United States, tariff debate in England, and the growth of Swiss and German competition, as all directly affecting Lyon.[5] The vicissitudes of the market caused rapid fluctuations in the state of the local economy. Between 1824 and 1826, for example, the amount of raw silk purchased and registered for weaving fell by 25 percent.[6] The result was recurrent financial crisis for many merchants and unemployment or lower rates for the weavers. "The *canuts,*" wrote one observer, "pass rapidly from excess of misery to prosperity and back again to distress."[7] The merchants were puzzled that the worker movement began to develop at a time when the *Fabrique* was emerging from half a decade of stagnation. From their point of view a relative abundance of contracts should have spelled general satisfaction.

Market fluctuations alone do not explain the precarious position of the average silk merchant. Equally important was the fact that there were too many firms. During the late Empire and the Restoration (roughly 1810–1830), the annual value of cloth production doubled while the number of *fabricants* grew tenfold.[8] While the major firms were able to withstand a temporary crisis, around them were clustered literally hundreds of small houses with little capital margin. The result, in the words of a spokesman, was "a continual war of merchant against merchant."[9] Such intense local competition made the average *fabricant* understandably hostile to demands for higher weaving rates. While publicly he would reject them out of a statesman-like concern for liberal principle and the health of the national economy, privately he might be attempting to prevent his business from going under.

In the merchants' minds, the future of their industry depended on maintaining high quality in the ornate, brocaded cloth called *façonnes,* and developing cheaper production methods for the plain cloth called *unies.* All of their innovative efforts pointed toward the achievement of these two goals. Firms that specialized in the sale of *façonnes* had their own designers who patented their intricate and beautiful creations. The municipal government supported an art school where local children were trained for employment by the merchants; a student with exceptional ability might even be offered a partnership in a firm.[10] Despite the fact that the mounting and weaving of *façonnes* required the work of a skilled artisan operating a special loom, the merchants considered these functions to be of secondary importance. As their newspaper stated, "The merchants compose the intellectual portion of the industry. The difference between a merchant and a master weaver is that between an architect and a construction worker."[11] Such a condescending attitude toward the work of all weavers severely poisoned relations between masters and merchants.

The market price of *façonnes* was also an important consideration in the merchants' minds. For this reason they applauded the introduction of the semimechanical Jacquard loom (named after the local master who invented it in 1804), which cut weaving time and production cost. Later in this essay we will examine how these iron frames altered the social structure and geography of the worker community. It is sufficient to say here that by 1830, only a quarter of the looms in the *Fabrique* were Jacquard models, and their owners constituted an elite group.[12]

The vast majority of the *canuts* continued to work the simple, wooden *unies* looms. Their livelihood was threatened by the fact that cheap foreign cloth used for handkerchiefs, hats, and simple clothing, was cutting deeply into what had previously been a secure Lyonnaise market. The merchants believed that the local *unies* houses could only survive by radically reducing production costs. Not only were all resolved to resist paying higher weaving rates even in the best of times, but many were also convinced that *unies* production no longer had a future within the existing structure of the *Fabrique*. A sensible solution from their point of view was to seek cheaper hand labor outside the city. Between 1825 and 1840, the period of the making of the worker movement, the percentage of rural looms out of the total number employed by the merchants rose from 21 to 52 percent.[13] The worker uprisings of 1831 and 1834 accelerated, but did not initiate this outward migration. With cottage industry growing at their expense the *canuts* in Lyon itself did not appreciate the irony of the fact that their fate at the hands of "economic progress" was the opposite of most nineteenth-century handloom weavers.[14]

The factory system had only begun to be anticipated in the Lyonnaise *Fabrique*. Mechanization (for winding thread) and large workshops (for printing designs on plain cloth) had been introduced, but in 1830 there was little weaving done outside the masters' shops. An important exception was the so-called *Grande Atelier* (literally, *large workshop*) established in a chateau on the edge of the city, where perhaps as many as five hundred men and women lived in model dormitories, ate meals in a common restaurant, and operated the owner's looms in shifts under the supervision of foremen. When this innovative, paternalistic experiment failed, the employees mourned their loss, but the master weavers were encouraged that theirs was a critical function, and the merchants concluded that the owner had been too "liberal" with the *canuts*.[15] Nonetheless, many *fabricants* were convinced that factories and machines were the wave of the future.[16]

The silk merchants believed themselves to be the central figures of the *Fabrique*. Commercial considerations dictated their decisions, whether to pay minimum weaving rates, to disperse, or to eventually mechanize the looms. From their point of view the existing structure of the *Fabrique* was archaic and the destruction of the traditional workshop form of production was to be desired because the master weavers had become little more than "parasites" and "useless intermediaries" between themselves and the journeymen.[17] The *canuts*, on the other hand, saw matters another way.

"The *canuserie*, or class of weavers, is divided and subdivided like society," wrote the master weaver, Pierre Charnier. "It has its rich and its poor, its aristocrats and its humble subjects."[18] While the fundamental distinction among those who worked the looms was between journeymen and master weavers, significant differences existed within the latter group itself. Among Lyon's eight thousand *chefs d'atelier,* the "aristocrats" were the handful of masters who owned several looms. Acting as virtual subcontractors for the merchants, in theory nothing prevented them from amassing enough capital to become *fabricants* themselves. Although such a step was far more difficult than it had been during the boom years of the late Empire and Restoration, the merchants continued to employ the prospect of social mobility as a scourge with which to chastise the *canuts* for their "idleness."[19]

The middle rank of master weavers was composed of those (less than one in eight) who owned four or more looms.[20] Eligible for election as representatives on the board of labor conciliation (the *Conseil des Prud'hommes*), these men were the "active citizens" of the worker community.[21] The average *chef d'atelier,* on the other hand, owned one to three looms, which he operated in his home workshop with his family and perhaps one or two journeymen. Socially proud and fiercely defensive of the fact that he was not an *ouvrier,* a simple worker, his absolute dependence on the merchants' rates brought the "humble subject" close to the economic position of a piecework laborer. The ambiguous role of the master weaver—the threatened loss of his independent economic and social status—was to be a critical element in the formation of the worker movement in Lyon.

An important theme weaves itself persistently through contemporary descriptions of the Lyon silk industry around 1830: the "typical" *canut,* a colorful, docile, and diligent sort of local character, had disappeared. In his place was to be found a belligerent idler, spouting political slogans (supplied him by the meddlesome Republicans, since the "typical" *canut* presumably never had a thought in his head), and declaring himself at war with the merchants. Local writers enjoyed slumming in the worker neighborhoods in search of some toothless old wreck whom they could proudly unveil to their readers as (the quote here is remarkable) "the last of the Mohicans."[22] Since worker strikes and riots had actually been a part of Lyonnaise life for more than a century, in one sense these observers were seeking to paint over the harsh present with a mythical golden past.[23] In another sense, however, they were correct. At the same time that the mode of production remained constant, the nature of the worker community had significantly changed. The *canut* of 1830 was different from the one of 1789.

This transformation was produced by two interwoven sets of pressures: legal and institutional on the one hand, technological and demographic on the other.

The Revolution swept away the traditional corporate structure of the silk industry that had been called the *Grande Fabrique.* A series of new laws and institutions gave the silk merchants greater power, and the master

weavers less, than they had enjoyed under the Old Regime.[24] The chamber
of commerce (1802), the *Condition Publique* (1804), and the commercial
court (1791) were all special institutions through which the merchants regulated the quality of the cloth and promoted trade. The *Conseil des Prud-
'hommes* (1804) was theoretically a restoration of the traditional board of
labor conciliation; whereas merchants and masters had formerly been
equally represented, the new statutes awarded a permanent majority to the
merchants. Such inherent inequality reflected the general character of post-
Revolutionary French law with regard to the workingman.

The labor legislation of the Revolution and the Empire, written according to the principles of individual and economic "liberty," remained
intact until 1848.[25] The law of 14–17 June 1791, better known as the *loi le
Chapelier,* denied all citizens the right to strike or associate in any manner
in order to advance "their pretended common interests." That the interpretation of this law blatantly followed class lines may be seen in the fact that
while workingmens' associations were forbidden as obstacles to a free economy, employer organizations such as chambers of commerce were permitted.
Napoleonic legislation also made a series of specific distinctions between the
rights of workers and employers. The Penal Code (1810) forbade all "coalitions" to raise or lower wages; penalties for workers, however, were more
severe than for employers. The Civil Code (1803) permitted courts to accept an employer's word in a wage dispute, while a worker was obliged to
produce some evidence to support his claim. Articles 291 through 294 of
the Penal Code prohibited all unauthorized associations of more than twenty
members for "religious, literary, political, or any other purpose." Armed
with these measures, the authorities were able to prevent the legal formation of effective worker associations. Finally, each worker was obliged to
carry with him an identification booklet called a *livret,* in which his employer noted the terms of his service, his conduct, and his debts. In France
as a whole, these laws were commonly used by master tailors, cobblers, and
other artisans to regulate the activities of their journeymen. The unique
structure of the Lyonnaise *Fabrique,* however, meant that they applied to
the master weavers as well as journeymen. Each *chef d'atelier,* for example,
had a special book called a *livret d'acquit,* in which the terms of his weaving contracts were recorded. If upon reading it a merchant determined that
a man was rebellious or a poor risk he would simply refuse to give him
work.[26] Such were the Lyonnaise merchants' weapons for social control.

The cumulative effect of this legislation was to deprive the *canuts* of
the protection, frequently exaggerated in their minds, that they had enjoyed under the Old Regime, and to send them legally defenseless into the
world of laissez-faire. In 1830, their community and their nation were still
in the midst of a conflict-ridden transition from traditional to modern society. Little wonder that the preindustrial worker movement was Janus-like:
looking backward toward the supposed "moral order" of the world that had

been lost; searching at the same time for the collective means of survival in the new competitive age.

The fundamental demographic alteration of the Lyonnaise worker community between 1789 and 1830 was produced by the interaction of technological innovation (principally the Jacquard loom) and the legal, social, and economic effects of the Revolution. In order to state matters as simply as possible, let us begin by describing the physical transformation itself, and then briefly discuss its causes.[27]

As Lyon and the silk industry grew in the half-century following the Revolution, a strong centrifugal force was in operation in the worker community. In 1789, the majority of the looms were concentrated in the five old quarters spread along the right bank of the Saône river (marked *A* on the map and today called *Vieux Lyon*). Workshops were also scattered throughout the city so that the weaver, the merchant, and even the aristocrat often lived side by side. There were virtually no looms in the immediate suburbs *(faubourgs)* or rural areas outside Lyon. If we discount for the present discussion the development of peasant weaving and cottage industry we described earlier, by 1830, Lyon had approximately twice as many looms as in 1789, but the majority were to be found either in the suburbs or in new areas within the city itself. Nearly a quarter of them were still housed in *Vieux Lyon,* but these were overwhelmingly the old, outmoded *unies* frames; out of 1,956 looms in the Gourgillon quarter, for example, only 39 were Jacquard models. Furthermore, the *canuts* were no longer familiar faces in the bourgeois neighborhoods. As late as 1825, for example, 128 looms remained in the wealthy Orleans quarter; by 1834, there were only two, and these were likely operated by widows. As the workshops moved out from the urban center, Lyon was becoming socially and economically polarized. Perhaps the most obvious and fundamental way in which the "typical" *canut* of 1830 differed from pre-Revolutionary counterpart was that he lived neither in *Vieux Lyon* nor as the neighbor of the silk merchant.

Four factors seem to have caused this demographic transformation. The first was the manner in which the Revolution stimulated urban growth and opened new land for development. In 1789, for example, the broad plain (marked *B* on the map) that lay directly across the Rhône river from the center of Lyon was governed from the city of Grenoble, 60 miles away. The Revolutionary reorganization of local and national administration brought this area into the new Rhône department, with Lyon at its center, and thereby stimulated the growth of the suburbs of Les Brotteaux and La Guillotière. Similarly, the confiscation and public sale of church property enabled private real estate speculators to construct entire neighborhoods with buildings specifically designed to accommodate silk workshops. In 1789, the land on the slopes of the steep Croix Rousse hill (marked *C* on the map) was the property of religious orders. In 1834, for example, the 1,427

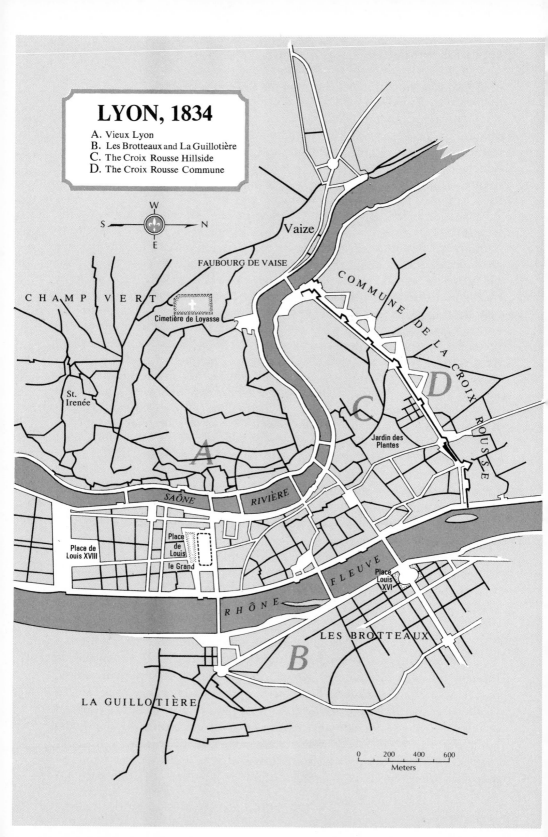

LYON, 1834

A. Vieux Lyon
B. Les Brotteaux and La Guillotière
C. The Croix Rousse Hillside
D. The Croix Rousse Commune

W
S   N
E

Vaize

FAUBOURG DE VAISE

CHAMP VERT

Cimetière de Loyasse

St. Irenée

COMMUNE DE LA CROIX ROUSSE

C

D

A

Jardin des Plantes

SAÔNE   RIVIÈRE

Place de Louis XVIII

Place de Louis le Grand

RHÔNE

FLEUVE

Place Louis XVI

LES BROTTEAUX

B

LA GUILLOTIÈRE

0   200   400   600
Meters

residents of the *rue Tolozan* operated 678 looms where the orchards of the Capuchin monastery had stood forty years earlier. Finally, the rapid expansion of the city up this hillside made the independent Croix Rousse commune at its peak virtually a contiguous part of Lyon (marked *D* on the map). On the eve of the Revolution, the total population of all of the city's suburbs had been around six thousand persons; in 1830, the Croix Rousse commune alone had 17,475 residents and 6,763 silk looms.

The second factor was an indirect response to the introduction of the Jacquard loom. Many of the buildings of *Vieux Lyon* had been constructed in the sixteenth and seventeenth centuries and were physically incapable of housing the new looms. Apartments in the new buildings outside the central city, on the other hand, were specifically designed to have tall ceilings and reenforced floors. The result was a steady migration of the best-equipped *façonnes* workshops into those neighborhoods that had been opened since 1789. In 1829 (a year for which we have complete fiscal census information), over 40 percent of the 5,035 looms on the Croix Rousse hillside were Jacquard models as compared with less than 10 percent of the 5,847 looms in *Vieux Lyon*. Much of the industry's muscle remained in the old quarters, but its heart had been transplanted.

The cost of living was the third factor that explains the centrifugal pressure felt by the *canuts*. The central quarters of Lyon were undoubtedly the most expensive place for a workingman to live in all of France.[28] Contemporary observers agreed that Lyonnaise rents were high, particularly when compared with the situation of silk weavers elsewhere (double those in Avignon, for example), and fuel and food far too expensive.[29] The principal reason for high prices was the *octroi*, the municipal tax on all goods that entered the city. The *octroi* was so strictly collected that workers returning to Lyon after a Sunday afternoon in the country had their market baskets inspected at the toll barriers.[30] While only a successful *chef d'atelier* could afford to install a Jacquard loom in a new building on the Croix Rousse hillside, even a poor *unies* master was able to move to the suburbs, where he not only escaped the *octroi* but also was able to cultivate a green garden for his family. Only the poorest of the *canuts* remained trapped in the old city. As the Prefect of the Rhône reported in 1833: "The suburbs are in the midst of prosperity; the town suffers. People are leaving the sober, humid, stuffy town and seeking breathing space."[31]

The fourth and final factor resulted from the abolition of professional requirements, which disappeared along with the Old Regime. The *chef d'atelier* of 1830 was no longer a person who had been admitted to the select circle of the masters' guild after years of apprenticeship and training. In the age of laissez-faire, anyone who could afford to purchase or rent a loom might call himself a "master" weaver. To the horror of many older *chefs d'atelier*, the idea of apprenticeship itself was fast dying out. In its place came the era of the journeymen weavers, who arrived in Lyon by the thousands when the *Fabrique* florished and abandoned the city when it languished. Often untrained and with few roots in the community, the journeymen were called "the floating population" by the local authorities. Most of them came from the rural regions of France, but a considerable number came from abroad; according to statistics compiled by the Prefect in 1833, among the 3,297 journeymen living in the Croix Rousse commune only 547 had been born there, and 1,100 were foreigners.[32] The *canuts* themselves, or at least their leaders, sensed the fact that their community had become less stable and more fluid than it had been in 1789. One key to understanding the significance of Lyon during this traditional, preindustrial period of European history lies in the fact that much of the initial energy of the worker movement was internally directed, aimed at the self-regulation of masters and journeymen and defining the relations between the two groups. In this physically and socially transformed atmosphere, the complex result of a nexus of revolutionary, technological, and demographic change, the master weaver of 1830 plied his trade.

Conflict was a by-product of the daily operation of the *Fabrique*. The master weavers were constantly made aware of the legal and customary control the merchants held over their lives. Here is a dramatized conversation that appeared in the worker newspaper, *L'Echo de la Fabrique*. A poor *unies* master has just delivered a rush order to a merchant, who is sitting behind the iron grill (the cage, as the *canuts* called it) of his warehouse:

Chef d'atelier. *Here is the piece I've brought you.*

Fabricant. *Well, it's about time. It was due at eight o'clock this morning and it's already noon. Because of you I won't be able to send the order out today.*

Chef. *Please excuse me, Monsieur, but my wife and I have worked on nothing else for the last twelve days. We haven't even left the loom to eat. We had many problems because the thread was so poor and the weave so fine. And my wife, who is pregnant, intended to weave all night, but she fell asleep at the loom. That is why I am late.*

Fabricant. *That's all well and good. Nevertheless you've caused my order to be late. [Looks over the cloth.] Here's a stain. What did you do, eat your stew over the loom?*

Chef. *Oh, Monsieur! If it's there it's because we were so pressed for time. My wife didn't even have time to make soup. We haven't eaten anything but bread while we worked on your order.*

Fabricant. *Ah, here's a thread out of line. [To his clerk] Monsieur Leon, mark this man down ten centimes per aune for waste.*

Chef. *But Monsieur, have you no conscience? After we worked all night with such poor thread there are bound to be mistakes. It isn't fair to mark us down for that.*

Fabricant. *Fair or not, that's the way it's going to be. When I pay good money I expect good work. And if you're as poorly paid as you claim, let me remind you that you didn't have to take the job. You could have refused it.*

Chef. *But you know very well that I haven't worked for three months and that I took it because my savings are gone. I couldn't refuse it because my wife is pregnant.*

Fabricant. *That is not my affair. I'm in business to make money, not to give you charity. What you are saying means little to me.*

Chef. *Will you give me another order?*

Fabricant. *Give you another order? After the way you made me late on a com-mission! You dare ask for another order. No, my dear man. We only give orders to those who appreciate what we give them. Here is your payment.*

Chef. *Dog of a merchant! If good times come you'll hear from me again.*

Fabricant. *[To his clerks] Messieurs, you will be heads of commerce some day. I cannot recommend more highly such severity with the workers. . . . It is the only way to force them to weave well. It is the only way that our industry can prosper.*[33]

Such a confrontation was not pure fiction. We know, for example, that the harsh treatment given Pierre Charnier by a clerk of the Bouila silk firm in 1827, led directly to the founding of the masters' secret Society of Mutual Duty.[34]

Secure inside "the cage," the merchant was on guard against all of the familiar abuses and petty crimes of domestic manufacture, sloppy work, the theft of thread (in Lyon called *piquage d'once*), the artificial weighting or stretching of the cloth. From the *canuts'* point of view, however, the abuses the *fabricants* themselves built into the system were far more serious. Among the more vexing were the refusal either to permit the master to write the weight of the thread he received and the terms of the specific con-tract in the merchant's books or to weigh the finished cloth in his presence, although both were required by law,[35] the failure to return bobbins that were the property of the master,[36] and the rejection of the request for higher rates for rush orders necessitating nighttime weaving—work which cost the *canuts* extra oil for their lamps and coal for their stoves, as well as their sleep.[37] Furthermore, because the warehouses dispensed orders and received cloth only within fixed hours, masters who chose to dispute a merchant's decision risked angering their fellow weavers standing impatiently in line behind them.[38]

Owners of Jacquard looms had a special set of grievances against the merchants. By custom, the *chef d'atelier,* not the *fabricant,* bore the cost of mounting *façonnes* patterns on the loom. This was an operation that not only could idle the loom for a week or more, but also required a consider-able investment; in the case of an important order, an outlay of 100 francs in materials and special tools was not unknown; yet, should the merchant cancel the contract, the master was unprotected and simply lost his invest-ment.[39] Risks such as these reduced competition for the newest *façonnes* contracts. Not only did the merchants fine them severely for any damage to the cardboard forms *(cartons)* that transferred the pattern to the cloth, but the masters also knew that working with a new pattern increased the likeli-

hood of unexpected mounting costs and problems.[40] Little wonder that
some with the skill and equipment to work *façonnes* wove *unies* instead because the latter promised them more working days at less financial risk.[41]
These long-forgotten grievances may strike the reader as less than burning
issues. Nevertheless, they lay at the heart of the conflict between merchants
and masters in Lyon.

The master weavers were not a naturally homogeneous class. The
"aristocrat" who owned several Jacquard looms was united, however, with
the "humble subject" who owned only two or three *unies* frames by the
conviction that they performed the critical function in the manufacturing
process. The growth of the worker movement after 1830 rested on their
ability to convince the journeymen that it was the merchants and not themselves who were the real "parasites" of the *Fabrique*.

The fluid world of the journeymen weavers is difficult to recapture in
simple terms. The image of the true *compagnon*, a young bachelor who
lived in the shop, worked for half of the rate for the finished cloth, and
slept in the same room as the loom, simply does not work in the case of
Lyon. In a large workshop housing four or five looms, one might find the
master and his wife operating two looms, an apprentice being trained under
a four-year contract, an experienced journeyman renting a loom from the
master by the month, and an unskilled weaver signed on for the preparation of a single order.[42] In this hypothetical example, the apprentice could
have lived with the master and his family, the experienced journeyman with
his wife in a rented attic room, and the unskilled weaver in a boarding-
house with other new arrivals from his rural region or country. In the case
of the latter, moreover, he was as likely to take a job for the next week on
a construction project as to move to the shop of another master.[43] The
critical question concerning the complex "floating population" is why the
journeymen, despite the separation of social status and economic interest
that potentially existed between the two groups, did not see masters as "useless intermediaries," but instead recognized a sense of solidarity with them
against the merchants.

The answer revolves around the negative and positive poles of a single
problem. Seeking to explain the relative absence of industrial conflict
among immigrant laborers in nineteenth-century Boston, Stephan Thernstrom has observed that unskilled workers who had the greatest grievances
"are precisely those who never stayed put very long in any one place."[44] So
it was with the *canuts* of Lyon. While the journeymen weavers came and
went, strangers to one another and often not speaking the same language,
the masters remained to define and articulate the problems of the community. The *chefs d'atelier*, always concerned by the alleged "license" and "in-
subordination" in their shops, were to use their secret society to enforce
rules and regulations on the journeymen.[45] Later in this essay we will learn
that the journeymen initially modelled their own association after that of

the masters. It is appropriate to note here, however, that as their society matured—as the journeymen gained a sense of institutional continuity—they began to formulate demands on the masters.[46] The fact that all worker associations were abolished by the government in 1834 prevents us, however, from learning whether or not the solidarity between masters and journeymen would have survived.

A more positive explanation lies in the fact that the *canuts* not only experienced mutual hardships, but also shared social goals to a remarkable extent. If one were to regard the workshop roles in crude economic terms, the master would seem a petit bourgeois craftsman whose property, in the form of his looms, placed him in constant conflict with the journeyman, a sort of preproletarian, who had only his labor to sell. Yet, both men worked daily side by side and their income was determined by the weaving rates set by a third party, the merchant.[47] Although the journeyman might complain about the irregularity of his work or even demand a portion greater than the traditional half of the established rate for the work he had done, he could not accuse the master of idleness at his expense. It is significant that Joseph Benoit, a journeyman elected to the Chamber of Deputies from Lyon after the revolution of 1848, should refer to the *chef d'atelier* as "a worker [an *ouvrier,* a term which the masters themselves rejected as demeaning] and one of the most mistreated in our economic society," and describe the plight of the journeyman by saying that "his life, like that of the master weaver, is a continual struggle, a constant fear for the future."[48] To the merchants' charge that the masters were "parasites" who unjustly deprived the weavers of half of their earnings, the masters responded that the journeymen were satisfied with this traditional arrangement and that with hard work they could rise to become masters themselves.[49] If the latter argument has the same air of unreality about it as the merchants' contention that any *chef d'atelier* might become a *fabricant,* the fact remains that the journeymen held no set of social goals or values other than those articulated for them by the master weavers. So far as generalization is possible concerning such a diverse group, the journeymen reflected the masters' perception of the problems of the industry. And that view, as stated by the *Echo de la Fabrique,* was that "without contradiction, the most direct and scandalous [abuse] is *the immoral and arbitrary exploitation of the master weaver by the merchant,* . . . who by virtue of the laws which rule us . . . exploits the industry as he chooses."[50]

We have completed our trip "inside" the Lyon silk industry around 1830 and followed the merchants, masters, and journeymen through the manufacturing process. Equipped with some sense of the economic and social antagonisms that were present within the *Fabrique,* we can come to grips with the term "the 'preindustrial' worker movement." A careful reader may already have wondered why "preindustrial" has been set apart by quotation marks, and "worker movement" has generally been used instead of "working class." At the risk of belaboring the obvious, let us consider these questions in reverse order.

First, when applied to traditional or transitional (that is, nonmodern) society, Harold Perkin has noted that "the concept of class is a bludgeon rather than a scalpel, and it crushes what it tries to dissect."[51] Considering the occupational triad of the *Fabrique,* it seems obvious that to apply the familiar sociological or economic definitions of *class* to the case of Lyon in 1830 would likely confuse more than clarify any explanation of why the city became synonymous with labor agitation. If one adopts the looser, working definition offered by E. P. Thompson, that

class happens when some men, as the result of common experience (inherited or shared), feel and articulate the identity of interests as between themselves, as against other men whose interests are different from (and usually opposed to) theirs. The class experience is largely determined by the productive relations into which men are born—or enter involuntarily. Class consciousness is the way these experiences are handled in cultural terms: embodied in traditions, value systems, ideas and institutional forms. . . .[52]

we see that the *canuts* did develop something akin to class consciousness, a clear sense of "us" against "them." But to refer to their activities as those of a working class tends to obscure the fact that they were not a class, but members of a hierarchical community of artisans. The term "worker movement" serves to remind us of this distinction.

Second, although it spills from their pens with regularity, historians have yet to agree on a definition for the term "preindustrial" (hence the quotation marks). In part, this is a result of the fact that there is little consensus as to the meaning of "industrialization" as a historical process rather than a sociological concept. The *canuts* did not operate power-driven looms in factories under the supervision of the merchants or the foremen, but it would be semantic torture (to use E. P. Thompson's phrase) not to call the massive, highly developed, and technically alert *Fabrique* an industry.[53] And while the relations between the merchants and weavers were not those of a traditional artisan society, they cannot be accurately described as either modern or industrial; "preindustrial," for all of the problems it raises, seems the best term. Modern industrial relations are characterized by the institutionalization of conflict, the channeling of grievances into (usually) nonviolent strikes and/or their resolution through negotiated settlement. In the following section, we shall see that the *canuts'* attempt to organize their community clearly pointed in this direction. That the route before them was blocked and they twice resorted to a violent uprising suggests that they were a social group caught in transition. This is not to say that there was a single road that all workingmen took on the way to modern industrial relations, but to suggest why the *canuts,* on a continent that had scarcely begun to feel the effects of heavy industry, anticipated so much of the ideology and tactics of the future labor movement.

II

Economic and social antagonisms exist in every industrial setting. The worker movement in Lyon was not generated, therefore, solely because of the conflict between the merchants on the one hand and the masters and journeymen on the other. The principal explanation must be found in the cumulative effect of four factors: community continuity, occupational concentration, relative worker affluence, and a high level of literacy. We shall discuss each of them briefly since they go far toward telling us what was unique about the *canuts*.

First, Lyon was not a new industrial town like Manchester or other cities commonly associated with the origins of the working class.[54] The city and the silk industry had been associated for centuries with the result that customs and traditions existed in the *Fabrique*. In a rapidly changing world, the *canuts* lived with a sense of the past. Second, not only did the entire local economy revolve around a single industry, so that the crises of the *Fabrique* were shared by all workers, but also the continued dominance of shop production gave a rhythm and quality to the *canuts'* work that was far different from that of the factory system. Other historians have suggested that conflict of interest between rival artisan groups on the one hand, and the strangeness of factory life on the other severely retarded the development of an organized worker movement.[55] Neither case applies to Lyon. Third, although their future was uncertain, the *canuts* nevertheless constituted an elite among French workingmen in 1830. Contemporary writers were fond of noting that at the same time the cotton weavers of Lille wore wooden clogs and lived in caves, the silk workers of Lyon wore boots and lived in furnished rooms. "They believe themselves unfortunate," wrote the economist Villermé, who had observed conditions throughout France, "because they have created new habits for themselves, new needs. . . ."[56] But recognizing that the worker movement was a product of the *canuts'* relative affluence is to grasp only part of the answer; that the fulfillment of their social and economic goals was threatened also suggests that it resulted from what sociologists call "relative deprivation."[57] Fourth, at a time when three quarters of all Frenchmen were illiterate, a remarkably high percentage of the *canuts* were literate.[58] Illiteracy bore a social stigma among the master weavers; one member of the Executive Council of their secret society resigned because his opinion was ignored due to his inability to read or write.[59] That there were two worker newspapers in Lyon at a time when there were no others on the entire continent testifies to the important role literacy played in the lives of the *canuts*.

Building on the four factors cited above, the attempt to organize the worker community essentially followed three lines: the newspaper press, secret associations, and plans for the reorganization of the *Fabrique*. What bound them together were the shared goals of winning for the *canuts* (particularly the master weavers) the respect that they felt due them, and of wresting from the merchants the social and economic power that they wielded by their absolute control over the weaving rates.

In our age of electronic communications, we often underestimate the role newspapers played in the past in imparting information, identifying issues, and molding both opinion and values. Nineteenth-century Frenchmen, however, were aware of the power of the press, as the history of official attempts to censor or control it attests. In Lyon, every faction seemed to have a journal of its own. The silk merchants quoted the *Courrier de Lyon,* while the *canuts* read the *Echo de la Fabrique* (founded shortly before the uprising of November 1831) or its rival, the *Echo des Travailleurs* (begun in November 1833). Debated in the cafes, workshops, and meetings of the secret associations, the worker press helped establish the norms of their community.

The weaver, said the *Echo de la Fabrique,* seeks "to live by the fruit of his labor and not be subject to the humiliations of a Helot or a Muscovy serf."[60] Pride and humiliation were like magnetic poles in the self-conscious development of community solidarity. In 1832, for example, the paper promised a free subscription to the person who suggested the best word to describe all silk workers. Other "classes" had an "honorable" word for themselves, it explained, and because *canuts* was used by the merchants many weavers considered it insulting. Forty-one words were entered in the contest, most of them disappointingly pretentious ones with Greek or Latin roots, such as *textoricarien* and *bombixier*. Language, nevertheless, is central to group identity and it is significant that soon after the contest terms such as "proletarians" and "laborers" *(travailleurs)* began to be employed for masters and journeymen alike.[61]

The themes of pride and humiliation extended also into discussion of the problems of daily life. "Who has never seen," asked the *Echo des Travailleurs,*

these houses of seven or eight stories, veritable hives of activity. . . . Thousands of men, women, and children are crowded into these narrow, airless, dirty buildings and it is a pity to see in what holes live these ingenious workers, who produce velours, satins, gauzes . . . and all the other magnificient cloths. The nation does not know . . . how many men of genius are hidden in this glorious and unfortunate town of Lyon.[62]

The public water supply, a matter of serious concern to the teeming neighborhoods on the Croix Rousse hillside, serves as another example. During the summer months the hundreds of residents of the *rue Tolozan* drew water from a single fountain that delivered only forty liters an hour. In addition to the inconvenience, the danger of fire was always present when oil lamps were used around the looms. The Municipal Council promised that the money it charged for the use of these fountains would go for the construction of more wells and pumps. The worker community was outraged, therefore, when the *Echo de la Fabrique* informed them that the funds were actually financing a new theatre where the merchants could enjoy the opera.[63] Little wonder that the *Echo des Travailleurs* should proclaim,

Our goal . . . is social equality. . . . a uniform condition of well-being . . . an integral development in all men of their moral and physical abilities; this does not yet exist.[64]

The worker press also led the campaign to break the economic power of the silk merchants. In an industry as diffuse as the *Fabrique,* where there were hundreds of merchants, eight thousand workshops, and countless varieties of cloth, each woven according to a different rate, a central source of information was an essential step toward organization. Which merchants paid the highest rates? Which treated the masters like dogs? What were economic prospects for the coming month? Had the *Conseil des Prud'hommes* decided what should be done with an apprentice who broke his contract, a master caught stealing thread, or a merchant who refused to pay the agreed rate? The *canuts* learned the answers from their own journals. A letter to the editor of the *Echo de la Fabrique* was a weapon frequently used by disgruntled masters to attack the merchants.

The worker press not only presented the *canuts'* view of the problems and abuses of the *Fabrique,* but it also stated time and again their demand for a *tarif,* a fixed minimum weaving rate for every type of cloth. While the concept of a *tarif* was rooted in the "just wage" tradition of the Old Regime, the inconsistency of the post-Revolutionary governments made it a burning issue in Lyon. A *tarif* had twice been established by the Emperor Napoleon, but under the Bourbon Restoration it was alternately enforced or ignored, its legality seemingly resting on administrative whim.[65] The establishment of the July Monarchy, born on the barricades in 1830, raised the *canuts'* hopes. The government's subsequent decision to side with the merchants and to oppose the *tarif* as an obstacle to a free and competitive economy caused the workers to become quickly disillusioned with the rule of Louis Philippe. When their campaign for a *tarif* was officially frustrated, they resorted to other means of guaranteeing their future.

While the *Echo de la Fabrique* and the *Echo des Travailleurs* were in serious disagreement over the future scope of the worker movement,[66] they were united by the manner in which they articulated the benefits of secret associations and justified the illegal action that membership entailed. The weaver could no longer "resign himself to suffering and dying while singing psalms to the Virgin and praying that She will send him work." He must

realize that his work was a form of property, it was "the *capital* of the proletarian," and that all men had a "right to work."[67] Since the *canuts* had
a "moral obligation" to protect their property and rights, the human laws
that forbade unauthorized associations and strikes were superseded.[68] In an
article with the suggestive title "On the Industrial Revolution in France,"
the *Echo de la Fabrique* inquired whether another revolution was necessary
to raise the "property" of work to a status equal with those of land and
money.[69] And the *Echo des Travailleurs* proclaimed that "all advanced men
. . . profess their agreement on this point: that their only strength lies in
association."[70]

Adolphe Thiers, a government minister centrally concerned with political order and economic development after the Revolution of 1830, acknowledged the accuracy of this statement when he lamented, "Associations
are one of the maladies of our epoch."[71] Indeed, a characteristic of the times
was the manner in which dissenting groups throughout France held the
term "association" as a kind of messianic formula, the means of attaining all
goals, of solving all problems. In Lyon it became part of the ideology of the
militant worker movement. But only after a struggle. The *canuts'* societies
were not launched by "advanced men," rather by conservative master weavers; the founder of the Society of Mutual Duty, for example, was a monar-
chist who owned several Jacquard looms and believed that the demand for
a *tarif* was a less appropriate issue than restoration of order and respect in
the workshops.[72] The attempt to organize the worker community by means
of illicit associations was marked, therefore, by internal conflicts from which
the militants emerged with a fragile (and ultimately ephemeral) victory.

The structure of the worker associations was determined by the law
that forbade unauthorized groups of more than twenty members. Although
the government tolerated a few organizations that it considered little threat
(principally the ancient fraternity of artisans called the *compagnonnages*),
all others were obliged to form around small lodges that were secretly united
in a single association.

The master weavers' Society of Mutual Duty had a pyramidal structure with the individual lodges at its base.[73] Two men from each lodge
served on a central lodge composed of twenty-two delegates. The presidents
of the central lodges formed the Grand Council, or Council of Presidents,
of Mutualism. Although democratic in theory, in practice the latter was an
oligarchy, which acted as a constant brake against the more aggressive rank
and file. Membership requirements were strict, in keeping with the founders'
intention that Mutualism should be a force for social restraint in the community. Not until 1833, did unmarried masters become eligible and even
then they had to be proposed by two married members and have their
moral conduct come under scrutiny at four meetings. An initiation fee of
five francs and monthly dues of one franc further served to exclude the
riffraff.

The journeymen weavers' association, called the Ferrandiniers, after a mixed cotton and silk cloth, mirrored the Mutualists' structure and social concern; in fact, they referred to themselves as "the sons of Mutualism." The local authorities feared what might result from the organization of the volatile weavers and actually sent Pierre Charnier, the founder of Mutualism, to buy off the Ferrandiniers with 6,000 francs. To his delight the conservative master found they were not bent on violence and described them as "true and good journeymen."[74]

The Mutualists and Ferrandiniers played professional, social, and educational roles in the attempt to organize the worker community. The original purpose of both groups was to provide mutual aid. Their regulations permitted treasury funds to be used in the form of small loans (to allow masters to rent special tools or purchase an additional loom) and to help sick, injured, or temporarily unemployed members. Deceased members received dignified funerals (at which attendance was required of lodge members) and their widows were given a small pension. Dissension arose when militants sought to use the treasury as a strike fund or to turn funeral ceremonies into a public show of strength. Three·days before the uprising of April 1834, for example, 6,000 *canuts* marched in the funeral procession for a master weaver.[75]

The Sunday meetings of the Mutualist and Ferrandinier lodges were important events for their members. Although the discussion of politics and religion was formally barred (not only to avoid a crackdown by the police, but also because the members strongly disagreed on the former topic), the worker newspapers were read aloud in these sessions, the decisions of the *Conseil des Prud'hommes* debated, banquets and dances were planned, the visit of Saint Simonian "missionaries" announced, and collections taken for the striking coal miners of Anzin. For many *canuts,* socialization was achieved by means of their associations.

Yet from within and without came the criticism that these societies were too exclusive and conservative. The *Echo des Travailleurs,* for example, ridiculed those who believed "there is no salvation outside Mutualism."[76] In 1883, a campaign was begun to expand their influence and goals in order to improve the condition of all *canuts*. While the prefect deplored "this spirit of egotism . . . so fatal to our industrial class," the merchants' newspaper predicted that "when the organization of the workers into lodges is completed . . . they will be the masters of the *Fabrique*.[77]

The aggressive campaign had four stages. First, the Mutualists established a body of overseers called *Syndics,* whose task was to be informed of current rates offered by each merchant house in the several branches of the *Fabrique*. Second, a small number of firms notorious for their low rates were selected for a strike in July 1833, a period when the *Fabrique* was flourishing. Perhaps a thousand looms were idled. While members of the Ferrandiniers visited the workshops to convince their fellow weavers of the justice of this action, representatives of the Mutualists called on the merchants and demanded higher rates. The latter refused to talk with anyone but those masters with whom they had contracts.[78] The local authorities privately advised the merchants to make no concessions, and after ten days sent the police to raid the office of the *Echo de la Fabrique* and to arrest the fourteen men identified as leaders. The strike was broken, but there was widespread official frustration over the lack of a legal way of suppressing the worker associations themselves. "The Government has decided on repression," wrote the Minister of Commerce, "and the only hesitation is as to the means. . . ."[79]

The third stage was reached in December 1833, when an open rebellion against the conservative leadership of the Council of Presidents was staged by the Mutualist rank and file. An ad hoc Executive Council, elected by two delegates from each lodge, was created and its members, who represented a younger generation of master weavers, pledged themselves to a program of action. The older Council of Presidents continued to function, but power had passed to the new body.[80]

The final stage of the worker associations' shift toward militancy occurred in February 1834, when the Executive Council called for a general strike in a demand for a *tarif*. The Mutualists endorsed the decision by a vote of 1,297 to 1,044, and the Ferrandiniers followed their lead. Resorting to threats of smashed looms and slashed cloth where necessary, they were able to idle all of the 25,000 looms in Lyon and its suburbs. On February 14, the Mayor wrote to the Prefect: "I walked today in the St. Just quarter [*Vieux Lyon*] and the northern part of the town [the Croix Rousse hillside] where the workshops are found and I failed to discover a single loom in operation."[81]

Alarmed by the "occult power" that the Mutualist leaders wielded over the *canuts,* the Government refrained from arresting them for fear of triggering violence; the only recourse was to promise the merchants protection and hope that the strike would collapse under its own weight. It did not take long, for the worker associations had far exceeded their means. On February 19, despite the Executive Council's declaration that "our cause is that of the entire city, of all France, even of the universe," the Mutualists voted to end the general strike.[82] The militants' victory had been a Pyrrhic one.

The general strike marked both the success and the failure of the attempt to organize the worker community by means of secret associations. On the one hand, the Mutualists and Ferrandiniers had extended their influence, albeit only for a moment, over all the *canuts;* on the other hand, their failure to win concessions from the merchants caused many to lose faith in militant action. The Government took steps to assure that a general strike would not occur again. After arresting the members of the Mutualist Executive Council, it introduced a bill to make illegal all unauthorized associations, whether or not they were divided into lodges.

Plans for the reorganization of the *Fabrique,* the third part of the attempt to organize the worker community, were often discussed as a solution to troubled industrial relations in Lyons. We have already learned, for example, that the merchants considered either dispersing the looms into the countryside or concentrating them in factories; their intention was to undercut or abolish the role of the master weavers. The latter, on the other hand, proposed a plan designed to destroy the economic position of the merchants. Each group fundamentally believed that the other's destruction would guarantee future prosperity for themselves. Economic conflict can run no deeper.

The master weavers' plan called for the formation of a series of cooperative associations called central commercial houses, one for each of the principal branches of the *Fabrique.* Formed with the belief that it would permit the *canuts* to "battle against the inhuman merchants, who enrich themselves on our suffering and privation," each house was to be headed by an "active *fabricant"* (presumably an experienced master weaver), elected by the empoloyees' association and charged with supervising both the manufacture and sale of the cloth. The employees associated with each house were to work for a fixed daily wage and also receive a percentage of the annual profits.[83]

The plan for a central commercial house was an expression in positive terms of the *canuts'* perception of the problems of the *Fabrique.* The radical centralization of production would not only eliminate competition between merchant houses, but also increase efficiency and hold manufacturing costs to a minimum for the weavers. This, in turn, would have a twofold result: it would permit a lower market price, enabling Lyonnaise cloth to compete with foreign products; and it would allow the weavers a fixed rate, the equivalent of a *tarif,* for their work. In addition, the principles of self-administration and profit sharing would not only serve as incentives to the masters and journeymen, but would also furnish public proof that the *canuts* were not idlers, rather honest artisans trapped inside an exploitive system. Finally, the elimination of the merchants from the manufacturing process would end class conflict and restore tranquility to the city and the industry. The central commercial house would be "the simplification of the industrial mechanism . . . in the collective name of the master weavers."[84]

Such hopes may appear as pie-in-the-sky dreams of threatened artisans, implicit proof of the way "association" had become their messianic formula, but the idea of a central commercial house itself was no fantasy. In July 1833, nine master weavers from the Croix Rousse wrote to the newspapers to announce plans for such a project. By November they had published its statutes and had begun to seek worker-stockholders at 25 francs per share.

There are indications, moreover, that the Mutualists were contemplating using the funds in their treasury to found a model house.[85] A related project called the Commercial Society was actually launched by a group of master weavers in October 1834, but with the worker movement in a state of collapse following the April uprising, it saw little success.[86] Its failure, however, should not be read as a judgment on the idea of a central commercial house. One can only speculate as to its fate had the worker newspapers and associations continued to flourish.

The *canuts'* attempt to organize their community did not pass unnoticed elsewhere; the general strike, in particular, was the subject of widespread discussion. But it was their violent uprisings that riveted all attention on the second city of France.

III

"The barbarians who menace society are no longer to be found on the Tartar steppes; they are presently in the suburbs of our manufacturing towns."[87] This comment by the *Journal des Débats* accurately reflects the reaction of most Frenchmen to the events of November 1831 and April 1834. But the *canuts* were not a wild horde suddenly descended from the hills. As we explore the Lyonnaise context of violence, it will be clear not only that the resort to arms grew directly from the economic and social antagonisms of the *Fabrique,* but also that there are discernible patterns in the uprisings that reflect the structure and organization of the worker community.

The November 1831 uprising resulted from the perfidious treatment of the *canuts'* demand for a *tarif*.[88] In October, a worker group (with the Mutualists, although still in their conservative phase, taking the lead) successfully used a combination of mass rallies and petitions to pressure the Prefect to convene a commission to negotiate a *tarif*. On October 25, while several thousand *canuts* waited outside the Prefecture, a panel of merchants and masters reached a general agreement with regard to weaving rates. But the *canuts'* apparent victory was short-lived. The merchants ignored the date of implementation and complained to Paris about the Prefect's intervention. On Thursday, November 17, the announcement came from the capital that the agreement had been only "an engagement of honor" and was not legally binding. The *tarif* was thereby annulled.

Tension mounted during the weekend. A general work stoppage in the shops and a protest march from the Croix Rousse to the Prefecture in the center of the city were called for Monday, November 21. The Prefect responded by sending National Guard units, largely composed of silk merchants and clerks, to bar the *canuts'* descent. A column of weavers began to march down the hillside. Shots rang out and they retreated with their dead and wounded, crying "To arms! Vengeance! They have killed our brothers!" The November uprising had begun.

News of the skirmish on the Croix Rousse hillside spread quickly.

Fighting soon broke out in the other worker neighborhoods. The garrison was totally unprepared for such a revolt and by midnight of the next day the municipal council recommended that the Army evacuate the city. A band of insurgents seized the undefended Hôtel-de-Ville. The Prefect was a prisoner in the Prefecture. On November 23, 1831, the *canuts* controlled Lyon.

They had no idea what to do with their unexpected triumph, however. Grasping this fact, the Prefect appointed a commission of sixteen wealthy and influential masters to govern the city. This act successfully defused the power of a radical group seeking to proclaim a Republic at the Hôtel-de-Ville. Under the supervision of these conservative masters, order was restored in the city; squads of workers were sent to guard the silk warehouses and the municipal treasury. And when the army returned, led by the minister of war, Maréchal Soult, and the King's son, the Duc d'Orléans, the city gates were open for their arrival. The November uprising ended with a whimper. But its implications were staggering. As one of the merchants' spokesmen wrote:

The moral influence of the November insurrection will be immense: their victory, so singularly the result of a succession of accidents and the incapacity of the authorities, will make them [the workers] more demanding. . . . Perhaps for a hundred years the marvelous tale of the defeat of the National Guard and the garrison of Lyon by the unarmed workers will charm the leisure of the workshop; this tradition will pass from generation to generation; a son will say with pride . . . , "My father was one of the conquerors of Lyon."[89]

As we have seen in our discussion of the July 1833 and February 1834 strikes, the lessons drawn by the government and merchants were vigorously applied during the next three years: official intervention in economic disputes only spelled trouble, all worker attempts to press their demands by means of collective action must be resisted, and never again be militarily unprepared. The rejection of negotiation and the evolution of confrontation as a conscious policy at the precise time the *canuts* set about organizing their own community went far toward making a second uprising inevitable.

On April 5, 1834, a crowd of weavers awaiting the verdict in the trial of the leaders of the February general strike disarmed a squad of troops guarding the courtroom. The authorities responded with a firmness that belied their panic. The *Fabrique* had been caught in an unexpected crisis; unemployment was widespread among the *canuts*. In addition, the government in Paris, whipped by the hysterical conviction that the Republicans had infiltrated the worker societies and were prepared to use them as the cutting edge of another revolutionary upheaval, had steered passage of a special law giving the police the power to suppress any undesired association, no matter what its structure or professed goals. Seizing this unexpected opportunity for alliance with the workers (something which, I have argued elsewhere, they had failed to accomplish as a result of their own efforts[90]), the Lyonnaise Republicans called for massive demonstrations to protest the law on associations on the day the trial reconvened. Unemployed, their demand for a *tarif* rejected, their strikes broken, their leaders on trial, and their associations in mortal danger, many *canuts* heeded the call. The government, meanwhile, prepared to meet this challenge with a show of force.

On the morning of April 9, 1834, thousands of troops patrolled the streets of Lyon. Fighting broke out when soldiers were twice provoked into firing on the unarmed crowds. Once the demonstrators had been dispersed, resistance was confined to isolated pockets; all but one were in distinctly worker neighborhoods. Although fighting continued for six days, there was never any doubt as to the outcome; the difficulties of street fighting and the military's mistaken belief that the rebels were well armed largely explain the delay. Eventually the uprising was crushed under the weight of 1,729 artillery rounds and 269,000 musket shots. The Army suffered almost three hundred and fifty casualties (civilian casualties are impossible to calculate, but certainly were higher), but the minister of war's personal investigator proudly proclaimed that the garrison of 1834 had avenged the humiliation of 1831.[91]

News of the second Lyon uprising—the largest domestic rebellion between the revolutions of 1830 and 1848—sparked minor troubles in a number of other towns. The government, believing (or claiming to believe) itself the victim of a national conspiracy, made thousands of arrests and later tried hundreds of radicals for sedition. Because Lyon was associated with the "April events," a myth was born that while the uprising of November 1831 had been economic in character, that of April 1834 was a political insurrection.[92] A few Republicans did play a role in the second uprising, but to accept this interpretation is to distort seriously the Lyonnaise context of violence.

Three significant patterns emerge from a comparison of the two Lyon uprisings. First, both revolts were triggered by a government decision to deny the *canuts* precisely that protection they believed would guarantee their future. The rejection of the *tarif* is related to November 1831 in the same manner as the threatened suppression of the worker associations is linked to April 1834. Those who have argued that the latter was political fail to asks the critical question: Would the *canuts* have rebelled if their leaders had not been on trial and only the Republican associations had been threatened? Both uprisings sprang directly from the particular antagonisms of the *Fabrique*.

Second, the critical personnel in both uprisings was essentially the same: the journeymen weavers. The warning that they would close their shops and turn the *compagnons* loose in the streets was the masters' ultimate threat in their struggles with the merchants and local authorities. This tactic was often used in the troubled decades before 1789, during the local revolutionary events in 1830, and again in 1831 and 1834.[93] We do not have accurate documentation concerning the composition of the crowd in November 1831, but the dossiers of the hundreds of persons arrested in April 1834 make such an analysis possible for the second uprising. They reveal that over 90 percent of the insurgents were members of the local worker community. Nearly four out of every ten persons arrested were silk workers, a clear refutation of the government's contention that only a handful of *canuts* participated in the fighting.[94] The fluid world of the journeymen is further reflected by the fact that only one in three of all persons arrested was born in Lyon or the Rhone department, two-thirds were bachelors, and nearly 90 percent were under the age of forty. Only two men out of the hundreds arrested confessed they had no trade or occupation and only a handful (2.5 percent) admitted having a previous criminal record. One must conclude that the insurgents of 1831 and 1834 were young, mobile, and employable, men who had come to Lyon seeking work. Far from constituting a mob of barbarians or revolutionaries, they fought only when their future appeared gravely threatened.

Third, the worker neighborhoods formed the backbone of resistance in both uprisings. By means of illustration, let us focus our attention on a single street already mentioned for its concentration of *canuts*.[95] The *rue Tolozan* was a center of worker militancy on the Croix Rousse hillside. A placard was displayed there announcing the mass meeting of November 21, 1831, and when the National Guard fired on the marching weavers its residents took up the cry "To arms! Death to the merchants!"[96] In the period between the two revolts, M. Falconnet, the editor of the *Echo de la Fabrique,* lived in the *rue Tolozan* along with many members of the Mutualist and Ferrandiniers societies. During the general strike in February 1834, the Mayor was obliged to send a squad of soldiers there to protect the life of a master weaver who had announced his intention to resume work.[97] And in April 1834, the street exploded. According to the official government report, the fighting in this area of the city was the most highly organized of all the rebel strongholds. Nonetheless the resistance was a neighborhood affair. A majority of the persons arrested on the entire hillside lived in a four-block area around the *rue Tolozan*. Typical of these insurgents was Claude Clocher, a young native of Savoy, who worked as a journeyman in a shop directly above the cafe that served as rebel headquarters. When he was arrested and charged with having manned an observation post at the end of his block, Clocher's only weapon was a sword given him by a neighbor who was a former member of the National Guard. When asked by the police to explain the uprising, he replied that "misery caused it all."[98]

The intentionally limited scope of this essay prohibits an extended discussion of the *canuts'* resistance. This brief account of the two uprisings and their common patterns, nonetheless, should have revealed the Lyonnaise context of violence. November 1831 and April 1834 mark the moments when the complex social and economic compounds of the *Fabrique* reached the

flash point. Hopefully the reader now understands the particular antagonisms that caused the explosion.

By way of an epilogue it is important to note that the *canuts* did not
remain in the vanguard of the worker movement throughout the nineteenth
century. As the railroad arrived (ironically the line connecting Lyon with the
coalfields of Saint Étienne was completed in 1834) bringing the metal and
chemical industries in its wake, the *Fabrique* lost its overwhelming importance in the local economy. The emigration of *unies* looms continued and
façonnes production fell victim to the "democratization" of taste after midcentury.[99] The era of the journeyman weaver came to an end, replaced over
the next decades by that of the industrial factory worker. The master weavers
remained, but the Revolution of 1848 was their last hurrah, a final fling at
violence. Increasingly preoccupied with protecting their artisan status and
contemptuous of the slavish proletarians, the *chefs d'atelier* became solidly
conservative. During the Lyonnaise Commune in 1871, the factory workers
belonging to the First International sent out the call to arms. The neighborhoods of the Croix Rousse, the *canuts* of the *rue Tolozan*, failed to respond.

NOTES

1. Gwyn A. Williams, *Artisans and Sans-Culottes* (New York, 1969); E. P.
   Thompson, *The Making of the English Working Class* (New York, 1966);
   P. H. Noyes, *Organization and Revolution: Working-Class Associations in the
   German Revolutions of 1848–1849* (Princeton, N.J., 1966); and the more
   recent Maurice Agulhon, *Une ville ouvrière au temps du socialisme utopi-
   que: Toulon de 1815 à 1851* (Paris, 1970).

2. "Critical Notes on 'The King of Prussia and Social Reform' (1844)," in L. D.
   Easton and K. H. Guddat, eds., *Writings of the Young Marx on Philosophy and
   Society,* 2nd ed. (New York, 1967), p. 355.

3. George Rudé, *The Crowd in History: A Study of Popular Disturbances in
   France and England, 1730–1848* (New York, 1964) stands as the best popular
   example of this activity. It includes a valuable bibliography.

4. Charles Beaulieu, *Histoire du commerce de l'industrie et fabrique de Lyon
   depuis leur origine jusqu'à nos jours* (Lyons, 1838), pp. 144–46.

5. *Les archives municipales de la ville de Lyon: documents Gasparin* (hereafter
   cited as *AM Doc. G.*), tome 1: Chamber of Commerce to Gasparin, 20 September 1832. The thirteen volumes of the official papers of Comte Adrien de
   Gasparin, Prefect of the Rhône from 1831 to 1835, are a rare source of information on the daily administration of France's second city under the early
   July Monarchy.

6. *Archives statistiques du ministre de travaux publics* (Paris, 1837), p. 267.

7. M. Villermé, *Tableau de l'état physique et moral des ouvriers employés dans les manufactures de coton, de laine, et de soie,* 2 vols. (Paris, 1840), 1:361.

8. E. Pariset, *Histoire de la fabrique lyonnaise: étude sur la régime social et économique de l'industrie de la soie à Lyon depuis le XVIe siècle* (Lyon, 1901), pp. 303–04. According to Beaulieu (*Histoire du commerce*, p. 172), there were about 500 merchant houses with two or three partners in most of them.

9. J. B. Monfalcon, *Histoire des insurrections lyonnaise de 1831 et de 1834 d'après des documents authentiques, précédée d'un essai sur les ouvriers et sur l'organisation de la Fabrique* (Paris and Lyon, 1834), p. 47.

10. Great Britain, House of Commons, *Report of the Select Committee on the Silk Trade* (London, 1832), p. 533.

11. *Le Courrier de Lyon,* 17 July 1833.

12. *AM Doc. G.,* t. 1: "Rapport sur la situation industrielle de la ville de Lyon et les moyens de l'améliorer," 29 November 1833.

13. Maurice Lèvy-Leboyer, *Les banques européenes et l'industrialisation internationale dans le première moitié du XIXe siècle* (Paris, 1965), p. 143.

14. David Landes, *The Unbound Prometheus: Technological Change and Industrial Development in Western Europe from 1750 to the Present* (Cambridge, England, 1969), pp. 43–44. The development of factory production in textiles generally had three stages: (1) small workshop manufacture in towns; (2) the putting-out system; (3) reconcentration in factories. The size of the Lyonnaise *Fabrique* and the luxury nature of silk cloth both suggest, however, that the dispersion of looms in this case (stage 2) was more than an example of economic retardation.

15. Beaulieu, *Histoire du commerce,* p. 140.

16. *Le Courrier de Lyon,* passim. This newspaper, edited by J. B. Monfalcon (see Note 9), was established in January 1833 as a house organ of the Orleanist silk merchants.

17. "Rapport sur la situation industrielle."

18. Fernand Rude, *Le mouvement ouvrier à Lyon de 1827 à 1832* (Paris, 1944), p. 49. *Canuserie* is a little used variation of *canuts.* Rude's classic dissertation, long out of print, has recently been republished by Editions Anthropos, Paris.

19. There is as yet no general study of the silk merchants as an economic and social group. Several young French historians, such as MM. Henri Pensu and Pierre Cayez, are preparing theses on this topic under the direction of Professor Pierre Léon of the University of Lyon.

20. In 1832, only 778 of the 8,000 master weavers owned four or more looms.

Number of looms	13	12	11	10	9	8	7	6	5	4
Number of masters	1	4	0	2	2	12	8	53	82	614

(House of Commons, Silk Trade, p. 541).

21. Under the July Monarchy all men had equal social rights, but only those who paid 100 francs direct taxes annually had the right to vote. The latter group were called active citizens.

22. A. Audiganne, *Les populations ouvrières et les industries de la France dans le mouvement social du XIXe siècle,* 2 vols. (Paris, 1854) 1:234.

23. See Louis Trenard, "The social crisis in Lyon on the eve of the French Revolution," reprinted in translation in Jeffrey Kaplow, ed., *New Perspectives on the French Revolution* (New York, 1965). Nor had things changed much. Trenard cites the Comptroller General of France in 1786: "Lyon is the only city in which the merchant has imperiously laid down the law and has always denied the artisan his fortune, a just and legitimate wage."

24. P. Truchon, "La vie interieure de la fabrique lyonnaise sous la Restauration," *Revue d'histoire de Lyon,* 9(1910):409–34.

25. J. P. Aguet, *Les grèves sous la monarchie de Juillet, 1830–1847* (Geneva, 1954), pp. xvii–xx.

26. Beaulieu, *Histoire du commerce,* p. 150.

27. The information presented here is built on data I have collected from the tax censuses of the city, the logbooks for which are currently stored in the attic of the *Hôtel-de-Ville* (series K. *Recensement de la population*). For a detailed discussion of the demographic transition, see my forthcoming book, *The Lyon Uprising of 1834.* It should also be noted that the shift from the central city to the suburbs is a pattern familiar in the development of preindustrial urban ecology.

28. See the comparative figures presented by Claude Aboucaya, *Les structures sociales et économiques de l'agglomération lyonnaise à la veille de la Révolution de 1848* (Lyon, 1963), p. 15 n.

29. P. Truchon, "La vie ouvrière à Lyon sous la Restauration," *Revue d'histoire de Lyon,* 11 (1912): Monfalcon, *Histoire des insurrections* p. 35; Villermé, *Tableau de l'état physique,* 2:364.

30. *Le Précurseur,* 3 January 1833.

31. *AM Doc.* G., t. 1: "Rapport sur la projet de réunion des communes suburbaines à la ville de Lyon," 27 November 1833.

32. "Rapport sur la situation industrielle."

33. *L'Echo de la Fabrique,* 26 August 1832.

34. Fernand Rude, "Pierre Charnier, fondateur du mutuellisme à Lyon," *Revue de 1848,* 35(1938):18–49, 65–117, 140–79.

35. *L'Echo de la Fabrique,* 26 February 1832.

36. Ibid., 13 May 1832.

37. Ibid., 5 February 1832.

38. Ibid., 25 March 1832.

39. Ibid., 5 February 1832.

40. Ibid., 1 April 1832.

41. Villermé, *Tableau de l'état physique*, 1:380.

42. *L'Echo de la Fabrique,* 11 August 1833. It would be inaccurate to suggest that only men wove the cloth. According to at least one expert (Monfalcon, *Histoire des insurrections* p. 31), there were a large number of female journeymen. In addition, a large shop also employed young boys, called *lanceurs,* whose task was to throw the shuttle back across the loom. In times of crisis the *lanceurs* were as prone to violence as the *compagnons* were.

43. *AM Doc. G.,* t. 1: Mayor of the Croix Rousse to Gasparin, 19 March 1832.

44. "Urbanization, Migration, and Social Mobility in Late Nineteenth Century America," in Barton J. Bernstein, ed., *Towards a New Past: Dissenting Essays in American History* (New York, 1968), p. 168.

45. *L'Echo de la Fabrique,* 6 May and 26 October 1833.

46. The *Réglement* of the journeymens' association mentions regulation of working hours, the limitation of the number of apprentices, and the exclusion of female weavers from the shops, and the abolition of night work as future goals.

47. According to Villermé (*Tableau de l'état physique,* 1:355), the number of masters who no longer worked a loom themselves was "too small to mention."

48. Joseph Benoit, *Confession d'un prolétaire* [1871] (Paris, 1969), p. 67.

49. *L'Echo de la Fabrique,* 18 August 1833.

50. Ibid., 23 August 1833: "On the abuses within the *Fabrique.*"

51. "Social History," in H. P. R. Finberg, ed., *Approaches to History* (London, 1962), pp. 64–65.

52. *The Making of the English Working Class,* pp. 9–10.

53. "Time, Work-Discipline and Industrial Capitalism," *Past and Present,* n. 38 (December 1967), pp. 79–80. One of the most brilliant articles ever written on the transition from traditional to modern forms of labor.

54. Asa Briggs, "Social structure and politics in Birmingham and Lyon," *British Journal of Sociology,* 1(1950):67–80.

55. For a discussion of the first point, see I. Prothero, "Chartism in London," *Past and Present,* n. 44 (August 1969); for the second, see Peter N. Stearns, "Patterns of Strike Activity in France during the July Monarchy," *American Historical Review,* 70 (January 1965).

56. Villermé, *Tableau de l'état physique,* 2:371.

57. Walter Runciman, *Relative Deprivation and Social Justice: a study of attitudes in 20th century England* (Berkeley, 1966).

58. Nearly 70 percent of the workers arrested following the April 1834 uprising were literate according to the statements that they made to the police and that are recorded in their dossiers.

59. *Les archives nationales de la France* (Paris) (hereafter cited as *AN*), CC 558, dossier Serre.

60. *L'Echo de la Fabrique,* 13 May 1832.

61. Ibid., 28 October, 2 and 11 November 1832. For a discussion of the changing worker vocabulary, see Jean Dautry, "De la première revolte des canuts à la mort de Blanqui," *Pensée,* n. 82 (1958), 95–102.

62. *L'Echo des Travailleurs,* 1 March 1834.

63. *L'Echo de la Fabrique,* 8 and 22 July 1832.

64. *L'Echo des Travailleurs,* 9 November 1833.

65. Truchon, "La vie ouvrière a Lyon."

66. The former favored the exclusive organization of the master weavers, while the latter supported the eventual union of all workingmen (*L'Echo des Travailleurs,* 3 and 20 November 1833).

67. *L'Echo de la Fabrique,* 24 March and 14 December 1833.

68. Ibid., 8 December 1833; *L'Echo des Travailleurs,* 7 December 1833.

69. *L'Echo de la Fabrique,* 6 October 1833.

70. *L'Echo des Travailleurs,* 30 November 1833.

71. *AM Doc. G.,* t. 3: Thiers to Gasparin, 2 December 1832.

72. Rude, "Pierre Charnier," pt. 1, p. 45.

73. The standard account of these associations remains Octave Festy, *Le mouvement ouvrier au début de la monarchie de juillet, 1830–1834* (Paris, 1908).

74. Rude, "Pierre Charnier," pt. 3, p. 146.

75. Monfalcon, *Histoire des insurrections,* p. 218.

76. *L'Echo des Travailleurs,* 20 November 1833.

77. *AM Doc. G.,* t. 1: Gasparin to Minister of Commerce, 18 March 1833; *Le Courrier de Lyon,* 17 July 1833.

78. For a detailed discussion of the July 1833 and February 1834 strikes, see my article, "Aspects du conflict des classes à Lyon, 1831–1834," *Le mouvement social,* 76 (1971):5–26.

79. *AM Doc. G.,* t. 1: Minister of Commerce to Gasparin, 22 July 1833.

80. The best source of information on this coup is the testimony of the members of the Council of Presidents. This is found in *AN* CC 558, dossier Rivière cadet.

81. *AM Doc. G.,* t. 13, Prunelle to Gasparin, 14 February 1834.

82. Ibid., Mutualist *ordre du jour,* 17 February 1834.

83. *Le Précurseur,* 5 March, 3 and 21 July 1833; *L'Echo des Travailleurs,* 23, 27, and 30 November 1833.

84. *Le Précurseur,* 6 December 1831.

85. This was the opinion of Anselme Petetin, the Republican editor of *Le Précurseur,* who was closely involved with the project for a central commercial house. Petetin's unpublished memoirs are found in the *Archives Nationales* (*AN* CC 567).

86. Office du travail, *Les Associations professionelle ouvrières,* 4 vols. (Paris, 1905), 4:256–57.

87. 8 December 1831.

88. The standard source for the first Lyon uprising in F. Rude, *Le mouvement ouvrier à Lyon.*

89. Monfalcon, *Histoire des insurrections,* pp. 98–99.

90. *The Lyon Uprising of 1834* (forthcoming), chaps. 3 through 5.

91. *Les archives du ministère de la guerre* (Vincennes), E5 51, Aide de camp du ministre en mission to Minister of War, 18 April 1834.

92. Monfalcon, *Histoire des insurrections,* p. 101. This is also the conclusion of the official report to the government, written by Girod de l'Ain, *Rapport fait à la cour des Pairs,* 4 vols. (Paris, 1834).

93. Trenard, "The social crisis in Lyon on the eve of the French Revolution," passim.

94. *The Lyon Uprising of 1834* (forthcoming), chap. 7. These interrogations are found in the *Archives Nationales,* CC 554–72.

95. See pp. 99–101.

96. Rude, *Le mouvement ouvrier à Lyon,* pp. 342 and 359.

97. *AM Doc. G.,* t. 13: Prunelle to Gasparin, 17 February 1834.

98. *AN* CC 563, dossier Clocher: interrogation.

99. S. Maritch, *La vie ouvrière à Lyon sous le second empire* (Lyon, 1929), p. 59. The export value of *façonnes* fell to 2 million francs in 1872, from a level of 84 million francs in 1858.

I FATTI DI MAGGIO: THE WORKING CLASS OF MILAN AND THE REBELLION OF 1898

Louise A. Tilly

The Italian political and economic crisis of the 1890s reached its most acute point in 1898. In that year, a wave of popular unrest washed over the country. Like earlier movements of rebellion from the Risorgimento onward, the wave of 1898 began in Sicily, spread through the South, and only then moved north. Because of high grain prices, many protests focused on demands for "bread and work." (These high prices resulted from a poor harvest and the exceptionally high prices of imports, which in turn resulted from the heavy Italian grain tariff and the reduction of shipments from an America involved in war.) But the central issue varied with the local situation. Some of the southern protests included demands for land distribution; others, complaints about particular taxes. Everywhere, however, the authorities reacted sternly. Police and troops moved against demonstrators through much of Italy; they killed and wounded hundreds of Italian civilians.[1]

The troubles continued from January into May. On May 6, Milan, Italy's center of industry and business, was the scene of a fateful demonstration. A group of Milanese gathered outside a police station in the industrial section of the city to demand the release of several men who had been arrested while distributing socialist manifestos. The prominent socialist deputy, Turati, and various factory owners hastened to negotiate with the authorities for the release of the prisoners. The municipal council, meeting in extraordinary session, immediately rescinded the local tax on grain and flour. Beyond these attempts to calm the mounting protest, the official response to the demonstration was harsh. Troops went to the station house, and eventually their gunfire dispersed the demonstrators. One policeman was killed because he didn't move out of the line of fire. Several workers were wounded, some fatally. A group of their fellows started to take one of the critically wounded men to the hospital of the Fatebenefratelli; when he died on the way, they continued to the Piazza del Duomo with his corpse. Police patrols prevented the regrouping of demonstrators in any numbers downtown. Finally a rain storm sent home the hangers-on.

The next day a strike (one witness felt it was at least in part a lock-

Louise A. Tilly is completing her doctorate at the University of Toronto and teaches at the University of Michigan at Flint.

out)² spread in the industrial neighborhoods. Demonstrating workers again skirmished with troops who were by then stationed at the city gates. Many of the industrial workers lived in the suburban area, outside the old walls; that is where the factories were located, and where the first day's demonstration had taken place. The seventh of May saw attempts by some of these workers to march down to the center of the city via the big avenues leading to the cathedral square from the gates, picking up other workers to support their protest and strike. The accompanying map shows, in a simplified, schematic version, the walled city, its significant avenues and squares, and the suburban area where the important metal and chemical factories were located. In view of the readiness of the military and the police for confrontation, both the Socialist party leadership and the officials of the Chamber of Labor did what they could to calm the situation. In the morning, there were fights between workers and soldiers—mostly in the northern half of the city, through which demonstrators were attempting to move toward the center. Barricades were built, defended, and destroyed. Although there were frequent reports of sniping, it seems that the weapons of the battling demonstrators were stones and roof tiles to throw at their antagonists, boards and iron bars to break up street cars, and heavy furniture and metal grilles to form the barricades.

By afternoon, violence had spread throughout the city. There was another series of barricades from the Ticinese Gate on the south toward the cathedral square. A state of siege was declared. The military established their superiority; they spent the next two days (employing heavy artillery and enjoying blanket orders to shoot) rooting out real and imagined troublemakers, against sporadic resistance from the workers. Most workers returned to their jobs on Monday, May 9. Yet there remained a final absurd military reaction, which went far to discredit the army with most groups within the city. It was the bombardment of a monastery, where a group of beggars had gathered for their daily soup. The officer in charge was told that the monks and the beggars were dangerous revolutionaries in disguise. He took the monastery by frontal attack, blasting through its wall with cannon.

These were the Fatti di Maggio, a rebellion that has usually been considered in the context of Italy as a whole in 1898. Milan was seen as a special case by contemporary commentators such as Olivetti and Colajanni: it represented the epitome of northern, industrial, anti-regime, anti-corruption, anti-militaristic opinion. They labeled Milan the "moral capital" of Italy. Yet the Fatti are generally seen as the capstone of a national popular movement in response to high prices and dissatisfaction with government policy. The purpose of this paper is to reduce the scale of the problem in two ways. First, by concentrating on individuals involved in the rebellion, then by placing it in the context of local history and politics. This approach can be summed up in terms of the orientations and techniques of "history from below."

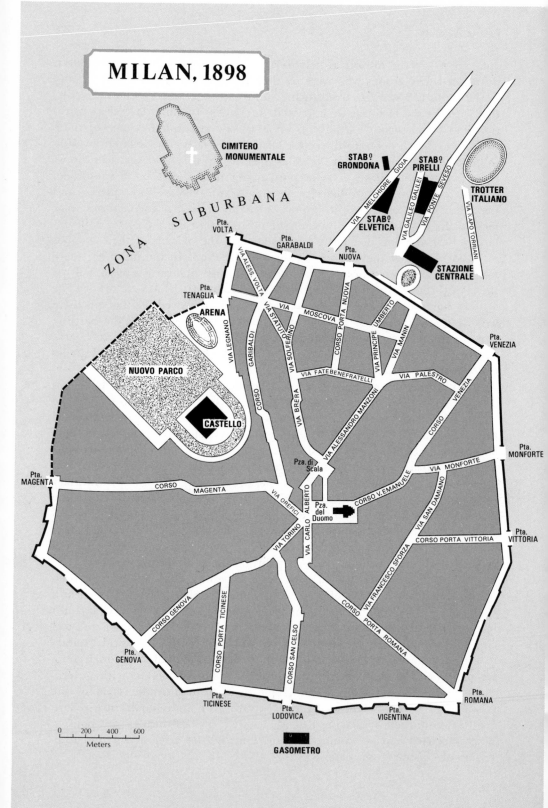

Popular history, as practiced by its English masters, George Rudé, Edward P. Thompson, and Eric Hobsbawm,[3] sees violence and rebellion as the political weapons of those whose role in ordinary politics is curtailed or even nonexistent. By studying the personnel of riots and examining their targets, proclaimed motives, and justifications, these historians have demonstrated how seldom riot or rebellion is the aimless threat to law and order it is so promptly labeled. Employed, respectable persons often take part in such violence; furthermore, their action is often based on real grievances, is motivated by hope for recourse, and has defined goals. To complicate matters, violent attack on persons or property is sometimes a calculated move, but such violence often grows out of official reaction to initial peaceful claims. Violence often achieves its short-run aims and contributes to change in the long run through the development of consciousness in the act of participation by groups and individuals. The words attributed to the Socialist deputy Filippo Turati, speaking at the Porta Venezia on May 7, 1898, sum this up: "The dead do count for something; they are milestones for the conquests to come of the people."[4]

The Fatti di Maggio were a milestone in the political progress of the working class of Milan. They also had national significance because what happened in Milan, the prime industrial city of Italy, both mirrored and shaped the industrialization of Italy. The growth of heavy industry in Italy as a whole was in a large part the measure of the great change occurring in Milan during the years 1890 to 1910. Along with structural transformation came increased political consciousness on the part of the working class, expressed through demonstrations, illegal strikes, and demands for political participation. Eventually, its increasing potency brought political recognition for the working class, legitimacy for the Socialist party, working-class representation in national and local government, legalization of strikes, and a voice in government policy and legislation. The experience of working-class activism in Milan in the 1890s also shaped the ideology and tactics of socialist and union leaders and rank-and-file members in the years before World War I. The Fatti, seen from the point of view of local, popular history, were integral to the economic and political formation of the Milanese working class over these years of rapid industrial growth. Because of Milan's crucial importance, the Fatti also subsume, in the sense of an ideal type, a process at work in Italy as a whole, the transformation of the working class by industrialization and its entry into politics.

The following discussion falls into four parts: (1) a review of contemporary and historical judgments about the Fatti di Maggio from which I have drawn a series of questions about the participants; (2) an analysis of the structure of the working class, its age and sex distribution, occupations, wealth, literacy, place of birth, and spatial distribution in the city; (3) with this structure as a base, an examination of the characteristics of about 600 persons who were wounded, arrested, or tried for their part in the Fatti; (4)

suggestion of an alternative explanation by a review of similar violent and nonviolent confrontations in the preceding years and an account of working-class organizational activity just before May 1898.

Views of the Rebellion; Unanswered Questions

Contemporary interpretation of the Fatti was quick to come; it was only weakly factual and strongly based on ideological preconceptions. Much recent Italian historical writing about the Fatti starts similarly with world views and not many more facts. The explanatory theories that most often underlie these world views could be grouped under these headings: the outsider agitator–marginal participant theory, the misery theory, and the repression theory. By contrast, American and British commentators—none of whom have done detailed work on the subject—have tended toward sociological explanations, which could be labeled an alienation–frustration theory. All of these approaches rest on unproven assumptions, which can be tested by asking a series of simple but concrete questions about who was involved in the Fatti.

The contemporary conservative view immediately discerned outside agitators or marginal or criminal persons as the chief perpetrators of the violence, and, behind it all, scheming subversive propagandists. The *Corriere della Sera* described "savage scenes," women shrieking unbelievable obscenities, shouting and hissing mobs of unruly children, complete abstention by the disciplined workers of prosperous Milan. The editorial of May 7–8, 1898 gave the following quick analysis: "The movement prompted by the high price of bread which began with a spontaneous outburst of the underprivileged masses has now passed under the domination of the subversive parties, which are inciting popular violence in the hope of gaining from it." By the tenth of May, the *Corriere* was expressing satisfaction with the efficiency of the repression, and declared, "We know by this time that the working population is foreign to the riots and wants nothing more than to return to work."

A similar combination of outrage, hurt disbelief, and equation of rioters with bums manipulated by sinister plotters appears in the speech of the conservative mayor, Vigoni, which opened the municipal council meeting on June 2, 1898:

Our city—our poor Milan—has been submitted to a hard test. It has been subjected to a crisis over which I would wish to draw a veil of forgetfulness. . . . This was all the work of rascals whom we shall leave to the courts to judge and punish, but toward whom we cannot resist a word of moral condemnation. . . . The uprising was repressed, and I congratulate myself that the government was strong and aware of its proper course so that it repressed the inauspicious acts of the enemies of order and prevented any renewal of that web of intrigue and conspiracy which prepared the way for the shocking event.[5]

The council joined him in voting thanks to General Bava Beccaris and his troops for the restoration of order, with only three members refusing to vote for the motion.

Liberal commentators were by no means alone in protesting the fierce repressiveness of government action, but this aspect of their interpretation is what quickly divided them from their conservative and moderate fellows. So we have the managing editor of the *Corriere della Sera,* Torelli Viollier, announcing his disagreement with his own newspaper's editorial policy in a letter to *La Stampa* of Turin on June 12, 1898. Whereupon he resigned to protest the excesses of the military repression. Salvemini charged that this resignation was a trick to preserve his liberal reputation while allowing the *Corriere* to express the most reactionary views. Nevertheless, Torelli Viollier's views were representative of one section of liberal opinion about the Fatti. In this interpretation, there was no rebellion; the killings were a monstrosity imposed upon the populace by vengeful troops and police. In a letter to a friend, Torelli Viollier described the Corso Venezia barricade, the most serious incident, but wrote that beyond this, there was only a game of hide and seek between workers and troops. He quoted his concierge: "Saturday [May 7] was the people's revolution; today [May 9] it is the soldiers' revolution."[6]

The explanation from misery is not the monopoly of socialist commentators, but it was most eloquently stated by them in the contemporary period. Niccolo Badaloni delivered this impassioned analysis to the Chamber of Deputies on June 17, 1898, the day the Di Rudinì government was forced to resign:

The shouts of misery, embittered by the high price of bread, reached out to you from all sides, but these voices, revealing the exhaustion of our working classes, were not enough to persuade the Italian government to suspend the grain tariff: the revolt of the proletariat was necessary.[7]

He continued with a review of high food prices and the movement of protest, then attacked the government claim that the protest was political in the North, specifically in Milan, and the result of a plot of "enemies of our institutions."

Although it would be an exaggeration to say that there was no unemployment and no misery [in Milan], the working classes did not lack bread, but they had to pay dearly for their bread, and that expense was recognized as resulting from the poor administration of this ministry.[8]

Badaloni concluded that repression of workers' rights was a central cause and placed the fault on Di Rudinì and his government. Many modern historical arguments also bow, perfunctorily or elaborately, to the explanation from misery. The historian of 1898 in Tuscany, Pinzani, is so intent on fitting protest into the context of extreme misery that he expresses surprise that there should have been trouble at Prato, where there had been no crushing rise in bread prices and no rural unemployment.[9] The twentieth century Marxist historian, although he presents a more complex explanation, feels the obligation to present increased bread prices, unemployment, and misery as the essential background for revolt in Milan.[10]

Napoleone Colajanni, a positivist sociologist of the nineteenth-century variety, and also a popular lecturer, journalist, and member of Parliament attacked Socialist analysis like that of Badaloni for oversimplification: "Aren't the Socialists reducing the social question to absurdity because some of them are making it a simple 'question of the stomach'?"[11] The main thrust of Colajanni's analysis is that the Fatti were essentially political, a "moral" protest against immoral government policies. He also argued a more subtle thesis of misery, emphasizing relative deprivation. The rising expectations theory is offered as a "canon of popular psychology": "The influence of unfavorable economic setbacks are suffered from more quickly and more intensely where prosperity is greater."[12] Colajanni goes on to argue that an important number of the rioters were furnished from the uprooted, alienated, newly arrived peasants, "elements without work and stable residence."

Similar notions of frustration and alienation lie behind several American comments on the Fatti. Neufeld says, "Lombard and Venetian peasants, in their search for factory work, had shifted from quiet village life to an urban atmosphere of political turmoil. These country men, without willing it, upset the social equilibrium in Milan."[13] The sociological overview of Italian working class history and ideology by Surace concludes, "During these years of violence, the social structure was changing and many tensions were generated by rising aspirations."[14]

Much of the evidence that could support or disprove the theories illustrated above, namely, the outside agitator–marginal participant, misery, repression, or alienation–frustration theories, lies in careful identification of the participants in the Fatti di Maggio.

Were there indeed many women and children among casualties and arrestees, which there should have been if the *Corriere* was right in identifying them as chief instigators and participants? Or was the impression an artifact of the youthfulness of the industrial work force and the heavy participation of women in certain kinds of work? Did other marginal persons—criminals, hoodlums, bums, the unemployed—play an important role?

If repression was the principal shaper of events, as liberal witnesses argued, the people who were arrested or wounded should reflect a random sample of persons likely to be in the streets of Milan on a spring day. Does analysis of those involved bear this out? The argument that emphasizes repression also belittles the participants (Torelli Viollier called them a *canaglia,* a rabble) and postulates a lack of consciousness of group identification, felt injustice, or program for change. Were the participants merely swept along by a movement out of control or were their actions the outgrowth of peaceful political action and organization?

To judge the adequacy of the misery theory, those who actually were involved in the Fatti will be compared with those who were most poorly paid, least secure economically. What is the fit between the occupations of rebels and the relative wealth of these occupations? If the persons with the lowest wages, those most likely to suffer from increased food prices, were not overrepresented among those involved in the Fatti, the explanatory value of the explanation from misery is vitiated.

Uprootedness and alienation as causative factors would be revealed if large numbers of country-born peasants as contrasted with native Milanese were among those involved. A majority of Milan residents were not native-born, however, and if the nativity of the rebels does not differ substantially from that of the population at large, the alienation argument disappears, because it cannot account for participation or nonparticipation.

In order to make judgments about the persons involved in the Fatti di Maggio, or the casualties and arrests, we need a clear and detailed picture of the occupational structure of Milan. The numbers of arrested persons of one occupation or another constitute curious facts but no more, until they are given a solid base by comparing them to the population at risk. The population at risk is the total population that could possibly share a given characteristic, such as occupation. The same principle, comparison to population at risk, is also crucial for characteristics other than occupation, whether demographic (age and sex), social (nativity and literacy), or economic (relative wages).

The analysis of those involved in the Fatti di Maggio will show that many of the assumptions of the commentators just reviewed are false. An alternative view is available, however. It stresses how violence can grow out of everyday politics, as movements take on internal dynamism quite apart from the directions imposed on them by their leaders, a dynamism that is often shaped in response to official government reaction. There had been mass demonstrations, illegal propaganda, destruction of property, confrontations of workers and troops in Milan before. The scenario at the police station in the Via Napo Torriani was a familiar one. What made the difference in May 1898? On the one hand, national tension and anxiety from four months of unrest led to determination to put a quick end to the protest. On the other hand, the workers were at the crest of a period of rapid growth of organization, increased propaganda, and mobilization around issues such as the grain tariff, freedom of assembly, and the right to strike. These two circumstances differentiated the situation of 1898 from other seemingly similar moments, and accounted to a large degree for the transformation of a street demonstration into a rebellion that transfixed the nation.

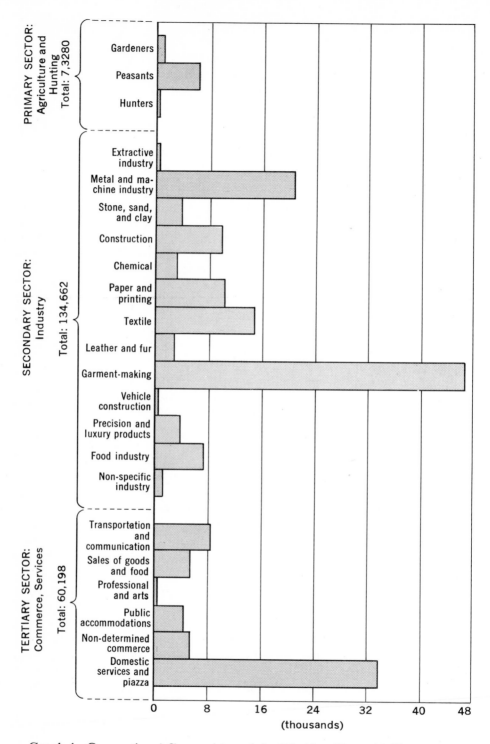

Graph 1 Occupational Composition of the Working Class of Milan, 1901

The Structure and Characteristics of the Working Class in Milan

Fortunately for the social historian, nineteenth-century Milan kept excellent records about its population, so we have both a continuing register of population, the Anagrafe, and the decennial national census. The scheduled 1891 census, however, was never taken because of financial difficulties of the central government. Therefore, the 1901 census is the census closest in time to the Fatti and the source of the occupational and social information about the population of Milan that follows. The statistical office of the city of Milan profited greatly from the fact that this census was done by local officials under the supervision of the national Direzione generale della Statistica. The census report issued by the city, referring to Milan only, gives a more detailed picture of the characteristics of its population than is available for any other part of the Italian population in the national census publications.[15]

Of the 270,654 persons aged 6 and over who were counted in 1901 according to occupation or condition (not including the garrison), 202,188, or 73 percent, fit the definition below of working class and appear in Graph 1, "The Occupational Composition of the Working Class of Milan." "Working class" designates those persons who do physical work for wages, a definition that arises from the form of presentation of the census tables. Occupations were first classified by economic sectors, then by finer categories within sectors, and finally by status groups within each category: owners, directors, and workers (operai e facchini). In the commercial sector, store clerks were not included in the working class as defined here, because they were grouped with supervisors and differentiated from porters and manual workers.

Industrial workers dominated the Milanese working class, as the graph shows, amounting to 48.63 percent. Industry, however, covered a variety of conditions of work apart from large-scale factory work. The largest number of industrial workers (almost 17 percent of the labor force as a whole) was occupied in "garment making," which by the 1901 census definitions included 8,056 workers in personal services of "hygiene"—hairdressers, laundresses, barbers. In the various garment trades, many workers, including dressmakers, shirtmakers, tailors, glovemakers, and shoemakers, worked in small shops or their own rooms. The same was true to some extent of the food, leather and fur, precision instrument, and luxury products industries.

The metal and machine industry, the characteristic industry of Milan, stood only second in numbers employed within the industrial sector. It included not only large factories (in the 1890s, there were a steel mill, employing 275 men, and nine machine shops that built locomotives and heavy equipment, employing 3,000 but also smithies and small shops that were quite small-scale. The closest date for which information about number of men employed per establishment is available is an 1896 survey by the chamber of commerce in reply to government inquiries. From this statistic

I calculated the ratio of workers to plant (that is, average size of establishment) for the metal and machine industry as only 28.91. In contrast, for the textile industry, the ratio was 49.36, and in the chemical industry, it was 33.05.[16] The third largest group of industrial workers were those in textiles, which in Milan had always been more specialized (producing braid, ribbons, and elastic) than the large spinning mills in the Lombard hills. Although the chemical workers were relatively few in numbers, about half of them worked for Pirelli, a relatively new, vigorous company that produced rubber objects and insulation.

Beyond the rather diffuse industrial sector, there were also 7,328 persons engaged in agriculture, the greatest number of whom called themselves peasants for the census. Finally, although the commercial sector as a whole contributed only 21.74 percent of workers, the second largest occupational group in the city was domestic service and street service workers, amounting to almost 12 percent of the labor force.

In its occupational composition, Milan was largely industrial; within industry, there was an important modern sector, but the work experience of most Milanese in 1901 was still mostly in skilled trades in small-scale shops or in unskilled manual work or domestic service.

This flat, two-dimensional description of working-class composition in Milan can be enriched by looking at the following characteristics of individuals *within* occupations: (1) the geographic distribution of the occupations within the city; (2) basic demographic characteristics, age and sex distribution; (3) economic condition through relative wages; (4) social characteristics such as literacy, nativity, and role in patterns of migration.

In the 1890s, Milan was very large in area, its territory going far beyond the still walled inner city and including both populous and very sparsely inhabited suburbs. At the period of the 1901 census, the geographic divisions used for administrative and descriptive purposes were three concentric circles: a central core, and a suburban and a rural ring. Through these outer rings in pie-slice fashion were cut the *Mandamenti communalii,* the basic administrative units.[17]

The density of the population naturally decreased as distance from the center increased, and in the rural zone, density was very low. The spatial distribution of occupational groups was not a random matter. First of all, of persons 16 years old and older, the percentage working in industry increased as a function of distance from the center, up to a maximum concentration of industrial workers in the suburban zone, the area around the old walls. In the center of Milan, 30 out of 100 were occupied in industry, in the suburban zone, 45 percent were. Most of these industrial workers lived close to their plants, so we find many pottery workers living in the southwestern rural zone of the city, where the Richard Ginori factory was located. Similarly, glass workers lived in the South and Southwest, where there were important glass works. The most important and visible concen-

tration of modern (that is, factory) industrial workers was in the northern
suburban region, where most of the rubber workers lived, close to the
Pirelli factory, and many metal and machine workers, close to the large machine shops. In the central core were concentrated especially skilled workers such as printers, lithographers and precision instrument makers, and
also the garment workers, the unskilled personal service workers, and those
working in the production and sale of food.[18]

   Population pyramids are used in this section to represent schemat-
ically the age and sex distribution of given populations; the numbers of
persons by sex are distributed on the horizontal axis, age groups on the
vertical axis. As a point of reference, the first population pyramid shows
the age-sex distribution by five-year age cohorts of the entire population

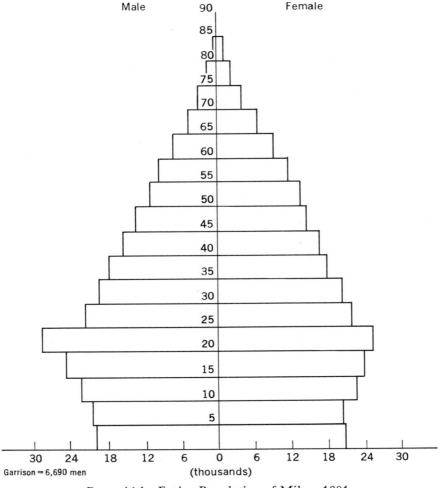

Pyramid 1   Entire Population of Milan, 1901

of Milan in 1901. The fact that the population cohorts between ages 10 and 30 are consistently larger than those of the population under 10 is the result of immigration. The city, as is typical of a fast-growing industrial city, was growing largely by immigration rather than by natural increase. The garrison, which is included in this pyramid, amounted to some 5,785 men and 470 officers, almost all aged 21 to 40. Therefore, another part of the large male population aged 20 to 25 was due to the effect of the garrison on the population distribution. Even on the female side, however, that age cohort was the largest, which shows how important immigration was in that age group.

For the purposes of illustrating the variation in age-sex distribution in sections of the working class, selected population pyramids with larger age blocks, 6 to 20, 21 to 40, and over 40, were constructed. As seen in Pyramid 2 for the working class only, women were a very important com-

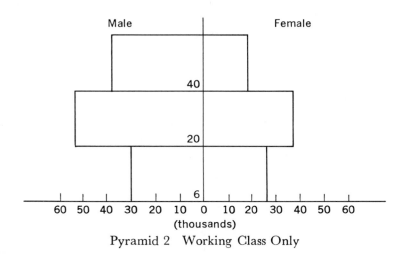

Pyramid 2   Working Class Only

ponent, 41.33 percent. Although women were 36.67 percent of the aggregate labor force, they were more important in working-class occupations, and their participation was strongly concentrated between the ages 20 and 40. Women obviously withdrew from active work earlier than men, mostly with marriage and children in late twenties.

The pyramids for sectoral breakdowns show a variety of patterns. Agriculture and hunting occupied only 2.65 percent of the labor force, of whom about one quarter were women. These were elderly people, the peasants of an industrial city, almost half were over 40. The workers in the industrial sector, unsurprisingly since they amounted to almost half the labor force, fall into an age distribution more like that of the working class as a whole. Women provided an even larger proportion of industrial workers, 42.19 percent. The largest census industrial worker category, the

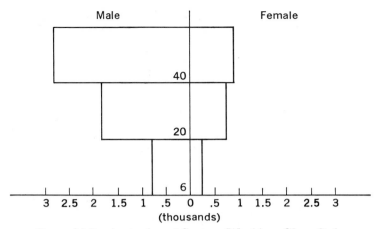

Pyramid 3   Agricultural Sector: Working Class Only

garment workers, was heavily dominated by young female workers. Metal and machine workers were almost all male, and also relatively young. These two most diverse industrial categories, in terms of age-sex distribution, are illustrated by pyramids 5 and 6. Most of the other industrial categories had a pattern of few women and predominant age cohort 21 to 40. Paper and printing, precision, and luxury are the exceptions to this generally predominant age distribution, with slightly more workers in the age 20 and under category than in any other age group. The chemical workers were the only exception to the predominant sex distribution, employing 51.58 percent women, almost all below the age of 41. This again reflects the employment

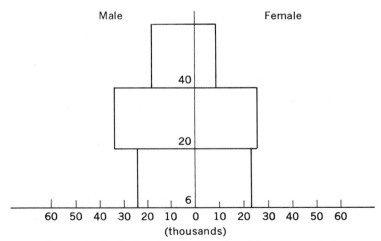

Pyramid 4   Industrial Sector: Working Class Only
134,662 persons, 48.63% of labor force, 42.10% women

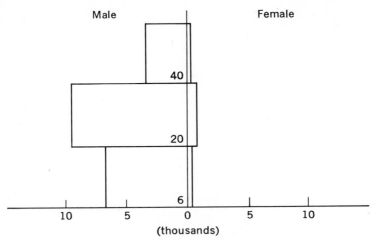

Pyramid 5   Mineral, Metal, and Machine Category: Working Class Only
20,513 persons, 7.41% of labor force, 3.49% women

pattern of the large Pirelli factory, which employed, in 1898, 858 women
and 809 men.[19]

In the tertiary sector, 41.23 percent of the workers were women, but
the individual categories range in sex distribution from domestic service,
with 66.79 percent women, to transportation and communications, in which
only 0.31 percent were women. The age distribution of the tertiary sector
workers included many fewer under age 21 than in industry, and also does
not go down steeply after age 40. This is true for all categories, regardless

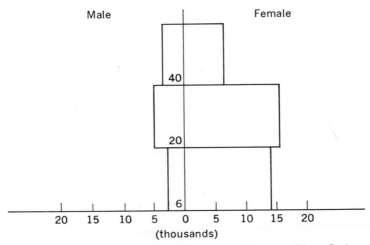

Pyramid 6   Garment-Making Category: Working Class Only
46,885 persons, 16.93% of labor force, 77.57% women

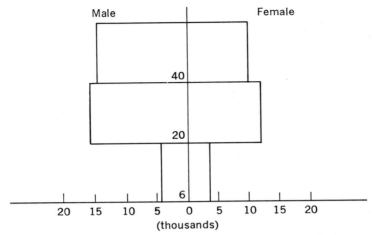

Pyramid 7   Commerce, Services: Working Class Only
60,198 persons, 21.74% of labor force, 41.23% women

of sex distribution: for transport workers only 3.31 percent of the men were under 21, 52 percent were 21–40, 44 percent over 40. In the domestic service category, 9.30 percent were women under 21; 31 percent, women between 21 and 40; 27 percent, women over 40.

For Milan, the first broadly based wage figures from which comparative economic well-being of various categories of workers can be deduced were collected in 1903. The Società Umanitaria, a Milanese foundation whose mission was both social action and collecting information about working-class conditions, conducted a survey in which 112,171 workers reported their wages.[20] Although wage levels were higher in 1903 than in 1898, scattered wage information from the earlier period indicates that the relative position of occupations was similar in the two periods.

The highest wages were in the tertiary sector, earned by workers in transportation and communications. This same sector also included the more humble domestic service workers whose wages had the lowest average of any category. The top industrial wage earners, who were printers, vehicle builders, the metal and machine workers in heavy industry and construction workers, had wages in the same range as transportation and communications workers, although averaging slightly lower. The craft workers held a middle position as far as wages went, and the bottom of the wage fan was occupied mainly by female occupations. The chemical industry had a low overall average wage because about half its workers were women, and poorly paid. Qualified male workers in the Pirelli rubber factory were making an average daily wage of L 2.80 as early as 1896; at the same time women in a similar skill category were making L 1.50.[21] A similar case lies hidden in the low average wages of garment workers; within this category the best paid workers were the shoemakers, all men. These last points reiterate the message of any wage comparison for Milan at the end of the nineteenth century. The largest wage differential was a sex differential, not a purely occupational one; female workers were uniformly paid wretchedly.

To complete this picture of the working population of Milan, the 1901 census provides our information about literacy and nativity. Illiteracy was overall a minor phenomenon in Milan, but it was also distributed differentially in the working class. Agricultural workers were much more likely to be illiterate than any other category of worker. Among industrial workers, the stone, sand, clay, and construction workers had the highest rate of illiteracy. Persons in both of these categories lived in the rural zone of Milan and sometimes were part-time agricultural workers, so we are probably seeing the same effect here of little schooling in rural areas. The most highly skilled male workers were the most literate also; poorly paid and relatively unskilled women, the most illiterate. The category of paper and printing grouped together two occupational categories that showed this large skill and sex differential in literacy. These were the highly literate male printing workers and the less literate female workers in paper or cardboard mills.

Turning to nativity, the 1901 figures in Table I show the following pattern by economic sector.

TABLE I. NATIVITY FIGURES BY ECONOMIC SECTOR, 1901

| | Percentage born in Milan | |
Sector	Male	Female
Agriculture	22.02	20.85
Industry	37.38	48.37
Commerce and service	21.70	12.78
Total working class	32.02	37.13

Clearly, industrial workers in numbers well above the mean for the working class as a whole were likely to be native-born Milanese. Women were more often natives than were men in the categories in which they were most often employed—garment-making, textile, and chemical industries—so almost half of the women industrial workers were native-born. The most skilled and best-paid male categories in industry had important city-born percentages. The anomaly, at least among well-paid workers, was the chemical industry, where only 16 percent of the men were native, 33 percent of the women. Here we are dealing again with the preponderance of one business, Pirelli, and the fact that it was a relatively new enterprise, the first of its kind in Italy. The other skilled and well-paid industries had old roots in the city and recruited among native-born men, perhaps the sons of their own workers. Pirelli's deliberate policy was to employ immigrants in the hope that their rustic innocence would discourage labor militancy in his factory.[22] The highest proportions of immigrants were found in agriculture and commerce and the services. These categories included, on the one hand, the skilled railroad workers, employees of a large system who were transferred by their company in and out of big rail centers like Milan. The peasants, workers in inns and cafés, and domestic servants, on the other hand, were representative of the newly arrived, unskilled workers for whom service work was the only opportunity.[23]

This pattern of immigrants entering nonindustrial occupations can also be deduced from the immigration figures by occupation over time. The occupations that contributed the greatest number of net immigrants annually between 1893 and 1903 were all working-class occupations; they were largely unskilled or required artisanal skills previously practiced in conjunction with farming (See Table II).[24]

TABLE II. NET IMMIGRATION, ANNUAL AVERAGE, 1893–1903

Occupation	Male	Female
Peasants	586	535
Workers in general	207	121
Shoemakers	121	. . .
Construction workers	109	. . .
Servants, concierges	103	206
Carpenters	98	. . .
Blacksmiths	71	. . .
Seamstresses	. . .	98
Tailors	67	210
Cooks, bakers	59	. . .
Coachmen, carters	57	. . .
Porters	54	. . .
Messengers	55	. . .
Mechanics	50	. . .

The yearly immigration was chiefly of young people, with the 16- to 35-year-olds running consistently about 45 percent in the years around 1898. These young unskilled immigrants did not come from far, however. There was a trend after the 1880s for immigrants to come from farther than the immediate hinterland of Milan, but the effect on the working-class population, as shown by the breakdown from the Società Umanitaria survey of 1903, was minimal. Only about 10 percent of the workers surveyed came from farther away than Lombardy.[25]

In the 1890s the average migrant was young, relatively unskilled, and came from close by. The occupations in which these immigrants worked often had brief or seasonal terms of employment, allowing movement between city and countryside. The immigrant was not as common in the skilled work force or in the factory-organized industrial sector, with the exception as always of the rubber industry.

Casualties and Arrests in the Fatti di Maggio: Who Was Involved?

We turn now to the variously labeled rabble, hoodlums, alienated peasants, hungry workers, whose involvement in the Fatti di Maggio has left historical traces. The description of the various demographic, social, and economic characteristics of the Milanese working class, the spelling out of the numbers of persons who shared these characteristics, has established the population at risk. The analysis of the demographic and social characteristics of persons involved in the Fatti follows. Comparisons between the two populations will test the assumptions of observers and historians and answer the questions that grew out of their descriptions.

The question of involvement is not as precise as it could be, given the nature of the protest and the overkill that characterized the official reaction. Some people were doubtless caught on the street unaware of the deadly nature of the conflict. Once wounded, arrest was likely; a good deal of police effort went into tracking down wounded persons and investigating their role in the disorders. Because of these uncertainties, I have designated my combined list of casualties, arrested, and tried, as "persons involved," rather than "rebels" or "rioters."

Names and biographical information were gathered from two newspapers: the moderate-to-conservative *Corriere della Sera,* and the non-partisan liberal *La Lombardia.* Police records in the Archivio di Stato di Milano are very thin for the May events, partly because many records were lost by fire in World War II and partly because the trials were handled by a military court. (As for any centrally stored records of this Tribunale di Guerra, the historical office of the General Staff of the Italian army searched for some trace of them at my request but reported no success in locating the papers.)[26] The miscellaneous scraps of paper, reports, protocols, orders, and checklists in the police box were concerned mostly with identification of the dead and investigations of the "political and moral character" of a disappointingly small number of casualties and other suspects. In general, this archival material added few names or information to newspaper accounts.

As far as I know, no official complete list of casualties was ever issued, although the newspapers carried allegedly complete lists of the dead. For casualties, I have culled from newspaper accounts 236 male names, and 27 female names, one of unknown sex (excluding police and military casualties.)[27] For 94 men and 11 women and the unknown, name was the only piece of information found. For arrests (which came close to 1,700, according to the *Corriere della Sera*), I identified 602 men and 25 women who appeared to be residents of Milan and were involved in incidents in the city between May 6 and May 10, 1898. There was more information about arrestees because most of the persons reported in the press as arrested eventually came to trial. In the trial reports, age, occupation, and sometimes place of birth and paternity were mentioned. Grouped with the arrests I included 30 people who were tried in contumacy, most of them convicted, but not actually arrested at the time, because they fled Milan and Italy. These were mostly socialist and anarchist activists who were tried for conspiracy and incitement to revolt. Among those arrested, the tiny middle-class contingent is drawn largely from a group of newspaper editors and publicists representing the entire range of the antiregime press from socialist to clerical, and three members of the Chamber of Deputies.

Looking at age and sex, the simplest demographic characteristics of those involved, we can see immediately that the number of women was insignificant, 8.5 percent of casualties, 4 percent of arrests. The median age of male and female casualties was 24, that of women arrests 22, men arrests, 25. These facts question the heavy involvement of women that contemporaries reported but confirm in a general way the youth of those involved.

I have prepared two tables that compare the occupational categories of the casualties and arrests to the total population in these categories: Table III gives participation rates per 100,000 for the categories, and Table IV gives the ratios between the number of persons of a given age and occupation in census and rebellion. This ratio has the effect of standardizing the occupational categories by the varying age distributions within them, which, as I have shown, differed significantly. Both tables list the categories in declining order of participation.

Most of the persons involved in the Fatti di Maggio were employed workers; only 4.03 percent of those whose occupation was given were listed as unemployed. There are no precise figures of unemployment rates in Milan for 1898. Discussions from the general period tend to put ordinary unemployment at about 3 or 4 percent. Exactly 41 of the men brought to trial were identified as having previous convictions (some were for political offenses), a rate of 6.81 percent. Even after publishing the names of all those tried and the identifying information on which these quantitative statements are based, La Lombardia summed up: "The population of Milan is dedicated to productive work and turns away from rash agitation; this was proved by the general abstention of the working class from any part in the riots, which were the deed of the lowest and most loathsome dregs of society."[28] They were wrong, as were most of the contemporary analysts, who could not imagine wide-based participation in such an affair.

Industrial workers as a group were the most heavily involved, but even the industrial category covered a range of patterns of life and work. Nevertheless, there was no correspondence between comparative economic

TABLE III.   PARTICIPATION RATES BY OCCUPATION: FATTI DI MAGGIO, MILAN, 1898

(Per 100 thousand persons involved)

Category	Male Number	Male Ratio	Female Number	Female Ratio	Total Number	Total Ratio
Working class as a whole	429	361	19	23	448	216
Industrial workers	308	395	10	18	318	236
1. Stone, sand, clay	40	1168	0	0	40	1060
2. Chemical	14	933	6	375	20	521
3. Construction	49	501	0	0	49	500
4. Metal, mechanical	85	429	0	0	85	414
5. Wood, straw	42	422	0	0	42	394
6. Paper and printing	23	338	1	44	24	264
7. Garment making	31	295	3	8	34	73
shoemakers	16	323	0	0	16	323
8. Food	14	230	1	79	15	204
9. Precision, luxury	5	166	0	0	5	128
10. Leather, fur	3	120	0	0	3	104
11. Textile	3	93	0	0	3	20
12. Vehicle construction	0	0	0	0	0	0
Commerce and service workers	82	232	3	12	85	141
1. Sales	51	1057	0	0	51	960
2. Banks, finance	1	240	0	0	0	240
3. Transport, communications	19	226	0	0	19	226
4. Domestic service	7	65	2	9	9	27
Agricultural workers	4	76	0	0	4	55
1. Gardening	1	112	0	0	1	91
2. Peasantry	2	46	0	0	2	32
3. Fishing	1	2703†	0	0	1	2703
Students	5	17	0	0	5	9
Persons on assistance	1	116	0	0	1	63
Housewives	0	0	4	5	4	5
Pensioned persons	2	77	0	0	2	53
*White-collar, owners**	73	138	1	6	74	108
1. Professions, arts	42	309	1	19	43	228
2. Commerce, proprietorships	19	83	0	0	19	66

* Summary figures by sector includes otherwise unclassifiable persons.
† This large rate is not significant since the base population is under 100, and hence rate is inherently unstable.

TABLE IV. AGE, SEX, AND OCCUPATIONAL DISTRIBUTION OF PERSONS INVOLVED IN THE FATTI DI MAGGIO, MILAN, 1898

(Ratio of casualties and arrests to base population times 100 thousand)

Population Category	Age 6–20 Male	Age 6–20 Female	Age 21–40 Male	Age 21–40 Female	Age over 40 Male	Age over 40 Female
Total population over 6, excluding garrison	329	16	468	21	109	5
Total casualties only	62	6	81	6	25	1
Total arrests only	267	10	387	15	85	4
Working class as a whole	420	27	472	24	117	15
Industrial workers	385	22	516	16	127	11
1. Stone, sand, clay	1386	0	1488	0	426	0
2. Chemical	2740	649	1125	328	0	0
3. Construction	536	0	746	0	733	0
4. Metal, mechanical	474	0	487	0	88	0
5. Wood, straw	485	0	565	0	140	0
6. Paper, printing	200	0	481	0	91	0
7. Garment making	261	14	365	6	174	0
8. Food	139	0	218	0	338	223
9. Precision, luxury	0	0	407	0	0	0
10. Leather, fur	166	0	521	0	0	0
11. Textile	0	0	226	0	0	0
Commerce, service	421	0	306	9	86	20
1. Sales	2155	0	1516	0	255	0
2. Transport, communications	358	0	297	0	80	0
3. Banks, insurance	0	0	0	0	610	0
4. Domestic service	98	0	69	10	37	11
Agriculture	0	0	166	0	37	0
White collar, owners, professions	54	0	116	0	58	19
1. Professions, arts	134	0	173	0	131	80
2. Commerce, proprietorships	49	0	433	0	142	0

malaise and rate of involvement. The most actively involved men and women were employed in occupations with wages in the middle range. The most poorly paid workers, that is, the unskilled peasants, servants, and garment and textile workers, were seldom involved. Nor were the best-paid workers. Women chemical workers are the only exception to this statement, being poorly paid and active in the Fatti. As will be shown later, a poor pay–misery–rebellion chain of causation would be oversimplification. Any development of the misery argument would have to show that those with the poorest wages and fewest resources were most affected by the increase in bread prices that did occur in Milan. Yet these people were not most often involved; the argument from misery does not stand.

What conclusions can be made about the roles of women and the young from the age-adjusted participation ratios in Table IV? Overall, the young do not seem terribly important. However, in the occupational groups that were proportionately most involved, as the brick-kiln workers, the Pirelli workers, and those in commerce, there were important contingents of males under 20. These are the unruly youths of the news stories, crucial initiators and participators in the action, but those most gainfully employed. The many young metal workers who also were on the streets are less important proportionately because of the younger age distribution of that occupational category.

The role of women, as seen in Table IV, still looks unimpressive, except for the chemical workers. It is possible that women were not as likely to be arrested as men, although no contemporary accounts suggest this. Furthermore, even if they were arrested less, if women were in the front lines of the demonstrations, as reported, they should have appeared more often in the casualties since gunfire from the troops reportedly swept the ranks of demonstrators randomly and at close range. The same was true of gunfire at the rooftops from which stones and tiles were thrown. Women were well under 10 percent of the casualties, even though all casualties reported (including some clearly accidentally involved) were taken into account in this calculation. Women were surely in the street during the first day's demonstration, for over 800 of them worked at the Pirelli plant, outside of which the demonstration started. They also took part in the May 7 demonstrations, since they were, after all, an important part of the work force of the city, and much of it was involved in the strike. I conclude, however, that their importance has been overestimated, and that observers whose attention was attracted by flamboyant and noisy women assigned them too great a role.

What about the nativity argument, that alienated newcomers fed the fires of rebellion? (We can discount in advance the hysterical reports of the conservative *La Perseveranza* that from the countryside to join the troubles came "tattered, barefoot peasants, hatless and with twisted faces." Colajanni gave this "news" report as fact to support his analysis.)[29] One contemporary pamphlet gave the place of birth of the 80 dead: 28, or 35 percent, were native-born, a percentage remarkably like that of the population as a whole.[30] There are two ways of examining the importance of immigrants among those involved by using the nativity information I was able to collect (see Table V). One is simply to compare the occupations in which migrants were most common with the participation rates in Table III. The three industrial groups most involved stand below the mean of nativity for

TABLE V. COMPARISON OF NATIVITY BY OCCUPATIONAL CATEGORIES OF POPULATION OF MILAN WITH PERSONS ARRESTED IN FATTI DI MAGGIO, 1898

Occupational Category	Percent Born in Milan			
	1901 Census		1898 Arrests	
	Male	Female	Male	Female
Agriculture	20.02	20.85	....	....
Industry	37.38	48.37	34.51	33.33
1. Metal, mechanical	41.93	31.47	51.43	....
2. Stone, sand, clay	35.51	51.71	20.00	....
3. Construction	32.15	47.83	33.33	....
4. Chemical	16.66	32.85	20.00	33.33
5. Wood, straw	36.31	30.66	40.00	....
6. Paper, printing	55.85	47.04	20.00	....
7. Textile	41.15	42.45	0	....
8. Leather, fur	38.76	32.82	....	....
9. Garment making	28.31	51.59	0	....
10. Precision, luxury	59.69	44.40	66.67	....
11. Food	20.66	62.19	28.57	....
Commerce, services	21.70	12.78	20.45	0
1. Transport, commun.	16.96	11.54	0	....
2. Sales	27.66	20.78	33.33	....
3. Domestic service	15.52	11.35	16.67	....
Total working class	32.02	37.13	35.03	28.57
White collar, owners, professions, total	33.70	40.65	34.29	....
1. Commerce	33.25	38.25	42.86	....
2. Professions, arts	29.98	41.34	35.29	....

the population as a whole, the chemical workers strikingly so. The fourth place metalworkers, however, were more likely to be native-born than the average Milanese worker. Of the occupational categories in the commercial sector, the food and goods sellers who stand highest in participation were more likely than the others to be native-born. No discernible pattern arises from this comparison, and it would obviously be more meaningful to compare the nativity of individuals among those involved with the respective working-class populations at risk.

This kind of category-by-category comparison between the percentage born in Milan in the population at risk with that among arrests is presented in Table V. I found a birthplace (whether Milan or elsewhere) for only 283 arrested persons; it was so seldom mentioned in casualty reports that only arrests appear in this table. Overall, 96 men were born in Milan, or 33.92 percent, while only 27.32 percent of the male population over 6 was native-born. For women, almost half the arrestees whose birthplace was given were Milanese. Category by category, arrestees were more likely to be native-born than population at risk in the cases of the metal-machine, construction, chemical, wood and straw, precision and luxury, and food industries. They were less often native-born in the case of stone, sand and clay, textile, and garment workers. In the first two cases, the number of men for whom place of birth is known is very small; any sweeping generalization is thereby inhibited. The case of the garment workers is more intriguing; twelve shoemakers were arrested, all born outside Milan. The frequency of the special place shoemakers occupy in this kind of analysis has been remarked on by Rudé and Hobsbawm, who consider the shoemaker radical a familiar figure in nineteenth-century rebellion. In Milan at least, the job description covered many relatively unskilled immigrants who had done cobbling in rural settings in their homes. Shoemakers were the third largest occupational category of immigrants in these years, as shown in Table II. In Milan, they continued work at home, either directly for customers, or more likely, for jobbers who provided materials. They were considered a rough and undisciplined group; nevertheless there were efforts to organize them into a craft union, and to promote self-help, and at least two of the shoemakers arrested were accused political activists.[31] The shoemakers are the only strong exception to the lack of connection between nativity outside of Milan and arrest in the Fatti.

Despite the failure of the traditional explanations to explain, overall it is clear that the persons involved in the Fatti di Maggio were not a random assortment of the population of Milan (See Table III). Although metal and machine workers were most involved in absolute numbers, in proportionate terms the stone, sand, clay group heads the list. This arises from one large incident—derailing a tram and knocking down telegraph poles at Gratosoglio, in the southern rural area. Because of the comparatively small population at risk, the 23 brick and tile makers who were tried for this episode alone become statistically important. This should serve as a reminder that there was a wider base to the rebellion than the workers in factory-based industry represented by the Pirelli and the machine shop workers who triggered the first days' demonstrations. These comparisons of persons involved in the Fatti di Maggio with the population at risk have demonstrated that none of the explanatory theories discussed earlier, namely, the outside agitator–marginal participant theory, the misery theory, the repression theory, or the alienation–frustration theory, is valid. To make sense of the Fatti, we must return to the political arena in which the working class as a whole was an imposingly large group with limited channels for action. Behind the Fatti lay a tradition of street protest with wide participation by various occupational groups, and a period of intense organizational activity that centered on the more modern industrial workers but reached into most occupational categories.

Street Protest and Working-Class Organization

Despite the romantic distortions with which commentators persisted in describing the workers of Milan as interested only in productive work and politically passive, street protest was an important part of local politics. Milan had been one of the few northern Italian cities to have violent revolution in 1848, against the Austrians, to be sure, but it was five days of street fighting with broad involvement of workers and others that threw the Austrians out. The Five Days of Milan were commemorated yearly by men of all shades of political opinion, because of their significance for the Risorgimento and the achievement of political unity.

Not so the "Revolt of the Micca" of 1886, the 1893 anti-French demonstrations, the antiwar demonstration of 1896 which had ended in the sack of the railroad station. These episodes elicited much critical comment in the newspapers, which concluded that they were the work of outside agitators, foreign to the loyal workers of Milan. Whether or not such workers had ever existed, in the 1890s the work force was being transformed by migration, and the working class was a rich mixture of native-born Milanese and newer arrivals. If outsiders seemed important in protest, it was to a large degree due to their important numbers in the labor force. Most of those arrested in these smaller affairs were employed, stable residents of the city. Furthermore, we can see a pattern in the earlier incidents of violence growing out of political conflict that was being worked out also in peaceful ways, with the violence finally succeeding in bringing home the final point that action had to be taken. It is not my intent to retell the long and complex history of working-class protest in Milan. Rather, I propose to sketch some high points in this history immediately preceding 1898, to illustrate how the Fatti slip easily into what can only be called a tradition of violence.

The Micca Revolt was named for the large loaf of bread that workers who lived in the suburban area carried into the walled city for their lunches when they went to work. Before March of 1886, although this quantity of bread was legally subject to the consumption tax when it was carried through the city walls, the regulation was only loosely enforced. Then, in a drive to increase revenues, the city decided to collect the *dazio* on the bread in the workers' lunch pails.

Contemporaneously, the prefect and the police chief were carrying on their customary campaign to contain and reduce working-class activity. By a typical arbitrary decision, the League of the Sons of Labor was forbidden to hold a public meeting to dedicate its new banner, emblazoned with this quintessential workers' motto: "The emancipation of the workers can be the accomplishment only of the workers themselves." As a compromise, a "private" meeting was held, with admission by ticket. The police made extensive preparations to see that nobody stepped beyond the limits they had drawn. There were agents in the meeting taking notes, and a patrol stood at the ready, outside. At the meeting, orators mixed platitudes with allusions to the injustice of the communal plan to tax the workers' very bread.[32]

Confusion increased each morning at the Porta Tenaglia as tax collectors tried to collect the few cents due on the *micca* carried in for workers' lunches. On April 1, about five hundred men gathered around the station, determined not to pay. One man who threw his bread inside the walls over the heads of the guards was grabbed and locked up. The crowd attacked the guard house with rocks, but the guards managed to hold their prisoner, and take others, using their pistols to keep the crowd back.

The liberal *La Lombardia*, which opposed the strict enforcement of tax collection, nevertheless deplored the violent events and appealed to the "real workers" of Milan not to let themselves be misled by the "false workers" trying to harvest disorder from the misery of the real. Violence, concluded the newspaper, can only damage the cause.[33]

The agitation continued nevertheless, and broadsides were posted advertising an evening meeting in the cathedral square to protest. Troops and police were mustered to protect the city hall in the close-by Piazza Scala. The spring evening promenade of the good bourgeois of Milan around the Piazza del Duomo and through the Galleria was interrupted by a gradually coalescing column of demonstrating workers moving toward the center, shouting "Bread, bread! Down with the city government." Store and café owners started to shutter their windows and close up when the first rocks began to fly. The police moved in, driving the demonstrators south to the via Torino. The police and military patrols scoured the streets, arresting many. Demonstrators regrouped as patrols passed and actually attacked patrols with rocks, freeing some prisoners and injuring police agents. Fighting continued for some time, and a final total of 80 were arrested that night. The next morning, there was a repetition of troubles at the *dazio* collection station, and in the evening there were demonstrations and fights downtown. On April 3, the communal council met and formally requested the ruling *giunta* to allow free entry for workers' meals on the job of up to 800 grams of bread.[34]

The newspaper list of the persons arrested and held (many were released in short order) showed that all were employed, most in working-class occupations. They were young; their age ranged from 17 to 42, with the greatest number in their twenties. They were not members of any organization and in fact both the Consolato Operaio and the Milan section of the Partito Operaio disclaimed connection with the demonstrators, although they had criticized the original decision to collect the *dazio*, and had tried to shape public opinion against it. The demonstrations grew out of the political activity of the workers' organizations, but went beyond rhetoric to tactics of violence. In the course of the mutation from talk to action, a larger population was drawn into involvement than the cautious organizational leadership that originally questioned city policy. The reason for the escalation of tactics was at least in part the anxiety of city officials to curb and limit debate, and, if possible, of course, to retain their unpopular policy.

Another series of workers' protests arising from economic crisis illustrates similar disagreement of leaders and followers over tactics, and the temptation to move to street demonstrations, given government attempts to limit and define the channels for working-class expression of dissatisfaction. In this case, in early 1890, unemployment was great and increasing; there was evidence of real suffering in working-class families. Consequent events show how severe economic dislocation nevertheless seemed to dampen violence, not promote it. The problems started with layoffs in the big machine shops in February. On February 10, about 100 of the laid-off workers from the Grondona and Elvetica plants went to the Invitti factory and called out the workers there to join them in a demonstration; the enlarged group went on to the Miani Silvestri plant nearby. Miani, the owner, and also a municipal council member, spoke to his men, urging them not to follow their fellows, because it could lead only to violence. Although the Invitti workers stayed out, and three persons were arrested for urging them to strike, the movement was transformed in the next days as Miani organized a joint worker-owner effort to pressure government for contracts to build railroad locomotives in the Milanese factories. The economic situation was so tight that the workers' meetings concerned themselves largely with raising money to help the unemployed, and then arguing about how to distribute the money.

Meanwhile, in the workers' meetings, dissent was growing, as an anarchist group tried to mobilize discontent and promote revolt. At a meeting of twelve hundred unemployed workers on February 26, several self-proclaimed anarchist spokesmen urged that the talking stop, and they move into the piazza to take bread by force. The meeting fell into an uproar; the more conservative leader of the metal workers, Brando, was hissed when he tried to speak but eventually he was able to get his message across. His opinion represented an important segment of working-class judgment: "We are few, we are mostly fathers of families; at home our wives and children need bread. We must let ourselves be guided by calm . . . violence would be our complete ruin."[35] There were other noisy meetings with disagreement over tactics, but the timidity born out of economic necessity triumphed, and the men stayed off the streets except for one clash with the police when one of their spokesmen was arrested.

Within the month, however, another agitation was mounted by masons and other construction workers, including again, some moments of violence. Their problems also rose out of the generally poor business situation, and the ensuing building slump. Masons from the countryside between Milan and Novara were being hired by those contractors who had work in preference to the Milanese masons who demanded higher wage rates. The workers daily impatiently crowded the streets where the traditional morning shape-up was held while their leaders, city officials, and the contractors negotiated over how to divide up the little work there was. The union leadership argued that demonstrations would be "dangerous" given the number of unemployed potentially involved, but the men marched spontaneously on several occasions. By mid-March, meetings of both unemployed machinists and masons were banned after the police dispersed an especially noisy ("seditious" shouts were reported) shape-up on March 10.[36]

Unemployment became a problem in new groups of workers—the brickmakers, weavers, shoemakers, and even domestic servants, who were dismissed by their wealthy patrons making economies. To cap the troubled spring, this was the first year for the May Day workers' holiday, so there was another burst of meetings and debate in late April. At the first meeting, the socialist organizer Casati defined their task: to plan a demonstration, not a revolution.[37] As usual, there was disagreement even on this fundamental orientation; when the meeting reconvened the next evening, the anarchist Brambilla declared that the time was ripe for revolt. His views did not carry the meeting, which decided not to encourage strikes, but to hold evening meetings May 1, and sponsor a demonstration on Sunday, May 4. Then the government intervened, and forbade the demonstration. The workers' representatives met again, with much disagreement. Brambilla offered his analysis: "With violence we can get something, with calm, we get nothing."[38] A baker, speaking as a "slave who works at night," reminded the audience that "Italy was made in blood, and we should follow this example." The meeting again refused to move any concerted plan, but the police and military were deployed in force ~on May Day, ready for anything. Thousands of workers did strike, and some four thousand tried to assemble in the Piazza del Duomo in the afternoon, only to be dispersed without violence but with arrests of those who did not move quickly enough to satisfy the troops.

In 1890, as in 1886, we can see the tension between workers and their leaders, the delicate balance of violence between police and would-be demonstrators, although in this case there was no dramatic outburst. Concern with keeping scarce jobs probably reduced the level of street action but even so, important numbers took part in spontaneous and illegal demonstrations that spring. There was an almost permanent struggle going on as long as the channels of working-class activism were severely limited and strikes were illegal, leading to dismissals and blacklists as well as arrests. Organizations were few; they were constantly harassed by police surveillance; meetings were forbidden. Association among workers had no legitimacy but depended on haphazard willingness of government or factory owners to work with them. With this situation, obtaining collective bargaining by riot, or threat of it, was a normal way of life.

Alongside this tradition of street violence the years right before 1898 were characterized by an enormous increase in organizational activity among workers. Again, turning to an aspect of local history, that of working-class associations, gives the proper perspective to the Fatti, beyond their national significance.

There had been an initial spate of new workers' organizations after the formation of the Chamber of Labor in 1891, but this had slowed down drastically after the decrees against the Workers' Party and against associations in 1894. During 1895 and 1896, the movement resumed, and fifty-one workers' leagues were founded, joining the twenty or so that had come into being over the thirty preceding years. By 1898, almost all workers were touched to some degree by organized working-class activity.[39]

Illustrations of this growth of association and mobilization of hundreds of workers are available from the very groups who turned out to be especially active during the May Fatti.

The *fornaciai,* the brick makers, organized their League of Resistance in 1891, to prevent wage-rate cuts, and they succeeded, after a seven-week strike. Nevertheless, they were faced with recurrent attempts by their employers to cut wages, and there were smaller strikes on similar issues in 1894 and 1897.[40] The metalworkers had a web of specialized organizations by 1898, but the most active and powerful was the League of Resistance of Metallurgists, founded after a lost strike in 1891. At the time, despite 15,000 strikers, the Elvetica machine shops had broken the strike in ten days, completely refusing to even speak to the workers' delegation. The new league had sponsored smaller strikes at more propitious moments in 1895 and 1896, so had some successes for its record. The employers had agreed to a joint owner-worker arbitration board. The balance was still not on the side of the union, however. Early in 1898, a strike at Stigler over the laying off of workers and union recognition had lasted three months, ending in a compromise. Five of the most active union leaders were fired. The strike was marked by much bitterness, and the strikers were blacklisted with all other machine shops. The police kept close tabs on the strike; they based their readiness to intervene on the right to work for nonstriking workers.[41]

The rubber workers did not have a long tradition of organization but were the object of intense proselytization just before May 1898. The League of Rubber Workers was founded May 3, 1898, after a series of meetings led by the socialists Dell'Avale and Anna Kuliscioff. Of the initial 1,000 members, 700 were women.[42] Commander Pirelli testified later that even the old faithful leadership of the mutual aid fund was replaced in the election that April by militants. One of these newly active workers had told him that their organization would lead to his feeling their strength.[43] The gas workers also had struck in April 1898, over a change in equipment that meant a drastic reduction of the number of workers employed by the Union del Gas.[44] Their only organization at that time was a mutual aid society, which despite its limited objectives had led an economic action in 1898 to get better wages for some categories.

This kind of revamping of organization, changing over the moderate mutual aid societies to leagues of resistance, or alternatively, leagues of improvement, and extension of organization and strike pressure against employers reached a peak in the spring of 1898. At the same time, the unions sponsored new cooperative ventures, like the cooperative restaurant in the Via Ponte Seveso, in the factory neighborhood. Pirelli accused this institution of contributing to the breakdown of discipline among the workers; 180 were eating there each day.[45] Finally, there was a deliberate campaign of some unions and the Socialist party to focus public discontent about the price of bread on revision of the tariff system and removal of the municipal *dazio*. For example, on January 18, 1898, the League of Masons sponsored a meeting at which D'Aragona, a socialist, spoke, blaming the high cost of bread on the existence of private property, which led to "parasitism and speculation." He called for adoption of the plank of the minimum program of the Socialist party, which demanded abolition of the grain tariff and immediate municipal action to reduce bread prices. This kicked off a round of similar meetings, faithfully attended by police agents, who took the high price of bread as a potential threat to public order.[46]

As it worked out, the question of bread prices receded into the background for several months, and the petition that a working class committee presented to the communal council on May 1 mentioned it not at all. Since May Day fell on a Sunday, there was no question of a strike, and the government forbade a demonstration, so similar meetings were addressed by orators who attacked the government.[47] In the first few days of May, police records include several warnings of threats to public order. On May 2 and 3, orders went out to police to watch for republican demonstrations. On May 5, the prefect warned the police to be prepared to guard grain merchants and grist mills against public attack.[48] The clash came in a different way than anticipated. It grew out of police efforts to end socialist propagandizing at the factory gates. The manifesto being distributed protested the police shooting down a demonstrator the day before in Pavia. It called for workers to join the Socialist party to work for universal suffrage and political rights. The right to demonstrate, the right of the workers to organize, the right to participate in the political process were the issues. If they were to make economic gains by their own efforts through building associations, workers needed the elementary political rights of petition and assembly.

The city responded partly in its usual way, banning the manifesto and forbidden meetings; partly in a sterner version of its usual way, sending troops with orders to shoot. When the troops fired, the die was cast. The government interpreted the demands of workers as revolutionary, and treated a demonstration as a revolution, thus transforming it into something that comes close to being revolutionary. The demands that socialist propaganda had set into motion led to a popular involvement and violence that the socialist leaders opposed. Turati warned the demonstrating workers outside the Pirelli factory not to let the authorities "choose the day of revolt."[49] But the violence was not a new departure in working-class politics. It grew out of the clash between the claims of workers for the right to demonstrate and the guns the state assembled to deny those claims.

NOTES

1. Antonio Gramsci, *La Questione meridionale* (Rome: Edizioni Rinascità, 1953), p. 83, remarks on the south-to-north direction of waves of popular protest in the Risorgimento and after. For a general treatment of 1898, see the contemporary report of Napoleone Colajanni, *L'Italia nel 1898 (Tumulti e reazione)* (Milan: Società editrice lombarda, 1898), and the recent Marxist interpretation of Renzo Del Carria, *Proletari senza rivoluzione. Storia delle classi subalterne italiane dal 1860 al 1950* (Milan: Edizioni oriente, 1966).

2. Lucio Villari, "I fatti di Milano del 1898. La testimonianza di Eugenio Torelli Viollier," *Studi Storici,* 8(July–September, 1967):542.

3. George Rudé, *The Crowd in History: A Study of Popular Disturbances in France and England, 1730–1848* (New York: John Wiley & Sons, 1964). Edward P. Thompson, *The Making of the English Working Class* (New York: Pantheon Books, 1963); E. J. Hobsbawm, *Primitive Rebels,* 2nd ed. (New York: Praeger Publishers, 1963).

4. Filippo Turati and Anna Kuliscioff, *Carteggio. I. Maggio 1898–giugno 1899* (Torino: Einaudi, 1949), p. xxxii. This statement is not in the correspondence but is quoted in the introduction by Alessandro Schiavi. It also appears in the official charge against Turati, on which he was tried and convicted at the end of July, 1898, by the Tribunale di Guerra. Turati, it should be noted, denied in his trial having made this "banal statement" and recalled his words as: "You know to what end these bodies will serve: to alienate the people even more from the government." (*La Lombardia,* 28 July 1898, pp. 1–2.)

5. Milano, *Atti del Municipio di Milano. Annata 1897–1898,* (Milan, 1899), p. 814.

6. Villari, "I fatti di Milano" p. 546. Salvemini's accusation is in Gaetano Salvemini, "I partiti politici milanesi prima e dopo il 1890," originally printed in *Critica sociale,* 1899; excerpt in Luciano Cafagna, *Il Nord Nella Storia d'Italia* (Bari: Laterza, 1962), p. 324.

7. Nicola Badaloni, *Atti del Parlamento Italiano. Camera dei Deputati,* Session 1897–98, vol. VI (Rome, 1898), p. 6298.

8. Ibid., p. 6303.

9. Carlo Pinzani, *La crisi politica di fine secolo in Toscana* (Florence: Barbèra, 1963), p. 131.

10. Rafaele Colapietra, *Il novantotto: La crisi politica di fine secolo (1898–1900)* (Milan-Rome: Avanti!, 1959), pp. 79–80; Del Carria, *Proletari* p. 323; Cafagna, *Il Nord,* p. 295.

11. Colajanni, *L'Italia nel 1898,* p. 246.

12. Ibid., pp. 225.

13. Maurice F. Neufeld, *Italy, School for Awakening Countries* (Ithaca, N.Y.: New York State School of Industrial and Labor Relations, Cornell University Press, 1961), pp. 219–20. See also Dennis Mack Smith, *Italy,* rev. ed. (Ann Arbor, Michigan: University of Michigan Press, 1969), p. 189, who sees urbanization and migration of the surplus rural population to cities as the context for the troubles.

14. Samuel Surace, *Ideology, Economic Change and the Working Classes: The Case of Italy* (Berkeley and Los Angeles: University of California Press, 1966), p. 118.

15. Comune di Milano, *La Popolazione di Milano secondo il Censimento del 1901* (Milan: Reggiano, 1903).

16. Italy, Direzione generale della Statistica, *Statistica industriale, Lombardia* (Rome, 1900), pp. 470–74. This evidence reduces the importance of large-scale industry, in contrast to Del Carria's judgment that "in Milan, at the end of the century, we are in the presence of a confirmed machine industry of modern type, in which there was significant capital investment, increasing improved mechanization, large concentration of the proletariat in the place in which they worked and a final cutoff of temporary employment or of families with close connection with the peasant world and domestic industry. In Milan these marked the qualitative jump from manufacture to industry." (*Proletari,* p. 321).

17. *La Popolazione di Milano,* pp. 19–20.

18. Ibid., pp. 22–24. It is not clear from the text whether these figures refer only to workers (*operai e facchini*) as the rest of my figures do, or to all persons working in industry, which would include owners, managers, and white-collar workers.

19. Alberto Geisser and Effren Magrini, "Contribuzione alla storia e statistica dei salari industrali in Italia nella seconda metà del Secolo XIX," *La Riforma Sociale,* 14(1904):866.

20. Società Umanitaria, *Le condizioni generale della classe operaia in Milano: Salari, giornate di lavoro, reddito, ecc.* (Milan, 1907). I arranged the 139 job titles in Table N85, pp. 250–53, into the census categories, then calculated average daily wages weighted by the number of persons receiving that wage. The wage listed in the Società Umanitaria table was already an average calculated from answers given by 112,121 workers surveyed by them in 1903.

21. Geisser and Magrini, "Contribuzione," p. 866.

22. Villari, "I fatti di Milano" p. 540. Torelli Viollier wrote that Pirelli had bragged to him three years before that his workers were "impervious to socialism, because they were peasants, young women all rough and exceedingly ignorant."

23. The city statistical office's first volume of its *Data Statistici*, 1884, closed the section on migration, p. 123, with this statement: "These poor folk do not fit the demand for labor, since they have nothing to offer but strong arms; therefore because of this they increase the competition for jobs in the manual services." By 1898, there was also a more skilled and professional immigration, but there was still a concentration of immigrants in the service occupations. See also the *Condizione generale*, p. 27, which shows that their surveyed sample was more likely to be native-born than the general population according to the 1901 census, and A. DeMaddalena, "Rilievi sull'esperienza demografica ed economica milanese dal 1861 al 1915," in *L'Economia italiana dal 1861 al 1961* (Milan: Giuffrè, 1961), p. 85 and passim.

24. *Condizione generale*, pp. 38–39.

25. Tables on migration in the *Dati Statistici* (Comune di Milano) for 1895, 1897, 1898 for age distribution of immigrants; *Condizione generale*, p. 28, for province of origin of immigrants. See also Guido Tagliacarne, "Il progresso economico di Milano negli ultimi cinquant'anni," in *Nel Cinquantenario della Società Edison*, 1884–1934, p. 40.

26. Letter dated 1 April 1971 from Col. Vittorio de Castiglioni, Capo Ufficio, Ufficio Storico, Stato Maggiore dell'Esercito.

27. A list of the names of the 80 identified dead and their places of birth appears in *I disordini di Milano e le sentenze del Tribunale del Milano. Dati riassuntivi* (Milan: Tipografia ambrosiana, 1898). Military and police casualties were 2 dead, about 50 wounded.

28. *La Lombardia*, 2 September 1898, p. 1.

29. Colajanni, *L'Italia nel 1898*, p. 298.

30. *I disordini di Milano, op. cit.*

31. See G. Montemartini, *L'industria delle calzature in Milano* (Milan: Editore l'Ufficio del Lavoro, 1904), passim, and Società Umanitaria, *Origini, vicendi e conquiste delle organizzazioni operaie aderenti alla Camera del Lavoro in Milano* (Milan, 1909).

32. *La Lombardia*, 26–29 March 1886, passim.

33. Ibid., 2 April 1886, pp. 2–3.

34. This narrative of the Micca Revolt is derived from newspaper reading of *La Lombardia*, 2–6 April 1886.

35. *Corriere della Sera*, 26/27 February 1890, p. 2. The narrative for 1890 is taken from reading the *Corriere* for the first six months of that year.

36. Ibid., 11/12 March 1890, p. 2.

37. Ibid., 22/23 April 1890, p. 2.

38. Report of workers' meeting in Archivio di Stato di Milano (ASM) Fondo Questura, Cartella 58, folder of notes on Primo Maggio, 1890–1899. Also in *Corriere della Sera*, 29/30 April 1890, p. 2, a slightly different version of the same meeting.

39. *Origini e vicendi*, p. viii.

40. Ibid., p. 57.

41. Ibid., pp. 3–5, *La Lombardia*, 24 February 1898, p. 3, and ASM, Fondo Questura, Cartella 53, the thick folder of police notes of the Stigler strike.

42. *Origine e vicendi*, p. 165. ASM, Fondo Questura, Cartella 53, for police reports on organizational efforts at Pirelli.

43. *Corriere della Sera*, 29/30 July 1898, p. 2.

44. *La Lombardia*, 5 April 1898, p. 3; *Origini e vicendi*, p. 31. ASM, Fondo Questura, Cartella 53, police report on *gasometro* strike.

45. *Origine e vicendi*, p. 27; *La Lombardia*, 24 April 1898, p. 3; *Corriere della Sera*, 29/30 July 1898, p. 2.

46. *La Lombardia*, 19 January 1898; p. 2, ASM, Fondo Questura, Cartella 53, folder on Rincaro dal Pane.

47. *La Lombardia*, 1 May 1898, p. 3.

48. ASM, Fondo Questura, Cartella 53, folder on Fatti di Maggio.

49. Franco Catalano, "Vita politica e questioni sociali (1849–1900)" in *Storia di Milano*, vol. 15 (Milan: Fondazione Treccani Degli Alfieri per la Storia di Milano, 1962) p. 311; also in newspaper accounts: *La Lombardia*, May 7, 1898, and *La Lombardia*, July 28, 1898 (report of Turati trial).

III. PEASANTS

One of the most persistent myths of modern European history is that of the uniformly dull and conservative countryside. It has been nearly fifty years since Georges Lefebvre's Les paysans du Nord pendant la Révolution française *(original edition, Paris, 1924; New edition, Bari: Editori Laterza, 1959) revealed the remarkable variety that existed in the social structure of the French peasantry at the time of the Revolution. While the book itself has been revered, its message was generally lost except on a handful of scholars. Historians have recently been awakened by a double alarm, however. The emergence of peasant guerrilla warfare as a dominant mode of twentieth-century conflict on the one hand, and the contention by anthropologists and sociologists that rural peoples have played a critical role in shaping modern political and social change on the other, have reminded them that there is more "action" in the countryside than their urban-oriented minds had assumed. Social historians have now taken a leading role in the important task of integrating rural peoples, until recently the overwhelming majority in every society, into our total picture of the past. The essays in this section focus on the peasantry of a single nation, Spain. Taken together they tell us a great deal about the ways Spanish rural social structure and culture have affected her political, economic, and social development. They also suggest the vast amount of work that remains to be done on the rural history of other nations, as well as for Europe as a whole.*

Glen A. Waggoner's "The Black Hand Mystery: Rural Unrest and Social Violence in Southern Spain 1881–1883" concerns the history of an alleged secret society in the province of Andalusia at the end of the nineteenth century. When a series of mysterious crimes occurred in 1882 and 1883, the Spanish authorities were quick to blame a murderous band of conspirators, the so-called Black Hand, and used the occasion to suppress the anarchist farm labor movement. But did the Black Hand really exist? Seeking an answer to the question Waggoner begins by reviewing the evidence compiled by the press, the military police, and the courts. He next examines the economic and social structure of rural Andalusia and attempts to fit the timing and types of crime attributed to the Black Hand within the larger pattern of unrest in the region. Real or not, Waggoner concludes, the significance of the Black Hand lies less in what it was, than in what it was not. It was not an effective rural working class weapon, rather the sort of primitive social move-

ment that expresses the inherent limitations on organization in such a society. In this sense, at least, the Black Hand was no mystery at all.

Edward Malefakis's "Peasants, Politics, and Civil War in Spain, 1931– 1939" examines the social and economic phenomena that lay behind the political and military turning point of modern Spanish history. While its title suggests that the essay deals only with the twentieth century, Malefakis begins by describing the historical origins of Spain's extraordinarily divergent rural property systems. Readers should note how he selects and uses statistical information to reveal the strong coincidence of social class and property in the various regions. Turning to a discussion of the Spanish Republic, Malefakis shows how the conflicting interests over the question of land reform, perhaps an insoluble problem in the infant democracy, played a critical role in the breakdown of support for the regime. During the Civil War, he contends, the rural populations continued to influence political and military events, as much by what they did not do as by what they did. The majority of the Spanish peasantry was under the control of the Nationalist forces, yet there was no effective guerrilla resistance to Franco's army from behind its own lines. And in those rural areas under Republican control the issue of land reform continued to sap support for the government (again the result of the divergent interests in Spain's social and property structures). In this essay Malefakis has forcefully demonstrated the contributions that a knowledge of social structures can make to our understanding of political history.

THE BLACK HAND MYSTERY: RURAL UNREST AND SOCIAL VIOLENCE IN SOUTHERN SPAIN, 1881–1883

Glen A. Waggoner

The tavern owned by Juan Nuñez differed little from other poor roadside bars in the countryside around Jerez de la Frontera, the economic capital of the province of Cádiz. The low, rectangular structure, located two kilometers northwest of Jerez on the Trebujena road, had only three rooms. The owner, his wife, and their infant son slept in the smallest room. Another room served as kitchen, parlor, and dining area. The third and largest contained a wooden bar, a few tables and chairs, unlabeled bottles of red and white wine, and two sixteen-gallon barrels of *amontillado* and *manzanilla,* both of the poorest quality. The white stucco walls outside contrasted sharply with the red tiles over the sleeping area and the brown thatch covering the remainder of the building. Thick cactus plants on three sides of the structure blocked from view the gently sloping wheat fields, which in the early winter of 1882 were dry and barren throughout western Andalusia.

Although their meanness attracted few travelers and no wealthy guests, taverns like the one owned by Juan Nuñez usually maintained a steady clientele from among agricultural workers employed from time to time on nearby estates. Laborers temporarily affluent after finishing a stint of work stopped in to drink a few glasses of cheap wine, report the latest outrages committed by their erstwhile employers, and swap rumors about where new jobs might be found. Throughout 1882, the conversation was both more bitter and more hopeful than usual—bitter because of the extended drought that left *braceros,* or day laborers, with less work than normal; hopeful because of the new workers' organization, the Federation of Workers of the Spanish Region *(Federación de Trabajadores de la Región Española),* which many said would solve all their problems. In the taverns and in the barracks of the estates where they worked, Andalusian *braceros* listened to local *sabios,* or "wise men," as they read aloud from the anarchist newspaper, *La Revista Social,* or one of the many pamphlets then being published in Barcelona. While they did not understand all the words and ideas they heard, they did learn that they must organize, join with other workers, and fight their oppressors. Conversations that began with complaints about this foreman or that owner often ended with talk of organized resistance, the *Federación,* and revolution.

Glen A. Waggoner studied at Columbia University. He now teaches at the University of Michigan.

Because his customers undoubtedly talked of such things too frequently and too loudly, Juan Nuñez may have learned a great deal about the *Federación,* about its meeting places, its plans, and its local leaders. If so, he probably realized how valuable such information would be to the local *Guardia Civil,* who paid informers well. With his own business suffering because of the high rate of unemployment in the region, he may have sold bits of information to the police. If he did, it cost him his life.

Near midnight on December 3, 1882, Nuñez was awakened by calls for service from outside the tavern. Apparently recognizing one of the callers, he admitted five or six men into the bar and served them wine. They paid for it and drained their glasses. Then, without warning, one of them grabbed Nuñez and accused him of being a spy for Captain José Oliver y Vidal, commandant of the *Guardia Civil* post in Jerez. The day before, Oliver's men had arrested 75 workers to question them about recent acts of vandalism and about the growth of working-class organizations in the Jerez region. Nuñez's accusers charged the tavern owner with informing Oliver about the anarchist association to which some of the arrested men belonged.

Verbal abuse soon gave way to physical attack. Nuñez, who seemed to be expecting the attack, drew a gun from behind the bar and killed one of the intruders, a twenty-year-old *bracero.* But after a few moments of scuffling and confusion, the other assailants overpowered Nuñez and stabbed him to death. Then they rushed into the kitchen and killed Nuñez's wife, who had come from the bedroom to investigate the disturbance. The attackers left her dead body crumpled against the wall, where she had huddled to shield her fourteen-month-old son from injury. Finally, after ransacking the place and stealing a few bottles of wine, they left.

Unfortunately for the assailants, they did not notice the only witness to their crime. A young boy employed at the tavern had been asleep in the kitchen when Nuñez answered the summons at the front door. When the violence broke out, the boy ran into the bedroom to awaken Nuñez's wife. He watched helplessly from the bedroom as the woman was killed, then crawled through the window and ran for help. The police arrived too late to save Nuñez and his wife; but the boy had recognized one of the murderers, an unemployed *bracero* named Juan Galán. Within hours Galán and four other suspects were arrested and charged with the double murder.

The savage and apparently pointless slayings horrified the residents of Jerez who were already on edge because of the recent outbreak of violent crimes in the region. Many owners of medium-sized estates and some upper-level executives of the sherry industry for which Jerez was famous had already left to live in Seville or Madrid until the current spell of disturbances should pass. The great landowners, the *latifundistas,* did not live in the region, and the English owners of the sherry *bodegas* rarely visited Spain except in the springtime. But those Jerezanos who remained were even more upset the following February when they learned from the police that the murders of

Nuñez and his wife had been decreed by a secret organization "whose name alone produces fearful disquiet in Andalusia."[1] That organization was *La Mano Negra,* the Black Hand.[2]

The Black Hand was alleged to be a band of revolutionary terrorists that thrived throughout western Andalusia in the early 1880s. Virtually every case of rural violence—crop burnings, bread riots, assaults, property destruction—plus a series of lurid murders in 1881–83 were popularly believed to be the handiwork of this secret society of Andalusian anarchists. For half a year Spanish journalists made the Black Hand the most sensational news item in Spain, and for even longer Andalusian authorities used the threat of this band of murderers and revolutionaries as a pretext for repressing working-class activities in the south.

The Black Hand is one of the least understood rural "rebellions" in Spain, but it is only one in a series. As E. J. Hobsbawm has pointed out, violent uprisings in Andalusia occurred on a regular, almost cyclical, basis in the nineteenth century;[3] the Black Hand was only one manifestation of extreme social discontent. Each of these revolts was swiftly and easily repressed by Spanish authorities. Far from being serious revolutionary threats to the social and political order in Andalusia, outbreaks of social violence like the Black Hand were no more than slave revolts, short-lived and easily suppressed.

Still, the persistence of rural violence in Andalusia suggests important questions for the social historian. What was the relationship between rural social structure and patterns of rural violence? How did economic fluctuations affect the timing and extent of rural rebellion? What was the reaction of Spanish political and social elites to the growing social tensions in southern Spain? How did the Black Hand episode affect the fortunes of the anarchist movement in Andalusia? In this essay, I shall tell the story of the Black Hand "mystery" with these questions in mind.[4]

In the following essay, Professor Malefakis makes clear the general causes of rural unrest in nineteenth-century Andalusia. Material impoverishment nurtured by psychological discontent caused the frustrations and anger of desperate men to spill over periodically in the form of violent, uncontrolled attacks against the existing social order. Uprisings in the villages of Arahal in 1857, Loja in 1861, Montilla in 1869, and Jerez in 1892 were only four in a series of social upheavals that included the Black Hand. These convulsive attacks were spawned in Andalusia by the interaction of three factors discussed by Professor Malefakis: the extension of the system of land tenure known as *latifundismo;* a sharp rise in population with a concomitant increase of pressure on the agricultural productivity of the land; and the difficult working conditions and low wages that prevailed in the south of Spain. With these factors insuring that social discontent would be chronic, the particular timing of the violent outbreaks was determined by the periodic economic crises that plagued the region.

As an economic system, *latifundismo* perpetuated inefficient use of natural and human resources. Great landowners felt no pressure to introduce artificial fertilizers, machinery, or modern agricultural techniques. So long as their access to an endless supply of cheap labor was not threatened and tariffs kept out foreign competitors, the *latifundistas* could afford to cultivate their land with no concern for efficiency of production. In the wheat-growing regions of western Andalusia, this meant that rich land that had been irrigated and farmed intensively by the Moors was, in the nineteenth century, cultivated *al tercio*—a third of the land fallow, a third of the land in scrub, and a third of the land planted. No wonder that travelers in Andalusia in the nineteenth century remarked at the apparent desolation of the southern countryside and spoke of "a land without people, a people without land."

For the people without land life became increasingly difficult in the course of the century. Where once the Church had offered at least the last resort of charity, now new *latifundistas* created by the redistribution of church lands in the 1830s managed the property and people of the south. These middle-class entrepreneurs, absentee landlords almost by definition, eschewed the patronal customs that, when the land was owned only by nobles and the Church, had helped soften class relationships somewhat. The change in attitude was sometimes subtle, sometimes direct, as for example, with the slow but steady elimination of gleaning rights, or with the spread of piece work *(trabajo á destajo)* to almost all important jobs on the *latifundios*.

Though the land seemed desolate and barren, population growth in the nineteenth century imposed continually greater pressure on the antiquated agricultural system in southern Spain. The population of Andalusia grew at double the rate of other nonindustrialized regions. This population growth was not accompanied by an increase in industrial activity in the south. Indeed, textile mills in southern Spain that had lingered on in the early nineteenth century in spite of competition from more efficient Catalonia factories began, after the penetration of railroads throughout the country, to succumb to that competition. Population growth in Andalusia meant that towns became even more swollen with landless *braceros* and their families, poor people who sought work in nearby wheat fields or vineyards or olive groves.

Because of monocultivation and the emphasis on extensive rather than intensive agriculture, frequently work was not to be found. Even when times were good, *braceros* and their families in wheat-producing regions could count on regular work only during summer harvests and spring planting. During the remainder of the year, *braceros* competed with one another for occasional jobs of short duration. Work patterns in vineyards and olive fields might vary in timing but not in duration; no Andalusian *bracero* could depend on working more than six or seven months of the year.

An ordinary day for an Andalusian *bracero* in search of work began an hour before dawn, when he joined other men in the town square of his *pueblo*. There they awaited the arrival of foremen from nearby estates, who came periodically to supplement their small permanent work forces with men from the town. Anyone not hired by dawn had virtually no chance of finding work that day. Unemployed *braceros* generally congregated in the town square or local taverns rather than return home. Although they could rarely afford even the cheapest wine, they could sit and speculate about the chances of finding work in other *pueblos,* discuss the merits of working under one foreman or another, and listen to someone read aloud from a newspaper or pamphlet about a perfect world in which all men shared equally in the wealth of the land.

The *bracero* had to be cautious about such activities, of course; a man could be denied work for reasons other than bad weather or a dearth of jobs. Foremen made it clear that any *bracero* suspected of agitating the other workers with wild ideas about unions and workers' organizations had no chance of being hired. Once blacklisted in a given *pueblo,* a worker had no choice but to travel to another town in search of work, and even then he had no assurance that his reputation as a troublemaker would not precede him.

A man lucky enough to be hired during the slow season walked from the town square to the estate that had employed him. Sometimes the trip took as long as two hours, during which time he learned how much a foreman intended to extract from his wages in return for giving him the job. The *bracero*'s day ended twelve to fourteen hours later, thirty minutes or so after sunset. Some jobs lasted only a few days, others a few weeks. Usually the *bracero* would be separated from his family for the duration of the job, with his living quarters furnished by the landlord. These mean barracks sheltered angry and frustrated men, who frequently took part in passionate discussions about the great day when the land would be theirs and about the new workers' organizations that would make that day possible.

A *bracero* working in the wheat fields around Jerez de la Frontera received four or five *reales* per day during the off season, a sum slightly less than the wage of an adolescent apprentice in the building trades in Madrid or a child working in a textile factory in Catalonia. At harvest time the Andalusian *bracero* could expect to double that figure at piecework rates, albeit at the cost of a greatly increased pace of work. During such times of *trabajo á destajo,* a surveyor assigned a given amount of work as the base unit for a team of workers *(cuadrilla)*. Friction frequently developed when the surveyors came to assess the quantity of work done by the *cuadrilla*. Workers were entitled to additional pay for anything above the basic unit of work, but surveyors and foremen padded their own meagre wages by undervaluing the amount of work done and pocketing the difference. Traditionally, workers had the right to request a second reckoning if the first valuation seemed too low, but few did since the second count was invariably lower than the first. *Braceros* received, in addition to their wages, two meals a day (three during harvest time), which consisted of soup, vegetables, and bread of the poorest quality. This arrangement, too, was a source of income for unscrupulous foremen, who received a set food allowance for each worker and then cut the quantity and quality of the food provided in order to make a profit.

Wages varied according to season and type of work. *Braceros* employed in vine and olive cultivation, for example, earned slightly more than workers in cereal production and other agricultural endeavors; and, more important, they could usually count on somewhat more than the 200 days of work per year that was the maximum for a worker in the grain-producing areas of western Andalusia. A *bracero* and his family supplemented their basic income in a variety of ways. Older daughters worked as domestic servants, children joined adults and adolescents in gleaning the fields or orchards after the harvest, and women took in laundry or worked as seam-stresses. In addition, the whole family took care of a small garden plot and rabbit hutch or chicken coop; these adjoined practically every worker's hut. But the Andalusian *bracero* could not usually expect to earn extra money by working a strip of land subleased or rented from someone else. Although common in central and northern Spain, this practice was followed only occasionally in the olive orchards and vineyards of eastern Andalusia and rarely in the western part of the region, where grains predominated.

In times of widespread economic depression, municipal governments traditionally employed jobless *braceros* on public works projects such as the repairing of roads and bridges. And in times of acute crisis, they distributed food to the poor or decreed an *alojamiento,* in which needy families were assigned to wealthy landowners for temporary upkeeping. But neither of these emergency measures constituted a supplement to regular income. They were employed only when the *bracero*'s normal sources of subsistence failed completely.

To survive between jobs, the *bracero* was frequently forced to borrow money at high rates of interest. A man with nothing else to offer as security for a loan would pawn his hoe for four *reales* in order to eat. Redemption of the hoe would soon cost eight to twelve *reales,* so the *bracero* was fre-quently forced to forfeit it. Then, when he found work, he had to pay the foreman one *real* per day to rent a hoe. The vicious cycle of unemployment, loans at usurious rates, and forfeiture of his tools contributed to the perpetual poverty of the *bracero*.

If life was hard for Andalusian *braceros* in normal times, it was es-pecially difficult during the periodic crises that plagued southern agriculture in the nineteenth century.[5] Landlords shielded themselves from foreign competition with high tariffs and import restrictions, but they had no such protection from their own inefficiency. Monocultivation of a single cash crop and inefficient land use left southern agriculture vulnerable before the extreme climatic fluctuations common in the region. Too much or too little rain at the wrong time could wipe out a crop. These periodic crises were no more than minor irritants to the great landlords, who experienced no difficulty in surviving until the next harvest. As a general rule, they simply instructed their agents to curtail normal farming operations for the time being and to make sure that tenants (*labradores*) did not default on their rents. This caused the few *labradores* with medium-sized holdings to be even harsher in their efforts to extract more work for less pay from their *braceros*. Unlike the great landlords or the *labradores* who leased large tracts of land, these "middle peasants" found it difficult to ride out even a short-term crisis. For the Andalusian *braceros*, of course, an economic crisis meant a desperate fight for survival. Caught in the cruel vise of unemployment and higher bread prices as a result of widespread crop failures, these landless laborers clamored frantically for "bread or work," the traditional rallying cry of social unrest in Andalusia. Not surprisingly, their desperation often culminated in violence directed against the most obvious symbols of their wretched condition: the property of the great landlords and *labradores*. This was the case in 1857, 1861, 1869, 1892, and in 1881–83.

The crisis of 1881–83 in western Andalusia was particularly severe. An extended drought ruined crops in 1881 and again in 1882. Rapidly rising wheat prices provided a graphic measure of the crisis. In normal times wheat sold for 22 to 24 *pesetas* the hectolitre in Jerez, Seville, and Cadiz. In the spring of 1882, the price soared to 35 to 39 *pesetas* and remained there for over a year. Prices were high elsewhere because of shortages resulting from the widespread drought, but nowhere did prices remain so high for so long as in western Andalusia. These inflated prices were not indicative of prosperity; instead, they reflected severe crop failures, in which farmers considered themselves lucky if they salvaged enough seed grain for planting the following year.

The crop failure of 1881 caused extensive suffering, as landlords and *labradores* stopped hiring workers except for the most essential jobs. When the crops failed a second time, the acute misery of landless agricultural workers sparked violent manifestations of social discontent. Occasional robberies of bakeries and granaries soon gave way to regular forays into the countryside by armed bands of men in search of food and money. Throughout the summer and fall of 1882, angry workers gathered in town squares to demand "bread or work" from harassed municipal governments. When neither was provided in adequate quantity, the anger of the hungry was turned against the property of the rich. Livestock was killed, barns burned, and vines destroyed in a dramatic escalation of what seemed to be a social war.

It was to this tinderbox of social discontent that organizers for the

Federación de Trabajadores brought the message of social revolution in the fall of 1881. That message sparked a great wave of anticipation and exultation in Andalusia. Whole communities seemed to be consumed by the words "anarchism" and "collectivism," even if their precise meanings were not comprehended. According to contemporary observers, virtually all the workingmen in some of the mountainous areas of western Andalusia joined the *Federación*. In September 1882, only one year after its formation, the new working-class organization claimed almost 60,000 members, with 38,000 of them in Andalusia. This could not be verified by outside observers because of the secrecy that characterized the operations of the *Federación* in rural areas, a secrecy made necessary by the hostility of the landlords, police, and public officials in the south. Whatever the precise dimensions of the movement in Andalusia, however, it was clear that a wave of revolutionary fervor was sweeping the countryside.

Andalusian laborers responded to the revolutionary appeal of the *Federación* with such enthusiasm because they had no place else to turn. Politically and economically they were powerless. The proclamation of universal manhood suffrage after the Revolution of 1868 offered the illusion but not the reality of political status to Andalusian workers; the restoration of limited suffrage along with the monarchy in 1875 merely confirmed their impotence. Economic resistance was virtually impossible because of the vulnerability of the Andalusian working classes. The ruling oligarchy forcefully resisted all attempts to organize trade unions and workers' associations, even when such groups had legal authorization from the national government. Strikes had no chance of success in rural Andalusia except at harvest time, when landowners depended on the labor of large numbers of *braceros*. Even then, landowners could go outside the local area to tap the seemingly endless supply of manpower in other parts of Andalusia, or they could import workers from Portugal, or in cases of extreme crisis, they could employ soldiers on assignment from the national government.

The *braceros* had few options in this one-sided struggle. They could submit for a time to their grinding poverty; but, as Professor Malefakis has noted, the logic of their circumstances could only lead to sporadic outbursts of violence:

The miserable lot of the day laborers under the latifundio *system ensured that they would protest; their powerlessness to improve their condition through normal channels ensured that this protest would assume violent forms.*[6]

In Andalusia in the early 1880s, the most extreme form of violent protest was the Black Hand.

From the first, police and provincial authorities in Andalusia sought to establish that the Black Hand was a great network of crime and terrorism, with national and perhaps international implications. Leaders of the *Federa-*

ción de Trabajadores were equally eager to deny the Black Hand's existence, or at least to cleanse themselves of any responsibility for its acts. Sagasta's liberal government in Madrid blamed its predecessor, Canovas's Conservative party, for the Black Hand, while the Conservative opposition insisted that the horrible association had been spawned by two years of liberal rule. *Cortes* deputies made ponderous, self-serving speeches about the allocation of blame; and newspaper readers thrilled to the lurid accounts of Black Hand atrocities that eager journalists provided in profusion.

This confusion, which perhaps was the result of police efforts to create a pretext for repression of working-class activities, or perhaps the consequence of urban misunderstanding of rural discontent and violence, is only compounded by a careful study of contemporary accounts and what little archival evidence exists. As the following narrative makes very clear, the paucity of solid evidence and the myriad contradictory accounts of the Black Hand episode prevent the historian from answering a basic question: Did the Black Hand actually exist? Curiously enough, one's only solace is that the question may not be vital to our understanding of the episode's importance.

On February 6, 1883, Captain Oliver of the *Guardia Civil* post in Jerez announced the arrest of sixteen men suspected of murdering a *bracero* in a nearby village. According to Oliver, the suspects belonged to a secret revolutionary organization, as their victim had also, a man known as "El Blanco de Benaocaz." Not until February 17 did Oliver inform the Madrid Government of his discovery, but his telegram prompted the minister of the interior to convene a special cabinet meeting that night to discuss "the terrifying association of assassins and robbers which is centered in Jerez but which has branches in various Andalusian *pueblos*."[7] Only then did newspapers and public officials begin to use the name that would gain immediate notoriety, *La Mano Negra*.

Confusion and mystery enshrouded the discovery of the Black Hand, with numerous contradictory accounts of precisely how Captain Oliver discovered the organization. According to one report, Captain Oliver had the good fortune to find documents concerning the secret society hidden under a rock. Another claimed that officers of the *Guardia Civil* seized the incriminating evidence on December 26, 1882, while conducting routine investigations of recent robberies. A third report insisted that Tomás Pérez de Montforte, head of the *Guardia Rural* in Jerez, had known about the Black Hand since 1878. Still another said that an alert policeman discovered a black imprint on the door of a man who had been threatened by suspicious characters in Villamartin, a small village east of Jerez.

Two accounts insisted that the authorities had known about the Black Hand for some years. Leopoldo Alás ("Clarín"), the literary critic and journalist who was writing a series on Andalusia for the liberal newspaper *El Día,* traced the Black Hand to the August 1878 trial of suspect members of a secret, illegal, anarchist organization.[8] Clarín said that the case consisted of over six thousand portfolios of evidence that had been turned over to the special judge appointed in February 1883 to investigate the Black Hand revelations. One prominent document in that case, a pamphlet entitled "The Honorable Poor Versus the Tyrannical Rich," allegedly linked the conspirators of 1878 with the Black Hand. Another reporter added that Captain Pérez de Montforte, who had been chief of the Jerez municipal police force from 1868 to 1875 before assuming command of the *Guardia Rural,* first became aware of "a secret association with sinister goals" in 1874.[9] In 1878, he made the arrests that led to the trial reported by Clarín. And in 1880, Pérez de Montforte supposedly captured three men who confessed to the murder of a fellow worker who had refused to join their secret organization, presumably the Black Hand.

The immediate sensation produced by the discovery of the Black Hand nourished wild speculations about the organization's historical origins. According to Spain's largest newspaper, *La Correspondencia,* the Black Hand originated in Seville in the first decade of the nineteenth century. During this epoch of war and social upheaval the society committed "crimes as horrible and mysterious as those committed recently in this region."[10] When police finally discovered the meeting place of this precursor of *La Mano Negra,* they were horrified to find, according to another paper,

a human hand, blackened with age, hanging from a rope attached to the center of the ceiling. The members swore oaths before this black hand to carry out loyally and honorably the plans which they agreed upon.[11]

Remnants of this macabre brotherhood presumably survived official repression and eventually revived the Black Hand later in the century.

Less sensational but more credible were contemporary speculations that the Black Hand was a nationwide conspiracy with international connections. *La Correspondencia* argued that Andalusian *braceros* were incapable of conceiving or maintaining the intricate structure uncovered by Captain Oliver:

The source of the evil from which this region suffers is not to be found here: it comes from elsewhere. The so-called socialists in this area are blind instruments of others of superior intelligence who care nothing about the deplorable consequences for Andalusian laborers of their internationalist propaganda.[12]

Evidence captured by the police added weight to this theory. In the mass arrests that began as soon as the discovery of the Black Hand was announced, the police confiscated letters sent to Andalusian organizers from all over Spain, books and pamphlets printed in Barcelona, and copies of *La Revista Social,* which was printed in Madrid. Captured documents referring to the Bakunist International in Geneva and the arrest in Andalusia of a Polish anarchist suggested international connections.[13] A socialist newspaper that was hostile toward the anarchist-dominated *Federación* noted the similarity between the alleged terrorism in Andalusia and the program adopted by anarchists at the 1881 congress of the "Black International" in London. A twentieth-century investigator with access to police and army archives claims that an "Italian specialist in plots and violence" named Alfredo Baccherini ignited "the spark which caused the flare-up of the Black Hand in Jerez."[14]

The idea of an international terrorist organization received further corroboration from the remarkable similarity between the Black Hand and a clandestine group discovered in France the previous autumn. In August 1882, a band of 150 French miners dynamited a church and set fire to a convent near Montceau-les-Mines. This incident culminated a brief but violent campaign, during which roadside crucifixes were destroyed and threatening letters were sent to mayors, priests, and wealthy citizens of this mining region in south central France. Police intervened "with energy" and soon captured twenty-three suspected leaders of an organization named "La Bande Noire," or the Black Band.[15] When Captain Oliver announced the existence of *La Mano Negra* six months later, the Spanish press immediately recalled *La Bande Noire* and suggested that the two were "fruits from the same evil tree."[16]

For the anarchist leaders of the *Federación de Trabajadores,* the Black Hand was both an embarrassment and a threat. Many of them were skilled craftsmen in the printing trades, most were Catalans, and all were relatively well educated. As a consequence, they had little in common with the Andalusian *braceros* who constituted two-thirds of the *Federación*'s membership. Dedicated revolutionaries in theory, the *Federación* leaders were earnest reformers in practice; and they opposed the more militant tactics Andalusian dissidents had advocated since the summer of 1882.

Now the Black Hand episode revealed the incompatibility of the *Federación*'s avowed goal to be a legal, public working-class organization with the social and political conditions prevailing in southern Spain. A public federation of trade unions and workers' societies might have some chance of success in Catalonia; such an organization was certainly doomed in Andalusia. There the hostility of the police and public authorities, the power of the great landlords, and the economic vulnerability of Andalusian laborers precluded the development of a working-class movement along the guidelines set down by the executive body of the *Federación,* the Federal Commission *(Comisión Federal).* The tenuous alliance of Catalans and Andalusians would soon collapse along the fissure opened by the Black Hand.

Leaders of the *Federación* sought to dissociate their organization from rural violence in general and the Black Hand in particular. The *Comisión Federal* demanded that the bourgeois press stop linking their organization with common crimes committed by the Black Hand. Haphazard reporting by the metropolitan press made such a demand seem clearly justified. For example, the second largest daily newspaper in Seville reported on March 3, 1883, that

as a result of recent disclosures, we now have a more precise idea of the number of members of the Black Hand. The number is 49,910 with the membership divided into 190 federations and 800 sections.[17]

Indeed, these figures were more precise than earlier speculations; but they referred to the membership of the entire *Federación de Trabajadores* in the summer of 1882, not to the Black Hand in 1883.

But *Federación* leaders did not content themselves with correcting careless journalists and repudiating the Black Hand. They explicitly rejected all Andalusian deviations from the pure line of Catalan anarchism. In the fall of 1882, the anarchist press and the *Comisión Federal* criticized the bread riots that had broken out throughout Andalusia, even though they did acknowledge the desperate straits of Andalusian laborers. In December, they castigated "turbulent and microscopic groups" in Andalusia for their advocacy of "a program of illegitimate actions which no organization dedicated to the success of dignified and honorable ideals could accept."[18] A month later, in a report on schismatic tendencies within the Andalusian branch of the movement, *La Revista Social* warned that

those who do not agree completely and without qualification with the programs of the Barcelona and Seville congresses are our enemies, and we shall combat them without truce or rest.[19]

In an effort to save their fragile creation, *Federación* leaders severed all ties with their erstwhile Andalusian compatriots. In March 1883, the *Comisión Federal* circulated a solemn resolution condemning crimes of violence and extolling the *Federación*'s own commitment to legal resistance. This moralistic pronouncement was not tempered with an explanation of the special circumstances that spawned social violence in Andalusia, nor did it mention the brutal harassment of the *Federación* itself that accompanied police investigations of the Black Hand. After the March manifesto, *Federación* leaders and the anarchist press said no more about the Black Hand, the *braceros* who were herded into Andalusian jails, or the repression of all working-class activities in southern Spain. Silence made their point.

Despite partisan interpretations of the origins and meaning of the social upheaval in the South, one thing was terrifyingly clear to all observers: the Black Hand seemed an ominous threat to life and property in Andalusia. Captured documents referred to a "popular tribunal" established to punish the bourgeoisie for their crimes. Members of this "large and formidable war machine" met secretly once a month to devise new and better ways of "burning, killing, poisoning, and inflicting injuries. . . ."[20] Some landlords hired gangs of armed thugs to protect them, and all called for more police and applauded the well-publicized efforts of Captain Oliver to purge the countryside of terrorists and incendiaries.

Rumor was accepted as fact in an atmosphere of growing panic. According to one widely reported story, the Black Hand had a list of "enemies of the people" and planned to murder ten "bourgeois" for each "socialist" executed. Police reported the disappearance of one young man who refused to carry out the Black Hand's order to kill his own father, and a leading Madrid newspaper claimed to know of at least 14 death sentences decreed by the "popular tribunal." In Jerez, the capital of Spain's sherry industry, Captain Oliver reported a plot to destroy vineyards by "cutting the buds of the vines at the moment when they first appear, when they are so delicate that the least blow will ruin them."[21] And the mayor of Jerez, inundated with rumors and demands for action, learned that the Black Hand intended to poison the water supply of the city.

That most of these and other rumors were patently unfounded seemed irrelevant in the winter and early spring of 1883, especially when daily reports of new crimes exacerbated the worst fears and fantasies of respectable Andalusians. Most of these crimes were against property, that is, robberies, burning of crops, and destruction of vines and orchards. On April 1, four masked men stole 1,500 *pesetas* from an estate near Arcos de la Frontera, 25 miles east of Jerez. On April 4, forty armed *braceros* assaulted two foremen at an estate near Jerez and stole bread, grain, and money. Two nights later ten men attacked one estate while twenty vineyard workers were sacking another. Subsequent investigations failed to link robberies of this sort to any organized conspiracy. Nonetheless, the wave of robberies and vandalism was popularly considered to be the work of the Black Hand.

Even more frightening were the brutal murders attributed to the Black Hand. Captain Oliver announced the discovery of the Black Hand and the murder of Blanco de Benaocaz in February 1883. Newspapers speculated and the investigating judge confirmed that the Black Hand was considered responsible for the slaying of the innkeeper Nuñez and his wife the preceding December. A *bracero* in Arcos de la Frontera who killed a fellow worker on February 28 was assumed to be operating under orders from "a secret revolutionary organization."[22] When a suspect being held in a Cádiz jail killed a fellow prisoner on March 6, a police spokesman announced that the Black Hand had silenced a potential informer. Two days later the *Guardia Civil* in Arcos arrested two *braceros* and charged them with the murder of a night watchman who had died on August 13, 1882, ostensibly from accidental injuries. Police said that the watchman had been executed by the Black Hand because of his refusal to join the "International." Also in March, police acting on an anonymous tip discovered a dead body buried under a pile of rocks in a dried creek bed near Jerez. Although the unidentified corpse had been dead four or five months and no other evidence was discovered, an official report said that "the examining judge attributes the crime to instructions or orders from the *Federación de Trabajadores*. . . ."[23] In the winter of 1883 in western Andalusia, all crimes of violence, no matter how "ordinary," were thought to be products of a systematic program of terror and intimidation, a program conceived and carried out by revolutionary anarchists.

Occurrences in the Andalusian *pueblo* of Grazalema seemed to confirm that the Black Hand was conducting a reign of terror in the southern countryside. Nestled in the rugged mountains of the Serranía de Ronda, east of Jerez, Grazalema was a notorious center of banditry, smuggling, and social unrest. Rocky, barren soil and uneven terrain made most agricultural pursuits unprofitable, while the town's isolation kept its nascent cork industry from expanding. The only good land nearby was contained in three large *latifundios,* which together composed 69 percent of the total area in the district. Shepherds tended sheep and goats on the surrounding hills, less than fifty workers were employed in two small textile mills, and some individuals managed to survive by selling *esparto* grass, which they harvested on nearby plains. But most *braceros* in Grazalema, unable to survive on what employment was available in their village, joined other landless workers in seeking work in the more fertile regions to the west. Together with Portuguese laborers imported under contract at harvest time, *braceros* from mountain villages like Grazalema kept the labor market flooded and wages depressed in the Jerez region.

Along with its export of unskilled workers, Grazalema produced a ready supply of converts to the cause of anarchism. In the fall of 1882, Grazalema had one of the largest local branches of the *Federación* in Andalusia, with 225 members in two sections (200 agricultural workers, 25 "manufacturers"). Documents captured by police the following April indicated that the membership had grown to almost 500. By this measure alone, the impoverished village of 6,700 inhabitants was a barometer of social and economic discontent in western Andalusia.

This discontent reached its apex in the spring of 1883. In one week alone, the bailiff of the local court was beaten, a woman was roughed up for refusing to allow members of the local branch of the *Federación* to use her house for a meeting, and a man was tied up and suspended from the ceiling of a barn, allegedly for his disloyalty to the local workers' organization. Threatening letters, poisoning of farm animals, property destruction, and assaults were "common currency" in Grazalema. Then, on April 25, the *Guardia Civil* discovered the body of the manager of a small vineyard in a nearby hamlet. The victim had first been tortured by his murderers—his neck and left arm had been charred by flames, and the fingers of his right hand had been cut off. The examining physician counted twenty-nine knife wounds, seven gunshot wounds, and two ax blows. Although five suspects were subsequently arrested, the case against them never came to court for lack of evidence. The police in Grazalema could arrest suspects, but they could not obtain evidence from people afraid of being marked for extermination by the Black Hand.[24]

Captain Oliver and the *Guardia Civil* did their job almost too well in the late winter and early spring of 1883. Prisons throughout the province of Cádiz were quickly filled to overflowing as the police brought in batches of new suspects. Municipal officials, initially exultant at the vigilance of the police, soon began to worry about the mounting cost of feeding and guarding so many prisoners. Estimates varied considerably, but no account placed the number of imprisoned suspects at less than 2,000. Some reports claimed that jails in Cádiz and surrounding provinces contained more than 5,000 suspected members of the Black Hand. Nor was prison overcrowding the only problem associated with the roundup of suspects. Rumors spread that bands of terrorists believed to be roaming the countryside were planning terrible reprisals. City officials in Jerez feared an armed assault on their jail, a converted monastery, whose walls were in a state of disrepair; the army accordingly agreed to their request for a squadron of cavalry to reinforce the municipal police assigned to guard the edifice.

Newspaper reports insisted that cases against the Black Hand would move shortly from the preliminary investigation *(sumario)* to the public trial *(juicio oral)*. But in mid-March the minister of justice removed the prosecutor from the criminal court of Jerez and transferred him to another province. The new prosecutor then announced a delay of unspecified duration in the judicial proceedings so that he could familiarize himself with the cases on the docket. Although the government offered no explanation of its actions in the matter, the change in prosecutors may have been a ploy to gain time, since the prosecution was obviously finding it difficult to prove a direct link between specific crimes committed in the region and any working-class organization.

Eventually, the Black Hand was officially implicated in three murder trials in the province of Cadiz, although a number of other murders committed in 1882–83 were commonly attributed to it. In the three main Black Hand trials, the prosecution made a diligent effort to define the murders as "social crimes." The anarchist movement in Andalusia was thus on trial along with the individual defendants.

The most important Black Hand trial took place in June 1883, when sixteen men were tried for the murder of Bartolomé Gago Campos, a *bracero* known as "El Blanco de Benaocaz." Blanco was killed on December 4, 1883; but police did not discover his body until two months later, probably as the result of a tip from one of the accused murderers. Blanco's murder had been the first crime officially attributed to the Black Hand in February, and the trial of his alleged slayers became something of a showcase for the government's evidence concerning the threat of revolutionary anarchism in Andalusia.

Little is known about the accused men. Nine of the sixteen were in their thirties, five in their twenties, only two over forty years of age. At least eight were married and had children. All lived in or near the village of San José del Valle, although none had been born there. Two of the men were landowning farmers, two were shepherds, one an artisan, one a night watchman, one the teacher of an unofficial school for working-class children, and nine were day laborers. Seven of the sixteen claimed to be able to read and write, a relatively high number given the 25 percent literacy rate for adult males in Andalusia as a whole. Only two had previous criminal records, both for assault. Francisco and Pedro Corbacho, the two landowning brothers, were president and vice president, respectively, of the local branch of the *Federación de Trabajadores* in San José del Valle. Juan Ruíz, the schoolteacher, was secretary. Aside from these bare biographical facts contained in the transcript of their trial, nothing certain is known about the backgrounds, the political views, and the activities of the accused men.

Most of the defendants openly admitted their role in the murder but claimed they acted out of fear of Pedro Corbacho, the dominant figure in the group. Bartolo Gago de los Santos, Blanco's cousin and one of the two men who lured Blanco into the ambush on December 4, said he felt compelled to take part in the execution:

The only reason I had for killing Blanco was that I received an order signed by Pedro Corbacho; and even though Blanco was my cousin, I had no choice but to follow the order. If they had asked me to murder my father, I would have done it.[25]

The others confirmed this. The order came from Corbacho; they were afraid not to follow it.

The prosecutor, Pascual Domenech, questioned their reason for accepting the order and referred repeatedly to documentary evidence introduced in the preliminary investigation. One document in particular, entitled the "Regulations of the Popular Nucleus," allegedly linked the defendants to the Black Hand. These bylaws described a revolutionary organization devoted to the destruction of the bourgeois order, "whether by fire, by cold steel, by poison, or by whatever means." Each member of the *Nucleo Popular* was to comport himself in a manner befitting a dedicated revolutionary, with deviation from prescribed behavioral patterns being grounds for expulsion. Because of the knowledge they possessed, expelled members were to be watched with care:

It is necessary to keep expelled members under continual observation in order to punish them with death should they reveal any of our secrets. One ordered to kill a traitor must do so even if the person is his friend, his brother, or even his father. The life of a traitor is worth nothing.[26]

Domenech tried to make each witness admit that he had helped commit the murder of Blanco because of this section of the "Regulations." None would do so, though all except the two Corbachos confessed to the crime itself.

While the defendants could not explain their blind obedience or the depth of their fear, they had no difficulty in explaining contradictions between testimony given in the public trial and earlier confessions in which some admitted being members of the Black Hand. One defendant testified that he had perjured during preliminary questioning because he was so tired of being beaten that he had finally "said whatever they wanted me to say."[27] Ruíz also attributed his confession during the *sumario* to beatings and threats he received from his interrogators. He added, in what could only have been an ironical tone, that

just because I have said these things you should not believe that I hate the Guardia Civil. *Nothing of the sort. They did very well, they discharged their duty; I would have done the same myself. All they did was do their duty.*[28]

Pedro Corbacho denied everything. He denied signing an execution order; he denied knowing anything about Blanco's death; and he denied seeking revenge for any affront. He had owed Blanco 150 *pesetas*, "more or less," which had been held back from Blanco's wages at his own request during the ten months that he had worked for the Corbachos; but he scorned that debt as a possible motive for murder. Corbacho repeated the denials he had made during the *sumario* and ridiculed the others for changing their stories: "I have always told the truth, and I swear before God and this Tribunal that I have never belonged and do not belong to any organization of any kind."[29]

In his summation, the prosecutor reiterated his assertion that the defendants belonged to a secret society in which "all submitted to a terrible and mysterious power which obliged them to commit the most atrocious crimes."[30] Domenech conceded that the documents concerning the Black Hand that he had introduced as evidence had not been captured in the possession of the defendants. The "Regulations of the Popular Nucleus" and other papers had been captured in 1879 during police investigations of robberies in the countryside around Jerez. But, Domenech argued, the documents were still relevant in the case at hand: "In 1879 they laid their plans and now they have carried them out."[31]

Although he sought death sentences for each of the defendants, Domenech focused special attention on the roles played by Pedro Corbacho and Juan Ruíz. Corbacho was a "man of iron, of profound conviction, with the true character of a *jefe*. . . ."[32] He had planned the murder, then forced his cohorts to carry it out according to the dictates of the rules that bound them. Afterwards, he had allowed his older brother to confess to planning the murder on the grounds that Pedro could best provide for both families if Francisco were executed. But Pedro Corbacho was the real leader of the

San José del Valle organization and the man most responsible for the death of Blanco de Benaocaz.

Ruíz represented a more subtle but more insidious threat to the established social order. He was the *sabio*, the man who "knew things" in a community of ignorant men, the dedicated anarchist who used his intellectual superiority to confuse and convert others to his criminal cause. As ideological mentor of the Corbachos and the others, Ruíz interpreted articles from *La Revista Social*, undertook the local federation's correspondence with regional and national organizations, and tried to educate his coreligionists in the intricacies of their faith. Newspaper accounts ridiculed Ruíz's description of himself as a *maestro de escuela*, and the prosecutor took care to point out that he was not an officially certified teacher. But by giving rudimentary instruction to the children of *braceros* and poor peasants for whatever small sums they could pay, Ruíz undoubtedly built up a considerable moral credit in the community; and this in turn contributed to his influential role in the local anarchist organization. Because of the importance of this role, Domenech argued, the court must ignore Ruíz's repudiation of his confession in the *sumario*. On the basis of that confession three months before the public trial began, Ruíz "was a socialist; he was a member of a society of criminals; he was the secretary of that society; and he wrote and countersigned the order which decreed the death of one of his erstwhile comrades. . . ."[33] He was, therefore, as guilty as Pedro Corbacho.

Because of the complexity of the case, the sixteen defendants were divided into five groups, each of which was represented by a court-appointed lawyer. The lawyers pursued divergent lines of defense and frequently came into conflict with each other because their clients had played different roles in the murder. But in spite of these disagreements in strategy and tactics, all of the defense lawyers sought to descredit the prosecutor's insistence on the "social nature" of Blanco's murder.

Salvador Dastis e Isasi, a well-known Jerez lawyer who defended four of the accused men, blamed a state of public panic for the "unfounded accusations" about the Black Hand. The judges had an opportunity to restore calm in Andalusia, he argued; they could demonstrate "with good will and profound conviction that the alarm is unfounded, that the much-discussed 'criminal society' does not exist, and that people are not really threatened by the evils which they feel surround them."[34] Fears engendered by irresponsible rumors had distorted the perspective of a just but impressionable people:

The mere name of the so-called society, "the Black Hand," is horrifying enough for everyone to focus his attention on a common crime, no different from any other. Everything is somehow "explained" because of that name. . . .[35]

With the feverish sensationalism of the press coverage, Dastis asked, "is it strange that we believe ourselves to be living on top of a volcano? Is it strange that there has been no crime committed here in a long time which has not been attributed to the Black Hand?"[36] But, Dastis insisted, the Black Hand did not exist. No further documents relating to the Black Hand had been captured since 1879 despite numerous arrests of Andalusian workers suspected of belonging to various secret organizations. If the Black Hand actually was the extensive network envisaged by the prosecution, why had no more evidence been discovered and produced? Most important, the documents introduced as evidence had not been found in the possession of the defendants in the Blanco case. Dastis concluded that the prosecution had not proved either that the Black Hand existed or that the defendants belonged to it.

On June 13, 1883, after three days of deliberation, the judges announced their verdict. One of the defendants was acquitted; the other fifteen were found guilty. Eight, including Ruíz, were sentenced to prison terms of seventeen years. Seven, including the two Córbachos, were sentenced to death. Ten months later the Supreme Court in Madrid heard appeals from the fifteen men convicted of murdering Blanco de Benaocaz. The seven who had been sentenced to death asked that their sentences be reduced to life imprisonment. The other eight asked for reduced sentences and specifically challenged the documentary evidence used by the prosecution to connect the accused men with the Black Hand. But these were not the only appeals. Under Spanish law the prosecution—in effect, the ministry of justice—also had the right to appeal sentences in cases where it felt that the lower court had been too lenient.

The public prosecutor before the high court, Manuel Azcutía, claimed that the Jerez judges had erred in considering eight of the defendants as mere accessories. They had had foreknowledge of the crime, and they should be punished as severely as the others. Azcutía made clear, as had Domenech in Jerez, that the stakes were higher than in a simple case of murder:

This case involves a secret and illegal organization, a clandestine and mysterious "court," whose means for carrying out its barbarous and iniquitous projects are fire, bullets, and poison. If the popular tribunal so ordains, then a father is lucky indeed if he can avoid a dagger thrust in the heart from his own son, and a son is fortunate if he does not have to bathe his hands in the blood of his own father.[37]

All the defendants belonged to this secret society, "whose powerful and irresistible voice disrupts the countryside, burns the crops, and destroys property in all the unfortunate districts around Jerez. . . ."[38] And all were murderers. In an impassioned peroration, Azcutía insisted that none should be granted mercy by the civilized world:

A horde of savages would not have acted any more brutally. A horde of Aztecs, or Bedouins, or cannibals who have fallen upon their human prey in order to drink his blood and devour him. Aztecs, Bedouins, or cannibals—from them it would be

expected; but these were Christians, sons of Christians, born and bred and edu-
cated in a civilized country. . . . One's heart is torn to shreds upon recalling, con-
sidering, and trying to explain such scenes of crime and brutality; scenes,
unfortunately, which are Spanish scenes—so cruel, so atrocious, so inhuman, so
barbarous.[39]

The Supreme Court agreed with the prosecutor's argument, though not perhaps with his excessive rhetoric. On April 5, 1884, the Court issued its verdict. All fifteen of the defendants were guilty of murder. All fifteen were to be executed.

When the verdict was made public, government officials and civic leaders in Jerez protested strongly. By the spring of 1884 the countryside was calm again, the Black Hand a bad memory, and the economic crisis over. An editorial in the leading Jerez newspaper said that the crimes of the Black Hand should be considered a terrible sickness whose cure could not— "a thousand times, no!"—be effected by the executioner:

the pueblo *of Jerez, so loyal, so noble, always so Christian, begs with sincerity, with passion, that the shade of the scaffold not be seen here.*[40]

Such pleas for mercy were partially rewarded. In May, 1884, the Council of Ministers in Madrid commuted six of the death sentences to life imprisonment. One man had already been declared insane and had received a commutation to life. The remaining eight, including Juan Ruíz, who had originally received a prison sentence, were garroted in Jerez de la Frontera on June 14, 1884.

The trial of Pedro Corbacho, Juan Ruíz, and their compatriots cast little light on the Black Hand mystery. The prosecution insisted that the sixteen defendants had acted in unison because of their membership in *La Mano Negra,* but the only documents offered in evidence had been captured four years before. While there was no doubt that the defendants had in fact murdered Blanco, there is considerable doubt as to why they committed the crime. Three possible motives emerged during the preliminary investigation. Pedro Corbacho owed Blanco a large sum of money and had him killed rather than repay it; Blanco had seduced a teen-aged cousin of the Corbachos and was murdered as a consequence of this violation of a primitive code of honor; and Blanco was executed by the *Nucleo Popular* because he was suspected of being a traitor to the Black Hand. Each of these motives was plausible, but two of them would have weakened the prosecutor's insistence of the subversive implications of the murder. Understandably, Domenech argued that the precise motive was less relevant than the nature of the crime, a brutal murder on command by members of a clandestine anarchist organization.

Despite the weakness of the prosecution's case, Domenech's primary contention may have been correct. All the defendants except for the Corbachos admitted to being members of a workers' organization; and, given the atmosphere of repression that reigned in Andalusia, that organization was necessarily clandestine. Moreover, the defendants themselves had personal qualities that set them apart from the majority of *braceros* in the *Federación*. Half were literate, and one was relatively well educated. Two owned land, albeit small parcels. In addition, dissident groups within the *Federación* had emerged in the region as early as the summer of 1882; and the San José del Valle group may well have come under the influence of radicals who had recently been expelled from the local federation in nearby Arcos de la Frontera.

Unfortunately, the dearth of evidence makes such speculation an exercise in frustration. The Black Hand may have been concocted by Andalusian authorities as a pretext for attacking the anarchist movement in the south; or it may have existed as a secret cell of radicals within the *Federación* in Andalusia. The trials of alleged members of the Black Hand did not resolve the question.

The Blanco de Benaocaz trial and two other murder trials involving the Black Hand in the early summer of 1883 attracted wide attention. All the chief Madrid newspapers sent reporters to cover the trials, and published transcripts of the trials sold well. Deputies in the *Cortes* debated the implications of the Black Hand and of the agrarian unrest in general, and the government promised to take stern measures to insure that there would be no recurrence of the Black Hand in Andalusia.

At the end of the summer, another murder trial received little notice from the press, the politicians, or the public. Juan Galán, a *bracero* from Jerez, was tried and convicted for murdering the innkeeper Juan Nuñez and his wife in December, 1882. The robbery and murders, so widely considered to be the work of the Black Hand in the spring of 1883, were, by late summer, treated in perfunctory fashion as ordinary crimes. The prosecutor made no effort to connect the robbery and murders with the Black Hand or any other working-class organization, even though Galán had earlier admitted to being a member of the *Federación de Trabajadores*. Galán claimed he had been drunk at the time of the crime and did not know what he was doing; his codefendants testified that he had planned the robbery and then committed the murders when things did not go according to plan. Galán was convicted. On April 19, 1884, he was executed.

The trial and conviction of Galán aroused so little attention in September, 1883, because by then the anarchist movement had been crushed throughout Andalusia. The summer harvest had been bountiful, an abortive strike by *braceros* had been easily crushed, and wheat prices were back to normal. In the first half of the year, official prosecution and unofficial persecution of the anarchist movement had taken their toll. By the end of the summer, the *Federación de Trabajadores* had virtually ceased to exist in southern Spain.

Official harassment took the form of formal prosecution of local sections of the *Federación* that did not abide by the letter of the law governing political associations. To obtain official recognition, an organization had to register formally with provincial authorities by giving the Civil Governor's office a list of the organization's members and a copy of its bylaws. Failure to do so was considered prima facie evidence of criminal intent, and police rounded up Andalusian workers by the hundreds on suspicion of belonging to illegal organizations.

One example will suggest the devastating effect on working-class activities of a rigid interpretation of this law. On February 24, 1883, shortly after the discovery of the Black Hand, police broke up a meeting in the *pueblo* of Juzcar (Málaga) and arrested 39 *braceros* on charge of belonging to an illegal organization. Among the incriminating documents captured at the time were copies of *La Revista Social,* the proceedings of the Barcelona Congress of 1881, and various papers identifying the captured men as members of the agricultural workers' section of the Juzcar branch of the *Federación.* In the summer of 1883, the accused men were convicted of belonging to a criminal organization. One sixteen-year-old boy was fined 130 *pesetas* (almost a full year's wages); thirty-seven others received sentences of two months imprisonment; and one man, considered by the court to be the leader of the group, was fined 250 *pesetas* and sentenced to two years and five months in jail.[41]

The fact that the *Federación de Trabajadores* was considered a legal organization by the national government made no difference in the outcome of the case. The Juzcar group had failed to follow the letter of the law by seeking official recognition from provincial authorities, and as a consequence their local section of the *Federación* was held to be illegal. To have sought such authorization would, of course, have been equally disastrous. Names of workers seeking official permission to form an organization were routinely sent by the Civil Governor's office to municipal authorities, who in turn informed local landlords and the *Guardia Civil.* Troublemakers and agitators would then be dealt with unofficially at the local level while their petition for formal recognition was being considered in the provincial capital. In an appeal before the Supreme Court the Juzcar group argued that belonging to an organization dedicated to the lowering of hours, raising of wages, and improving of working conditions was not illegal; they also noted that their organization was officially tolerated in other parts of Spain. But the Supreme Court upheld the decision of the lower court and let the convictions stand.

Such cases were frequent in the spring and summer of 1883. While it is impossible to determine precise figures, an estimated 300–400 Andalusian workers were sentenced to prison during this period for belonging to "illicit organizations," organizations that elsewhere in Spain existed legally, publicly, and with relatively little official harassment. Hundreds more were arrested, kept in jail for days or even weeks, then released without trial. Police found that such tactics were effective in dealing with all but the most zealous working-class militants in the region. Poor men in prison had no way to feed their families, so many rank-and-file members of the *Federación* destroyed their membership cards and severed all connections with the organization.

Even more devastating than the judicial proceedings carried out against members of the *Federación* was the systematic but unofficial harassment of the Andalusian anarchist movement by police, landlords, and public authorities. Meeting places were raided, funds and papers confiscated, and workers arrested arbitrarily throughout the region. Mail to suspected members of the *Federación* was "lost" by postal authorities (in one month alone in 1883, seven packets of *La Revista Social* failed to reach their Andalusian destinations), and requests for public meetings were routinely denied. A letter to *La Revista Social* from a *Federación* member in Jerez summarized the situation:

This region, dear friends, has become a living hell. No one feels secure. The horrors of hunger have been succeeded by a reign of terror even more terrifying. The proletarians, and especially the farm workers, do not have a moment's rest. With the pretext of this or that crime, of the kind which are always committed in these parts, the police try by all sorts of illegal methods to secure confessions and documents from us. Our meeting places, our homes, our persons, even our beds are inspected at all hours of the day and night. And anyone unlucky enough to be found with a copy of La Revista Social *. . . in his possession is considered to be the greatest criminal in the world and is thrown into jail.*[42]

Harassment of the anarchist movement in Andalusia reached its peak during a strike by agricultural workers in the Jerez region in the early summer of 1883. Only at harvest time could Andalusian *braceros* hope to exert pressure on landowners by withholding their labor; and even then the harvesters, who counted on making enough money during the three summer months to carry them through the rest of the year, had much more to lose than the *latifundistas* and large tenant farmers. But after two successive crop failures, the bountiful harvest predicted for 1883 seemed to offer the *braceros* a bit more leverage, since no proprietor wanted to lose still another crop. Strike organizers for the *Federación* hoped to capitalize on this situation by convincing workers that they could exercise their potential strength if only they would stand together.

Landowners fought back through their own spokesmen, the provincial and municipal governments. These public officials made clear that the *Federación de Trabajadores* would no longer be tolerated in western Andalusia.

In response to reports of the attempt to organize the Jerez strike, the Civil Governor of the province of Cádiz said in an official edict that this "unqualified attack on the sacred right of property imposes on all public authorities the duty of repressing it with energy and punishing it without hesitation."[43] He ordered all mayors and public officials in the province to guarantee "the liberty of contact between workers and proprietors. . . ."[44] This meant, of course, that they should make every effort to break the strike. Individuals whose names were on file with the *Guardia Civil* for their bad conduct or their questionable background *(antecedentes desfavorables)* were to be watched closely and arrested immediately if fires, assaults, or "any disturbances" occurred near their places of residence. A curfew was imposed on the countryside throughout the province; anyone outside village or city limits after 10 P.M. was subject to arrest. Wagon drivers were required to carry receipts and shipping instructions, presumably to facilitate checking for stolen goods. Finally, the Civil Governor issued a sweeping warrant that in effect gave police *carte blanche* is disrupting the activities of the *Federación*:

Any damage or fire thought to be accidental will be presumed to be the work of individuals discovered in the immediate area; or, if no one is found, of those individuals who compose the local junta *of the nearest branch of the* Internacional *or the* Federación de Trabajadores.[45]

This was the first agricultural strike in the history of a region where not even city workers employed the strike effectively or frequently. In short strikes two years before, bakers in Jerez won a slight reduction in their working hours; and barrelmakers in the sherry industry gained a slight increase in the piece rate at which they were paid. But this was the first serious attempt to organize an agricultural strike in the Jerez *campiña,* the richest agricultural region in western Andalusia.

Strike organizers played down ideological questions and emphasized the one issue that might unite unsophisticated Andalusian *braceros.* That issue was *trabajo á destajo,* or piecework. During harvest time *trabajo á destajo* meant three months of driving, uninterrupted work. Men, women, and children competed with each other in the fields under the broiling Andalusian sun. Sickness or injury could ruin one's hopes for survival during the remainder of the year, and the old and the lame were forced to work at a killing pace merely to earn a marginal existence. Piecework had been introduced in the 1860s and 1870s by middle-class landowners anxious to increase productivity. The strikers sought to replace *trabajo á destajo* with the more traditional daily wage, which from their point of view meant exchanging a tension-charged race with other workers for a steady, tolerable work pace.

From the first, the strikers faced insurmountable odds. Agricultural laborers were not well organized, they had no tradition of cooperative actions of this sort, and they had no resources in reserve. For these reasons their early success shocked local landlords and amazed everyone. At first *braceros* stayed away from the fields in passive resistance, much to the surprise of foremen who came to town plazas each day looking for workers. This forced the region's landowners to look to their other traditional sources of labor, men from mountain villages in the eastern part of the province and Portuguese laborers who were brought in by the wagonload. These two groups of workers were even more desperate and less organized than *braceros* in the Jerez region. Yet, to the consternation of local officials and landowners, many joined the striking Jerez laborers and refused to work *á destajo*.

But the strikers' early successes were short-lived. Local landowners, annoyed more than threatened by the strike, decided to play their trump card: they asked the national government in Madrid for permission to hire soldiers to harvest the crops. The Council of Ministers agreed, soldiers were dispatched to Jerez, and the strike was quickly broken.[46]

The Black Hand trials, the extralegal harassment of the *Federación*, and the breaking of the Jerez harvesters' strike crushed the anarchist movement and the *Federación de Trabajadores* in Andalusia in the summer of 1883. Symptoms of the collapse appeared in a familiar pattern in the anarchist press. First came the passionate exhortations not to be intimidated, the pleas to attend the night-school sessions and meetings at the local "workers' center," and the urgent requests that all members pay their dues at once. Then, reports of documents seized, meeting places closed down, and members arrested. Finally, silence. By the end of the summer the page of *La Revista Social* devoted to reports from local federations contained virtually no news from Andalusia. This silence, not the strident rhetoric of *Federación* leaders who promised great new gains, indicated the true fate of the anarchist movement in Andalusia.

The third congress of the *Federación de Trabajadores*, held in Valencia in September 1883, was a hollow replica of the exuberant meetings of 1881 and 1882. Leaders dutifully denounced the Black Hand and affirmed their legal and moral rectitude before a small gathering of less than 90 delegates, only four of them from Andalusia. The Civil Governor of the province attended the public meetings to make sure that the proceedings were not inflammatory in tone or content, but he need not have bothered. Delegates routinely approved resolutions endorsing the work of the *Comisión Federal*, and they agreed to minor modifications in the bylaws. But no issues of importance were resolved or even discussed. No mention was made, for example, of emergency relief for the wives and families of Andalusian members of the *Federación* who were in jail. The usual manifestos and revolutionary appeals were issued, but brave words could not hide the fact that the *Federación* was in a shambles.

Various factors contributed to the rapid disintegration of the *Federación*. In western Andalusia a good harvest in the summer of 1883 meant employment and cheap bread for *braceros* who had barely survived the crop failures of the two previous years. These enticements, plus the harsh repression of working-class activities throughout the south, drove many Andalusian workers away from the *Federación*. In Catalonia a rash of poorly planned strikes in 1882 and 1883 had seriously weakened Catalan trade unions, and many workers simply stopped paying their dues and dropped out of the *Federación*. But clearly the most important reason for the breakup of the *Federación* was the Black Hand affair, which had dramatically illustrated the fundamental contradictions within the anarchist movement in Spain.

Anarchist leaders of the *Federación* had sought from the first to dissociate their organization from the Black Hand. Once again at the Valencia congress they made clear that the rural violence of Andalusia was not their doing:

We want to emphasize that our organization has never advocated robbery, arson, vandalism, or assassinations; we do not have and we have never had anything to do with the "Black Hand," nor the "White Hand," nor any secret society dedicated to the perpetration of common crimes.[47]

But some elements of the Catalan branch of the movement were not so quick to denounce "propaganda of the deed," especially since trade union activities in Catalonia bore the stigma of reformism as well as of failure. Others agreed that the *Federación* should pursue a nonviolent, legal course but did not feel that anarchist leaders should be so harsh in their denunciation of the movement in Andalusia. Factional disputes became more open and more frequent, and by the end of 1883 the anarchist press was filled with bitter charges and recriminations. The Black Hand affair and its aftermath thus opened a breach within the *Federación* between its two constituent parts. And with the Andalusian faction completely shattered, the Catalan branch of the anarchist movement was unable to maintain more than the shell of a national organization. The *Federación de Trabajadores* was not officially dissolved until 1888, but it was effectively defunct by the end of 1883.

The Black Hand episode evoked a popular response bordering on hysteria in Andalusia; it elicited extended and fanciful speculations on its nature and origins by the Spanish press; and it served as a convenient pretext for the crushing of rural working-class activities by Andalusia authorities. In addition, rural unrest in Andalusia prompted a formal national inquiry into the nature and causes of the "social question." The Commission for Social Reforms, founded in 1883 as a direct consequence of the disturbances in the South, never carried out its charge to investigate social and economic conditions in Andalusia; but it did serve as a precursor of the Institute of Social Reforms, an organization founded in 1903, which did function as an important element of the movement for orderly social change in Spain. That much is clear.

But the Black Hand itself remains a mystery. Police, army, and prison records are closed to outside researchers; judicial records have been either burned or lost. Only one document has been found in Spanish archives that makes specific reference to the Black Hand. And that document, copies of which are in Madrid and Jerez archives,[48] establishes no clear link between rural violence in Andalusia in 1882–83 and the Black Hand. The date of its discovery by Spanish authorities is not clear, but internal evidence indicates that it was written at least as early as 1881, and perhaps 1879. Did the Black Hand ever exist? The available evidence does not permit a verdict.[49]

That the Black Hand mystery remains unsolved is frustrating and troublesome; and it emphasizes how little is known about rural unrest in the nineteenth century and how difficult is the task facing the historian of rural society. But the unsolved mystery does not detract from what the Black Hand episode reveals about the pattern of rural unrest and the context of rural violence in Andalusia. Indeed, the importance of the Black Hand is independent of the question of its existence.

The history of peasant unrest in nineteenth-century Spain is virtually unknown. Why were some regions centers of chronic unrest while others were never touched by rural disturbances? Why, within a given region, were certain villages always ready to explode while others remained quiet through the worst of times? What were the motives of the men and women who picked up guns and pitchforks with the cry of "Viva la anarquía"? These are only a few of the questions about Spanish peasants in the nineteenth century that remain unanswered. Our uncertainty is, as E. J. Hobsbawn and George Rudé put it in *Captain Swing,* a consequence of "their inarticulateness, our ignorance. . . ."[50]

That ignorance is difficult to overcome. As noted above, certain important archives in Spain are closed to historians. Newspapers offer impressionistic, fragmentary, and erroneous information, more trap than clue. Anarchist publications are marginally more useful; but the urban, industrial, Catalan orientation of anarchist leaders in Spain affected their perceptions of rural, agricultural, Andalusian society. Demographic questions are hard to answer because of the primitive nature of Spanish census reports for the late nineteenth century: for example, the census of 1887 lumps all people engaged in any way in agriculture under one general occupational category. Most important, the people who took part in the rural violence of the early 1880s were unable to write, and thereby speak for themselves. We have no memoirs, no letters, no firsthand accounts except for those by observers, not participants. What we can learn about peasant unrest, therefore, is of a tentative and speculative nature.

Fabrication by the police or actual organizations? No matter; the Black Hand mystery exemplifies an unvarying pattern of rural unrest in nineteenth-century Andalusia. Physical misery and psychological alienation; a sharp economic crisis that made the misery especially acute; initial enthusiasm for the millenarian visions of "outsiders" (before 1868, radical republicans; after 1868, revolutionary anarchists); acts of violence against property, sometimes spontaneous, sometimes organized by small, secret bands of dedicated revolutionaries; and inevitably, defeat and repression. This pattern suggests the powerlessness of Andalusian *braceros* and their vulnerability to the economic crises that precipitated their short-lived rebellions in the nineteenth century. When, as in the 1880s, they lashed out violently against the symbols of a social and economic order that despised them, they did so out of frustration. The acts of violence and terrorism in the early 1880s, whether spontaneous or planned by groups like the Black Hand, were symbols of failure. As in the "Captain Swing" uprising in England in 1830, terrorism was "the active response to defeat."[51] And, given the social and economic structure of Andalusian society in the nineteenth century, defeat for the *braceros* was inevitable.

NOTES

1. *El Guadalete* (Jerez de la Frontera), February 27, 1883.

2. This reconstruction of the Nuñez murders is based on contemporary newspaper accounts.

3. E. J. Hobsbawm, *Primitive Rebels* (Manchester, England: Manchester University Press, 1960), pp. 74–92. For general accounts of the history of the anarchist movement in Spain, see Max Nettlau, *La Première Internationale en Espagne (1886–1888)* (Dordrecht-Holland: D. Reidel, 1969); José Termes Ardevol, *El Movimiento Obrero en España (1864–1881)* (Barcelona: Publicaciones de la Cátedra de Historia General de España, 1965); and Stanley Payne, *The Spanish Revolution* (New York: W. W. Norton, 1970). A fine introduction to rural anarchism in Spain is Gabriel Jackson, "The Origins of Spanish Anarchism," *Southwestern Social Science Quarterly*, 36 (September, 1955):135–47. The best books on the subject—and two of the best books in any language on modern Spanish history—are Gerald Brenan, *The Spanish Labyrinth*, 2nd ed. (Cambridge: Cambridge University Press, 1960), and Juan Diáz del Moral, *Historia de las Agitaciones Campesinas Andaluzas: Córdoba* (Madrid: Revista de Derecho Privado, 1929).

4. This essay is based on the following sources: national and provincial newspapers; official publications (including transcripts of three Black Hand trials); anarchist newspapers, books, and pamphlets; a large number of books and pamphlets dealing with the "social question" in Spain; and materials in local archives in Jerez de la Frontera, Arcos de la Frontera, and other towns in the provinceof Cádiz.

5. For the general pattern of economic crises in Spain in the nineteenth century, see Jaime Vicens Vives, *Historia Social y Económica de España y America,* vol. 5 (Barcelona: Editorial Teide, 1959), pp. 233–305. The crisis of 1857 is studied in detail by Nicolás Sánchez-Albornoz, *La Crisis de Subsistencias de España en el Siglo XIX* (Rosario, Argentina: Instituto de Investigaciones Históricas, 1963).

6. Edward E. Malefakis, *Agrarian Reform and Peasant Revolution in Spain* (New Haven: Yale University Press, 1970), p. 110.

7. *El Eco de las Provincias* (Madrid), 17 February 1883.

8. *El Día* (Madrid), 23 March 1883.

9. Eusebio Martínez de Velasco, "La Mano Negra," *La Ilustración Español y Americana* (30 March 1883), p. 189.

10. Quoted in *El Eco Nacional* (Madrid), 9 March 1883.

11. Ibid.

12. Quoted in *El Guadalete* (Jerez de la Frontera), 10 March 1883.

13. All I know about the Polish anarchist is her name, Sofia Pereskaia. Rumors of "strange-looking foreigners" in the region were probably a consequence of the natural desire to blame the area's troubles on outsiders. No other arrests of foreigners were reported in the papers (nor did any of the arrested have identifiably Cátalan names).

14. Eduardo Comín Colomer, *Historia del Anarquismo Español (1836–1948)* (Madrid: Editorial R. A. D. A. R., n.d.), p. 84. Currently the head of the Spanish secret police, Comín Colomer is more policeman than historian, so the potential advantage of his access to secret archives must be discounted.

15. For *La Bande Noire* and its aftermath, see Jean Maitron, *Histoire du Mouvement Anarchiste en France (1800–1914)* (Paris: Societé Universitaire d'Editions et de Libraire, 1951), pp. 139–40. For typical responses in the Spanish press, see *El Día* (Madrid), 23 October 1882, and *El Porvenir* (Madrid), 28 October 1882.

16. *El Guadalete* (Jerez de la Frontera), 1 March 1883.

17. *El Porvenir* (Seville), 3 March 1883.

18. *Crónica de las Trabajadores de la Region Española,* Book One (December 2, 1882), p. 4. This was the official "newsletter" of the *Federación de Trabajadores.*

19. *La Revista Social* (Madrid), 4 January 1883.

20. *El Porvenir* (Madrid), 26 February 1883.

21. *El Guadalete* (Jerez de la Frontera), 2 March 1883.

22. *El Porvenir* (Madrid), 8 March 1883.

23. *El Liberal* (Madrid), 5 March 1883.

24. Grazalema is the real name of the village ("Alcalá de la Sierra") portrayed in the anthropological study, J. A. Pitt-Rivers, *The People of the Sierra* (Chicago: University of Chicago Press, 1961).

25. *Los Procesos de la Mano Negra,* vol. 2 (Madrid: Imprenta de la *Revista de Legislación,* 1883), p. 155. The transcripts of two Black Hand trials were bound together and published by the Royal Academy of Law and Jurisprudence. Most of the *sumario* is excluded; all of the public testimony in the *juicio oral* is apparently here.

26. Ibid., p. 99.

27. Ibid., p. 132.

28. Ibid., p. 172.

29. Ibid., p. 174.

30. Ibid., p. 239.

31. Ibid.

32. Ibid., p. 251.

33. Ibid., p. 249.

34. Ibid., p. 279.

35. Ibid.

36. Ibid.

37. Quoted in Georges Clemenceau, ed., *El Proceso de "La Mano Negra"* (Toulouse: Ediciones CNT, 1958), p. 9. This is the Spanish translation (by Jose Peirats) of two pamphlets first published in France in 1903: *La Mano Negra* (Paris: *Les Temps Nouveaux,* 1903), and *La Mano Negra et l'opinion française* (Paris: *Les Temps Nouveaux,* 1903). Material contained in the two pamphlets first appeared in Clemenceau's Toulouse newspaper, *La Dépêche* (7 and 15 December 1902), as part of a campaign mounted by ex-Dreyfusards to free prisoners held in Spanish jails subsequent to the Black Hand trials in 1883. The coalition in search of another unifying cause held public meetings, circulated petitions, and published these two pamphlets, which contain accounts of the trials, excerpts from the official transcripts, and letters from the prisoners.

38. Ibid., p. 17.

39. Ibid., p. 18.

40. *El Guadalete* (Jerez de la Frontera), 8 April 1884.

41. The case is reviewed in *Sentencias del Tribunal Supremo, 1884,* no. 83 (28 January 1884), pp. 239–44.

42. *La Revista Social* (Madrid), 15 March 1883.

43. "Edicto de 4 Junio 1883—Eduardo de la Loma y Santos, Gobernador Civil," Municipal Archive of Jerez de la Frontera, *Edictos,* 46:163.

44. Ibid.

45. Ibid.

46. Material for this description of the 1883 strike was drawn primarily from *El Guadalete,* one of two daily newspapers in Jerez; and a collection of documents entitled "1881—Órden Público—Huelgas," Municipal Archive of Jerez de la Frontera, Legajo 8, Sección II, Expediente 12591. Many of the documents in this curiously marked folio pertain to the harvesters' strike of 1883.

47. *La Revista Social* (Madrid), 23 March 1883.

48. *Cf.* "La Mano Negra—Sociedad de Pobres contra sus Ladrones y Verdugos—'Reglamento: Europa, Siglo XIX'" Municipal Archive of Jerez de la Frontera, Legajo 8, Sección II, Expediente 12591. This document was discovered in the same general folio entitled "1881—Órden Público—Huelgas." It is a copy from the original, but it is undated. A virtually identical document was discovered in the General Archive of the Royal Palace in Madrid by Professor Clara E. Lida; cf. her article entitled "Agrarian Anarchism in Andalusia: Documents on the *Mano Negra*," *International Review of Social History,* vol. 14, pt. 3 (1969), pp. 315–52. The Royal Palace document is also a copy; a covering letter from the head of the *Guardia Civil* is included.

49. Professor Lida does not agree: she assumes that the Black Hand did exist more or less as described in the cited document, as a secret "internal security" force within the anarchist movement in Andalusia. I feel that this lonely document is not adequate proof of the Black Hand's existence; certainly there is no direct link between it and any known group of individuals (such as the defendants in the Blanco case). Indeed, neither of the two copies makes clear when—or where—the document was discovered. To be sure, the secret society described in the contemporary press and in the "Black Hand document" is precisely the kind of organization one would expect to find in western Andalusia, given prevailing social, economic, and political conditions. But this does not prove that the Black Hand itself actually existed, or eliminate the possibility that it was a fabrication woven from whole cloth by Andalusian police.

50. E. J. Hobsbawm and George Rudé, *Captain Swing* (London: Lawrence and Wishart, 1960), p. 11.

51. Ibid., p. 288.

PEASANTS, POLITICS, AND CIVIL WAR IN SPAIN, 1931–1939

Edward Malefakis

The human mind has a tendency to regard objects that are unfamiliar to it as uniform wholes, forgetting that like everything else in life they are fraught with complexity. Because of the fundamentally urban orientation of Western society over the past century, this tendency is strongly evident in much of what is written about the peasantry. An extraordinarily diverse group, often constituting the majority of the population in a given society and almost always divided within itself by a multiplicity of factors both natural and man-made, is indiscriminately encompassed by a single term. We read of the "conservatism" of the French or German "peasant" in the nineteenth century, or of the "revolutionary temperament" of the Mexican, Russian, Chinese, Algerian, and Vietnamese "peasantry" in the twentieth, and are consequently led to assume a far greater homogeneity of attitudes and actions than existed. Our understanding of great historical events suffers as a result, and richness of analysis becomes more difficult.

This conceptual defect is a universal and largely unavoidable one; in order to function, the human mind seems to require not only the categories of thought described by Kant, but also other, lesser modes of organizing its mental processes. However, since none of these lesser modes are *in themselves* inherent in the mind, as the Kantian categories are, man can free himself of at least some of them through considerable effort. For the historian, the effort is worth making to the degree that a particular generalization distorts and misrepresents the reality it is attemping to organize. From this point of view, the conclusions drawn about the specific peasantries mentioned in the preceding paragraph, while not conducive to subtlety of analysis, are not especially misleading. Although by no means uniform, the

Edward Malefakis received his Ph.D from Columbia University. He is now teaching at the University of Michigan.

This article consists of three parts: an analysis of the rural social and property structures in Spain during the early part of the twentieth century; an examination of the Spanish Republic's failure to reform those structures by normal legislative means from 1931 to 1936; and, finally, a discussion of the role played by the peasantry in the Spanish Civil War of 1936–39, a war in large part caused by the failure of the Republic's agrarian reform programs. Although they contain new data and interpretations, the first two sections of the article are based chiefly on my recent book, *Agrarian Reform and Peasant Revolution in Spain: Origins of the Civil War* (New Haven: Yale University Press, 1970). The last section presents preliminary results of research that I am now beginning on the Civil War period.

conditions of life and the attitudes of a sufficiently large majority of the
rural populations mentioned were probably sufficiently alike in decisive
periods to admit of a certain type of mental shorthand. The same is not true
for the Spanish peasantry in the twentieth century. Far less homogeneity
and far greater diversity existed within it than in the other national peasantries cited. It possessed no majority groups or attitudes on the basis of
which a single generalization can be drawn even with the limited degree of
validity that is possible for its counterparts elsewhere. Precisely because
there was so much diversity, the Spanish story ended uniquely. The occurrence of civil war is not its distinguishing feature for such wars also ravaged
Mexico, Russia, China, and Vietnam. What is unusual about the Spanish
case is that the peasantry, instead of lending the bulk of its support to one
side or the other, remained so divided within itself that it is impossible to
determine which side a majority of its members favored in the conflict. To
fall back into the generalizations I have been warning against, the other
civil wars mentioned can be interpreted primarily as struggles by the peasantry against other social groups. In Spain, although this type of struggle
was not lacking, the Civil War was also to a very significant degree a
fratricidal conflict of peasant against peasant.

I

In what ways did Spanish peasants differ from each other? The most fundamental difference, which conditioned everything else, was undoubtedly the
extraordinary divergence of the property systems that prevailed in the regions in which they lived. Spain is not a homogeneous country either geographically or historically. Its climate, because of Spain's position between
the Atlantic and the Mediterranean, and also between Europe and Africa,
causes its relatively small land area to experience a variety of conditions
equaled only by nations of continental proportions. Wheat, oats, and
barley, the temperate zone crops par excellence, are grown in this country,
but so are such subtropical crops as citrus fruits, sugar, and rice. Its northern coastal zone has rainfall as heavy as that of Scandinavia or the British
Isles, but along its southeastern coast, aridity approaches that of the Sahara
desert. The human consequences of these climatic divergencies are frequently reinforced by Spain's topography. Aside from Switzerland and some
of the Balkan nations, Spain is the most mountainous country in Europe;
indeed, if the lightly populated nations of the Himalayan and Andean
chains are left aside, it is probably among the five or six most mountainous
countries in the world. Mountain barriers, therefore, encourage each region
to develop in isolation.

Climate and topography contributed to *some* of the divergencies that
existed in the property structures of Spain. Far more important, however,
were historical factors, for these not only intensified the differences that
climate and topography initiated, but also created new divergences among

and within regions that climatically resembled each other. Few nations have sprung forth whole, like Athena from the brow of Zeus; but fewer still have gone through a process of nation-building of so many discrete stages as Spain has. The nation as it is now organized was conquered step by step from the Moslems over a period of eight centuries (711–1492), one of the longest historical processes known to man. In each step, different problems had to be faced and radically different policies of resettlement followed. As a general rule, the Castilian kingdom, which reconquered about 60 percent of present-day Spain, increasingly favored large-scale over small-scale settlement as it expanded from north to south, whereas Catalan-Aragonese royal policy remained more committed to the small-scale solution in the lesser conquests it made along the Mediterranean coast. The initial decisions taken proved of lasting significance because, once established, the property systems in each region reinforced themselves and survived all future historical vicissitudes. This was true even during the great transformation in property that occurred in the mid-nineteenth century, as Spanish agriculture shifted from traditional to capitalist modes of production. Although vast quantities of land changed hands everywhere, the net result of this *desamortización* was to reinforce the property structures that had appeared in earlier centuries. Where small property had prevailed in the precapitalist era, the enormous quantities of church, municipal, and noble lands that were put up for sale went mostly to small buyers; where large estates had been dominant, a new economic oligarchy replaced the old.

The divergences that resulted from this multiplicity of factors are summarized in the third column of Table I. The index of property concentration used in that column attempts to take into account both the *amount* of land held by large owners and the *value* of that land. Either of these two traditional measurements used by itself can be misleading: the owner of large tracts of wasteland does not monopolize any important resources; the owner of a medium-sized tract who increases its value by farming it unusually well has gained his wealth less by denying others access to a community's resources than by adding to them. When the two measurements are averaged in a single index, we approach somewhat more closely the true extent to which wealthy owners controlled the chief means of agricultural production in each region.

As can be seen in the column, there is an exceedingly low degree of property concentration along the northern coast of Spain, the region in which rainfall is heaviest and in which Christian kingdoms established their rule before their social orders began to rigidify. The vast region of Old Castile, with moderate rainfall, conquered during the second stage of Christian expansion, is also characterized by small properties. The Mediterranean littoral, in parts of which ancient irrigation systems more than compensate for extreme aridity, and which was reconquered by the Catalan-Aragonese rather than by the Castilian medieval kingdom, also is predominantly a

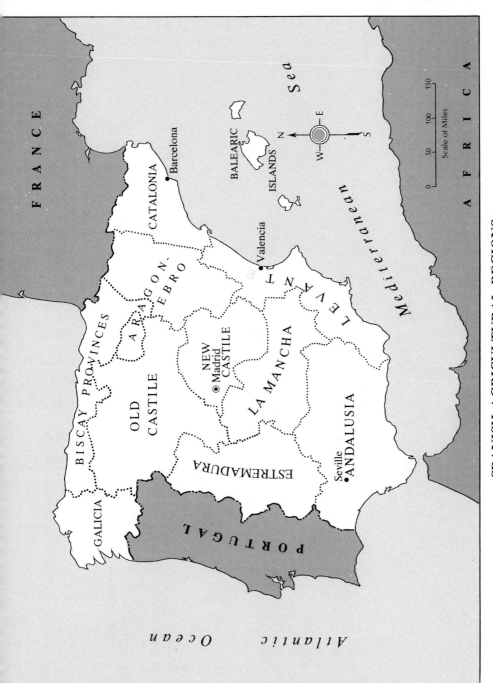

SPANISH AGRICULTURAL REGIONS

TABLE 1. PROPERTY AND RURAL SOCIAL CLASS STRUCTURE IN SPAIN

Region	Total Area (In Thousands of Hectares)	Males Employed in Agriculture (Thousands of Persons)	Index of Property Concentration (Percentage)	Percentage of Males by Occupation	
				Peasant Proprietors	Day Laborers
Atlantic littoral	*6,296*	*913*	*13.7*	*53.2*	*7.3*
Galicia	2,944	613	9.9	55.9	6.6
Biscay provinces	3,352	300	20.8	47.3	9.1
Mediterranean littoral	*7,533*	*986*	*23.0*	*28.1*	*26.0*
Catalonia	3,193	279	22.2	30.1	11.9
Levante	4,340	706	23.2	27.3	31.5
North Central Spain	*17,176*	*873*	*27.4*	*41.3*	*16.1*
Old Castile	8,181	447	24.8	45.5	13.0
New Castile	3,725	165	29.5	33.9	23.6
Aragon-Ebro	5,270	261	30.2	38.9	16.8
Subtotals: small and intermediate property regions	*31,005*	*2,772*	*23.8*	*39.6*	*16.6*
Southwestern Spain	*18,241*	*1,557*	*46.2*	*14.3*	*43.3*
La Mancha	4,998	314	39.5	15.8	34.1
Estremadura	5,394	369	51.4	15.9	37.2
Andalusia	7,850	874	45.6	13.1	49.1
Spain as a whole (including islands)	*50,747*	*4,545*	*33.4*	*31.0*	*25.7*

Note: Population figures are drawn from 1956, and land tenure figures partly from 1959, but both are indicative of pre–Civil War conditions, because Spanish agriculture changed very little prior to the 1960s. The proportion of the population in secondary occupational groups not listed above was as follows for Spain as a whole: labor-employing farm entrepreneurs, 19.2%; small tenants and sharecroppers, 15.1%; permanent hired hands, 9.0%.

small-property zone. The situation begins to change as we move inland and southward. In Aragon proper, and in New Castile (that is, reconquered later than "Old" Castile), we are in areas whose property structures are intermediate between small- and large-scale. Only when we move further south and west, to La Mancha, Estremadura, and the enormous region of Andalusia, do we reach the large-property zone par excellence. In these regions (because of a combination of semiaridity and late reconquest in Estremadura and La Mancha, and because of reconquest after the medieval Christian social order had achieved its pinnacle of rigidity in the case of Andalusia), we arrive at the antithesis of the property structure of the two coastlines and of Old Castile. In terms of the index, almost half of the land-value ratio is controlled by a handful of large owners (0.8 percent of the active male rural population in both Andalusia and La Mancha; 1.3 percent of that population in Estremadura). For technical reasons that we cannot go into here, economic life in these regions is even more oligarchical than the index suggests.[1] It is safe to assume that immediately prior to the Civil War less than 1 percent of the agricultural population controlled about two-thirds of all agricultural resources in southwestern Spain.

The property structures of each region in turn determine to a large extent its rural class structure. Where small properties flourish, so too do small peasant-proprietors who work their lands with their families; where large estates predominate, there is little land left over for small owners and the biggest social group becomes that of the landless laborers who work the large estates. The only indeterminate group is that composed of tenant farmers and sharecroppers, who may appear within either a small-scale or a large-scale property system.

As can be seen from the fourth and fifth columns of Table I, the correlation between property and class is almost perfect in Spain. The Atlantic littoral, where property concentration is least, has the highest proportion of peasant proprietors and the lowest proportion of day laborers in its rural population. Old Castile, another small-property region, constitutes a close second in both categories. Aragon and New Castile once again occupy an intermediate position. In southwestern Spain, home of the large estate, class structure is the reverse of that of the Atlantic littoral and Old Castile, as landless day laborers outnumber peasant proprietors by three to one. The Mediterranean littoral alone fails to show a close correlation, partly because in Catalonia an unusually large number of small properties are tilled by tenant farmers rather than by their owners, and partly because irrigation has made the Levante so exceptionally productive that it can provide employment to numerous day laborers even within a small property system.

Property and class coincide closely. But what does this coincidence mean in the sociopolitical terms that interest us most in this article? Eric Wolf, the anthropologist, has recently advanced a theory based on a study of the Mexican, Russian, Chinese, and Vietnamese experiences that it is the "middle peasants," that is, those who own some land, who are most prone to revolution. This, Wolf hypothesizes, is because such peasants are more affected by the market fluctuations brought about by the commercialization of agriculture, more exposed to ideas of protest through closer ties to the cities, and better able to risk acts of rebellion because of the relative security they enjoy as owners of some land, however small.[2] Wolf's theory may be applicable to Spain in the sense that middle peasants sometimes provided the leadership in local revolts. Most of the evidence we have suggests otherwise,[3] but this is one of the many topics in Spanish history that has not yet been sufficiently studied for anyone to speak with much confidence. Wolf's theory is not applicable to Spain in any other sense, however. Rather, the more sentimental view that revolution is the product of intolerable misery seems closer to the mark. The Atlantic littoral and Old Castile, the strongholds of the middle peasantry, did not take the lead in Spanish rural revolt. Although the accidents of the Civil War have led many observers to assume the contrary, neither did regions like Aragon and New Castile, in which middle peasants were mixed with other rural classes. The birthplace and chief sanctuary of Spanish peasant revolt were Andalusia and Estremadura, precisely those regions in which "low," not "middle," peasants predominated because so much land was monopolized by so few owners.

Why was this so? One exceedingly important reason is the reverse of an argument used by Wolf. The commercialization of agriculture over the past two centuries affected the peasant proprietors of northern Spain far less drastically than it did the landless day laborers of the south. First, many peasant proprietors in the Biscay provinces, Old Castile, and, above all, in Galicia engaged primarily in subsistence farming; their contacts with the market were infrequent, and market fluctuations therefore did not affect them as severely as they would have if their entire livelihood had depended on the sale of crops. Second, because of climatic conditions, there is less crop variety in northern than in southern Spain, The chief marketable crop, particularly in Old Castile, is wheat; this was sold almost entirely in the domestic Spanish market, where it was usually protected against foreign competition by tariffs and import quotas. Third, because few important commercial possibilities existed, a kind of medieval peasant democracy persisted into the capitalist era; few men could rise significantly above their fellows, and village common lands survived in greater quantities than in the south because there was nobody powerful enough to appropriate them.

The opposite was true for the southern day laborer. The large estates on which he worked depended almost entirely on the sale of their produce and provided employment in direct proportion to their success in satisfying this purpose. Since more varieties of crops are grown in the south, and most of them did not enjoy protected domestic markets, a bad year could result if prices or production fell in any one of them. Because there were so many economically powerful owners seeking to add to their possessions, village commons practically disappeared.[4] Nor did the day laborer have any resources to fall back on in time of emergency since he possessed no property. He was entirely at the mercy of his masters and of the market that they, in their turn, served.

Yet it would be a mistake to make an abstraction and hold "commercialization of agriculture" responsible for the unique misery of the southern day laborer's life. As important as commercialization itself was the fact that it did not go far enough. This can be seen by comparing the lot of the southern day laborer with that of his counterpart in the Levante, the other main region where landless laborers were especially numerous. It was not the fact that the Levante laborer usually served smaller property owners that made the difference; as many recent studies of industrialization have proven, small employers may be considerably more rapacious than are large precisely because of the paucity of their reserves and the consequent precariousness of their position. Rather, partly because of extensive irrigation, partly because of climate, and partly because of a more highly developed entrepreneurial tradition, agriculture in the Levante was more completely and effectively commercialized than in Andalusia. The day laborer there could find more diversified and continuous employment than in the south. Consequently, although he was by no means immune to revolutionary yearnings, he never showed as great a propensity toward protest as his southern counterpart did.

A second important reason for the difference in revolutionary orientation of various regions in Spain is related somewhat less directly to rural class structure. As can be seen in the first column of Table II, where I have summarized the population growth of *nonindustrialized* Spain during the crucial period from 1860 to 1930, each region underwent a quite distinct demographic evolution. The small and intermediate property regions seem to show no consistent pattern at first glance. The population of rural Catalonia and of the north central region grew at an exceedingly slow rate, that of the Atlantic littoral somewhat faster, and that of the Mediterranean littoral faster still. Yet on closer examination, two patterns emerge. First, despite the differences among them, the small property zones all increased their populations much more slowly than southwestern Spain did.[5] Second, the slower growth was due mainly to conscious choices made by the peasant proprietors and small tenant-farmers who predominated in those regions. In north central Spain and rural Catalonia, peasants followed the practice of their counterparts in France during the same period and deliberately limited the size of their families to prevent their small properties from excessive fragmentation. In Galicia, where severe overpopulation already

TABLE II. SOCIAL INDICATORS
IN NONINDUSTRIALIZED SPAIN

Region	Percentage of Population Growth, 1860–1930	Infant Mortality Rate, 1920 (Per 1,000 Live Births)	Illiteracy Rate, 1920 (Percentage of Total Population)	Estimated Percentage, Rural Males, Anarchist or Socialist Unions, c. 1932
Atlantic littoral	*29.5*	*102*	*48.8*	*2.6*
Galicia	24.0	103	56.3	2.9
Rural Biscay provinces	38.1	100	38.2	2.0
Mediterranean littoral	*32.7*	*101*	*57.7*	*11.3*
Rural Catalonia	4.5	76	44.4	5.7
Levante	46.2	106	62.6	13.5
North Central Spain	*16.9*	*139*	*43.6*	*12.0*
Old Castile	17.2	144	36.8	8.9
Rural New Castile	18.2	152	56.3	18.2
Aragon-Ebro	15.9	118	50.1	13.4
Subtotals: small and intermediate property regions:	*28.9*	*118*	*50.1*	*8.0*
Southwestern Spain	*60.6*	*133*	*64.5*	*22.9*
La Mancha	68.8	132	67.1	24.8
Estremadura	55.3	156	58.6	21.1
Andalusia	60.2	125	65.8	22.9
Nonindustrialized Spain as a whole	*38.8*	*125*	*55.7*	*13.2*

Note: Since urbanized areas differed so strikingly from rural, I have not included in my calculations for the first three columns the four heavily industrialized provinces of Barcelona (Catalonia), Madrid (New Castile), and Guipúzcoa and Viscaya (Biscay provinces).

existed because of excessive population growth in the seventeenth and eighteenth centuries, massive emigration to other parts of Spain and abroad prevented social pressures from increasing. In southwestern Spain, the day laborers who constituted the bulk of the population did not employ either of these defences. Family planning and emigration were exceptional practices, not the rule. Whether this was caused by the crushing of the human spirit and the ignorance that the large-property system produced, or whether it served as an unconscious psychological means of protest against that system, we do not know. What is important for our present purposes is that population in southwestern Spain grew at *more than double* the rate of the three other principal regions combined (60.6 percent as against 28.9 percent). Since economic growth in southwestern Spain did not keep pace (in contrast to what happened in the Biscay provinces and the Levante, the only other areas that even remotely approached the southern population rise), the pressure of people on the land constantly increased.

With high population growth added to the monopolization of most economic resources by a tiny oligarchy, great poverty for the majority of the population was the inevitable result. The wages paid southern day laborers were always considerably below those paid either to urban workers or to day laborers in the Levante. So far as it can be determined, the average annual income of the southern peasantry as a whole was also considerably below the average for the small and intermediate property regions. As can be seen in the second column of Table II, the south also lagged tragically far behind the average for the small-property regions in one of the most significant of all social indicators, the infant mortality rate. Some 13 percent more children died in their first year of life in the Southwest than in the rest of nonindustrialized Spain on the average.

Yet material poverty alone does not explain the revolutionary orientation of the southern peasant. As can be seen in Table II, infant mortality in Old Castile, a bastion of peasant conservatism, far exceeded that of most of southwestern Spain. Because of severe overpopulation in Galicia, it also seems likely that peasants in that small-holding region had to survive on even lower incomes than southern day laborers did; the same may be true for portions of Old Castile, because of poor agricultural conditions.[6] Within southwestern Spain itself, it was not the poorest regions, Estremadura and La Mancha, that were the most rebellious, but the richest, Andalusia.

As important as material poverty were the psychological grievances felt by the southern rural population. These grievances were more quickly and acutely experienced than they might otherwise have been because of the greater-than-average proximity of many southern peasants to cities that had developed revolutionary traditions of their own. Such proximity seems to act as a catalyst in all peasant societies, as Wolf noted. In Spain, it is one of the several reasons why Andalusia became revolutionary sooner than Estremadura and La Mancha, and helps explain why Old Castile remained even more conservative than one would expect on the basis of the social indicators we have been discussing. Yet, as proven by the relative conservatism of the peasantry in the two most industrialized regions of Spain, Catalonia and the Basque provinces, cities do not act as catalysts of rural rebellion unless the surrounding peasantry has already developed reasons of its own for protesting.

The sources of the psychological grievances *independently* experienced by the southern peasant were many and diverse. At their core lay the fact that he lacked the security and sense of independence that the northern peasant proprietor gained from his small plot, or that most northern tenant farmers obtained from the long-term leases under which they worked the land. The southern peasant, whether day laborer or tenant farmer, was at the mercy of the economic oligarchy that ruled his village. Employment was uncertain, and to obtain it the worker had to move from farm to farm. Wages were low and hours long because so many persons competed for the same jobs. Normal trade-union tactics like the strike were ineffective because there were so many migrant laborers who could be used as strikebreakers, because agriculture is more flexible in its productive processes than industry and permits owners to dispense with many nonessential tasks rather than give in to striker demands, and because the monetary reserves of the workers were so scant that they could not afford the luxury of long walkouts. Moreover, because of the seasonal nature of agricultural production, even should a strike be won, the gains could be enjoyed for a short time only; when the next agricultural season rolled around, the same battles would have to be fought all over again.

Because of social inequalities, the constant movement in search of jobs, and the lack of any property to which to root oneself, community life as it functioned in northern Spain also had little parallel in the south. We have already noted how southern villages were powerless to stop the almost complete destruction of their common lands, whereas villages elsewhere managed to retain considerable portions of them. Another indication of the weakness of southern community life appears in the illiteracy figures presented in Table II. Except for the Levante, where day laborers also abounded, illiteracy in southwestern Spain far exceeded that of any small-holding region. In comparison with illiteracy in Old Castile, the largest and politically probably the most important of the small-holding regions, the southern rate was more than double.

To some degree, the discrepancies in the illiteracy rates also reveal the different role played in each region by the Church, probably the chief agency of community in traditional Spanish rural society. Illiteracy was especially rife in the southwest partly because the Church there did not fill in the educational gap left by the sluggish Spanish state to the degree that it did in regions like Old Castile. The Church also remained an active force in the daily life of the peasants of Old Castile and the Basque provinces in that it organized a vast network of cooperatives, credit funds, and insurance programs to help protect them against economic vicissitudes. In Andalusia, Estremadura and La Mancha, whose rural populations had been rendered rootless by the large property system under which they lived, such institutions were exceedingly rare. On several occasions, liberal Catholics attempted to organize them, but since Catholic emphasis on class reconciliation was at variance with the profound class divisions that existed, at best they were disregarded by the southern peasants and at worst earned their enmity. Consequently, a cultural gap also separated segments of the Spanish peasantry; in several important northern regions, the rural population was extremely pious; in the southwest, anticlericalism was a powerful force.

To fill the social void and express the grievances of the southern peasants, philosophies of life other than Catholicism were necessary. These began to appear in the 1870s, when anarchism first gained a foothold in Spain. Its growth during the next half century closely followed the pattern we would expect from the regional property and class analysis we have just completed. Rural anarchism first took hold in Cadiz and Seville, provinces where property was especially heavily concentrated, day laborers were particularly numerous, agriculture was unusually commercialized, and large cities existed to serve as catalysts. In the anarchist federation of the early 1870s, most of the rural locals founded were either in these two provinces or in the Catalan countryside surrounding Barcelona, Spain's most industrial city. By the early 1880s, when a new anarchist federation was established, the Catalan peasants had permanently abandoned the anarchists; by contrast, the anarchist peasant following had increased in Cadiz and Seville and had spread to Malaga, another Andalusian province containing a large port city. By 1903, anarchism had become a significant force in Cordoba, still another Andalusian province. At about the same time, the Socialists, who had failed dismally to establish themselves among the peasant proprietors of the Biscay coast, where their industrial unions were then concentrated, began to find more fertile ground for rural recruitment in Estremadura, La Mancha, and the northern and eastern fringes of Andalusia.

In the decade after 1910, working-class movements made their first real gains outside the large-property region of southwestern Spain as the anarchists increased their followers in the Levante, where day laborers were numerous, and (to a lesser extent) in Aragon, an intermediate property region. This early phase of development reached its culmination during the "Bolshevik triennium" of 1917 to 1920, when peasant strikes without precedent swept Spain in the immediate aftermath of the First World War. Both anarchists and Socialists strengthened their positions, and the main regional divisions that would carry over into the Spanish Republic of the 1930s were clearly laid out. As can be seen from the last column of Table II, where anarchist and socialist peasant membership circa 1932 is presented as a percentage of the male rural population in each region, three quite distinct rural Spains had emerged. Most of northern Spain remained untouched by the working-class movements and was politically conservative. A large proportion of the population in southwestern Spain had joined the movements and was inclined toward revolution. Aragon, New Castile, and the Levante were in an intermediate position.

These divisions, of course, are crude ones; we do not have the space to go into the many local variations that existed. In particular, Galicia, because of severe overpopulation and the complex *foro* problem, and Catalonia, because of the even more complicated *rabassaire* controversy, form special cases.[7] The same is true of peasants in the Biscay province of

Navarre, among whom Carlism, a radical rightist mass movement that had plunged Spain into civil war from 1833 to 1840 and again from 1873 to 1876, continued to exert a lingering influence. Yet the central fact I have been attempting to establish is quite clear. There was no true majority group and little homogeneity among the Spanish peasantry. Rather, Spain was divided into at least three main political segments, chiefly according to the property and class structures that prevailed in each region.

II

The Spanish peasantry had engaged in many isolated acts of rebellion since the early nineteenth century, but had never launched a revolution. There was nothing in its history like the "great fear" of 1789 in France, the peasant rising in Austrian Galicia in 1843, the Rumanian *jacquerie* of 1907, or peasant participation in the Russian revolutions of 1905 and 1917. Nor did any leftist rising receive rural support remotely comparable to that given by the northern peasantry to the reactionary Carlist movement in the 1830s and 1870s. To be sure, acts of rebellion had become more frequent over time, and the wave of peasant strikes during the "Bolshevik triennium" had seriously upset social and economic life in Andalusia. But no overwhelming tide of peasant revolution had gathered force at the time of the establishment of the Spanish Republic in 1931. The Bourbon monarchy was overthrown in municipal elections held in April of that year primarily on the strength of urban votes and out of fear of urban risings. The peasantry played practically no part in this process. Republican majorities were much smaller in the rural than in the urban balloting; the changeover of political regimes was not accompanied by the takeover of villages by excited peasant groups; the first attempt to seize land did not occur until a month after the elections. Nevertheless, the Provisional Government, which exercised power from April until July 1931, immediately committed the Republic to carrying out an agrarian reform for three central reasons. First, land reform had gained respectability as a goal even among the middle-class Republican parties because of the writings of certain intellectuals and because it was considered part of the general Republican effort to "regenerate" Spain. Second, the Socialist party, a principal component of the Republican coalition, was trying to recruit the peasantry, and demanded reform as the price of its continued collaboration. Finally, although no peasant revolt had yet occurred, the Republican coalition feared that the Anarchosyndicalist CNT (Confederación Nacional de Trabajo), up to this time by far the most powerful peasant union, would soon succeed in organizing one as part of its struggle to overthrow the Republic and establish a new anarchist society. Thus, out of a combination of idealism and fear, the Republic set out to solve Spain's chief social problem by legal means.

During the first two months, rapid progress seemed to be made. Although the Provisional Government, because of its commitment to democratic procedure, decided to postpone resolution of the central issue of land redistribution until a parliament could be elected, it introduced an unprecedented amount of legislation in favor of the peasantry by means of decrees. Tenant farmers benefited considerably when existing leases were frozen at existing rents to prevent mass evictions by owners who feared application of the reform to their lands. The position of day laborers improved even more because of two key edicts. One, the municipal labor decree, laid the basis for an increase in wages and the development of strong peasant unions by proclaiming, in effect, a closed shop in each of Spain's 9,000 rural municipalities. The second decree, which created arbitration boards to handle rural labor disputes, had similar effects. Because the balance of power on the boards was held by appointees of the Socialist-controlled Ministry of Labor, they usually favored workers' demands for higher wages; because labor unions were alloted permanent seats on the boards, unionization of the countryside was further encouraged. As a result of these two edicts, farm wages rose by an average of perhaps 40 percent during the first year of the Republic and almost doubled during the first two years. Similarly, peasant membership within the Socialist union, the UGT (Unión General del Trabajo), increased approximately tenfold between April 1931 and June 1932; by June 1933, the UGT had almost half a million peasant members.

Ironically, however, the extraordinary success of these early edicts ultimately handicapped the enactment of a truly radical program of land redistribution. On the one hand, it intensified the already basically reformist orientation of the Socialists and caused them to rely almost exclusively on traditional parliamentary and political maneuvering rather than on mass demonstrations and strikes by the peasantry. Even more significant, the concessions made by the decrees seem to have reinforced the nonrevolutionary mood that had characterized the peasantry during the overthrow of the monarchy. Although the Anarchosyndicalist CNT expanded its rural membership somewhat and tiny Communist locals were established in a few scattered villages, the gains of these revolutionary organizations were insignificant in comparison to those made by the reformist UGT, which quickly replaced the CNT as by far the largest peasant union. The effective power of the CNT even in its traditional stronghold of lower Andalusia was laid open to question in July 1931, when it failed to recruit peasant support for a general strike in the city of Seville. Although there were several village upheavals in the mountainous regions of Andalusia in the late summer and early fall, these did not develop into the general rising the Republicans had so feared when they first assumed power. With the failure of the threat of rural revolution to materialize, the excessive fears of the Republicans were gradually replaced by excessive confidence in the essential tractability of the southern peasantry.

The inaction of the peasantry during the first months of the Republic, when the political situation was most fluid, weakened one of the main pressures on the new regime for decisive agrarian reform. The self-satisfaction of the Socialists with the apparent effectiveness of their reformism weakened another. The widening of the political arena that occurred with the election of the first Republican parliament, or Cortes, further diluted the impetus of the early months. Only a few rightist deputies were elected, but since strong center parties were established and political power became far more dispersed than it had been so long as it remained with the handful of men who made up the Provisional Government, the political situation was transformed. Moreover, the elections gave new proofs of the lack of homogeneity of the Spanish peasantry. Although peasants in southwestern Spain voted for the Socialists in sufficient numbers to establish them as the largest single party, the rightist deputies were elected almost entirely by the small peasant proprietors of Old Castile and Navarre, while the center groups owed their victories in great part to the rural vote in the intermediate-property regions.

Under these circumstances, parliamentary debate on land redistribution bogged down almost immediately. Four major bills and several minor ones were presented to the Cortes but none could generate enough support to have any hope of approval. Nor did the situation improve significantly after the Republic took an apparent step leftward in December through the formation under Manuel Azaña, a middle-class intellectual, of a coalition between the left Republican parties and the Socialists. The left Republicans were far more radical in their anticlericalism and their concern for the regional autonomy of Catalonia than in their social policies, while the Socialists did not enjoy as much leverage over them as they otherwise might have because there was no other group with whom the Socialists could ally to maintain the cabinet positions to which they had increasingly become addicted. Consequently, the new coalition could not agree on a land redistribution bill to present to the Cortes until late March 1932. And once debate on that bill began in early May, the left Republicans were so passive in defending it that debate could be obstructed for three months by the determined opposition of the handful of rightist deputies elected from Old Castile, and by the technical objections of the larger center groups. Thus, by August, instead of the prompt breakup of the large estates that had been expected when the Republic was proclaimed, almost a year and half had passed in complicated but ineffective maneuvering.

The parliamentary stalemate was not ended by peasant action. A gruesome incident that occurred at the turn of the year in Castilblanco, a village in Estremadura where peasants massacred four civil guards, had stirred only a momentary outcry. New CNT efforts to rouse the Andalusian peasantry through provincewide work stoppages in Seville in May and June were easily crushed by government repression. The number of agricultural strikes in 1932 doubled over the previous year, but none was of sufficient magnitude to sway parliament or the Azaña government. The stalemate was broken, rather, by General Sanjurjo's ludicrously ill-planned attempt at a coup on August 10, 1932. Although rapidly defeated, the military rising temporarily served to revive middle-class radicalism both within the Azaña coalition and among the center parties that had helped bring the Republic into being. Within a month, the land redistribution bill had become law and the Institute of Agrarian Reform was established soon afterward to carry it out. In November, as will be explained in greater detail shortly, the Azaña government anticipated some of the provisions of the law by passing out land on a temporary basis to approximately 40,000 peasants in Estremadura under the "Intensification of Cultivation" decrees.

It would be wonderful to be able to record that this turn of events proved permanent and the Azaña coalition went on to redistribute land at a sufficiently rapid rate to satisfy the Republican dream that "a profound transformation of society could be accomplished" by legal means so as to spare Spain "the horrors of social revolution."[8] Unfortunately, fundamental attitudes require a more profound shock than one such as that provided by the Sanjurjo revolt before they can change, and complex problems do not lend themselves to easy solutions. The impetus toward reform had once again been dissipated by the spring of 1933, and governmental paralysis when dealing with agrarian affairs became even more complete than it had been immediately prior to the Sanjurjo revolt. The reasons for this renewed failure are manifold. They include the incompetence of Marcelino Domingo, the left Republican leader entrusted with implementation of the reform, the higher priority Azaña placed on a balanced budget and further anticlerical legislation, the reluctance of the great Spanish private banks to help finance land redistribution, the continued lack of leverage of the Socialist ministers because of their refusal to contemplate abandonment of the coalition, and the general Republican obsession with time-consuming legalistic procedures. What interests us most in this article, however, is the way in which the heterogeneity of the Spanish peasantry in itself affected the fate of the Azaña government's agrarian program.

The main beneficiaries of the Republic's legislation as of 1933 were the day laborers, who constituted a major proportion of the rural population only in southwestern Spain and to a lesser degree in the Levante. Nevertheless, even this class had not been won over completely to the Republic. This was partly because the Agrarian Reform Law of September 1932 had been so long delayed and was implemented so slowly that little land had actually been transferred under it. The tenacious hold that the Anarchosyndicalists retained over certain localities in lower Andalusia also contributed to the Republic's failure to take root among the day laborers. Probably more important than either of these factors, however, were the contradictory effects produced by the eminently successful Provisional Government decrees to increase rural wages and encourage unionization. The doubling

of farm wages between 1931 and 1933 in a depression period when the price
of farm produce was falling created a profound economic contradiction
that farm owners resolved by dispensing with many marginal tasks and
hiring fewer laborers. Consequently, the higher wages day laborers earned
when they could find jobs were in large part nullified by longer periods of
unemployment. Union members were especially affected since farm owners
preferred to hire the more docile unorganized workers. Protests against
unemployment and demands that job discrimination be stopped by re-
quiring owners to hire workers in the order of their registration with the
local unemployment offices mounted as a result, particularly among the
Socialist unions that encompassed the largest number of day laborers and,
unlike the Anarchist unions, still hoped to be able to work within the
system. The deterioration of conditions was reflected in a huge increase of
agricultural strikes; these once more doubled in 1933 to become more than
four times as numerous as they had been when the Republic was established
in 1931.

Ineffective though pay raises and unionization had been in securing
the firm support of the day laborers, they nevertheless helped estrange from
the Republic many small proprietors and tenant farmers, both in southwestern Spain and in other regions. Although often primarily subsistence
farmers, both of these occupational groups employed a certain amount of
labor at peak periods of the year and sold some of their produce on the
market. The wage gains made by the day laborers therefore reduced their
profit margins, which had always been small and were in any case falling
because of the decline in agricultural prices. This source of conflict among
major sectors of the peasantry became particularly acute after the autumn
of 1932 when a bumper wheat crop, the largest in Spanish history, caused
a sharp drop in the price of by far the most important agricultural product.
The tenant farmers and sharecroppers might have maintained their faith
in the Republic despite this crisis had the early promises to give them
possession of the land they leased been carried out. But attention had come
to be concentrated so exclusively on the day laborers and the breakup of
the large estates of southwestern Spain that their interests had been mostly
ignored.

This combination of factors contributed to the development of two
separate tendencies in the Spanish countryside by 1933. On the one hand,
many peasants, particularly in southwestern Spain, became far more radicalized than before. This radicalization manifested itself in the huge rise in
strikes mentioned earlier, in somewhat greater peasant participation in the
two Anarchosyndicalist attempts at revolt that occurred in 1933, in an increased number of farm invasions and violent local conflicts, and in the
greater rebelliousness of Socialist local unions. Particularly important was
the radicalization of the *yunteros* of Estremadura, a unique group that was
something of a cross between impoverished tenant farmers, in that it cul-

tivated land more or less independently, and day laborers, in that the land tilled changed yearly and there was no security of tenure whatsoever. Owner attempts to deny the *yunteros* land in the fall of 1932 had provoked local disturbances and the Intensification of Cultivation decrees mentioned earlier. A new and greater wave of *yuntero* farm invasions in January and February 1933 caused amplification of the decrees, so that a total of 40,000 peasants were temporarily settled under them. Although social tensions in Estremadura diminished subsequently, this Socialist stronghold never recovered its always fragile equilibrium.

On the other hand, a strong countercurrent toward greater conservatism also appeared, not only in Old Castile and Navarre, but in several of the intermediate property regions as well. Carlism, long quiescent in Navarre, began to re-emerge as a militant force in 1933. Municipal elections held in 2,653 rural townships of Old Castile, New Castile and Aragon, which contained perhaps a fifth of the total Spanish peasantry, resulted in a resounding defeat for the Azaña government and a huge increase in the vote for center and rightist candidates. During the summer and fall of 1933, the newly created Catholic conservative party, the CEDA, attracted hundreds of thousands of peasants to its organizational rallies in such widely scattered regions as Old Castile and the Levante.

The Azaña coalition began to fall apart under the strain of these contradictory pressures. Segments of it, particularly within the Socialist party, wanted to cast aside legalistic procedures and implement the agrarian reform in a radical fashion. Other important segments advocated left Republican abandonment of the Socialists, alliance with the center groups that had remained outside the coalition, and reversal of the agrarian reform so that it would primarily benefit the small proprietors and tenant farmers rather than the day laborers. Support for the coalition also began to disintegrate in the country at large as rural disorders mounted. The most decisive single blow to government prestige was undoubtedly the massacre by state police of twenty peasants in Casas Viejas, one of the dozen or so Andalusian villages that had supported the January 1933 CNT attempt at a national uprising. But the cumulative effect of the government's inability to control the hundreds of minor incidents that occurred throughout the year was also a factor in lowering its reputation to the nadir to which it had fallen by the autumn of 1933, when the president of the Republic decided that new parliamentary elections had become mandatory. The Azaña coalition's noble hope to restructure rural society by democratic means through legislative action had been frustrated by its own timidity, mistaken priorities, and technical incompetence. But the complex and contradictory interests of the Spanish peasantry had also contributed to the failure.

The Azaña parties were routed in the November 1933 elections for two fundamental reasons. First, the radicalization of the rank and file Socialist membership had finally begun to influence the national party leadership and resulted in a Socialist refusal to form electoral alliances with the left Republicans. This meant sacrificing the extra Cortes seats that the electoral law (drafted by the Azaña coalition itself) awarded to large electoral blocs. Second, although the Socialist and left Republican vote in the cities remained more or less steady in comparison to 1931, it dropped significantly in all rural areas. The Anarchosyndicalist boycott of the elections was responsible only to a minor degree, since the CNT at this time was primarily urban based. Far more important was the opposition that agrarian reform had aroused among small proprietors and many tenant farmers, and the disillusionment it had engendered among day laborers. The national left Republican parties were practically wiped out, dropping from slightly more than 100 to 13 Cortes seats. Somewhat more fortunate was the Catalan left Republican party, the Esquerra, which retained 20 of its 32 seats because of regional loyalties and its closer ties to the *rabassaires*, the predominant Catalan peasant group. The Socialists also fared a bit better because of their union following, but their parliamentary delegation was nevertheless halved, from 117 to 59 seats. The rural backlash affected them with special severity. While the number of Socialist deputies from the five most indutrialized provinces in which the party was represented rose from 18 to 19, despite the lack of electoral coalitions with the left Republicans, in its seven most important rural strongholds (all of which were in southwestern Spain) it fell from 44 to 14.

The elections were won by the center parties, which picked up many of their votes among the disillusioned peasants of southwestern Spain and the Levante, and the right, whose greatest successes were registered among the peasant proprietors of Old Castile, Galicia, the Biscay provinces and Aragon. Leadership of the government was assumed by the largest center party, the "Radicals," but it was forced to rely on the acquiescense of the slightly more numerous Catholic CEDA for its parliamentary majority. The alliance between these two parties was an uneasy one. The Radicals were a nonideological, basically opportunistic group that did not seek totally to reverse the liberal orientation the Provisional Government (of which the Radicals had formed part) and Azaña had given the Republic; the CEDA, though primarily rightist, contained within it social Catholic deputies who dreamed of carrying out humanitarian reforms of their own. At the outset the Radicals wielded more power since leftist deputies still constituted about a fourth of the Cortes and the CEDA was excluded from the cabinet as a gesture of appeasement toward leftist sensibilities. Although it was not likely that cabinet exclusion of the CEDA could long be maintained since it was the largest single party, the new parliamentary constellation was so diffuse as to make it probable that the Republic was about to settle down into a relatively uneventful mediocrity in which there would be no great new initiatives and a few of the changes wrought earlier would be abandoned, but in which no important assault on the Azaña heritage could be

launched. Developments in the Socialist party and the autonomous region of Catalonia changed all this. In both sets of developments the agrarian question played a principal role.

The disastrous election results of November intensified the radicalization of the Socialist party. Although many moderates associated with Julián Besteiro resisted the new drift, they were ousted from their posts in the UGT union hierarchy in January 1934 by followers of Francisco Largo Caballero, the Minister of Labor during the Azaña period who had abandoned his earlier reformism and emerged as leader of the militant cause. Indalecio Prieto, the third principal Socialist chief, supported Caballero, though it was probably partly due to his restraining influence that the change in Socialist policy was not more immediate and complete. Simply stated, the Socialists disavowed their past reformism, determined to rely on mass action rather than parliamentary negotiations to achieve their ends, repeatedly threatened to launch a revolution if pressed too hard, and specifically demanded the permanent exclusion of the CEDA from the government on the grounds that it was a fascist party whose leader, José María Gil Robles, would destroy democracy in Spain as Hitler and Dollfuss had done in Germany and Austria a short time previously. Although the Socialist threats remained primarily verbal in nature, there was secret arming of party militants. The Socialists also sought alliances with the Anarchosyndicalists and other, smaller labor groups, but these bore fruit only in a few regions because the CNT usually refused to collaborate with persons it had come to regard during the Azaña era as traitors to the workers' cause.

The first important application of the new Socialist policies was made by the peasant federation of the UGT, out of a mixture of defensive and aggressive motives. The federation was by far the largest socialist union, with over 40 percent of total UGT membership. Its new leaders were particularly militant young men who convinced themselves that they held irresistible power in that they could stop harvesting of the wheat crop, without which Spain would starve, by calling a nationwide strike of their nearly half-million followers. Provocation for such action seemed present in that the agricultural workers, who had made the greatest gains under Azaña, now bore the brunt of the limited reaction that was instituted by the new government. Land redistribution, although not halted by the center-right coalition, was being carried out at the same snail's pace as under Azaña; farm wages had fallen somewhat as landowners sought to recover their losses of the previous two years and the Socialist appointees who had controlled the rural arbitration boards were replaced; most important of all, the Municipal Labor Act, which all other groups (including the left Republicans and Anarchosyndicalists) detested for its inequities but which the Socialists regarded as the indispensable basis for the survival of their rural unions, was repealed by the Cortes in May 1934.

Amid much haste and confusion, the leadership of the UGT peasant federation called the national harvest strike on June 5. Their decision accurately reflected peasant opinion to a far greater extent than the three recent Anarchosyndicalist calls to revolution had, since in contrast to the support from a handful of villages that the CNT was customarily able to muster, strikes were declared in 1,563 villages, approximately four-fifths of them in southwestern Spain. Yet the strike was doomed from the start. Strikes were proclaimed in 1,563 villages, but there were another 7,500 in which either the UGT local refused to follow the lead of the national federation or no local existed. Moreover, the strike call could be enforced in only 435 villages; elsewhere, Socialist militants were either too weak or unenthusiastic to prevent work from proceeding. The UGT industrial unions offered only verbal support, and did not order sympathetic walkouts. Finally, non-Socialists opposed the strike almost unanimously because of the fear loss of the wheat harvest had engendered[9] and because the UGT, in its attempt to make the strike total, tried to prevent even those small peasants and tenant farmers who did not employ outside labor from collecting their crops.

The result was catastrophic. Although strikes continued in some villages for as long as fifteen days, the main struggle was over within a week. The chief consequence of this gamble on which so much had been staked was a drastic weakening of the UGT peasant federation. Local police closed union headquarters and arrested peasant leaders wherever they could do so without excessive adverse publicity; members abandoned the federation by the tens of thousands out of disillusionment and also fear of economic reprisals from the triumphant farm owners. The full extent of the disaster became apparent only in October, however, when the Socialists launched their long-threatened revolution in response to the government's decision to grant three of the fourteen cabinet seats to the CEDA. The revolution failed miserably everywhere except in the coal-mining region of Asturias, the only place where an effective workers' alliance among Socialists, Anarchosyndicalists and Communists had been forged. The failure was particularly great in the rural areas that had formerly provided the UGT with its greatest number of followers. Because peasant strength had been uselessly squandered in the June strike, no more than a handful of villages supported the October revolution.

The other principal remaining source of strength of the Spanish left after the November 1933 elections, the Esquerra-controlled autonomous government of Catalonia, also collapsed in the October 1934 revolution. In Catalonia, where small properties predominated, the chief dissatisfied rural class consisted of tenants and sharecroppers called *rabassaires*, who although they enjoyed a prosperity and security of tenure that would have been the envy of Spanish peasants elsewhere, felt that the landowners had begun to encroach on their rights and demanded that they be forced to sell them the land on favorable terms. The conflict was therefore one between two more or less "bourgeois" groups, not one of the truly impoverished against the excessively wealthy as in most of the rest of Spain. Precisely because they were not proletarians, the *rabassaires* did not join either the Anarchosyndicalist or Socialist unions, but constituted a mainstay of support for the left Republican Esquerra.

As the national government failed to keep its promise to transfer the land they leased to tenants and sharecroppers, the *rabassaires* began to pressure the regional government to provide such legislation in Catalonia under its own authority. After a series of well-organized demonstrations in 1933, a law was enacted that was to go into effect in April 1934. Opposition groups brought suit before the Spanish equivalent of the Supreme Court, which struck down the law as unconstitutional. Pressed by the *rabassaires,* the Catalan government threatened to implement the law in defiance of the court ruling. A severe constitutional conflict ensued that continued throughout the summer of 1934 and created the extraordinarily complex set of circumstances that led the Catalan president to take advantage of the crisis produced by the Socialist October revolution to declare Catalan independence from Madrid. The Catalan regional revolt was even more ill-conceived than the workers' revolt to which it attached itself. Lacking armed forces of its own as well as support of the CNT, the strongest urban force in Catalonia, the Catalan government was obliged to surrender within hours, before the few *rabassaires* who tried to come to its aid could reach Barcelona. Regional autonomy was immediately suspended, the Catalan president jailed, and the *rabassaire* legislation, which had never actually been applied, voided.

The October defeats temporarily wrecked the left, but the center-right coalition used its new found power in so shortsighted a fashion that their ultimate effect was to lay the basis for a great leftist revival. Hypocrisy was not the least of the coalition's sins. Having always professed great sympathy for tenant farmers, the coalition subverted an intelligent lease law that Manuel Giménez Fernández, a social Catholic who fought desperately against the reactionary tide while Minister of Agriculture from October 1934 to March 1935, succeeded in pushing through the Cortes. This subversion was accomplished by simultaneously ending the freeze on leases and rents that the Provisional Government had instituted, thus permitting landowners to carry out mass evictions and rent hikes during the transitional period before the new law came into effect. Having attacked the September 1932 Agrarian Reform Law as too exclusively favorable to day laborers, the Cortes revised it after Giménez Fernández had been forced out of office in such a way that it stopped land redistribution to the workers without increasing it for the small proprietors and tenants. Since another bumper wheat crop in 1934 brought about a new price crisis, by the end of

1935 the center-right coalition had managed to alienate many of the peasant entrepreneurs who had previously supported it and who it claimed as objects of its special concern.

The day laborers, meanwhile, had been completely alienated. The self-destruction of their unions in June 1934 harvest strike and in the October revolution left them defenseless before the retaliation of the landowners. Since the government did not attempt to fill the power vacuum that had appeared in the countryside by offering the day laborers its protection, their wages fell drastically, often to levels lower than those that had prevailed under the Monarchy. The most radicalized group of all, however, were the *yunteros* of Estremadura. Although Giménez Fernández had been able in November 1934 to secure a one-year extension of the temporary land grants the Azaña government had made to them, this was not renewed in 1935 after he had been forced from office, and *yunteros* by the thousands were thrown off the land they had received.

The price for these several acts of blindness was paid by the coalition in the parliamentary elections of February 1936, elections that could be held because the coalition, although it became reactionary after the October revolution, was never fascist, as is often asserted. Peasant conservatism in Old Castile, Navarre, and much of the rest of northern and central Spain remained sufficiently solid to give the CEDA even more votes than it had received in 1933. But the center groups were nearly wiped out both because of financial scandals in which they had become involved and because the rural vote that had gone to them in the intermediate-property regions and southwestern Spain in 1933 now swung back to the left. Since the left had also sufficiently absorbed the lessons of the 1933 balloting to form an electoral alliance known as the Popular Front, it gathered the premiums awarded by the electoral law to large coalitions and thus secured a much greater parliamentary majority than its popular vote alone would have warranted.

The Popular Front, both prior to and during the Civil War, papered over but did not heal the enmities that had divided the left since 1933. Leftist parties shared a common opposition to the more reactionary elements of the right, but the divisions among them persisted and became more intense with the passage of time. The two main tendencies that existed in the spring and early summer of 1936 were new manifestations of the old division between reformism and revolution. The left Republicans, supported by the moderate wing of the Socialist party now led by Prieto, rejected the excessive legalism and timidity that had hampered the first Azaña government, but still sought to operate within a legal, parliamentary framework. The radical wing of the Socialists under Largo Caballero continued to press a revolutionary course, as well as formation of workers' alliances with the CNT and the small but rapidly growing Communist party. Because the CNT still rejected Caballero's advances, and the Communists (who had previously opposed the Republic even more violently than the CNT) had adopted, with Comintern approval, a policy of overt, though not necessarily genuine or long-lasting, support of the Popular Front, the workers' alliances that were a prerequisite to successful social revolution did not materialize. Nevertheless, the Caballeristas maintained their revolutionary rhetoric, which while never so indiscriminate as that practiced by the Anarchosyndicalists, was indirectly aimed against their nominal Popular Front allies as well as against the center and rightist parties.

The split within the Popular Front was reflected both in Socialist refusal to participate in the cabinet, which had to be staffed entirely by left Republicans, and in constant Caballerista promptings of the working classes to disregard the government and take matters into their own hands. Given the profound radicalization that had occurred during the rightist reaction of 1935 as well as the catastrophic crop losses and increased agricultural unemployment caused by the extraordinarily heavy rains of the winter and early spring of 1936, these promptings did not long go unheeded. The vast expansion of peasant union membership that took place benefited the CNT almost as much as the UGT, brought stronger labor units into existence in intermediate property regions like New Castile, and gained the support of many tenant farmers and poor proprietors as well as day laborers. In late March, a series of small-scale land seizures that the government had tried to head off by a decree authorizing it to turn over to the peasants any farm in Spain it deemed to be of "social utility," reached its culmination in a well-organized seizure of huge quantities of land by some 60,000 *yunteros* and day laborers in Badajoz (Estremadura). Speedier government land grants and the end of the spring planting season prevented, for the time being at least, a repetition elsewhere of the Badajoz experience, but peasant anger began to express itself in other ways. The period from early May, the beginning of the harvest season for crops planted the previous fall, until July 18, the outbreak of the Civil War, witnessed by far the most severe epidemic of agricultural strikes in the history of the Republic. No single strike achieved the proportions of the 1934 Socialist harvest walkout, but a provincewide work stoppage in Malaga (Andalusia) came close, and the cumulative impact of at least 200 other less important walkouts was far greater.

Although sentiment for an open break with the Caballeristas and a crackdown on labor agitation gained strength among many left Republicans (and perhaps even with some members of the Prieto wing of the Socialists), the government continued its desperate efforts to appease the peasantry. During the preceding four years, the Republic had redistributed only about 130,000 hectares to approximately 13,000 peasants, if the temporary land grants to the *yunteros* are left aside. In the six months between the Popular Front elections and the Civil War, something like 900,000 or a million hectares were transferred to some 225,000 peasants. Wages also rose dramatically to exceed by a considerable margin even the high levels they had attained in 1933. Strong measures were instituted by the national government to aid tenant farmers, and by the newly reestablished Catalan government to assist the *rabassaires*. Finally, a previously untouched issue of the greatest importance was opened as the Popular Front government decided to help villages recover the common lands they had lost in the nineteenth-century *desamortización*.

Because there are so many contradictory signs, it is impossible to say with any confidence what would have occurred had events been allowed to play out their course. The Spanish peasantry as a whole had unquestionably become far more radicalized than at any previous time in its history. Nevertheless, the old regional and class divisions continued intact. The revolutionary current clearly predominated only in southwestern Spain. Estremadura had been the sole site of massive land seizures, although some minor ones had also occurred in the provinces of Madrid (New Castile), Toledo (La Mancha), and Murcia (Levante). The great rural strike wave had its center in Andalusia; otherwise, only Estremadura, La Mancha, and the Levante, the other regions in which day laborers were numerous, experienced significant walkouts. The government itself seems to have been concerned primarily with the threat of peasant revolt in southwestern Spain since, to judge from the incomplete information available,[10] 98.8 percent of the land it redistributed in its attempt to calm peasant passions was located in this region.

The other rural areas of Spain were much less agitated. The peasantry of Old Castile and Navarre stayed firmly conservative. Peasants in Galicia seem to have remained isolated in their own little-understood orbit, without obvious signs of either profound conservatism or significant radicalization. The small-property region of the Levante and the intermediate regions of New Castile and Aragon moved to the left, as indicated by a rapid increase in peasant union membership, greater strike activity than before, and occasional small-scale farm seizures. Nevertheless, the shift in these regions was neither so rapid or complete as to warrant the common assumption among later observers that peasant sentiment there had become overwhelmingly revolutionary. As to Catalonia, the *rabassaires*, assured that they would receive property rights to the land they cultivated by the restoration of the Esquerra-controlled regional government, returned to the orderly habits one would expect from such relatively prosperous individuals.

On balance, then, because rural society conditions in Spain had never been so uniformly harsh and unjust as they were in Mexico, Russia, or China on the eves of their revolutions, there was no universal mood of rebellion among the peasantry. To be sure, sufficient militancy existed in enough regions that a nationwide rural rising might have been set off either by a massive revolt among the southwestern peasantry or by revolution among the city workers, who supported the revolutionary labor organizations more unanimously than the peasants did. But it is by no means certain that either of these events would have occurred had not the military insurrection of July 18 taken place, and they probably would easily have been defeated even if they had occurred had not the insurrection removed from government control the traditional instruments of state coercion. So it was above all the generally unsuccessful Nationalist military revolt that provided rural social revolution with its great opportunity.

Briefly freed from the restraints imposed by state power because of the political vacuum created by the military insurrection, peasants throughout Spain were momentarily at liberty to do whatever most accorded with their perceived interests. In Navarre and Old Castile, they flocked to the support of the military insurrection that sought to preserve against leftist encroachments a social and property structure they regarded as favorable. In Galicia they appear to have remained neutral, offering no serious resistance to the military or to local police forces that joined the rising. Aragon suffered a mixed fate that perhaps best exemplifies the general rule that prevailed during these first fatal days, whereby dominion in a region was determined by which side seized control of the large cities in or near it. Even though the upper Ebro river basin included the strongly Anarchosyndicalistic farm area of La Rioja, it fell to the Nationalists almost immediately because it was delimited by the rebel-held provincial capitals of Pamplona, Logroño, Huesca, Teruel and Saragossa. The lower Ebro basin and eastern Aragon, by contrast, were saved for the Republic by CNT columns that streamed out of the nearby metropolis of Barcelona. Along the Mediterranean coast, none of the urban military coups was successful so that the countryside was never given the chance to show the degree to which it would have resisted the Nationalist rebels. The same was true in most of the Biscay provinces, where agriculture was in any case relatively unimportant.[11] The fate of New Castile and Catalonia was also decided almost exclusively by the failure of the military coup in Madrid and Barcelona.

Peasant revolution was a powerful force only in the single great region whose recent history would have led us to expect it, southwestern Spain. None of the provincial capitals in Estremadura or La Mancha fell to the rebels, but the peasants nevertheless displayed their revolutionary spirit by immediately seizing all of the large estates as well as many medium and small properties.[12] In Andalusia, where the military coup succeeded in four of the five most important provincial capitals, the general rule that prevailed in the rest of Spain was broken and peasant revolution nevertheless proceeded. In short, the outbreak of open conflict had not brought about any miracles, unless they were those of the surprisingly effective popular resistance to the coup in such cities as Barcelona and Madrid, and the equally surprising collapse of principal Anarchosyndicalist urban centers like Cadiz, Saragossa, and Seville. The peasants of the various regions continued to display under the new circumstances characteristics similar to those they had been manifesting since the nineteenth century. In south-western Spain they were intensely revolutionary; in Old Castile and Navarre, deeply conservative; and in the rest of the nation, either mixed or neutral.

III

We cannot analyze the role of the peasantry during the Civil War with anything approaching the precision possible for the peacetime Republic because no systematic study of the countryside during the war has yet been made. The printed sources available deal mostly with the conflict that arose between the Communists and the CNT over collectivization in that portion of Aragon that stayed under the Republic; moreover, the information these sources present is highly untrustworthy because it was usually intended to serve polemic ends. A smaller body of literature on the agrarian revolution in Catalonia and the upper Levante suffers from similar defects. Almost nothing has been written on the peasantry either in the rest of Republican Spain or in the Nationalist sector.

We can, however, make a few observations with a fairly high degree of certainty. Perhaps the most fundamental and frequently overlooked fact is that for most of its duration, the Civil War was fought between a primarily urban Republican zone and a predominantly rural Nationalist zone. The Nationalists, not the Republicans, controlled a majority of the peasants for most of the war. Except for the first three and the last two months of the conflict, peasants never constituted even so much as 40 percent of the Republican zone's population.

These assertions are documented in Table III. The percentages listed are only approximate for several reasons, among them the fact that refugees from conquered regions altered to some degree the peacetime occupational

TABLE III. RURAL POPULATION OF THE OPPOSING SIDES DURING THE CIVIL WAR

	Percentage of Peasants in Population of:		Percentage of Total Spanish Peasantry in:	
Period	Republican Zone	Nationalist Zone	Republican Zone	Nationalist Zone
July–Oct. 1936	44.3	56.7	57.6	42.4
Nov. 1936–Feb. 1937	39.1	58.7	40.5	59.5
March–Sept. 1937	37.9	58.4	36.1	63.9
Oct. 1937–June 1938	38.1	56.2	31.7	68.3
July 1938–Jan. 1939	36.0	56.5	27.6	72.4
Feb.–March 1939	44.3	50.3	22.4	77.6

Note: All figures are only approximate. They are calculated on the basis of the 1950 census, since earlier censuses were less detailed and trustworthy and the occupational distribution of the population in 1950 remained practically identical to that of the 1930s.

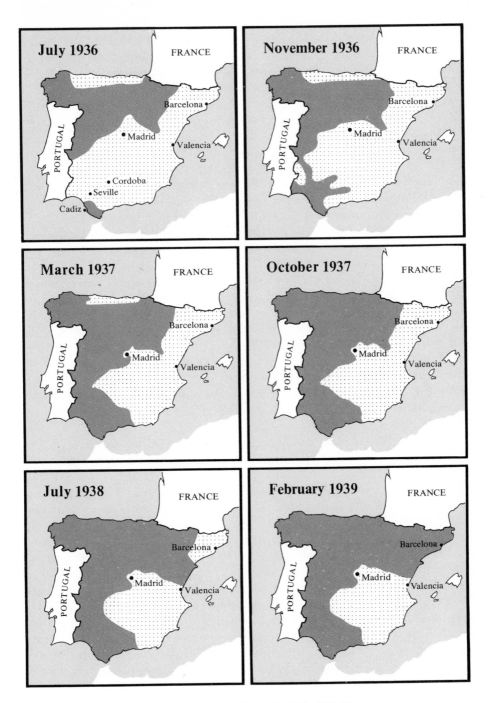

STAGES OF THE CIVIL WAR

Republican Zone   Nationalist Zone

composition of both zones, and minor frontier changes occurred within the major time periods listed. Nevertheless, the main trends shown are indisputable. During the first three months of the war, so long as the Andalusian peasantry maintained its revolution despite the Nationalist seizure of most Andalusian cities, the Republic retained a large rural contingent within its ranks as well as control of a majority of the total Spanish peasantry. However, since the Andalusian peasantry was too disorganized to withstand for long even the minuscule urban columns sent against them, and since the Estremadura peasants collapsed almost immediately once small units of the Nationalist army entered the field in August, this situation had been radically altered by late October, when the Nationalists completed their mopping up operations in Estremadura and western Andalusia.

The successful Republican defense of Madrid temporarily stopped the rebel advance in November. A new equilibrium appeared that survived until February 1937, when southeastern Andalusia fell to a concerted Nationalist drive. From March until September 1937, the rebel army focused its attack on the primarily industrial Biscay provinces, whose gradual conquest caused a slight rise in the proportion of peasants in the Republican zone, though Republican control over the total Spanish peasantry was still further diminished. The new class distribution of the two zones persisted until the next important Nationalist advance from April to July 1938, which split the Republican zone in two by occupying eastern Aragon, parts of rural Catalonia, and the uppermost portion of the Levante. Deprived of an important part of its surviving rural sector, the Republican zone became even more predominantly urban than before.

The rough balance that had maintained itself since November 1936, whereby the peasantry in the Republican zone oscillated between one-third and two-fifths of the population, was more seriously altered in January 1939, when the Nationalists conquered heavily industrial Catalonia. Only then did the Republic, which many observers assume always to have been primarily rural, once again begin to approximate the rural-urban population distribution that was characteristic of Spain at large. But by this time it controlled so small a proportion of Spain's total peasantry that it no longer made any difference.

A second observation about the war that can be made with a high degree of certainty is that nowhere did the peasantry display revolutionary spirit and organization to such an extent that the Nationalists were denied effective use of the human and military resources of the regions they conquered. Even in Andalusia, the Nationalists did not merely neutralize the peasantry when they conquered it, but benefited enormously from the dominion they had gained.

Three points are relevant in this connection. First, unlike what occurred in Algeria, Russia, China, and Vietnam (as well as in Spain itself during the Napoleonic invasion and Carlist wars of the nineteenth century), there was no important peasant guerrilla activity behind Nationalist lines. Spain's human geography and relatively high degree of economic development were no longer conducive to such action. The Nationalists enjoyed sufficient popular support even within Andalusia to prevent the development of that alien "human sea" able to sustain guerrilla bands of which the Chinese Communists speak. Finally, the Nationalists applied a systematic terror that cut off all revolutionary stirrings before they were able to gather force. In consequence, the country which had given the world the word *guerrilla* in the nineteenth century was not able to generate an important guerrilla movement in its civil war of the twentieth century.

If there was no open peasant resistance in the Nationalist zone, neither was there much hidden sabotage. Agricultural production figures from both zones deserve more study than they have thus far received, but it is clear that such production remained at a sufficiently high level in Nationalist Spain not only to maintain an ample food supply (which one would expect since the food-consuming cities mostly had remained with the Republic), but also to accumulate considerable reserves. From all indications, the conquered regions contributed to the food surplus as much as those that had joined the Nationalists from the start.

The peasants also acquiesced to the Nationalist cause in that they supplied it with its primary source of troops. Contrary to common assumptions and to what is occurring in the Vietnamese war, the Spanish Civil War was fought primarily by Spaniards. Foreigners rarely exceeded ten percent of the total troop strength of either side. By the end of the war, the Nationalist army had recruited approximately a million men. A far greater percentage of them were peasants than in the Republican army because the Nationalist zone was more rural and, in contrast to the Republican zone, enjoyed such abundant food supplies that it did not hesitate to draft peasants.[13] Although no figures on the regional distribution of Nationalist recruits are yet available, it seems probable that by at least mid-1937 they were drawn more or less equitably from all regions under rebel control, including Andalusia and Estremadura. Yet, whether because of the popularity of the Nationalist cause among the northern peasants with whom draftees from southwestern Spain were often mixed, or because potential resistance could not become effective under the systematic discipline that was maintained, the Nationalist army was never handicapped by its extensive reliance on persons who earlier presumably had been its enemies. During the entire history of the war, there were no important instances of Nationalist units cracking under pressure or of mass desertions to the Republican side, even along the Andalusian front where desertions would have been particularly easy.

The final important observation I want to make on the war will have to await development in a subsequent article since we are both lacking in space and reaching the limits of my present knowledge. Because of the inability of the Andalusian and Estremadura peasantry to maintain its initially successful revolution, the Republic quickly lost control of most of that single great region, southwestern Spain, where the peasant population was sufficiently homogeneous and the pre-existent property structure so unjust as to make profound agrarian reform both relatively easy and highly desirable. Ironically, the advocates of reform were left primarily with small and intermediate property regions in which the chief victims of any land redistribution could not be tiny groups of excessively wealthy landowners, but large numbers of modest farm owners or operators. The situation was made still more difficult because the Anarchosyndicalists, having finally secured an opportunity to establish their long-awaited new society, abandoned in practice the tolerance toward small-scale agriculture they always professed in theory, and tried to impose a strictly collective solution wherever defeat of the military coup had left them in control.

The magnitude of the problems that confronted the Republic as a result of these two factors can best be illustrated by examining the case of Aragon. This was an intermediate property region, where the land-value index used in Table I to measure land concentration was 30.2 percent, as against 46.2 percent in southwestern Spain and an average of about 20 percent in the small property regions. Day laborers constituted a sixth of the peasant population, but were far outnumbered by small proprietors (38.9 percent) and tenant farmers or sharecroppers (14.5 percent).[14] The peasants were mostly unorganized prior to the war, but approximately 13 to 14 percent of them had joined labor unions, two-fifths of these the Socialist UGT and the remaining three-fifths the Anarchosyndicalist CNT. The CNT was considerably stronger among urban workers, both in Saragossa (where it may have included as much as 25 percent of the population) and in several secondary Aragonese cities. The mixed heritage of Aragon is revealed by the fact that although the unsuccessful December 1933 CNT revolution was centered there and Saragossa was one of the greatest Anarchosyndicalist strongholds, the combined power of the entire left was not sufficient to prevent rightist parties from gaining 17 of Aragon's 28 Cortes seats during the 1936 elections,[15] despite CNT abandonment of its customary electoral boycott and the leftist sweep in much of the rest of Spain.

The political complexion of the region was decisively altered in July 1936 when the rebels immediately took control of western Aragon, including Saragossa and La Rioja, but the CNT nevertheless emerged as the dominant force in eastern Aragon because its militia columns from Barcelona established themselves as the main military force in that area. The ascendancy of CNT was at first reluctantly accepted by the other Republican factions and given official recognition through the creation of an

Anarchist-dominated regional government known as the Council of Aragon. By the spring of 1937, however, the Communist-led drive for a centralization of power and a more thorough militarization of the Republic had gained sufficient support to reverse this early tolerance. After street-fighting in Barcelona and the ouster from office of Largo Caballero (who, though neutral when he became prime minister in September 1936, increasingly favored the CNT against the Communists), the Council of Aragon was dissolved in August 1937, and the CNT-organized collectives that had monopolized Aragonese rural life since the preceding summer were disbanded.

There were several reasons for the CNT-Communist clash, but the one that interests us here is related to agriculture. Basically, the CNT position was that a spontaneous rural revolution had occurred in eastern Aragon in which the peasantry had freely decided to organize itself into collectives. Some peasant proprietors and tenants may have preferred to divide the large estates seized among themselves, the CNT admitted, but the merits of collective farming so quickly became apparent that they changed their minds and accepted not only loss of the extra lands they would have received if property redistribution had proceeded on an individualistic basis, but also incorporation into the collectives of the farms they already held when the war started. The Communist counterargument, which ironically contradicted the position adopted during the collectivization drive in Russia a few years earlier, was that the Aragonese peasantry vastly preferred an individualistic land reform and had been forced into the collectives only because of early CNT military domination of the region.

Some evidence can be found in support of the CNT stance. This includes a set of statistics that shows a considerable rise in Aragonese wheat production during the year of collectivization,[16] and the subsequent admission by a Communist official that the decollectivization had been "a very grave mistake . . . [because it enabled peasants] who were discontented with the collectives . . . [to take] them by assault, carrying away and dividing up the harvest and farm implements, without respecting those collectives that had been formed without violence or pressure, that were prosperous, and were a model of organization. . . ."[17] There is also some truth in the Anarchist contention (strongly supported by the Caballero Socialists who ran the UGT peasant federation) that Communist agrarian policy was influenced by the fact that, having been by far the smallest of the worker organizations prior to the war, the Communists now sought to create a mass following by catering to the individualistically oriented peasant proprietors and tenants. Finally, the Anarchists assert that the unpopularity of decollectivization was proven during the following year, when the Nationalists were able to conquer eastern Aragon with little effort because the morale of the peasantry had sunk so low.[18]

Nevertheless, the Communist position, shared by the Prieto Socialists and the left Republicans, was probably more accurate. The CNT prior to the war had been the most important worker organization in Aragon, but its strength lay mainly in the cities. If peasant acceptance of the CNT was indeed voluntary, why had not more of them joined it in peacetime? The wheat production statistics mentioned above are not entirely trustworthy, and even if correct, may reflect unusually favorable climatic conditions rather than peasant enthusiasm for the collectives since they are for only one year.[19] The collapse of the Aragon front in April and May 1938 proves nothing, since collectivized Estremadura and Andalusia had fallen as rapidly to much weaker Nationalist forces in August and September 1936. The Communists, as the most Machiavellian of all modern political forces, may indeed have had ulterior motives in pursuing decollectivization, but this argument misses the point that their policies would have been unsuccessful had they not corresponded to the interests of large numbers of peasants. For example, in La Mancha and easternmost Andalusia, the only portions of southwestern Spain that remained under the Republic, the Communists did not seriously try to overturn the very widespread collectivization that had occurred because there were so few small proprietors and tenants to whom their policies could appeal that they would have failed miserably. As to the Communist admission cited earlier that the decollectivization had been at least partly mistaken, the very completeness with which peasants "who were discontented with the collectives" dismantled them may only suggest their fury at having been forced to join them in the first place.

Whatever the ultimate validity of the two arguments, the fundamental point remains that property systems were so varied and the peasantry so heterogeneous in most of Spain that agrarian reform continued to divide Republicans even more bitterly than it had prior to the war. In eastern Aragon, although the small proprietors and tenants may indeed have proven different from their Russian and Eastern European counterparts and have eventually come to accept collectivization, their first impulse was probably to expand their own individual holdings and they were stopped only by the CNT's military dominion. But this small entrepreneur's vision of agrarian reform conflicted with the needs of the day laborers, who had no property to expand and could not obtain enough (since there were few large estates to divide) unless the holdings of small proprietors and tenants were made available to all by being pooled into collectives. The clash between the Communists and the CNT therefore reflected a deeper clash between the basic interests of sizable peasant groups. Its particular manifestations varied according to the pre-existent social and property structure of each locality. Among day laborers and those proprietors or tenants whose lands were so minuscule even by Spanish standards that they had little to lose by incorporating them into collectives, the Anarchosyndicalist policies were undoubtedly popular. In the more numerous villages where slightly more comfortable proprietors and tenants predominated, the Communists were undoubtedly regarded as saviors from a local CNT dictatorship.

Although the conflicts produced by the difficulties of carrying out an equitable land reform in Aragon were not equaled elsewhere, they also were frequent in the Levante and some sectors of Catalonia. Even in La Mancha and the remaining portions of Andalusia, where property concentration was high and the peasantry relatively homogeneous, there were many disputes. We do not have the space to discuss these regions or the complex situation in New Castile, but the basic points I have been trying to make in this article should by now be clear.

Because Spain's rural society was so varied, the peacetime Republic never gained general peasant support and the Azaña government of 1931–33 was discouraged from pursuing agrarian reform more actively by the contradictions its policies immediately raised even among their intended beneficiaries. The military insurrection was actively supported from the start by the peasants of Navarre and Old Castile, and passively accepted by those of Galicia. Although it unleashed a massive social revolution in what became the Republican zone, this revolution was violent in form only in some localities, particularly in southwestern Spain. Elsewhere it often involved nothing more than peasants taking advantage of the power vacuum that had appeared to stop rent payments or encroach on temporarily vacated lands. Although nobody ever seriously attempted to restore the previous status quo, the new social and property relationships established were themselves so disruptive that to some extent they retroactively justified the vacillations of the left Republicans while in office. Had not the Communists paradoxically emerged as champions of individual liberty because of the sorry state to which the war had reduced the left Republicans, this new conflict might have remained hidden as the labor groups with a vested interest in the collective solution imposed a façade of unity. With the Communists willing to help give it political expression, it emerged into the open and led to divisions of the type we have described in Aragon.

Whether hidden or open, the conflict produced by the inability to find a universally acceptable solution to the agrarian problem seriously weakened the wartime Republic and hastened the Nationalist victory. Social harmony did not follow social revolution because the Spanish peasantry was so diverse that what constituted a positive revolutionary action for one sector was regarded as a negative, antirevolutionary act by another. Had Spanish rural society been more homogeneous, the Spanish peasantry might have followed the course of its Mexican, Russian, Chinese and Vietnamese counterparts and added another saga of triumphant peasant war against external enemies to twentieth-century history. Since it was not, we are left only with the much grimmer reality of a peasant civil war within the broader Spanish internecine conflict.

NOTES

1. For further details, see my book, *Agrarian Reform and Peasant Revolution in Spain: Origins of the Civil War* (New Haven: Yale University Press, 1970), pp. 25–33, 73–77, 404–5.

2. Eric R. Wolf, *Peasant Wars of the Twentieth Century* (New York: Harper & Row, 1969), pp. 291–92. Despite my occasional disagreements with it, Wolf's book is pioneering and merits careful reading.

3. Malefakis, *Agrarian Reform,* pp. 118–29.

4. In 1959, municipal commons occupied only 7.7 percent of the land in south-western Spain, as against 23.0 percent elsewhere.

5. The contrast is even more striking than the column indicates since it probably overstates rural population growth in the Biscay provinces and the Levante, regions in which urban growth cannot be as easily separated from rural growth as elsewhere.

6. For example, in 1950, the per capita income from agriculture of everyone engaged in farming in Galicia averaged about 6,300 pesetas, as against 9,750 pesetas in Andalusia. Because of the maldistribution of income under the large-property system, however, the advantage of the Andalusian day laborer was undoubtedly much smaller than these averages suggest, if indeed it existed at all.

7. The *rabassaires* are discussed briefly later in this article. The *foro* system, which had lost most of its earlier political importance because of reforms instituted in the 1920s, is described in Malefakis, *Agrarian Reform,* pp. 124–25.

8. Azaña's speech of February 14, 1933, as quoted in A. Ramos Oliveira, *Politics, Economics and Men of Modern Spain: 1808–1946* (London: Victor Gollanz, 1946), p. 472.

9. There was never any chance that the entire wheat harvest would be lost, but repeated Socialist threats had convinced most people of the contrary—another of the many historical incidents in which exaggerated revolutionary rhetoric proves counterproductive.

10. Detailed statistics exist on only 573,190 of the 900,000 or so hectares that were redistributed between February and July 1936.

11. An indication of the low level of peasant rebelliousness in the Biscay provinces, however, is that the Asturian miners, not the peasants, carried out the long and unsuccessful siege of Oviedo, the only provincial capital seized by the Nationalists.

12. In *The Spanish Cockpit* (Ann Arbor: University of Michigan Press, paperback edition, 1963), pp. 97–98, 141–42, Franz Borkenau, one of the few objective and truly competent persons who traveled in the Spanish countryside immediately after the social upheavals of July, depicts revolutionary fervor as far greater among the peasantry of Estremadura and La Mancha than of Aragon.

13. There was no formal exclusion of peasants from the draft in the Republican zone, but some evidence suggests that they were often exempted in practice.

14. Even if only the poorest of the small proprietors and tenants are taken into account, and permanent hired hands are included alongside day laborers as "workers," as was done in an Institute of Agrarian Reform census of the rural proletariat conducted between 1933 and 1936, landless workers made up less than a third (32.2 percent) of the total number of impoverished persons in the Aragonese countryside.

15. In all the above statistics, I include the province of Logroño as part of Aragon, even though it fell in its entirety to the rebels and wartime Aragon for the Republicans consisted only of the eastern portions of Huesca, Saragossa, and Teruel provinces.

16. These government statistics, as summarized in an Anarchist paper and reprinted by Hugh Thomas, "Anarchist Collectives in the Spanish Civil War," in Martin Gilbert, ed., *A Century of Conflict: 1850–1950* (New York: Atheneum, 1967), pp. 253–54, show a 20.0 percent increase in the Aragonese wheat crop over 1936, as against an increase of only 4.0 percent in the rest of Republican Spain. On the other hand, the Aragonese production record for wines was worse than that of other regions.

17. Cited in Burnett Bolloten, "The Parties of the Left and the Civil War," in Raymond Carr, ed., *The Republic and the Civil War in Spain* (London Macmillan, 1971), p. 147.

18. This Anarchist contention has been most recently restated by Noam Chomsky in his provocative *American Power and the New Mandarins* (New York: Vintage Books, 1969), pp. 74–124.

19. The same reservation does not apply with equal force for the production statistics employed earlier to suggest peasant acquiescence in Nationalist rule since these are for three years rather than only one.

IV. PERSONAL BEHAVIOR AND SOCIAL CHANGE

"No one would argue," writes Robert Neuman, "that historians devote more attention to how people feed, clothe, house, govern, and destroy themselves than they do to the customs and institutions surrounding the way in which they reproduce themselves." It is certain that the history of population growth (and decline) and sexual behavior are topics that touch everyone in a society; in many respects they are fundamental to any attempt to write the history of society. But how to study them? As Edward Shorter laments: "The difficulty in bringing evidence to bear on a subject as private and intimate as sexual behavior is overpowering. . . ." The purpose of this section is to demonstrate the ingenuity with which social historians have begun to confront these problems.

Edward Shorter's "Sexual Change and Illegitimacy: The European Experience" examines the explosion of illegitimate births that occurred throughout Europe between 1750 and 1850 within a conceptual framework provided by current theories of the process of modernization. Blending theory and evidence drawn from demography and sociology, Shorter establishes a rough measurement of the dimensions of the illegitimacy explosion and discusses some of its implications. He then proposes a general model linking the modernizing forces in society to sexual change and illegitimacy and draws on his own considerable skill as a statistician to test it with evidence he has gathered on the Kingdom of Bavaria. Readers are encouraged to consult Shorter's footnotes. They indicate not only the high degree to which the infant discipline of historical demography is a joint effort depending on close consultation among its practitioners, but also the extent to which the research hitherto reported remains at a local, sometimes microscopic level. His essay should be read, therefore, as an exploratory contribution; an attempt to make a general statement in a field where few can be found to date.

Robert Neuman's "Industrialization and Sexual Behavior: Some Aspects of Working-Class Life in Imperial Germany" disputes the familiar proposition that the lives of urban, industrial workers were of a substantially inferior moral quality when compared with those of their country cousins. Neuman develops his argument by means of an unusual set of sources: rural and urban worker autobiographies, as well as contemporary surveys and interviews concerning the background and attitudes of prostitutes, and working-class opinions about contraception and family life. His

229

analysis of this evidence concerning sexual behavior and attitudes leads to the conclusion that what appears in one context to be "the demoralization of workers under the impact of industrialization and urbanization" is better explained as "the result of a growing rationalization and demystification" in the sexual lives of rural and urban workers alike.

These two essays can be read as a set. While the first seeks to make a general statement, the second examines a related aspect of the same broad topic in more detail. Neuman suggests that worker autobiographies and interviews may be used to "round out statistical data." Indeed the insight they provide into the character of popular culture enhances our appreciation of Shorter's model of the linkage between modernization and illegitimacy. When we read of the rural swain Franz, who finally agreed to marry his sweetheart, Dora, one month before the birth of their first child, the statistics suddenly acquire a personalized dimension. It is equally important to note, moreover, that Shorter and Neuman agree that the study of individual sexual behavior cannot be isolated, but must be seen as an aspect of change in an entire society.

SEXUAL CHANGE AND ILLEGITIMACY: THE EUROPEAN EXPERIENCE

Edward Shorter

Sex has gotten into everything nowadays but the study of modernization. While scholars have investigated how political institutions, social structure, economic systems, and family life have been transformed by the social changes of modernization, they have left the realm of sexual behavior and values pretty much unexamined. Only in the plastic-wrapped volumes of the "dirty" bookstores may one find a set of explanatory hypotheses and an accumulation of evidence bearing on sexual change.

The failure of social scientists to study sex in the context of modernization is puzzling to a European historian. One of the signal changes in popular life in Europe during the last two centuries has been a revolution of sexual mores. European society has passed from the rigid prudishness which hallmarks traditional life to the hedonistic self-indulgence characteristic of modern sexual attitudes. Indeed, the much discussed "sexual revolution" of our own times is, I would argue, merely the most recent development in a process of secular change two centuries old. The rapid evolution of sexual values and behavior which both Europe and North America —although only the former will be discussed here—experienced starting around 1750 is the subject of this paper.

To be more precise, only one of the manifestations of sexual change will occupy us here: a rapid increase in the incidence of illegitimate births between the mid-eighteenth and mid-nineteenth centuries. I shall make the case that this explosion in illegitimacy is one sign that sexual attitudes and behavior were swiftly changing, becoming "modernized," if one will. We may bring to bear other kinds of evidence as well upon sexual history, such as the observations of contemporaries, various "medical" surveys of the population conducted by the cameralist governments of western and central Europe, court records on sexual crimes and aberrancies, or the study of pornography. And in an investigation currently in progress I am studying these kinds of data as well in an effort to illuminate changing sexual patterns. Yet in this paper, I wish to present the evidence of illegitimacy alone.

First, we examine potential objections to illegitimacy data as a measure of real sexual attitudes and practices; second, we briefly discuss the dimen-

Edward Shorter received his Ph.D. from Harvard University. He now teaches at the University of Toronto.

sions of the increase in illegitimacy between mid-eighteenth and mid-nine-teenth centuries; third, a review of some current theories about sexual behavior and illegitimacy is in order; fourth, a general model linking modernizing forces to sexual change and illegitimacy will be proposed; finally, I shall present empirical data confirming some of the linkages in this model from a region of central Europe which participated in the illegitimacy explosion—the Kingdom of Bavaria.

I

Clearly one may use the incidence of illegitimacy to study sexual behavior only with some important reservations in mind. What we are really interested in is the level of premarital intercourse, a substantial increase in which is central to sexual change in western Europe.[1] And to find out about this, we must sort out some thorny measurement problems.

In this paper I am going to argue that the *propensity* to illegitimacy rises greatly over the years, which is to say the likelihood that the average unmarried woman will bear an illegitimate child increases, for I think that the values and mentalities of the average unmarried woman underwent an important change starting around 1770. Yet the historical data to which I have access fit poorly with the kind of explanation I wish to make. Only the illegitimacy *ratio* is available from parish registers or from aggregate government statistics. (The ratio is the percentage of illegitimate births to total births at a given point in time.) Yet the illegitimacy *rate* must be consulted in order to talk about changes in the propensity to bastardy, for the rate is the number of illegitimate births per 1,000 unmarried women at a given period. An increase in the ratio may be solely due to an increase in the number of unmarried women in the population, without the behavior of those women having changed at all. Or an increase in the ratio may come from a decline in marital fertility, for as fewer legitimate births occur, the importance of the same number of illegitimate ones is inflated. The rate, therefore, is manifestly preferable to the ratio, yet the sad fact is that census data on the number of unmarried women in the population are required to compute a rate, and only exceptionally do such data exist before 1850. The history of illegitimacy may either be studied with the ratio, or not at all.

This disjunction between evidence and argument forces me into some logical slippage. I shall suggest that the illegitimacy rate climbed between 1750 and 1850, even though I know for certain that only the ratio went up. And I ask the reader to suspend disbelief at this argumentative looseness only because in the few instances where information on the number of unmarried women is available—especially in Sweden since 1750—the illegitimacy rate increased right along with the ratio. Let us assume, therefore, that we are dealing with a genuine rise in nonmarital fertility, not merely with a change in the ratio resulting from some "compositional" factor. Yet even then our logical problems in determining shifts in mentalities are not entirely resolved, for the illegitimate fertility rate is by no means a perfect mirror of levels and changes in premarital sex. Many circumstances can interpose themselves to prevent premarital coition from resulting in the birth of an illegitimate child, duly registered as such by the authorities. A demographer might think of these as the intervening variables in illegitimate fertility.

The first such intervening variable is contraception. If the population is practicing birth control, intercourse may not lead to conception. We may be dealing with a situation in which young people are sleeping around as much as ever, yet fewer girls are getting pregnant because they have begun to employ contraceptive devices or to follow the "rhythm" method intelligently. This objection, I believe, commands caution in attributing a fall in illegitimacy to changing sexual behavior, but would not apply to the rise we are concerned with here. One cannot argue that around 1750 the European population started to forget an accumulated lore of contraceptive information. Yet even if people do not practice contraception, other variables may intervene to prevent the act of premarital intercourse from issuing in an illegitimate birth. For example, the woman must be fecund, able to conceive. An increase in fecundity would result in higher illegitimate fertility even though no change at all in the level of intercourse had taken place: the same amount of coition would produce a greater incidence of conception. There is, in fact, some evidence of increasing fecundity with improvements in the diet of the European population. And I readily concede that some proportion of the new illegitimate births stemmed from newly fecund but unmarried women. Yet it strains credulity to think this enhancement of fecundity sufficient to cause the illegitimacy boom. After all, no counterpart explosion in marital fertility took place, though perhaps there was a modest rise in the legitimate birth rate. In short, improved fecundity was probably not behind higher illegitimacy.

Pregnancy interruptions, both spontaneous and induced, constitute another intervening variable. If, for some reason, the rate of foetal deaths declined, more prebridal conceptions would culminate in illegitimate births —without a change in intercourse. Suppose, for example, that abortion came increasingly into disfavor within popular folkways, or was pursued with greater relentlessness by the state; an apparent increase in illegitimacy would result. The evidence, fortunately, all goes the other way, pointing to an increase in abortion during the nineteenth century rather than a decrease. And there is no reason why the rate of spontaneous abortion should have altered over the years. Thus we may rule out a decline in pregnancy interruptions as the cause of rising illegitimacy.

A more important intervening variable, which may distort illegitimacy as an index of sexual behavior, is the possibility that many children conceived out of wedlock will be born legitimate because their parents got married in the interim period. In other words, one might argue that the level of premarital intercourse in a society is really more or less constant, and that changes in illegitimacy are merely a function of changes in the marriage rate. This, of course, is a weighty objection. Ideally, one would consult the incidence of prebridal pregnancies to find out about premarital intercourse. Yet such information becomes available only through detailed monographic studies of individual parishes and towns, and clearly is not to be found among published aggregate statistics.

There are several reasons why one should not seek to explain illegitimacy primarily in terms of the inability of the couple to get married. If we ask why the parents didn't wed before the child was born, we have probably made two implicit assumptions about the situation of its conception. Either we assume that the couple are a devoted pair whom fate, in the form of bad harvests or financial penury, prevented from sanctifying their relationship at the altar; or we assume that the girl was, for some reason or another, unable to *compel* her seducer to wed her. A scholar who thought illegitimacy could best be studied through the negative question of "why no subsequent marriage?" would therefore attempt to account for the illegitimacy explosion in terms of a change over time either in economic conditions or in the social controls that the fallen woman and her family could exert upon the seducer.

I argue that these two assumptions do not exhaust the possibilities. We may envision a situation where the couple is not at all a stable, devoted pair but rather two people who casually cohabit and then go their separate ways. Getting married later would not have occurred to them, high grain prices or not. And even after the girl became pregnant, forcing the man to wed her would have appeared either undesirable or unrealistic. This third assumption about the background of the premarital conception defines, I think, the situation that came to predominate in Europe. Behind part of the mechanism of sexual change there is a certain unlinking of sex and marriage, the creation of a value system that prizes sex for the sake of physical or romantic gratification and that does not see all sexual actions in marital terms. This means that in theory we may account for changes in illegitimacy with arguments that have little bearing upon the ability of the parents to get married.

In practice the marriage and illegitimacy rates, observed over time in various areas of Europe, are not correlated in any neat inverse way. During the 1840s, for example, a time of poverty and disaster for much of Europe's population, the marriage and illegitimacy rates simultaneously fell. One would have expected a decrease in marriage to have produced an increase in illegitimacy, if illegitimacy were a smooth function of marriage. The opposite in fact happened.[2]

Just as there is little evidence that marriage delayed for economic reasons produced illegitimacy, there is no evidence that normally high ages at marriage resulted in illegitimacy. E. A. Wrigley points out that historically in Europe no association has existed between late marriage and illegitimacy. Rather it was probably the other way around: "Where early marriage was widely countenanced, extramarital intercourse was often also common and the percentage of illegitimate births rather high, whereas if a community set its face against early marriage illegitimate births were nevertheless usually few in number."[3] (If we assume that knowledge of contraception was minimal, at least among the lower classes, we may only conclude that in *traditional* society people remained continent until marriage.) This further suggests we should not try to write a history of illegitimacy as a history of marriage customs alone.

Another point: it may be demonstrated that relatively few of the couples who produced illegitimate children did in fact marry later. In Europe only one-third of the illegitimate children born each year were later legitimated by the subsequent marriage of their parents.[4] Now, if illegitimate children are the work of young people devoted to each other but who, for some economic reason perhaps, are unable to get married just then, one would expect the legitimation rate to be much higher.

State marriage laws also help to make illegitimacy a useful indicator of premarital sexual activity, not just of difficulty in getting married. Until the last half of the nineteenth century, government restrictions in central Europe made marriage a difficult goal for the lower classes to attain: if they did succeed in winning official authorization for marriage it was only after a long, arduous battle with officialdom. The central European governments were obliged by municipal officials to impose these curbs on marriage. The local authorities feared that if the lower orders were permitted to marry freely, their numerous families would swamp local poor-relief resources in the event of bad times. So for many people marriage became possible only as they advanced toward middle age, when communal consent could finally be obtained. These restrictions themselves helped skyrocket the illegitimacy rate, which is part of the story.[5] The point is that even if a girl were to become pregnant, official regulations made a quick, honor-saving marriage out of the question. And so her child would be illegitimate. As long as these regulations prevailed in force, and variations in the severity of their administration did not take place, we may assume that many premarital conceptions among the poor and working classes would lead to illegitimate births.

A final objection which could be offered to using illegitimacy data as a reliable measure of behavior is the quality of the reporting of such statistics. More particularly, might one not interpret the increase in illegitimacy from 1750 to 1850 as a statistical artifact resulting from an improvement in the official collection of demographic data? If illegitimacy appears to have risen, is that not partly because people became more meticulous about recording such births? I think some improvement in the reporting of vital statistics did take place during this period as a consequence of increasing governmental centralization and awakened interest in gathering reliable social statistics. Yet I think that whatever sharpening in official observation of illegitimacy occurred would contribute only marginally to the tripling and quadrupling of illegitimacy we commonly find. Possibly such reporting improvements might account for a leap in illegitimacy rates just as official statistical services are established. Yet it is difficult to maintain that, once established, the European statistical offices dramatically increased their reporting reliability as the nineteenth century progressed. In the course of a thorough study of census reporting and data gathering in one European state—the Kingdom of Bavaria—I found no hint in the administrative correspondence that the actual determination and registration of which births were illegitimate might be a problem. Either these officials were obtuse, which I doubt, or the quality of official illegitimacy statistics in Bavaria after 1825 was excellent.

Having dealt with these potential objections to illegitimacy as a valid and reliable indicator in the evolution of sexual behavior, I again state the main case I wish to make: the rapid increase in illegitimacy, between around 1750 and 1850, measured as the number of illegitimate children born each year per 100 total births, suggests that the populations of Europe, and of North America as well, were undergoing a revolution in the sexual attitudes of young people toward one another, a revolution manifest in a great increase in premarital sexual intercourse.

II

The scattered illegitimacy data available for Atlantic society since the eighteenth century show an explosion of illegitimate births taking place in virtually every country from Prussia to the American colonies. Past scholarly inattentiveness to illegitimacy means that few compilations of aggregate statistics exist; fewer still are the local studies which present time-series data on bastardy. Our survey of the development of illegitimacy over time, then, rests upon a wide variety of sources.

Yet these various sources reveal marked similarities in the historical development of illegitimacy in Western society. Before the eighteenth century relatively few children were born of unwed mothers. The illegitimacy ratio was perhaps 1 percent of the total births. Then a great increase in prebridal pregnancies and illegitimate births began sometime during the eighteenth century in every region or society for which demographic data have become available, accelerating during the years of the French Revolution and the Napoleonic Wars. Illegitimacy continued to rise throughout the first half of the nineteenth century, peaking in the 1850s and 1860s. Then the trend reversed itself. Around 1880 a great decline in illegitimate fertility commenced, continuing until the 1930s. In every European country except Ireland and Bulgaria, illegitimacy dropped sharply in these years. The illegitimacy ratio also fell somewhat during this time, though often not as rapidly as the rate, for marital fertility plunged downward even more rapidly, keeping the ratio at a deceptively high level. Thus the secular pattern of illegitimacy over the last three centuries has assumed a rather mountainous appearance: the upward slope of the mountain was the period 1750–1850, a likely rise in illegitimate fertility betokened by a universal increase in the bastardy ratio; the mountain's downward slope was between 1880 and 1940, as everywhere both marital and non-marital fertility plunged dramatically, yet bottoming out at a level still above that of pre-1750 traditional Europe. I have discussed in detail the post-1880 fall in illegitimacy elsewhere, in collaboration with John Knodel and Etienne van de Walle; here I wish merely to account for the 1750–1850 rise.[6]

Let us examine the development of ratios country to country, going clockwise around Europe. Illegitimacy data available for long periods of time have been reproduced in Figure 1. They are calculated as a percent of total births.[7]

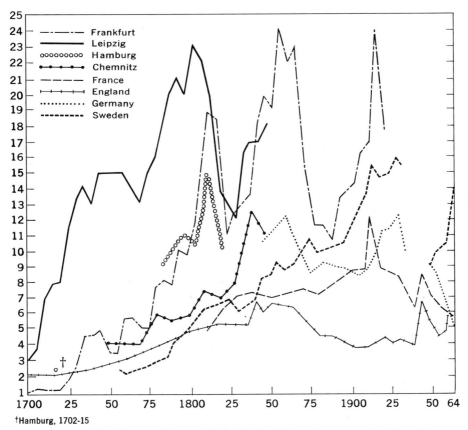

†Hamburg, 1702-15

Figure 1   Illegitimacy Rates, 1700–1964: 5 Year Averages in Most Cases
(Number of Illegitimate Births/Total Number of Births × 100)

In Sweden and Germany, bastards were an infinitesimal number before the eighteenth century: on the whole less than 1 percent of all births in seventeenth-century Frankfurt am Main, less than 2 percent in Lychen, Erfurt, and Halle. Then in the eighteenth century the increase began: a jerky upward movement in Frankfurt starting in the 1720s, peaking at 19 percent in the Napoleonic Era and at 23 percent in the 1860s. The increases in Sweden, Leipzig, Hamburg, the countryside around Halle, Chemnitz, and Styria were roughly similar, the take-off and peak decades different from one case to another, but everywhere the pattern of rapid late-eighteenth and early-nineteenth century increase. German illegitimate fertility then fell off dramatically after the 1890s, a fact concealed by the meandering ratio.

Swedish illegitimate fertility declined somewhat later than the German, and also unlike the central European, has risen abruptly since World War II.[8]

Serial data on Italy appear only in the last quarter of the nineteenth century. The figures of that time and the shards of information for earlier periods are highly unreliable because of the Mediterranean custom of making unwanted children foundlings. The Italian foundling rate is extremely high, and one does not know how many of these abandoned children are illegitimate. In any event, published figures put Italian illegitimacy at around 7 percent late in the century and at 2 or 3 percent since World War II.[9]

As for France, isolated reports of the illegitimacy ratio in one village or another at various fixed points in time indicate that the Old Regime knew very little bastardy. Several authors attribute this to a strictness of morals in rural France, where both illegitimacy and premarital conception rates appear to have been very low. Yet premarital sexual activity, as measured by the incidence of prebridal conceptions at least, was quite high in some *urban* places. In Sotteville-les-Rouen, with minimal illegitimacy, the incidence of premarital conceptions was sometimes 30 percent of all first births. A great increase in foundlings in Paris from 1709 to 1789 may also point to rising urban illegitimacy, most foundlings being of illegitimate parentage; yet that measure must be used with caution. Finally, in urban Bordeaux bastardy increased from 4 percent early in the seventeenth century to 20 percent in 1784, to 35 percent in 1840. Official statistics indicate that by the first decade of the nineteenth century French illegitimacy, following the widespread pattern, had risen to 5 percent, fluctuated then at around 7 percent until the turn of the century, and has declined since.[10]

The Anglo-Saxon world also participated in the illegitimacy explosion late in the eighteenth century. Although data are scarce (the American and English administrations not sharing the central European penchant for collecting social statistics), some intriguing local results emerge. P. E. H. Hair, after studying a number of different parishes, concludes that bridal pregnancy increased considerably in England after 1700.[11] Before the eighteenth century perhaps one-fifth of all brides were pregnant, thereafter two-fifths. This result is particularly interesting in view of the general superiority of premarital pregnancy to illegitimacy as an index of sexual activity. By studying a sample group of parishes, E. A. Wrigley and Peter Laslett have discovered a temporary upturn in bastardy early in seventeenth-century England. As in other countries, a major rise then took place in the course of the eighteenth century, leveling off at a high plateau throughout much of the nineteenth century.[12] Official British statistics show that illegitimacy declined from these heights to a constant level of 4 percent or so from the 1870s to the 1950s. In the 1960s British illegitimacy has again been on the increase.[13]

In the United States the eighteenth century was also a period of increasing illegitimacy and prebridal pregnancy. John Demos has pointed out that no couple in Bristol, Rhode Island, had a child within eight months after marriage between 1680 and 1720; between 1720 and 1740, 10 percent of the newlyweds did; between 1740 and 1760, 50 percent did! Demos attributes this dramatic increase to a "significant loosening of sexual prohibitions as the eighteenth century wore on. . . ." Furthermore, "It is my own guess that when the subject of American sexual behavior is more fully explored, the middle and late eighteenth century may prove to have been the most 'free' period in our history."[14]

Finally, a quick look at the growth of illegitimacy in Bavaria is required, for we shall shortly return to that country for a more detailed empirical examination of some of the assertions presented in this article. Bavaria followed a pattern common in Europe: acceleration of bastardy from almost nothing to perhaps one-fifth of all births by the 1850s, then an equally precipitous decline of illegitimate fertility rates from late nineteenth to twentieth centuries.

The source of Bavarian illegitimacy data for the years before 1825, when official reporting of such statistics began, is the baptismal registers of sixteen rural communes in the province of Oberbayern, 1760 to 1825.[15] The statistics are displayed in Figure 2. These selected communes had a relatively low, constant level of illegitimacy in the mid-eighteenth century: 4 percent in 1760 and 1770. With the 1780 data, when illegitimacy soared to 12 percent of all baptisms, a rise commences. Between 1795 and 1825 bastardy climbs in an unbroken progression from 5 to 18 percent.

In 1825 official statistics begin, revealing, as Figure 2 further points out, that the ratio for Bavaria as a whole was similar to that of these sixteen selected communes. Between 1825 and the early 1850s Bavarian illegitimacy hovered near the 20 percent mark, a final dramatic peaking of 24 percent taking place around 1860. The decline commenced in 1868–69, with the repeal of legislation which made marriage for the lower classes dependent upon municipal consent. By the end of the century the ratio had stabilized at around 14 percent, while the rate continued to fall. Bavarian illegitimacy

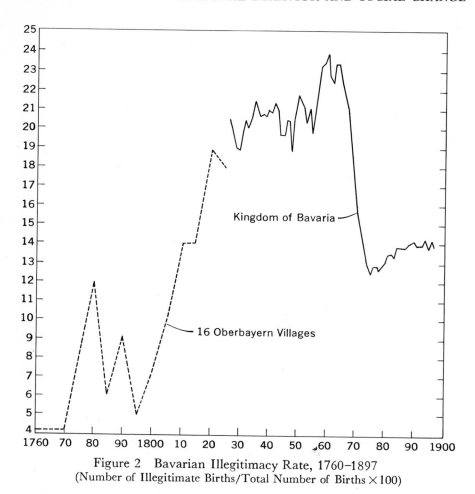

Figure 2   Bavarian Illegitimacy Rate, 1760–1897
(Number of Illegitimate Births/Total Number of Births × 100)

in the 1960s, although still the highest in West Germany save West Berlin's, was 7 percent of all births.[16]

I do not wish to extend this recitation of statistics into the tedious. The point is that all the regions of western and central Europe, the United Kingdom, and colonial America seem to have experienced a similar explosive increase in illegitimacy, starting sometime in the eighteenth century, followed by an equally dramatic decrease, starting late in the nineteenth century. Of course, further investigation will turn up considerable variation in what now appears to have been a uniform, homogeneous process: important differentials in the timing and pacing of the increase will emerge, or factory industrial, cottage industrial, and agricultural districts will turn out to differ in significant ways. At this point we note merely that an extraordinary quantitative change in illegitimate births occurred around the time of the Democratic Revolutions.

III

We may make sense of these transformations in illegitimacy rates only if we are able to construct hypotheses linking modernization with sexual change. And in this area the existing literature in the social sciences is weak. Until now scholars have pursued the social dimensions of sexual questions haphazardly, and no clearly defined body of literature provides a theoretical core of hypotheses from which future research might depart. Here work on the illegitimacy explosion may prove useful, for the historical facts I have just recounted suggest a model which will take us from fundamental modernizing social changes such as urbanization and industrialization to changes in sexual behavior and values. First, I examine current sociological theories about sex and illegitimacy; then, I present a tentative model.

Recent research emphasizes a common thread of social class in accounting for differences in sexual behavior. Stratification influences may make themselves felt in the form of differentials by class in the need for ego gratification and assurance of status. One researcher tells us that among the upper and middle classes sex is thought of as a means of self-enhancement and personality development.[17] Ira Reiss points out that differences in sexual behavior are traceable to class differences in family and courtship patterns, these latter factors being the true variables which determine sexual behavior. Reiss also observes that whatever libertinism may exist among the lower classes does not result from the "disorganized atmosphere of poverty," an assertion shortly to be of relevance to us.[18] Other well-known research links social class to sexual behavior via class differences in role segregation between husband and wife: in lower-class families the functions of husband and wife are usually highly "segregated." A negativeness or indifference to sexual relations among lower-class women, for example, is associated with this rigid compartmentalization.[19] The only recent sociological study of sexual patterns without a class emphasis is Harold Christensen's work on international differences in sexual permissiveness: Christensen thinks cultural differences strategic.[20]

These are useful findings, for they permit us to see that variations in sexual behavior are not distributed in some random way among the population, and to reject the notion that such matters do not vary at all from group to group. Rather we realize that sexual mores are systematically linked to such basic and familiar forces as social class. What previous research does not permit us to do is relate social change to the realm of sex. We need to know how modernization *changes* sexual practices, not merely how such practices are found among already "modern" populations.

A more substantial literature on the specific subject of illegitimacy will help to formulate hypotheses on the history and sociology of sex. During the nineteenth century, when illegitimacy first became a major social problem, a number of writers gathered statistics and speculated on the causes of the phenomenon. And in the 1970s, when events taking place within the black ghettoes again cause illegitimacy to emerge as a signal concern, a second round of writings on the subject appears. Two different theoretical approaches to illegitimacy may be discerned in existing writings.

One group of authors sees illegitimacy as the product of enduring common-law type unions within the context of a stable culture. For one reason or another, the culture does not demand that all those who live and sleep together get married, and so an informal style of marriage, perfectly durable and sanctioned by the society, may come to be the dominant form of cohabitation. Of course the children born of these unions are legally registrable as illegitimate, but that doesn't mean their conception resulted from some kind of social pathology. The point is that the parents of these illegitimate children either think of themselves as married for most intents and purposes, or they shortly do in fact get married. William J. Goode, while rejecting this "stability" interpretation in general, applies it to the peasant cultures of northwestern Europe. An instance of it has been found in the numerous prebridal pregnancies of Denmark. And one sociologist interprets Caribbean illegitimacy in light of the "consensual union" hypothesis.[21] It says, to sum up, that there is nothing pathological about illegitimacy, no aura of social disorganization around its apparition. Rather bastardy is a statistical artifact, arising solely from the fact that the parents, who represent a stable union within a stable culture, have not yet decided to legalize their intimate relationship.

An alternative group of writers takes a diametrically opposed position: illegitimacy is a product of social disorganization. It occurs when the normal processes which regulate courtship and family life break down, when social disaster hits the society and things start to fall apart. This view is in line with classical sociological theories which emphasize the disintegrating effects of social change, predicting that modernization will result in instability and disorientation, social alienation and individual anomie. It is when people lose a sense of what is right, of what manner of behavior society expects from them, that they begin to have premarital sex—which of course eventuates in illegitimacy. This point of view characterizes the "moral statisticians" of the nineteenth century, such as Alexander von Oettingen and Georg von Mayr. It characterizes as well such twentieth-century observers as Louis Chevalier, who in his study of the "dangerous classes" in Paris of the early nineteenth century attributed an upsurge in illegitimacy to the disorganizing effects of social change.[22]

A persuasive, sophisticated version of this thesis is advanced by William Goode, who argues that high Latin American illegitimacy rates may be explained in terms of the disorganization arising from the clash and interpenetration of two different cultures. A breakdown in community creates some anomie, and the ensuing confusion about cultural values leads to premarital intercourse, and thence to illegitimacy.[23] In a similar vein Daniel Patrick Moynihan, in his famous report on the Negro family, argued that the social disorganization black people experience in northern industrial cities has devastated family life, causing illegitimacy to become almost the norm.[24]

Within the general social disorganization explanation of illegitimacy there is a subgroup of authors who see economic deprivation and the ruin of the workingman's life brought about by industrial capitalism as chiefly responsible for illegitimacy. This interpretation goes back to Friedrich Engels, who noted in the industrial slums of England a trend to "sexual license" among the working classes. But the writers who indict capitalism and industrial society for producing illegitimacy are by no means all Marxists. Many conservative nineteenth-century observers claimed that the working classes were both demoralized and impoverished by industrial growth, thus unwilling and unable to marry—hence illegitimacy.[25]

The social disorganization approach to illegitimacy is important because it represents the only cluster of theories within the area of sex research able to connect sexual evolution with social change. As we have seen, current sex research has a timeless quality about it, and is unconcerned with how large-scale societal changes operating over time alter sexual behavior. The social disorganization school, at least, hooks up the two by claiming that modernization causes traditional moral values and stable behavioral patterns to break down, with the consequences of libertine sexual mores and illegitimacy.

Can we not combine the two approaches? The stable-union theorists rightly point out that the presence of illegitimacy need not betoken social disorganization, as it may arise from "normal" conditions, from integrated societies with unchallenged value systems. The social disorganization people rightly see social change as resulting in illegitimacy, a fact we know historically to be true because during a time of great turmoil Western illegitimacy rates did indeed soar. Might one argue that modernization has fostered illegitimacy in Western society by creating new social groups or subcultures which look benignly upon the permissive sexuality from which illegitimacy springs?

IV

Let us for a moment climb down from these arid theoretical plateaus and consider the situation of a young girl deciding whether to sleep with a young man. Understanding this microscopic situation will permit a better specification of the macro-sociological forces which bear upon it.

The young unmarried woman, contemplating having sex with her boyfriend, will probably ask three questions: 1) Who will know? 2) Who will be hurt? 3) What will my friends say? She will probably not start sleeping around if the local parson or Mom and Pop will find out about it; she will be loath to have premarital sex if becoming pregnant would mean disappointing family expectations in her forthcoming arranged marriage with

Farmer Huber's lad; and she will not have intercourse if her girl friends would strongly disapprove and think her a deviate, a cheap little hussy, as one used to say. On the other hand, she probably will shed her qualms about premarital sex if the questions could be answered the other way: if she could keep her activities secret from those who know her well; if becoming pregnant would not mean ruining the elaborate economic arrangements about land inheritance and dowries predicated upon her arranged marriage; if her friends would either be indifferent to, or actually applaud, the boldness in shaping her own life and the readiness to develop her personality she has expressed by going to bed with Laborer Meier's son. This third question is necessary because even if anonymity and innocuous consequences were guaranteed the girl, religion, and other internalized value systems would make her pull back from "sin" unless her peers approved as well.

The answers to these questions do not remain constant over the years, but instead change on the basis of differences in the world view and the social situation of young people. Accordingly, the level of premarital sex in society is not steady, but varies with changing answers to these questions. Assuming for the moment that these propositions are valid, we go on to determine what large-scale social changes might alter the willingness of this young girl, and millions like her, to participate in sex before marriage.

We now raise our sights to a macro-societal view. These three questions suggest that premarital intercourse and illegitimacy will be furthered by social changes that do three kinds of things: 1) enhance anonymity, making it possible for young people to do as they please without the censuring eyes of parents or social authorities upon them; 2) create a propertyless proletariat among whom the rigid familial controls on sexual behavior which prevail among burgher and peasant populations need not apply (personal skill and talent, rather than family position, become the means through which the lower classes advance themselves, if at all, in the world); 3) reorient value systems from "traditional" to "modern," creating specifically a youth subculture in which qualities like self-expression, ego development and individuality are prized. I shall argue that the forces that bring out these three conditions are those primarily responsible for the sexual revolution and its accompanying illegitimacy explosion.

How may these considerations be linked together in a model which will explain the course of events in Europe? Figure 3 traces out the rough steps which get us from modernization to illegitimacy. Various modernizing social changes, to be more closely identified in a moment, altered the structure of traditional society in several critical ways. For one thing, the European population in the late eighteenth and early nineteenth centuries was both much larger and much younger than ever before. For another, the class structure was swiftly changing during this time due to the accumulation of great numbers of landless laborers in both urban and rural areas,

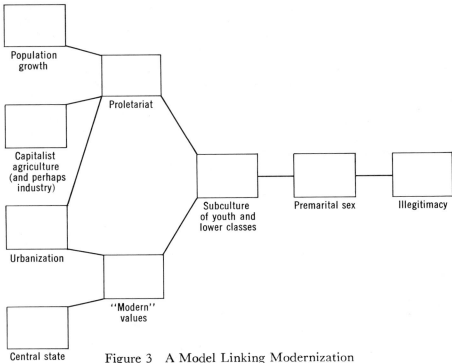

Figure 3   A Model Linking Modernization
to Sexual Change in Europe, 1750–1850

in short as a result of the growth of a proletariat. Thirdly, the center of gravity of Europe's population began to shift from the countryside to the city. And finally, the tentacular growth of the modern state altered the structure of society, as government bureaucrats, emissaries of centralist rule, began to weaken the authority of the traditional local elites.

Next step in the model: these structural changes lead to the growth among the young and the lower classes of a new subculture, different from the traditional culture in devotion to "modern," specifically urban values. This new value system exalts individualism, opening the door for romantic love, at the cost of traditional values of obedience to the dictates of the family and of the communal social authorities, agencies that command sexual abstinence before marriage.[26] Further step: the values of this new subculture lead to a great increase in premarital intercourse, now sanctioned as a legitimate means of ego development ("true love"). Final step: this higher incidence of coitus leads to an explosion in illegitimate births.

Before the particular developments which "modernizing social change" entails are specified, an earlier warning about the role of poverty and marriage in this matter should be reiterated. It is a mistake to say that immiseration caused the original illegitimacy explosion by making the founding of a family more difficult. Instead I suggest that young people participate in intercourse for reasons having little to do with the prospect of later marriage. Rather there are positive cultural reasons why they might engage in such activities. The lack of correlation between economic disaster and illegitimacy, or of one between illegitimacy and marriage rates, are empirical reasons for caution in linking together poverty, marriage, and illegitimacy. My model finds the critical relationships in the area of new social classes and new value systems, not in that of economic crisis and postponed marriage.

Four major kinds of social change proved strategic in transforming European patterns of sexual behavior: the growth of population, the advent of capitalist agriculture and industry (both domestic and factory), the growth of cities and the ensuing diffusion of urban values into society as a whole, and finally the spread of the modern, centralist, bureaucratic state. We now consider the impact of each of these.

The turbulent growth of Europe's population, beginning around 1750, stimulated illegitimacy by creating a landless proletariat. The traditional agricultural system was based upon the single family farm, which is to say upon peasant subsistence agriculture. And the traditional family demanded chasteness of its daughters in order to marry them off in a way economically advantageous to the family. Thus economic exigencies made the peasant family an agency of rigorous sexual control. The need for such controls vanished with a rising population, as more and more people appeared for whom no individual holding could be made available. Landless laborers, they could behave sexually as they wished: it was a matter of indifference to the family.[27]

Agricultural capitalism, another of the great historic forces which upset traditional European society, also promoted illegitimacy by further breaking down the peasant family farm. The engrossment of fields into unitary market-oriented holdings meant the displacement of the cottagers and the yeoman smallholders. Formerly independent peasants lost their holdings and became landless laborers in the employ of the modernizing agriculturalists.[28] So here again the economic considerations which formerly had induced sexual restraint disappeared.

Industrial capitalism must also be counted an important variable, probably boosting illegitimacy in two ways. One, by providing an alternative to staying down on the farm or in the craft shop under the father's watchful eye, industry offered young people a means of physically liberating themselves from the controls upon their lives inherent in traditional occupations. Two, by promoting "modern" value systems among the population caught up in this mode of production, industry—and especially the domestic system or "putting out" system—encouraged sexual adventure. Rudolf Braun has demonstrated how the outworking population in the Zurich highlands became more open to individualism, to the gratification of personal desires as an acceptable social goal, in consequence of finding work in the putting out system.[29] A similar transformation of traditional, peasant value systems seems to have gone on in other places as well where cottage industry spread. Whether factory industry will prove to be related to the spread of illegitimacy is a separate question which only further research will clarify.

I have built the city into this model, even though I am uncertain exactly how urbanity influences sexual behavior, or indeed whether it alters mentalities and psyches at all. The city clearly increased the sheer number of children born illegitimate by drawing together in one place so many unmarried women. But the city seems to have had no predictable, recurrent pull upon the propensity of the average single woman to have premarital intercourse (and therewith to bear illegitimate children). In some areas of the continent urban illegitimacy rates were higher than rural, in some lower.[30] What is lacking is regularity in the relationship between sex and the city. The one consistent association between illegitimacy and urbanity is that almost everywhere in the eighteenth century the illegitimacy ratio seems to have risen first in the cities, only later in the countryside.

Unquestionably, in some great cities illegitimate fertility rates were higher and increased more rapidly than in the surrounding countryside. Leaving aside for the moment cities where this was not true, how might we link urbanity to "immorality"? A moment of speculation may be in order. For one thing, urban growth meant the sheer transplantation of much of the agricultural population into the cities. There, where industrial or commercial work was available, the migrants were definitively removed from the sexual controls and property considerations of the peasant family and of the local village authorities. So to the extent that people moved to the city we should expect to see illegitimacy increase, up to a point. But the quality of urban life itself, the values of the city, also stimulated illegitimacy. A city is a place where anonymity lets the individual experiment with his life, strike out in new directions if he wishes. It is a place where a premium is placed on individual freedom and the cultural values which accompany this personal liberation, as Georg Simmel pointed out. Thus the city is a place where the pastor's censuring eye does not extend, and where true love flourishes.[31] At least, some cities are.

But the city changed the world view not only of the people who moved to it: the urban way of life reached out in the nineteenth century to permeate the countryside as well. Urbanization means not merely the physical growth of cities, it means the spread of "urbanism" to the entire society. In Europe the great cities like London and Paris—and Munich in Bavaria—represented nodal points for communication. Most activities came to be channeled through them, which meant that sooner or later news of the urban way of life would penetrate to the most distant hinterland village.[32] Between 1750 and 1850, as a result of increased circulation of goods and people, of the exposure to the wider world through military service, or of the widespread distribution of popular magazines and novels, the cultural horizon of the agricultural village expanded to reach the black smokestacks and busy wharves of Europe's great cities. And the swelling proletariat in these villages liked the image of urbanity newly offered to them.

The last of the great social changes which directly influenced illegitimacy was the rise of the modern state. The liberal, rationalistic, bureaucratic colossus grew up everywhere between 1750 and 1850, sending into the hinterland tax officials, subprefects, forestry agents, gendarmes, and a host of other officials, who now would be close to local populations which formerly had only the most ephemeral contacts with deputies of the state. At the hands of these men the structure of moral society in the villages suffered a devastating blow. Everywhere the secularization of church property and other forms of anticlericalism damaged the status of the regular and secular clergy who formerly were of such influence. The bureaucratic state, with its notions about civil liberties, equality before the law and the like, abolished such administrative paraphernalia of sexual control as the "fornication penalties" and sartorial regulations, which had been of such utility to the local authorities. The local reeves and aldermen now saw their administrative authority curbed by a straightjacket of government regulations and possibilities of appeal to higher authorities.[33] I would argue that their ability to control sexual behavior—either by penalizing premarital intercourse or by compelling the seducer to wed the hapless girl—suffered grievously through the expansion of the central government.

This, then, is a model which may serve to explain how the various social changes Europe experienced between 1750 and 1850 resulted in a transformation of patterns of sexual behavior, and therewith in a surge of illegitimate births. The model is, to be sure, still highly tentative and underelaborated, doubtless failing to take note of many nuanced relationships or forces for change. Perhaps it will be drastically modified in the course of future research. Yet it may be the beginning of understanding.

V

These general speculations receive some empirical confirmation in the Kingdom of Bavaria, which had one of the highest illegitimacy ratios in Europe. We examine briefly the experience of that state in the nineteenth century in order to demonstrate that the model proposed above fits the facts in at least one instance.

Until 1871, when the kingdom joined Bismarck's new German Empire, Bavaria was an independent state, the third largest after Austria and Prussia in central Europe. The kingdom combined within its own borders much of the social and economic diversity found in Europe as a whole. "Old Bavaria," the former electoral state of the eighteenth century, was part of the country between the Danube and the Alps, largely agricultural with farms of considerable size on which labored live-in farmhands (*Dienstboten*) and day laborers (*Taglöhner*). The great city of Munich dominated this part of the country, a focus for all commerce and transportation. During the Napoleonic era parts of the regions of Swabia and Franconia had been added to the old electoral state, and the new political construct became in 1806 the Kingdom of Bavaria. In contrast to Old Bavaria, these provinces to the north and west were rich in industry. During the eighteenth century the putting-out system had infiltrated much of the Franconian countryside, with its center around the city of Hof. And in the nineteenth century factory industry appeared in the artisanal cities of Nürnberg, Würzburg and Augsburg. This meant that a "modern" population involved in commerce and industry would be mixed in among the peasant subsistence farmers of Franconia and Swabia.[34]

Bavaria was well known to the moral statisticians and philosophers of nineteenth-century Europe for its great illegitimacy, which amounted at its height, as we have seen, to a quarter of all births. This high level was probably due to two factors: the kingdom's strict regulations for marriage and practicing a handcraft, and the "impartible" inheritance system in agriculture, which meant the family farm would not be subdivided among the children, passing intact to the eldest instead. (The younger children would be bought off with money payments, and either stayed around as farm help or migrated away.) Both circumstances worked to stimulate illegitimacy. Young journeymen would be denied for years the right to marry and to set up an independent livelihood as master craftsmen because the municipal authorities who rejected their requests feared the burden of poor relief if these men, together with their new families, were to require assistance. Also the existing master craftsmen, who spoke a powerful word in the town halls, feared added competition, and so encouraged the rejection of young journeymen. In agriculture the impartible nature of inheritance meant that the younger sons of a peasant could not acquire sufficient land to become "independent," and lacking such independence they were kept from marriage by both rural custom and law. As a result of these laws, then, both urban and rural proletarians were consigned to bachelorhood, and sired hordes of illegitimate children.[35]

But these facts do not explain the original upturn in illegitimacy. In order to understand the change over time, which we observed above, we must seek out other factors. Here the general model already outlined will be of service. One may observe how well the relationships it identifies hold up in reality by looking at Bavaria's experience between 1750 and 1850.

Late in the eighteenth century Bavaria had to face the problem of surplus rural population, people for whom no farmstead could be found. The problem of the rural poor, of course, had always been with that country, as with all of Europe. Yet the first stirrings of population growth exacerbated it. While the population of Old Bavaria seems to have stagnated throughout much of the eighteenth century, several local studies have demonstrated significant population increases in Franconia toward the end of the century. And certainly during the first half of the nineteenth century the Bavarian population everywhere increased at a rapid clip, rising from an estimated 3,060,000 around 1812 (excluding the Palatinate) to 4,029,000 in 1860, an increase which averages out to seven-tenths of a percent growth per year. One must keep in mind that perhaps a quarter of the gross increase in population during this time was siphoned off by emigration, so the growth is all the more impressive.[36]

Meanwhile, cottage industry was transforming the countryside. Starting in the 1790s cottage cotton weaving became an important means of subsistence in much of rural Oberfranken, and other provinces too shared in the expansion of the domestic system.[37] So late in the eighteenth century a rural underclass was rising outside of the framework of traditional peasant subsistence agriculture. Itself landless, this proletariat would not be subject to the constraints upon sexual experimentation which the peasant family normally imposed.

Another of the social changes responsible for illegitimacy which made itself felt both in Europe as a whole and in Bavaria was urbanization. It is impossible to attribute the original impetus for sexual change to the shift of population from the countryside to the city, for urban migration became a substantial force for change only after 1830. And Bavaria did not become urbanized land, in the quantitative use of the term, until the twentieth century, for in 1855 only 14 percent of her population lived in communities larger than five thousand people.[38]

Yet amidst Bavaria's torpid urban burghs was the dynamic city of Munich, which experienced accelerated growth starting with the Napoleonic era. Munich's population doubled from an estimated 63,000 around 1812 to 132,000 in 1852—a quarter of the land's urban population. And the city's importance in society as a whole increased at an even faster pace, for Munich became in the early nineteenth century the national marketplace, and the centerpoint for culture, communications, and transportation. The spread of Bavaria's government bureaucracy out from this state capital also enhanced the city's importance. I would argue that Munich did much to spread "urban" values through the Bavarian population by virtue of its central position alone.[39] These values were to become the cultural norms of the new lower classes whom social change was causing to appear, deforming the symmetry of traditional social structure.

Bavaria was turned topsy-turvy by the fourth of the great social changes at work upon Europe: the advance of the centralized, bureaucratic state. Between 1799, when Maximilian I became elector of Old Bavaria, and 1817, when Count Maximilian von Montgelas resigned as the king's first minister, Bavaria transmuted itself from a sleepy Old Regime principality into a dynamic modern state. Montgelas was one of a breed of enlightened administrators, devoted to French precepts for organizing and ruling a centralized country, who descended upon Germany in these years.

He caused the judiciary and legal code to be reformed, the state bureaucracy to be professionalized, and government control over local fiefdoms to be asserted. Every aspect of public life underwent a wrenching reorganization in these years, something which simultaneously happened in much of the rest of Europe as well.

These governmental changes shook the old hometown elites, though not entirely displacing them. Bavarian small towns and villages had traditionally been run by an oligarchy of the wealthy and established citizens: the prosperous master craftsmen in elite trades, the merchants, peasant farmers with substantial holdings, and the local cleric—most likely Protestant in Franconia or Swabia, Catholic in Old Bavaria. In the Old Regime the state government in Munich, or Ansbach or wherever, was so remote and its authority so intermittent that these local types could act pretty much as they chose in enforcing local standards of behavior upon the citizenry, punishing miscreants, and in general arranging the moral and social environment of their communities to suit themselves.[40]

The reforms of the Montgelas era changed all this. Local citizens who felt themselves abused by the arbitrary exercise of municipal authority could appeal to echelons of the national government hovering just above the communal administrations, avid for a chance to reach into the local arena and intervene. In a period of secularization the churches were stripped of much of their property, the clerics of much of their influence and authority. There would, for example, be no more compelling people to go to church on Sundays. The controls which master craftsmen could exert upon the journeymen and apprentices who lived with them, as well as the controls which farmers could apply upon the servants and agricultural laborers housed in their garrets, became circumscribed. The entire range of penalties for premarital intercourse, illegitimacy, and adultery, which formerly civil authorities had employed against "immorality," were abolished. An ordinance of 1808 stated specifically that the "fornication penalties" were outlawed. Henceforth no criminal or civil sanction could be invoked against those who had sex outside of marriage, aside from seldom used provisions which permitted the authorities to put "chronically immoral" women in workhouses and to break up "concubinage." These were the means with which traditional society compelled obedience to its codes of sexual morality, and they were all swept away.[41]

Thus the Napoleonic era left the local elites, not only in Bavaria but in all of western and central Europe save England, in a very much different situation than it had found them. The traditionalists believed in a value system which stressed curbing "egoism," keeping chaste until marriage, and exalting the inheritance requirements of the family above all personal considerations. After the Napoleonic era they continued to believe in these things, but they had lost the power to impose their own views of moral righteousness upon a younger generation—and upon a swelling mass of lower orders in general—which was rapidly acquiring different social values and moral standards.

The next step in the argument is to demonstrate how these major social changes—population growth, rural and perhaps industrial capitalism, urban migration and the urban way of life, and government centralization —transformed sexual morality with a consequent increase in illegitimacy. I believe that they made themselves felt by creating new lower classes who participated in a new subculture, further that this subculture stressed individual self-development and experimentation. Here we run into major evidential problems. It is not difficult to demonstrate a population increase or the growth of cities, these things being quantitatively ascertainable. It is difficult to verify the emergence of a subculture among an inarticulate social class, and to specify the content of this new culture. The lower classes have left few personal testimonials behind, written historical evidence being generated almost solely by members of the upper orders. So if we wish to find out what the lower classes and the young were thinking, we must read the accounts of their activities handed down by middle- and upper-class observers, people who had every cause to be hostile to these subcultural developments. This is much like trying to study the heresies of the Middle Ages through the writings of the theologically correct, the heretical materials themselves having long been destroyed.

Whatever the reality of lower-class culture early in the nineteenth century, the fact is that upper-class observers certainly thought that a new subculture was emerging. They believed a decisive historical change had taken place, in which the lower classes rejected the modesty of dress, the humility of behavior, and the propriety of morals traditionally expected of them for high-quality, fashionable apparel, an assertive demeanor, and libertine moral standards. I have made no attempt to quantify these judgments, impressionistically asserting the existence of this strain in nineteenth-century thought. Yet such evidence may have some validity.

We may examine some samples from an enormous literature on the "immorality" question. In the province of Oberbayern it was customary for "masses" of single women to appear at dance locales, wishing to be asked to dance, and hoping to find a man to escort them home. The district poor-relief board of Landshut thought this practice repugnant to public morality, and the source of much illegitimacy. The observer who reported these facts noted that "the daughters of respectable peasants, millers and such—in general of well-to-do landowners—are not permitted to take part in this practice." Or there is the "dying sister" story from the Bamberg official newspaper: "How far the demoralisation of the lower classes of people has progressed is seen in the following incident in a nearby village. A young man sitting in a tavern was called by his mother to hurry to the bedside of his dying sister. He however replied: 'You run ahead and tell her to wait until I have finished my beer.' "[42]

Finally, we note the report of a provincial official in 1859 on the condition of the lower classes in the province of Oberfranken. He observed that the severe economic crises of earlier years had by now largely vanished and the land was prospering. Nonetheless the "moral misery" of the past years had not receded.

The damage egoism causes in public and social life through overweening ambition (Selbstüberhebung) and megalomania (Grossmanssucht) appears in private and family life through status-seeking (Standesüberhebung) and pleasure-seeking (Genussucht). . . . The population of Oberfranken does not lack alertness, industriousness and perseverance. But it lacks indeed the moral power to oppose inner passions and bad examples which corrode and undermine discipline and custom.[43]

The writer concluded that the frivolity and immorality of the population had led to great increases in illegitimate births.

This middle-class perception of immorality pervades government reports, newspaper accounts, political pamphlets, social writings, parliamentary speeches, and diary observations. Whether the lower classes were acquiring a subculture of their own, with the above-mentioned qualities, remains to be definitively established. Beyond dispute is that the middle classes thought a radical departure from traditional patterns was taking place.

The last part of my argument is the assertion that the new value systems which prevailed among the young in fact meant more sexual intercourse and a higher incidence of illegitimacy. This may be indirectly demonstrated in several ways. Contemporaries agreed that the cities were the seedbed of immorality. And independent of their outraged assertions, I have suggested that urban life did promote a new subculture by aggregating together people naturally open to new moral standards, by guaranteeing them anonymity, and by imbedding within the very fabric of the environment a different view of life. So we would expect urban illegitimacy rates and ratios to be higher than rural ones.

And in fact they are. The level of illegitimacy in the larger Bavarian cities was considerably higher than that of the surrounding countryside. Between 1879 and 1888 an average of 30 percent of all births in Munich were illegitimate; only 16 percent were illegitimate, however, in the rural districts of the province of Oberbayern, where Munich was located. This difference is not due merely to the fact that the cities had more unmarried women available for illegitimate conceptions than the countryside. Such women actually became involved in premarital intercourse leading to an illegitimate birth more often in Munich than in the countryside: there were 80 illegitimate children for every thousand unmarried women in Munich, 60 in the country districts of Oberbayern. Such results obtain for most of the other Bavarian cities as well, and not just in the 1880s but throughout the nineteenth century since 1835–36, when data on such matters first became available.[44]

Another type of statistical technique will also permit us to relate illegitimacy not just to cities, but to "modern" occupations and proletarian social constellations. Bavarian census data taken by district from the censuses of 1840 and 1880 permit us to spot an ecological relationship between the presence of illegitimate children and of socio-economic characteristics of the district. The technique employed was multiple curvilinear regression. The relationship between the dependent and independent variables was derived using the backward elimination procedure. This will be gibberish to any reader not versed in statistics. The technique simply involves calculating correlations between different independent variables, such as the percent of farmers in the district, and the dependent variable of illegitimacy. Each variable is observed in simultaneous conjunction with all others. The trick is to determine which combination of independent variables will explain a maximum amount of the variation in the dependent variable. At the same time, one tries to keep the number of independent variables to a minimum. The procedure lets us construct the ideal-typical profile of a district with high illegitimacy.

The census of 1840 reported for all the rural districts and the towns of the kingdom a large number of socio-economic characteristics: marital status of the population, a crude age breakdown, religion, economic structure with reference to whether agricultural, whether self-employed, and whether propertied. In addition it asked whether the children under fourteen years were of legitimate birth. Multiple curvilinear regression analysis was applied to these data.[45] Let me emphasize that of the fifteen or so census variables originally used in the regression analysis, I report in the following pages *only* those found to correlate closely with illegitimacy.

Interesting results were obtained for rural areas, using the number of illegitimate children per 1,000 juvenile population as the dependent variable. As Table I demonstrates, 54 percent of the variation was explained on the basis of the following characteristics:

1. the absence of married couples
2. the absence of Catholics
3. the absence of people exclusively in agriculture (we are observing here the square of the variable)[46]
4. the presence of landless laborers (*landwirtschaftliche Taglöhner ohne Grundbesitz*)
5. the presence of farmhands (*Dienstboten*)
6. the absence of propertied craftsmen (*Gewerbetreibende mit Grundbesitz;* this observation is based on the square of the variable)
7. the presence of smalltown lower-class types (*städtische Taglöhner.* I am, again, going by the square of the variable. Small towns count as rural for census purposes.)

The results obtained for rural areas when the dependent variable was the number of illegitimate children per 1,000 unmarried women were not substantially different from those just reported.

To summarize, Table I permits the construction of an ideal type of rural county with high illegitimacy in whose profile some kinds of social characteristics are prominent, others conspicuously absent. I emphasize that such a county must combine all of these qualities simultaneously. The district will, of course, have some obvious distinguishing characteristics: few married couples and numerous common-law unions, to take the evidence of rural rate 2. Most important, however, the district will be abundant in the landless lower classes, agricultural laborers, farmhands and similar types. I have hypothesized that the illegitimacy explosion is partly a consequence of the growth of these orders of people, not tied in their sexual activities to the inheritance patterns of the traditional family farm. Here appears to be empirical confirmation.

The relationship between illegitimacy and these various characteristics drops way off in urban areas. Table I shows that when the dependent variable is the permille of illegitimate children in the juvenile population, the most propitious combination of independent variables accounts for only 22 percent of the variation. In urban areas some of the correlations we noted in the countryside either disappear or are reversed: the presence of Catholics becomes positively, not negatively correlated with illegitimacy; the presence of widows means a positive, not a negative correlation. (Urban widows have illegitimate children after their husbands' deaths; rural ones don't, apparently.) And so on.

The point about urban areas is that relationships which held up well in the countryside, accounting in a significant manner for illegitimacy there, almost vanish in the city. This means that *some quality of urban life itself,* not just some feature of the socio-economic mix of the urban population, produces the high levels of urban illegitimacy. That is perhaps the major conclusion of this particular analysis.

I have examined a few of the figures Friedrich Lindner published from the census of 1880 using the same technique.[47] Lindner gives data on only a few variables, adding to our knowledge solely the average amount of arable land per farm by district. The dependent variables are the number of illegitimate births per thousand total births, and the number of illegitimate children in the population per thousand unmarried women, for both indices the 1879–88 average. The independent variables are the percentage of the population in agriculture, the percentage in agriculture who also practice a craft, the hectares of both land in general and arable land per landowner, and whether inheritance in the district was partible. The results are reproduced in Table II. I observe at once that this latter variable turned out to be unimportant because the land was generally not split among inheritors anywhere in Bavaria except the province of Unterfranken. And among the counties in that province a wide range of illegitimacy levels existed.

TABLE I.　THE RESULTS OF MULTIPLE REGRESSION ANALYSIS APPLIED TO 1840 CENSUS
(260 Census Districts)

Rural Rate 1 (illegitimate children/total population of children × 1,000)

Variable	Partial Regression Coefficient (b_i)	T-Test	Standard Partial Regression Coefficient (B_i)
X1　The percent of married couples in the population	−1.6407	−9.88***	−0.5010
X1^2　The percent of married couples squared	0.0155	2.77***	0.1258
X2　The percent of Catholics	−0.0409	−5.81***	−0.3065
X3　The percent of population exclusively in agriculture	0.0027	0.10^{NS}	0.0060
X3^2　The percent of population exclusively in agriculture squared	−0.0004	−2.96***	−0.1566
X4　The percent of landless laborers (Landbau-Taglöhner ohne Grund- oder Hausbesitz	0.3098	3.83***	0.3022
X4^2　The percent of landless laborers squared	−0.0011	−1.74*	−0.1254
X5　Live-in farmhands (Gesinde)	0.1682	4.82***	0.2597
X6　Self-employed tradesmen with property	0.0278	0.71^{NS}	0.0423
X6^2　Self-employed tradesmen squared	−0.0007	−2.60**	−0.1422
X7　Smalltown laborers (Städtische Taglöhner)	−0.0494	−0.36^{NS}	−0.0264
X7^2　Smalltown laborers squared	0.0020	2.51**	0.1683

% of variation explained ($R^2 \times 100$) = 53.68%

Rural Rate 2 (illegitimate children/unmarried women [widows excluded] × 1,000)

X1　The percent of married couples in the population	−1.2789	−5.15***	−0.2612

NS not significant at 10% level　　　　　　　　** significant at 5% level
* significant at 10% level　　　　　　　　　*** significant at 1% level

Table I (*continued*)

Variable	Partial Regression Coefficient (b_i)	T-Test	Standard Partial Regression Coefficient (B_i)
X2 *The percent of common law unions*	18.4657	3.25***	0.1599
X3 *The percent of widows*	−1.1679	−1.88*	−0.0935
X4 *The percent of Catholics*	−0.0864	−7.28***	−0.4240
X5 *The percent of population exclusively in agriculture*	−0.0587	−1.39NS	−0.0864
X5² *The percent of population exclusively in agriculture squared*	−0.0005	−2.30**	−0.1236
X6 *The percent of landless laborers (Landbau-Taglöhner ohne Grund- oder Hausbesitz)*	0.4016	4.91***	0.2620
X7 *Self-employed tradesmen with property*	0.0089	0.15NS	0.0090
X7² *Self-employed tradesmen squared*	−0.0012	−3.01***	−0.1664
X8 *The percent of urban laborers*	−0.3062	−1.44NS	−0.1095
X8² *The percent of urban laborers squared*	0.0032	2.63***	0.1816

% of variation explained ($R^2 \times 100$) = 50.49%

Urban Rate 1 (illegitimate children/total population of children × 1,000)

Variable			
X1 *The percent of married couples in the population*	−0.5420	−3.04***	−0.2945
X2 *The percent of widows*	0.6487	1.25NS	0.1330
X2² *The percent of widows squared*	0.0629	2.32**	0.2561
X3 *The percent of Catholics*	0.0408	2.79***	0.2968
X4 *The percent of landless laborers (Landbau-Taglöhner ohne Grund- oder Hausbesitz)*	0.3131	2.48**	0.2443
X5 *The percent of servants*	−0.2972	−1.68*	−0.1748

TABLE I *(continued)*

Variable	Partial Regression Coefficient (b_i)	T-Test	Standard Partial Regression Coefficient (B_i)
X6 *The percent of apprentices*	0.2093	2.65***	0.2625

% of variation explained $(R^2 \times 100) = 21.77\%$

Urban Rate 2 (illegitimate children/unmarried women (widows excluded) $\times$ *1,000)*

Variable	(b_i)	T-Test	(B_i)
X1 *The percent of married couples in the population*	−0.4764	−1.53NS	−0.1590
X1² *The percent of married couples squared*	0.0147	2.71***	0.2745
X2 *The percent of widows*	2.5238	2.99***	0.3179
X2² *The percent of widows squared*	0.1343	3.04***	0.3364
X3 *The percent of Catholics*	0.0691	1.95*	0.3086
X3² *The percent of Catholics squared*	0.0003	2.68***	0.4097
X4 *The percent of landless laborers (Landbau-Taglöhner ohne Grund- oder Hausbesitz)*	0.7745	3.97***	0.3712
X5 *The percent of servants*	−0.5444	−1.94*	−0.1967

% of variation explained $(R^2 \times 100) = 28.62\%$

The key predictor variables were the percentage of the population in agriculture, the percentage simultaneously practicing a craft, and the hectares of arable land per landowner. The first two were negatively correlated with both dependent variables, the latter one positively, up to a point. These three independent variables explained 44 percent of the variation for each dependent one.

These results confirm the findings of the 1840 census. Illegitimacy does not flourish in heavily agricultural areas because of the continuing moral grip of the single family farm. Yet when the average farm size starts to increase, illegitimacy also rises for the obvious reason that a rural proletariat, highly prone to illegitimacy, is required to run big farms.

VI

In conclusion let me summarize these results. The problem was to account for the gradual, massive liberalization of the sexual mores of much of Europe's population over the last two centuries in terms of modernization. The difficulty in bringing evidence to bear on a subject as private and intimate as sexual behavior is overpowering, but I have claimed that, taken with a number of grains of salt, we may use illegitimacy statistics as evidence of sexual activity. The phenomenon we are trying to judge, of course, is the

TABLE II. THE RESULTS OF MULTIPLE REGRESSION ANALYSIS APPLIED TO 1880 CENSUS
(126 Census Districts)

Rate 1 (illegitimate births/total births × 1,000)

Variable	Partial Regression Coefficient (b_i)	T-Test	Standard Partial Regression Coefficient (B_i)
X1 *The percent in full time agriculture*	−0.1128	−2.60**	−0.2060
X1² *The percent in full time agriculture squared*	0.0056	2.04**	0.1545
X2 *Hectares of arable land*	1.8287	7.89***	0.6255
X2² *Hectares of arable land squared*	−0.4733	−5.43***	−0.4438
% of variation explained $(R^2 \times 100) = 44.2\%$			

Rate 2 (illegitimate population/unmarried women × 1,000)

Variable	Partial Regression Coefficient (b_i)	T-Test	Standard Partial Regression Coefficient (B_i)
X1 *Percent in full time agriculture*	−0.0434	−2.82***	−0.2149
X2 *Percent in part time agriculture*	−0.0591	−1.95*	−0.1786
X3 *Hectares of arable land*	0.5134	4.71***	0.4758
X3² *Hectares of arable land squared*	−0.2051	−6.06***	−0.5212
% of variation explained $(R^2 \times 100) = 43.8\%$			

* significant at 10% level
** significant at 5% level
*** significant at 1% level

incidence of premarital intercourse, for its acceleration was essential to the sexual revolution. A good measure of this phenomenon would be the frequency of prebridal pregnancies. Yet because arduous local digging is required to turn up such data, perhaps illegitimacy may stand as a surrogate. The data on illegitimacy seem accurate for the most part, and certainly in central Europe some significance for sexual behavior may be attached to fluctuations in illegitimacy because official delay of lower-class marriages often made it impossible to mask an illegitimate conception with a shotgun wedding.

The major empirical finding of this paper is an explosion in illegitimate births between 1750 and 1850, taking these years as rough guideposts, not precise turning points. An upsurge in illegitimate births from the negligible levels, perhaps 1 or 2 percent, of traditional Western society to the 10 or 20 percent of mid-nineteenth century Europe constitutes a remarkable occurrence. This increase occurred sooner or later in every Western country for which data are available, although the precise timing of the increase varied. I argue we may explain this increase in illegitimacy as a consequence of a fundamental transformation of the sexual attitudes of the lower classes: they abandoned the sexual abstemiousness prescribed for them in traditional society for a more easy-going style of interpersonal relations, coming to see sexual experience as an important part of personality development. This emphasis upon social class in accounting for differentials in sexual activity is fully in keeping with empirical sociological research on sex. If recent work has taught us anything, it is that styles of sexual activity, differences in attitudes towards and frequency of sexual relations, are not distributed randomly throughout the population; they are rather a close function of social class.

I submit that four of the major social changes, which together make up much of Europe's experience with modernization, caused this shift in sexual attitudes. Population growth and the advent of capitalist farming and of cottage industry caused the ranks of the lower orders to swell rapidly: a great class of landless proletarians began to appear for whom there was no place in the family farm, the traditional social and economic unit of rural Europe. Inheritance considerations meant the European family, concerned about the future of its little farm and about making advantageous marriages for its daughters in particular, enforced a sexual puritanism upon its offspring. With the appearance of propertyless groups, the need for such controls vanished.

At the same time, the expansion of the centralized state caused many of the traditional elites in the villages and small towns of Europe to suffer a loss in status and authority. More particularly they were deprived of the administrative devices, such as the "fornication penalties" with which they once commanded sexual conformity within the community as a whole. So two sets of inhibiting factors—the controls of the family and those of the village elders—become seriously weakened in the course of modernization.

Yet the argument has a further step. A sexual revolution is not produced merely by dropping mechanical controls on the opportunity for intercourse, or by abandoning civil and criminal penalties for premarital pregnancies. A positive change in the internalized values of the population must also accompany the abandonment of these social controls. Here I suggest that capitalism and urbanization encouraged people to reorient their value systems. The freer, easier life of the city militated against the repressiveness and fear of one's inner emotions, evaporated the hostility to self-understanding and rational analysis one finds in traditional society. And the logic of the marketplace stimulated a sense of self. Numerous investigations have discovered the value transformation which involvement with modern situations brings about: people become more eager for ego gratification, more concerned to develop their personalities at the cost of their formerly strong identification with the community. True love, a sign of strong ego development, blossoms.

So as the cities of Europe waxed and news of their way of life spread out into the countryside, the lower-class youth of the late eighteenth century embraced a new subculture. The rational destruction of traditional institutions which the Enlightenment represented, and the development of individualism which comes with romanticism, conspired to replace the old culture with a new one. Part of this culture asserted a positive value to sexual experimentation. And its consequence was illegitimacy.

NOTES

Glen Jones and Joan Baker assisted in preparing the data on which this article is based. Among those who suggested changes in earlier drafts are Rainer Baum, Natalie Davis, David Hunt, John Knodel, Peter Laslett, W. H. Nelson, Paul Robinson, Ann Shorter, Lawrence Stone, Charles Tilly, Etienne van de Walle, Mack Walker, Barry Wellman, and E. A. Wrigley.

1. Other quantitive changes, such as an increase in extramarital intercourse or in homosexuality, must also be considered in chronicling the revolution in sexual behavior, as must *qualitative* shifts in the kinds of sexual things people do, such as oral intercourse or fetishism. At this stage in my researches I have little concrete evidence on these matters, however, and so limit the discussion to premarital heterosexual relationships.

2. See the data presented by Friedrich Lindner, *Die unehelichen Geburten als Sozialphänomen: Ein Beitrag zur Statistik der Bevölkerungsbewegung im Königreiche Bayern* (Leipzig: A. Deichert, 1900), p. 57. The Thüringen Statistisches Bureau noted this inverse correlation between falling illegitimacy and

rising grain prices during the late 1860s. "Zur Statistik der unehelichen Geburten in den Thüringenschen Staaten," *Jahrbücher für Nationalökonomie und Statistik*, 22 (1874):337–58, especially p. 346.

3. The Wrigley citation is from *Population and History* (New York: McGraw-Hill, 1969), p. 119.

4. The legitimation rate varies considerably over time and place. In Bavaria on the average between 1857 and 1862 some 15 percent of illegitimate births were subsequently legitimated. (Note that this statistic merely relates the number of children legitimated in a year to the number born illegitimate; it does not say how many of a year's crop of bastards were themselves later legitimated.) See "Bewegung der Bevölkerung, 1857/58 bis 1861/62," *Beiträge zur Statistik des Königreichs Bayern*, 11 (1863):87. Results for Saxony and Austria around the turn of the century point to a legitimation rate of around 30 percent. But unlike the Bavarian data, these figures exclude from consideration the illegitimate children who died before legitimation. See Ludwig Elster, ed., *Handwörterbuch der Staatswissenschaften*, 4th ed., vol. 8 (Jena, 1928), pp. 394–95. In Dresden during the 1890s around 60 percent of the illegitimate children who survived until age five were legitimated. See Eugen Würzburger, "Zur Statistik der Legitimationen unehelicher Kinder," *Jahrbücher für Nationalökonomie und Statistik*, 3rd ser., 18 (Berlin, 1899):94–98. According to the statistician Bertillon, in Paris one-quarter of the illegitimate children were "recognized" by their natural fathers in 1880, which is perhaps the functional equivalent of legitimation. Cited in Louis Chevalier, *Classes laborieuses et classes dangereuses à Paris pendant la première moitié du XIXe siècle* (Paris: Plon, 1958), p. 381, n. 1.

5. On these marriage and settlement laws see Karl Braun, "Das Zwangs-Zölibat für Mittellose in Deutschland," *Vierteljahrschrift für Volkswirtschaft und Kulturgeschichte*, 20, iv (1867), pp. 1–80; Eduard Schübler, *Die Gesetze über Niederlassung und Verehelichung in den verschiedenen deutschen Staaten* (Stuttgart, 1855); John Knodel, "Law, Marriage and Illegitimacy in Nineteenth-century Germany," *Population Studies*, 20 (1966–67):279–94; Mack Walker, "Home Towns and State Administrators: South German Politics, 1815–30," *Political Science Quarterly*, 82 (1967):35–60; and Edward Shorter, "Social Change and Social Policy in Bavaria, 1800–1860," Harvard Diss., 1968.

A government official explained in the Bavarian legislature in 1840 how such laws caused premarital conceptions to become illegitimate births. He said that an elderly man had approached him in his office, desperate "because he had the misfortune to see his only child, his daughter, dishonored. To be sure, the seducer was prepared to marry her, but the communal officials had thundered against him with their veto." After the official explained that the royal government could not possibly overturn the communal decision, the old man "collapsed in desperation, tearing his hair, beating his head against the wall, and threatening to kill himself." Bavaria. *Verhandlungen der Kammer der Abgeordneten des Königreichs Bayern*, 1840, 4:428–29.

6. See Edward Shorter, John Knodel and Etienne van de Walle, "The Decline of Non-Marital Fertility in Europe, 1880–1940," a paper presented at the

Center for the Interdisciplinary Study of Science and Technology conference on "The Social Consequences of Industrialization" at Northwestern University, 22–25 March 1971.

7. It makes little difference whether one takes live births or total births—still-births included—as the denominator in these calculations, for although the stillbirth rate among illegitimate children was generally higher than among legitimate, the difference will affect our figure only marginally.

   The sources for the illegitimacy ratio by country since 1906 are: Henri Bunle, *Le Mouvement naturel de la population dans le monde de 1906 à 1936* (Paris: Editions de l'Institut National d'Études Démographiques, 1954), pp. 73–77; United Nations, *Demographic Yearbook: 1959*, pp. 218–38 for 1949–58; *Demographic Yearbook: 1965*, pp. 516–30 for 1959–64. These sources have been used for all countries in Figure 1 after 1906; the data are for five-year periods. For data on *rates* during these years see Shorter–Knodel–van de Walle.

8. The source of Swedish data is Gustav Sundbärg, *Bevölkerungsstatistik Schwedens, 1750–1900: Einige Hauptresultate,* 2nd ed. (Stockholm: P. A. Norstedt, 1923), p. 117. Data represent five-year averages. Sundbärg also makes available the illegitimacy rate.

   Pre-1900 data for individual German cities and regions come from W. Hanauer, "Historisch-statistische Untersuchungen über uneheliche Geburten," *Zeitschrift für Hygiene und Infektionskrankheiten*, 108 (1927–28):656–84; German national data for the nineteenth century are from the Federal Republic of Germany, Statistisches Bundesamt, *Statistisches Jahrbuch für die Bundesrepublik Deutschland, 1965*, p. 58; data are for single years taken at five-year intervals since 1875.

9. Italian data before 1900 come from Alexander von Oettingen, *Die Moralstatistik in ihrer Bedeutung für eine Socialethik*, 3rd ed. (Erlangen: A. Deichert, 1882), pp. 303 and xxxv.

10. For a few lonely statistics on eighteenth-century France see Etienne Gautier and Louis Henry, *La population de Crulai: Paroisse normande: Étude historique* (Paris: Institut national d'études démographiques, 1958; cahier no. 33), p. 67, which data in fact show an increase in bastardy during the last half of the century; Pierre Girard, "Aperçus de la démographie de Sotteville-lès-Rouen vers la fin du XVIIIe siècle," *Population*, 14 (1959):485–508, and especially 494; M. Terrisse, "Deux monographies paroissales sur la population française au XVIIIe siècle. I, Un faubourg du Havre: Ingouville," *Population*, 16 (1961): 285–300; Ingouville had an average illegitimacy ratio of 6 percent in 1774–90. Pierre Goubert comments on the low level of bastardy in France, mentioning "a certain strictness of morals, particularly in the countryside." "Recent Theories and Research in French Population between 1500 and 1700," in *Population in History: Essays in Historical Demography*, eds. D. V. Glass and D. E. C. Eversley (London: Edward Arnold, 1965), pp. 457–73 and particularly p. 468. For foundling data on Paris see Marcel R. Reinhard, et al., *Histoire générale de la population mondiale,* 3rd ed. (Paris: Eds. Montchrestien, 1968), p. 268; M.-Cl. Murtin, "Les abandons d'enfants à Bourg et dans le département

de l'Ain à la fin du XVIIIe siècle et dans la première moitié du XIXe," *Cahiers d'Histoire*, 10 (1965): 135–66. Bordeaux data come from private information with which Robert Wheaton has kindly supplied me, and from a notice in the *Annales de Démographie Historique, 1968*, p. 182. Nineteenth-century illegitimacy data are summarized in Wesley D. Camp, *Marriage and the Family in France Since the Revolution: An Essay in the History of Population* (New York: Bookman, n.d.), p. 108; data are for ten-year averages. The yearly number of illegitimate births is published in France, Institut National de la Statistique et des Etudes Economiques, *Annuaire Statistique de la France, 1966: Résumé rétrospectif*, pp. 66–75.

11. P. E. H. Hair, "Bridal Pregnancy in Rural England in Earlier Centuries," *Population Studies*, 20 (1966–67):233–43, especially 237–40.

12. Mr. Laslett kindly communicated these findings to me in a letter. For a preliminary report of Laslett-Wrigley illegitimacy data see also the revised French edition of Laslett's *World we have lost (Un monde que nous avons perdu* [Paris: Flammarion, 1969], p. 149.)

13. Data for England and Wales after 1840, which I have turned into five-year averages, are from B. R. Mitchell and Phyllis Deane, *Abstract of British Historical Statistics* (Cambridge: At the University Press, 1962), pp. 29–30, and from United Kingdom, Central Statistical Office, *Annual Abstract of Statistics*, no. 102 (1965), pp. 20–21. D. E. C. Eversley finds a "marked increase" in illegitimacy in a group of Worcestershire parishes after 1789, peaking in 1815–19. "A Survey of Population in an Area of Worcestershire from 1660 to 1850 on the Basis of Parish Registers," in *Population in History*, eds. Glass and Eversley, pp. 394–419, especially p. 413. On recent developments see Shirley M. Hartley, "The Amazing Rise of Illegitimacy in Great Britain," *Social Forces*, 44 (1966):533–45. K. H. Connell discusses the low Irish ratio in "Illegitimacy Before the Famine," in his *Irish Peasant Society: Four Historical Essays* (Oxford: Clarendon, 1968), pp. 51–86; an absence of time-series data makes it impossible to say if Ireland participated even hesitantly in the original illegitimacy explosion.

14. "Families in Colonial Bristol, Rhode Island: An Exercise in Historical Demography," *The William and Mary Quarterly*, 3rd ser., 25 (1968), pp. 40–57, especially 56–57.

15. I am indebted to Dr. Michael Phayer for these data. Dr. Phayer spent many hours culling church records in the archive of the episcopal chancellery of the archdiocese, and most generously made the results of his researches available to me.

16. The official statistics are summarized in Lindner, *Uneheliche Geburten*, p. 217. 1963 data are reported in *Statistisches Jahrbuch für die Bundesrepublik Deutschland, 1965*, p. 61.

17. Clark E. Vincent, *Unmarried Mothers* (New York: Free Press, 1961), p. 92 and passim.

18. Ira L. Reiss, *The Social Context of Premarital Sexual Permissiveness* (New York: Holt, Rinehart and Winston, 1967), pp. 177–78.

19. Lee Rainwater, "Some Aspects of Lower Class Sexual Behavior," *The Journal of Social Issues*, 22, ii (April, 1966):96–108; see also his *And the Poor Get Children: Sex, Contraception, and Family Planning in the Working Class* (Chicago: Quadrangle, 1960).

20. Harold T. Christensen, "Cultural Relativism and Premarital Sex Norms," *American Sociological Review*, 25 (1969):31–39.

21. William J. Goode, "Illegitimacy, Anomie, and Cultural Penetration," *American Sociological Review*, 26 (1961):910–25, especially 912; Sydney H. Croog, "Aspects of the Cultural Background of Premarital Pregnancies in Denmark," *Social Forces*, 30 (1951–52):215–19; Hyman Rodman, "Illegitimacy in the Caribbean Social Structure: A Reconsideration," *American Sociological Review*, 31 (1966): 673–83.

22. Oettingen discusses illegitimacy in *Moralstatistik*, pp. 289–346; Georg von Mayr, *Statistik und Gesellschaftslehre*, vol. 3: *Sozialstatistik* (Tübingen: J. C. B. Mohr, 1909), pp. 127–50; Chevalier, *Classes laborieuses*, pp. 380–97; Chevalier takes up illegitimacy within a section entitled "Un état pathologique."

23. "Illegitimacy, Anomie, and Cultural Penetration."

24. See the original report and comments on it in Lee Rainwater and William L. Yancey, *The Moynihan Report and the Politics of Controversy* (Cambridge, Mass.: MIT Press, 1967), pp. 39–124. Moynihan's views are, of course, in a tradition dating back at least to E. Franklin Frazier, who thought illegitimacy a consequence of social disorganization and a cause of personal demoralization. On Frazier see Charles A. Valentine, *Culture and Poverty: A Critique and Counter-Proposals* (Chicago: University of Chicago Press, 1968), pp. 20–24.

25. Friederich Engels, *The Condition of the Working-Class in England in 1844* (London: Allen and Unwin, 1892), p. 128; see Pierre Pierrard's discussion of worker concubinage and illegitimacy in a French industrial city: *La vie ouvrière à Lille sous le Second Empire* (Paris: Bloud et Gay, 1965), pp. 118–35; for a typical conservative account linking industrialization to "immorality" and illegitimacy, see Ernst Fabri, *Der Notstand unserer Zeit und Seine Hebung* (Erlangen, 1850); some of the popular polemical writing in mid-nineteenth-century Germany on this subject has been summarized in Edward Shorter, "Middle-Class Anxiety in the German Revolution of 1848," *Journal of Social History*, 2 (1969):189–215.

26. In using such expressions as "lower-class subculture," I follow Walter B. Miller, who has demonstrated how juvenile delinquency, commonly considered pathological, is accepted, normal behavior among the strata from which most delinquents come. "Lower Class Culture as a generating Milieu of Gang Delinquency," *Journal of Social Issues*, 14 (1958):5–19. In employing "individualism" I have Robert A. Nisbet in mind, who restated the thesis that

Western man's growing sense of individuality sent the institutions of traditional society into disrepair. See *Community and Power (formerly The Quest
for Community)* (New York: Oxford U. P., 1962; Galaxy edition), passim.

27. Of the enormous literature on social life under subsistence agriculture several
titles may be mentioned by way of example: Pierre Goubert has defined the
peasant morality of small-farm areas in *Beauvais et le Beauvaisis de 1600 à
1730: Contribution à l'histoire de la France du XVIIe siècle,* 2 vols. (Paris:
S.E.V.P.E.N., 1960); Goubert previewed some of his findings in "The French
Peasantry of the Seventeenth Century: A Regional Example," *Past and Present,* no. 10 (Nov., 1956), pp. 55–77; on England see Peter Laslett, *The World
We Have Lost* (New York: Scribner's, 1965); Laslett notes the probity of rural
sexual mores, and comments: "If the shape of the society was to be maintained,
Pauline morality had to be enforced" (p. 130). The fact of Europe's enormous
population growth requires no citation. A recent challenging treatment of the
subject is by William Langer, "Europe's Initial Population Explosion," *American Historical Review,* 69 (1963):1–17, who argues that the cultivation of the
potato stimulated the subdivision of land, therewith the founding of new
families, all of whose offspring constituted the population explosion. It seems
clear that when farm sizes dropped beneath a certain level, inheritance and
chastity would no longer be social problems: the holdings were simply too
tiny. On the social consequences of population growth see also Wrigley,
Population and History, pp. 135–43.

28. E. J. Hobsbawm and George Rudé have recently shown how agricultural capi-
talism proletarianized England's rural laborers in *Captain Swing* (New York:
Pantheon, 1968), especially pp. 11–93. Helmut Bleiber traces the social impact
of capitalist agriculture in a region of Germany in *Zwischen Reform und
Revolution: Lage und Kämpfe der schlesischen Bauern und Landarbeiter im
Vormärz, 1840–1847* (East Berlin: Akademie-Verlag, 1966), especially pp. 57–81.

29. *Industrialisierung und Volksleben: Die Veränderungen der Lebensformen in
einem ländlichen Industriegebiet vor 1800 (Zürcher Oberland)* (Erlenbach-
Zurich: Eugen Rentsch, 1960), passim; a companion volume takes the story
into the twentieth century: Braun, *Sozialer und Kultureller Wandel in einem
ländlichen Industriegebiet (Zürcher Oberland) unter Einwirkung des Mas-
chinen und Fabrikwesens im 19. und 20. Jahrhundert* (Erlenbach-Zurich:
Eugen Rentsch, 1965).

30. The relationship between the city and illegitimacy is discussed in detail in
Shorter–Knodel–van de Walle, *op. cit.*

31. Adna F. Weber, *The Growth of Cities in the Nineteenth Century: A Study
in Statistics* (New York: Macmillan, 1899; Cornell reprint, 1963), is still the
standard quantitative treatment of Europe's urbanization. Of recent research
on the growth of European urban populations, Wolfgang Köllmann, "Zur
Bevölkerungsentwicklung ausgewählter deutscher Grosstädte in der Hochindus-
trialisierungsperiode," *Jahrbuch für Sozialwisenschaft,* 18 (1967):129–44; and
Philippe Pinchemel, *Géographie de la France,* 2 vols. (Paris: Colin, 1964),
especially, II, 560–640, may be mentioned.

Simmel's "The Metropolis and Mental Life" is conveniently reprinted in *Classic Essays on the Culture of Cities,* ed. Richard Sennett (New York: Appleton-Century-Crofts, 1969), pp. 47–60. J. A. Banks, in a recent important article, argues that urban migration took place because of the cultural attractiveness of English cities for young people: the city became a site for individual emancipation and personality development. He rejects the horror-story approach to urbanization in England, arguing instead that countrymen flocked to the city for positive reasons. Banks' insight is akin to my assertion that one should not attempt to explain the illegitimacy explosion as a consequence of the economic deprivation and social disorganization which accompanied the industrial revolution. "Population Change and the Victorian City," *Victorian Studies,* 11 (1968):277–89.

32. See E. A. Wrigley, "A Simple Model of London's Importance in Changing English Society and Economy, 1650–1750," *Past and Present,* no. 37 (July 1967), pp. 44–70; ". . . A city like London in the later seventeenth century was so constituted sociologically, demographically and economically that it could well reinforce and accelerate incipient change" (p. 54).

33. On this process in Germany see Mack Walker, "Napoleonic Germany and the Hometown Communities," *Central European History,* 2 (1969):99–113. Charles Tilly sees the penetration of the centralized state into the most backward hinterland and the most routine areas of daily life as profoundly important in European social history; he argues specifically that the sprawl of central authority altered the nature of collective violence in the course of the nineteenth century from a "primitive" pattern to a "reactionary" one. "Collective Violence in European Perspective," in *Violence in America: Historical and Comparative Perspectives,* eds. Hugh Davis Graham and Ted Robert Gurr (New York: Bantam Books, 1969), pp. 4–45, and especially pp. 16–24.

34. For an introduction to the Bavarian economy and society in the nineteenth century, the reader is referred to M. Doeberl, *Entwicklungsgeschichte Bayerns,* vols. 2, 3 (Munich: Oldenbourg, 1928–31); Wolfgang Zorn, "Gesellschaft und Staat im Bayern des Vormärz," in *Staat und Gesellschaft im deutschen Vormärz,* ed. Werner Conze (Stuttgart: Ernst Klett, 1962), pp. 113–42; Zorn, *Kleine Wirtschafts- und Sozialgeschichte Bayerns, 1806–1933* (Munich-Pasing: Verlag Bayerische Heimatforschung, 1962).

35. On these laws, customs, and their consequences for illegitimacy, see Knodel, "Law, Marriage and Illegitimacy in Nineteenth-Century Germany," Shorter, "Social Change and Social Policy in Bavaria," and Lindner, *Uneheliche Geburten.*
Large-scale agriculture had traditionally prevailed in many regions of Bavaria, and with it a rural proletariat of farm laborers. And while the numbers of such people increased during the first half of the century in consequence of general population growth, their ranks were not augmented by the specific process of agricultural capitalism. On the lack of market orientation before 1850 see Christoph Borcherdt, *Fruchtfolgesysteme und Marktorientierung als gestaltende Kräfte der Agrarlandschaft in Bayern* (Kallmünz/Regensburg: Michael Lassleben, 1960), p. 31. On the rural laboring classes, see Hanns

Platzer, *Geschichte der ländlichen Arbeitsverhältnisse in Bayern* (Munich, 1904).

36. Friedrich Lütge, citing Schmelzle's study of Old Bavaria, claims the eighteenth-century population of the electoral state did not increase. *Die Bayerische Grundherrschaft: Untersuchungen über die Agrarverfassung Altbayerns im 17.–18. Jahrhundert* (Stuttgart: Piscator, 1949), p. 10. But various authors find evidence of substantial population growth in Franconia in the eighteenth century. See Valentin Steinert, *Zur Frage der Naturalteilung: Eine Untersuchung über die bäuerlichen Verhältnisse des fränkischen Grabfeldgaues,* in the series Wirtschafts- und Verwaltungsstudien . . . Bayerns, 23 (1906):53; Wieland Kindinger, *Beiträge zur Entwicklung der Kulturlandschaft in der zentralen Rhön vom Dreissigjährigen Krieg bis 1933* (Würzburg, 1942; Fränkische Studien, NF 4), pp. 86–91; Ludwig Schmidt-Kehl, "Wandel im Erb und Rassengefüge zweier Rhönorte, 1700–1936," *Archiv für Bevölkerungswissenschaft,* 7 (1937):176–99, especially 179; Carl Hofmann, *Die Hausweberei in Oberfranken* (Jena: Gustav Fischer, 1927), p. 22; Friedrich Kästner, *Die Oberfränkische Handweberei* (Diss. Munich, 1918), p. 7. For national population growth data, see "Geschichte der neueren bayerischen Statistik," in *Beiträge zur Statistik des Königreichs Bayern,* 86 (1914):269.

37. See Hofmann, *Hausweberei,* and Kästner, *Handweberei.*

38. Bavaria. Königliches Statistisches Landesamt, *Bayerns Entwicklung nach den Ergebnissen der amtlichen Statistik seit 1840* (Munich: K. Statistisches Landesamt, 1915), p. 3.

39. The population of Munich, and of all other Bavarian municipalities, since 1840 is reported in "Historisches Gemeindeverzeichnis: die Einwohnerzahlen der Gemeinden Bayerns in der Zeit von 1840 bis 1952," *Beiträge zur Statistik Bayerns,* 192 (1953):14. For the cultural impact of cities we have the testimony of the anonymous author of "Suggestions as to how Barriers may be Placed Against the Vice Spreading to the Countryside": "The curse of vice . . . is creeping out from its previous abode—the cities—in order to inundate the countryside and its thriving fields with ravaging torrents. Young flowerlike maidens by the thousand have been seized in this wild current and thrown to the ground." *Vorschläge wie dem auf dem Lande um sich greifenden Uebel der Unzucht könnten Schranken gesetzt werden* (n.p., 1814), p. 3.

40. On the quality of social control under the Old Regime, see Jos. von Destouches, *Ueber den Verfall der Städte und Märkte und die Mittel, ihnen wieder aufzuhelfen* (Ulm: Verlag Stettinischen Buchhandlung, 1803), passim; Mack Walker, "Reform Invades the Hometown Communities" (draft paper of December, 1967). See also Felix Joseph von Lipowsky, *Bayerns Kirchen und Sittenpolizei unter seinen Herzögen und Kurfürsten* (Munich, 1821), especially pp. 123–44.

41. Among the few competent studies of administrative reorganization and centralization of this time, Horst Clément's may be especially recommended. *Das bayerische Gemeindeedikt vom 17. Mai 1818: Ein Beitrag zur Entstehungs-*

geschichte der kommunalen Selbstverwaltung in Deutschland (Diss. Freiburg i. B., 1934). Revisions in the administrative law on social control may be followed in Georg Döllinger, *Repertorium der Staats-verwaltung des Königreichs Bayern,* 6 vols. (Munich, 1814–17); and Döllinger, *Sammlung der im Gebiete der inneren Staats-verwaltung des Königreichs Bayern bestehenden Verordnungen, aus amtlichen Quellen geschöpft und systematisch geordnet,* 33 vols. (Munich, 1835–54), especially vols. 11, 12, 14, 26 and 27; the 1808 ordinance abolishing fornication penalties may be found in vol. 5, 179–80. Fornication penalties were abolished in the Franconian principalities of Ansbach and Bayreuth in 1795.

42. For these quotations, see Munich Hauptstaatsarchiv, MI 46556, memo of 22 Feb. 1837; clipping from *Bamberger Regierungsblatt* preserved in MI 46560.

43. MI 46560, 7 April 1859.

44. Lindner, *Uneheliche Geburten,* pp. 81–112, 226–38.

45. The 1840 census data are from "Stand und Bewegung der Bevölkerung, 1818–1846," *Beiträge zur Statistik des Königreichs Bayern,* 1 (1850):30–113.

46. Using the square of a variable in a regression model rather than the variable itself is a crude way of spotting curvilinear relationships among the independent and dependent variables. On this technique see Jerome C. R. Li, *Statistical Inference,* vol. II (Ann Arbor: Edwards Brothers, 1964), pp. 215–18, and Robert A. Gordon, "Issues in Multiple Regression," *American Journal of Sociology,* 73 (1968):592–616 and especially 611.

47. *Uneheliche Geburten,* pp. 132–68.

INDUSTRIALIZATION AND SEXUAL BEHAVIOR: SOME ASPECTS OF WORKING-CLASS LIFE IN IMPERIAL GERMANY

R. P. Neuman

Some years ago, Gordon Rattray Taylor observed that "the assumption of historians seems to be that sexual manners are something which exists in a watertight compartment, almost independently of historical trends as a whole, and that it would no more throw light on the general problem of interpreting history to open this compartment than it would be to study the development of, say, cooking."[1] No one would argue that historians devote more attention to how people feed, clothe, house, govern, and destroy themselves than they do to the customs and institutions surrounding the way in which they reproduce themselves. But historians have not been quite as indifferent to the relationship between historical trends and sexual manners as Taylor suggests. There have appeared in the last fifty years alone a number of very broad surveys of sexual customs over long periods of time and in several countries. However, many such studies tend to foreshorten changes and overgeneralize, giving to such periods as the Renaissance and the Protestant Reformation their own distinctive set of sexual manners and mores.[2] In somewhat the same genre are those polemical works that interpret broad aspects of human sexual life in terms of Marxist ideology.[3]

Some historians have given considerable attention, along with these general studies, to the sexual customs and behavior among the working classes during periods of industrialization. Many of the problems they examine (the "breakdown" of the family, the demoralization of the working classes in an urban factory setting, and the contrast between sexual habits in town and country) derive from the observations of a variety of nineteenth-century conservative and radical critics of industrial capitalism and big-city life.[4] Late in the last century, as more and more women entered the factories, earlier criticisms were repeated and elaborated by socialists in outright condemnation of capitalism.[5] The views of many of these critics reflected their own class and educational backgrounds, moral codes and political ideologies. Deeply impressed and often disturbed by the rather sudden emergence of the urban industrial working classes, early observers often seem to have exaggerated the nature and rapidity of the changes in sexual behavior and family life among these classes.

Robert P. Neuman received his Ph.D. from Northwestern University, and is now teaching at the State University College in Fredonia, New York.

More recent students of industrialization have tried to criticize, extend, and sometimes correct these early analyses. Among English historians, for example, the relationship among industrialization, sexual morality, and family life has for some years been the subject of a historical debate running parallel to the better-known "standard of living" debate.[6] Helmut Möller's excellent study of the eighteenth-century petit bourgeois German family shows that much of the concern over sexual behavior usually associated with the industrial working classes already existed among respectable artisans before 1800.[7] In general, these studies modify earlier interpretations and revise them to show that the changes placed under the rubric of "modernization" were more subtle and complex, and not so rapid or dramatic as previously believed.

In spite of such refinements in the study of changes in sexual and family life in the period of industrialization, it is striking that the testimony of workers themselves as found in their autobiographical writings has been largely ignored. Although the life stories of German workers written by themselves are comparatively few in number, they provide a valuable source for the social historian on how the workers perceived and described their own lives. With the help of these writings this essay will examine some of the sexual attitudes and practices of the working classes in Imperial Germany. The aim of doing so is first, to introduce the reader to working-class autobiographies and some of the problems involved in using them as historical sources. Second, and more important, to make some tentative observations on the similarities and differences between sexual customs in the city and factory and village and farm; in this I hope to contribute to the larger question of urbanization and social change in an industrializing society. To be specific, the essay suggests that the differences between urban and rural sexual habits in Imperial Germany were not so great as is often believed. Both contemporaries and historians have exaggerated the "evil" influence of the city as contrasted with the "natural purity" of the countryside.[8] In addition, changing sexual attitudes and practices are seen not so much as the results of urban industrial life after 1870, but rather as a secular trend including industrialization, which might be termed simply modernization. Life and work in urban factory surroundings did not directly undermine sexual attitudes and behavior. They provided the framework in which the growing demystification of the worker's life and worldview took place. To illustrate this demystification in the sexual sphere, we must supplement the autobiographies on certain questions (illegitimacy, prostitution, and contraception) with some contemporary statistical data, sociological surveys, and psychological studies. Wherever possible, however, the working-class autobiographers have been allowed to speak for themselves.

Limiting this study to only the working classes and to the period of Gemany's great industrial and urban growth in the decades after 1870 is in part determined by the nature of the sources. Most of the worker autobiographies appeared after 1900 and concentrate largely on the half-century after 1860. This limitation gives this essay a certain static quality that can only be overcome by extending the period under consideration back beyond 1860 and forward past 1914. It would be necessary in addition to compare the sexual ideas and habits of German workers with those of Germans in other social classes and with workingmen in other countries. Such a study lies in the future. In full recognition of the shortcomings and difficulties involved, the present study is offered as a first step toward revealing some elusive and often ignored facets of human life in the past.[9]

Illuminating these facets with writings produced by members of the working classes presents several problems for the historian. Some of these have already been encountered by earlier students using the autobiographies for purposes other than those of this essay. Because the books are mainly concerned with living, working, and political conditions as perceived by the workers themselves, they have been used to study the "psychology of anti-capitalistic mass movements,"[10] the breakdown of community feelings among the working classes,[11] the history of German artisans and society,[12] group consciousness and group structures among workers,[13] and, recently, the early history of German Social Democracy.[14] These and other studies deal with the historical and methodological problems presented by the autobiographies and the following discussion of the sources draws on a number of these earlier works.[15]

The definition of the term *working classes* as used in this essay is dictated by the occupations of the autobiographers: farm laborers, factory lathe operators, unskilled workers in bottle-making plants, waiters and waitresses, domestic servants, cigar- and brickmakers, coal miners, casual day laborers, and the like. It is clear that the workers were very conscious of differences in pay, skills, and status among themselves. Perhaps the chief common denominator among the writers is the feeling that they belong to a lower stratum of German society. All of the books suggest an awareness of the gap between "them up there" and "us down here." Beyond this, it is very difficult and dangerous to generalize about the workers' attitudes on various subjects.

Can the writings produced by a handful of workers be regarded as representative of the German classes at large? Even a complete bibliography of autobiographies written by members of these classes between 1890 and 1930 would scarcely total eighty titles. Of these, only a few were written by women, which gives a male slant to any study based on them. Furthermore, the very fact that a worker took the time, and had the patience and ability, to write down his life story would seem to set him apart from the rank and file. Indeed, many of the working-class autobiographers were autodidacts who may have stood above their fellow workers in intelligence, initiative, and perhaps pretentiousness. However, the autobiographers spent much time describing the conditions of their lives, the difficulties of finding and keeping a job or a suitable place to live. Certainly these were problems faced by the majority of working-class people. In spite of these shared experiences, it is hard not to agree with one commentator on these working-class autobiographies, Hans Gruhle, who suggests that the authors were to a certain extent outsiders who stood on "the margin of the class."[16] However that may be, the autobiographers are an indication of the growing articulateness and sense of individuality among German workers around the turn of the century. Whether the working-class writers were also sexual outsiders in comparison with their fellow workers is difficult to decide. I have tried to overcome this problem in two ways. First, by looking for common sexual themes within the autobiographies. Second, by a comparison wherever possible of what the autobiographers say with some contemporary sociological and statistical studies. In the words of an early student of this genre, Adelbert Koch, "as a source of information, the memoirs of the worker do not replace, but rather round out, statistical data."[17]

Another important problem concerns the reliability of the testimony of the authors. Here the question of motivation is important. Many of the books were written by men and women who rose from their working class positions to become functionaries of some standing in the trade unions and the Social Democratic Party. For such writers the intimate facts of private life are usually secondary and subordinate to their part in S.P.D. and trade-union history. Sexual matters are either totally absent or only alluded to, which may be an indication of the autobiographer's growing sense of respectability.

Those authors who did not rise far beyond their origins through the union or party hierarchy and who were either retired or still employed in their usual job at the time of writing seem to have been motivated by very different reasons. Chiefly, they sought to bring the plight of the worker, his or her "struggle for existence," to the attention of a larger reading public. Whether or not they exaggerated the conditions of working-class life can be checked against contemporary studies of income, cost of living, housing conditions and the like. But in sexual matters perhaps the best test of reliability is to read a number of autobiographies and try to acquire a sense for truth and fantasy. Naturally some allowance must be made for the shortcomings of memory and vividness of imagination, although even fantasies can be instructive. Significantly, earlier studies of working-class autobiographies regard the frankness of the writers on their sexual life as an indication of the overall reliability of their testimony, the assumption being that a man who admits for example, that he masturbated for several years is also likely to be frank and honest in less sensitive matters.[18]

Who, then, produced these working-class autobiographies? The authors can be divided into the two groups suggested above. The first includes those who rose above their origins through the trade unions and S.P.D. Among these can be mentioned the autobiographies of August Bebel,

Ottilie Baader, Wilhelm Bock, Nikolaus Osterroth, Julius Bruhns, and Adelheid Popp.[19] While these books add a little to our knowledge of working-class family life, they offer little direct sexual information. They would lend themselves more to a study of the transmutation of workers into party or union functionaries.

The second and principal source of materials for this study are those autobiographies written by workers who at the time of writing had not risen far, if at all, beyond the lives they had known since childhood.[20] Several of the books in this group were edited by Paul Göhre, an Evangelical pastor with socialist sympathies, who wanted to bring the life of the working classes before the German reading public. The first one that Göhre edited was the autobiography of Karl Fischer, published in no less than three volumes between 1902 and 1905.[21] Fischer, born in 1840, was the son of a master baker living in a small Thuringian town. During his life Fischer worked at a wide variety of jobs, ranging from railroad construction to unskilled factory work. His life seems to have been uneventful, not to say drab, and his writing style is leaden and colorless. More than any other of the autobiographers used here, Fischer justifies Hans Gruhle's criticism that most workers' memoirs are written in the style of "there was one, and there was another one, and there came one, etc."[22] Fischer took practically no interest in political affairs, and even less in Social Democratic propaganda. As Göhre notes in his introduction, Fischer "today still has complete respect and awe for the Kaiser."[23]

In 1905, Göhre edited another autobiography, that of Moritz Bromme, born in 1873, the son of a railroad worker.[24] After growing up in a small Saxon town, Bromme became a semiskilled lathe operator in a number of machine-making plants in and around Leipzig. Married, the father of six children, Bromme wrote his memoirs while he was a patient in a clinic for the tubercular. Unlike Karl Fischer, Bromme was an ardent Social Democrat, active in local electoral organizations. Younger than Bromme, but like him a metal lathe-operator, was Eugen May, whose autobiographical sketch appeared in 1922.[25] Down to the time of writing, May claimed to have worked at more than fifty locations in southwestern Germany, Switzerland, and northern Italy. Though May exhibits a strong streak of "antibossism," it is not clear whether he supported any particular political party.

Wenzel Holek, a German-speaking Czech born near the German-Bohemian border, published his autobiography in 1906.[26] Born to a Catholic family in 1864, Holek later became an avid member of local Czech nationalist and socialist discussion clubs. He divided his working life between seasonal work in Bohemian sugar-beet processing plants and brickmaking or unskilled factory work in Germany. Holek's son, Heinrich, born in 1885, also published his own life story.[27] His book is especially interesting because it recounts some of the same family events described by his father, but from a son's point of view. Like the elder Holek, Heinrich became a socialist and his book describes his work in factories, towns, and schools, in both Germany and Bohemia.

Very useful for the information it gives about rural life is the autobiography of Franz Rehbein, the only longtime farm laborer included in this study.[28] Although born in Eastern Pomerania, Rehbein spent much of his life working on farms in Schleswig-Holstein. His book includes a detailed description of farm life and also of his three-year tour of duty as a cavalryman stationed at Metz. After his discharge in 1890, he returned to farm life, increased his interest in Social Democratic ideas first introduced to him by some of his fellow soldiers, lost an arm in a threshing-machine accident, and eventually became a reporter for *Vorwärts*, the Berlin socialist newspaper.

Another fervent Social Democrat, Franz Bergg, was born in Königsberg in 1867.[29] After two years as an apprentice cigarmaker in Hamburg, he wandered into Bavaria and finally Italy. Illness forced him to return to Germany, where he spent some time in jail for stealing from the cigarmakers' union funds. He later stayed in Paris for a time and booed the Czar during his state visit to France in 1898. Franz returned to Germany where he wrote and recited poetry when he was not rolling cigars. Bergg's book is at once the most sexually explicit, not to say mildly erotic, of all the autobiographies, and for that reason it is suspect. His vivid imagination seems to have got the best of him at times, as in the description of his elaborate seduction of a concert singer, complete with wine, soft lights, and a beautiful girl in a sky-blue Japanese kimono.[30] Some interesting sexual fantasies also appear in the work of Georg Meyer, a native of Cologne who served in the French Foreign Legion before moving to the United States early in this century.[31]

The youngest of the male autobiographers, Ludwig Tureck, was born in 1898.[32] Tureck's father was a Hamburg cigarmaker and a socialist. Ludwig became a typesetter's apprentice and in 1912 joined the Socialist Workers' youth organization. Drafted into the army in the First World War, Tureck was wounded in 1917; he recovered, deserted, and was arrested and imprisoned, and released in time to join a communist militia group in the Ruhr after the war. In his autobiography he declares that both he and his wife are members of the Communist party, share Marxist views, and have no children thanks to "scientific birth control measures."[33]

Working women are not well represented among the autobiographers. In addition to Adelheid Popp's book mentioned above, only two have been used. The first, by the stolid Doris Viersbeck, describes the life of a domestic servant in Hamburg of the 1880s and 1890s.[34] The other is a very interesting anonymous life story, also centered in Hamburg, of a woman who worked successively as a factory worker, a domestic servant, and a barmaid.[35] Her descriptions of the characters in some of Hamburg's sleazier bars are reminiscent of Brecht's *Three Penny Opera*. Two further books, not written by working-class women, also give some insights into the lives of working women. The first is by a middle-class woman who worked "underground" disguised as a worker in several Chemnitz textile factories early in the 1890s.[36] The other is a book by a Lutheran minister based on seventy hours of discussions with a sixty-nine-year-old East Prussian mother and ex-factory worker.[37] Although the good pastor saw fit to edit out the old woman's "most pungent remarks" on marriage, the family, and sexual behavior, some interesting comments managed to escape his blue pencil.

Finally, I have found useful three works by Adolf Levenstein, the first two consisting of short life histories and the letters of workers, and the third a rather sophisticated sociological study of working-class life prepared by Levenstein, himself a worker and a talented amateur sociologist.[38] Two other works, both anonymous, one by a Vienna orphan boy,[39] and the other by a woman confined to a Swiss asylum,[40] help to round out the sources of information.

These then are the primary sources for our discussion. The average age of the authors in 1900 was between thirty and forty. None of them had any formal schooling beyond age fourteen, at least at the time of writing. All, except Karl Fischer and the servant, Doris Viersbeck, had some socialist sympathies if they did not actually support the S.P.D. Apparently all of them, except for Adelheid Popp and Wenzel Holek, both Austrian-born Catholics, were raised in Evangelical Lutheran families. But only the stolid Karl Fischer attended church conscientiously, if irregularly, and continued to profess his childhood faith. All, again excepting Fischer, a lifelong bachelor, were either married or living in common-law at the time they wrote their memoirs. Apart from the farmhand Franz Rehbein and the domestic servant Doris Viersbeck, all worked in industrial occupations or home "industries" (like cigarmaking) for rather extended periods of time. Almost all of the men did military service, even when this conflicted with the socialist principles. None of the writers came from Berlin, and there seems to be a larger number of them from northern and eastern Germany than from the south and southwest.

If it is hard to generalize about such matters as age, geographic origins, and occupations, it is even more difficult to generalize about the sexual experiences related in the autobiographies. Adelbert Koch is correct in saying that "the authors express themselves with great frankness concerning their sexual and love lives."[41] This is not to say that they border on the pornographic or that sexual anecdotes are deliberately inserted to shock or titillate the reader, although this may be the case in certain of Franz Bergg's recollections. Rather, such information usually appears in a natural context where the author wishes to supply what he or she evidently considers a necessary part of a well-rounded picture of a life otherwise devoid of history-making events. It seems best here to recount some of the sexual experiences of the workers and then to apply them to a discussion of the similarities and differences between urban and rural sexual manners.

Early sexual knowledge comes to the autobiographers chiefly from their young friends. Ten-year-old Moritz Bromme, who believed that the stork brought babies, was amazed when an apprentice a few years older than him told him "how people are made." The apprentice got his knowledge firsthand by observing his master and his wife in the bedroom he shared with them.[42] Three years later Moritz refused to join his friends when they smeared birchbark sap on their faces and pubic regions in order to induce the growth of hair, the sign of "manliness."[43] Franz Rehbein mentions his first sexual enlightenment at the age of thirteen. Still in school, Rehbein served as a "fox," a general servant for a club of older high school students. At one of the meetings of this club, Franz saw a collection of obscene photographs of men and women. He was particularly impressed by the fact that they were not drawings, but photographs of actual people. They changed his way of looking at things. "I dreamt about them [the photographs]. From that time on I looked at grown women and girls with entirely different eyes. It always seemed to me as if I had to look right through their clothes."[44] Franz took the trouble to steal several of the pictures and share them with some of his friends.

Wenzel Holek's sexual education was more direct. As a twelve-year-old boy, he worked in a sugar-beet processing plant near his home in Bohemia. One day at the plant he came upon a foreman having intercourse with an eighteen-year-old female worker in a storeroom. Shocked and embarassed by what he had seen, Wenzel was told by an older worker that some of the girls submitted themselves to the foreman hoping for better wages and hours, "something I had never thought about."[45] A year later Holek and his father worked as diggers in clay pits that provided raw materials for an adjacent brickmaking plant. Holek considered the men and women who worked in the pits and the plant as the coarsest he ever met. He recounts the following typical exchange between some male workers and a twenty-year-old girl from the brick plant:[46]

"Anna, was the tomcat stuck in the drainpipe last night?"

"How many times did you —— yesterday?"

"What's the matter with you pigs? You stupid louts, I can do whatever I want."

"Can I take you out tonight, Anna?"

"Yes, if you haven't messed you pants."

"Bravo! Bravo! She told you!"

During a lunch hour at the same place Holek describes some crude horseplay in which a male worker held a woman down on the ground and imitated the motions of sexual intercourse. The woman spit in the man's face, but he continued. Holek remarks that the other workers cheered approvingly " 'Bravo! Bravo! Franz, that's a real masterpiece!' But I was ashamed because I had to see such a thing while sitting beside my father, so I crept off between the big piles of clay as though I had seen none of it."[47]

Holek's own son, Heinrich, recalls that at age eight he got his first lessons in sex from older school boys who drew obscene words and drawings on walls. The schoolchildren also made up jingles suggesting that the local priest preferred sleeping with his housekeeper to praying.[48] Holek, like a number of other autobiographers, reports the sexual advances of transient workers who rented rooms and beds from his parents. This testimony might lend some support to those who spoke about the "breakdown" of the family, for it was very common for German working-class families to take in one or more boarders in order to supplement their income.[49] But only Franz Bergg, characteristically, suggests that the innocent stroking of his cheek by an eighteen-year-old servant girl boarding in his parents' house led him to a premature sexual awakening at age six.[50]

Early exposure to sexual intercourse also appears in the autobiographies. In spite of the fact that many of the writers seem to have shared rooms and even beds with their parents, sexual intercourse between mother and father is never mentioned, which may or may not be surprising. Heinrich Holek reports that at age ten or eleven he was seduced, or rather raped, by a twenty-year-old girl one day when he delivered his father's lunchpail to a brickmaking plant.[51] When Moritz Bromme was a fifteen-year-old working in a rather large machine-making plant a pregnant girl four years older than him who also worked there tried to attract his attention by ostentatiously lifting her skirts to adjust her garters. Because of her bad reputation and the fact that she had legs like "a pair of water pails" Bromme ignored her advances.[52] A ten-year-old boy in a Vienna orphanage came upon one of the attendants and a servant girl having intercourse and was shocked by what he saw.

The following night I could not fall asleep for a long time. Again and again the picture of how the attendant and the girl wrestled came before my eyes and I often felt a hot flush running over my body. In the morning it struck me that I now knew something about the attendant that could hurt him very much if I revealed it. This thought made me extremely happy.[53]

With the coming of adolescence some of the autobiographers begin to describe their own sexual life. Ludwig Tureck recounts in detail and with almost Joycean precision his first nocturnal emission. When Ludwig was seventeen he took a girl ice-skating. On the way home they kissed, Ludwig was somewhat aroused, but went no further. Later that night, which Tureck specifies as that of January 5-6, 1915, he dreamt about the girl and "suddenly there was a rushing crash; the whole world crashed along with me."[54] When he woke he was seized by guilt, and felt himself to be as unclean as those boys who masturbated and then bragged about it. He fell asleep resolved to have nothing more to do with girls. But he experienced another emission on March 9 and claims to have made his first sexual "conquest" on April 14: "Masturbation [*der Onanie*] was a waste of time, only for weaklings, cowards, fools and stupid kids. I became a Don Juan."[55] It is interesting to note Tureck's desire to date precisely his first nocturnal emissions; extraordinary that he should remember the exact dates—and if he does not remember exactly—extraordinary that he should think precision so important.

Sexual dreams also play a part in the story of Georg Meyer, who offers the following interesting comments on two dreams inspired by his adolescent crush on an eighteen-year-old bar maid. Meyer was sixteen at the time and loved from afar.

Thus I loved. The animal that always pulls at its chain and is never satisfied, the starved beast in me, stretched out its claws. The "demon of fleshly lust" won control over me. When I lay down to sleep, it climbed unsummoned through the window; an undraped female figure floated voluptuously next to my meagre bed, bent over me, laid down at my side in sumptuous nakedness; she nestled against me, embraced me, pressed me to her full breasts; and in the sultry, suffocating embrace I inhaled her hot breath. Because of a pretty face I had become a fool.[56]

In keeping with the animal imagery of this passage, Meyer further recounts a dream in which he sees a tiger pouncing on a lamb. The lamb is suddenly transformed into a naked girl whose "full, heaving breasts" are mauled and bloodied by the tiger's claws. Then the tiger sees his reflection in the eyes of his dying victim. "It is my own distorted visage!" He awakes from his dream as a voice like thunder calls out the command "Be a man!"[57] Other working-class autobiographers sometimes share Meyer's opinion that the sexual drive is like a chained animal, but few of them express this view in such savage imagery or in such purple prose.

References to masturbation appear quite often in the autobiographies. The authors usually share the common nineteenth- and early twentieth-century view that it is at once a shameful and a harmful practice.[58] An exception to this view was expressed to Moritz Bromme when he surprised a friend masturbating in his room. The fourteen-year-old Moritz asked his friend what he was doing and his friend replied that he had been unable to visit a prostitute in some time and "still wanted to stay healthy."[59] This is an echo of a curious nineteenth-century medical debate over the good and bad effects of sexual abstinence on (particularly male) physical health. Those who favored sexual abstinence argued that semen contained vital elements essential for good health and growth. These vital elements must therefore be retained within the body until full sexual "maturity" is reached at age twenty-four. Sexual intercourse, masturbation, or even an "excessive" number of nocturnal emissions before this age was supposed to lead to lifelong mental and physical ailments.[60] The antiabstinence school believed, like Bromme's young friend, that the release of sexual tensions was a prerequisite of good health. Some doctors concurred with the popular folk belief that periodic ejaculation in some form was as necessary for good health as other eliminative functions.[61]

Moritz Bromme himself later masturbated for some time until an older worker advised him of the "harmfulness" of the practice.[62] When Bromme was nineteen and working in a factory, he saw a particularly coarse worker in his middle twenties who, during the morning breakfast halt, often lay down on a workbench and masturbated "without concealing himself in the least from the many younger people standing around. . . . Nevertheless, he was one of the best lathe operators in the town."[63] Evidently Bromme did not consider the habit totally debilitating. Max Lotz, a thirty-two-year-old married coal miner, recalled that as a fourteen-year-old working in a Ruhr factory, "I became acquainted with the diabolical blight of masturbation, and for a long, long time, until very recently, this fire has burned in my nerves."[64] Franz Bergg says that he began masturbating before he went to grade school.

Even at that time I was no longer pure. I was familiar even then with the child's vice [that is, masturbation]. No actual seduction had ever taken place. Nature had simply given me an innate curiosity about such matters. Therefore how surprised I was when I got to school and discovered how this game was practiced by most of the children. The higher I went through the grades, the more I was convinced that the "innocent pleasures of children," as one doctor foolishly called the [sexual] drive, was generally widespread.[65]

Speaking as an adult, however, Bergg seems to have felt guilty about masturbating and proclaims "Oh, guard your treasure, you budding youth! So that you need not blush before yourself and before those who slumber in your semen!"[66] Again, it should be remembered that Bergg appears to have been sexually precocious, for according to him even Bible stories about Joseph and Potiphar's wife, and David and Bathsheba, excited his sexual interest as a schoolboy. And "in catechism instruction the danger is even greater."[67]

The tyranny that the condemnation of masturbation and its imaginary telltale symptoms could exert is shown in the life of the Vienna orphan boy mentioned earlier. After leaving the orphanage he lived with foster parents. One day when he was about twelve his schoolmaster began calling him a *Schwein,* and asking him privately why he was so pale and had blue rings under his eyes. The boy says that he had not masturbated before this time and did not know these were supposed to be the physical signs of "self-abuse." After several weeks of this harassment during which the boy racked his brain for an explanation of his teacher's accusations, his foster mother was called to school for a conference. "Shaking in a fever of anxiety" the boy was dragged home by the woman and soundly beaten. The whole class found out about the incident and the reason for it and "in a very short time half of the class yielded to the vice of onanism. Now the teacher noticed nothing."[68] Oddly enough, when the same boy was fifteen his stepmother saw fit to have him share a bed with her niece, a servant girl some years older than the boy, who lived with them. When the boy tried to fondle her as she slept, she awoke, there was a scene and thereafter he slept on a hard cot in another room.[69]

Explicit references to homosexuality appear in only three of the autobiographies. As a student in a military preparatory school, Otto Krille recalls being caressed one night by another fourteen-year-old boy, an experience "which awoke feelings in me for which I had no name."[70] He also remembers seeing two of his schoolmates lying in bed together and kissing. Moritz Bromme says that his mother was forced to evict two women textile workers who rented a room from her when she discovered that they were lesbians.[71] The anonymous authoress of *Im Kampf ums Dasein!* describes masked costume balls in a Hamburg dance hall attended by prostitutes and lesbians dressed in men's clothing complete with false mustaches and canes.[72]

Having gained a general impression of the style and contents of these worker autobiographies, we may now seek to apply them to a question that deeply concerned late nineteenth-century observers of social change and that still interests the modern social historian—the influence of rapid industrialization and urbanization on the sexual attitudes and behavior of the German working classes. Did the conditions of factory life, with men and women working together for long hours engender a new, looser, and somehow "lower" set of sexual manners than those found among the rural laboring population? This is a difficult question to answer. Some tentative suggestions can be made, however, by concentrating on the comparison of rural and urban sexual customs and their relationship to the process of modernization.

Many nineteenth-century German observers regarded the shift from a rural agrarian to an urban factory environment as unsettling, unnatural, and crisis-ridden for the maintenance of traditional society.[73] Paul Göhre, a theology student working "under cover" in a Chemnitz factory, observed that for workers from a rural background, the new urban factory surroundings "unfailingly become the source of severe intellectual and religious crisis, in which the old order of things was almost always swept away to be replaced by a new order."[74] The same theme is echoed by a Lutheran minister from Posen who felt that factory work, with men and women working together and walking together to and from work, the "rest pauses," the greater economic freedom of young workers, and the cramped housing conditions found among the working classes all made for a perceptible decline in moral standards. Worse still, factory workers come under the influence of Social Democratic ideas "which do not put much stock in chastity."[75]

Another pastor from Braunschweig believed that the factory system with its "changed daily routine and the Sunday work connected with it, revolutionizes the entire existence. Generally a locality where a factory is built is, within a few years, changed significantly in its religious, moral, and social physiognomy."[76]

Such contemporary views could easily be multiplied. Nor is it difficult to find modified versions of the same ideas today. Thus, in the words of the social historian Peter Stearns, "rampant immorality was a minority phenomenon. But the standards of family life and of morality itself were changing. Particularly when contrasted with rural customs these changes indicate clearly the novelty and confusion of worker life."[77] This is a cautious statement, more moderate and probably nearer the truth than earlier observations. Yet we are still left with the central question: How different were the sexual attitudes and behavior of urban workers from those of their country cousins? That there were differences is undeniable. But it can be argued that there were also many similarities and that rural sexual attitudes often carried over into the urban industrial setting, albeit with different results. Finally, it can be suggested that both urban and rural workers in Imperial Germany were experiencing a growing rationalization and demystification of their sexual lives as traditional religious and social sanctions lost their force.

This is an important point. For centuries the Christian church had much to say on the subject of human sexuality, most of it negative. Sexual intercourse outside marriage was generally condemned and even intercourse between man and wife for reasons other than procreation was suspect. Pregnancy was seen as an act of God, a normal part of life in this vale of tears and beyond man's control. Contraception, because it ignored the biblical command to multiply and replenish the earth, was rejected by the Church.[78] But birth control had great attractions: it offered the chance of freeing husband and wife from the burden of too many children, and at the same time made sexual intercourse a source of pleasure without the nagging fear of conception. Thus life might be freed of one of its oldest burdens and uncertainties. The individual could try to take control of what had hitherto been in the hands of the Deity. Secularism, the belief that man could enjoy pleasure in this life and control over his environment in this world, an idea implicit in the rise of modern science since the seventeenth century, came much later to the realm of human sexuality. Only when much of the physical world around them had been demystified and rationalized by science and industry, did working-class people in the late nineteenth century begin to demystify and rationalize their own sexual lives. The indications of these changes can be found by examining three separate but not altogether unrelated areas: illegitimate births, prostitution, and contraception. Once more it must be emphasized that only suggestions, not solid conclusions, in these matters can be offered at the present time.

There seems to be an assumption that factory and urban life stimulated an increase in illegitimate births during the nineteenth century. This increase might be interpreted as the result of changing and presumably "looser" codes of premarital behavior. It is not possible here to examine in detail this cause-and-effect relationship, riddled as it is with demographic and semantic problems. Rather we can better approach the subject of illegitimate births at that time with the help of some contemporary German statistics on illegitimacy, leaving aside for the moment the question of morality.[79]

We can begin by comparing the illegitimacy rates of what can be called urban and rural areas. In 1900, the number of illegitimate children (that is, those born to unmarried women, a rather unsophisticated but common definition) born in German cities with populations of 2,000 and more was 9.14 per 100 live births, while that of smaller towns and the countryside averaged 6.16 per 100.[80] With just this data, it might be argued that there was some causal relationship between city life and illegitimacy. But these raw figures are deceptive. It is significant, for example, that the illegitimacy rate in the Rhineland-Westphalia industrial region as a whole was only 4 percent between 1896 and 1900, a fact partly attributable to the higher ratio of men to women living and working there. Thus in a region where one might expect to see most clearly the "loosening" effect of industrial and urban life on morality as indicated by illegitimacy, we find a level more than two percentage points lower than in the countryside.[81] Admittedly, it is difficult to distinguish between "urban" and "rural" simply by town size and the presence of a few large factories. Also, it is possible that by 1895 the most unsettling effects of industrialization were beginning to fade while newer, more stable patterns of sexual life were established.

Some evidence that these patterns were "leveling out" in the three decades after 1867 emerges from a study of the fecundity rate (the ratio of those women who actually have children to all women in the population between the ages of fifteen and fifty). An examination of the period from 1867 to 1897 reveals that the fecundity rate of married women (like the actual numbers of marriages) appears to fluctuate roughly in accord with economic conditions. However, the fecundity rate of unmarried women, which supposedly should increase during this period of German social and economic transition and expansion, remains very nearly constant (see Table I).[82]

In general, these figures simply indicate that the illegitimate fecundity rate does not seem to be as closely tied to economic changes as the legitimate rate, a point already noted by earlier social historians.[83] At present, nothing conclusive can be said about the relationship between industrialism, urbanization, and illegitimacy. Nevertheless, it must be stressed that the traditional view of illegitimacy as one of the outstanding characteristics of urban sexual life cannot be accepted without a good many qualifications.

TABLE I. FECUNDITY RATE OF MARRIED AND UNMARRIED
GERMAN WOMEN, 1867–1897

	Number of Live Births to Every 100 Married Women between Ages 15 and 50		Number of Live Births to Every 100 Unmarried Women between Ages 15 and 50	
Years	Germany	Prussia	Germany	Prussia
1867–1871	. . .	27.3	. . .	2.47
1872–1875	29.7	30.0	2.90	2.49
1879–1882	27.4	28.8	2.98	2.61
1889–1892	26.5	27.2	2.83	2.51
1894–1897	26.7	26.9	2.92	2.48

Turning from these quantitative measurements back to the autobiographers, we find indications that the sexual behavior of the urban working classes may not have differed radically from those of agrarian workers. Citing the farmhand Franz Rehbein's autobiography, Adelbert Koch concludes that "a false impression prevails about the influence of village morality. Among agricultural workers, intercourse with the other sex is as free as among factory workers."[84] For example, Rehbein noted the same kind of overcrowded living conditions among farm workers that was once given as a cause for the looser sexual morality of urban workers.[85] Furthermore, Rehbein describes an event that took place on a large Pomeranian estate where he worked as a fourteen-year-old that lends support for the German adage *Ländlich, Schändlich* (literally, rural = shameful). At the close of the potato harvest the farm workers, men and women alike, celebrate a "potato marriage." In a scene reminiscent of a Breughel painting, the workers provide their own music with fiddle and harmonica, while couples disappear from time to time into the haylofts and stalls of the barns.[86] All of this seems to take place in an atmosphere of peasant exuberance unmarked by any twinges of conscience.

Later, while working as a hired hand on a farm in Holstein, Rehbein started courting Dora, a servant on a neighboring farm. Unable to marry, according to Rehbein, because of his low wages, he began to make nightly visits to his sweetheart, where "the bedroom window of my Dora was not obstructed by a nasty lattice."[87] Rehbein got into the habit of spending the night with Dora and then returning to his job early the next morning. This went on for nearly a year. Then, when Rehbein was twenty-six, Dora became pregnant. Marriage, which earlier seemed out of the question for economic reasons, suddenly became imperative. Dora and Franz married just a month before the birth of their first child.

Rehbein's account lends some support to the impression that sexual intercourse between men and women intending to marry one another was a common occurrence in the countryside. In a survey conducted by the Evangelical Church's Morality League in the mid-1890s, approximately half of the women married in country parishes were considered "fallen brides," which was usually, but not always, the same thing as unwed mothers. Referring to premarital intercourse, one pastor from Schleswig-Holstein remarked that it took place "sometimes after the public betrothal has taken place, sometimes before; the latter as frequently, yes, probably more frequently than the former.[88]

Of course, this premarital behavior and Rehbein's experience may only have been representative of the sexual behavior of a certain group of farm-hands. Nevertheless, Rehbein's premarital sex life and his manner of entering into marriage can be usefully compared with several other urban autobiographers. Like Rehbein, Moritz Bromme did not marry until his sweetheart became pregnant. He confesses that "if I hadn't got my 'bride' pregnant, I probably wouldn't have married for a long time."[89] Wenzel Holek and his "wife" lived together "on trial" for seven years before deciding to get married and give their two children a "legal father."[90] Eugen May also lived in a common-law arrangement, but for a much longer time. As May puts it, he had "provided" a girl for himself when he was seventeen in 1904. Seventeen years later he was able to announce in his autobiography that "we now intend, in the very near future, to finally get married."[91] It would be going too far to conclude from these few examples that most working-class men in town and country only married after the intended wife became pregnant or after several years of living together. The autobiographies simply indicate that premarital sexual intercourse and common-law marriages were not at all unusual among factory and farm workers alike. Hence, it can be suggested that, in this sphere at least, men and women from both areas shared some common sexual behavior patterns.

Prostitution is another subject that can illuminate the similarities and differences between urban and rural sexual life. Although the world's "oldest profession" has been a common literary theme and many nineteenth-century reformers regarded it as *the* social evil, social historians have as yet given prostitution and its practitioners scant attention. This is not surprising, for prostitution, its nature, extent, and causes, is an extremely complex social and psychological phenomenon. Students of prostitution in the last century often took a simplistic view of the subject, attributing it to a decline in "morality" (a view popular with conservative social critics), poor wages for women in home and factory industries (the common socialist view), or innate mental degeneracy among certain women (the conclusion of Cesare Lombroso, the Italian criminologist).[92] Today authorities on the subject give some weight to each of these factors and add to them a variety of psychological nuances involving the learning of sexual roles and the sexual experiences of women in childhood.[93] In addition to these problems of interpretation, there is a shortage of reliable quantitative and qualitative data on nineteenth-century prostitutes, not to mention their customers. In spite of these difficulties it is time to begin a serious investigation of prostitution, for it leads into several interesting and hitherto little explored areas of the past. In the remarks that follow I rely on several contemporary studies prepared before the First World War.

Before we begin, however, the reader should understand that in Imperial Germany prostitution as such was not prohibited by law.[94] Rather it was tolerated. That is, prostitutes were required to register themselves with the police in their place of residence. They were issued a special identification book, prohibited from living in or frequenting certain parts of the city, and expected to report for weekly or biweekly medical examinations. Those suspected of having a venereal disease were placed into hospital until "cured" and then they usually went back on the streets. Since these prostitutes lived under police control they were known as "supervised girls" (*Kontrollmädchen*). Although it seems clear that these *Kontrollmädchen* represented only a minority of the active prostitutes in most cities, it is from studies of them that we get our most reliable information.

In view of the extent of immigration from the countryside to urban centers in late nineteenth-century Germany, it is not surprising that less than half of the registered prostitutes were natives of the cities where they lived and had usually lived there less than five years. This was the case with 2,224 Berlin prostitutes in 1872–73 and also in Hamburg and Cologne early in the present century.[95] It was often presumed (especially by socialists) that these *Kontrollmädchen* were predominantly farm girls who came to the big city seeking work as domestic servants, then were seduced by their masters (or master's son), and finally turned into the streets.[96] Although it is true that a very high percentage of registered prostitutes gave domestic service as their former occupation, the romantic notion of the "daughter of the people" corrupted by the master of the house is not supported by the available evidence, which is not to say that it never happened. To begin with, not many *Kontrollmädchen* seem to have been from farm family backgrounds. If we use the occupation of the prostitute's father as a rough guide to social origins we find that about half of them came from artisan (that is, craftsmen like shoemakers, carpenters, plasterers, and the like) and factory backgrounds. Table II offers some general information on the occupational backgrounds of prostitutes' fathers,[97] but it can only serve as a very rough guide owing to the imprecision with which various job categories were defined by officials and also incomplete knowledge of the geographical origins of the prostitutes themselves.

Although this information must be used cautiously, it does seem clear that not many daughters of farm owners or farm laborers became registered prostitutes. When they did, however, it is possible that they did so not after seduction by their social betters, but rather by carrying over into an urban setting their rural sexual code. It has been shown from the auto-

TABLE II. OCCUPATIONS OF FATHERS OF REGISTERED PROSTITUTES

(Percentage of Total)

Occupation	Berlin (1872–73)	Breslau (1901)	Frankfurt a. M. (1911)	Hamburg (1912)	Cologne (1913–14)
Artisans and craftsmen	47.9	72.0	33.0	22.2	30.0
Factory workers	22.0		20.0	30.6	12.8
Farm owners and workers	4.1	4.2	. . .	3.2	7.0
Miscellaneous and unknown	26.0	23.8	. . .	44.0	50.2

biographies of farm laborers that premarital sexual intercourse and lengthy "affairs" were not unheard of in the German countryside. What happened if a country girl came to the big city as a domestic servant (as so many did, having no other skills to offer[98]), took a lover almost always from her own class background, and perhaps became pregnant? Back home on the farm she could expect to marry the child's father sooner or later. But in the city this solution was not nearly so certain.[99] The servant girl might find herself without a job and with a child to support. Already an outcast in a society that condemned bastardy, such a girl might resort to prostitution.[100]

It is possible to compare the experience of these farm girls with that of the daughters of artisans and factory workers. Before doing so, it is worth noting that here it is difficult to differentiate clearly between urban and rural backgrounds, because many artisans and factory workers lived in towns of less than 2,000 people and might therefore be classed as rural. This is a problem that might be overcome by correlating a variety of factors concerning prostitutes (place of birth and its population size, parental occupation, and so forth), but for the purposes of this essay it will be assumed that artisans and factory workers can be defined as nonrural in the sense that they do not work on the land.

The high percentage of the daughters of artisans among *Kontrollmädchen* was interpreted by some contemporaries as an indication of the declining economic and social position of this social group in Imperial Germany.[101] It should be understood that through most of the nineteenth century, German artisans considered themselves to be eminently respectable citizens, closer to the middle class than to the emerging factory proletariat. Certainly it is difficult to imagine a daughter of a puritanical, not to say prudish, German artisan of the late eighteenth century ever becoming a prostitute.[102] After 1870, German artisans found that their once proud position was being undermined by the factory system. They could not always support their daughters at home until they married. It seems likely that the daughters of artisan fathers (particularly from small towns) moved to larger towns and cities looking for work as servants. The life stories of prostitutes from the nonrural artisan and factory backgrounds follow a common pattern, whereby girls drift into, rather than deliberately choose, prostitution as a way of life: the girl leaves school at fourteen without any skill in hand; within a year or so she takes a job as domestic servant, waitress, or barmaid, often in a location other than her home town; after another year she is going steady with a boy from her own social class, not infrequently someone from her own home town or even a distant relative; sexual relations begin casually, often after a few beers on the way home from a dance; the girl becomes pregnant, and for one reason or another, the boy friend refuses (or cannot afford) to make an "honest woman" of her; she has a child, who usually dies before his first birthday; the girl enters into a more permanent "relationship" with another man and becomes a semi-kept woman, that is, she may be living in common-law with a working-class man while she earns money as a barmaid.[103] washerwoman, or other; this relationship eventually ends and the girl drifts into affairs more and more transitory until she finally decides to turn "professional" and registers herself as a prostitute with the police.[104]

Are there any common factors here? One seems to be that the premarital affairs of rural areas could and usually did lead to marriage. In the countryside, social pressures could be brought to bear on a man who left a pregnant girl in the lurch. But the same kind of affairs in the city, with its increased anonymity and different moral codes, might gradually evolve into professional prostitution. In addition, prostitution among women from either urban or rural origins seems to have been the end point of a process more or less free from moral compunctions about premarital sexual intercourse. Again and again prostitutes recount their life stories with an air of innocence and matter-of-factness devoid of any qualms of conscience usually associated with traditional moral codes. It is perhaps the decline of the authority of these codes that is the key to the "loosening" of morality, sexual or otherwise, in the German working classes after 1870. Instead of talking about the "impact" of industrialization on working-class morality, the social historian might better regard changes in sexual attitudes and behavior as an integral part of the gradual secularization and rationalization of society already under way before Germany began its period of rapid industrialization after 1870.

Perhaps this theme can be enlarged and clarified by looking at the practice of contraception among the German working classes. That pregnancy was so frequently a forerunner of working-class marriages and part of the prostitute's evolution would seem to indicate ignorance and/or indifference about contraception in these classes. Information on this subject is now very sketchy, but with the help particularly of several hundred interviews conducted by Max Marcuse in 1917 on the nature and extent of contraception in working-class marriages, several points can be made.[105]

First, contraception is rightly regarded as being a phenomenon associated with a rather well-developed stage of industrial and urban life. This seems to be true of Imperial Germany, although it must be emphasized that even in the 1890s a variety of folk and scientific methods of contraception was available to rural workers. Coitus interruptus, or withdrawal, was of course the most common, if the most unreliable, method for those who wished to prevent conception. "Rubber articles," probably condoms, were available in some rural areas, especially around larger towns and cities. Elsewhere mothers nursed their children up to age three in the hope of remaining infertile, while other women brewed up extracts of various barks and leaves for either contraception or abortion.[106] Knowledge of more sophisticated and reliable means of contraception seems to have spread to the countryside through men returning from military service or from women returning from domestic service in the city, or even through advertisements in the popular press.[107] Nevertheless, many people in the countryside continued to look upon a large family as "natural" and sometimes as a positive economic factor. Such people tended to regard contraception, even in the form of coitus interruptus, as a "citified" custom. Thus, in an interview in 1917, a twenty-nine-year-old North German farm laborer, the father of three (only one of which was still alive) declared that he and his wife did not practice birth control: "My wife is far too stupid for that. She doesn't understand it, and wouldn't want it at all. [I] also don't want it. It's not the fashion by us. They do that in the city."[108] In spite of this attitude, the knowledge and practice of birth control seems to have spread perceptibly in rural Germany before 1914.[109]

Secondly, the ability and the desire to limit the number of one's children, to regulate the interval between births, or to have no children at all are all indications of a sophisticated level of social, economic, and most important, intellectual development. The decision to use contraception indicates that the users are trying to exercise control over a part of their lives that traditionally lay beyond their control. As people become more conscious of their socioeconomic status, of their sense of individuality, and their chances for ego gratification they begin to rationalize and demystify their sexual lives with the help of contraception. Children are no longer the usual and often feared result of sexual intercourse. Pleasure rather than conception can become the aim of the intercourse. Those who use contraception with these aims in mind, even when efforts to prevent conception fail, are already breaking away from older, religious traditions. They are also showing that they believe that they can influence their own destiny in very significant ways. In the words of Lee Rainwater,

a sense of stability about and trust in the future . . . is one precondition for consistent [family] planning. Closely related to this is the belief that one can affect one's future, can determine to some extent what will happen. . . . In addition . . . a person has to be able to assume that he can be effectively assertive in [the] world, and that he can mold the future closer to his heart's desire.[110]

In keeping with these observations, in the working classes of Imperial Germany it appears to have been the better paid, skilled industrial workers, many of whom held "advanced" or socialist views, who increasingly assumed that they could indeed assert some influence over their lives and practiced birth control most effectively. So a thirty-four-year-old Berlin master mechanic, an agnostic married five years and with one child, said during an interview in 1917 that his wife used a diaphragm to limit births because "we want to get ahead and our daughter should have things better than my wife and sisters did."[111] Among the autobiographers Moritz Bromme, an ardent Social Democrat and metal lathe operator, and Ludwig Tureck, communist typesetter, speak of their desire and efforts to limit their family size so that they and their wives will be less vulnerable to economic privation.[112] Another class-conscious worker, a thirty-seven-year-old Berlin factory foreman and father of three, told Max Marcuse during the First World War that coitus interruptus was the form of birth control used by him and his wife. The reason for doing so was because "a person owes it to his future to limit births. . . . We workers are no longer as stupid as before, when we supplied children for the rich and for the state—factory and cannon fodder—that doesn't go anymore, and if our wives ever go on a birth-strike [*Gebärstreik*] we'll see if everything doesn't get better."[113] The point here being that contraception forms an integral part of a secularized, demystified world view held by some German workers.

The emergence and evolution of this secular world view is the positive way of expressing what is usually called the "demoralization" of the working classes. I have suggested that perhaps "demystification" might be a better descriptive term. It can be argued that what was once regarded as the demoralization of workers under the impact of industrialization and urbanization was really a part of and another stage in the decline of traditional religious and social sanctions that antedates the rapid changes of the post-1870 period. In negative terms German workers showed less respect for the old proscriptions against premarital sexual intercourse, illegitimacy, and contraception. In positive terms, within a social setting increasingly urbanized and industrialized, they developed a more secular set of standards stressing the enjoyment of this life rather than the next as well as a conscious desire to control and improve the conditions of their lives. It seems clear that in the years before 1914 the old religious beliefs and the growing secular concerns lived side by side in the world views of many working class Germans. The process of demystification incorporating the decline of old traditions and the creation of new ones operated at different tempos in town and country. The visible manifestations of this process may only have become noticeable in the mushrooming cities of Imperial Germany. But to overemphasize the contrast between urban and rural sexual behavior and attitudes is to risk overlooking the common elements and the evolution of both.

Seen from another perspective, contraception and even prostitution in Imperial Germany can be interpreted as ways in which the working class responded to a social existence largely beyond its control. The prostitute has usually been regarded as a criminal, a threat to society; but she can also be interpreted as a woman rationally trying to relate to a socioeconomic system that, in Imperial Germany, offered few attractive positions to women. This is not to say that prostitution was the most sensible or appealing response to a variety of social controls; but it can be said that the prostitutes (and ordinary criminals too) may be usefully interpreted as people struggling to order and control their own lives in a highly structured and authoritarian society. Contraception seems to be a similar response. Together, prostitution and birth control, the archenemies of traditional sexual and moral codes in the last century, may, in the long view, be seen as two facets of the desire of "little people" to control their own lives.

German working-class autobiographies provide a good deal of support for these various hypotheses. They offer a possible starting point for the yet unwritten "analytical history of moral behavior and attitudes" called for by the German historian, Thomas Nipperdey.[114] Such a history has been a long time coming and is only beginning to be in sight. Until very recently historians have neglected some of the basic structures of society (marriage and the family) and the value systems around which people organize their private lives, while devoting extraordinary energy and ingenuity to the study of political and economic man. The importance of the latter cannot be denied, but if historians show the same ingenuity in investigating moral and sexual behavior of the past, we might not only find that the research problems are not insurmountable, but also discover answers to questions that now confound us. When such investigations are made, the writings of working-class autobiographers can play an important role.

NOTES

1. G. Rattray Taylor, *Sex in History* (London, 1954), p. 4.

2. Taylor's book belongs to this category. See also Karl Saller, "Sexualität und

Sitte in der vorindustriellen Zeit," in Ferdinand Oeter, ed., *Familie und Gesellschaft* (Tübingen, 1966), pp. 113–140.

3. See Leo Schidrowitz, *Sittengeschichte des Proletariats: der Weg vom Leibeszum Maschinensklaven* (Vienna-Leipzig, n.d., ca. 1925); Otto Rühle, *Illustrierte Kultur- und Sittengeschichte des Proletariats* (Berlin, 1930).

4. See, for example, P. Gaskell, *Artisans and Machinery* (London, 1835); Friedrich Engels, *The Condition of the Working Class in England* (London, 1969; orig. pub. 1845); Robert Mohl, "Ueber die Nachteile, welche sowohl den Arbeitern selbst als dem Wohlstande und der Sicherheit der gesamten bürgerlichen Gesellschaft von dem fabrikmässigen Betrieb der Industrie zugehen, . . . " (1835) reprinted in Carl Jantke and D. Hilger, eds., *Die Eigentumslosen. Der deutsche Pauperismus und die Emanzipationskrise in der Darstellungen und Deutungen der zeitgenössischen Literatur* (Freiburg-Munich, 1965), pp. 294–318; W. H. Riehl, *Die Familie* (Stuttgart, 1854).

5. In Germany the best-known example is August Bebel's *Die Frau und der Sozialismus,* first published in 1879, revised and reprinted many times thereafter.

6. See W. F. Neff, *Victorian Working Women* (London, 1966; orig. pub. 1929); Ivy Pinchbeck, *Women Workers and the Industrial Revolution 1750–1850* (New York, 1930); Margaret Hewitt, *Wives and Mothers in Victorian Industry* (London, 1958); Neil J. Smelser, *Social Change in the Industrial Revolution* (Chicago, 1959); Harold Perkin, *The Origins of Modern English Society 1780–1880* (London, 1969), pp. 149–75.

7. Helmut Möller, *Die kleinbürgerliche Familie im 18. Jahrhundert. Verhalten und Gruppenkultur* (Berlin, 1969).

8. For the larger question of nineteenth and twentieth century German "cultural despair," see Klaus Bergmann, *Agrarromantik und Grossstadtfeindschaft,* Marburger Abhandlungen zur Politischen Wissenschaft, vol. 20 (Meisenheim am Glan, 1970).

9. For discussions of related problems see William J. Goode, "Industrialization and Family Change," in Bert F. Hoselitz and W. E. Moore, eds., *Industrialization and Society* (Mouton, 1966), pp. 237–55; and the same author's "The Theory and Measurement of Family Change," in E. B. Sheldon and W. E. Moore, eds., *Indicators of Social Change. Concepts and Measurements* (New York, 1968), pp. 295–348; Lee Rainwater, "Some Aspects of Lower Class Sexual Behavior," *The Journal of Social Issues,* 22(April, 1966):96–108; and the same author's "Sex in the Culture of Poverty," in C. B. Broderick and J. Bernards, eds., *The Individual, Sex, and Society* (Baltimore, 1969), pp. 129–40.

10. Robert Michels, "Psychologie der antikapitalistischen Massenbewegungen," in *Grundriss der Sozialökonomik* (Tübingen, 1926), vol. 9, pt. 1, 271–74.

11. Cecilia A. Trunz, *Der Autobiographien von deutschen Industriearbeitern* (Freiburg i. Breisgau, 1934).

12. Wolfram Fischer, *Quellen zur Geschichte des deutschen Handwerks: Selbstzeugnisse seit der Reformationszeit* (Göttingen, 1957); W. Fischer, "Arbeitermemoiren als Quellen für Geschichte und Volkskunde der industriellen Gesellschaft," *Soziale Welt*, 9(1958):288–98.

13. Leo Uhen, *Gruppenbewusstsein und informelle Gruppenbildungen bei deutschen Arbeitern im Jahrhundert der Industrialisierung* (Berlin, 1964).

14. Richard Reichard, *Crippled from Birth. German Social Democracy 1844–1870* (Ames, Iowa, 1969).

15. Theodor Klaiber, *Die deutsche Selbstbiographie* (Stuttgart, 1921), pp. 270–71; Hans Gruhle, "Die Selbstbiographie als Quelle historischen Erkenntnis," in Melchior Palyi, ed., *Erinnerungsgabe für Max Weber* (Munich, 1923), 1:155–77; Adelbert Koch, "Arbeitermemoiren als sozialwissenschaftliche Erkenntnisquelle," *Archiv für Sozialwissenschaft und Sozialpolitik*, 61(1929):128–67; Anthony Oberschall, *Empirical Social Research in Germany 1848–1914* (Hague, 1965), pp. 80–82.

16. Gruhle, "Die Selbstbiographie," p. 176.

17. Koch, "Arbeitermemoiren," p. 166.

18. Ibid., pp. 151–52; Uhen, *Gruppenbewusstsein*, pp. 28–29. It is difficult to say how much stock can be put in this argument. Masturbation certainly is not a theme mentioned very often in modern autobiographies, J. J. Rousseau's *Confessions* are an exception in this regard, as is the more recent *Autobiography of Bertrand Russell 1872–1914* (New York: Bantam edition, 1968), pp. 40–41.

19. August Bebel, *Aus meinem Leben* (Berlin, 1961; orig. pub. 1910); Ottilie Baader, *Ein steiniger Weg* (Berlin, 1921); Wilhelm Bock, *Im Dienste der Freiheit* (Berlin, 1927); Julius Bruhns, "*Es klingt im Sturm ein altes Lied!*" (Berlin, 1921); Adelheid Popp, *The Autobiography of a Working Woman* (London, 1912); Nikolaus Osterroth, *Vom Beter zum Kämpfer* (Berlin, 1920).

20. For very brief selections from some of the following books, see Georg Eckert, *Aus dem Lebensberichten deutscher Fabrikarbeiter* (Braunschweig, 1953); for brief summaries of the lives of some of the working-class autobiographers see Inge Diersen et al., *Lexikon sozialistische deutschen Literatur von den Anfängen bis 1945. Monographisch-biographische Darstellungen* (Leipzig, 1964).

21. Karl Fischer, *Denkwürdigkeiten und Erinnerungen eines Arbeiters*, 2 vols. (Jena, 1902–1904); and *Aus einem Arbeiterleben: Skizzen* (Jena, 1905).

22. Gruhle, "Die Selbstbiographie," p. 173.

23. Fischer, *Denkwürdigkeiten*, 1:xi.

24. Moritz Bromme, *Lebensgeschichte eines modernen Fabrikarbeiter* (Jena, 1905).

25. Eugen May, "Mein Lebenslauf, 1887–1920," in Eugen Rosenstock, *Werkstattsaussiedlung: Untersuchungen über den Lebensraum des Industriearbeiters. Sozial-psychologische Forschungen*, 2(Berlin, 1922):16–72.

26. Wenzel Holek, *Lebensgang eines deutsch-tsechischen Handarbeiters* (Jena, 1906).

27. Heinrich Holek, *Unterwegs. Eine Selbstbiographie* (Vienna, 1927).

28. Franz Rehbein, *Das Leben eines Landarbeiters* (Jena, 1911).

29. Franz Bergg, *Ein Proletarierleben* (Frankfurt a. M., 1913).

30. Ibid., pp. 85–90.

31. Georg Meyer, *Die Lebenstragödie eines Tagelöhners* (Berlin, 1909).

32. Ludwig Tureck, *Ein Prolet erzählt: Lebensschilderung eines deutschen Arbeiters* (Berlin, 1930).

33. Ibid., p. 337.

34. Doris Viersbeck, *Erlebnisse eines hamburger Dienstmädchens* (Munich, 1910).

35. *Im Kampf ums Dasein! Wahrheitsgetreue Lebenserinnerungen eines Mädchens aus dem Volke als Fabrikarbeiterin, Dienstmädchen und Kellnerin* (Stuttgart, 1908).

36. Minna Wettstein-Adelt, *3½ Monate Fabrikarbeiterin* (Berlin, 1893).

37. C. Moszeik, *Aus der Gedankenwelt einer Arbeiterfrau: von ihr selbst erzählt* (Berlin, 1909).

38. Adolf Levenstein, *Proletariers Jugendjahre* (Berlin, n.d., about 1909); *Aus der Tiefe: Arbeiterbriefe* (Berlin, 1909); *Die Arbeiterfrage* (Munich, 1912).

39. *Erinnerungen eines Waisenknaben. Von ihm selbst erzählt* (Munich, 1910).

40. E. Bleuler, *"Dulden!" Aus der Lebensbeschreibung einer Armen* (Munich, 1910); of further interest, see Franz Lüth, *Aus der Jugendzeit eines Tagelöhners* (Berlin, n.d., about 1908); Christian Mengers, *Aus der letzten Tagen der Zunft. Erinnerungen eines alten Handwerkers aus seinen Wanderjahren* (Leipzig, 1910); Robert Köhler, *Erinnerungen aus dem Leben eines Proletariers* (Reichenberg, 1913); Wilhelm Reimes, *Durch die Drahtverhaue des Lebens. Aus dem Werdegang eines klassenbewussten Arbeiters* (Dresden, 1920).

41. Koch, "Arbeitermemoiren," p. 151.

42. Bromme, *Lebensgeschichte,* p. 58.

43. Ibid., p. 98.

44. Rehbein, *Das Leben,* p. 32.

45. Wenzel Holek, *Lebensgang,* pp. 82–83.

46. Ibid., p. 115.

47. Ibid., p. 118. Compare Holek's remarks with those of Karl Marx on the English brick- and tile-making trades in *Capital* (London, 1967), 1:464.

48. Heinrich Holek, *Unterwegs,* pp. 70–72.

49. Ibid., pp. 85, 90; Bergg, *Proletarierleben*, pp. 26–28; Popp, *Autobiography*, pp. 41–42; Bromme, *Lebensgeschichte*, pp. 82–83.

50. Bergg, *Proletarierleben*, p. 26.

51. Heinrich Holek, *Unterwegs*, p. 123.

52. Bromme, *Lebensgeschichte*, p. 124.

53. *Erinnerungen eines Waisenknaben*, p. 41.

54. Tureck, *Ein Prolet erzählt*, p. 87.

55. Ibid., p. 88.

56. Meyer, *Lebenstragödie*, p. 69.

57. Ibid., pp. 69–70.

58. See Alex Comfort, *The Anxiety Makers. Some Curious Preoccupations of the Medical Profession* (London, 1967), pp. 69–113.

59. Bromme, *Lebensgeschichte*, p. 100.

60. See Anton Nyström, *Sexualleben und Gesundheit*, 2nd ed. (Berlin, 1911) for a discussion and critique of this position.

61. See Wilhelm Reich, *The Sexual Revolution*, 4th ed. (New York, 1962), pp. 102–15. Late in the eighteenth century a German artisan said that young journeymen believed that masturbation was not harmful "because through it evil humors went away." See Möller, *Die kleinbürgerliche Familie*, p. 64.

62. Bromme, *Lebensgeschichte*, p. 100.

63. Ibid., p. 201.

64. Levenstein, *Arbeiterbriefe*, p. 12.

65. Bergg, *Proletarierleben*, p. 26.

66. Ibid., p. 27.

67. Ibid., pp. 27–28. Curiously, Luther's catechism plays a part in the weekly sexual ritual of an elderly masochist who has a prostitute play the role of stern schoolmistress in a mock religion lesson in a mild German version of *Fanny Hill*, J. Zeisig, *Memoiren einer Prostituierten, oder die Prostitution in Hamburg* (Hamburg, 1847), pp. 133–34.

68. *Erinnerungen eines Waisenknaben*, pp. 104–06.

69. Ibid., pp. 69–70.

70. Otto Krille, *Unter dem Joch* (Berlin, 1914), p. 70.

71. Bromme, *Lebensgeschichte*, pp. 81–83.

72. *Im Kampf ums Dasein!*, pp. 156–60.

73. See the remarks scattered throughout C. Wagner, *Die Sittlichkeit auf dem Lande* (Leipzig, 1895).

74. Paul Göhre, *Three Months in a Workshop* (London, 1891), p. 148.

75. C. Wagner, ed., *Die geschlechtlich-sittlichen Verhältnisse der evangelische Landbewohner im deutschen Reiche,* Allgemeinen Konferenz der deutschen Sittlichkeitsvereine, (Leipzig, 1895–96), 1:218.

76. Ibid., 2:224.

77. Peter Stearns, *European Society in Upheaval* (New York: 1967), p. 133.

78. See John T. Noonan, *Contraception* (Cambridge, Mass., 1965).

79. On the subject of illegitimacy in Imperial Germany, see R. Kuczynski, "Zur Statistik der Fruchtbarkeit," *Jahrbücher für Nationalökonomie und Statistik* (III. Folge), 35 (1908):229–41; Max Taube, *Der Schutz der unehelichen Kinder in Leipzig* (Leipzig, 1893); Friedrich Lindner, *Die unehelichen Geburten als Sozialphänomen. Ein Beitrag zur Statistik der Bevölkerungsbewegung in königreiche Bayern* (Leipzig, 1900); Othmar Spann, *Untersuchungen über die uneheliche Bevölkerung in Frankfurt am Main* (Dresden, 1905); Max Marcuse, *Uneheliche Mutter,* Grossstadt-Dokumente, Nr. 27 (Berlin, n.d., about 1906); K. Oldenberg, "Ueber die Rückgang der Geburten- und Sterbeziffer," *Archiv für Sozialwissenschaft und Sozialpolitik,* 32 (1911):319–77; 33 (1912):401–99; John Knodel, "Law, Marriage, and Illegitimacy in Nineteenth Century Germany," *Population Studies,* 20 (March, 1967):279–94.

80. Friedrich Prinzing, *Handbuch der medizinischen Statistik* (Jena, 1906), p. 75.

81. Othmar Spann, "Die Bedingungen der Unehelichkeit, statistisch betrachtet," *Neue Generation,* 6 (1910):30.

82. F. Prinzing, "Die uneheliche Fruchtbarkeit in Deutschland," *Zeitschrift für Socialwissenschaft,* 5 (1902):37.

83. Hilde Weiss, "Materialen zum Verhältnis von Konjunktur und Familie," in Max Horkheimer, ed., *Autorität und Familie,* Studien aus dem Institut für Sozialforschung (Paris, 1936), pp. 579–81.

84. Koch, "Arbeitermemoiren," p. 151.

85. *Die geschlechtlich-sittlichen Verhältnisse,* 1:i, 103, 125, 214, 233, 2:ii, 16, 44, 143–44, 150.

86. Rehbein, *Das Leben,* pp. 53–57.

87. Ibid., p. 213.

88. *Die geschlechtlich-sittlichen Verhältnisse,* 1:181.

89. Bromme, *Lebensgeschichte,* p. 219.

90. Wenzel Holek, *Lebensgang,* p. 235. Holek's son, Heinrich, also only married when his girl friend became pregnant. See his *Unterwegs,* p. 280.

91. May, "Lebenslauf," p. 16.

92. For a discussion of these various views, see Paul Hirsch, *Verbrechen und Prostitution als soziale Krankheitserscheinungen,* 2nd ed. (Berlin, 1907).

93. See Kingsley Davis, "The Sociology of Prostitution," *American Sociological Review,* 2 (1937):744–55; Harry Benjamin and R. E. L. Masters, *Prostitution and Morality* (New York, 1964).

94. Alfred Blaschko, "Prostitution," in J. Conrad, ed., *Handwörterbuch der Staatswissenschaften,* 3rd ed. (Jena, 1910), 6:1227–49.

95. H. Schwabe, "Einblicke in das innere und äussere Leben der Berliner Prostitution," *Berliner Städtisches Jahrbuch für Volkswirtschaft und Statistik* (Berlin, 1874), pp. 68–69; E. von Grabe, "Prostitution, Kriminalität und Psychopathie," *Archiv für Kriminologische-Anthropologie und Kriminologie* (Gross' Archiv), 48 (1913):142; Kurt Schneider, *Studien über Persönlichkeit und Schicksal eingeschriebener Prostituierter,* Abhandlungen aus dem Gesamtgebiete der Kriminalpsychologie (Heidelberger Abhandlungen), no. 4 (Berlin, 1921), p. 177.

96. See August Bebel, *Die Frau und der Sozialismus* (East Berlin, 1961), pp. 16–17, 232.

97. Schwabe, "Einblicke," pp. 64–65; von Grabe, "Prostitution," p. 155; Max Sichel, "Geisteszustand der Prostituierten," *Zeitschrift für die gesamte Neurologie und Psychiatrie,* 13 (1912):449; Schneider, *Studien über Persönlichkeit,* p. 179.

98. Johannes Schult, *Geschichte der Hamburger Arbeiter, 1890–1919* (Hamburg, 1967), p. 67.

99. H. Neumann, "Die uneheliche Kinder in Berlin und ihr Schutz," *Jahrbuch für Nationalökonomie und Statistik* (III. Folge), 62 (1893):519–20, and the same author's *Die uneheliche Kinder in Berlin* (Jena, 1900), p. 24.

100. See Oscar Stillich, *Die Lage der weiblichen Dienstboten in Berlin* (Berlin, 1902), and the same author's "Die Sittlichkeit der Dienstboten," *Mutterschutz: Zeitschrift zur Reform der sexuelle Ethik,* 3 (1907):230–41.

101. Schwabe, "Einblicke," p. 65.

102. Möller, *Die kleinbürgerliche Familie,* p. 293.

103. On barmaids, see Arthur Cohen, "Die Lohn- und Arbeitsverhältnisse der münchener Kellnerinnen," *Archiv für soziale Gesetzgebung und Statistik,* 5 (1892):97–131; Karl Schneidt, *Das Kellnerinnen-Elend in Berlin* (Berlin, 1893); Heinrich Peter, "Zur lage der Kellnerinnen im Grossherzogtum Baden," *Archiv für Sozialwissenschaft und Sozialpolitik,* 24 (1907):558–612.

104. See Schneider, *Studien über Persönlichkeit* for the life stories of seventy prostitutes as well as the same author's "Die Kindheit der Prostituierten," in *Festschrift zur Feier des zehnjährigen Bestehens der Akademie für praktische Medizin in Cöln* (Bonn, 1915), pp. 77–78. Also Wilhelm Hammer, "Zehn

Lebensläufe Berliner Kontrollmädchen," in Hans Ostwald, ed., *Gesammelte Grossstadt-Dokumente: Das erotische Berlin* (Berlin-Leipzig, n.d., about 1905), 1:1–104.

105. Max Marcuse, *Der eheliche Präventivverkehr, seine Verbreitung, Verursachung und Methodik. Dargestellt und beleuchtet an 300 Ehen* (Stuttgart, 1917) provides an invaluable source of information on working-class contraception, as based on detailed interviews with soldiers during the First World War.

106. *Die geschlechtlich-sittlichen Verhältnisse*, 1:67, 119, 174–75; 2:43, 92, 121.

107. Marcuse, *Der eheliche Präventivverkehr*, pp. 132–35.

108. Ibid., pp. 41, 90.

109. Ibid., pp. 132–34.

110. Lee Rainwater, *And the Poor get Children. Sex, Contraception and Family Planning in the Working Class* (Chicago, 1960), p. 52.

111. Marcuse, *Der eheliche Präventivverkehr*, p. 36. The desire to improve the conditions of life with the help of contraception also existed in rural areas, as is shown in the post–First World War study by Elsbet Linpinsel, "Familien- und Geschlechtsbeziehungen," in Leopold von Wiese, ed., *Das Dorf als soziale Gebilde*, [Ergänzungshefte zu den Kölner Vierteljahrsheften für Soziologie] (Munich, 1928), p. 66.

112. Bromme, *Lebensgeschichte*, pp. 224–25; Tureck, *Ein Prolet erzählt*, p. 337.

113. Marcuse, *Der eheliche Präventivverkehr*, p. 84.

114. Thomas Nipperdey, "Kulturgeschichte, Sozialgeschichte, historische Anthropologie," *Vierteljahrschrift für Sozial- und Wirtschaftsgeschichte*, 55 (1968): 159–160.

V. FORMS OF SOCIAL PROTEST

The desire that history be "relevant" is one of the clearest messages now being received on college and university campuses. Certainly the presumption that a person can better comprehend the present with knowledge of the past is one that most historians, particularly social historians, would hasten to agree with. Their agreement rests, however, on a set of assumptions that students often misunderstand.

Historians feel uncomfortable hearing their profession defended with the popular slogan that those who fail to learn from the past are condemned to repeat it. Few of them believe that history repeats itself, or that there exist historical "laws" that can be mastered and applied by analogy to the present. Is history not relevant, they ask, if it instead makes us sensitive to our present condition by means of an understanding of how and why other men made certain political and social decisions within the context of their own times? In an essay called "Detachment and the Writing of History," Carl Becker wrote:

The value of history is . . . not scientific but moral: by liberalizing the mind, by deepening the sympathies, by fortifying the will, it enables us to control, not society, but ourselves—a much more important thing; it prepares us to live humanely in the present and to meet rather than to foretell the future.

The questions historians think it important to ask are often conditioned by the events of their own day, but it is critical that they seek answers from the past on its own terms. In this sense, the three essays in this section, each of which deals with a form of social protest familiar in our own times, are offered as being relevant.

Anthony Esler's "Youth in Revolt: The French Generation of 1830" looks at the currently popular topics of youth, ideology, and generational conflict in a historical setting. While concentrating his attention on the story of one of the most exciting and colorful periods of French history, Esler also carefully discusses such important concepts as social generations and birth cohorts, reviews the scholarly literature concerning them, and speculates broadly on the role of rebellious generations over the past century and a half. Particularly suggestive is his contention that withdrawal is as characteristic an ideological response on the part of a social generation as rebellion is. Readers should also seriously consider the implications of Esler's bold statement that "neither class nor nationality, perhaps not even race—has a more powerful effect on the growing human animal than the forces that mold a generation."

Michael R. Marrus' "French Jews, the Dreyfus Affair, and the Crisis of French Society" is concerned with the manner in which a religious or racial minority perceives and handles the problem of its identity within a professedly liberal, assimilationist society. When one of their fellows, Captain Dreyfus, was accused of treason, why did some French Jews either remain silent or rush to assert their patriotic loyalty, while others felt compelled to raise the bitter issue of anti-Semitism? In what subtle ways were Zionists and anti-Dreyfusards, many of whom were anti-Semites, united in rejecting the values of secularized French society? (Readers will discover a connection here with Judson Mather's discussion of the Assumptionist response to secularization in the first section of this volume.) In answering these questions, Marrus implicitly suggests a model with regard to social and cultural assimilation that might be applied to the case of minority groups in other societies.

Amy Hackett's "The German Women's Movement, 1890–1914: A Study of National Feminism" examines the third largest feminist movement in the period before the Great War and contrasts it with the better known American and British versions. Although German women actually received the right to vote before their Anglo-American sisters, Hackett contends that many feminists consciously rejected suffrage as the central goal of their movement. The combined impact of specific legal restrictions and cultural and political values, she finds, caused most German women to regard the tactics and arguments of the suffragettes as "too American" and no model for themselves. The women members of the German Social Democratic party did, however, see suffrage as a direct goal and readers should note the socialists' interesting debate as to what women would do with the ballot once they received it. Finally, Hackett's emphasis on "national feminism," the manner in which cultural differences determine the forms of social protest, suggests that there exist inherent limitations on the success of all international movements.

YOUTH IN REVOLT:
THE FRENCH GENERATION OF 1830

Anthony Esler

The young men of the revolution handed their list of demands to Monsieur Guizot on his way to the Palais-Royal one hot August day in 1830. That middle-aged liberal statesman remembered vividly in later years how passionately the revolutionary youth pressed the paper upon him, how they "recommended it in an extremely emotional tone of voice to my most serious attention." Guizot kept the document long enough to include it in his *Mémoires*.[1] It is unlikely, however, that he ever gave any serious consideration to acting on the demands contained therein.

He knew them by heart by this time anyway, these "demands" of the young heroes of the July Revolution. They wanted a new "declaration of rights," a constitution that would turn Louis Philippe, the new "King of the French," into a mere figurehead for a second French Republic. They wanted a wholesale rejection of the Bourbon Restoration, and sanguinary punishment for those who had imposed it upon France. They wanted an international crusade to liberate other oppressed peoples from the death grip of the Old Regime. And they wanted it all now.

For these were the young extremists of 1830, "the enemies of established order," "the revolutionists at any price."[2] Guizot and the other liberal leaders of the bourgeois monarchy would have none of them.

But the revolutionary younger generation was everywhere in evidence during those exciting days after the July Revolution. "The July days," as one contemporary recalled, "had heated the brains, overexcited the youth of France . . . ."[3] Or, as a member of the Chamber of Deputies put it: "The students are always ready to revolt . . . revolution against all constituted and recognized authority having become in their eyes 'the first of duties and the sweetest of pleasures!' "[4]

Balzac described the archetypal "modern conspirator" of the time, not as a truculent peasant or an oppressed artisan or proletarian, but as an eighteen-year-old student. Typically, wrote that alert observer of the human comedy, the young revolutionary was committed to his cause, recklessly brave, and bright enough too "when he does his studying somewhere besides the public square." He sported a "Robespierre waistcoat," a "Marat-style

Anthony Esler received his Ph.D. from Duke University. He currently teaches at the College of William and Mary.

hat, a rallying sign in his buttonhole and a club for a cane. . . ." He had "an arsenal of instant principles," most of them vaguely republican in tone. Above all, he "agitates against every conceivable order of things."[5]

Rebellious youth came in all sorts and conditions in the months and years after *les trois glorieuses,* the "three glorious days" in July. You could generally tell them apart by the cut of their beards. Legitimists—there were a few even of this persuasion among the young—displayed a simple fringe of hair along the jaw line. Bonapartists wore an arrogantly "imperial" mustache. Young republicans like Balzac's "conspirator" often sported full beards. Saint-Simonian socialists gloried in both full beards and shoulder-length hair. The more or less apolitical bohemians of the Latin Quarter also tended toward long hair and beards; the public often found it difficult to distinguish them from their more militant generational contemporaries.

The solid citizens of the July Monarchy were clear on one thing, however: there were revolutionaries loose in the land that summer of 1830, and an astonishing number of them were young.

I

The revolt of the younger generation is a familiar phenomenon of our own time. It has become increasingly familiar in the Western world, and latterly around the globe, ever since the early nineteenth century. The French generation that came of age in the revolutionary year 1830 was in fact one of the first of a long succession of ideologically driven younger generations who have taken up arms against the modern world.

The essay that follows is intended as a case study in generational history. It will analyze the tumultuous early years of the reign of Louis Philippe from a purely generational point of view. More specifically, it will attempt to demonstrate that at least some of the seething ferment of opposition to the citizen king can best be understood as a generational revolt, a rebellion of the young against their parents' world.

The notion of the generation in history, however, remains an unfamiliar one to many readers. It may be well, therefore, to devote a few introductory pages to the theory of social generations itself, before plunging into the present analysis.

The French youth of 1830 were far from isolated in the early decades of the nineteenth century. In those days of youthful secret societies and romantic younger generations in the arts—of Mazzini's Young Italy, of Heine and the Young Germany movement in literature—this generation of youthfully rebellious Frenchmen was clearly part of a trend.

Youth revolts had in fact sputtered and exploded sporadically across Europe throughout the fifteen years since Waterloo. The first student revolt in Western history, for instance, was likely that of the German *Burschenschaft* movement of 1815. The Russian Decembrists, the young army officers who revolted against the tsar in 1825, probably represented a generational phenomenon. In France itself, the *Charbonnerie* of the years around 1820, a secret society organized originally by students after the model of the notorious Italian *Carbonari,* clearly revealed the response of liberal youth to the Restoration of the Bourbons.[6]

Subsequent decades of the nineteenth century, furthermore, were to see repeated outbreaks of generational insurrection in Europe. The Europe-wide revolutions of 1848 alone provide a number of illustrative examples of the important role played by the young in the politics of the barricades. Russia in the 1860s and '70s, the home of Turgenev's *Fathers and Sons,* bred generation after generation of rebellious youth. The decades before the First World War swarmed with generational discontent: from the hippie-style *Wandervögel* of Wilhelmine Germany to the *Yellow Book* Decadents of Oscar Wilde's London; from Lenin's generation of revolutionary Russians to the bomb-throwing anarchists and riotous young Dreyfusards of *fin-de-siècle* Paris.

The nineteenth century thus saw the emergence of the rebellious younger generation as a force in the shaping of modern history.[7] Not surprisingly, that century also produced the first groping efforts to comprehend this strange new phenomenon.[8]

Throughout the period from 1815 to 1914, sensitive observers grappled more or less intuitively with the increasingly important role that self-conscious youth groups and clearly generational upheavals were playing in the troubled history of their own times. Novelists and poets, critics, philosophers, social thinkers of various sorts, and even a few historians all recorded their insights and analyses. Such celebrated nineteenth-century intellects as Goethe, Hegel, Ranke, Dilthey, Mill, Comte, Balzac, Flaubert, Sainte-Beuve, Taine, Turgenev, and Tolstoy offered casual comments or detailed dissections of the phenomenon of generational unrest.

Only in the twentieth century, however, has generational theory begun to find exponents and practitioners equal to its potential importance as a tool of social and historical analysis. Public interest also has grown apace, naturally enough considering the almost continuous generational turbulence of the five decades since World War I.

In the 1920s, then, José Ortega y Gasset in Spain and Karl Mannheim in Germany offered thoughtful, if often conflicting, theories of generational development.[9] Mannheim, Ortega, and their successors, furthermore, began to explore some of the many theoretical difficulties that still confront the would-be generational historian. And Mannheim in particular began to give substance and structure to what had thus far been more commonly a matter of intuitive response and flashes of impressionistic insight than of coherent history.

Over the decades since Ortega and Mannheim, separate Spanish and German "schools" of generational theorists developed. At the same time, a number of historians of literature and the arts have seized upon the generational approach, often, apparently, quite independently of the theorists. So have countless analytical journalists, repentant revolutionaries, and other students of the restlessly insurgent youth of our own century. Not until the 1960s, however, did social scientists begin to call for wider application of one form or another of the theory of social generations in their respective disciplines.[10] This theory, as briefly summarized below, will be employed in the present investigation of the tumultuous early years of the reign of Louis Philippe.

A social generation is, of course, essentially an age group.[11] It is a band of coevals, people born during the same brief span of years, growing up together, conditioned by the same social institutions and the same historical events.[12] It is as real and important an element in society as the social class, the religious sect, and the racial or national group.[13]

Members of the same social generation are thus more than merely coevals. They are a birth cohort born and bred in what Mannheim calls a common generational "location" in society.[14] They have been raised in similar sociologically defined circumstances, by members of the same caste or class. Their psyches have been shaped by common child-rearing methods and by similar educational institutions. They have faced the big crises of the life cycle together. And they have finally been flung out of the nest into much the same shaping matrix of social institutions. Perhaps most important, they have been shaped by the same span of history.

Major historical trends and great events, namely, wars and revolutions, booms and busts, and even such intangibles as shifting value systems and changing world views, of course have some effect upon people of all ages. But coevals, and particularly coevals raised in the same generational location in society, experience such historic earth tremors at the same point in their common psychosocial development. They thus share these experiences in a peculiarly intimate way impossible for people of differing ages.

"For some," wrote Ortega, " 'today' is a state of being twenty, for others, forty, and for still another group, sixty. . . . [Mere] contemporaries are not coevals. . . . Dwelling in the same external and chronological time, they live together in three very different periods of life."[15] An important depression, for example, may weigh heavily on even an established man of forty; but it can be fatal to the career of a young man in search of his first job. The outbreak of war is one thing to a man of sixty; it is quite another for one of twenty.

People of like age who are also products of the same generational location share the historical currents of their times even more closely. In a very real sense, they discover the world together. Members of the same generation revel in the same fads and fashions during their formative years. They hail their own "new wave" in the arts, and discover their own generation's new truths together. They may be recruited as enthusiastic sign-carriers in movements for social change launched by their elders. And they will experience the same bitter feeling of disillusionment when utopia is not forthcoming, a bitterness their elders seldom understand.

These successive shocks of history, then, impinging on a birth cohort already bound by common psychological and sociological influences, forge bonds of "generationhood" strong enough to last a lifetime. The resulting "group mind" is united at least in its underlying assumptions; in its main categories of thought and emotional response; in its angle of approach to living. Neither class nor nationality, perhaps not even race in our race-conscious age, has a more powerful formative effect on the growing human animal than the forces that mold a generation.

Ortega has, perhaps a bit too poetically, likened the group mind of a generation to a desert caravan:

a caravan within which man moves a prisoner, but at the same time a voluntary one at heart, and content. He moves within it faithful to the poets of his age, to the political ideas of his time, to the type of woman triumphant in his youth, and even to the fashion of walking which he employed at twenty-five. From time to time he sees another caravan pass with a strange and curious profile; this is the other generation.[16]

There are quarrels even within the caravan, of course—differences between generational contemporaries sizable enough to make the whole notion of the social generation seem dubious to many. Here, fortunately, Mannheim's judicious concept of the "generation unit" provides a vitally needed corrective.

"Within any generation," says the German sociologist, "there can exist a number of antagonistic generation units." These clearly distinguishable, often conflicting subgroups are nevertheless parts of a larger generational whole: "They are oriented toward each other, even though only in the sense of fighting one another." The key quality that unites each generation unit, and sets it off from all others, is "an identity of responses, a certain affinity in the way in which all move and are formed by their common experiences." Thus

youth experiencing the same concrete historical problems may be said to be part of the same actual generation; while those groups within the same actual generation which work up *the material of their common experiences in different specific ways constitute separate generation units.*[17]

The French younger generation of 1830, for instance, certainly had its share of strikingly different generation units. We have met some of them already, clearly distinguishable by the cuts of their beards.[18] And yet, all of them remained members of a single social generation, bound together by their upbringing in a common generational location, and by the tremendous historical experience they all shared at a crucial moment in their young lives.

Only two or three essential theoretical points remain before we get back to the proper business of the historian—the confrontation of empirical reality. These main points concern ideology, youth, and the patterns of generational revolt.

Perhaps the single most important identifying characteristic of the rebellious generations of the past century and a half is their dedication to ideology. This ideological motivation distinguishes the generational insurrection of today from the mindless student rioters or club-swinging apprentices of medieval times, or from such aimless acts of youthful defiance as vandalism, gang-fighting, or panty-raids in our own time. The young revolutionaries of the nineteenth and twentieth centuries have been almost compulsively ideological rebels.[19] They are fighters for ideas.

It is not surprising, therefore, that given this fundamentally ideological impetus, the social generations that have made their mark in history have typically been younger generations. That is a truism, but worth emphasizing nonetheless; generational ties are strongest and the psychological capacity for ideological commitment most powerful when a birth cohort is in its teens and twenties.[20] "The young men," as a shrewd old preacher put it, "hear the word."[21] In this age of ideologies, the 150 years since 1815, the youth have found plenty of new words to listen to.

Most frequently, the word that has reached the young seems to have been in the nature of a call to revolution.[22] Shaped by influences very different from those that formed their elders in that other world of several decades back, some social generation units, at least, find themselves at war with the aging institutions and ideas that those elders still hold dear. Such conflict between the children of today and those of yesterday is perhaps inevitable. Certainly it has become increasingly common these last two centuries. For as rebels against the status quo—in politics, in the arts, in morality and style of life—the social generations have thrust themselves most aggressively and visibly on the modern world.

Among the more extreme forms of ideologically motivated youth revolt, finally, two types seem to predominate. These may be simply characterized as *rebellion* and *withdrawal*.[23] Both the active rebel and the passive withdrawer from society are reacting against an unsatisfying status quo. Both types oppose the system, and do so for reasons rooted in their common generational experience. Only the form of their revolt differs. The activist rises in open rebellion: he is the eternal militant, the barricade builder and the street fighter. The withdrawer, by contrast, simply drops out, turns his back on society at large and seeks refuge, most often in his own bohemian subculture. Both are familiar types. Both have a history that goes back at least as far as that tumultuous time a century and a half ago when the French generation of 1830 first took to the streets of Paris.

This, then, is the famous younger generation in revolt. An ephemeral, transitory thing, a minority even among its age mates, the social generation yet remains a powerful force for change. It is a growing force in modern history and deserves more attention than it has had from modern historians.

II

The reality of the French youth revolt of the 1830s seems to have been clear enough to contemporaries. And yet this great generational upheaval has somehow almost vanished in the stream of history.

We have subdivided and subsumed a whole generation in revolt, scattered its substance among half-a-dozen hazily related isms and trends. There was the rise of utopian socialism, for instance. There were the republican clubs, journals, and secret societies. There was the rapid increase in Bonapartist feeling, perhaps more a mood than a movement. There was the Catholic revival in its various forms. There was the romantic period in the arts. There were certain colorfully bohemian aspects of the social history of the time, matters of dress and custom perhaps best left to the "buttons and bows" school of popular social historians.

All these ideologies and trends flourished in the 1830s. They jostled each other in the streets of Paris in those frantic years after the July Revolution. But only if we look very closely will we notice the most obvious fact about them all: they were, by and large, the creeds and customs of the young.[24]

If we are to recapture something of the vivid reality of this forgotten youth revolt, we must begin with a backward glance at the years that preceded the sudden accession of the "king of the barricades." For the revolt of the young generation of 1830 began, like all generational upheavals, long before the historic event that set off the explosion (in this case, the July Revolution). To understand the intoxicating impact of the revolution on this generation of French youth, we must go back to their childhood and adolescence, back to the decade and a half of the Bourbon Restoration. We must, in short, embark on a brief generational biography of the generation that came of age in 1830, the birth cohort of 1810.

A great many children were born in France in the years around 1810, and most of them are of no concern to us. What we are seeking here, after all, is not some spurious "consensus" of the views of all those Frenchmen who happened to be in their late teens or early twenties in the year of the July Revolution. We are after a social generation, a group raised in a common generational location, and hence shaped by similar experiences into the multifaceted dissenting force of the early thirties.

Hence, peasant children, who in their profusion outnumbered children of all the other segments of society, are of no interest here. Neither are those fortunate infants born to silver spoons and monogrammed teething rings in the elegant *faubourg Saint-Germain*. The half-literate peasant majority and the fading aristocratic elite of French society played only a minor role in the explosive youth revolt of the early 1830s. This, like most modern generational rebellions, was primarily a revolt of the children of the bourgeoisie.[25]

The revolutionary street fighters and the long-haired bohemians of 1830, then, were raised in the solidly middle-class homes of Paris and the provinces during the eighteen-teens and -twenties. A brief glance at the homes and schools that shaped their early years will give us a good start toward understanding their subsequent rebellion.

"The child," writes Philippe Ariès, "unnoticed in the seventeenth century, discovered in the eighteenth, became almost tyrannical in the nineteenth." By the early 1800s, as a celebrated statesman wrote unhappily to a colleague, "the bonds of subordination have been loosened everywhere to such an extent that in the family, the father considers himself obliged to humor his children!"[26] It was a disturbing reversal of values, yet one which found increasing numbers of converts among the French middle classes in the early decades of the nineteenth century.

The shrinking size of the family, the influence of *Émile* and much other childhood literature, perhaps the romantic cult of the simple, uncorrupted souls—the noble savage, the peasant, the child—all contributed to this startling new ascendancy of the young. As a result, the family in which the generation of 1830 grew up was increasingly built about the child himself. His health, his education, his future career were prime concerns to his elders. Tender family festivals and an almost cloyingly sentimental "togetherness" prevailed in the middle-class home.[27] From the child's infancy until he was sent away to school, he was coddled, petted, made much of by his indulgent parents.

The schools of the Restoration, by contrast, emphasized discipline and strict obedience. Both the church schools and the new system of public education, whose primary innovation was the *lycée,* put stern discipline high on their list of priorities. Schoolboys were birched, marched about, confined to the newly popular boarding schools in rooms "more like cells with their barred windows," and generally treated with "regimental methods and barrack-room style . . . ."[28]

The pattern was thus one of doting overindulgence of childish impulses followed by sudden, sharp repression of them. This pattern of permissiveness in childhood yielding abruptly to repressiveness in adolescence surely helped to create the smoldering sense of injustice that burst out at last in the generational rebellion of the 1830s.

This generation of young bourgeois Frenchmen had, however, yet another singular cross to bear. They were the victims of what can perhaps best be described as a massive deprivation of believable ideals.[29] Religious ideals had long since been laughed to scorn by Voltaire, and the Church had been thoroughly compromised by its continuing involvement with the Old Regime. The secular idealism of the Revolution of 1789 had soured into disillusionment before the generation of 1830 was born. The inspiring splendor of Napoleon, which had once awed a continent, had shrunk to the chafing confines of St. Helena before this generation was well aware of the world around it. The result was a very considerable dearth of ideals during the years when the birth cohort of 1810 was growing up.

Certainly the bourgeois *père de famille* had few exalted ideals to pass on to the next generation. He had seen too many noble visions tarnished, too many self-justifying regimes rise and fall since 1789. The father of the "professional revolutionary" Auguste Blanqui, for instance, had once sat in the councils of the Convention. But he had languished in prison through the Terror, had married a shrewish *déclassée* noblewoman during the Directorate, and had ended as a henpecked bureaucrat under Napoleon. No wonder the elder Blanqui turned his face away when young Auguste in his turn joined the revolutionary movement against the Restoration.[30]

The schools, by contrast, had plenty of official ideals to inculcate in the young. Their best efforts were undermined, however, by the harsh methods they employed and by the antiquated nature of the notions they had to peddle. A sensitive adolescent like the bohemian writer Petrus Borel, whether he attended a Catholic *collège* or one of the new national *lycées,* was quite likely to emerge with a hot-eyed contempt for church and state in France. What his father had not taught him to admire, the schools had quickly taught him to despise.[31]

Thus starved for ideals they could believe in, the sons of the bourgeoisie reached their late teens as the decade of the 1820s drew toward a close. At this point there came, for the more talented of them at least, a significant turning point in their young lives.

When he left secondary school, the young man of brains and initiative was more than likely to be bustled off to Paris, if he was not a Parisian already. For his drained and disillusioned father retained at least one drive intact: the bourgeois urge to "make good," and to see that his son made it even better after him. And Paris was the only place in the nation where a talented youth could hope for the kind of high achievement this young man had been raised to expect.

Paris drew the brightest youth of the provinces like a magnet. It was the center of higher education as the home of the Sorbonne, the Polytechnic, and the chief legal and medical schools. It was the throbbing heart of French politics, finance, and the fashionable life of the dandy. It was also, for those whose secret yearnings turned that way, the home of French culture, of the literary journals and the publishers, of the artists' ateliers, the academies, and the art galleries. The bright young man in France needed little urging from an ambitious father to send him scurrying up to the capital when his schooling was done.

By thus dispatching his son to Paris, however, the bourgeois father unwittingly played straight into the hands of the generational process that would soon turn the youth angrily against everything his father stood for. The father of the family was sending his offspring up to swell the milling cohorts of disaffected youth already growing rapidly in the City of Light. He was also, quite unintentionally, helping to intensify this youthful disaffection by condemning his son to the probable frustration of his exalted career aspirations. And he was unconsciously offering his offspring up, an empty vessel longing to be filled, into the hands of the ideological prophets of Paris. Each of these points deserves a moment's further development.

A self-conscious social generation does not spring up spontaneously, the pentecostal flames of generationhood leaping up suddenly over a thousand heads across the land. Generational consciousness is ignited in the first instance "within *concrete groups* where mutual stimulation in a close-knit vital unit inflames the participants . . . to develop integrative attitudes" latent in the social generation of which they are a part.[32] Or, as the anthropologist S. N. Eisenstadt puts it: "Everywhere the nucleus of an age-group organization is a small, usually face-to-face primary group of peers with a strong sense of solidarity. . . ."[33]

Just such "concrete groups" collected in Paris as provincial youth swarmed to join their Parisian peers at the university or the professional schools of the 1820s. And, thanks to the expansion of educational opportunities begun by Napoleon and accelerated by the restored Bourbons, the graduating classes grew larger year by year.

From this last fact came yet another turn of the screw in the inexorable preparation of this generation for its revolutionary destiny. The object of an advanced education was to make a young man's fame and fortune. But fortunes, as it turned out, were a good deal harder to come by than the talented provincial or Parisian youth had been led to expect. In France during the 1820s and '30s, there were simply not enough prestigious posts in law, medicine, engineering, the civil service, or the academic world to go around.[34] It was the sort of situation that frequently breeds "deviant" youth groups: a situation in which "intellectual development has been much more advanced than the economic. . . . For this reason, the economic and professional opportunities open to young people are inadequate. . . . This is especially true," Eisenstadt adds, "of the more intellectual youth. . . ."[35]

Certainly it proved to be true of a noticeable proportion of the French generation of 1830. Many a bright young man, thus overeducated and underemployed, quickly sank into one of those "intellectual proletariats" that have proved to be so troublesome to the modern world.[36] The smoldering discontent of this growing army of the young needed only a spark to set the powder alight. And the flame that ignited this faith-starved generation was most often that most intangible of historical agents, a new idea.

The new and liberating truth might come to him at any time as he wandered the colorful streets of the Latin Quarter in the late twenties. The air of the capital, after long decades of Restoration stuffiness and Napoleonic discipline, was vibrating once again with subversive new ideologies. And if there is one defining characteristic of the youth revolution of the past century and a half, it is the central role of ideology.

"I would honestly have died for an idea," recalled a former schoolboy rebel of 1830, "though I would no doubt have been much embarrassed if I had been asked to explain what I meant by that pretentious word. Oh," the aging one-time radical continues, "that four-letter word *Idea,* with a big *I,* a capital *I,* how many poor heads has it addled, and what evil has it not done to my unfortunate country!"[37]

This sort of ideological commitment distinguishes modern revolutionary youth from the youthful hell-raisers of the past. It is "common values" and "common symbols," shared "integrative attitudes and formative principles" that produce the new "generation style" of the revolutionary younger generation.[38] In Paris during the last years of the Bourbon Restoration, such new values, new symbols, new integrating *Gestalten* were everywhere at hand.

The out-at-elbows, underfed young intellectual proletarian of the *rue St. Jacques* could readily enough pick up a copy of Théodore Jouffroy's "new liberal" journal, the *Globe,* with its titillating hints of subversive republicanism. He might come across Victor Hugo's new manifesto lambasting the literary establishment, namely, the notorious Preface to *Cromwell,* in any bookstall along the Seine. He might drop in at a Saint-Simonian meeting to hear the ardent young disciples of the master, who was dead only a couple of years, orating on the technocratic utopia of the future.[39] Whichever of these insurrectionary ideologies the disillusioned young man seized upon, he was almost sure to find theoretical reinforcement for his own simmering sense of an unjust world.

The concrete core of a social generation had been created by the magnetic pull of Paris on the young and talented sons of the French bourgeoisie. In the capital, the apostles of the new creeds were soon busy sorting out the core groups of the various generation units, groups bound by a particular response to the common generational experience. From these nuclei in turn, this multifaceted youth revolt would spread back to the provinces in the early thirties. Cells of the great republican secret societies would be established in a number of cities. Duels would be fought in the provinces over Hugo's *Hernani.* Saint-Simonian missionaries would soon be carrying the new gospel, not only into the Midi, but across the frontiers into foreign lands. The heart of the matter would remain at Paris throughout, but there was some feedback to the social generation at large even this early in the long history of the modern youth revolution.

But the culminating event in the process of reeducation that turned the petted, overdisciplined, and finally disillusioned child of the bourgeoisie into the ideological rebel of the thirties was yet to come. It came with the explosion of July.

It is, according to Mannheim, "the trigger action of the social and cultural process" that produces a new "generation style."[40] The July Revolution of 1830 was the climax of just such a process. The outbreak of revolutionary street violence that toppled Charles X from the throne of France completed the spiritual liberation of the younger generation. It also catapulted the youth of 1830 into a revolutionary trajectory of its own that would shake the nation for half-a-dozen years and would echo for decades into the future. For the young, the July Revolution began with victory and ended in defeat.

In three glorious days of barricades and bloodshed—so ran the heroic legendry of the revolution—the "sacred people," led by the crusading youth, overthrew the government by force and smashed the Old Regime.[41] Power lay in the smoky midsummer streets of Paris. But before the victorious barricade fighters could pick it up, new and even more nefarious enemies of hope intervened. Bustling onto the scene as soon as the bullets stopped flying, these new villains snatched up the fallen crown before the victorious revolutionaries could grind it under heel. The unctious intruders on the battlefield hastily dusted off the golden symbol of royal tyranny, ceremoniously draped it in the tricolor of '89, and placed it on the head of Louis Philippe d'Orleans.

"We no sooner get rid of one king," protested the young street fighters who had occupied the Hotel de Ville, "then they give us another one." "It's all to do over again!" cried the wild-haired radical Pierre Leroux. "Light up the matches again, and cast some more bullets!"[42]

The revolutionaries had been betrayed, as they saw it, their revolution hijacked. And the villain, as so often seems to be the case, was that archenemy of the root-and-branch revolutionary, the reforming liberal: solid middle-class men of business, politics, and the professions who believed in orderly progress and moderate reform; men who, as Guizot said, were "resolved not to become revolutionaries even while making a revolution;"[43] men like Guizot himself, like the journalist Thiers, like the bankers Lafitte and Casimir Périer, like the old intriguer Talleyrand.

The exhilarating heroics of the "three glorious days" were thus followed by the unrevolutionary and totally unheroic "bourgeois monarchy" of Louis Philippe. Once again the youth had been allowed the most intoxicating hopes, only to have the golden prize snatched from them in the end.

The glory and the betrayal of 1830 had a two-fold impact on this social generation. On the one hand, the dazzling victory of July exalted them as nothing else in their young lives had. If the government really could be overthrown by force in the streets, anything might be possible. So at least it seemed to some of these newly converted true believers. For others, however, the impact of the betrayal of the revolution apparently outweighed the enthusiasm for change kindled by the revolution itself. For them, the new idealism must find some other outlet than foredoomed campaigns for significant political or social change. As far as this wing of the generation of 1830 was concerned, political involvement was a mug's game.

Almost all the ideologically based generation units of the rising generation of 1830 were affected in one way or the other. Those whose great expectations for change survived the debacle of July became the militants of the early 1830s. The most important of these were the revolutionary republicans, led by the street fighters of July themselves. But there were growing numbers of youthful converts to the Bonapartist cause too, embodied after 1832 in the person of young Louis Napoleon. And there were the handful of young legitimists who idolized the mother of the Bourbon heir, the romantic young Duchesse de Berry. Among these activists, we might even include the abortive liberal Catholic movement centered around that stormy petrel of the French church, Lamennais, and his new journal, *l'Avenir*.

But there were also those whose disillusionment with the outcome of the Revolution of 1830 led them to turn from the national stage to their own back gardens, to do what good they could and save their own souls in the process. Such were the youthful Catholic founders of the *conférence* of St. Vincent de Paul, dedicated in an almost medieval way to self-sacrificial service to the poor. Of this sort also was the colorful socialist cult set up in the name of Saint-Simon, a communal brotherhood that, while preaching technocracy to come, for the present provided a passionate religious experience for the religion-starved children of the bourgeoisie. Such were the bohemian dropouts of the next generation of French romanticism, who rejected all social crusades to become the apostles of *l'art pour l'art*.

It would be impossible, within the brief confines of this essay, to follow the further development of all these generation units of the birth cohort of 1810. In the succeding part of this paper, therefore, we shall focus on two specific units of this generation, tracing each in turn through the early thirties, from the zenith of this youth revolt through its decline and eventual extinction. One of these subgroups has been selected to illustrate the aggressively militant, sometimes even violent response to the event that was the hinge of fate for this generation, the Revolution of 1830. The other has been chosen to exemplify the equally common pattern of withdrawal from a despised society, in this case, the grubby realities of life under the July monarchy. In each case, the youth of these movements will be stressed, and the common patterns beneath apparent differences will be duly emphasized. For diverse as its many manifestations might be, this was a single generation in revolt, and the fate of one of its component subgroups was by and large the fate of all.

III

Certainly there was violence enough in the early years of the reign of Louis Philippe. There was the Carlist (legitimist) peasant revolt in the Vendée. There were the strikes and insurrections of working men in Lyon and other industrial towns. There was the turbulence that repeatedly swept the streets of the capital itself. Law and order were not easily restored to France in the months and years after the July Revolution.

Unrest among peasants, artisans, and the new proletariat during this period is widely recognized. Such upheavals among the lower orders are readily comprehensible in terms of traditional dynastic loyalties and the economic pressures of the depression of 1828–32. The role of ideologically driven youth, however, was equally self-evident to contemporaries. And though such vocal and vigorous dissent among the children of the very classes who profited most from the new regime may at first seem more perplexing, it is quite easily understood when seen in the context of the generational biography outlined above.

The most militant of all the generation units of this young cohort were the revolutionary republicans. The present section will attempt to trace the rise and fall of this young republican wing of the generation of 1830. According to the police spy Lucien de la Hodde, "almost all" the leaders of the first great republican secret society of the 1830s were young, "a generation of young men" among whom "July fell like a bomb. . . ."[44] These leading spirits seem most typically to have been in their thirties, dynamic young men like Cavaignac, Garnier-Pagès, Armand Carrel, and Armand Marrast. But young and vigorous though they might be, these were clearly members of the birth cohort of 1800, not that of 1810. Theirs was the generation that came of age in the 1820s, the generation of Victor Hugo, Prosper Enfantin, Théodore Jouffroy, and others who provided inspiration and leadership for the new youth of 1830.

Youths a decade younger than Cavaignac and Carrel, however, provided much of the manpower and more of the delirious enthusiasm for the conspiracies and *émeutes* of the early thirties, youths like those described by a correspondent in Paris writing to a provincial prefect in August of 1830:

The present time is perilous. We will have some bad days to get through yet, under the fire of all the exalted absurdities of the students. . . . Here the populace, the shopkeepers, even the workers are excellent; without the schoolboys (écoliers), *everything would be perfectly calm.*[45]

One *émeutier* of the thirties recalled that he was drawn into his first street riot when he was only fifteen years old. Another describes vividly how he first charged a line of troops, carried away by "the intoxication of the *émeute*," while he was still "a boy of school age."[46]

Balzac's "modern conspirator," it will be recalled, was only eighteen. Real-life revolutionaries like Blanqui and Barbès, leaders of the far left wing of the republican societies, were in their twenties at the time of the July Revolution. Somewhere in this age range, between the late teens and the early twenties, would probably be found the typical young republican of the first years of Louis Philippe.

Youthful militance of many kinds was widely in evidence in the aftermath in July. Some students, for instance, turned upon the rigid, stultifying educational routines of the French secondary schools. Rebelling usually over such apparent trivia as harsh discipline or unappetizing food, some of the schoolboys went so far as to expel their masters and "occupy" the schools themselves. Supporters in the streets below kept them fed by flinging bread and sausages up to crowded windows of the barricaded buildings.[47]

In Paris particularly, the young thrust themselves even more arrogantly to the center of the national political stage. The students especially were widely admired in the capital for the part they were believed to have played on the barricades. Those who had fought in July were given medals by the government. "The schools" were lustily cheered by the populace when they paraded through the streets *en masse*. They were the "ardent youth," the "glorious youth," the petted darlings of the revolution.[48]

All of this rhetorical admiration seems to have gone somewhat to their heads. "The youth of the schools" appear to have developed a rather exalted view of their own place among the builders of the new nation. They sent manifestos and policy statements up to the Chamber of Deputies and were surprised and embittered when liberal politicians like Guizot, an ex-professor, failed to act on their advice. As their frustration and disillusionment grew, some of these young ideologues carried their commitment beyond petitions and parades. They went on to agitation and propaganda, to radical organizations, to conspiracy and violence.

The political ideals of the new generation were hazy enough, and often impractical, but they were nonetheless ardently felt. There were emotional Bonapartists among them, eager devotees of the burgeoning Napoleonic legend. There were some who were feeling their way toward socialism, a far more militant socialism than that preached by the contemporary cults of Saint-Simon and Fourier. But the core of their revolutionary creed lay in the lofty ideals generated by the French Republic of forty years before.

The young radicals were immense and uncritical admirers of the Revolution of 1789 and of the republican dream fostered by the legendary leaders of the 1790s.[49] Robespierre, for them, was not the evil genius who presided over the Terror of '93, but the Incorruptible, the radical idealist who dared to demand a French Republic dedicated to a better life for all its citizens.[50] The Republic of Reason and Virtue, the reign of liberty, equality, fraternity—these exalted aims of the men of the nineties were also the goals of the young republicans of the 1830s.

They sang the *Marseillaise* with unexampled passion, falling on their knees at the last verse. They bore the tricolor through the streets as though it were a holy icon. They idolized the "sacred people," the victims of all oppressive establishments, the heroes of all revolutions. They demanded universal public education, universal manhood suffrage, and even some measure of economic relief for the poorest of their fellow citizens. For a time, at least, they seem to have gained a certain ascendancy over the working men of Paris, enough so that the government even called upon the students, on at least one occasion, to cool off a potential revolt of the lower orders.

Young activists with this central republican orientation thronged the Paris political clubs that sprang up in the wake of the July Revolution. When the authorities finally moved in to break up these frequently tumultuous meetings, the youth joined the more structured seances of the *Amis du Peuple*. When that group was suppressed in 1832, many of them went on to Godefroy Cavaignac's *Société des Droits de l'Homme,* the most notorious and most formidable of all the republican secret societies. The tentacles of the Rights of Man reached from Paris to Marseille, Lyon, Grenoble, and other provincial cities. The society made serious efforts to reach the working class, both the established guilds and the new industrial proletariat, and in fact succeeded in forming a number of working-class sections. The left wing of the *Droits de l'Homme,* led by the twenty-five-year-old veteran, Auguste Blanqui, worshiped at the shrine of Gracchus Babeuf, demanded a welfare republic, and grimly accepted the necessity of violence to achieve their ends.

The young republicans published their views openly to the world in newspapers like Armand Carrel's *National* and Armand Marrast's *Tribune,* and also in provincial papers like the *Emancipation* of Toulouse and the *Sovereign People* in Marseille. They lambasted the establishment in pamphlets like *The Debauchery of the Clergy* and *The Crimes of the Police.* They chuckled happily over the jokes and sneers and savage cartoons that filled the opposition press and its readers with contempt for their new ruler. And increasingly the young radicals brooded on "the next time," the coming Third French Revolution, which would crush the infamous thing once and for all and bring in the Republic of Virtue at last.

For it was an article of faith with a substantial proportion of this social generation that "1830" had been that abortion in nature, "a revolution stopped halfway." Even so moderate a republican as Armand Carrel insisted that "the revolution of 1830 was not an end, but a beginning." The militant leader Cavaignac declared darkly that "we only gave way [in July] because we were not strong enough. Later on it will be different."[51]

Some of Cavaignac's less judicious young followers felt that "later on" was too long to wait. They wanted revolution now, and they drifted repeatedly into violence. In September of 1830, for instance, "a crowd of young patriots" proceed to "liberate" the Pantheon by filling it with the busts of all the long-proscribed heroes of '93 they could get their hands on. After the furious demonstrations surrounding the trial of Charles X's ministers, a score of National Guard officers and others—"young men," the judge lamented, "full of generous feelings who were not born for the humiliation of the dock"—were brought to trial as ringleaders of the mob. The sacrilegious rioters who smashed up the church of Saint-Germain-l'Auxerrois and looted the palace of the Archbishop of Paris in February of 1831 were, according to an eyewitness, not "workers" but "the young men of the schools."[52]

In the larger, more nearly organized *émeutes,* youth was also prominent. Thus the half-dozen conspirators who tried to trigger a large-scale revolt by setting fire to the towers of Notre Dame in January, 1832, were "all in their first youth," no more than nineteen or twenty years of age. One was a mere boy who burst into tears when he was seized by the police. Youth was also prominent at the funeral of General Lamarque, a popular revolutionary hero, whose huge funeral procession in June of 1832 turned into the bloodiest uprising since 1830. Three hundred young men drew the casket through the streets, while large numbers of students and young members of the secret societies, hardly troubling to conceal their weapons or their insurrectionary intentions, marched in the van. The youth of the *École polytechnique,* the special heroes of the July Revolution, had been forbidden to march; but they broke out of the engineering school and joined the mob, to the acclamations of the thronging tens of thousands. Soon after their arrival, the first shots were fired and the barricades went up once more.[53]

These young men, "apprentices fashioned in the nurseries of insurrection," combined rather hazy ideological commitment to their cause with a growing contempt for "the king of the greengrocers."[54] They shouted threats at him through the gates of the Tuileries. They scrawled silhouettes of his rotund figure and notoriously pear-shaped head on walls and used the caricatures for target practice. During the years 1832 to 1836 alone, four serious attempts were made to assassinate the king.[55]

Louis Philippe, of course, died comfortably in bed; nor was his government overthrown by the young militants of the 1830s. Their most desperate efforts, like those of the peasants of the Vendée or the silk workers of Lyon, were doomed to failure. It appears that the activist wing of the generation of 1830 did itself more harm than good by the increasingly desperate violence of its assault on the status quo. In this, of course, it was typical of youth revolts, indeed, of revolutions of all sorts, in many times and places.

At the beginning of the decade, the young dissidents enjoyed a considerable amount of public prestige. Their widely publicized heroism in July had, as we have seen, won much admiration for their courage and idealism. It was not long, however, before the new government saw the error of taking this flattering tack with the forces of anarchy. Within less than a year, hard-lining Casimir Périer and the "party of resistance" had replaced the amiable but ineffectual government of Lafitte.

But repression was not so easy for the new government as it had been for the old. Efforts to put down the young militants were repeatedly frustrated by the fundamentally liberal mood of the political nation. The republicans, after all, spoke the rhetoric and cherished the symbols of the Revolution of 1789, as almost everyone else did in the wake of that second overthrow of the house of Bourbon. In 1830, the most unrevolutionary bourgeois citizen wore a tricolor cockade in his buttonhole, and the citizen king himself emerged regularly on his balcony to sing the Marseillaise with surging crowds of demonstrators.

Lacking the support of the moderately liberal majority of the literate population, Louis Philippe and his ministers found it almost impossible to stop the street violence and the conspiracies. In 1831, '32, and '33, juries repeatedly acquitted rioters, revolutionary plotters, and even young men accused of trying to kill the king. The most serious charge of which the government could convict even so professional a revolutionary as Auguste Blanqui was something on the order of contempt of court.[56]

By the middle years of the decade, however, the insurrectionary zeal of the young activists had exhausted their store of public sympathy. The rash of rebellions that broke out in 1834, the last on such a scale before 1848, proved to be the final straw. By the end of 1835, the violent years were over for this generation of French republicans.[57]

The opening gun in the regime's final assault on the enemies of order was the Law on Associations, passed early in 1834. The primary target of this measure, which enabled the authorities to suppress unauthorized societies of any size, even the smallest, was the Society of the Rights of Man, which was in fact divided into small autonomous cells not legally provided for under the penal code. The effect of the new law was to make some impetuous young members of the society talk wildly, despite the warnings of wiser heads, about "taking up the gauntlet" thus flung at their feet by the royal government.

The great revolt of 1834 began, however, not in the secret societies of Paris, but among the artisans of the silk manufacturing city of Lyon. This provincial city, which had exploded once before, three years earlier, had remained a tinderbox ever since. In April of 1834, what had begun as a bread-and-butter strike rooted in a recession in the silk industry turned into a political confrontation when the government intervened against the strikers. For five days, French troops fought their way through the working-class sections of the city, making use of artillery where necessary. The uprising at Lyon, furthermore, sparked outbreaks in a number of other cities as well—in Marseille, Grenoble, Poitiers, Vienne, Clermont, Chalons, Auxerre, Arbois, and Paris itself. In the capital, tens of thousands of troops were deployed to restore order in the streets.

Cavaignac and other radicals had been in Lyon organizing the year before, and some young republicans apparently did fight beside the workers in April.[58] In Paris, many republicans of the most nonviolent sort felt compelled to accept a share of the "moral responsibility" for the deeds of their "brothers" in Lyon.[59] Cavaignac and scores of other leaders of the Rights of Man were rounded up before they could bring themselves to take any action in the common cause. Others, however, did fling up barricades and launch their own ill-fated rebellion just as that in Lyon was sputtering out.

The republicans had neither sanctioned the strike nor ordered the insurrection at Lyon. The government, however, made the most of what republican involvement they could discover, or fabricate. A nationwide revolutionary conspiracy was alleged, with the young republican ideologues at the heart of it.[60]

Little admiration was left for the young militants of 1830 when the "monster trial" of 1835 convened in Paris. In the public mind, the typical republican was no longer an impetuous young idealist, a youth "full of generous feelings . . . not made for the humiliation of the dock," but a bloody-minded fanatic. A popular jingle summed up the "insane schemes" of the revolutionaries:

> *With blood we'll sprinkle the festive meats,*
> *In blood we'll wash our hands;*
> *How sweet to see the high heads fall—*
> *That's why we are republicans!*[61]

The monster trial of 164 young radicals constituted in itself a final, striking confrontation between the generations. The accused were tried before the Chamber of Peers, who themselves, as it happened, numbered 164. On one side were ranged some of the most distinguished elder statesmen in the nation. Facing them on the benches of the accused sat some of the most militant leaders of the generation of 1830—"almost all of them young."[62] But the gulf that divided them was greater than years or narrowly political principles: it was a cultural chasm that spanned every aspect of their respective world views and value systems. One young defendant admirably summed up this yawning generation gap:

We do not feel the same, we do not speak the same language. Our country, humanity, its laws and its needs, duty, religion, the arts and sciences . . . none of the things that constitute a society, not the heavens and the earth look the same to us. There is a whole world between us.[63]

The conclusion was forgone. Cavaignac, Marrast, and some others did escape from prison before the trial was over, but they soon fled into exile. Of those that remained, 121 of the "cream of the republican movement" were duly convicted and imprisoned. The *Société des Droits de l'Homme* was dissolved, the *Tribune* and other republican journals closed down. The dashing young republican editor Armand Carrel was killed in a duel the following year. Two years later, the abortive revolt of Blanqui's Society of the Seasons was crushed, and Blanqui and Barbès were flung into prison for the balance of the reign. The meteoric career of this unit of a young generation in revolt thus quickly drew to a close. Politically speaking, the "years of silence" settled down over Orleanist France.[64]

IV

There were other reactions among the young to the debacle of 1830 besides the open rebellion of the republican secret societies. At the opposite extreme on any spectrum of political activism, there was the apparently apolitical stance of the Left Bank bohemians. The bohemians of the 1830s built no barricades, launched no *émeutes* against the monarchy. Yet their alienation from French society was as complete as any revolutionist's.

There could be no question, at least, of the youth of this colorful new generation of rebels in the arts. Even more obviously than the republicans, the bohemians were young, young with a fury and a vengeance.

A modern authority puts the average age of the younger romantics whom Victor Hugo rallied in 1830 for the defense of *Hernani* at nineteen or twenty.[65] Contemporary observers saw the new generation of artists and writers as even more callowly youthful. "There is scarcely a boy so insignificant," snorted a literary visitor to Paris, "as to doubt his having the power and the right to instruct the world." Established literary circles, however, generally shrugged off "this 'new school' (as the *décousu* folks always call themselves)." The press also waxed sarcastic about the new generation in the arts: "These authors are sometimes [no more than] fifteen years old; the great number are even younger. . . . I know some who went to read plays before the selection committee of the *Théâtre Français* in their nurses' arms. . . ."[66]

The bohemians themselves frankly acknowledged their youth: indeed, they gloried in it. "In the army of the romantics, as in [Napoleon's] Army of Italy," Théophile Gautier joyfully recalled, "everybody was young."[67] They cheerfully accepted the label of *les Jeune-France* slapped on their "new school" by the newspapers. Their only terror, in fact was of growing old. "At twenty," as this intensely self-conscious youth movement saw it, "one was Young France, a handsome young melancholic. . . ." But it was all downhill from there. By twenty-five, one had become world-weary and cynical, a Byronic "Childe Harold" type. After thirty, decay set in rapidly.

At forty, one reached "the last stage of decrepitude" as an "Academician and Member of the Institute."[68]

The papers called them worse things than "Young France." The "bohemian" tag, for instance, applied for the first time to this generation of impecunious young writers and artists, was derived from a French word for *gypsy* and had nothing but negative connotations for their elders. The derivation of *bousingo,* another journalistic epithet for the new artistic youth, is even more obscure.[69] The almost untranslatable term is perhaps best rendered for the modern reader by some such equivalent as "beatnik" or "hippie." To the solid bourgeois citizen of 1830, however, the meaning was clear enough. A *bousingo* was a thoroughly disreputable individual, a young hooligan totally dedicated to wine, women, and song, to midnight revelry and window-breaking, to jeering at bourgeois morality and publicly flouting all the standards of civilized society.

At first glance, it might seem that all this hostility from the establishment was, if not undeserved, at least not reciprocated in kind by the otherworldly young aesthetes of the Latin Quarter. The bohemians professed to be entirely uninterested in social and political disputes, claiming to be a generation that had withdrawn from such mundane concerns to dedicate their lives to art.

The apolitical attitude of this generation unit of the birth cohort that came of age in 1830 was vigorously summed up by one of their chief spokesmen, the long-haired prophet of "art for art's sake," Théophile Gautier:

I know that you will tell me that we have an Upper House and a Lower House, and that we may soon hope to see every man a voter. . . . [But] what does it matter whether a saber [like Napoleon's], a holy-water sprinkler [symbol of church power under the Restoration], or an umbrella [Louis Philippe's famous bourgeois accessory] governs you? It's a stick all the same, and I am astonished that the Men of Progress should dispute so hard over the choice of the cudgel that will administer the beating.[70]

Gautier and his fellow artistic bohemians displayed, or seemed to display, a vast contempt for politics, revolutionary and establishment alike. They adhered to the lofty dictum laid down by their prophet, Victor Hugo: "Whatever may be the tumult of the public squares, let art persist, let art seek its own essence, let art remain faithful to itself . . . ."[71] In some bohemian circles, any attempt at serious discussion of political issues was loudly hooted down by the group as a whole.[72]

It is not perhaps surprising that artists should be apolitical. Indeed, profound social and political unconcern would seem to have been built into the aesthetic creed of these particular young artists. For this was the generation that promulgated the notion with which Gautier's name especially was to be indissolubly linked: the notion of *l'art pour l'art.*

The bohemians came by their creed quite legitimately: they were, after all, second-generation romantics. They had been stirred in their earliest youth by the rebellion of their immediate predecessors—Hugo, Dumas, Balzac, Mérimée, George Sand, Lamartine, Delacroix, Chopin, and the rest of what historians of French culture have dubbed the Great Romantic Generation. But that rebellion of the 1820s had been strictly an artistic one, a rejection of the dictates of the academies and the tyranny of classical rules and models. The new generation, some ten years younger than Hugo and his contemporaries, sought to carry this revolution to its ultimate consummation—to plumb the profoundest depths of Art, to ascend the loftiest peaks of Beauty. If Hugo chose to take up social reform, and Lamartine ran for political office, so much the worse for Hugo and Lamartine.

Form and structure, the correspondence of the arts and the canons of ideal beauty were the prime concerns of writers like Gérard de Nerval, Philothée O'Neddy, Petrus Borel, and Gautier himself, of graphic artists like Célestin Nanteuil and composers like Félicien David. No wonder the *Jeune-France* school had no concern with politics.

Or had they? A closer look at the pronunciamientos of this generation in the arts makes clear that the bohemian reaction to the bourgeois monarchy was just as virulently, contemptuously negative as that of the most aggressive streetfighter, and perhaps even broader in scope. The *émeutier*'s response to the ascendency of the bourgeoisie was to attack it; that of the bohemian aesthete was to withdraw from it, not passively, but fiercely and violently, as if from contamination. Both of these extreme elements of the youth revolt of 1830 were thus clearly products of the common generational experience: the spiritual liberation of the twenties, followed by the "betrayal" of July.[73]

"In Paris," declared Petrus Borel, the self-styled "Wolfman" (*Lycanthrope*) of French letters, "there are two caves, one full of robbers, the other for the murderers. The robbers' cave is the Stock Exchange; the murderers' is the Palace of Justice." The bushy-haired young poet Philothée O'Neddy declared open war on the financial and industrial magnates, "the second-hand junk-dealers" who were widely believed to be the masters of France under the bourgeois king. Romantic youth, O'Neddy announced, had launched a "metaphysical crusade against society." "Our dream," as Gautier himself recalled it, "was to turn the world upside down."[74]

Their revolution was real enough, though it did not take the form of political agitation or fighting in the streets. These young men really believed that the exalted idealism embodied in their cult of art and beauty could and would replace the grubby materialism of the bourgeoisie. It was a spiritual revolution they called for. "It seemed to us," as one of them wrote, "that one day Religion must . . . be replaced by Aesthetics."[75]

But there was more to the *Jeune-France* revolt than such unlikely preachments, however intensely felt. The young bohemians *lived* their revolution. And this bohemian life style itself—"the romantic life," as O'Neddy called it, "as turbulent, as adventurous, as free as the Arab tribes in their solitude"—was the purest expression of the alienation of the younger generation from the values and mores of their bourgeois elders.[76]

The very appearance of the bohemians was an affront to all the tidy instincts of bourgeois France. *Bousingos* affected shoulder-length hair and unkempt beards. Their hair and skin and fingernails were frequently filthy, and they reeked of strong tobacco. They often had a haggard look about them, the greenish, corpselike complexion and haunted eyes of the romantically dissipated soul, clearly doomed to an early grave.[77]

Their clothing was usually greasy, shabby, slovenly, with broken boots and a threadbare coat. For special occasions, however, such as all-night festivals, or romantic first-nights like that of *Hernani,* the bohemians broke out in a fantastic array of colorful costumes. They dressed like cavaliers and minstrels and corsairs, a gorgeous panoply of capes and trunk hose and medieval headgear borrowed from ages more exciting than their own drab, frock-coated century. They sported costumes defiantly reminiscent of Polish freedom-fighters (whom the new government of France had pusillanimously refused to rescue from the Russians) or wandering Algerian bedouins (whom French armies were then engaged in subjugating). Bright colors and weird combinations predominated, the more exotic and unlikely the better, so long as the result properly shocked the eye of middle-class conformity.[78]

The bohemians lived in the Latin Quarter around the university or in the dilapidated section near the Louvre, usually in ramshackle tenements or in old, ill-furnished houses rented communally. They littered their quarters with unfashionable art objects, medieval memorabilia, and perhaps exotic weapons allegedly intended for the great romantic war upon the bourgeoisie.[79] They ate poorly, dressed shabbily, had only the leakiest of roofs overhead, and didn't seem to care at all. Nothing could have been more galling to those solidest of nineteenth-century men of property, the French bourgeoisie.

These disreputable young outcastes seemed deliberately set upon outraging their elders in every conceivable way. The middle class, for instance, believed in hard work and moving up in the world. The *Jeune-France* writer or painter did only the minimum of paid labor necessary to keep body and soul together, devoting the rest of his time to his artistic vocation. Art, especially experimental coterie art, was not a line of business that was likely to move a young man up in the hustling, materialistic, money-conscious world of 1830.

The respectable bourgeois perhaps kept a mistress, but he kept her out of sight. He maintained due decorum and vociferously valued his family life. The *bousingo* drifted cheerfully from *grisette* to *lorette* and back again. He gave himself up to all-night revels, loud music, dancing in the streets, and mischievously shocking debauches around flaming bowls of punch or human skulls brimming with cheap wine.

The good citizen believed in God, even if his God was closer to Voltaire's Deist divinity than to that of traditional Christianity. The romantic bohemians claimed to be atheists, or even Satanists. Satan, after all, was the archetypal rebel, and they were all his subjects—outlaws, outcasts, the Byronically accursed of the earth. More than one probably followed the practice of Charles Lasailly the poet, who "never went to bed without offering choice bits of blasphemy to the God of the bourgeoisie."[80]

All good Frenchmen, of course, were loyal sons of *la patrie*. They ostentatiously honored the flag and eagerly served in the National Guard as staunch defenders of public order. The *bousingos,* of course, had no more respect for country than for God. "Wolfman" Borel showed his contempt for the flag by having a portrait of himself in his most outlandish *bousingo* costume gaudily framed in the tricolor. Théophile Gautier reported for compulsory military training in what he regarded as a far more aesthetically pleasing uniform than that provided by the state: green dresscoat, rose cravat, yellow waistcoat with blue flowers, a gendarme's hat perched on his curly, long hair and an exquisite antique musket on his shoulder.

And so it went, up and down the line. The top-hatted middle-class citizen of Paris believed in order and morality and decent respect for religion, in getting ahead personally, in the material progress of society, and in constitutional monarchy under the Charter of French Liberties. The slovenly, hairy bohemian of the Latin Quarter was disorderly, immoral, unambitious, antimaterialistic, blasphemously irreligious, and totally, viscerally contemptuous of the Charter of French Liberties. "I would cheerfully renounce my rights as a Frenchman and a citizen," Gautier assured all and sundry, "in order to see an authentic picture of Raphael's, or a beautiful woman naked."[81]

This was, in short, a genuine counterculture, a counterculture of the young, and one whose descendants are with us to this day. This first generation of bohemians, however, was foredoomed to failure. The public did not read their books nor hang their canvases. Victor Hugo was a great success by this time; but then, Hugo at least dressed like a gentleman, was a solid family man, and kept as sharp an eye out for profit and loss as any shopkeeper in Paris. The new generation was simply beyond the pale.

There were more specific and more concrete reasons for the failure of the first bohemians, of course. Reasons built into the structure of French society itself during the 1830s. Educational reforms under the Restoration had made literacy far more common than ever before in France, and wide-circulation newspapers and provincial lending libraries seemed to bring a potentially gigantic audience within reach of this second romantic generation. But it was a grammar-school level of literacy that was so widespread during the thirties, and grammar-school taste that dictated what the new media printed. The more select audience of the salon had largely faded with the Old Regime. What the huge new audience wanted was simple prose, suspense, humor, perhaps an inspirational theme or a bit of sentiment. The new public had no palate for anything so esoteric as aesthetic experimentation, or so shocking as sexual obsession, charnel-house horrors, iconoclastic jeers at society, and other staple subjects of the literary output of the *Jeune-France* school. An exciting historical novel out of Dumas's fiction factory might reach tens of thousands of readers through newspaper serialization alone. A slim volume of *Jeune-France* verse would be lucky to sell three hundred copies.[82]

So Philothée O'Neddy gave up poetry, cut his hair, and took up his father's old career in the government bureaucracy. Théophile Gautier so far betrayed his high aesthetic principles as to take a job working for the newspapers. "Wolfman" Borel, adamantly refusing to compromise, was finally driven from Paris by sheer poverty. For years he lived alone in a miserable shack in Champagne, sunk in deep depression, scribbling away at a horrific novel, which like all his works, failed to take literary Paris by storm. Borel, like Rimbaud after him, ended his life in self-imposed exile in North Africa.

Eighteen-thirty had brought a dazzling moment of total emancipation to this young generation in the arts. "At the very hour," wrote one who lived through that exhilarating time, "when the *émeutier* with a violent hand tore from the constitution of this country those pages which displeased him, the writer . . . freed himself also from the accepted rules, broke the yoke which weighed upon him, and, in his own world of prose or poetry, of the drama or the novel . . . accomplished his own little July Revolution."[83] By 1835, however, that first adventure in Bohemia was over. A generation that had defiantly seceded from French society now slipped almost sheepishly back into the fold. The bigger battalions, it seemed, were on the side of the philistines.

V

The pattern of development and decay after 1830 was not so clear for all the component units of this social generation.

As early as 1832, the legitimists suffered a near-fatal blow with the capture and subsequent disgrace of the duchesse de Berry. Lamennais and the young liberal Catholics of *l'Avenir* were formally condemned by the Pope in that same year. Many Bonapartists went down with their republican allies in 1834 and 1835; but Bonapartism itself, a sentiment enshrined in the living memories of many older Frenchmen, seems to have grown steadily, with the blessing of the bourgeois monarchy, through the rest of the decade.

Among those generation units of 1830 that rather withdrew from than rebelled against the increasingly bourgeois France of Louis Philippe, a simi-

lar diversity seems at first apparent. The Saint-Simonians were broken
by prison sentences in 1832; by 1834, a faithful remnant had fled France
entirely, heading East in search of the fabulous "Woman Messiah." The
Catholic revival sparked by the youthful founders of the *conférence* of St.
Vincent de Paul, by contrast, did not even get under way until 1833; like
Bonapartism, the movement influenced people of all ages and easily survived through the rest of the decade.

By and large, however, the basic pattern of youthful ideological insurgency and, in most cases, ultimate repression does seem to be maintained. A
generation pampered in infancy and overdisciplined in adolescence, first
starved and then surfeited with ideas, had been swept off its ideological
feet by the July Revolution. Through the early thirties, at least half-a-
dozen subgroups of this generation of the brightest sons of bourgeois
France had surged at full career across the uncertain firmament of the July
Monarchy. Thereafter, as the public at large grew weary of the endless
émeutes and eccentricities of the younger generation, inexorable repression
set in. As a coherent social generation, the French generation of 1830 hardly
survived the middle years of the decade.[84]

The youth themselves, feeling the failure of their generation, sensing
the impossibility of attaining the extravagant ends they had set for themselves, soon lost the exuberant enthusiasm of those early years. They abandoned their creeds, their crusades, their artistic careers and their communal
experiments. By the middle thirties, their leaders were in prison or in exile,
and they themselves, as lads not yet turned twenty put it, had "hearts as
worn as a whore's staircase." "Our youth," as another somewhat exaggerated
lament expressed it, "became age in a matter of months . . . our hair went
white in a single night. Hope vanished from our souls."[85]

Most of them survived the crisis well enough as individuals, of course.
Nor were the sparks of popular ideology kindled by this hectic generation
so easily snuffed out. Bourgeois France preserved and even fostered some
of the *isms* so passionately urged on the nation by the new youth—Bonapartism, for instance, and some of the spirit of the Catholic revival. Others
survived in spite of the establishment, brooding underground, simmering
in silence until their hour might come again. Henry Murger's famous version of the *vie de bohème,* for example, still lay ahead, in the 1840s; and
Auguste Blanqui would be back in the streets again in 1848. Socialism would
not die with the Saint-Simonian brotherhood, and France had more than
one republic in her future.

Like many rebellious younger generations, these young rebels of 1830
thus made solid contributions to the future. Some at least of the more
radical ideas they seized upon and flung into the teeth of the system were
to become potent forces for change in decades to come. Wasteful of its
resources and talents, brutally shocking to the public at large and clearly

reactionary in its short-range effects, this was nevertheless a generation that made a difference in history.

NOTES

1. François Guizot, *Mémoires pour servir à l'histoire de mon temps* (Paris, 1859), 2:31–33.

2. Ibid., 2:6.

3. Augustin Challamel, *Souvenirs d'un Hugolâtre: la génération de 1830* (Paris, 1885), p. 9.

4. André-Marie Dupin, speech in the Chamber, 21 September 1831, reprinted in *Révolution de Juillet, 1830: son caractère légal et politique* (Paris, 1835), p. 267.

5. Honoré de Balzac, in *La Caricature,* July 1831, reprinted in *Oeuvres diverses,* ed. M. Bouteron and H. Longnon (Paris, 1938), 2:399–400.

6. There were earlier instances of historically significant generational rebellion, of course. Among these precursors, the role of youth was probably most important in the sixteenth-century Age of the Reformation and the eighteenth-century Age of Democratic Revolutions. It is hard, however, to find earlier examples of generational rebellion that so clearly reflect the strength, scope, and bewildering variety of modern youthful insurgency as these revolts of the decades after Waterloo.

7. See Anthony Esler, "Rebellious Younger Generations as a Force in History," paper read at the American Historical Association meetings in Boston, December 1970.

8. On the history of the theory of social generations, see among others the two articles in the recent edition of David L. Sills, ed., *Encyclopedia of the Social Sciences* (New York, 1968): Julián Marías, "Generations—the Concept" (6:88–92) and Marvin Rintala, "Political Generations" (6:92–95); also Yves Renouard, "La notion de génération en histoire," *Revue historique,* 260 (1953):1–23; François Mentré, *Les générations sociales* (Paris, 1920); Pedro Laín Entralgo, *Las generaciones en la historia* (Madrid, 1945); and Detlev W. Schumann, "Cultural Age-Groups in German Thought," *Publications of the Modern Language Association,* 51 (1936):1180–1207.

9. See the relevant essays in Ortega's *El tema de nuestro tiempo* (Madrid, 1923) (trans. James Cleugh as *The Modern Theme* [London, 1931]) and in his *En torno de Galileo* (Madrid, 1933) (trans. Mildred Adam as *Man in Crisis* [New York, 1958]); and Karl Mannheim's crucial two-part article, "Das Problem der Generationen," *Kölner Vierteljahrshefte für Soziologie,* 7 (1928):157–85, 309–

29 (trans. as "The Problem of Generations" in *Essays on the Sociology of Knowledge,* ed. Paul Kecskemeti [New York, 1952], pp. 276–320).

10. See Marvin Rintala, "A Generation in Politics: A Definition," *Review of Politics,* 25 (1963):510–11; Norman B. Ryder, "The Cohort as a Concept in the Study of Social Change," *American Sociological Review,* 30 (1965):861; and Esler, "Rebellious Younger Generations" passim.

11. The social generation should be clearly distinguished from the biological or chronological generations with which it is often confused. What we may call biological generations are father-and-son related, and are usually separated in age by the traditional twenty-year interval. (See, for example, such demographic studies as Philip Greven's *Four generations: Population, Land, and Family in Colonial Andover, Massachusetts* [Ithaca, New York, 1970].) The term *generation* is also frequently used in a purely chronological sense to denote a span of time, most commonly twenty or thirty-three years. (As an illustration of this usage, see Carlton J. H. Hayes, *A Generation of Materialism,* [New York and London, 1941].)

    The social generation is neither a chronological unit nor a link in a genealogical chain. It is a concrete social subgroup that is distinguished, in the first instance, by contemporaneousness of birth. (As an example of generational history in this sense, see Anthony Esler, *Aspiring Mind of the Elizabethan Younger Generation* [Durham, N.C., 1966].)

12. The precise length of this "brief span of years" remains a much debated problem for the generationist. Ortega, for instance, postulated a generational span as long as fifteen years. Some very interesting computerized research, on the other hand, has been based on birth cohorts born over periods as short as three years. (See Marías, "Generations" for a brief summary of Ortega's system. For the computer view, see William R. Klecka, "The Use of Political Generations in Studying Political Change," read at the American Association for Public Opinion Research, Lake George, New York, May 1970.)

    Since, however, the social generation is the product of the pace of social change, a highly variable phenomenon, it is not surprising that the length of the generational span also varies considerably with time and circumstance. In the sixteenth century, men born fifteen years apart still clearly bore the mark of common generationhood. In the twentieth, youths whose ages differ by a mere five years often hardly seem to belong to the same generation. Marc Bloch has probably said the last and most sensible word: "There are in history some generations which are long and some which are short" (*The Historian's Craft,* trans. Peter Putman [New York, 1953], p. 186.)

    As far as the present investigation is concerned, a nineteenth-century generational span of somewhere between five and ten years seems most frequently to accord with the historical realities.

13. Such challenging comparisons are made by a number of students of the generational phenomenon. See, for example, Herbert Moller, "Youth as a Force in the Modern World," *Comparative Studies in Society and History,* 10 (1968):255–57; Bennet M. Berger, "How Long Is a Generation?" *The British Journal of*

Sociology, 11 (1960):20; Rintala, "A Generation in Politics," p. 511; and Ryder, "The Cohort," p. 847.

14. Mannheim, "The Problem of Generations," pp. 288 ff.

15. Ortega, "The Idea of the Generation," in *Man in Crisis,* pp. 42–43.

16. Ibid., pp. 44–45.

17. Mannheim, "The Problem of Generations," pp. 306, 304. Emphasis added.

18. See pp. 564–566.

19. On the central importance of abstract ideas in the integration of the un-formed personality of youth, see Erik H. Erikson, *Childhood and Society,* 2nd ed. (New York, 1963), pp. 262–63; and Karl Mannheim, "The Problem of the Intelligentsia," in *Essays on the Sociology of Culture,* ed. Ernest Manheim (London, 1956), pp. 163–65.

20. On the strength of generational bonds during youth, see Mannheim, "The Problem of Generations," pp. 298–301; Kenneth Keniston, *The Uncommitted: Alienated Youth in American Society* (New York, 1960), pp. 196–200; and Rintala, "A Generation in Politics," pp. 513–16.

21. Henry Smith, "The Young Man's Task," in *Sermons of Master Henry Smith,* ed. Thomas Man (London, 1611), p. 228.

22. The notion of the social generation itself seems to have first taken shape as a response to the revolutions of 1820, 1830, and 1848, in which the younger generation often played a prominent part.

23. See Kenneth Keniston, "The Sources of Student Dissent," *Journal of Social Issues,* 23 (1967):109–15.

24. Among the leaders of the chief movements of the early thirties, Prosper Enfantin, the Saint-Simonian *père,* was 34 in 1830; the duchesse de Berry, the mother of the Bourbon pretender, was 32; Armand Carrel, the Bonapartist-cum-republican journalist, was 30; Godefroy Cavaignac, the leader of the republican secret societies, was 29; and both Victor Hugo and the celebrated Catholic preacher Lacordaire were 28. There was also a whole cadre of lesser leaders, who were significantly younger men. Blanqui, for example, was 25 in 1830; Barbès was 20; Montalembert, 20; Ozanam, 17; Michel Chevalier, 24; Considérant, 25; Gautier, 19; Borel, 21; Gérard de Nerval, 22; and so on. Among the rank and file of many of these groups, furthermore, the average age must have been considerably closer to 20 than to 30. See pp. 312–313 and 315.

25. To limit ourselves to the two generation units that will be considered in some detail, it may be said that most of the republicans of the early 1830s were middle-class in background, and that many of the bohemians of those years came from solid bourgeois families. (See John Plamenatz, *The Revolutionary Movement in France, 1815–71* (London, 1952), pp. 37–45; and Malcolm Easton, *Artists and Writers in Paris: The Bohemian Idea, 1803–1867* (New York, 1964),

pp. 67–68. Lewis Feuer in his study of student movements emphasizes that most modern youth revolts involve the children of the middle classes (*The Conflict of Generations: The Character and Significance of Student Movements* (New York and London, 1969), pp. 15–17).

26. Philippe Ariès, *Histoire des populations françaises, et de leurs attitudes devant la vie depuis le XVIIIe siècle* (Paris, 1948), p. 475; Villèle to Polignac, 31 October 1824, quoted in Philippe Ariès, *Centuries of Childhood: A Social History of Family Life* trans. Robert Baldick (New York, 1962), p. 403.

27. Ariès calls attention to the sentimental pictures of family get-togethers, on birthdays and at Christmas, playing in the garden, visiting grandmother, and the like, reproduced in A. D. Toledano's *Livre sur la famille au début du XIXe siècle* and in his *Vie de famille sous la Restauration et la Monarchie de Juillet.*

28. A. D. Vandam, *An Englishman in Paris, Notes and Reminiscences* (New York, 1892), 1:27–28; Ariès, *Centuries of Childhood*, p. 266. The boarding-school system had a great vogue in France in the early nineteenth century: as many as 80 percent of all *lycée* pupils were boarders during the first three-quarters of the century (*Centuries of Childhood*, p. 282).

29. Perhaps the best descriptions of this spiritual deprival are to be found in fiction. See Alfred de Musset's famous second chapter of the *Confessions d'un enfant du siècle*, and the celebrated antihero of Stendhal's *Le rouge et le noir*.

30. See Noel Stewart, *Blanqui* (London, 1939).

31. See Enid Starkie, *Petrus Borel the Lycanthrope: His Life and Times* (London, 1954).

32. Mannheim, "Problem of Generations," p. 307.

33. S. N. Eisenstadt, *From Generation to Generation: Age Groups and Social Structure* (Glencoe, Ill., 1956), p. 184.

34. Lenore O'Boyle, "The Problem of an Excess of Educated Men in Western Europe, 1800–1850," *The Journal of Modern History*, 42 (1970):487–94. It was widely felt that youth in particular was discriminated against by an older generation that had come in at the time of the Restoration and had not yet died off. (See James Fazy, *De la gérontocracie, ou de l'abus de la sagesse des vieillards dans le gouvernement de la France* [Paris, 1828], quoted in Bertier de Sauvigny, *The Bourbon Restoration*, trans. Maurice Allem [Paris, 1960], pp. 238–39.) The result of this overeducation was believed to be a "floating mass of unemployed and inconstant persons who form an army always available to . . . the instigators of revolt." (Saint-Marc Girardin, *De l'instruction intermédiaire et de son état dans le midi de l'Allemagne* [Paris, 1835], quoted in O'Boyle, p. 489.)

35. Eisenstadt, *Generation to Generation*, p. 314.

36. Maurice de la Hodde, who spent many years as a police spy among the radicals and revolutionaries, described many of them as doctors without patients,

lawyers without clients, writers without readers, and so on. (*Histoire des sociétés sécrètes et du parti républicain de 1830 à 1840* [Paris, 1850], pp. 13–14.)

37. Amedée Achard, *Souvenirs personnels d'émeutes et de révolutions* (Paris, 1872), p. 6.

38. Eisenstadt, *Generation to Generation,* p. 184; Mannheim, "Problem of Generations," p. 305.

39. On this multifaceted new generation, see Sébastien Charléty's chapter on the subject in *La Restauration* (Paris, 1921), pp. 198–228.

40. Mannheim, "Problem of Generations," p. 310.

41. The traditional emphasis on the role of the youth in the barricade fighting of July has been called in question by David H. Pinckney, who has sensibly suggested that grizzled Napoleonic veterans were more likely leaders than enthusiastic schoolboys ("The Crowd in the French Revolution of 1830," *American Historical Review,* 70 (1964):6, 14–16). Pinckney's statistics, however, do indicate that more than half, or 54 percent, of those killed or wounded on the revolutionary side were in their twenties or early thirties. Contemporaries quickly built a whole legendry around this "jeunesse ardente." See, for instance, the parade of heroic feats appended to F. Rossignol and J. Pharaon, *Histoire de la Révolution de 1830 et des nouvelles barricades* (Paris, 1830), pp. 287–382, anecdotes whose heroes are frequently described as "a student of the *École polytechnique*," "a young medical student," "an apprentice," "a young worker." and so forth. The young *émeutiers* of the next few years seem to have been much influenced by the *legende dorée* of their own heroism in July.

42. Quoted in Paul Reynaud, *Les trois glorieuses: 27, 28, 29 Juillet, 1830* (Paris, 1927), p. 113.

43. Guizot, *Mémoires,* 2:7.

44. De la Hodde, *Histoire des sociétés sécrètes,* p. 35.

45. M. de Barante to the Baron Sers, 7 August 1830, in Jean André Sers, *Souvenirs d'un préfet de la monarchie: Mémoires du baron Sers, 1786–1862* (Paris, 1906), p. 243.

46. Adolphe Chenu, *Les conspirateurs* (Brussels, 1850), p. 7; Achard, "Souvenirs," pp. 12, 8, 5. Plamenatz points out that the majority of the more moderate republicans were also "the younger liberals . . . young men tired of their elders" and disturbed to see "the republicans do the fighting and the old men exploit their victory." (*Revolutionary Movements,* pp. 39, 38, 37.)

47. Challamel, *Souvenirs,* pp. 21–22.

48. Chateaubriand, quoted in J. Lucas-Dubreton, *Louis Philippe* (Paris, 1938), p. 153; Louis Philippe, quoted in Paul Thureau-Dangin, *Histoire de la Monarchie de Juillet* (Paris, 1897), 1:154.

49. Godefroy Cavaignac, himself the son of an exiled member of the Convention, repeatedly urged revolutionaries to study their heroic predecessors for advice

and inspiration. (See his Introduction to *Paris révolutionnaire* (Paris, 1848), p. 46.)

50. The *Société des Droits de l'Homme* shocked bourgeois France by printing Robespierre's notorious Declaration of Rights, a document so revolutionary that Robespierre himself had never dared to put it in print.

51. Victor Hugo, quoted in Godfrey Elton, *The Revolutionary Idea in France, 1789–1871* (New York, 1969), p. 110; Carrel, quoted in Louis Fiaux, *Armand Carrel et Émile de Girardin*, (Paris, n.d.), p. 106; Cavaignac, quoted in Frederick B. Artz, *Revolution and Reaction, 1814–1832* (New York, 1934), p. 270.

52. Pierre de La Gorce, *Louis Philippe (1830–1848)* (Paris, 1931), p. 36; Thureau-Dangin, *Histoire,* 1:585; 220, n. 2. (Cf. Lucas-Dubreton, *Louis Philippe,* p. 186.)

53. Louis Blanc, *Histoire de dix ans, 1830–1840* (Paris, 1844), 3:164; De la Hodde, *Histoire des Sociétés secrètes,* p. 66; Thureau-Dangin, *Histoire,* 2:120–30; Lucas-Dubreton, *Louis Philippe,* p. 266; La Gorce, *Louis Philippe,* p. 96.

54. Lucas-Dubreton, *Louis Philippe,* pp. 300–31.

55. La Gorce, *Louis Philippe,* p. 117. T. E. B. Howarth counts eight attempts altogether, but the pace slackened appreciably after 1836 (*Citizen-King, The Life of Louis-Philippe King of the French* (London, 1961), p. 162).

56. Blanqui was one of the defendants in the 1832 Trial of the Fifteen. All were acquitted of the subversive activities charged against them. Blanqui and four others, however, were given one-year sentences for preaching sedition at their own trial.

57. Plamenatz, *Revolutionary Movement,* p. 50.

58. "All types of revolutionaries" had been organizing in Lyon as early as 1831, and the Rights of Man Society had made converts in the city and in the surrounding countryside in 1833. (See M. D. R. Leys, *Between Two Empires: A History of French Politicians and People between 1815 and 1848,* London, 1955, pp. 196, 200.)

59. Plamenatz, *Revolutionary Movement,* p. 55.

60. See Robert Bezucha's forthcoming volume on *The Lyon Uprising of 1834* for a confutation of this "conspiracy theory" of the 1830s.

61. The Chamber of Deputies, in an address to the Throne, angrily denounced republican doctrines as "these insane schemes which would substitute an elective government for the hereditary, constitutional monarchy. . . ." (M. J. Mavidal and M. E. Laurent, eds., *Archives parlementaires de 1787 à 1860,* 2nd series, vol. 85 [Paris], p. 384.) The jingle is quoted in Georges Weill, *Histoire du parti républicain en France de 1814 à 1870* (Paris, 1900), p. 137, n. 1.

62. Philibert Audebrand, *Nos révolutionnaires: pages d'histoire contemporaine 1830–1880* (Paris, 1886), p. 88.

63. Trélat, quoted in Charléty, pp. 118–19.

64. Plamenatz, *Revolutionary Movement*, p. 55.

65. Easton, *Artists and Writers*, p. 57.

66. Frances Trollope, *Paris and the Parisians in 1835* (New York, 1836), pp. 52–54; *Figaro*, quoted in Marcel Hervier's Introduction to Théophile Dondey, *Feu et flamme* (Paris, 1926), p. xvi.

67. *Histoire du romantisme* (Paris, 1927), p. 102.

68. Théophile Gautier, *Les Jeune-France: romans goguenards*, (Paris, 1875), p. 87.

69. The root word seems to be *bousin*, a loud noise, and one explanation of the term relates it to the chorus of a drinking song:

> *Nous allons faire du bouzingo,*
> *du bouzingo, du bouzingo . . .*
> *"We're going to make a lot of noise,*
> *lot of noise, LOT OF NOISE . . .*

(Starkie, *Petrus Borel*, p. 92) Another explanation, however, relates the nickname to the rough leather seaman's cap, called a *bousingot*, which was affected by "the most ferocious" of the *Jeune-France*. (Francis Dumont, *Nerval et les bousingots* [Paris, 1958], p. 18.)

70. Preface to *Mademoiselle de Maupin* (Vienna, n. d.), p. xxxviii.

71. Quoted in Albert Joseph George, *The Development of French Romanticism: The Impact of the Industrial Revolution on Literature* (Syracuse, N. Y., 1955), p. 70. Hugo himself changed his tune in the 1830s and began to preach the gospel of art as a bully pulpit, of the artist's duty to join the fight for social justice. The new generation, however, clung to the master's earlier pronouncements.

72. Leo Larquier, *Théophile Gautier* (Paris, p. 1948), p. 78.

73. Malcolm Easton emphasizes the influence of the young artists, who had long entertained a "whimsical grievance" against their toplofty bourgeois patrons, in spreading the passion for "shocking the burghers" among their literary confrères (*Artists and Writers*, p. 59). But Easton also agrees with other authorities, including the young bohemians themselves, that "the Revolution of July spelt disillusionment for this group, as for others," and that "the Revolution of 1830 left a mark on this community, for it changed baiting the bourgeois from a light-hearted studio prank into a serious demonstration" (pp. 57, 60).

74. Petrus Borel, *Champavert: contes immoraux*, in *Oeuvres complètes* (Geneva, 1967), 3:35; Théophile Dondey, *Feu et flamme*, pp. 3–4, 19; Gautier, quoted in Maxime du Camp, *Théophile Gautier* (Paris, 1895), p. 33. "Philothée O'Neddy" was Dondey's characteristically exotic *nom de plume*.

75. Théophile Dondey, *Lettre inédite de Philothée O'Neddy, auteur de Feu et flamme, sur le groupe littéraire romantique dit les bousingos* (Paris, 1875).

76. *Feu et flamme*, p. 4.

77. For contemporary descriptions of the first bohemians, see William Makepeace Thackeray, *The Paris Sketchbook of Mr. M. A. Titmarsh* (Boston, 1891), p. 53; Honoré de Balzac, "Un Prince de Bohème," in *La Comédie humaine* (Paris, 1914), 18:372; Gautier, *Histoire du romantisme*, p. 31.

78. Contemporary accounts of *bousingo* costumes may be found in Gautier, *Histoire du romantisme*, p. 74; Thackeray, *Paris Sketchbook*, p. 53, and Vandam, *An Englishman*, 1:12–13. Models for the bizarre costumes and wild behavior of the *bousingos* may perhaps be found as far back as the groups of art students known as "Primitives" and "Meditators" of the years around the turn of the century. (See Easton, *Artists and Writers*, pp. 11–12, 18–19, 52–53.) Between the early years of the century and the 1830s, however, there seems to have been a lengthy hiatus, even among the artists; and young writers do not seem to have entertained the "bohemian idea" at all before the latter decade.

79. This struggle to the death with the bourgeoisie was perhaps not always as seriously intended as it seemed. But the *bousingo* student club known as the *Badouillards*, for instance, did spend a good deal of time practicing with fists and duelling swords, as well as rehearsing bawdy songs, for the great confrontation. (See Cesar Graña, *Modernity and Its Discontents: French Society and the French Man of Letters in the Nineteenth Century* [New York, 1964], p. 76.)

80. George, *French Romanticism*, p. 82.

81. Preface to *Mademoiselle de Maupin*, p. xxviii.

82. George, *French Romanticism*, p. 73.

83. Jules Janin, *Histoire de la littérature dramatique* (Paris, 1853), 1:154.

84. Starkie dates the *Jeune-France* period as 1830 to 1835, the year of Borel's retreat from Paris and of Alfred de Vigny's *Chatterton*, with its wildly applauded message that the artist is doomed in a philistine world.

85. Maxime du Camp, "Souvenirs litteraires," *Revue des Deux Mondes*, 1 October 1881, and Edgar Quinet, *Avertissement à la Monarchie de 1830* (Paris, 1831), cited in Thureau-Dangin, *Histoire*, 1:371; 386.

FRENCH JEWS, THE DREYFUS AFFAIR, AND THE CRISIS OF FRENCH SOCIETY

Michael R. Marrus

In human life there must always be place for love of the good and love of one's own. Love of the good is man's highest end, but it is of the nature of things that we come to know and to love what is good by first meeting it in that which is our own. . . .*

    The Dreyfus Affair, it is generally recognized, prompted a crisis in French society, a crisis whose dimensions extended widely, whose passions were not easily calmed, and whose meaning was profound. Beyond this, however, there has been not only little agreement, but remarkably little precision. How did the conviction of a Jewish staff officer for selling military secrets to the Germans, a conviction generally considered now to have been a colossal frame-up, how did this become a *cause célèbre,* which was unsurpassed in France at the end of the nineteenth century? What was the character of the crisis in French society at the time? What were the elements of French life that were subject to such strain? The enormous attention historians have given to the Dreyfus *case,* to the endless sifting of documents and letters relating to the alleged selling of secrets to the Germans, has tended to obscure these larger questions, and has drawn attention away from a more general analysis of the nature of the crisis. This paper does not propose to give a definitive answer to this problem. It does, however, by referring to a seldom discussed aspect of the Affair, the reactions of French Jews, hope to provide some tentative suggestions.[1] It will be seen that the Dreyfus Affair threatened the most fundamental assumptions of the Jewish community in France, that it challenged their loyalty to the republican regime, their commitment to France as the "apostle nation" with a special example to set for Jews all over the world, and their alliance with the forces of liberalism, which were everywhere in Europe the chief guarantors of civic equality for the Jews. In each of these cases, what Jews were responding to was not simply a threat to the rights and the allegiances of their particular community. In each case, questions raised during the Dreyfus Affair seemed to raise doubts about the foundations of French society itself. France, whose

Michael R. Marrus received his Ph.D. at the University of California at Berkeley. He now teaches at the University of Toronto.

* George Grant, *Technology and Empire: Perspectives on North America* (Toronto, 1969), p. 73.

social foundations at last permitted a liberal, parliamentary order with a sense of national mission—this France was commonly seen by contemporaries to be at some kind of crossroads. Jews were affected by a society that in some sense seemed to be doubting itself. Highly assimilated into that society, and yet never completely becoming at one with it, French Jews found themselves faced with questions that assimilated communities seldom have to confront. Significantly, some of those who most clearly and forcefully raised these questions for the Jewish community were Jews themselves.

I

At the center of this crisis in France was a small community of Jews. Numbering perhaps as many as 80,000, French Jews were widely scattered throughout the country. They lived, however, overwhelmingly in urban centers: in the west, about Bordeaux, Bayonne, and other areas settled by Sephardic refugees of the Spanish monarchy; in the east, in what was left to France of the province of Lorraine, close to the much older communities of Ashkenazic Jews of Alsace; in the south, near the former papal sanctuaries of Avignon and Comtat Venaissin; and, of course, in the larger cities of France such as Lyon, Marseille and Lille.[2] But well over half of this community lived in Paris, in the capital from which Jews had been officially excluded in the years before the French Revolution. In Paris were to be found the chief state-supported governmental organizations of the Jewish community; in Paris there was an active Jewish press, with two weekly periodicals; and in Paris there was located the formidable network of charities, self-help organizations, and other agencies that together provided the framework for a coherent and identifiable community. Here the Jews could feel at home. In Paris, moreover, the work of assimilation, which had been the pride of French Jewry since the Revolution, was on display to an extent not imaginable elsewhere. Jewish academics, politicians, artists, and professional men frequently made their mark there. In the splendid synagogue of the *rue de la Victoire*, Jewish high society and aristocracy could encounter the Jewish poor; former refugees from the ceded territories of Alsace and Lorraine could meet the newly arrived refugees from eastern Europe. Paris had become the headquarters of Jewish institutional life in France, the focus of Jewish religious activity, and the center of Jewish social life. Its Jewish community, the Grand Rabbi of France once said, was "the standard bearer of Judaism, the beacon whose light spreads far and wide."[3]

Yet the strength of the Jewish community of Paris suggests some of the weaknesses of the Jewish community as a whole. Paris was, of course, the intellectual core of the country, the pole from which were generated the currents of positivism and secularism that reached considerable strength during the 1880s and 1890s. Paris was a traditional melting pot in which the old communal ties of a preindustrial or rural society were invariably subject to erosion. Thus the Jewish community of France found that its most important institutions and its most distinguished members were subjected in an immediate, proximate way to the corrosive effects of antireligious modernism. The continual migration of Jews from various parts of France to the capital set the stage for what one Jewish commentator called a process of "selection in reverse," by which Judaism was losing her most gifted sons.[4] There was a constant lament among rabbis and other Jewish leaders, as the nineteenth century drew to a close, that secularism and assimilation, both fruits of the Jewish emancipation wrought by the French Revolution, were undermining what had once been a vigorous though materially impoverished community of believers.[5]

Jewish life in France, then, could be viewed with mixed emotions by sincere Jews. On the one hand, the Jews in France had achieved remarkable successes in many areas and in many fields of endeavor. From being an oppressed people of outcasts before the Revolution, they had won a secure place in the busy, creative France of the nineteenth century. French Jews had made ample use of the citizenship granted to them in 1790 and 1791; they had proven that Judaism was fully capable of adapting to the modern world, and that Jews were indeed useful, productive contributors to national life. On the other hand, a price was being paid to the forces of modernization; the Jewish community had lost most of its old cohesion, and the distinctiveness that was built into the Jewish religion itself was growing increasingly faint. Yet spokesmen tended, in looking at the matter as a whole, to play down the negative effects of their experience in France. From the Grand Rabbi of France to the local *rabbins communaux,* from the Baron Alphonse de Rothschild, president of the Consistoire Central, to the Jewish vaudevillian Albin Valabrègue, there was general agreement that the previous century in France had been a critical milestone for Jewsh progress.[6] French Jews were leading the way for Jews the world over; Jews in France were providing a magnificent example for their more primitive and superstitious coreligionists of eastern Europe. Jews considered it a privilege to be living in France. "The time of the Messiah," wrote one enthusiast, "had come with the French Revolution."[7]

Yet this is perhaps not the best note on which to close this brief description of the Jewish community in France. For along with the general optimism, the complacency and the self-satisfaction, all of which existed in the years before the Dreyfus Affair, one can detect a newly developed element of unease. The end of the nineteenth century in Europe saw the rise of anti-Semitism as an organized mass movement of formidable proportions. In the period with which we are concerned, French Jews witnessed in 1886 the publication of Edouard Drumont's explosive and wildly popular anti-Semitic book *La France juive;* they saw the growth and spread of an antagonism toward the Jews that evoked memories, some long since forgotten, of the earlier period of persecutions.[8] Elsewhere, particularly in eastern Europe, the anti-Jewish tide reached a fearful and bloody crest. Streams of

Jewish refugees began to trickle into France after 1882, and settled French Jews found themselves uncomfortably faced with a reincarnation of their own, pre-emancipation image. Many worried that these unassimilated victims would give French Jewry a bad name.[9] In the light of these developments, prominent Jews advised a special form of prudence. Théodore Reinach, a well-known poet and classical scholar, warned a meeting of a Jewish philological society in 1887: "Being, as we are, the smallest religious sect, being, as we are, strangers newly arrived in the French household, we are especially subject to jealousy and criticism." What was necessary, above all, was circumspection. "Our merchants must all be honest, our rich men all unassuming and charitable, our scholars all modest, our writers all disinterested patriots."[10] Leaders of the French Jewish community were highly conscious of the image they presented to the community at large. Matters were further complicated, after 1891, by the rapprochement of the French and Russian governments, a diplomatic move of enormous popularity in France. In the unsettled and somewhat threatening climate of European politics, many argued that France needed all of the friends she could get. Could there now, as in the past, be public protests against a diplomatic irrelevancy like tsarist pogroms?[11] And, even more important, could French Jews expect that France would continue to shower upon them the blessings of the nineteenth century? Could France escape the paroxysm of anti-Semitism that was occurring elsewhere? Few, of course, faced these questions openly. These new and troublesome questions were seldom put before the larger Jewish community. But by the end of 1894, when Jewish Captain Alfred Dreyfus was arrested for selling military secrets to the Germans, the basis for such doubts at least existed.[12]

II

The Dreyfus Affair began in a quiet way, with not even a hint of the great confrontation that was later to occur.[13] With military dispatch the alleged traitor was arrested, convicted and sent to Devil's Island to suffer what was to be four years of anguish and physical privation. Meanwhile the Dreyfus family, aided by a small group of friends, worked quietly and behind the scenes to secure his release. Not until the beginning of 1898, however, thanks in part to the persistence of another staff officer, Major Picquart, did the Affair become an *affaire*. Emile Zola thundered forth with his famous *J'Accuse,* the public became inextricably involved, and the dramatic events with which we are familiar began to unfold. Early in 1898, too, there began an anti-Semitic storm in France of unparalleled ferocity. Beginning with a serious outbreak in Algeria the previous spring, a torrent of mob violence and hatred swept across the towns and cities of France. Everywhere, the fate of Dreyfus was linked to the fate of the Jews as a whole. Everywhere, the Jews met forms of abuse they thought had been reserved for Jews of other, more backward countries. By the beginning of 1898, in addition, the

Michael R. Marrus

forces working on behalf of Dreyfus came fully into the open, and their campaign passed from the small circle of intimates about the family to the larger and more vocal group of public campaigners: Labori, Reinach, Clemenceau, and eventually Jaurès. And, for the Jews of France, what was once for some a vague unease was transformed into a general state of anxiety.

What was put at issue, so far as the Jews of France were concerned, was their patriotism, their general commitment to the nation that had befriended them by making them citizens, that offered them the rights of other Frenchmen, and that even, since 1831, paid their clergy. The anti-Semitic chorus, supported now by some influential Catholic opinion and by others in high places, charged the Jews with gross ingratitude. The accusations were repeated in an increasingly shrill refrain—that the Jews were mostly traitors or *sans-patrie;* that their first loyalty was to a cosmopolitan "syndicate"; and that Jewish greed and Jewish gold were working to undermine the French state. For Jews, of course, these developments could scarcely be ignored. The critical problem for them was to evaluate the forces that had so explosively been released and to assess the significance of the upheaval over Dreyfus as it related generally to Jewish life in France.

It is difficult, of course, to generalize on the "Jewish" reaction to this crisis. Jews were, as we have seen, highly assimilated into French society and to a certain extent their response simply followed that of other Frenchmen of various social and political *milieux.* But there can be no doubt that Jews were affected in a special way. Contemporary accounts, by both Jews and non-Jews, seem agreed on the fact that French Jewry was deeply touched by the outbreak of the Dreyfus crisis. "Who among us has not suffered from it?" wrote the editor of the *Univers israélite:*

Who among us can say that it has not profoundly altered our social relations with our fellow citizens of other religions? Have we not all noticed, as we meet socially with non-Jews, that the conversation falls off suddenly because one has just mentioned the Dreyfus Affair? What Jewish officer and what Jewish official has not wondered at any given moment whether the condemnation of the ex-Captain would hinder his own career? . . . Truly, this lamentable story weighs heavily upon the situation of the Jews in France.[14]

Moreover, there is a great deal of testimony to the effect that French Jews preferred to remain aside from the swelling controversy, as they had tended to keep apart from the particularly sensitive issue of "clericalism" in the 1880s and early 1890s.[15] What Charles Péguy referred to as the Jewish "politique," what one Jewish writer even less kindly described as the "politique d'autruche" (an ostrich policy) dictated that Jews maintain what is now called a "low profile," and that they avoid placing themselves in the exposed ranks of the Dreyfusards.[16] Throughout most of 1898, for example, the Orientalist Silvain Lévi maintained a strict silence over the Affair, judging, he said, that the cause of Dreyfus could only lose by the adhesion of a Jew.[17] During the entire crisis Jewish writers such as Julien Benda or Emile Durkheim muted the specifically anti-Jewish dimensions of the Affair.[18] Even the Dreyfus family, it could be argued, relied heavily on influence and "backdoor maneuvers" in part because they were sensitive to their position as Jews.[19] Summing up the Jewish response, the American writer Mark Twain observed that "the Jews did wisely in keeping quiet during the Dreyfus agitation."[20] Quiet, after all, would give the anti-Semites little to feed upon; Jewish passivity would allow others, who were less "suspect," to take up the cause of the convicted Jewish officer.

Certainly this was the stance adopted by official circles within the Jewish community. The French rabbinate, it was complained by one Jewish writer, showed "la plus grande réserve" in the face of anti-Semitic attacks.[21] Zadoc Kahn, the Grand Rabbi of France, considered that his primary duty was to maintain the most complete discretion in the matter.[22] The reason for this quiescence is not hard to find. As *fonctionnaires,* as paid officers of the state, the rabbis felt bound by their office to keep silent on any issue of public controversy. As representatives of the Jewish community, moreover, they would offend their coreligionists least by a prudent noninvolvement. Similarly the *consistoires,* the government-sponsored agencies set up to govern Jewish community affairs, drew themselves into the protection afforded by bureaucratic routine. They had little to say about the Affair in their *procès-verbaux,* and they considered the crisis as something in which they could not directly get involved.[23] Likewise, the Alliance Israélite Universelle, a well-established Jewish organization based in Paris and opposed to anti-Semitism the world over, virtually ignored the outbreak in France, and continued to direct its efforts elsewhere.[24] Generally speaking, Jews in France were reluctant to discuss the Affair or the anti-Semitism associated with it.

At the same time, however, Jews were frequently to be heard declaring their patriotism and protesting their loyalty to the republican regime. Such difficulties as Jews were experiencing at the time were held to be transitory and unconnected with the true character of the society. "Do not confuse France with the foam which tosses wildly but temporarily on the surface of the waves," one scholar told a group of Jewish school children in 1898. "Continue to love her, this France, with all your strength, with all your heart, as you would a mother, even though she be [momentarily] unjust or led astray, because she is your mother, and because you are her children."[25] The dominant note here, which one finds so frequently elsewhere, was one of optimism, of faith that the France of 1789 would soon reassert itself. Public statements continued to reflect the expectation that, in the words of Zadoc Kahn, the country would "remain faithful to her natural genius, so wonderfully made up of reason, good sense, loyalty and generosity."[26] Such optimism, perhaps out of place during the dark days of 1898 and 1899, was based on the traditional Jewish attachment to the existing regime in France.

It drew its confidence from the ample evidence of success that surrounded the Jewish community, and it fed on the growing realization that something much larger was at stake, during the Dreyfus crisis, than the fate of French Jews. Because it appeared that French society as a whole was entering a profound ideological crisis, because Jewish interests were seen to be tied closely to the interests of the liberal parliamentary order, it was considered safest to remain unobtrusive and to rely upon more powerful forces to preserve a secure Jewish existence. For the Jews who held such a position, then, the work of assimilation had gone far indeed. Jewish interests and French interests were held to be one; specifically Jewish activity, apart from the most ostentatious declarations of patriotism, were held to be suspect.[27]

Not all Jews, of course, remained on the sidelines. Among the most prominent of the Dreyfusards there were a few Jews who stood out, in no sense as defenders of "the Jewish cause" (that was certainly to be avoided) but rather as Jewish defenders of a certain view of France. The most prominent of these was the journalist and politician Joseph Reinach, well-known in liberal circles and considered to be the political heir of the popular statesman and one-time French Premier Léon Gambetta. Reinach certainly did not lack courage. In the teeth of vicious anti-Semitic attacks, he pursued the Dreyfusard arguments, carrying the battle into the heart of the military and nationalist camp. Like other Jewish Dreyfusards such as Michel Breal, Alfred Berl, and Gustave Kahn, Reinach argued that the Affair was much more than an explosion of anti-Semitism, and that the very future of the country was in jeopardy.[28] According to Berl, the Jew was being attacked because the entire liberal underpinning of the state was being eroded; the conclusion to be drawn from this was that the defense of the Jews could best be effected through the defense of liberal society itself.[29] France was seen, in this view, as being a natural haven for the Jews, a bastion of liberal enlightenment that was currently under assault. In a similar vein, Jewish Dreyfusards drew on the commonly held notion that anti-Semitism was not really a part of French tradition at all; it was rather a particularly insidious influence of Imperial Germany, an influence that had begun to make itself felt following France's defeat at the hands of the Germans in 1871. Anti-Semitism, it thus could be argued, was an ideology of "foreigners," an attempt to import German ideology and practices into France.[30] In this way, Jewish Dreyfusards did not distinguish themselves in any notable way from their non-Jewish counterparts. On the contrary, while they may have felt the anti-Semitic dimensions of the Affair more keenly than most, they took pains not to show any sign of this. For them the greater battle was being fought for possession of France itself; from their perspective, the Jewish aspect was clearly secondary.

The traditions of French liberalism, which these Jews prized so highly and which they considered to be so vital for their own security, did not really permit any independent political organization of French Jews. Nor did they permit, during this time when Jews were being so cruelly singled out, any proud and independent assertion of a specifically Jewish identity. In France, each Frenchman was a citizen, with the rights and duties of citizenship; the Revolution, it was considered, had broken the old system of corporate rights and privileges that came to be associated with the *ancien régime* and that was held to be an anachronism in the modern state. The liberal traditions associated with the Revolution implied that the national patrimony should belong to every citizen; individuals, conversely, would identify themselves as Frenchmen first and above all. In the new France the old, semiautonomous communities such as that of the Jews (and, of course, orders of the Catholic Church) were held to be suspect. During the latter part of the nineteenth century, moreover, as France became increasingly preoccupied with the German enemy, the liberalism that became the official ideology of the Republic retained virtually none of the eighteenth-century universalism that had previously coexisted, to a greater or lesser extent, with the homogenizing thrust of French nationalism. The fact that the established Jewish community was so heavily committed to this liberal ideal made it extremely difficult for Jews to respond differently from the manner we have described.

In the early days of the Affair, for example, a number of Jews did attempt to set up a Comité contre l'Antisémitisme, a committee of Jews that would act, not secretly, but openly to protect specifically Jewish interests. But this idea soon met with widespread resistance among Jews. In the end it was decided to keep the committee secret, to keep its membership restricted to a small Jewish elite, and to keep its activity strictly limited to influence behind the scenes.[31] The established community of Jews disliked any hint of what was pejoratively referred to as an "action confessionnelle"; having accepted the restrictions implied in the liberal ideal of French citizenship, there was little left for them but to defend that ideal as the sole principle at stake during the Dreyfus crisis. Little was said, therefore, of the Jews' right to be left alone or their sense of inner obligation to continue to remain Jewish. Virtually nothing was done to question why anti-Semitism had won so wide a following in France. And Jews were reluctant to link their cause with that of Jews elsewhere, outside of France.

III

The alternative for Jews in France lay outside the liberal frame of reference. This was to say that the Jews were not simply or even primarily French citizens, but that they had an identity that transcended national boundaries, that reached out beyond France and extended back in time. It was to put a higher priority on the historic community of the Jewish people than on the obligations of citizenship in the modern and secular French state. It was further to argue that Jewish identity was a value in itself, a value well worth preserving in the modern age and that, particularly when it was under attack, Jews had a moral duty to assert that identity and to focus their attention upon their own distinctiveness. This was the nationalist alternative, one that had few Jewish followers in France, but that was nevertheless to take shape during the Affair, and was to constitute a considerable embarrassment to the established Jewish community.

No one did more to further the Jewish nationalist idea in France than the journalist and *littérateur* Bernard Lazare.[32] Born Lazare Bernard in the small town of Nîmes, in 1865, the young anarchist and literary critic first made his name in Paris as a pugnacious and politically involved writer. During the period immediately preceding the Affair, Lazare underwent a profound metamorphosis concerning his perspectives on Jewish identity. Earlier in his career Lazare had shared many of the common anti-Semitic assumptions of his time, particularly those common among the militants of the extreme left.[33] But by the time he was approached by a member of the Dreyfus family looking for support for the cause, early in 1895, Lazare's position had changed dramatically. From being a Jewish anti-Semite, he was well on the way to becoming a Jewish nationalist. The reasons for this transformation are somewhat unclear. Lazare may have been led by his anarchist and revolutionary politics to reject the liberal assimilationist ideology so loudly trumpeted by French Jews. He was always estranged from the Jewish "establishment," such as it was, and his adoption of the nationalist stance meant in part the championing of the Jewish underprivileged against what he considered to be their maltreatment at the hands of their coreligionists. Lazare may also have had some contact and discussion with the future Zionist leader Theodore Herzl, who was living in Paris at this time and who was coming to a similar position simultaneously. It is possible that the two men worked out their ideology of Jewish nationalism together.[34] In any case, by the time Lazare made his most important contribution to the Affair, namely, an explosive pamphlet published in Brussels in the autumn of 1896, he was the chief spokesman in France for a full-blown doctrine of Jewish nationalism.

Unlike the assimilationist leaders, whose tendency was to play down the anti-Semitic dimensions of the Affair, Lazare declared these to be paramount. Dreyfus, he held, belonged to "a class of pariahs"; because Dreyfus was a Jew, and for this reason alone, he was arrested, prosecuted, and unfairly condemned.[35] Dreyfus, moreover, was a symbol of Jewish suffering throughout the world:

He incarnates, in himself, not only the centuries-old suffering of his people of martyrs, but their present agonies. Through him I see Jews languishing in Russian prisons, striving vainly for a bit of light and air, Rumanian Jews, who are refused the rights of man, those of Galicia, starved by financial trusts and ravaged by peasants who have been made fanatics by their priests. . . . He has been for me the tragic image of the Algerian Jews, beaten and pillaged, the unhappy immigrants dying of hunger in the ghettos of New York or of London, all of those whom desperation drives to seek some haven in the far corners of the inhabited world, a haven where they will at last find that Justice which the best of them have claimed for all of humanity.[36]

Dreyfus, Lazare argued, was typical of the persecuted Jew; perhaps for this reason French Jews, who believed that they had left such persecution behind, were reluctant to identify with him and were unwilling to stand out in his defense. But Lazare believed that these Jews were thus rejecting what was an indelible aspect of their being. The long years of suffering and the centuries of common Jewish experience had built a national entity of the Jewish people, and this could not be destroyed by a century of merely nominal acceptance by the French. The Dreyfus explosion in France was simply one aspect of the continuing hostility of society to this Jewish nation that attempted in vain to live in peace amongst others.[37]

Lazare thus accentuated the anti-Semitic aspects of the Affair, and criticized the established Jewish community for what they were attempting to obscure. But Lazare did more than this. In drawing attention to what he considered the true cause of anti-Semitism—the fact that the Jews constituted a nation—he presented an analysis with important political and social implications. The Jews were persecuted, Lazare contended, largely because of the character of their nationalism. The Jews were persecuted, not because they were a people of capitalists or moneylenders, such as the socialists frequently maintained, but rather because, historically speaking, they were a people of revolutionaries. Built into the Jewish spirit there was a tradition of resistance to the established authority, wherever it was unjust, and wherever it oppressed other peoples. It was no accident, for example, that the Church considered the Jews as enemies.

[The Church] knows better than anyone what this race has been, how many times in the past, on the soil of its ancestors, it worked for Justice. She knows that the terrible injunctions against the rich, the powerful, the tyrants came from the mouths of the Prophets. She knows that the Jewish aspect of Jesus is not that of resignation or of contentment with the human condition, but on the contrary that of revolt. . . .[38]

Jews had an obligation to carry on this spirit of revolt, and to free themselves from the self-denying passivity of French society. This was the only way the Jews could free themselves to live once again as men, and the only way in which they could make some genuine contribution to humanity at large:

We must work to liberate ourselves and thus we will help to liberate others. We must live as that people [of Biblical times], that is to say as a free collectivity, but on the condition that that collectivity does not reflect the image of the capitalistic and oppressive states in the midst of which we live.[39]

What was involved here was more than an existential search on Lazare's part for an authentic expression of Jewishness. What was involved, explicitly, was a rejection of French society as it was then constituted. Jewish nationalism implied less a cultural than a social aspiration, and one that related directly to the societies in which Jews found themselves. Jewish liberation was particularly necessary in France because the Jews had become so corrupted since the time of their emancipation. And this corruption came from France. Just as colonialists brought the worst aspects of their societies to the savages they exploited, so the French had transmitted their materialism and their degeneracy to those Jews who were most successfully assimilated.[40] In recovering their former, independent identity, however, Jews would be able to make their contribution to the more general task of human liberation. In becoming authentic Jews once again, they would help other peoples to be free.

One returns, in examining Lazare's approach to the question of Jewish nationalism, to his anarchist politics. As an at least nominal revolutionary, Lazare believed, of course, in the overthrow of the French political and social order. But what he believed should replace French society was not a unified national community such as that which the liberals had accepted and which even the radicals had argued, in the Jacobin tradition of the French Revolution, was France's great mission in the world. Rejecting both the liberal and, to a certain extent, the socialist models, Lazare believed in a federation of free, autonomous social groups in which the Jews would find their place.[41] This was the larger context for his nationalism, and the meeting place of his anarchist and Jewish nationalist perspectives. Lazare appears, therefore, essentially as a *révolté*, as one who rejected the liberal France so loudly praised in the established Jewish community, and who saw in Jewish tradition both an effective antidote to the poisonous effects of assimilation and a powerful catalyst for the libertarian transformations of the future.

This was the position of a small minority of Jews in France during the Dreyfus Affair, a minority that has left little trace of its activity and little evidence of its social character. Yet shreds of material can be found. At the height of the anti-Semitic violence in 1898, an organized group of Jewish workers met together and published a long open letter to the Parti Socialiste Français, condemning the parliamentary socialists for their inactivity. The Jewish workers who were thus aroused drew on the nationalist rhetoric of Bernard Lazare; like him they considered their prospective revolutionary activity within a specifically Jewish context.[42] These Jews took considerable pains to point out, as Lazare had, that the Jews were far from being a people of bankers and capitalists; rather they were, numerically, overwhelmingly working-class. This was a principal theme of the only Jewish protest meeting ever held against anti-Semitism during the entire Dreyfus Affair, a gathering organized by Jewish workers in the autumn of 1899. At that meeting a number of spokesmen rejected the assimilationist position taken by Jewish leaders in France, and argued instead for a revolutionary solidarity of all

Jews in the face of oppression. To these Jews, Jewishness signified a kind of autonomous counterculture that resisted the seductive offerings of a liberal, bourgeois society. To them, remaining true to some Jewish identity signified a proud affirmation of their individuality, which they felt was in danger of being submerged in the cult of French, liberal humanitarianism.[43]

IV

In the later stages of the Dreyfus Affair, during 1898 and 1899, these ideas formed the core of the emerging Zionist program. The Jews who participated in the articulation of Zionist strategy began with a nationalist orientation, and prepared on this basis a political solution to the problems the nationalists had identified. Jews, it was agreed, were oppressed the world over, particularly, at that moment, in France. French Jews, at the same time, were being increasingly drawn into the French orbit and were being induced into rejecting their cultural heritage. In order to organize an effective opposition to this process, and in order to prompt a mass "relèvement" (revival) of Jews of all countries, it was essential that Jews construct a political alternative to the politics of assimilation. This alternative was a Jewish state. Zionism, of course, was beginning to develop elsewhere in Europe at this time, and drew support largely from the impoverished Jewish masses of central and eastern Europe. In France, Zionism became the sole preoccupation of a small group of Jews, mainly Russian or Polish students and immigrants living in Paris. Including Bernard Lazare, who became the unofficial leader of the group in France, and Max Nordau, a somewhat eccentric psychologist of European reputation, the Zionist movement took root, organized about a number of periodicals, and formulated a militant Jewish alternative to the politics of the established Jewish community. Understandably, perhaps, their attack was often directed as much against the assimilationist tradition as against French society and the anti-Semitism it had spawned. A small band of generally youthful, alienated intellectuals, they drew little mass following in France during the Dreyfus years. Nevertheless, they made a considerable impression.

Beginning with the nationalist assumption, namely, that the Jews constituted an oppressed but distinct nationality, Zionists linked their cause with the struggles of oppressed peoples generally. The Jewish nationalist movement, wrote one of their number,

is simply one of the numerous manifestations of the human spirit liberated by the Great Revolution from the old shackles that bound it for centuries. This movement is characteristic of our nineteenth century; it is an expression of the general tendency towards individual liberty, a tendency that is accentuated day by day, spreading all over the globe, embracing in its irresistible current all peoples, great or small, all classes and all individuals. The time has passed when resignation [and] the tacit consent to suffer submissively the domination of brute force was exalted as the indispensable virtues of all honest men.

What the Zionists demanded, the writer contended, were basically two things. First, it was essential for Jews to have "the right to develop freely," to assert "our individuality," "our national spirit." Second, Jews must have "a small corner of the earth, where we can develop our faculties freely, without bothering anyone, and without being bothered by anyone."[44] Once again, it was emphasized, Jews were facing a threat to their existence; even in France, one hundred years after what was supposed to have been their emancipation, Jews were being made outcasts. The fact that this was occurring in France simply confirmed the contention that it was impossible to solve the problems of the Jewish people by deferring to the beneficence of the liberal state.

While the established Jewish community tried to minimize or even to ignore the seriousness of the anti-Semitic campaign, Zionists seemed to feel it with a sensitivity that made their condition practically unbearable:

It seems to us that it would be very dangerous for us to remain in this hostile milieu, with our activity paralyzed, deprived of our most precious qualities, of our individuality, placed in the position of slaves, imploring the condescension, the benevolence of our masters. . . . We can no longer tolerate this condition of slavery. We can no longer tolerate it, because it humiliates us, it degrades us, because it assaults our sense of dignity and self-esteem.[45]

Because they had succumbed to the pressures of assimilation, because they had accepted the humiliating role of suppliants before the French, most Jewish leaders had lost all credibility in the eyes of the Zionists. French Jewish leaders were frequently designated "juifs honteux," Jews who were ashamed of their heritage; one writer referred to Zadoc Kahn and his assistant as "messieurs les chanoines de la cathédrale de Notre Dame de l'Assimilation."[46] "The Jewish bourgeoisie," concluded another, "which until now has claimed to lead the [entire] Jewish people, has played its final card. Already its favorite theories, so cruelly tested by recent events throughout Europe, are crumbling, and soon nothing will be left of them but a memory."[47]

It is apparent that these spokesmen were not, in criticizing the established community of Jews, condemning any lack of religious fidelity. Their attitudes toward religion were seldom made explicit, and their general orientation was overwhelmingly secular. To the Zionists, drawing on both their nationalist ideology and their sense of revulsion toward the society that they felt had enslaved them, the assimilationist betrayal consisted in a rejection of Jewish cultural and, even more important, social independence. These Jews wanted their community to be separate; they wanted to emancipate themselves from French society, and from all that they detested in French life. Jewish authenticity thus implied a Jewish capacity to build their own social order. It may be argued, of course, that their "Jewishness" was largely symbolic, and that its content was purely negative. To some extent this is true. But there can be no denying their nationalist fervor, or their efforts to find in Jewish traditions the core of their social outlook.

Support for this position was never, needless to say, very strong within the Jewish community in France. The Zionists attracted Jews who had not yet been assimilated into French society, and who were unable or unwilling to adopt the French way of life as their own. To a certain extent, therefore, Zionism in France was a class phenomenon, a movement of a class of Jewish outcasts. These Jews had never felt that they were openly received in France, and were in no position to celebrate the liberal traditions of the Third Republic. More probably they felt like Jehudah Tchernoff, a Russian student in Paris, alone, impoverished, and unwelcome. Tchernoff sensed, typically, that he was rejected as much by French Jews as by the rest of French society. When the anti-Semitism of the Dreyfus Affair brought to him a brutal reminder of the pogroms he had experienced as a child in Russia, Tchernoff was shocked by the indifference with which French Jews faced the same phenomenon:

I only wondered why, with freedom of the press, the counterattack was taking so long in coming. This was what struck me, the complete inertia of my coreligionists in France, the passive attitudes of my Jewish associates, the impossibility of getting together with my French friends to protest my outrage at the propagation of such doctrines.[48]

Young Jews such as Tchernoff accepted the Zionist contention that France was not worthy of their veneration. They had little reason to praise a government that had allied with tsarist persecution abroad, and that even failed to protect its Jews at home. They were disillusioned with a French Jewry that seemed both weak before the anti-Semites and condescending towards themselves. These Jews supported the small French delegation to the First Zionist Congress in Basel in 1897, and were to be instrumental in launching the Université Populaire Juive, which emerged after the euphoria of the Dreyfus Affair. In so doing they virtually cut themselves off from their coreligionists in France. Morally isolated in French society, they continued to find something attractive in the appeals against assimilation.

Most French Jews, quite rightly, considered that this Zionist program went contrary to their own most fervent hopes for the Jewish community in France. Where the leaders of French Jewry glorified in their association with the Third Republic, the Zionists spoke of France as degenerate and corrupt. Where Zadoc Kahn and the leaders of the *consistoires* advocated that Jews should champion France's mission in the world, the nationalists referred to the Jews' own national mission, which was in conflict with that of France. Where liberalism and a faith in universal progress through civic equality was the civic ideal of a man like Joseph Reinach, Bernard Lazare urged Jews to recover more ancient traditions of community. In short, there emerged in the course of the Dreyfus Affair two very different ideals of social and political organization for Jews to follow. The one, of course, was patterned on the model set down by the traditions of French republican liberalism after 1871; the other was based on a rejection of these values, and on a search for an alternative form of social existence. The one drew its support from those who were essentially satisfied with life in France, from those for whom assimilation had brought tangible benefits. The other was an ideology of *révoltés*, of those who, for various reasons, were profoundly dissatisfied with conditions in France.

But here we return to the suggestion made at the outset—that the Dreyfus Affair represented a crisis that called into question something very basic about the France of the 1890s. It would be rash to argue that the lines of division in the Jewish community, the lines between the assimilationist majority and the Zionist minority, were simply a somewhat ironic reflection of the divisions between Dreyfusards and anti-Dreyfusards in French society at large. The rift in the Jewish community was not unique, either to French Jewry or to the Dreyfus period. The anti-Dreyfusards, with what was often their violent xenophobia and their cult of authority, could not have been further, in many ways, from the ideals and example of those Jews who stood apart from assimilation. Yet there were common elements. Common to them both was a profound sense that all was not well with France, and that the forces at work in the modern, progressive society in which they lived were not to be trusted. Both groups doubted that France was a success. Common, too, was a deep suspicion of the Dreyfusard idealization of liberal traditions. Both Zionists and anti-Dreyfusards rejected the specifically liberal heritage of the French Revolution, with its pressing of formerly independent groups into the service of a modern, secular state. The passionate repudiation of this heritage by such apparently divergent political and cultural segments of French society ought to give pause to the historian of the Dreyfus period. Perhaps we have tended to be too kind to the Dreyfusards, impressed as we are by their heroic struggles of 1898 and 1899. Perhaps the ringing and sometimes prophetic words of the Zionist minority of that period, along with the difficulties of liberalism in our own time, should lead us to reexamine the faith Jews and other Frenchmen once placed in the liberal ideals of the Third Republic.

NOTES

1. For a more extensive treatment of many of the issues touched on in this paper, see Michael R. Marrus, *The Politics of Assimilation: A Study of the French Jewish Community at the Time of the Dreyfus Affair* (Oxford, 1971).

2. See Zosa Szajkowski, "The Growth of the Jewish Population in France: The Political Aspects of a Demographic Problem," *Jewish Social Studies*, vol. 8, no. 3, July 1946, pp. 179–96, and no. 4, October 1946, pp. 297–318.

3. Zadoc Kahn, *Sermons et allocutions*, 3 vols. (Paris, 1894), 3:62. On the role of Paris in the French Jewish community, see Léon Kahn, *Les juifs de Paris depuis le VIe siècle* (Paris, 1899); Hippolyte Prague, "Le culte en province," *Archives Israélites*, 11 August 1898, p. 258; Jules Bauer, "Le judaisme de province," *Univers Israélite*, 12 March 1897, pp. 790–91.

4. R. T., "Les carrières libérales et la religion," *Univers Israélite*, 29 January 1897, pp. 594–96; 12 February 1897, pp. 657–58.

5. See Hippolyte Prague, "Coup d'oeil sur l'état présent du judaisme en France," *Archives Israélites*, 10 September 1896, pp. 298–99; id., "Contre la décadence," *Archives Israélites*, 12 January 1897, pp. 17–18; Simon Debré, "The Jews of France," *Jewish Quarterly Review*, 3 (April 1891):367–435.

6. See Zadoc Kahn, *Sermons*; Benjamin Mossé, ed., *La révolution française et le rabbinat français* (Paris, 1890); on the Rothschilds see especially Jean Bouvier, *Les Rothschild* (Paris, 1960).

7. Maurice Bloch, "La société juive en France depuis la Révolution," *Revue des Etudes Juives*, 48 (1904):xx.

8. See Robert F. Byrnes, *Antisemitism in Modern France,* vol. 1, *The Prologue to the Dreyfus Affair* (New Brunswick, N.J., 1950); Léon Poliakov, *Histoire de l'antisémitisme*, vol. 3, *De Voltaire à Wagner* (Paris,1968). For the significance of the crash of the Catholic banking house, the Union Générale, in 1882, in the rise of French anti-Semitism see Jeannine Verdès, "La presse devant le krach d'une banque catholique: l'Union Générale (1882)," *Archives de la sociologie des religions*, no. 19, January–June 1965, pp. 125–56, and Jean Bouvier, *Le krach de l'Union Générale, 1878–1885* (Paris, 1960), p. 146.

9. See Mark Wischnitzer, *To Dwell in Safety: the Story of Jewish Migration since 1800* (Philadelphia, 1948); Zosa Szajkowski, "The European Attitude to East European Migration (1881–1893)," *Publication of the American Jewish Historical Society*, 41 (December, 1951):127–62.

10. Théodore Reinach, *Actes et Conférences de la Société des Etudes Juives* (1887), p. cxxxii.

11. See Daniel Lévy, "Les persécutions russes et la presse parisienne," *Archives Israélites*, 4 June 1891, p. 178; Zadoc Kahn, "Lettre pastorale du Grand Rabbin de France," *Univers Israélite,* 1 December 1891, pp. 163–65; Albin Valabrègue, "Appel aux israélites," *Le Matin*, 14 September 1893; "Prières publiques," *L'Eclair*, 21 October 1894; "Actualité: le service pour le Tsar à la synagogue," *Archives Israélites*, 11 June 1896, p. 195.

12. See Lazare Wogue, "Une séance mémorable," *Univers Israélite*, 1 July 1893, p. 611; Isidore Singer, "L'apathie des juifs et la campagne antisémite," *La Vraie Parole*, 28 June 1893; Hippolyte Prague, "Revue de l'année israélite 5653–54," *Annuaire des Archives Isaélites 5655* (1894–95), p. 31.

13. There is, of course, an enormous literature on the Affair. For the best account in English, see Douglas Johnson, *France and the Dreyfus Affair* (London, 1966). An interesting recent interpretation, from a Marxist point of view, may be found in Jean-Pierre Peter, "Dimensions de l'Affaire Dreyfus," *Annales: économies, sociétés, civilisations*, November–December 1961, pp. 1141–67.

14. B.-M., "M. Scheurer-Kestner et l'Affaire Dreyfus," *Univers Israélite*, 12 November 1897, p. 230. Cf. I. Déhalle, "L'assimilation des israélites français," *Univers Israélite*, 16 August 1901, p. 683.

15. On the Jewish response to the anticlerical campaign, see for example, Isidore Cahen, "Les cultes en guerre civile," *Archives Israélites*, 1 January 1885, p. 1; idem, "La marée montante," *Archives Israélites*, 26 November 1885, p. 381; idem, "Les jésuites et les juifs," *Archives Israélites*, 31 October 1889, p. 359; Adolphe Franck, "Le rôle du judaisme dans le mouvement politique contemporain," *Archives Israélites*, 19 August 1886, p. 258.

16. See Louis Lévy, "L'antisémitisme et la France," *Univers Israélite*, 25 February 1898, pp. 715–16; Léon Blum, *Souvenirs sur l'Affaire* (Paris, 1935), pp. 25–26; Daniel Halévy, "Apologie pour notre passé," *Cahiers de la quinzaine* (Paris, 1910), p. 23; Charles Péguy, *Notre Jeunesse* (1910) in *Oeuvres complètes* (Paris, 1916), 4:104.

17. *Univers Israélite*, 2 December 1898.

18. See, for example, Julien Benda, "L'Affaire Dreyfus et le principe d'autorité," *Revue Blanche*, 20 (1899):190–206; Emile Durkheim, "L'individualisme et les intellectuels," *Revue Bleu*, July 1898, pp. 7–13. Cf. Julien Benda, *Dialogues à Byzance* (Paris, 1909), pp. 71–73; Henri Dagan, ed., *Enquête sur l'antisémitisme* (Paris, 1899), pp. 60–61.

19. Hannah Arendt, *The Origins of Totalitarianism* (Cleveland, 1958), p. 105. Cf. Robert Gauthier, ed., *"Dreyfusards!" Souvenirs de Mathieu Dreyfus et autres inédits* (Paris, 1965), pp. 52–53; Johnson, *Dreyfus Affair*, pp. 60–62.

20. Letter to Simon Wolf, 15 September 1899, in Simon Wolf, *Some Presidents I Have Known* (Washington, 1918), p. 149.

21. R.T., "Les fonctionnaires religieux," *Univers Israélite*, 21 January 1898, p. 551.

22. Salomon Reinach, "Conférence de M. Salomon Reinach," *Bulletin de l'Association Amicale des anciens élèves des Ecoles Halphen et Lucien de Hirsch*, April 1908. Cf. Julien Weill, *Zadoc Kahn, 1839–1905* (Paris, 1912), p. 202.

23. H. Prague, "Réflexions sur le Consistoire Central," *Archives Israélites*, 20 August 1896, p. 274; B.-M., "Elections consistoriales," *Univers Israélites*, 9 October 1896, p. 71; H. Prague, "L'organisation du culte israélite en France," *Archives Israélites*, 16 September 1897, p. 290; Archives of the Consistoire Central and the Consistoire de Paris, 1896, 1897, 1898, 1899.

24. André Chouraqui, *Cent ans d'histoire: l'Alliance Israélite Universelle et la renaissance juive contemporaine, 1860–1960* (Paris, 1965), pp. 140–1; Zosa Szajkowski, "Conflicts in the Alliance Israélite Universelle and the Founding

of the Anglo-Jewish Association, the Vienna Allianz and the Hilfsverein," *Jewish Social Studies*, 9 (January–April 1957):39; "Fausses accusations," *Bulletin de l'Alliance Israélite Universelle*, 1897, pp. 25–26; ibid., 1898, pp. 74–88; ibid., 1899, pp. 65–108.

25. Théodore Reinach, "Discours prononcé à la distribution des prix des écoles consistoriales israélites de Paris," *Univers Israélite*, 25 July 1898, p. 595.

26. "Quelques voeux d'intellectuels," *Le Siècle*, 1 January 1899.

27. See "Une lettre de M. Fernand Ratisbonne," *Le Gaulois*, 25 January 1898; Gaston Pollonnais, "Le syndicat," *Le Soir*, 1 April 1899; idem, "Il faut choisir," *Le Soir*, 18 November 1899; Arthur Meyer, "A bas les juifs," *Le Gaulois*, 7 February 1895; H. Prague, "Les israélites, le Sainté-Siège et M. Arthur Meyer," *Archives Israélites*, 14 February 1895, pp. 50–51.

28. See Charles Péguy, *Notre Jeunesse*, 4:226; Jean France, *Souvenirs de la Sûreté générale* (Paris, 1936), p. 132; Isidore Cahen, "Une profession de foi," *Archives Israélites*, 21 April 1898; Joseph Reinach, *Histoire de l'Affaire Dreyfus*, 7 vols. (Paris, 1901–8), 3:542–49.

29. Alfred Berl, "L'eclipse des idées libérales," *Grande Revue*, 1 May 1900, pp. 291–316.

30. See Daniel Lévy, "La guerre de 1870–71 et le patriotisme," *Archives Israélites*, 12 June 1890, pp. 187–88; H. Prague, "La guerre de 1870; ses conséquences morales et sociales," *Archives Israélites*, 12 September 1895, p. 290; Berl, "L'eclipse," p. 316; I. Levaillant, "La genèse de l'antisémitisme sous la Troisième République," *Actes et Conférence de la Société des Etudes Juives* (1907), p. lxxxiv; Emile Durkheim in Henri Dagan, ed., *Enquête sur l'antisémitisme* (Paris, 1899), pp. 60–61.

31. *Univers Israélite*, 5 December 1902, pp. 332–37; Weill, *Zadoc Kahn*, pp. 169–71. Cf. A. de Boisandré, "Un nouveau syndicat juif contre l'antisémitisme," *La Libre Parole*, 26 November 1902.

32. On Bernard Lazare see especially Marrus, *Politics of Assimilation*, chap. 7; Nelly Jussem-Wilson, "Bernard Lazare's Jewish Journey: From Being an Israélite to Being a Jew," *Jewish Social Studies*, 26 (July 1964):146–68; Baruch Hagani, *Bernard Lazare, 1865–1903* (Paris, 1919).

33. See Bernard Lazare, "Juifs et israélites," *Entretiens politiques et littéraires*, 1 (September 1890):174–79; id., "La solidarité juive," ibid., 1 (October 1890): 222–32. On leftist anti-Semitism in France, see especially George Lichtheim, "Socialism and the Jews," *Dissent*, July–August 1968, pp. 314–42.

34. See Israel Cohen, *Theodore Herzl: Founder of Political Zionism* (New York, 1959), pp. 57–58; Alex Bein, *Theodore Herzl: A Biography* (Cleveland, 1962), chaps. 4–5; Pierre Van Passen, "Paris, 1891–1895: A Study of the Transition in Theodore Herzl's Life," in Meyer W. Weisgal, ed., *Theodore Herzl: A Memorial* (New York, 1929), pp. 37–39.

35. Bernard Lazare, *Une erreur judiciaire: la vérité sur l'Affaire Dreyfus* (Brussels, 1896), p. 9.

36. Id., "Lettre ouverte à M. Trarieux," *L'Aurore,* 7 June 1899.

37. Id., *Le nationalisme juif* (Paris, 1898).

38. Id., "Le prolétariat juif devant l'antisémitisme," *Le Flambeau,* January 1899, p. 13.

39. Ibid., 14.

40. Id., *Le nationalisme juif,* pp. 7–9.

41. Ibid., p. 4.

42. *Le prolétariat juif: lettre des ouvriers juifs de Paris au Parti Socialiste Français* (Paris, 1898). Cf. Edmund Silberner, "French Socialism and the Jewish Question, 1865–1914," *Historia Judaica,* 16 (April 1954):15.

43. See "Le Groupe des Prolétaires juifs," *L'Aurore,* 18 September 1899; "Le Groupe des Ouvriers juifs de Paris," *L'Echo Sioniste,* 20 September 1899, p. 27; Maître Jacques, "Prolétaires juifs," *Les Droits de l'homme,* 17 September 1899; "Les réunions: meeting des prolétaires juifs," *Le Journal du peuple,* 18 September 1899.

44. Adolphe Raskine, "Ce que nous demandons," *Zion,* October 1897, pp. 77–78.

45. Ibid., p. 79.

46. Pinhas, "Le torchon brule," *Le Flambeau,* March 1899, p.18. Cf. Henri Dhorr, "Le droit d'être juif," *Le Libertaire,* 24 September 1899; La rédaction, "Notre programme," *Kadimah,* 15 February 1898, pp. 1–3; Jacques Bahar, "Sionisme et patriotisme," *Le Flambeau,* February 1899, pp. 13–15.

47. Léon Paperin, "La banqueroute," *L'Echo Sioniste,* 5 December 1899, p. 97.

48. J. Tchernoff, *Dans le creuset des civilisations,* vol. 3, *Le destin d'un émigré* (Paris, 1937), p. 31.

THE GERMAN WOMEN'S MOVEMENT AND SUFFRAGE, 1890–1914: A STUDY OF NATIONAL FEMINISM

Amy Hackett

The women's movement would seem to have been about suffrage. The long struggle of American feminists for the right to vote is the most chronicled episode in women's history. Tales of British suffragettes storming Parliament and being force-fed in prison are also well known. American and British women did win the ballot, but the feminist movement apparently exhausted itself on the suffrage issue.[1] Women in these nations today are not so optimistic about receiving equality with men through legislation, and "Women's Liberation" itself is a manifestation of the limitations of their earlier victory. Nevertheless, the Anglo-American movements did ex-exemplify a sort of feminism that shared the trust in political rights of their surrounding cultures.

Feminism in Wilhelmian Germany did not conform to this paradigm. The land of *Küche, Kirche, und Kinder* produced a notable women's movement in the feminist heyday before the Great War. In the International Council of Women (ICW), German membership was third in strength to membership from the United States and England. German feminists probably turned out more pages of analysis and argument than the other two nations combined. But they rarely overrated the importance of suffrage. Bourgeois feminists long circumlocuted the very word.[2] The minor emphasis on political rights in German feminism as against the contemporary Anglo-American movements invites comparative treatment.

Prewar feminism was an international phenomenon, yet a meaningful comparison of the German and Anglo-American movements is possible only if we employ the concept of "national feminism." We may agree that women were oppressed everywhere, but their traditional family role centrally involved them in the transmission of specific values from one generation to the next. Women and women's movements must be viewed, therefore, within the social and cultural context of a particular nation. Profound divisions within nations further complicate any treatment of a feminist movement. Feminists everywhere are confronted by issues that touch them in that sensitive (and extensive) area where they are women "as such," and like men, nationals of a country, adherents of a political view, members of a socioeconomic class, and confessors of a religious faith. (Depending on

Amy Hackett studied at Columbia University, where she currently teaches.

354

the individual and the issue, these factors and others are variously decisive.)
Women's competing allegiances inevitably disturb a feminist movement.
In Germany, their multiple identities thwarted all attempts to devise a
"women's" politics.

Mirroring Wilhelmian society at large, the deepest split in German
feminism was between Social Democratic and bourgeois women. The latter, moreover, were not a monolithic force. In the mid-1890s a more
politically oriented "left wing" of these bourgeois women set about distinguishing itself from the "moderate" majority. And after the turn of the
century there emerged a conservative "right wing," opposed to woman
suffrage beyond the community level.

Legal restrictions on women's political activities in several states in
the German confederation abetted hesitancy of the women in demanding
the vote.[3] Nonetheless, when an imperial law governing associations and
assemblies superseded state rules in 1908, women's public activities had
rendered these rules largely unenforceable. The most significant injunc-
tion, given Prussia's size and importance, was paragraph 8 of that state's
association law of 1850, which barred women (also apprentices and schoolboys) from political organizations and their meetings. (The election period
was technically exempt.) "Politics" legally included "the constitution, administration and legislation of the state, civil rights of subjects and the
international relations of states."[4] Scrupulously applied, paragraph 8 permitted only kaffeeklatsches. Application was arbitrary and unscrupulous in
the broader tradition of Prussian, indeed imperial, justice. Particularly
between 1895 and 1900, women who were also Social Democrats suffered
most. Women could officially discuss politics at meetings called by individuals. Until an 1898 reform, official interpretation made the Bavarian law
even harsher. In Mecklenburg, which resisted the formation of the representative body constitutionally expected of German states, political rights
were ambiguous for either sex. In the city-state of Hamburg, bourgeois
women ran afoul of general laws protecting public order and morality
when they attacked state-sanctioned brothels. Ironically, they fled to
neighboring Prussian Altona to assail Hamburg's pandering city fathers.
Almost anywhere, bourgeois or socialist meetings might be graced by police-
men, who assiduously noted everything said. In Prussia they often sat,
uniformed, on the podium; if offended, the officer stood up and declared
the meeting dissolved. Anglo-American feminists did not confront such
autocratic governments.

The German women's movement was not seen as an outright danger
to the state. The feminist "left wing" often met in the Reichstag building.
Mayors and other government officials were increasingly evident at feminist
assemblies. (Such gentlemen pro forma voiced dismay at "certain manifestations" of the movement.) Police practice was consistent in its intent to
inhibit threats to the existing order. While Socialist women called them-

selves enemies of the state, bourgeois feminists only wanted to make the existing order more viable. Hence there was a double standard in law enforcement, unless, as in Hamburg, reformers became too critical or embarrassing; or unless, as happens in a bureaucratic, police-minded state, some official decided it was time to assert authority.

Class consciousness and class justice protected socialist women from many illusions about some "one, united woman's movement which hovers above the cloud of party struggles—the highest social justice and wisdom become flesh and blood."[5] Clara Zetkin, the party's feminist theoretician, dubbed the rhetoric of universal sisterhood *Harmoniedüselei* (sentimental simpering about harmony).

Socialist women had one huge edge over bourgeois suffragists: the Social Democratic Party (*Sozialdemokratische Partei Deutschlands,* or SPD), whose platform included woman suffrage.[6] They also had August Bebel, the party patriarch, whose classic *The Woman and Socialism*[7] gave a special imprimatur to women's emancipation in the SPD. Yet despite official support for women's equality, a point of theory complicated the identity confusion to which socialist women were susceptible. Was there a "woman question"? Wilhelm Liebknecht denied it at the 1890 party congress. The platform need not specify woman suffrage because Social Democracy's wish for human equality subsumed women's equality as a "simple matter of course. For Social Democracy there isn't any woman question, period; the woman question is simply part of the social question, which will solve itself with the transformation of present social and productive relationships."[8] Emma Ihrer retorted that socialist women wanted "no extra movement for women, no games; we only want to support the general workers' movement. . . ." She denied any female intrigues, yet reminded the party that it had done "almost nothing" for women, who had a "right to be treated by you as fully equal comrades."[9] Fervent socialists like Ihrer were hurt and outraged when not taken seriously by fellow-strugglers in a sacred cause. Defensiveness and bitterness were comprehensible. Socialist women's extravagant self-abnegation is fair proof of a "woman question" *within* the SPD. Socialist feminist doctrine itself denied the reality of a "woman question," but it rarely sounded quite the same coming from a man.

Theoretical adherence to scientific socialism did not erase masculine supremacy from every comrade's heart. Women often remarked the absence of party leaders' wives from SPD women's activities. Still, the SPD was notable among socialist parties in its honest support of women's equality; with German bourgeois parties there was no comparison. Legal restrictions complicated women's accommodation in the party. Despite attacks on women's separatism, association laws necessitated extra organizations. Educational groups for women and local women's representatives (so-called *Vertrauenspersonen*) with a central office and representative in Berlin helped create a network among socialist women throughout the empire.[10] A political party rarely advances a principle if it is thought that the realization might cost it power. Despite a nagging suspicion that women would not reward socialists with their votes, the SPD alone among German parties promoted woman suffrage in the Reichstag. Socialists must be given primary credit for its inception when the empire collapsed and revolution superseded ordinary parliamentary procedures in 1918. The suspicions were well founded: socialists' reputed hostility toward religion stood them in especially bad stead with the new voters.[11]

This principled behavior was in ironic juxtaposition to the expediency that purportedly determined proletarian support for woman suffrage. At the founding Paris International in 1889, Zetkin demanded political rights despite their insignificance. Even countries with universal suffrage had their "social questions." Women, like all mankind, would only be liberated by the "emancipation of labor from capital."[12] Suffrage was more highly valued as the socialist women's movement grew. (The lapse of the antisocialist law in 1890 also made parliamentary battles seem more useful.) At the SPD congress in 1892, women proposed efforts to win more members of their sex for socialism: unionization should be pushed; women should be urged to join party organizations where it was legal; the rights of assembly and association had high priority; finally, elections should be used to awaken and educate women and to protest their lack of rights. Political rights were a useful weapon. Zetkin, defending the proposals, avoided any hint of feminism. It was wasted energy to "incite against men's privileges"; the worker's wife suffered less from "slavery to her husband than from her dependence upon capitalism." The now ritual denial of separatism drew cheers. Zetkin supported the demands "not because I'm a woman, but because I feel myself to be first a comrade, and only because of the value and importance of the feminine sex for winning over the proletariat." She did not ask for justice or fairness, to which *no* political party responded. Rather she asked "in the interest of the whole proletariat," so that, for example, women's labor would not forever undersell men's.[13]

When, the next year, the Reichstag was dissolved and elections called, the SPD made the first open and concerted effort to use feminine persuasion in the service of a political party. Where possible, women held their own meetings or attended regular campaign meetings. They passed out leaflets, climbed up and down proletarian stairwells to discuss candidates and issues. On election day, women carried placards with candidates' names through the streets (in Magdeburg they carried red umbrellas that read "Elect W. Klees"), passed out ballots, pulled lazy or forgetful voters to the polls.[14]

The election was also used, if incidentally, to demand women's rights. Zetkin's women's journal *Die Gleichheit* (*Equality*) described campaign work as a "certificate of qualification" for the vote, as proof of political "maturity." The lowliest woman laborer would, it was claimed, become a "champion of the highest ideals" as practice instructed her in politics and economics. Women would also show how well they subordinated their particular interest to that of the working class.[15] Male socialists would, in other words, see that woman suffrage was a good thing. The hint that women should prove they deserved suffrage recalls the arguments used by most bourgeois feminists. Both cases seem to involve uncertainty whether women would vote the "right" way. Bourgeois feminists subordinated suffrage to the greater good of society; socialist women subordinated it to that society's overthrow. The gist of the bourgeois feminist line was that given women's "immaturity," suffrage lay just as well in the far future. Socialist women never drew this conclusion. The ballot could be used to gain political power. For the working class was a political majority. Once they had power, socialists would totally revolutionize society. Only then would German women—and men—be free.

Qualms about women's voting behavior were, for Zetkin, ultimately overcome by faith in Marxian economic determinism. For centuries, women's exclusion from politics had harmed neither them nor society. Nationalism, cosmopolitanism, and above all a world market had changed this. For proletarian men, political changes had dutifully followed shifts in productive relationships. In women's case, a classic contradiction emerged. Even a housewife was at the mercy of a world market. Her simplest purchases were cheap or dear depending on colonial wars and tariffs; new machines might mean unemployment for her husband. Working women, directly exploited by capitalism, of course felt their dependence on politics more clearly. Their economic lives hardly differed from men's except that their economic weakness too often meant prostitution. Working women above all needed the vote. They hadn't even a clear-cut right to organize.

Zetkin admitted that women themselves must change in light of their objective condition. "Woman can no longer crawl off behind the family hearth, she must live in society; her one-sided, narrow-minded, deeply egoistic *love of family* must be replaced by the *general feeling of solidarity* now so very lacking in women." Women's increasing economic independence demanded political and social rights. Nor did voting require some arcane "maturity." One needed only "healthy human understanding, a practical sense, clear insight into one's own interest and its intimate connection with the general welfare." Women would not receive political and economic education in front of their stoves. Custom, masculine egotism, and their own indifference had inhibited them. But when more than one in four women were involved in the production process, woman's rights became inevitable "with or against the will of men, *yes, even against her own will.*"[16]

Economic determinism was also used to show the enlightened self-interest in SPD support for woman suffrage. Sheltered and intellectually indolent as middle-class and petit bourgeois women were, it was "ten against one" they would even vote. Women of the "upper 10,000" were correspondingly few. The great majority of women were of course proletarians. Most women who were employed (and thus, it was argued, politically aware) were proletarians. Numbers should speak to the SPD. In case they did not, Zetkin evoked the danger that bourgeois parties might try to use women as "voting cattle" (*Stimmvieh*) against the SPD. Ignored by the party, their class consciousness dim, proletarian women would be backward and conservative. Woman suffrage could "mobilize the whole proletarian family and lead it onto the battlefield of class struggle." Now proletarian wives sometimes thwarted their husbands' political activity.[17]

It would seem that Zetkin underestimated the voting potential of middle-class housewives. Under the Weimar Republic in the 1920's most of them voted either for their husbands' party or more conservatively. This subsequent fact does underline, however, the concern of prewar Socialist women for the educational significance of the family and the need to develop socialist mothers; they realized that wives who did not think about politics were a detriment. A social revolution that bypasses the family, keeping women home-oriented, sheltered, ill-educated, and in hostage to Mrs. Grundy, will probably miscarry. Because of the character of their home lives, German women were unlikely material for socialism. In the longer run, the more sexual equality is realized, the more the argument that woman suffrage was opportune is persuasive, assuming the SPD's own premise that it was the party with the brightest future in any case. Sexual differences in political behavior are finally insignificant in the youngest generation of West German voters. The Federal Republic's long postwar domination by Christian Democracy was however largely caused by demographic imbalance; an inordinately high percentage of older women.[18] Socialism has of course been alert to the effects of work experience on personality. Unquestionably women's work beyond the home is related to their interest in the wider world of politics, though the link is more complex than was implied.[19]

Socialist women's usual line of argument had drawbacks. An ethical appeal to natural rights that would transcend possible or short-term vote losses was rejected as metaphysics. Moreover, as long as more strictly "feminist" approaches were eschewed—that is, those which recognized women's peculiarities as well as their likenesses with men—it was not altogether obvious why socialist men could not adequately represent working-class women. (They might even understand these women's real interests better than they could themselves.) In 1902, Belgian socialists provided a precedent by dropping their demand for woman suffrage when the clerical party promoted it.[20]

Zetkin took a new tack at the women's conference accompanying the 1906 party congress. The innovation bespeaks greater confidence, less fear of seeming separatist; it also reflects bourgeois feminists' increasing affirmation of women's uniqueness and cultural potential. After a nod at democratic principles, Zetkin noted that woman suffrage was based on more than equal duties. She specifically rejected the sexual egalitarianism of "certain feminist circles."

No, I am of the opinion that just as we are physically, so we are also emotionally and intellectually different . . . but different does not mean lesser and . . . we feel just this being different (Anders-Sein) *as an advantage in regard to the completion of man and the enrichment of society.*

(These remarks were greeted with "stormy applause.") Zetkin further claimed that women of *all classes* saw political equality as a way to freer and more rewarding lives in society.[21] Yet it was in the nature of things that the earlier non-"feminist" arguments remained paramount.

After the women's adamant approach to equal rights, it is enlightening and amusing to analyze August Bebel's defense on the notable occasion when the SPD first proposed woman suffrage in the Reichstag in 1895.[22] (The party demanded a general constitutional amendment to elect state parliaments by the democratic terms of its program: sheer bravado apart from woman suffrage.)

Bebel predicted that woman suffrage would triumph as all reasonable, just, and natural proposals did. The very discussion of an idea, he claimed, sounding still more like John Stuart Mill, broke down resistance. Even in Germany woman suffrage would prevail. Bebel emphasized the vanguard nature of the SPD's demand "in the name of *equal rights for the sexes*"; the most advanced bourgeois feminists were only petitioning for the rights of assembly and association.[23] Perhaps in part because of the nonparty audience, but also because he was free of the identity conflicts of socialist women, Bebel used a feminist line that they still shunned: men simply could not represent women. Living under different circumstances, men could never by themselves have much insight into women's needs. Sex rule was indeed very like class rule: a dominant group legislated to an oppressed group.[24] Bebel then returned to the more usual point about increased employment. (It was "sometimes frightening" how many women worked.) Millions of women were forced by social circumstances "to wander their way through life alone." Forced to work, they had every interest in industrial legislation and tariffs.

Bebel also took up the old but inevitable question of a female equivalent to man's duty "if the occasion arises to let himself be shot dead." He reminded the deputies that an army required that "boys must be born who later become soldiers." The parliamentary mirth this inspired was noteworthy in light of the grisly earnest with which the connection between maternity and the military was drawn in the prewar years when international tensions shot up and the birth rate slacked. If endangering oneself in the line of "duty" were a qualification for rights, Bebel continued, his colleagues might ponder the statistics on mortality and disabilities in childbirth. One wonders if the resultant "commotion" noted among the deputies arose from bad conscience over their prior laughter, indignation at such a parallel (childbearing being just disagreeable and no equivalent to service in the King's army), or some deeper discomfort.

To prove that woman suffrage was no utopian socialist scheme, Bebel listed the states that enfranchised women. He even used the classic feminist line on Wyoming, which gave women the vote while still a territory in 1869: there were no poorhouses and the jails were empty. Bebel admitted that other factors were involved, but thought that woman suffrage raised the cultural level. Sentimental feminist that he was, Bebel believed as much in women's goodness, superiority if you will, as in their equality: "Women *possess* a greater *feeling for justice* than men; I further claim that women *are* much *less corrupted* than men, that in every regard they constitute the morally higher element of society." And if he thought that politics ruined character, he would get out himself.

Touting the ultimate triumph of rational virtue, Bebel sounded like the only liberal in this first suffrage debate. (It was of course a Social Democratic commonplace that the party had to assume the historical tasks that immature and diffident German "liberals" botched.) Progressives of all stripes—the would-be, should-be parliamentary beaux of bourgeois feminism—were remarkable for their silence.[25]

Conservatives only laughed at Bebel's observation that "a very great majority" of women would vote for them or at most for the National Liberals. He believed, nonetheless, that woman suffrage would eventually undercut its Conservative sponsors as universal male suffrage had done to Bismarck. But the Conservatives just thought to preserve the status quo. They saw the role of women in society only in terms of a binder of wounds in "war and peace" and as a distributor of ecclesiastical charity. They were also concerned that "older unmarried girls from good families" should be able to support themselves, thereby avoiding exploitation by the Jewish owners of department stores and white slavers.[26] National Liberals also discounted the political gains they might make from suffrage reform.[27]

Woman suffrage was soon eclipsed by conflicting interpretations of Mecklenburg history. The real issue in 1895 was universal male suffrage in the states. (It still was when the war broke out.) Since virtually all bourgeois feminists seemed to think the subject unfit for polite society, the deputies' indifference to woman suffrage is no surprise. The respectable democratic-progressive *Frankfurter Zeitung* was prompted to a favorable article. But they were ahead not only of the progressive parties, but as they noted two years later, of most German feminists.[28]

Bourgeois feminism deviated significantly not only from socialist feminism, but also from the Anglo-American varieties. In 1890, an organized movement was a quarter-century old, yet a popular lexicon could report: "In Germany [as against England and the U.S.] a political feminist move-

ment has thus far been entirely absent; only immediately practical goals
are pursued here." (Which was as it should be according to the author of
the lexicon's entry on "The Woman Question": "The state for man, the
family for woman!")[29]

German feminism was timid for some of the same reasons that German
liberalism, to which it was historically and ideologically related, was. An
earlier feminist movement developed in the agitated 1840s; like liberalism,
it fell victim to the repression that followed the 1848 revolutions. (That the
American women's rights movement is usually dated from the 1848 Seneca
Falls conference makes the divergence of American and German feminisms
the more interesting.) General political excitement prompted speculation
about women's emancipation. When in 1843 a democratic paper in Saxony
raised the question of women's participation in affairs of state, Louise Otto,
24 years old and signing herself "a Saxon girl," replied that woman's love
for her fatherland was so great that "at least in heart and spirit" she must
be concerned with its fate.[30] Democratic women's clubs sprang up, and Otto
and other women helped political prisoners and refugees. She became a
democratic publicist, pledged to a program to educate girls and bring them
closer to their fatherland and to develop the economic independence of
women so that they might avoid marriages of convenience. Otto exposed the
plight of working women and demanded their organization. Her fiancé, Karl
Peters, was imprisoned for liberal revolutionary activities. Her writings suffered censorship. The 1850s were a sobering decade.

In 1865, Louise Otto-Peters called women from throughout Germany
to Leipzig to found a General Association of German Women's Organiza-
zations (*Allgemeiner Deutscher Frauenverein,* or ADF), with which organized feminism really began.[31] The ADF concentrated on increasing
educational and employment opportunities, particularly for middle-class
girls who might not marry.

German women were generally worse off than American and British
women.[32] This alone made German feminism less political. There were
many obvious goals more easily won than suffrage in 1890 when the women's
movement began to gain impetus. German universities were virtually
closed to women, who usually studied in Switzerland. Had they been admitted, girls had no equivalent to the boys' preparatory *Gymnasium.* The
höhere Töchterschule (upper girls' school) for young ladies of good family
notoriously turned out dilettantes who chattered pleasantly in society and
neither embarrassed nor bored their husbands. These schools were dominated by male teachers, particularly with regard to administrative positions.
Ever more middle-class women, unprepared for the world, had to find employment in keeping with their social status. Significant changes were made
in all these areas by 1914; most of them probably would not have been
without feminist pressure. In 1914, there was no foreseeable chance of
woman suffrage. Had feminists unequivocally demanded the vote since

the early nineties, they would hardly have won over a parliamentary majority. German women were, as it happened, enfranchised in 1918, before the far more insistent American women. This was less the result of their efforts than of the extraordinary circumstances of war and, still more, revolution.[33]

Even though there was no cause for suffrage to have absolute priority, German feminism's hesitant approach to politics has revealing aspects: the reluctance of many women to speak the word *suffrage,* much less demand the right; the implication that to demand suffrage outright was somehow "un-German"; the reasons given why women should vote; the significance attached to suffrage; the emphasis on local rather than Reichstag suffrage and on the contributions of woman's "nature" to politics and culture. Inseparable from feminists' treatment of suffrage were their private political sympathies, which often had little to do with their sex. These asexual partialities complicated feminist harmony. The problematic relationship between feminism and liberalism was central.

Legal sanctions on women's political activity do not fully explain feminists' reluctance to demand the vote. From the outset restrictions were breached to discuss topics other than suffrage. Social Democratic women were most threatened by the law, but never hid their desire for suffrage. (Of course their coyest circumlocutions would have cut little ice with the authorities.) Nor was there any clear correlation between the harshness or leniency of state laws and prosuffrage activity in those states.

The truth was that German feminists were skeptical about political rights. Tension between the concepts of rights and duties strangely echoed received ideas about women's "rights." A popular medical-moral guide for wives was concise: "A woman's rights are founded on her duties."[34] In his assault on nineteenth-century Europe's false morality, Ibsen was nowhere so subversive as with the virtuous tyrant Duty, notably in *The Master Builder* where Solness' wife, whose milk has become infected, poisons her twin sons. "She had to feed them herself. It was her duty, she said."[35] Ibsen's message is clear: Duty poisons the lives of everyone near those who subordinate themselves totally for others; the debt incurred weighs too heavy. No ideas were so basic to the feminine ethos as "self-sacrifice," "self-denial," and "giving oneself to others." With sources so diverse as Kantian ethics and authoritarian government, the German *Pflicht* was a more onerous imperative than the English "duty."

Revealing of German feminist mentality was a denial by Auguste Schmidt, feminist veteran and first chairwoman of the Union of German Women's Organizations (*Bund Deutscher Frauenvereine,* or BDF), the central federation of bourgois groups, that women wanted primarily something for themselves. Equal rights would enable women to promote the general welfare. She rejected "women's righters" (*Frauenrechtlerinnen*) as an appellation for feminists. Their watchword was "not '*Rights and Du-*

ties,' rather *'Duties and Rights.'* "[36] The sequence was crucial. (This attitude dovetailed with Social Democratic abuse of bourgeois feminism as *Frauen-rechtelei.*)

For not only was duty urgent; "rights" had unpleasant connotations. They suggested a willful selfishness unbecoming and even offensive to women. Nor were "rights" much valued in the surrounding culture. Demanding them would hardly endear feminists to authorities whose indulgence was desired.

America's debt to natural law ideology is immense. Nothing could have been more natural than that the women at Seneca Falls declared it was "self-evident: that all men and women are created equal; that they are endowed by their Creator with certain unalienable rights . . ." From this they inferred that women had a self-evident right to vote.[37] German women had nothing like a Declaration of Independence at hand nor had they such inviting ideology; natural law theories were superseded during the nineteenth century in Germany by an historical approach to law. Universal male suffrage was a calculated grant by Bismarck to maintain a balance of political forces. The closest thing to a popular view was the inaccurate belief that universal suffrage rewarded those who fought the wars of unification. (This did not help women.) The nondemocratic suffrage which existed in most of the German states at the regional level was not necessarily thought inconsistent with the more or less democratic suffrage for the national Reichstag.

Most bourgeois feminists viewed natural law ideology, helpful as it had been to women, as *passé.* Suffrage was a civil right, and whom a state enfranchised should not depend on principles, but should be decided "merely *according to considerations of political expediency.*" It was "contrary to duty" to give the vote to persons who would likely use it to "endanger the state or general well-being." Such remarks did not generally mean total rejection of woman suffrage. They might hint at property or educational restrictions or at the wisdom of delaying full suffrage until women were "ready" for the responsibility. The feminist herewith cited typically suggested that women first fight for municipal rights. "[Local] self-administration will be for the woman what it was for the man—the best school for political education. Once women are thus raised to citizenship they will be mature [enough] to be active in the welfare of the *state.*"[38] In 1904 Susan B. Anthony visited Berlin for an international women's congress, in conjunction with which an International Alliance for Woman Suffrage was founded. Gertrud Bäumer reflected on the American suffragist's "imperturbable enthusiasm for a cause," declaring that Anthony

almost puts to shame us who are more skeptical and more historically bound. There is something great in the naiveté of this belief in a program. . . . Into our cooler observation of political movements radiated from her personality something of the spirit of the first witness and everything seemed warmer, lovelier and more worth living for in this gleam.[39]

Patronization and perhaps a touch of envy are mixed. Anthony was most revered for her total dedication to and self-denial for a cause, as for her belief in the redeeming moral quality of women. Her tactics and approach to suffrage were deemed "American" and no model for Germany.

German and American women wanted suffrage for different reasons. Their varying priorities may be illustrated by noting ten theses composed by American suffragists in 1902 to serve as basic principles for the International Alliance. The first thesis asserted that men and women were "born as equally free and independent members of human society, equally gifted with reason and talent and equally entitled to the exercise of their personal rights and personal freedom." "Born free" is a concept nonexistent in German feminism. The theses that followed declared the relationship between the sexes to be one of "independence" and proclaimed "self-determination in the home as in the state" the "unquestioned right" of every normal adult. Economic disadvantages incurred through disenfranchisement came fifth in the American program, while German women, and not only socialists, accorded them utmost importance. Tenth and last, after the "tyranny" of demanding taxation and obedience without representation, Americans put women's better education and increased intellectual capabilities as well as their new economic role in industrial society. These historically determined factors, closely tied to the idea of readiness to vote, were favored by German feminists. Americans ignored other central German arguments: women's duty to the state and to culture, unique feminine contributions to national welfare and men's inability to represent women, particularly because of their less rigorous morality.[40]

Feminist organization and politics exacerbated ideological timidity about suffrage. The BDF was founded in 1894 to link all groups in the women's movement. Some of these were dubiously feminist; the concerns were as diverse as establishment of girls' high schools, better training in homemaking, abstinence from alcohol, encouragement of women physicians, and rewards for loyal female domestics. A discussion of suffrage was not allowed at the 1898 BDF assembly in Hamburg. Chairwoman Schmidt, though sympathetic to the "final achievement of suffrage," thought it a "tactical mistake to repulse many timid souls now. We have time before us." She thought the next biennial meeting would be a likely time to raise the "most important question of the woman's movement." (It was first raised in 1902.) Schmidt was especially worried by the effect of a discussion in Hamburg, where organized feminism was described as a tender young plant needing protection.[41] If it was feared that BDF members were so easily offended, what of the masses of women outside? German feminism was not alone in confronting large numbers of women, even within the movement, who wanted no part of suffrage. The percentage was however surely higher than in countries where suffrage movements had long defended the idea.

The BDF itself swore to an ideology of harmony, the *"Bund's* gospel of love," as it was dubbed in 1895. This policy, presumably copied from the American Council of Women (which did not approve suffrage either), permitted a stance on only those issues "where *all heartily* agree." Leaving the "solid ground of concord in order to risk a leap in the air toward a far goal" might, it was suggested, "bring the whole *Bund* to disaster."[42] "Far goal," like "last consequence," was a typical euphemism for the unmentionable suffrage.

A more political feminism emerged around 1895. In December 1894, Lily von Gizycki made the first public prosuffrage speech by a nonsocialist German woman. It was perhaps the most radical suffrage speech ever made by a bourgeois feminist. Relying on such sources as the French philosopher Condorcet and American feminists, she defined suffrage as "this fundamental right from which all others of necessity follow."[43] She even ended with a compliment to socialism. (It was characteristic of German feminism that this initial radicalism should not be repeated.) The address was first given under the auspices of the Ethical Culture Society, one of whose founders was Lily's husband Georg, whom she credited with helping her draw feminist conclusions from her own experiences. *Ethische Kultur,* edited by Gizycki, seems to have been the first German journal to treat woman suffrage favorably.[44] The public meeting where Lily spoke was called by Minna Cauer, whose Berlin "Frauenwohl" ("Women's Welfare") organization was a rival of Helene Lange's Berlin Women's Club. (A chance to outdo Lange may have overcome qualms about this radical step.)[45] In January 1895, Cauer, with Lily von Gizycki as coeditor, launched the polemical *Die Frauenbewegung (The Women's Movement)* to compete with Lange's more literary *Die Frau.* It supported suffrage virtually from the outset. Georg von Gizycki was chosen to make the first brave demand. He suggested that only inferior men, afraid of competition, would question women's qualifications. Gizycki drew heavily on English and American sources, making suffrage a simple matter of equity; it alone would bring a basic change in woman's position. Taxation without representation was "despotic." Women's peculiar gifts, especially "something of their pure love," were also needed by society. Morality, education and help for the poor were areas specially suited to women, who, properly educated, could fill "nearly all" public offices.[46]

Cauer, Gizycki, and Adele Gerhard soon petitioned the Reichstag to end restrictions on women's political activity. In 1896, Cauer helped organize an international women's congress in Berlin where suffrage was publically mentioned.[47] A larger petition drive followed in 1897. In Dresden, 1800 persons attended a meeting for a free association law.[48] In 1898, the BDF began its own petition campaign. Simultaneously women debated a new civil code. Feminists were pulled into the political arena if they did not go voluntarily.

The political women came to see themselves as radicals, a feminist "left wing." In 1899 they formed the Union of Progressive Women's Organizations (*Verband Fortschrittlicher Frauenvereine*) to support activities toward which they could not move the BDF. For example, the Union would "lead women to esteem political rights, in particular, woman suffrage."[49] This would be a fighting organization to agitate for big ideas.

The same radicals set up an official suffrage organization, the German Association for Woman Suffrage (*Deutscher Verein für Frauenstimmrecht*, or DVF) in January 1902. It occurred to Anita Augspurg, spurred by American suffragists' intention to found an international suffrage association, that a German suffrage group might be formed in a state such as Hamburg, which had no restrictive laws. The DVF promoted use of the few, albeit mostly indirect, local franchises that women had in some states, and political equality where they had no rights.[50] The DVF was accepted into the BDF, at whose assembly later in 1902, woman suffrage was not just discussed but proclaimed "urgently to be desired."[51]

Already in 1897 suffrage was in a way applauded at a national assembly of the oldest feminist organization, the solidly moderate ADF. The presence of vocal radicals in the BDF ironically helped maintain that organization's gag on suffrage talk; even as their insistence finally prompted the 1902 recognition of suffrage. The BDF's sisterly gospel reflected strong-handed control by such women as Schmidt and also Lange, a sharp-witted schoolmistress who added a disciplinarian touch to feminism. The ADF could lift the taboo on suffrage because its leaders, also Lange and Schmidt, knew that members could be trusted. Lange's report of the ADF event, a speech on "last goals," was revealing. That the "fully sanctioned cooperation in the cultural work of civil and ecclesiastical communities as well as in the life of the state could be brought to expression proves . . . that one can say anything if he knows how to find a worthy form."[52] Women who had concocted the "morality question" (*Sittlichkeitsfrage*) to discuss prostitution should not have been at a loss. The concern was characteristically with propriety, not to say aesthetics. Were political rights really demanded? Women wished to fulfill cultural duties. Allgemeiner Deutscher Frauenverein (ADF) members would abide by the rules of decorous speech. Their primary interests were education, employment, and reasonably quiet community work. They would not call open air meetings to demand rights. The radicals, harping on "agitation" and flaunting their political precocity, grated on Lange's nerves. They wanted to wrest control of the BDF from the old leadership and move it away from its "charity work" mentality toward "large goals." Lange's view of proper feminist activity and its rewards was nicely embodied in the motto "Not screaming, rather performance is needed."[53] She probably knew the ADF would support her long-range view on suffrage. Lange, for example, took issue with Schmidt's prediction that in a quarter-century women might be sitting in city halls.[54]

Schmidt was not impatient so much as optimistic. Like Lange, she saw feminism in the light of evolution. Schmidt did not care "whether a right is won one year sooner or later," so much as that its champions defended it with "energy and wisdom."[55] Lange too invoked the ultimate benediction of the nineteenth century when she could no longer avoid the suffrage issue. Leopold von Ranke unveiled for her "humanity's evolutionary process, which here and there is hastened or retarded by external events and individual personalities, but on the whole imperturbably continues on its great path and in the long run . . . makes external events subservient to itself." Though feminism was on evolution's schedule, the consequences Lange inferred as to suffrage tactics seemed at odds with the ineluctable sweep of history. Whether the "last consequence" came "sooner or later" was less important to humanity's progress than that change proceed "in tranquil pathways." Any anticipation invited confusion. Healthy feminism began with education, employment, and community activity, which then provided "schooling for further duties and rights."[56] As if a few radical feminists rocking the evolutionary boat might send feminism—and human progress with it—to a bottomless grave!

Indirections like "last consequence" and "far goal" involved more than a realistic assessment of the chances of the Reichstag's granting woman suffrage. Marie Stritt, BDF chairwoman from 1899 to 1910 and an outspoken proponent of suffrage,[57] perceptively explained the German mentality to the London international women's congress in 1899. German men, she reported, thought suffrage more a hard-won good, particularly a reward for military service, than a "right due every citizen." Earlier feminists had seen suffrage "not as the necessary means to achieve all other civil rights but as the *confirmation* and last public recognition of the full economic, legal, and social equality of women; not as the *foundation stone* upon which all else must be built, but as the protecting *roof* over woman's emancipation." Some women, seeing their "error," realized that nothing would be achieved without political rights. (Though such barriers as the laws of association meant that political equality would for long be only the "theoretical consequence" of feminism.)[58] Stritt was called on the carpet for attributing "error" to feminist notables.[59] Equally reprehensible, she had covertly acknowledged the radical position. A more representative feminist present at London observed: "A number of our women declare that the *final goal* of our efforts must be the gaining of political rights," but only a small "minority . . . see woman suffrage as the real and true *beginning* point of work."[60]

The suffrage debate as usually formulated was quite absurd. The vote's significance was given little thought—not only because of its unlikely attainment, but also for other considerations. The terms of the usual moderate argument were stated in an 1895 article in Lange's *Die Frau*. Lange carefully identified the author, a Dutch woman, as one who had "put her great talents entirely at the service of the social question"; that is, she was no suffrage agitator. Readers were further reminded that suffrage had little chance in Germany. In any event, "our most discerning and noble feminist leaders" believed that "the rights and duties of German women will for a long while lie in entirely different areas than that of political action." Still, the SPD had just brought the issue to the Reichstag and incipiently radical feminists were beginning to agitate and petition. Perhaps these events led Lange to conclude "that the German woman too should for once concern herself with this part of the woman question." The Dutch author disputed the priority Mill gave the vote. It was a "capstone." Women's immaturity also worried her. (The translator agreed it would hurt women and their cause to "pull the feminine sex blindly into impassioned election contests and the disagreeable party squabbles of the day," though it might seem desirable for a "few discerning and gifted women" to have a voice on matters concerning their own sex.) The Dutch author concurred: better prepare woman for the distant event than "toss the vote into her lap like an unripe fruit."[61]

The vote as "capstone" (or "roof" or "crown" as the German women generally preferred) or the vote as "foundation"? The debate suffered from unreal alternatives. The ballot as "crown" resembles being handed paddles once your canoe has reached land. (The journey to full equality would not of course end on the shore; the route is longer and far more devious.) But for the vote to be of much use, women would have to be politically awake and consciously feminist. The most common radical metaphor was aquatic: to learn to swim, one must jump in the water. This implied that were women granted the vote, they would then, and only then, learn how to use it; political rights and activities would produce responsible citizens. Yet suffrage has not automatically made women politically effective, either in general or as an interest group. Certainly prior feminist consciousness is necessary for the latter. (How far women really are an interest group is a touchy question to which I address myself later in this essay.) Some women might have considered the uses of suffrage less important than the insult of being classed with schoolboys and lunatics as political incompetents. Yet the vote gives at least potential power. (In Germany, the power of suffrage was of course limited. Had the Reichstag been less impotent, or more highly regarded, feminists might have been more anxious to vote.) Denied suffrage and otherwise legally enjoined from political involvement, most women, upon whom informal forces operated in the same direction, ignored the larger world and especially politics. They even accepted their circumstances in areas where legislation alone could have done little: for example, in the whole area of personal male-female relationships. The power of suffrage can surely be overestimated. If women could make no progress without suffrage, then woman suffrage would be impossible. Moderate feminists thought the ballot not of sufficient importance or use to risk the controversial consequences of demanding it. They did not think German women mature enough for the "crown." There are overtones here of the double standard. Not only should women's sexual criteria be higher than men's, they must uphold political purity as well. Less idealistic was the worry of the many liberal or progressive feminists that the masses of women would abstain or vote for the Catholic Center or Social Democratic parties.

The suffragist leader Anita Augspurg tried to avoid the two seemingly exclusive alternatives: either women were not ready for political rights, so could not demand them; or, given these rights, women would gain political wisdom. Though women weren't yet ready to vote, they could demand the right to do so. (Everyone ignored the fact that there was *absolutely no danger* that women would get the vote.) The time spent agitating for these rights could be used for political education. When rights were finally granted, women could then fulfill their duties. (Radicals could shamefacedly ask for rights, they could never completely do without duties.) Augspurg cited England, where women had been politically active for decades and where suffrage seemed imminent, as a model. The vote sounded like a "prize" for hard work and discipline. Augspurg's sense of "responsibility" and her concern for "maturity" were hardly less than the moderates'. She claimed that a voter needed a *good* general education as well as a "warm heart" for humanity and for one's own people. (She would not lower her standards because men did not meet them.) But, unlike the moderates, Augspurg thought that agitation and political activity were more effective preparations for politics than silent labor in moderate feminist vineyards.[62]

Zetkin found Augspurg's demand for what seemed to be universal knowledge "downright shocking."[63] Even Minna Cauer wondered if Augspurg's "high ideals" could be fulfilled.[64] Important as education was, suffrage, at least a truly democratic one, was a better reply to the woman question than a few academic high schools for girls. Germany's professors and academics were not model politicians; political work alone made mature citizens. Cauer criticized the "classroom" model for women's progress favored by moderates, whereby the qualified advanced to ever higher levels: first, one had education; then, the right of association and assembly; then maybe municipal suffrage; and so on. "That's not how man has been treated," she protested, "therefore it is unjust to prescribe such evolutionary stages for us, that is, to demand a proof of capability."[65]

Radicals were too prone to think that suffrage would easily "solve" the woman question. The underlying causes of women's disabilities were too often ignored. Radicals were rethinking the family and the relationship between the sexes, but they usually discussed political issues as separate and in a vacuum. Suffrage was often described as *the* goal. Hence Cauer's *Die Frauenbewegung* called suffrage "the solution to the woman question" and urged women to "fix your eye straight on the goal and plant it high on the mountaintop, that its gleam will be visible to all at a distance: this *goal is the full equality of woman as a citizen, woman suffrage.*" (Cauer had no gift for metaphor.) Women depended on men for the legislation that dominated the modern state. Full equality would be the "ineluctable" consequence, so Cauer thought, of historical development; whether it came sooner or later would, however, largely depend on how women demanded suffrage. The right to vote would not bring miracles overnight, but it would make women responsible for the laws that governed them. "Full equality in citizenship . . . will result in the fusion of women's interests with the interests of the whole, and thus will woman suffrage bring the solution of the woman problem."[66]

The 1902 BDF suffrage resolution urged member groups to "further, so far as within their power, understanding for the idea of woman suffrage, since only through woman suffrage will all efforts of the *Bund* be certain of success." Adoption was unanimous or nearly so.[67] Radicals had charged that suffragists were often disparaged by other feminists. They asked whether such hindrance was in keeping with BDF solidarity, indeed whether the BDF's concern for the general well-being and women's status had implications as to suffrage. The executive committee, led by Lange, stuck to noninterference with a group's internal affairs. But few protested the radicals' interpellation. Moderates like Julie Bassermann, wife of the National Liberal leader, suggested that discussion at least was warranted. Lange's attempt to squelch debate that would be "to no purpose," that is, controversial and a radical *coup,* was overruled.[68]

The BDF decision was an anticlimax. Even Lange supported suffrage in principle and BDF membership was more feminist than ever. Lange's defeat was more of an event. The suffrage resolution was at one with the usual feminist philosophy that some rights were necessary to fulfill duties properly. An amendment averted any obligation to support suffrage. Lange even construed victory from the upholding of the voluntary principle.[69] *Die Gleichheit,* in a fair assessment, credited the radicals with a victory even though the resolution was weak. The "logic of facts" was however ultimately responsible.[70] The idea of woman suffrage no longer shocked most feminists.

German feminists presented suffrage in a very unthreatening way. They calmed the fears of entanglement in impassioned Reichstag politics of many women by stressing their peculiar mission in the community, recalling not accidentally the charitable duties that were their traditional preserve. If woman's place was no longer exclusively in the home, her place in public life was at that level closest to and most resembling the home. Women's peculiar qualities were invoked for a "feminine" approach to politics. The woman's movement would, typically, "open the world of public life to [women's] maternal influence" while training them to a "consciousness of their duties to the whole."[71] Women's care was especially useful for the poor and orphaned. Guardianships provided a unique release for maternal energies and emotions. The "finer feminine eye" was closer to real life. Women's emotions were an advantage, keeping them from lifeless theorizing. These ideas sometimes smacked strangely of received ideas about woman's "nature": for example, women should not write laws because such activity involved intellectual abstractions; women were to be relegated to carrying out men's orders humanely. Women city planners would think of gardens. Surprisingly, statistical work could be "feminine," because it involved the "individual observation of masses."[72] Women were also demanded where special understanding of their sex was desirable. Women factory inspectors, for example, were needed because women would not talk with men about some problems. Women judges and juries were demanded. Some moral views were accessible only to women; or there were "certain vibrations of the feminine soul" that were "so to speak, sensed intuitively by women."[73] Masculine justice was inappropriate in cases of rape, for example.

The idea that women might personalize cold and faceless bureaucracy is appealing. Because the feminine ideology affected upbringing and behavior, many women probably had expertise and interest in the "feminine" areas of government. (Radicals, however, criticized the implication that women could treat public life like the family; they would only see individuals with problems, rather than underlying social causes.) It seems today outrageous that women had so little influence on the public education of girls. But feminists largely ignored their exclusion from the formal education of boys. (Women did teach in the often coeducational *Volksschule*, generally for the lower classes.) There was humor to be wrung from a deputation of bearded public officials nonplussed at having to investigate infant care. It was of course humorous largely because child care was unequally distributed in the family, the father hardly associating with a child until it reached the age of rational discourse. However, a male pediatrician was not regarded askance. Concern for immediate results may have commended stress on areas where women's "nature" converged with public life and needs. Few men could have pictured a woman writing tax laws. How many women were equipped to do so? It made sense to fill offices in sectors of public life with women when these offices dealt with other women who might be hurt by masculine insensitivity and hostility (or by their own modesty). Shared understanding and experience might sometimes mean sympathy. (Though it was likely that many women, given the rigorous moral expectations and education to which they were subjected, would have not viewed sympathetically, say, infanticide of an illegitimate child by its mother.)

There were pitfalls in the politics of "femininity." Women seem to be no more attracted by local politics than men are; they pay more heed to national issues.[74] Criticism by feminists rarely examined how the sexes were predefined. To accentuate "feminine" spheres probably reinforced customary opinions as to what women should and should not do. Even today women in public office remain concentrated in "feminine" ministries: health, education and family. These are crucially important concerns; in fact they are often neglected in favor of defense, which is everywhere virtually closed to women's influence. Women's insights into education may be acute, but if, as usual, they do not sit on committees which disburse finances, their ideas will be stillborn for want of monetary support. Women in government, too, often seem intended as guardians of mankind's better impulses, which are the more easily dismissed because expressed by women (and "idealistic" men).[75]

In line with their evolutionary bias, feminists claimed that priority given to the issue of local suffrage reflected an ideal pattern. The usual model was Britain, where women's community work and their use of local suffrage presumably had led Parliament to the brink of woman suffrage.[76] Even the radicals first petitioned for local suffrage.

The municipal offices that German feminists demanded were not necessarily elective and were sometimes dubiously political. More serious were the property qualifications usually tied to municipal suffrage. Because of marriage laws and their lesser earning capacity, women were especially hurt by these qualifications. Many local governments were controlled by a few notables. Socialist invective about "ladies' suffrage" was understandable. The empire's disunity made the issue of communal suffrage unwieldy for agitation. In England or Scandinavia, municipal suffrage was regulated for the whole country at once. In Germany, states, provinces, and municipalities divided jurisdiction over suffrage in local corporations. Most of the energy moderate feminists put into suffrage agitation was spent urging a handful of property-holding women to exercise the restricted vote they possessed in a few rural areas.[77] Their ballots were usually tendered by male "representatives" over whom the women had no control. This was hardly the stuff with which to inflame the hearts of masses of women. It did typify German feminism's gradualism and sense of "responsibility."

A considerable number of women held community positions when World War I broke out.[78] Yet the state of suffragism was neatly revealed in the remarks of a leader in the Silesian women's movement in 1911. Communal suffrage was the foremost task, "that once and for all . . . timidity be broken regarding suffrage for care of the poor and school administration." Women, who were "much easier to convince through practical work than through theories," would only demand the vote when they had learned to administer poor laws and the like. Interestingly, women remained "our greatest enemies."[79]

Women's local public service was supposed to prove their eventual value as full citizens of the state. (Most feminists would have deferred suffrage rather than have it prove detrimental to Germany's welfare.) Politicians, however, rarely admitted a link between women's community work and their ability to elect a parliament. When in 1902 the Prussian interior minister, von Hammerstein, observed that nothing on which women's rights impinged had changed for a half-century, he freely admitted that women's contributions, particularly care for the poor, were "indispensable for us all. . . . But whether this could be an equal blessing in the political arena, even in some distant future, I at least must energetically dispute."[80] In the Reichstag in 1902, the National Liberal leader, Ernst Bassermann, suggested that women be allowed limited public participation in "social-political efforts" germane to "women's interests." This was consistent with feminists' remarks—as no doubt he knew from his wife, Julie. "Gentlemen," he elaborated, "we demand above all women's participation for the weak, poor and ill. The soft hands of women are much better suited to intervene here." Bassermann himself would reserve galleries for women at political meetings and festivals "at which there is after all a good deal of patriotism." But he wanted a measure that might pass.[81] None did, however, until 1908.

Whatever the opinion of legislators and ministers, feminists were increasingly active in politics. Use of the women's movement as a political weapon was, however, severely limited by feminists' self-imposed curbs on political alliance. (Also by numbers: women working for suffrage probably never exceeded a few thousand. Their financial resources were meager too.) Feminism was, as socialists fondly pointed out, a middle-class movement. Feminists were constrained by the strongest forces in the political constellation. Drawn to liberalism, especially the progressive variety, they were repelled by the other political options open in Germany. A few feminists defected to the SPD, notably Lily von Gizycki (who made a second marriage to the revisionist leader Heinrich Braun) in 1896 and Tony Breitscheid, who, with her husband Rudolf, left progressivism in 1912. Cauer was so hopeful of a renewed and united liberalism that she occasionally flirted with socialist revisionism. Even Augspurg, inveterately disdainful of socialism, sometimes threatened progressives with mass feminist defections if they did not treat women with more respect, or at least seriousness. But few feminists would not have understood Anna Pappritz's reply to a suggestion that they be politically consequential:

If women . . . are advised to place themselves in the service of the party which promises to represent their demands, adherence to this advice would consequently lead them into the ranks of Social Democracy, the party which proclaims full equality of rights for women.[82]

No more needed to be said.

Overwhelmingly Protestant as well as liberal, feminists could not be attracted to the Catholic Center, the other mass party, even when churchmen and politicians began making overtures to the women's movement. (A separate Catholic women's movement developed in the early years of this century.) Feminism was urban. The German Conservative party was agrarian

(Junker and peasant) and basically hostile to feminism. The Free Conservatives, the party of industry and bureaucracy, though open to property rights for heiresses, were hardly more attractive.[83] Feminists were left with liberalism in its various manifestations; their sympathies led them there in any event.

German feminists understood that some things were more important than "women's issues," for example, the state's welfare and culture. Moderate feminists first spoke out on a non-"woman's issue" when in 1900 they backed proposed naval increases; they claimed the ships would make the world safe for German culture.[84] The concern with "maturity" was rooted in a concern for Germany's liberal well-being. According to Ika Freudenberg, leader of moderate feminism in Munich, who gave more credit to socialists' support of women than most feminists, it would also be a sin against the SPD to join for the sake of only one issue, however important. The women's movement was moreover contemporary in origin with liberalism, in which it had "always seen its natural ally." Freudenberg admitted that women's predestined partners had put them in the "typically" feminine situation of waiting to be claimed, but she thought this yet unrequited constancy showed sound political instinct. Women were naturally attracted to a party that did not bow to the status quo, yet had not deserted progress for revolution. Further proof of women's political acumen was their placing the general above the particular: for women, the whole fatherland was decisive. Social Democracy opposed the national state. Hence, Freudenberg asserted, liberalism, champion of intellectual and civil freedom, was women's only choice.[85] The Liberal People's party (*Freisinnige Volkspartei*) deputy, Müller Meinigen was only realistic when he replied to radicals' outrage over a party colleague's patronizing remarks about women: "According to its whole position on culture, the bourgeois women's movement can find protection of its justified interests only by progressive liberalism."[86]

These "justified interests" did not include suffrage, though a few progressive men were sympathetic. Despite the links between feminism and liberalism and although feminist leaders were overwhelmingly progressive, even left-liberals might well have opposed woman suffrage. They must have reckoned that they would become the main losers from this reform, because of women's conservative and religious tendencies and the relatively large number of organized socialist women. German liberal males may have been extremely closed to the idea of sexual equality. German liberalism saw itself as peculiarly the party of the academically educated. The disparity in education between the sexes must have been greatest in liberal circles, and thus "the conviction of the political immaturity and inferiority of women was so dominant. . . ."[87]

The classic liberal cause of low tariffs was the first nonspecifically feminist issue to unite women of all colors from moderate to socialist. (Radicals and socialists attacked moderate feminists' support for naval increases.) They used some general political arguments; for example, the poor suffered most from high tariffs, reactionary Junkers would profit from higher grain prices. But "women's" points were usually included. Even socialists appealed to the "woman as consumer," who would have to manage with her already tight budget. Low tariffs were almost unanimously regarded as "women's politics." (Junkers' wives were noticeably absent from feminist ranks.) The lone dissent came from Marianne Weber of the BDF executive, who warned against tying the bourgeois movement to any party or interest group. Weber saw feminism motivated by such ethical ideals as the realization of women's right to "self-determination and independence without regard to her peculiarity as a sexual being," which required "elimination of all external barriers which oppose her development to full humanity." Weber's vintage liberal rhetoric reveals the difficulty of "neutrality." (She herself thought these ideals indispensable to feminism's "stamp of universal validity.") Individual groups might have very different methods and programs, but the "goals of the woman's movement as such can only be those demands which are raised from woman's standpoint as such and for woman as such." Weber had uncovered, but not solved, the problem. Who was this noumenal woman? Whoever "she" was, Weber doubted that "she" would oppose higher tariffs. Grain at, say, 3.5 marks per ton, was not a "feminine" tariff. Nor was free trade the only imaginable policy. Unanimity among women regarding such material interests was impossible. She thought that women would, like men, ultimately join existing political parties.[88]

Socialists saw bourgeois feminists' tacit partisanship as a sign of maturity. Women must have political opinions if radicals urged them into politics. They would hardly work for a party because of one or two "women's issues." Political maturity would split bourgeois feminism because sisterhood could never obviate the contradictions among women. "Serious" feminists would soon realize that the woman question could not be isolated from other social questions. The more involved in politics feminists became, the more the forces that act on human beings in society would divide them.[89]

If socialists were right, feminist movements seemed to be condemned to disintegrate somewhat short of the goal of equality. Perhaps it is more apt to say that a women's movement must finally consist of alliances formed for issues that strike women as more or less germane to their condition. I am deliberately vague. "Woman's condition" is not easily sorted out from among the multiple identities of individual women. Maybe "women's issues" are only determined by women's decisions that they are such. One may, for example (with good arguments) claim that the right to abortions is patently in women's interest; all women do not support the abolition of abortion laws. It is likely that one's consciousness as a woman increases in conjunction with an increase in general consciousness. The differences among feminists may in many ways be greater than among women in general. The BDF's fiction of "sisterly love" was viable only while there were relatively few genuine feminists among its members. Feminism was not doomed by diversity so much as organizations like the BDF, which pretended to speak for a movement larger than itself. (Even from the outset the BDF could not accommodate socialist women.) Women's movements would have to live with plurality, with coalitions and temporary alliances.

Radical feminists' nonpartisanship rarely exceeded potential sympathy with any of the left-liberal parties. They first called women to participate in Reichstag elections in 1898; in 1903 the DVF made a similar effort.[90] Both appeals were ostensibly nonpartisan, yet the authors' progressive sympathies were transparent. At one DVF meeting, Augspurg censured a National Liberal spokeswoman. "Women" could not support that party's military and naval policy. The Liberal People's party, she insisted, "supports women in the Reichstag on every occasion."[91] This hyperbole expressed Augspurg's own politics. In 1898 and 1903, candidates were to be judged on their response to several feminist demands. In 1898 suffrage was included; in 1903 it was dropped (probably realistically). Written agreement was accepted from candidates unwilling to commit themselves publicly. Response to the earlier attempt was meager. In 1903, the DVF produced results in Hamburg, where local party organizations were asked to admit women as regular members. Progressives called a special meeting, which after a heated debate, approved the request by a nearly two-thirds majority. Women had shown their usefulness, virtually taking over the work in one electoral district.[92] Success was not so resounding elsewhere.

Moderates rejected the "test question" approach. They did not think the movement strong enough to persuade any party, and rejected the idea of choosing a party for its stance on women. The nation came first. In 1912, the BDF decided that at least until women could vote, politics was best influenced by individual women acting as feminist missionaries within the parties. Women's groups should remain nonpartisan. Within the BDF, political convictions were to be subordinated to unity. Women could do their politicking within the parties.[93]

Especially after 1908, the more political moderates became active in the parties. Gertrud Bäumer, who succeeded Stritt as BDF chairwoman in 1910, began with sympathies for Friedrich Naumann's tiny National Social party. When she could, she joined the progressive Liberal Union (*Freisinnige Vereinigung*) with which Naumann's group had merged in 1903. This was the party most open to women's demands. She entered the party's executive committee in 1909. In line with what became BDF policy, she and other women members pushed recognition of women's demands, including suffrage, when the various left-liberal parties coalesced as the Progressive People's Party (*Fortschrittliche Volkspartei*) in 1910. In 1912, the Progressive party congress urged those of its members who could to support full civil equality.[94]

Radicals meanwhile grew disenchanted with the parties. They preferred women's own suffrage organizations to party auxiliary committees. Moderates were increasingly aware of the political differences among women, while such suffrage leaders as Cauer and Augspurg continued to insist on the natural affinity between feminism and left-liberalism. Augspurg could assert that the very political redistribution of Reichstag seats to attain a more equitable rural-urban balance was a nonpartisan issue. Women had "the same interest as every man that the people be *equally* represented in the Reichstag." It was a mere affirmation of urbanization and industrialization.[95] Politics intruded most insistently in the question of what kind of woman suffrage was to be demanded. In socialist terminology, woman suffrage or lady suffrage? Cauer and Augspurg assumed that woman suffrage meant that all women voted. But particularly as suffrage became a more acceptable idea to women, its adherents were less unanimously disposed to progressivism. Beginning about 1909, new suffrage organizations for whom universal woman suffrage was either not acceptable or else unnecessary began to proliferate, destroying the unity of the DVF. Personal squabbles, discouragement, and organizational splits contributed to the impression of decline. And sex proved more scandalous than suffrage for the radicals' Progressive Union. Espousal of the "New Ethics," a combination of freer sexual morality (free marriages and the like), less hypocrisy, neo-Malthusianism, the right to illegitimacy, and the improvement of the species through scientific eugenics, lost them adherents.

The German Association of Protestant Women *(Deutsch-Evangelischer Frauenverein,* or DEF), founded in 1900, completed the feminist political spectrum as the nucleus of a right wing. Originally suspect by feminists skeptical of confessional politics, they entered the BDF en masse with relaxed membership requirements in 1908. They were welcomed to help stem incursions of the "New Ethics," specifically to defeat a resolution to liberalize abortion laws. Moderate feminists came to appreciate the conservative women because they made the women's movement more genuinely neutral. The Protestant women sympathized with a Conservative party that did not know quite what to do with their offers of help. The DEF came to support suffrage for the ecclesiastical community and municipality, but firmly and vocally stopped there. Joining the BDF, it acted as a brake on the suffrage issue. Success—or the enlistment of still more women in the women's movement—for the BDF as for the DVF meant conservatism. Feminism was becoming respectable.

World War I was, for feminism as for socialism, a blow to the ideology of internationalism. Certainly "woman's condition" and other such generalizations obscure as much as they explain. Although the "condition" of German, English, and American women was sufficiently uniform to generate feminist responses in all three nations, it was as culturally determined as the movements themselves. The concept of "national feminism," in other words, goes far towards explaining why avid suffragism was not a universal phenomenon in the women's movement.

Reference to "woman's condition" is all the more confusing because it reifies "woman" in precisely the same way as the old saw about "woman's nature." "Woman" does not exist for the social historian. There are women of diverse qualities, in each of whom the feminine component is inseparably bonded to all other components in a total cultural configuration. While "the woman question" has an undeniable antiquarian charm, questions about *women* will produce more answers concerning the feminist phenomenon.

NOTES

1. Kate Millet, *Sexual Politics* (Garden City, N.Y., 1970), pp. 80–85; William L. O'Neill, *Everyone Was Brave: The Rise and Fall of Feminism in America* (Chicago, 1969). For a comparative look at two feminisms, see O'Neill's introductory essay in *The Woman Movement: Feminism in the United States and England* (Chicago, 1971), pp. 14–97.

2. The differences between American and German movements were of course matters of degree, not absolute differences. O'Neill's "social feminists," more interested in serving than in voting, show similarities with moderate German feminists. The limited suffrage to preserve "social purity" that was wanted by the WCTU, largest women's organization in the U.S., resembled German emphasis on the "feminine" community suffrage. See p. 371. (A religiously based temperance movement of significant proportions did not exist in Germany.)

3. For a rundown of the association laws, see the documentation for the 1908 reform: "Entwurf eines Vereinsgesetzes," in *Verhandlungen des Reichstages,* XII Leg. Per., 2nd sess., Anlage 5:12–22 (Anlage 1a); 33–35 (Anlage 1b). (Hereafter cited as *Verh. d. Rtgs.*) See also Jacqueline Strain, *Feminism and Political Radicalism in the German Social Democratic Movement, 1890–1914* (Diss., University of California, 1964), pp. 55–62, 95–98.

4. 1887 Imperial Court decision, cited in Gertrud Bäumer, "Geschichte der Frauenbewegung in Deutschland," in *Handbuch der Frauenbewegung,* ed. G. Bäumer and Helene Lange, 1 (Berlin, 1901) 116.

5. *Die Gleichheit,* 10 (28 February 1900):54 (hereafter cited as *Gleich*).

6. The 1891 Erfurt program, official SPD platform until the Weimar Republic, substituted for the vague "citizen from the age of twenty," whom the Gotha program (1875) wished enfranchised, "all imperial citizens over the age of twenty without regard to sex." Suffrage was to be equal, direct and secret as well. These were the conditions set for Reichstag elections, except that the minimum age was 25 and women were excluded. Suffrage requirements for the

state diets were generally far more discriminatory. The Erfurt program also demanded an "end to all laws which put women at a disadvantage with men in regard to public and civil law." See SPD, *Protokoll über die Verhandlungen des Parteitages . . . , abgehalten zu Erfurt* (Berlin, 1891), pp. 45, 349–50 (hereafter cited *Protokoll*).

7. First published in 1879, *Die Frau und der Sozialismus* went through three revisions. A fiftieth edition was published in 1910.

8. SPD, *Protokoll* [Halle] (Berlin, 1890), pp. 169–70.

9. Ibid., p. 49.

10. See Strain, *Feminism and Political Radicalism*, pp. 63–68, 75–92, 160–77; see also Werner Thönnessen, *Frauenemanzipation: Politik und Literatur der deutschen Sozialdemokratie zur Frauenbewegung, 1863–1933* (Frankfurt, 1969).

11. Gabriele Bremme, *Die politische Rolle der Frau in Deutschland* (Göttingen, 1956), pp. 72–73.

12. *Protokoll des Internationalen Arbeiter-Congresses zu Paris* (Nürnberg, 1890), pp. 83–84.

13. SPD, *Protokoll* [Berlin] (Berlin, 1892), pp. 20–21, 275–76, 278.

14. See "Die deutsche Genossinnen im Wahlkampf," *Gleich.*, 3 (26 July 1893):119; and 31 March–26 July, passim. Activity seems to have been mainly in a few cities.

15. Ibid.; see especially "Wahlrecht-Wehrrecht," (14 June), pp. 89–90.

16. Clara Zetkin, *Die Arbeiterinnen- und Frauenfrage der Gegenwart* (Berlin, 1894), pp. 14–22. (Ser. 1, pt. 3, *Berliner Arbeiter-Bibliothek,* ed. Max Schippel.)

17. "Das Proletariat und das Wahlrecht der Frau," *Gleich.*, 4 (25 July 1894):113–14.

18. On women's political behavior in general, see Bremme, *Politische Rolle*; and Maurice Duverger, *The Political Role of Women* (Paris, 1955). Duverger (pp. 54–61) includes a table with the male-female distribution of votes during the Weimar period, when ballots were separately tabulated. On the high voting participation of married women (and men), ibid., p. 44. On present-day West Germany, where sexual equality is not of course yet complete, see "Unterm Joch," *Der Spiegel*, 23 (1 September, 1969):32–49; "Denn man tau," ibid. (27 October), 52–57.

19. The connection may be clearest with women in the professions and civil service, somewhat less clear with working-class women. It probably reflects free time, but may also be a commentary on the relatively greater emancipation of women with more education and higher-level jobs than working-class women. See Duverger, *Political Role*, pp. 39–43. In 1969, the SPD's greatest successes among women voters were with those who were highly educated and in responsible positions: "Denn man tau."

20. See Emile Vandervelde, "Nochmals das belgische Experiment," *Neue Zeit*, 20 (2) (1901–02):166–69.

21. SPD, *Protokoll* [Mannheim] (Berlin, 1906), p. 445.

22. *Verh. d. Rtgs.*, IX Leg. Per., 3rd sess., 1894/95, 1:856–58. (13 February 1895).

23. See p. 699.

24. See Friedrich Engels: "The first class opposition that appears in history coincides with the development of the antagonism between men and women in monogamous marriage and the first class oppression coincides with that of the female sex by the male." *The Origin of the Family, Private Property, and the State* (New York, 1942), p. 58. Socialist women rarely cited Engels' *Origin*, perhaps because it smacked too much of sexual divisiveness and hostility.

25. Heinrich Rickert of the Liberal People's party, long counted a friend of feminism, claimed that the states might interfere in imperial affairs if they were more representative than the Reichstag. *Verh. d. Rtgs.*, 845; also 2:1014.

26. Ibid., 1:864; 2:1004. The involvement of "Galician Jews" in white slavery was notorious in anti-Semitic circles.

27. Ibid., 1:862.

28. The *Frankfurter Zeitung* articles were cited in *Gleich.*, 5(20 March 1895):43, and 7(29 September 1897):160. The first article denied that women's voting would change the political balance. The later one called suffrage the "solution" to the woman question so far as it was insoluble without political participation, and because political rights broadened one's horizons.

29. "Frauenfrage," *Meyers Konversations-Lexikon*, 4th ed. (Leipzig and Vienna, 1890), 1:622.

30. Frances Magnus-Hausen, "Ziel und Weg in der deutschen Frauenbewegung des 19. Jahrhunderts," in *Deutscher Staat und deutsche Parteien: Friedrich Meinecke zum 60. Geburtstage dargebracht* (Munich and Berlin, 1922), p. 202.

31. On the early years of German feminism see ibid., pp. 201–26; Bäumer, Geschichte der Frauenbewegung," pp. 33–80; Margrit Twellmann-Schepp, *Die deutsche Frauenbewegung im Spiegel repräsentativer Frauenzeitschriften, ihre Anfänge und erste Entwicklung (1843–1889)* (Diss., University of Marburg, 1967); Zetkin, *Zur Geschichte der proletarischen Frauenbewegung Deutschlands* (E. Berlin, 1958), esp. pp. 15–59, 151–60.

32. On the German women's movement and the position of women, see Bäumer and Lange, *Handbuch der Frauenbewegung*, 5 vols. (Berlin, 1901–1906); Agnes von Zahn-Harnack, *Die Frauenbewegung: Geschichte, Probleme, Ziele* (Berlin, 1928). Both these accounts are biased against the "left wing" of feminism, on which see Else Lüders, *Der "linke Flügel"* (Berlin, [1904]).

33. Woman suffrage was granted through a decree of the *Rat der Volksbeauftragten* (Council of People's Delegates) on 30 November 1918, ordering elections

to a constituent National Assembly. Duverger comments on the frequency with which woman suffrage comes by revolution or executive decree. *Political Role,* p. 10.

34. "Des Weibes Rechte beruht auf seinen Pflichten": epigram for Dr. med. Hermann Klencke, *Das Weib als Gattin,* 13th ed. rev. (Leipzig, 1895), p. ii.

35. Solness in Act II. Henrik Ibsen, *When We Dead Awaken and Three Others Plays,* trans. Michael Meyer (New York, 1960), p. 174.

36. Schmidt, "Die Parteien in der Frauenbewegung," *Die neue Bahnen,* 33 (15 November 1898):233–34 (hereafter cited *N.B.*)

37. See Eleanor Flexnor, *Century of Struggle,* (New York, 1970), pp. 74–77.

38. Elisabeth Gottheiner, "Das Gemeindewahlrecht der Frau," in *Der internationale Frauen-Kongress in Berlin, 1904,* ed. Marie Stritt (Berlin [1905]), pp. 492–97. See n. 76.

39. Bäumer, "Eindrücke vom Internationalen Frauen-kongress," *Die Frau,* 11 (July 1904):578.

40. "Die Thesen des Internationalen Frauenstimmrechts-Komitees," "Parlamentarische Beilage" Die Frauenbewegung, 8 (1 December 1902):89 (hereafter cited "Parl. Beil" and *FB*). Americans did not of course eschew less idealistic justifications for women suffrage; arguments of justice yielded increasingly to those of expediency, for example, women's potential support for progressive legislation, though also their potential as a counterweight to immigrant voters.

41. See Schmidt's letters to Anna Simson, BDF executive member, (17 and 26 July 1898) in the BDF Archive (Schmidt folder), now held by the Berliner Frauenbund (hereafter cited BDFA).

42. Anna Simson, *Der Bund Deutscher Frauenvereine: Was er will und was er nicht will* (Breslau, 1895), pp. 9, 11–12, 15. (Pt. 1, "Schriften der BDF.")

43. Lily von Gizycki, *Die Bürgerpflicht der Frau* (Berlin, 1895), p. 8. Despite the carefully chosen title, Gizycki (citing Ibsen) made an unusual attack on the idea of duty, then incorporated it into her argument for rights.

44. Probably because of the dearth of German sources, Gizycki used an article by the American Wendell Phillips: "Frauenrechte," *Ethische Kultur,* 1 (3, 10, 17, 24 June 1893), 179–81, 189–90, 196–97, 205–07. Phillips considered suffrage the "cornerstone of our efforts" and used the arguments German women largely rejected.

45. For Lily von Gizycki's reminiscences of the speech and connected events, see Lily Braun, *Memoiren einer Sozialistin: Lehrjahre,* vol. 2 of *Gesammelte Werke* (Berlin, n.d.), pp. 505–15.

46. Georg von Gizycki, "Frauenstimmrecht," *FB,* 1 (1 February 1895), 17–18. This article was balanced with another opposing suffrage at least for the foreseeable future, by the feminist pioneer Henriette Goldschmidt. Nothing dire apparently resulted from their boldness, and the *FB* never printed another word against the vote.

47. Moderates boycotted the congress because it was "premature" for Germany. E. Vely, "Vom Internationalen Kongress," *Die Frau,* 4 (October 1896):50. The German women held their own with representatives from the classic lands of woman suffrage. Millicent Garett Fawcett, the British suffragist, who submitted a paper, could not emphasize enough how antirevolutionary women were; as a clincher she asserted that women wanted rights only to fulfill duties better. "The Suffrage Movement in England," in *Der Internationale Kongress für Frauenwerke und Frauenbestrebungen* (Berlin, 1897), pp. 23–34. Marie Stritt claimed it was an "open secret" that "we too . . . can attain our total rights only through our civil rights." "Die Frauenbewegung in Deutschland, ibid., p. 8.

48. Marie Stritt, "Die Protestversammlung der Dresdener Frauen," *FB,* 4 (15 February 1898):38.

49. "Die Delegiertenversammlung der Verein Frauenwohl," *FB,* 5 (15 October 1899), 173–74.

50. "Deutscher Verein für Frauenstimmrecht," *FB,* 8 (1 January 1902):1.

51. See p. 369.

52. Lange, "Der Frauentag in Stuttgart," *Die Frau,* 5 (November 1897):65–66.

53. "Nicht das Schreien, sondern das Leisten tut's." Lange, "Frauenwahlrecht," *Cosmopolis,* 3 (August 1896):194. Lange's first prosuffrage article was characteristically published in this multilingual journal published in England.

54. Lange, "Frauentag in Stuttgart," p. 66.

55. Schmidt, "Die Zeit und wir!," *N.B.,* 33 (1 January 1898):1–2.

56. Lange, "Altes und Neues zur Frauenfrage," *Die Frau,* 2 (June 1895):585–86.

57. Though hard to measure, Stritt's influence in pushing the BDF on suffrage (and to more advanced positions in general), must have been great. She was first accounted part of the "left wing," then gravitated toward the BDF establishment, where she was one of few women who tried to hold her own against Lange. Perhaps more than any German leader she deserved the name "feminist"; her single-minded regard for women's emancipation was fairly unique. Stritt's down-fall from power was precipitated by her inclusion under feminism of such BDF taboos as the so-called New Ethics (greater sexual freedom for women) and abortion.

58. Stritt, ICW report, *Centralblatt der Bund Deutscher Frauenvereine,* 1 (1 August 1899):69. Hereafter cited *CB.* That timidity was not unique to German feminism is indicated by the necessity of holding a public suffrage meeting separate from the London ICW conference and women's congress at the behest of more conservative British women.

59. She claimed to have been misunderstood: "It would not have occurred to me in a dream to characterize the conception of political maturity of our first champions as of itself 'in error,' rather I stated that it was *dictated* by circumstances." Letter to Schmidt (4 August 1899), BDFA (Stritt folder).

60. Gottheiner, "Der Internationale Frauenkongress in London," *N.B.*, 34 (1 August 1899):170–71.

61. Helene Mercier, "Das Wahlrecht der Frau," *Die Frau*, 2 (March 1895):731–34.

62. Augspurg, "Die politische Erziehung der Frau," *FB*, 8 (1 February 1902):18–19.

63. "Der 2. Verbandstag des Verbands Fortschrittlicher Frauenvereine," *Gleich.*, 11 (20 November 1901):189–90.

64. Cauer, "Die Tagung des Verbandes Fortschrittlicher Frauenvereine," *FB*, 7 (15 October 1901):154.

65. Cauer, "Antwort," *FB*, 12 (1 May 1906):66–67.

66. [Cauer], "Das Frauenstimmrecht—die Lösung der Frauenfrage," *FB*, 11 (1 September 1905):129–30.

67. "Die fünfte Generalversammlung des Bundes Deutscher Frauenvereine," *CB*, 4 (1 November 1902):116; and Lange, "Der Bund . . . in Wiesbaden," *Die Frau*, 10 (November 1902):68, had it unanimous. Cauer, "Stimmungsbilder," *FB*, 8 (15 October 1902):154, qualified the concord, as the *Frankfurter Zeitung* did (3. Morgenblatt, 7 October 1902). The report of total unanimity may well evince the preoccupation with hearty agreement.

68. *F.Z.;* Cauer, "Stimmungsbilder," p. 154; and *Gleich.*, 12 (19 November 1902):187, all have Lange acting as prime instigator in damping discussion. Stritt spoke on "politics and woman" at a big public meeting planned before the resolution arose. *Gleich.* (pp. 187–88) thought this public meeting the clearest expression of the BDF's increased maturity. (No report of it was made in the feminist press.)

69. Lange, "Der Bund . . . in Wiesbaden," pp. 67–68.

70. *Gleich.*, pp. 187–88.

71. Elisabeth Altmann-Gottheiner, "Grundsätze und Forderungen der Frauenbewegung auf dem Gebiet des öffentlichen Lebens," in *Grundsätze und Forderungen der Frauenbewegung* (Leipzig and Berlin, 1912), p. 30. ("Flugschriften der BdF," no. 1.) The same tendencies can be found within the radical wing. See Augspurg, "Die kommunale Ämter der Frau," "Parl. Beil.," *FB*, 5 (1 December 1899):61.

72. Natalie Rümelin, "Die Tätigkeit der Frau in der Gemeinde," in Elly Saul and Hildegard Obrist-Jenicke, eds. *Jahrbuch für die deutsche Frauenwelt* (Stuttgart, 1899), pp. 122–36.

73. Altmann-Gottheiner, "Grundsätze," p. 30.

74. See Duverger, *Political Role*, pp. 20–21, 26. Flexner mentions that partial suffrage in the U.S. did not bring enough women to the polls to constitute a convincing demonstration that the ballot was wanted. *Centuries of Struggle*, p. 177.

75. See Duverger, *Political Role*, pp. 95–101. The "feminine" fields are health,

family, welfare, children, women, social questions, or generally low-priority concerns. Finance, defense and foreign affairs are virtually off limits. In West Germany, the ministry of health and the family seems to be women's position: of late the CDU's minister has been Elisabeth Schwartzhaupt and the SPD's, Käte Strobel. Bremme, on the other hand, argues for concentration on 'feminine' areas that may otherwise be neglected; women should thus make themselves irreplaceable. *Politische Rolle,* pp. 224–25, 228.

76. Lange, "Frauenwahlrecht," pp. 190–92. In young nations, she suggested, where women's civilizing influence on masculine brutality might be needed, the first interest of women in public life was the right of women's suffrage. America was no model for Germany. The importance to Germany's political development traditionally attributed to municipal self-administration, one of Stein's reforms in early nineteenth-century Prussia, also played a role in the emphasis on local politics. See Hajo Holborn, *A History of Modern Germany,* 2 (New York, 1964), 401–05.

77. See Jenny Apolant, *Das kommunale Wahlrecht der Frauen in den deutschen Bundesstaaten* (Leipzig and Berlin, 1918).

78. The number increased particularly rapidly in the years before the war. In 1913, in 559 communities of over 6,000 population, 17,960 women were working in public welfare offices; 16,939 in honorary, 1,021 in paid positions. True to feminist ideology, most were involved with orphans, no doubt as unpaid guardians. Those involved with the poor came a close second. Ibid., p. 152.

79. Marie Wegner, "Der Schlesische Frauenverband," *CB,* 13 (11 May 1911), 20–21.

80. Prussia, Haus der Abgeordneten, *Stenographische Bericht,* XIX Leg. Per., 4th sess., 1902, 5:5319–20.

81. *Verh. d. Rtgs.,* X Leg. Per., 2nd sess., 1900/03, 4:3593–94. Ten Centrists signed the Bassermann proposal. Ibid., p. 3581.

82. Pappritz, "Die politische Betätigung der Frauen," *Die Frau,* 9 (November 1901):110.

83. The Free Conservative Wilhelm von Kardorff was the first nonsocialist to support suffrage publicly in the Reichstag; but he spoke only for himself. *Verh. d. Rtgs.,* X Leg. Per., 2nd sess., 1900/03; 4:3586–87. (22 January 1902).

84. "An die deutschen Frauen," *Die Frau,* 7 (March 1900):322–23. This appeal was signed by several women on the BDF and ADF executive committees, including Schmidt and Lange. See Lange, "Flottenbewegung und Friedensbewegung," ibid., pp. 321–22. Augspurg attacked the moderates' support of such a militaristic undertaking: "Die Flottenmanie," "Parl. Beil.," *FB,* 6 (15 February 1900):13–14. See *Gleich.,* 10 (28 February 1900):39–40.

85. Freudenberg, "Die Forderungen der Frauen an den bayrischen Liberalismus," *CB,* 7 (1 December 1905):129–30.

86. Ernst Müller-Meineger, "Offener Brief an die Herausgeberin," *FB,* 12 (1 May 1906):65.

87. Freudenberg, "Forderungen," pp. 130–31.

88. Weber, "Politik und Frauenbewegung," *CB,* 3 (1 December 1901):129–30. Perhaps she had it from her husband Max what the ideal-type "woman" wanted.

89. Lily Braun, in *Gleich.,* 8 (12 May 1897):77–78.

90. "Frauen Deutschlands!" *FB,* 4 (1 April 1898):73; "Rundschreiben des Deutschen Vereins für Frauenstimmrecht betreffend Wahlarbeit der Frauen, "Parl. Beil.," *FB,* 9 (1 May 1903):33–34.

91. *FB,* 9 (15 May 1903):78.

92. "Erfolge," "Parl. Beil.," *FB,* 9 (1 June 1903):41.

93. See Lange, "Die Aufgaben der Frauen in den politischen Parteien," *Die Frau,* 18 (May 1911):449–52; Bäumer, "Gotha und Mannheim," ibid., 65–67.

94. *Die Frau,* 18 (October 1912):51–52.

95. Augspurg to Käthe Schirmacher (29 July 1902). Schirmacher papers, Universität Rostock.